高等院校电子信息与电气学科系列教材

电子信息与通信工程专业英语

第3版

张雪英 刘建霞 桑胜波 王一平 编著

本书是为高等院校电子信息与通信工程类专业学生编写的专业英语教材。本书系统、全面地介绍了专业英语的基础知识，精心编选了与电子信息、通信工程专业相关的课文和阅读材料，不仅包括传统的专业基础知识，还包括近些年正蓬勃发展的新的专业知识。

　　全书共分三篇，分别为基础篇、专业篇、应用篇。基础篇介绍科技英语的基础知识；专业篇涵盖本科学习的主要专业基础课内容和热点技术，包括电路系统与设计、信号系统与信号处理、通信技术、人工智能等方面的内容；应用篇主要从阅读、翻译、写作等角度提高学生对专业英语的应用能力。每章后均附有书中专业篇课文及阅读材料对应的中文翻译，供学生和教师参考。

　　本书可作为高等院校电子信息与通信工程等相关专业的本科生"专业英语"课程的教材，也可用作相关专业研究生的课外读物，还可供相关科技人员学习和参考。

图书在版编目（CIP）数据

电子信息与通信工程专业英语 / 张雪英等编著．
3版． -- 北京：机械工业出版社，2024.11． -- （高等院校电子信息与电气学科系列教材）． -- ISBN 978-7
-111-76801-2

Ⅰ．G203；TN91

中国国家版本馆CIP数据核字第2024BB0499号

机械工业出版社（北京市百万庄大街22号　邮政编码100037）
策划编辑：刘松林　　责任编辑：刘松林
责任校对：陈　洁　　责任印制：常天培
北京机工印刷厂有限公司印刷
2024年11月第3版第1次印刷
185mm×260mm・20.5印张・541千字
标准书号：ISBN 978-7-111-76801-2
定价：69.00元

电话服务　　　　　　　　　网络服务
客服电话：010-88361066　　机　工　官　网：www.cmpbook.com
　　　　　010-88379833　　机　工　官　博：weibo.com/cmp1952
　　　　　010-68326294　　金　书　网：www.golden-book.com
封底无防伪标均为盗版　机工教育服务网：www.cmpedu.com

FOREWORD 前言

专业英语是目前我国大学非英语专业三四年级开设的一门专业必修课，其目的是使学生熟悉本专业的基本科技词汇，掌握相关专业术语，熟悉科技文章的英文表达方法，了解英语写作的一般规范，提高用英语阅读科技文献和表述科技成果的综合能力。本书2009年出版第1版、2014年出版第2版，一直受到广大读者和使用学校的欢迎与肯定。由于电子与通信技术的快速发展，新技术与新方法不断涌现，教材编写应以适应信息科学发展的角度组织，并展现新的专业知识；另外，《高等学校课程思政建设指导纲要》中指出，落实立德树人根本任务，必须将价值塑造、知识传授和能力培养三者融为一体、不可割裂。因此，编者对第2版的部分章节内容进行了调整，在信号系统与信号处理方面增加了语音情感识别的研究热点，在通信技术方面增加了移动通信和北斗卫星导航技术，旨在让学生了解我国卫星导航技术的发展，增强自信心；同时也新增了人工智能领域的相关知识，对模式识别、机器学习、计算机视觉等进行了介绍，以便让学生在学习专业英语的同时，了解科技前沿技术。

全书共分三篇，分别为基础篇、专业篇、应用篇。基础篇介绍科技英语的基础知识；专业篇涵盖本科学习的主要专业基础课内容和热点技术，包括电路系统与设计、信号系统与信号处理、通信技术、人工智能等方面的内容；应用篇主要从阅读、翻译、写作等角度提高学生对专业英语的应用能力。本书涵盖了电子信息与通信工程类专业本科基础课程的大部分内容及部分相关前沿技术发展的内容。

本书内容安排如下：全书共分7章，其中专业篇共12节，均包括课文（TEXT）和阅读材料（READING）两部分。每篇课文后均配有短语和专业词汇表、难句注释，并配以相应的练习题，帮助学生检查对所学内容的掌握情况，题型包括英译汉、汉译英、填空、根据课文回答问题四种形式。阅读材料的难度在课文的基础上有所提高，也配有短语和专业词汇表、难句注释，以进一步扩大学生的阅读范围。

建议本书教学时间为一学期（32~38学时），可根据实际教学要求选择、调整教学内容，建议本科生选择课文作为精讲内容，阅读材料部分为学生自学内容或研究生的速读材料。

本书由太原理工大学的张雪英、刘建霞、桑胜波、王一平编写，其中第3章由张雪英编写，第2、6、7章由刘建霞编写，第5章由张雪英、刘建霞共同编写，第1章由刘建霞、桑胜波共同编写，第4章由刘建霞、王一平共同编写，全书由张雪英统稿。本书的编写得到了太原理工大学信息与计算机学院部分博士、硕士研究生的帮助，在此表示诚挚的感谢。由于作者水平有限，书中难免有不足之处，敬请广大读者批评指正。

编者

教学建议 / INSTRUCTOR'S MANUAL

教学内容	学习要点及教学要求	学时安排 全部讲授	学时安排 部分选讲
Chapter 1 Fundamentals of English for Science and Technology （科技英语基础知识）	• 了解科技英语语法的特点 • 了解科技英语词汇的特点 • 掌握科技英语中常用的词缀及词根 • 掌握科技英语中常用符号和数学式的表达 • 掌握专业英语词汇、句子的翻译方法	4~8	4
Chapter 2 Circuit System and Design （电路系统与设计）	• 通过精读课文 Circuit and System，理解电子学中的基本概念，理解电路分析的基本定理、定律，掌握相关的专业英语词汇和工作原理的英语表述 • 通过精读课文 Analog and Digital Circuits Design，理解模拟电路、数字电路的基本工作原理与分类，掌握相关的专业英语词汇和工作原理的英语表述 • 通过精读课文 Radio Receiver Circuit，理解超外差接收机的基本组成模块、工作原理，了解接收机的特征参数，掌握相关的专业英语词汇和工作原理的英语表述 • 通过泛读阅读材料 Semiconductor Device、Operational Amplifier、RF/Microwave Theory，进一步理解半导体器件的类型及工作原理，了解运算放大器、微波技术的基本原理与分析方法，掌握相关的专业英语词汇和工作原理的英语表述	8~14	8~10
Chapter 3 Signal System and Signal Processing （信号系统与信号处理）	• 通过精读课文 Signal and System，理解连续时间信号与系统、离散时间信号与系统的基本概念，理解数字信号系统的基本特性，掌握相关的专业英语词汇和工作原理的英语表述 • 通过精读课文 Digital Signal Processing，理解傅里叶分析方法、FIR 数字滤波器的设计，理解窗函数的基本概念，掌握相关的专业英语词汇和工作原理的英语表述 • 通过精读课文 Speech Signal Processing，理解语音信号的特点，理解数字语音信号处理的基本技术，掌握相关的专业英语词汇和工作原理的英语表述 • 通过泛读阅读材料 Wavelet Transform、Compressive Sensing、Speech Emotion Recognition，进一步了解信号处理领域的新方法和新技术——小波变换、压缩感知、语音情感识别，掌握相关的专业英语词汇和工作原理的英语表述	6~12	6~8

（续）

教学内容	学习要点及教学要求	学时安排 全部讲授	学时安排 部分选讲
Chapter 4 Communication Technology （通信技术）	• 通过精读课文 Electromagnetic Fields Theory，掌握电磁场理论的基本词汇，理解电磁场基本原理的英语表述 • 通过精读课文 Development of Mobile Communication，理解移动通信的发展历史、1G～5G 的特点，掌握相关的专业英语词汇 • 通过精读课文 Optical Fiber Communication，理解光纤通信的发展历史、基本技术，掌握相关的专业英语词汇和工作原理的英语表述 • 通过泛读阅读材料 Antennas、Global Navigation Satellite System、Ultra-wideband Communication，进一步了解天线基本特征参数的英语表述、全球导航卫星系统和超宽带通信技术的基本概念，掌握相关的专业英语词汇和工作原理的英语表述	6～12	6～8
Chapter 5 Artificial Intelligence （人工智能）	• 通过精读课文 Pattern Recognition，了解模式识别的定义、系统设计及分类，掌握相关的专业英语词汇和工作原理的英语表述 • 通过精读课文 Machine Learning，理解机器学习的概念、工作原理及分类，掌握相关的专业英语词汇和工作原理的英语表述 • 通过精读课文 Computer Vision，了解计算机视觉的定义和任务，掌握相关的专业英语词汇 • 通过泛读阅读材料 Artificial Neural Network、Deep Learning、Digital Image Processing，进一步了解人工神经网络基本理论、深度学习模型、数字图像处理技术，掌握相关的专业英语词汇和工作原理的英语表述	4～8	4
Chapter 6 Textual Type of Special English （专业英语文本类型）	• 通过对专业原版书文体、专业论文文体、产品说明书等应用文体相关内容的学习，了解其基本构成和特点，掌握科技英语应用文体阅读方法 • 初步学会从文体中迅速了解基本信息的方法	2～4	2
Chapter 7 Writing of English Papers for Science and Technology （科技英语论文的写作）	• 通过标题、摘要、正文、结语和参考文献的内容及写作方法的介绍，了解科技英语论文的构成和写作方法 • 学会用英语完成摘要、简短的科技英语论文的写作	2～4	2
教学总学时建议		32～62	32～38

说明：1. 本教材为电子信息及相关学科本科专业"专业英语"课程教材，授课学时数为 32～62 学时，不同专业根据不同的教学要求和计划学时数可酌情对教材内容进行适当取舍。例如，对于电子信息工程、通信工程等专业，教材内容精读部分原则上可全讲，泛读部分作为课外阅读；对于其他专业，可酌情对教材内容进行适当删减。

2. 本教材建议授课学时数 32～38 学时，其中包含课文精读、习题课等必要的课内教学环节。

3. 若某些学科本科专业教学计划课时少于 32 学时，可对第 5～7 章的相关内容进行删减。

目录

前言
教学建议

基 础 篇

**Chapter 1　Fundamentals of English for Science and Technology
（科技英语基础知识）** ………… 2

1.1　科技英语语法的特点 …………… 2
1.2　科技英语词汇的特点 …………… 3
1.3　科技英语中常用符号和数学式的表达 …………………………… 7
1.4　科技英语的翻译 ………………… 11

专 业 篇

**Chapter 2　Circuit System and Design
（电路系统与设计）** …………… 28

2.1　Circuit and System ……………… 28
　　　READING：Semiconductor Device …… 35
2.2　Analog and Digital Circuits Design …… 43
　　　READING：Operational Amplifier …… 49
2.3　Radio Receiver Circuit ………… 57
　　　READING：RF/Microwave Theory …… 65
课文译文 ………………………………… 73

**Chapter 3　Signal System and Signal Processing
（信号系统与信号处理）** …… 87

3.1　Signal and System ………………… 87
　　　READING：Wavelet Transform …… 94
3.2　Digital Signal Processing ………… 100
　　　READING：Compressive Sensing …… 108
3.3　Speech Signal Processing ………… 114

　　　READING：Speech Emotion Recognition …………………… 122
课文译文 ………………………………… 130

**Chapter 4　Communication Technology
（通信技术）** ………………… 143

4.1　Electromagnetic Fields Theory …… 143
　　　READING：Antennas ……………… 149
4.2　Development of Mobile Communication ………………… 157
　　　READING：Global Navigation Satellite System ……………………… 167
4.3　Optical Fiber Communication …… 174
　　　READING：Ultra-wideband Communication ……………… 183
课文译文 ………………………………… 192

**Chapter 5　Artificial Intelligence
（人工智能）** ………………… 207

5.1　Pattern Recognition ……………… 207
　　　READING：Artificial Neural Network …… 215
5.2　Machine Learning ………………… 223
　　　READING：Deep Learning ………… 230
5.3　Computer Vision ………………… 239
　　　READING：Digital Image Processing …… 246
课文译文 ………………………………… 256

应 用 篇

**Chapter 6　Textual Type of Special English
（专业英语文本类型）** ……… 272

6.1　专业原版书文体 ………………… 272
6.2　原版图书结构 …………………… 273
6.3　专业论文文体 …………………… 277

6.4　产品说明书 ················· 284

Chapter 7　Writing of English Papers for Science and Technology
（科技英语论文的写作）··· 290

7.1　标题写作 ····················· 290

7.2　摘要写作 ····················· 292

7.3　正文写作 ····················· 296

7.4　结语和参考文献写作 ············· 298

练习参考答案 ························· 301

参考文献 ····························· 316

基 础 篇

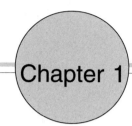

Chapter 1

Fundamentals of English for Science and Technology

（科技英语基础知识）

科技英语是指英语科技文体，包括英语科技论文、科技报告、科普文章、科技新闻和科技产品说明书等，它有别于一般英语和文学英语。科技文体崇尚结构严谨，概念准确，逻辑性强，行文简练，推理周密，重点突出，句式严整，段落章节分明。科技英语作为科技文体的信息传递工具，在写作和翻译过程中都要体现语言结构特色，具体而言，科技英语在语法结构、用词及表达方式上有其自身的特点。

1.1 科技英语语法的特点

科技英语的语法具有以下 4 个特点。

1) 多使用现在时和被动语态。由于科技文体描述的都是一般的客观真理、事物、过程和现象等，因此主语多为非人称代词。使用现在时和被动语态，在一定程度上提高了科技文体的客观性。如：

The signal levels inside power amplifiers are so much larger than these weak inputs that even the slightest "leakage" from the output back to the input may cause problem.

功率放大器中的信号幅度比微弱的输入信号大得多，即使输出中极微小的泄漏传输到输入端都会引发问题。

2) 多使用带有介词短语、形容词短语、分词短语、不定式短语、同位语从句、定语从句、状语从句等修饰语的长句。当阅读科技文体时，往往会遇到一个句子长达七八行，甚至整段文字是由一个英语长句构成的现象。

3) 科技英语中常常用两种语气，即虚拟语气和祈使语气。虚拟语气在科技英语中用来描述假设的条件，即假设有某种条件，就会产生某种结果。在公式化表达或不强调动作的执行者时常用祈使语气。如：

①If there were no attraction between the proton and the electron, the electron would fly away from the proton in a straight line.

倘若质子和电子之间不存在引力，电子就会沿直线飞离质子。

②Suppose $f(x)$ is a periodic continuous function.

设 $f(x)$ 是周期连续函数。

4）普遍使用能表示动作或状态的抽象名词或起名词功用的非限定动词，即名词化倾向。科技英语的名词化倾向是与科技文体的基本要求密切相关的。科技文体的任务是叙述事实和论证推断，要求言简意赅，表达客观，内容确切，这就要求语言结构的简化，而名词化正好有助于这几点的实现。名词化可以把句子变成短语，可使复合句变成简单句。如：

①Using of neural models can make simulation and optimization process less time-consuming, shifting much computation from on-line optimization to off-line training.

采用神经网络建模可节省仿真和优化的时间，将在线优化转为离线训练。

②Considering the fact that the activation functions of the neurons in the output layer are linear, we are trying to solve the problem with system of linear equations.

因为输出层中神经元的激活函数是线性的，所以我们尝试用线性方程组来求解该问题。

1.2 科技英语词汇的特点

在语言的发展过程中，旧词不断被淘汰，新词不断产生。科技英语尤其如此。随着科学技术的发展，新概念、新技术、新理论、新产品不断出现，因此新的技术词汇不断出现，许多日常用语也被赋予新的科技含义，缩略词的增加尤为迅速，技术词汇的相互渗透也日益增多。其特点主要表现在以下几方面。

（1）大量使用技术词

例如，bandwidth（频带）、flip-flop（触发器）、diode（二极管）、triode（三极管）、capacitor（电容）等。这些词的词意面都较窄，往往只出现在某些领域，甚至仅限于某一专业中出现。

（2）大量使用半技术词

例如，lead（导线）、series（串联）、relay（继电器）、conductor（导体）、power（功率）等。这类词在科技英语和普通英语中都能见到，在不同的学科领域含义有所不同，如 conductor 在日常生活中指售票员、乐队指挥，在电学中指导体。

（3）频繁使用缩略词

为了方便人们逐渐用几个字母来代替某些词汇，主要分为节略词、缩略词、首字词、缩写词等。

- 节略词：用前几个字母表示的词，如 del-delete，lab-laboratory，ad-advertisement 等。
- 缩略词：由每个词的首字母所组成的词，如 ROM 是 Read Only Memory 的缩写，IEEE 是 Institute of Electrical and Electronics Engineers 的缩写。
- 首字词：与缩略词相同，但必须逐字读出，如 CAD 表示 Computer Aided Design，IC 表示 Integrated Circuit，DSP 表示 Digital Signal Processing。
- 缩写词：大多数缩写词后都附有一个句号，如 Eq. 表示 Equation，et al. 表示 and other，Fig. 表示 Figure，sq. 表示 square，e.g. 表示 for example，etc. 表示 and so forth 等。

（4）组合词和派生词多

1）组合词：两个或两个以上的词结合成一个新词，包括有连字符和无连字符两种方式，如

feedback 反馈（*vt.*+*adv.*）

open-loop 开环 （*adj.* +*n.*）
zero-input response 零输入响应
step-by-step control 步进控制
copper end rings 铜端环 （*n.* +*n.*）
magnetic moment 磁矩 （*adj.* +*n.*）
alternating current 交流电 （ing 分词+*n.*）
printed circuit 印制电路 （ed 分词+*n.*）
forward-bias 正向偏置 （*adj.* +*n.*）

组合词的组合方法有名词+名词、形容词+名词、动词+副词、名词+动词、介词+名词、形容词+动词等。

2）派生词：即词根加上前缀或后缀构成新词，科技英语中大部分词汇由派生法得到。

表 1-1~表 1-4 给出了部分科技英语中常用的前缀、后缀和词根。

表 1-1 科技英语常用前缀

前缀	意义	词例
a-	不、无	asymmetry, asynchronous
anti-	反、逆、抗、非	anti-clockwise, anti-acid
auto-	自己、自动	automation, autoalarm
bi-, di-	二、双	binomial, dibit, binary
co-	共同、相互	cooperation, correlation
counter-	反、逆、对抗	counterbalance, countermeasure, counteract
de-	去、减、分、脱	decolor, decomposition, defuzzification
dis-	分离、除去、相反	disadvantage, discover
en-, em-	使	enable, enlarge, embed, embody
elec-	电、电的	electronic, electrical, electromechanical
equi-, iso-	等同的	equality, isochromatic
im-, il-, in-, ir-	不	imbalance, illegible, incorrect, irregular
inter-	在……之间、相互	interchange, interface, internet, interact
macro-	大、长、宏	macrocode, macroinstruction
micro-	微小的	microcomputer, microwave, microprocessor
mis-	不、失	miscount, mistake
multi-, poly-	多	multipurpose, polytechnic, multimedia
non-	非、无、不、未	nonlinear, nondestructive
out-	出	output, outline
post-	在后	postgraduate, posterior
pre-	预先	preset, preface
re-	再、反、重新	reaction, readjust, reverse
simili-, homo-	类似的、同类的	similarity, homogeneous
sub-	在下、次于	subroutine, subscript
super-	在上、超	superconductor, superposition, superhighway
sym-, syn-	相同	symmetry, synchronous
tele-	远程的	telephone, telegraph, teletext
trans-	跨、移	transmitter, transverse, transform
ultra-	外、极、超	ultrasonic, ultraviolet
un-	不	unbiased, unavoidable, unstable
uni-, mono-	单一的	unicode, monochrome

表 1-2 表示数量关系的常用前缀

前缀	意义	词例
pico- (p)	10^{-12}	picofarad
nano- (n)	10^{-9}	nanometer
micro- (μ)	10^{-6}	microhenry
milli- (m)	10^{-3}	millisecond
kilo- (k)	10^{3}	kilogram
mega- (M)	10^{6}	megahertz
giga- (G)	10^{9}	gigabytes
semi-, hemi-	半	semiconductor, hemisphere
uni-, mono-	一	monotone, uniform
bi-, di-, ambi-, twi-	二	bilateral, diode, ambiguous, twilight
tri-	三	triangle, tripod
quad-	四	quadruple
oct-	八	octagon
deca-	十	decade
deci-	十分之一	decigram, decimeter
hecto-	一百	hectowatt, hectoampere

表 1-3 科技英语常用后缀

作用	后缀	意义	词例
名词	-ance, -acity, -acy, -ancy, -cy, -ence, -ency, -ality	表示情况、性质、状态、程度等	resistance, capacity, determinacy, accuracy, inference, efficiency, conditionality
	-age, -al	表示抽象概念,如性质、状态等	voltage, removal
	-er, -or	表示人或物	amplifier, conductor, researcher
	-graph	记录仪器	telegraph, spectrograph
	-ic (s)	学科、学术	logic, electronics
	-ion, -tion, -sion, -xion	表示动作及其过程、状态和结果	distribution, conclusion
	-ing		readings, recordings
	-logy	科目、某某学、某某论(法)	methodology
	-ist	表示人	scientist, specialist
	-(i) ty	表示性质、程度等	reliability, confidentiality
	-ment	表示动作、状态等	measurement, development
	-meter	计量仪器	spectrometer, telemeter
	-scope	探测仪器	telescope, spectroscope
	-ship, -th	表示动作、性质、状态	relationship, growth
	-ture	表示性质、状态等	mixture, temperature
	-ness	形容词变成名词要加的后缀	hardness, robustness
	-ure	表示动作、状态等	measure
	-ware	表示部件	hardware, freeware, software

（续）

作用	后缀	意义	词例
形容词	-able，-ible	表示可能性	differentiable，countable
	-(c)al，-ic(al)	表示性质，……的	statistical，atomic，typical
	-ant，-ent	表示状态、性质等	convergent，important，independent
	-ar(y)	与……有关的	circular，secondary
	-ed	已……的、被……的	reduced，treated，refined
	-en	表示……质（制）的	golden
	-ive	表示性质、状态等	objective，relative，effective
	-ish	表示稍微有点	reddish
	-ful	充满……的	plentiful，useful
	-less	没有、无……的	useless，countless
	-logical	表示……学的	technological
	-ory	表示性状	selfoscillatory
	-proof	抗…、防…	water-proof，shock-proof
	-ous	有……性质的	numerous，various
	-y	表示性状	handy
动词	-en	使变成……	harden，broaden
	-ize，-ise	使成为、……化	modernize，stabilize
	-fy	使成为、……化	classify，verify
副词	-ly	地、每……（一次）地	closely，likely，imperfectly
	-ward(s)	表示方向	backwards，upward(s)
	-wise	表示方式、方向	clockwise，likewise

表 1-4 科技英语常用词根

词根	意义	词例
audi	听、听见	audibility，audiphone
aut，auto	自己	automation，automaton
cid，cis	切、杀	incise，excide，bactericide
circ	环、圆	semicircle，circulate
chrom	颜色	photochrome，chromatron
chron	时间	synchronism，chronic
cycl	圆、轮形	bicycle，recycle
dict	说	predict，maledictory
duc，duct	引导	conduct，reduce
fact，fac	做	manufacture，facile
free	无	rustfree
fold	……倍、成……倍	threefold
gram	写、画，文字、图形	diagram，program
graph	同 gram	telegraph，biography
graphy	图像学	photography
gress	走、行	progress，retrogress，ingress

(续)

词根	意义	词例
hydr（o）	水	hydromechanics, hydraulic
mens	测量	measurable, commensuration
meter	仪器、仪表	thermometer
mini	小、少	minimize, diminish
ology	学（科）	biology, geology
pan, panto	全部、泛	panorama, Pan-American
pens, pend	悬挂	suspension, append
pel	推动、驱动	impeller, propel
phone	声音	telephone, microphone
port	携带、拿	portable, import, export
proof	防……	waterproof
rot	轮、转	rotate, rotor
son	声音	supersonic, resonator
scope	观测仪	telescope
tele	远	telecontrol, telemeter
therm（o）	热	thermoelectron
tight	密、不透	airtight
vis	见	revise, previse, television

1.3 科技英语中常用符号和数学式的表达

1. 常用希腊字母

α	alpha	π	pi
β	beta	σ	sigma
γ	gamma	τ	tau
δ	delta	φ	phi
ε	epsilon	ψ	psi
η	eta	ω	omega
θ	theta	λ	lambda
μ	mu		

2. 小数、分数、百分比

1/2	a (one) half	0.2	0 (nought, zero) point two
1/3	a (one) third	0.0032	0 point 0 0 three two
1/4	a (one) quarter	63.57	sixty-three point five seven
1/9	a (one) ninth	49%	49pc, forty-nine percent
2/3	two-thirds	5‰	five per mill (thousandth)
5/16	five-sixteenths	$2\frac{1}{2}$	two and a half

3. 一般数学符号
（1）基本符号

+	plus, positive	$\neq$	be not equal to
-	minus, negative	$\approx$	be approximately equal to
$\pm$；$\mp$	plus or minus; minus or plus	$\propto$	be in direct proportion to
$\times$；$\cdot$	multiplied by; times	$n!$	factorial n
$\div$；$-$；/	over, is to, divided by	$\because$	because
:	(proportion) e.g, $a:b$ a is to b, or the ratio of a to b	$\therefore$	therefore
		<	be less than
%	percent	>	be greater than
( )	parentheses; round brackets	$\geqslant$	be greater than or equal to
[ ]	square brackets	$\leqslant$	be less than or equal to
{ }	braces	$\not>$	be not greater than
=	be equal to, equals	$\not<$	be not less than

（2）特殊符号

$\rightarrow$	result in, lead to	$\perp$	be perpendicular to
&	and	$\circ$	degree
$\angle$	angle	$\iint$	double integral
$\equiv$	be equivalent to	$\iiint$	triple integral
$\sim$	be similar to	$\int\cdots\int$	n-fold integral of
£	pound	$\int_a^b$	integral between limits a and b
¥	yuan		
μP	microprocessor		
μC	microcomputer	#	number
″	inches, seconds		
//	be parallel to	$	dollar

4. 符号与方程

$a+b$	a and (plus) b
$a-b$	a minus b
ab	a times (multiplied by) b
a/b	a over (divided by) b
$a=b$	a equals (is equal to) b
$a\neq b$	a is not (is not equal to) b
$a\approx b$	a approximately equals b
$a>b$	a is greater than b
$a\leqslant b$	a is less than or equal to b
$x\rightarrow\infty$	x approaches infinity
$a\equiv b$	a is equivalent to b
$a\propto b$	a is proportional to b
$a:b$	a to b

（续）

$90°$	ninety degrees
$90℃$	ninety degrees Centigrated
$90℉$	ninety degrees Fahrenheit
x^2	x square (squared)
y^3	y cube (cubed)
z^{-10}	z to the minus tenth power
$\sqrt{x}$	the square root of x
$\sqrt[3]{x}$	the cube root of x
$\log_n x$	log x to the base n
$\log_{10} x$	log x to the base 10, common logarithm
$\log_e x$, $\ln x$	log x to the base e, natural logarithm, napierian logarithm
e^x, $\exp(x)$	exponential function of x, e to the power x
$x^{\frac{1}{n}}$, $\sqrt[n]{x}$	the nth root of x, x to the power one over n
$\sqrt{4}$	the square root of four
$\sqrt[3]{a}$	the cube root of a
$\sqrt[5]{a^2}$	the fifth root of a square
a'	a prime
a''	a double (second, twice) prime
a_1	a sub one
f'_c	f prime, sub c
$y = f(x)$	y is a function of x
sin	sine
cos	cosine
tg, tan	tangent
ctg, cot	cotangent
sc, sec	secant
csc, cosec	cosecant
$\sin^{-1}$, arcsin	antisine
$\cos^{-1}$, arccos	anticosine
sinh	the hyperbolic sine
cosh	the hyperbolic cosine
Σ	the summation of
$\sum_{i=1}^{n} x_i$	the summation of x sub i, where i goes from 1 to n
Π	the product of
$\prod_{i=1}^{n} x_i$	the product of x sub i, where i goes from 1 to n
$|x|$	the absolute value of x
$\bar{x}$	the mean value of x; x bar
Δ	finite difference or increment
Δx, δx	the increment of x
dx	dee x, dee of x; differential x

(续)

$\dfrac{\mathrm{d}y}{\mathrm{d}x}$	the differential coefficient of y with respect to x; the first derivative of y with respect of x
$\dfrac{\mathrm{d}^2 y}{\mathrm{d}x^2}$	the second derivative of y with respect of x
$\dfrac{\mathrm{d}^n y}{\mathrm{d}x^n}$	the nth derivative of y with respect of x
$\dfrac{\partial y}{\partial u}$	the partial derivative of y with respect of u, where y is a function of u and another variable (or variables)
$\boldsymbol{F}$	vector $\boldsymbol{F}$
$E = \dfrac{p/a}{e/l} = \dfrac{pl}{ae}$	big E is equal to the ratio of p divided by a to e divided by l, is equal to the ratio of the product pl to the product ae
$M = R_1 x - P_1(x - a_1)$	M is equal to R sub one multiplied by x minus P sub one, round brackets opened x minus a sub one, round brackets closed
$b = \dfrac{1}{2} p \cdot \sec \dfrac{1}{2}\beta$	b equals half p secant half beta
$R = \sqrt{(\sum Px)^2 + (\sum Py)^2}$	R equals the square root of sigma Px all squared, plus sigma Py all squared
$1 \text{ rad} = \dfrac{180°}{\pi} \approx 57.3°$	one radian equals one hundred and eighty degrees divided by pi, which is approximately equal to fifty-seven point three degrees
$\displaystyle\int \dfrac{\mathrm{d}y}{\sqrt{c^2 - y^2}}$	the integral of $\mathrm{d}y$ over (by) the square root out of c squared minus y squared

5. 基本函数式

$a^2 - b^2 = (a+b)(a-b)$	a squared minus b squared equals open parenthesis a plus b close parenthesis times open parenthesis a minus b close parenthesis
$\dfrac{x+1}{x^2(x^3-4)^{2/3}}$	x plus one over the quantity x squared times the quantity x cubed minus four to the two-thirds power
$\displaystyle\lim_{n \to \infty} \dfrac{1}{n^2}(1 + 2 + \cdots + n)$	the limit as n approaches infinity of the quantity one over n squared times one plus two plus to plus n
$\dfrac{1}{2}\{a[b+(c-d)]\}$	one half open brace, a open bracket b plus open parenthesis c minus d close parenthesis close bracket close brace
$\displaystyle\sum_{n=1}^{5} a_n b_n \cos\left(\dfrac{n\omega}{2\pi}\right)$	capital sigma the quantity a sub n times b sub n times the cosine of n time omega over 2 times pi from n equals one to n equals five
$\displaystyle\prod_{n=1}^{\infty} a_n$	product of all a_n from n equals one to infinity
$\max(a_1, a_2, \cdots, a_n), \min(a_1, a_2, \cdots, a_n)$	maximum/minimum value of the series a sub one to a sub n
$\displaystyle\lim_{n \to \infty}\left(1 + \dfrac{1}{n}\right)^n = e$	limit as n approaches infinity of the quantity of one plus one over n to the nth power equals e
$\displaystyle\lim_{n \to \infty} \text{squa}\, a_n, \ \lim_{n \to \infty} \text{inf}\, a_n$	upper/lower limit of a sub n as n approaches/tends to infinity
$y' = -1/x^n$	y prime equals minus one over x to the nth power, the first derivative of y with respect to x equals minus one over x to the nth power

（续）

$\dfrac{d^2 y}{dx^2} = a^2 e^{-ax}$	the second derivative of *y* with respect to *x* equals *a* squared times e to the power of minus *a* times *x*
$\displaystyle\int \dfrac{a}{x-a} dx = a\log\|x-a\| + c$	the indefinite integral of the quantity *a* over *x* minus *a* with respect to *x* equals *a* times the quantity logarithm of the absolute value of *x* minus *a* plus *c*
$\displaystyle\int_0^{\frac{\pi}{2}} \dfrac{dx}{1+a\cos x}$	the integral from 0 to pi over two of the quantity one over one plus *a* times cosine of *x* with respect to *x*
$a^{-m/n} = 1/\sqrt[n]{a^m}$ （$a>0$, m, n 均为正整数）	*a* to the minus *m* over *n* power equals one over the *n*th root of *a* to the *m*th power, where *a* is greater than zero, and *m* and *n* are both positive numbers
$f(x) = 1 + \ln(x-2)$	the function of *x* equals one plus log the quantity *x* minus 2 to the base e
$\sin 3x = 3\sin x - 4\sin^3 x$	the sine of three *x* is equivalent to three times sine of *x* minus four times the quantity sine *x* cubed

1.4 科技英语的翻译

1.4.1 词汇的翻译

科技英语（English for Science and Technology，EST）是从事科学技术活动时所使用的英语，是英语的一种变体（科技文体）。科技英语自20世纪70年代以来引起了人们的广泛关注和研究，目前已发展成为一种重要的英语语体。科技英语词汇的特点是词义繁多，专业性强，在科技英语的学习过程中，我们需要把科技文体中的专业术语翻译成相应的汉语词语，翻译时必须根据专业内容谨慎处理，稍不注意就会造成很大的错误。

科技英语词汇包含大量的科技术语，科技术语是指科学技术领域里确定某个观点、概念时所使用的专门语汇。科技术语包含两层含义：字面含义（literal meaning）与学术含义（scientific meaning）。我们在阅读科技文章的过程中必须兼顾其字面含义与学术含义。

科技术语的概念与其相应学科或相应领域的整个概念系统彼此联系，并受其限定。一般认为，术语的选定可以概括为以下几条原则：准确性、一义性、系统性、简明性、稳定性和理据性。

1.4.1.1 科技术语的分类

科技术语通过渗透、派生、转变等途径产生大量的新词汇，这是它的一大显著特征。根据科技英语与普通英语的不同特点，可以将科技术语分为以下三类。

1. 纯科技或专业词（technical words）

这类词汇的使用范围局限于某些专业，例如 chlorophyll（叶绿素）、photosynthesis（光合作用）局限于植物学，motivator（操纵机构、操纵装置）、motor armature（电动机电枢）局限于机械学，而 chloromycetin（氯霉素）和 diuretic（利尿剂）则局限于药物学。就科技文章而言，专业词汇的使用率远在通用词汇和半专业词汇之下。过去人们往往存在一个误区，认为科技英语中的词汇主要为专业词汇，事实上通用词汇占第一位，半专业词汇占第二位，而专业词汇（专业术语）占第三位。由于绝大多数的专业词汇为单义词，使用范围狭窄，与其他词汇相比，在科技文章中出现的频率也较低，而且从翻译和学习的角度来说，也并非重点，因此在一般的翻译中不存在选择词义的困难，误译较少。对非专业学生来说，这些词乍看起来很麻烦，但实际上它们大部分是国际通用的，有统一、专门定义的名词。对于这种词汇，我们只须查出汉语对应的词汇以帮助理解课文，无须过多记忆，因为在将来的阅读翻译过程中遇到这类词完全可借助科技或专业辞典予以解决。不过，对一些各学科都常用的词，如 oxidation（氧化）、insulator（绝缘体）等，还是应当记一些，起码做到碰到认识，省得总查字典。

2. 半科技或半专业词（semi-scientific or semi-technical words）

半专业词是由普通词转化而来的，除了本身的一般词义外，在不同的学科中具有不同的专业词义。以 pencil 为例，在通用英语中它的词义为"铅笔"，但在光学中它的词义则为"光线锥""射束"，在热学中 colour pencil 为"测温色笔"，在机械专业中 metal pencil 为"焊条"，在气象学中 pencil rocket 则为"（高空气象观测用的）小型火箭"。再以动词 dress 为例，它的通用词义为"穿衣"，但在医学上为"包扎"，在农业上为"整地"，在矿冶方面为"选（矿）"。正因为许多普通英语中常用的单词在科技英语中因不同的专业、不同的搭配有不同的意思，这些词看似熟悉，却很麻烦，应认真对待，不可望文生义。在学习过程中，应尽可能多地了解其常见搭配，并结合单词本义进行联想，以区分其含义。

3. 科技用语（phraseology of science）

与日常英语相比，科技文章由于其严肃性及权威性的学术要求，常使用较正式的单词和习语。例如，不用 begin、spread、helpful、get rid of，而用 commence、propagate、conducive、obviate 等。这些词不像纯科技词那样为单一定义的名词，而是包括各种词类。许多词根据上下文有不同的意思，用法复杂多样，且拼法生僻难记，对学生来说是最难掌握的。例如，propagate 在下列两种语境中由于意思不同，用法就不同：①Trees propagate themselves by seeds. 树木靠种子繁衍；②Sound is propagated by vibrations. 声音是通过振动传送的。

1.4.1.2 科技英语词汇的翻译方法

随着科技的迅猛发展和信息的广泛交流，科技英语的翻译（尤其是科技英语词汇的翻译）越来越受到人们的重视。科技英语翻译的确存在着许多不同于一般英语翻译的方面，例如，同是 element 一词，一般英语译作"要素""成分"，但在化学中译作"元素"，在无线电学中译作"元件"等。这是科技英语词汇翻译的一个特点——专业性。又例如下面一个句子：Heat-treatment issued to normalize, to soften or to harden steels. 如果按一般字面翻译直译为"热处理被用来使钢正常化、软化或硬化"，实在令人费解。此句正确的译法应该是"热处理可用来对钢正火、退火和淬火"。因此，科技英语翻译必须讲究专业性，只有通过学习普通英语词汇的专业化译法才能把科技英语翻译得更科学、更严密、更完整。

翻译是一个理解与表达的过程，科技英语翻译也是如此。科技英语翻译的表达方法主要有直译和意译两种。

所谓直译，就是直接译出词汇所指的意义。科技英语翻译中大量使用的就是直译这种方法。但有的科技英语词汇却必须采用意译。意译通常使用的方法有推演（deduction）、引申（extension）和解释（explanation）等。直译的方法有移植译（transplant）、音译（transliteration）和象形译（pictographic translation）等。具体方法论述如下。

1. 音译（transliteration）

专有名词（如人名、地名等）通常采用音译法。此外，有些词在汉语中没有确切的对等译词，按照意译又比较费劲时，就只好借助于音译。这些词如新材料、药名、缩略词等等。例如，clone（克隆）、hacker（黑客）、nylon（尼龙）、aspirin（阿司匹林）、radar（雷达）等，这些词都是按音译进行翻译的。也有一些词是部分音译的，例如 topology（拓扑学）、Hellfire "海尔法"导弹等。

2. 象形译（pictographic translation）

所谓象形译实际上就是根据物体的形状进行翻译。例如，H-beam（工字架）、V-belt（三角带）、cross-bit（十字钻头）、twist drill（麻花钻）、U-steel（槽钢）、U-shaped magnet（马蹄形磁铁）等。象形译强调汉语"形象"比喻的习惯，将 V-belt 中的"V"译成"三角"。因为汉语中没有使用"V"表示物体形状的习惯。形译则不然，它照抄原文。例如，L-electron 译成"L 层电子"、γ-ray 译成"γ射线"、FORTRAN 译成"FORTRAN 语言"等。

3. 推演（deduction）

推演的词义是根据原文本或原文词典中的意思进行概括，推演出汉语的译义。译文不仅包含原词的字面意义，还必须概括出词语所指事物的基本特征。如 space shuttle 一词，如果按照移植的方法将其译成"太空穿梭机"显然不妥，很容易引起误解。其实，这里的 space 指的是 aerospace（航天），shuttle 指往返于太空与地球之间的形状像飞机的交通工具。因此，将 space shuttle 推演译成"航天飞机"。这种用推演法译出的词语更直观易懂，因此也更容易使人接受。推演法使用得当便能译出高质量的译文，这就要求译者不仅要有较好的专业基础知识，还必须具备两种语言的良好修养。

4. 引申（extension）

所谓引申就是在不脱离原文的基础上，运用延续与扩展的方法译出原文。通常的做法是：①将具体所指引向抽象泛指，如 brain，具体词义是"大脑"，抽象意义指"智力"，brain-trust 则可以引申为"智囊团"；②将抽象泛指引向具体所指，如 qualification，抽象泛指"鉴定"，具体可以指"通过鉴定所具备的条件"，因此 data qualification 可以引申为"数据限制条件"。

5. 解释（explanation）

若某个词用上述方法都难译好，则可采用解释法，即用汉语说出英语原文的意思而不必给出其汉语的对等词。如 blood type 可译为"血型"、blood bank 可译成"血库"。但 blood heat 却不能译成"血热"，用其他方法又很难译出其准确含义，此时可借用解释法，将其译成"人体血液的正常温度"。这一方法大多用于个别初次出现而意义比较抽象、含义比较深刻的名词或术语。

6. 形译

为了形象化，科技术语中常采用外文字母或英语单词来描述某种与技术有关的形象。翻译时可以将该外文字母照抄、改译为字形或概念相近的汉字，这种用字母或汉字来表达形状的翻译方法称为形译法。形译法可细分为以下三种：第一种保留原字母不译，如 O-ring（O 形圈）、S-turning（S 形弯道）、X-ray（X 射线）、A-bedplate（A 形底座）；第二种用汉语形象相似的词来译，如 steel I-beam（工字钢梁）、T-bolt（T 字螺栓）、O-ring（环形圈）、L-square（直角尺）；第三种用能表达其形象的词来译，如 U-bolt（马蹄螺栓）、V-belt（三角带）、T-bend（三通接头）、twist drill（麻花钻）。

7. 移植译（transplant）

移植译就是按词典里所给的词义将词的各个词素的意义依次译出。翻译派生词和复合词时多采用这种方法，如 microwave（微波）、information superhighway（信息高速公路）、magneto-hydrodynamics（磁流体力学）。这些专业词语比较长且复杂，往往是由一些基本的科技英语词素组合成的，因而大多采用移植译法。

1.4.1.3 复合词与缩略词

大量使用复合词与缩略词是科技文章的特点之一，复合词从过去的双词组合发展到多词组合；缩略词趋向于任意构词，用单词的第一个字母代表一个词组的缩略词，就叫作首字母缩略词。在科技英语中使用复合词与缩略词十分常见，下面列举出其中一部分，供读者参考。

1. 复合词

anti-armoured-fighting-vehicle-missile 反装甲车导弹（多词合成名词）
colorimeter 色度计（无连字符复合词）
cpd（compound）化合物
criss-cross 纵横交错（双词合成副词）
feed-back 反馈（双词合成名词）
FM（Frequency Modulation）调频（用首字母组成的缩略词）
ft（foot/feet）英尺
full-enclosed 全封闭的（双词合成形容词）
lab（laboratory）实验室
maths（mathematics）数学（裁减式缩略词）
on-and-off-the-road 路面/越野两用的（多词合成形容词）
P.S.I.（Pounds per Square Inch）磅/英寸
radiophotography 无线电传真（无连字符复合词）
SCR（Silicon Controlled Rectifier）可控硅整流器
TELESAT（TELEcommunications SATellite）通信卫星（混成法构成的缩略词）
work-harden 加工硬化（双词合成词）

2. 缩略词

ATM（Automatic Teller Machine）自动柜员机，又称自动取款机
BBS（Bulletin Board System）公告牌系统或电子公告板
BSS（Base Station System）基站系统，指移动通信中的空中接口部分
CATV（Cable Television）有线电视
CBD（Central Business District）中央商务区
CD-ROM（Compact Disk Read Only Memory）光盘只读存储器，即光驱
CEO（Chief Executive Officer）首席执行官
CPU（Central Processing Unit）中央处理器
DDN（Digital Data Network）数字数据网
DOS（Disk Operating System）磁盘操作系统
E-mail 电子邮件
GSM（Global System for Mobile communications）全球移动通信系统
HDTV（High Definition Television）高清晰度电视
HTTP（Hyper-Text Transfer Protocol）超文本传输协议
ISDN（Integrated Service Digital Network）综合业务数字网
ISO（International Organization for Standardization）国际标准化组织
MODEM（Modulator Demodulator）调制解调器
MS（Mobile Station）移动终端
MSC（Mobile Switch Center）移动交换中心

PDA（Personal Digital Assistant）个人数字助理
USB（Universal Serial Bus）通用串口总线

1.4.2 句子的翻译

由于专业英语专业性强，逻辑性强，注重客观事实和真理，表达要求准确、精练、正式，因此，正确地理解并翻译专业英语文章中的句子，并原汁原味地用汉语表达，除了要求我们熟练地运用汉语表达方式以外，还要求我们具有一定的专业水平。在句子翻译方面，我们要注意的是：在科技英语中有很多内容都由长句表示，在翻译长句时，不要因为句子太长而产生畏惧心理，因为无论句子多么复杂，它都是由一些基本的成分组成的。然后，要弄清楚英语原文的句法结构，找出整个句子的中心内容及各层意思，然后分析几层意思之间的相互逻辑关系，再按照汉语的特点和表达方式，正确地译出原文的意思，不必拘泥原文的形式。

虽然学好专业英语不是一件很容易的事情，但只要我们在学习专业英语时，能注意科技英语词汇、句法专业性强的特点，在我们原有的英语基础上，经过一定的专业英语训练，我们就能掌握专业英语的学习方法，提高我们阅读科技文章的理解能力和翻译能力。

1.4.2.1 谓语的译法

1. 直译

Voltage regulating devices maintains the voltage at receiving end within permissible limits.
电压调整装置保持接收端的电压在允许值内。

In machining, grinding processes are most often used as finish machining processes.
磨光法是机加工中最常用的精加工方法。

2. 谓语转译为主语

在翻译科技英语时，为了使疑问符合汉语的表达习惯，谓语除了仍然要译成谓语外，还可以把谓语动词译为汉语句子的主语，而原英文句子中的主语被转译成了汉语句子的定语，并常常译为"是……的"句型，这一点已在主语的译法部分有所阐述。如：

Compression formats are devised to greatly reduce file size, yet retain acceptable quality.
压缩格式的设计是为了大幅度减少文件所占用的空间，同时又维持可接受的质量。

Using a person's voice as an identifier is based on the fact that the geometry of the vocal tract differs greatly from person to person.
利用人的语音来验明身份的依据是每个人声道的几何形状大不相同。

3. 谓语转译为宾语

The power supply for the fire alarm system should be backed up by the emergency generator.
系统的供电应由应急发电机作为备用电源。

The tensile strengths vary tremendously with wire size.
拉抗强度随簧丝尺度的不同而发生显著的变化。

4. 谓语转译为定语或状语

More metal is removed when the feed is increased.
当进给量增加时，切除的金属更多。（转译为定语）

The speech synthesis process typically begins with recording a human voice and analyzing it to extract important frequency and amplitude data.
言语合成过程一般是先记录人的说话声并通过分析获得重要的频率和振幅数据。（转译为状语）

5. 谓语省译

Generators used in production have no bar magnets. Instead electromagnets are used.

生产上用的发电机不用条形磁铁，取而代之的是电磁铁。（省译了 are used）

The magnitude of the force is found to be inversely proportional to the distance between the conductors.

力的大小与导体间的距离成反比。（省译了 is found）

The alpha rays proved to be charged electrically with a positive charge.

α射线原来是带有正电荷的。（省译了 proved）

1.4.2.2 表语的译法

由于英语中名词、代词、数词、副词、动名词和不定式等都可以作表语，而且英汉两种语言表达方式存在差异，因此表语的汉译产生了如下不同的译法。

1. 直译

所谓直译，就是按照原句子系表结构的词语顺序进行翻译，表语大都译为"是"。如：

The feed to the shaft furnace is lump ore, sinter, or pellets, all preferably less than 64mm in diameter.

加入竖炉中的矿石可以是块矿、烧结矿或团矿，它们的直径最好小于64mm。

The odometer is mechanical, driven by a stepper motor.

里程表是机动的，由步进电机带动。

The purpose of the radiator is to get rid of heat from the engine.

散热器的用途是排放发动机产生的热。

2. 转译为主语

英语句子的主语有时可以转译为汉语的定语，在这种情况下，原句子的表语往往可以转译为汉语的主语，如果作表语的为形容词，则该形容词同时转译成名词。如：

The rotor is a well-designed structure consisting of a laminated core containing a winding.

转子的结构设计得很好，它由一个叠片铁心组成，铁心上面绕着线圈。

3. 主表倒译

顾名思义，所谓的主表倒译，就是把主语译成表语，把表语译成主语。常见的主表倒译有两种情况。

1）当名词作表语时，主语和表语表达的内容往往是一致的。这时为了符合汉语的修辞习惯，英语句子的表语常常被译为汉语的主语，同时，英语句子的主语被转译成汉语的表语。如：

Methane is the chief constituent in natural gas, and it is formed as a by-product in the petroleum industry.

天然气的主要组成成分是甲烷，它是石油工业的一种副产品。

Aerodynamics is my field of research.

我的研究领域是空气动力学。

2）第二种类型的主表倒译，通常是用来翻译 It+be+表语+主语从句或不定式短语句型的，也就是将作真正主语的从句或动词不定式译成表语，原表语译成主语。如：

It is note worthy that small as atoms are, they contain vast amounts of energy.

值得注意的是原子虽小，却具有很大的能量。（主语从句转译为表语）

It is desirable to use large units for measurement of large quantities and small units for small quantities.

最好使用大的单位来测量大的量值，使用小的单位来测量小的量值。（不定式短语作主语转译为表语）

4. 转译为谓语

在系表结构的句子中，如果表语是含有动作意义的形容词、副词或介词短语，则翻译时系词可以不译，把原句的表语直接译为汉语的谓语。如：

When the switch is on, the circuit is closed and electricity goes through.

将开关合上，电路就闭合，电也就接通了。（介词作表语转译为谓语）

5. 转译为宾语

当谈及某物质的特性时，英语常用系表结构的句型来表达，其中表语通常为形容词或 of+名词结构。这时，系词 be 可译为"具有""属于"等动词，作表语的形容词或作表语的 of+名词结构则转译为名词，在译文中作句子的宾语。如：

Cutting tools must be strong, hard, tough, and wear resistant.

刀具必须有足够的强度、硬度、韧性和耐磨性。

The early steam engines were of the piston-type.

早期的蒸汽机属于活塞型。

6. 转译为定语

如果形容词作表语且句子主语有定语的修饰，则翻译时为使译文自然、通顺，常常可以把表语转译为定语。如：

In this air mechanics laboratory, few instruments are valuable.

在这个空气动力学实验室里，贵重的仪器不多。

In this book, many theories are very important.

在这本书中，重要的理论很多。

1.4.2.3 宾语的译法

1. 直译

原句的宾语仍然译为汉语句子的宾语。如：

Hand forging tools comprise variously shaped hammers.

手锻工具包括各种形状的锻锤。

Heat used to melt a solid is called melting heat.

用于熔化固体的热叫作熔化热。

2. 译成汉语的主语

英语中的宾语在翻译时译为主语有两种情况。

1) have 作谓语的句子常常把 have 的宾语译成主语，把原句的主语转译为定语，整个句子通常译成系表结构，而 have 本身则省译。如：

Different metals have different coefficients of expansion.

各种金属的膨胀系数都不同。

Instructions and microinstructions do not have the same format.

指令和微指令的格式不同。

2) 在很多情况下，英语句子中介词的宾语可以转译为汉语的主语，这时英语的介词常略去不译。这在科技英语翻译中尤为常见。如：

The spores are very small and light in mass.

孢子很小且质量很轻。

Another type of lens is thinner in the middle than at the edges, and is known as a concave lens.

另一种透镜的中间比边缘薄一些，称为凹透镜。

Microwave electronic components and sub-systems are encountered during the development of systems such as those mentioned.

开发上述系统会遇到微波电子部件和子系统。

3. 译成汉语的谓语

如果英语句子的宾语（包括介词宾语）是由动词派生词或具有动词意义的名词，在翻译时可将宾语转译成汉语的谓语，原来修饰宾语的形容词可以转译为修饰谓语的状语。如：

Each organism owes its existence to genes it contains.

每个生物有机体因其含有基因而存在。

In selecting a material, the engineer must have a knowledge not only of what the material's properties are, but also of how they are determined.

在选择材料时，工程师不仅要知道材料的性能是什么，而且要知道性能是怎样测定的。

1.4.2.4 定语的译法

1. 顺译

定语的顺译同样按照词语顺序，将定语译为汉语的定语，单个的词作定语常采用此种译法。如：

The seeds of plants contain a small undeveloped plant, the embryo.

植物的种子里包含一个尚未发育的小植物体——胚芽。

The low-frequency motions are considered to be meteorologically significant.

低频运动在气象学上是很重要的。

2. 倒译

在英语中，当短语（包括介词短语、不定式短语、分词短语等）作定语时，往往把它放在被修饰词的后面。在翻译时可采取倒译法，先翻译后置的定语部分，再翻译被后置定语修饰的名词。如：

The equation for this chemical reaction is the reverse of one we have just been studying.

这个化学反应的反应式是刚才所讨论的反应式的逆转。（介词短语作后置定语）

The gas to be studied is admitted to the tube at a known temperature and at atmospheric pressure.

被研究的气体在已知温度和大气压力下充入管中。（不定式短语作后置定语）

The energy not consumed in the system will be stored up in the form of potential energy.

系统未消耗的能量将以势能的形式存储起来。（分词短语作后置定语）

3. 转译为主语

在 there be 句型中，如果主语后面有介词 of 引出的定语，在翻译时常常把 of 引出的定语译成汉语的主语。如：

There are many sizes of computers.

计算机有很多尺寸。

There are two kinds of video capture devices, analog and digital wares.

视频采集设备有两种，模拟采集设备和数字采集设备。

There are three states of matter: solid, liquid and gas.

物质有三态：固态、液态和气态。

4. 转译为谓语

1）当形容词作定语且句子的谓语是 have 等时，为了使译文更加明确、通顺，在翻译时常常把定语译成汉语句子的谓语。如：

A synchronous motor usually has a higher efficiency than that of a comparable induction motor.

通常，同步电动机的效率比相应的感应电动机的效率高。

2）在 there be 结构的句子中，如果主语后面有分词短语作定语，在翻译时可将作定语的分词短语译成汉语句子的谓语。如：

There are only two important chemical reactions involved in the combustion of any fuel, be it coal, wood, oil or gas.

任何燃烧的过程只包含两种重要的化学反应，不论燃烧材料是煤、木材、油还是煤气。

There is a board range of research interests in the department, including both traditional and emerging areas of chemical engineering.

该系的研究课题广泛，涉及化学工程的传统领域和新兴领域。

There has been no case of malaria found in this region for ten years.

这个地区已经十年没有发现疟疾的病例。

1.4.2.5 状语的译法

状语用来修饰动词、形容词和副词。英语中副词、介词、名词短语、不定式短语等都可以作状语。英语状语的译法主要有以下几种。

1. 直译

原句中的状语译成汉语的状语，可视情况在语序上进行个别调整。如：

The charge passes at the uniform rate.

电荷匀速通过。

The heat loss can be considerably reduced by the use of firebricks round the walls of the boiler.

用耐火砖包住锅炉壁可以大大减少热损失。

2. 转译为主语

英语中许多作状语的介词短语，在翻译时可译为汉语句子的主语，而介词本身则省译。如：

At this critical temperature, changes begin to take place in the molecular structure of the metal.

在这种临界温度，金属的分子结构开始发生变化。

Various types of standardized bearings are manufactured at the factory.

工厂生产各种不同类型的标准化轴承。

3. 转译为定语

英语中有许多介词短语（in 引导的介词短语最常见），从形式上看是状语，但意义上与句子中的某个名词关系密切，具有修饰或被修饰的关系。汉译时，这样的介词短语常可译为某个名词的定语。如：

In larger amounts, ozone is unpleasant with strong odor that irritates the eyes and lungs.

大量的臭氧都带有一种让人不舒服的强烈气味，对眼睛及肺有刺激作用。

1.4.3 词性转换翻译

英语和汉语最大的区别之一是英语讲究词性。英语中的词可分为十大词类（parts of speech），其中和词类转译密切相关的有名词、形容词、动词、副词、介词、冠词等。词性转换是专业英语翻译中常用的翻译方法。一般地说，英汉词性转换有一定规律，比如英语比较喜欢多用名词和介词，而汉语则是动词用得多一些。现将几个关键的词性转移问题列举如下。

词性转换几乎可以在所有词性间进行，如名词转换成动词，动词转换成名词，介词转换成动词，副词转换成动词，名词转换成形容词等。

1.4.3.1 转译成动词

1. 名词转译成动词

英语中有大量由动词派生的名词和具有动作意义的名词以及其他名词可转译成汉语动词。如：

Rockets have found application in the exploration of the universe.

火箭已经用来探索宇宙。

The sight and sound of our jet planes filled me with special longing.

看到我们的喷气式飞机，听见隆隆的机声，令我特别神往。

He has no knowledge of how electricity is generated.

他不知道电是如何产生的。

An acquaintance with world history is helpful to the study of current affairs.

读一点世界史对研究时事是有帮助的。

A careful study of the original text will give you a better translation.

仔细研究原文，你会翻译得更好。

The discovery of a new dish does more for the happiness of mankind than the discovery of a new star.

发明一道新菜要比发现一颗新星对人类幸福贡献更大。

There has been a tremendous expansion of nurseries and kindergartens in both town and villages.

在城市和乡村，托儿所和幼儿园都在大量地增加。

2. 介词和介词短语转译成动词

英语中介词的使用频率相对于汉语来说要高得多。实际上，英语中很多介词在语境中可带有明显的动作意味，例如across、against、past、toward、through、with等。因此在翻译的过程中为了汉语表达的通顺流畅，可以根据具体情况将一些介词转译为动词。如：

I found him at his book when I came into the room.

我走进房间，看见他正在看书。

The road to development is long but we are firmly on it.

发展的道路是漫长的，但是我们已经坚定地走上这条道路。

This proposal was against the spirit of group.

这个提议违背了集体主义精神。

3. 形容词转译成动词

英语中的形容词常常与系动词搭配构成"系表结构"。"系表结构"作谓语，从而使这些形容词具有了动作意味，翻译时需要转换为动词。这些形容词常常是表示知觉、情感、欲望等心理状态的形容词，常见的有：

1）与思维和知觉相关的形容词：aware、conscious、certain、sure、mindful、ignorant、alert等。

2）与情感相关的形容词：glad、pleased、cautious、careful、angry、happy、exhilarated、excited、confident、thankful、grateful、concerned、eager、afraid、doubtful、sorry等。

3）与欲望相关的形容词：desirous、hopeful、anxious、keen、enthusiastic、zealous等。

Scientists are confident that all matter is indestructible.

科学家们都深信,所有的物质都是不灭的。

We are not content with our present achievements.

我们不满足于我们现有的成就。

This solution is not acceptable.

这个解决办法无法让人接受。

4. 副词转译成动词

在英语中,副词常常用来修饰动词作状语,这样使得副词具有了动作意味。所以,副词也可以作为汉语的动词来翻译。如:

After careful investigation they found the design behind.

经过仔细研究之后,他们发现这个设计落后了。

Sorry I wasn't in when you rang me up.

很抱歉,你打电话来时,我不在。

She opened the window to let fresh air in.

她把窗子打开,让新鲜空气进来。

1.4.3.2 转译成名词

1. 动词转译成名词

英语中很多由名词派生的动词,以及由名词转用的动词,在汉语中往往不易找到相应的动词,这时可将其转译成汉语名词。如:

To them, he personified the absolute power.

在他们看来,他就是绝对权威的化身。

This kind of behavior characterizes the criminal mind.

这种举止是罪犯的心理特征。

Most U.S. spy satellites are designed to burn up in the earth's atmosphere after completing their missions.

美国绝大多数间谍卫星,按其设计,在完成使命后会在大气层中焚毁。

The electron weighs about 1/1850 as much as atom of hydrogen.

电子的重量约为氢原子的 1/1850。

2. 形容词转译成名词

1) 英语中有些形容词加上定冠词表示某一类人,汉译时常译成名词。如:

They are going to build a school for the blind and the deaf.

他们将为盲人和聋人修建一所学校。

Both compounds are acids, the former is strong and the latter is weak.

这两种都是酸,前者是强酸,后者是弱酸。

2) 有时候根据情况,可以灵活处理,把有些形容词转换成名词来翻译。如:

He was eloquent and elegant—but soft.

他有口才、有风度,但性格软弱。

They showed a sympathetic understanding of our problem.

他们对我们的问题表示同情和理解。

3. 副词转译成名词

It is officially announced that China has successfully launched her first manned spaceship.

官方宣布，中国已经成功地实现了载人航天。
He is physically weak but mentally sound.
他身体虽弱，但精神很好。

1.4.3.3 转译成形容词

1. 名词转译成形容词

1）形容词派生的名词往往可以转译成形容词。如：

This issue is of vital importance.

这个问题至关重要。

The pallor of her face indicated clearly how she was feeling at the moment.

她苍白的脸色清楚地表明了她那时的情绪。

2）当有些名词加不定冠词作表语时，往往要转译成形容词。如：

The music is a gas.

这音乐妙极了。

Independent thinking is an absolute necessity in study.

独立思考对学习是绝对必须的。

2. 副词转译成形容词

由于英语中的动词在翻译时可以转换成汉语名词，因此修饰该动词的副词往往转译成形容词。如：

He was deeply impressed by what they did in the critical moment.

他们在关键时刻的行为给他留下了深刻的印象。

The President had prepared meticulously for his journey.

总统为这次出访做了十分周密的准备。

1.4.3.4 转译成副词

1. 形容词转译成副词

由于英语中的名词在翻译时可以转换成汉语动词，因此修饰该名词的形容词往往转译成汉语副词。如：

We must make full use of existing technical equipment.

我们必须充分地利用现有的技术设备。

At last, he whispered a hurried good-bye to his host and darted toward the door.

最后，他匆匆地向主人轻声道别，大步地走向门口。

2. 名词转译成副词

I had the fortune to meet him.

我幸运地遇到了他。

When he catches a glimpse of a potential antagonist, his instinct is to win him over with charm and humor.

只要一发现有可能反对他的人，他就本能地要用他的魅力和风趣将这人争取过来。

1.4.4 实例练习

eg. 1 Both CW and pulse modulation may be classed as analog modulation.

译文：连续波调制和脉冲调制都归类于模拟调制。

这里"*modulation*"重复多次。

eg. 2   I had experienced oxygen and /or engine <u>trouble</u>.

译文：有可能是氧气设备或引擎出故障，或两者都出故障。

在英文原文的表述中，能够清楚地由"*trouble*"这一个词将"麻烦"表达清楚，而在翻译过程中，为了能够将译文含义描述清晰，就多次重复了"故障"。但译文并不拖沓、烦琐。

eg. 3   Under ordinary conditions of pressure, water <u>becomes</u> ice at 0℃ and steam at 100℃.

译文：在常压下，水在0℃时变成冰，在100℃时变成蒸汽。

增加了动词"变成"，使句子的含义更加明确。

eg. 4   While stars and nebulae look like <u>specks</u> or small patches of light, they are really enormous bodies.

译文：星星和星云看起来只是斑斑点点，或者是小片的光，但它们确实是巨大的天体。

用"斑斑点点"来描述"天体"的小，更符合汉语的思维。

eg. 5   The <u>pure scientists</u> study phenomena in the universe.

译文：从事理论研究的科学家研究宇宙中的各种现象。

不可译为"纯的科学家"。

eg. 6   The major <u>contributors</u> in component technology have been in the semi-conductors.

译文：半导体元件是很重要的电子元件。

eg. 7   To <u>achieve</u> its function, a video amplifier must operate over a wide band and amplify all frequencies equally and with low distortion.

译文：为了实现这一功能，视频放大器就必须在宽频带、能够对所有频率进行同样的放大且失真很小的环境下运行。

"*achieve*"的原意是"达到"，在这里引申为"实现"，是为了和后面的"功能"相搭配。

eg. 8   Oscillators are used to produce audio and radio signals for a wide variety of <u>purposes</u>.

译文：振荡器用于产生音频和视频信号，用途广泛。

"*purposes*"是"目的"的意思，这里引申为"用途"更为贴切。

eg. 9   This CD-ROM feature over 100 applets for you to learn from the <u>master</u>.

译文：此光盘提供了一百多个程序，供你向专家学习。

"*master*"原意是"主人"，这里为版权所有者，译为"专家"。

eg. 10   The instrument is used to <u>determine</u> how fully the batteries are charged.

译文：这种仪表用来测定电池充电的程度。

本句中的"*determine*"一词译作"确定"不符合专业规范，而应译为"测定"。

eg. 11   Then hundreds of years from now, billions and billions of miles away, the embryos will be thawed and their hearts will start beating. These <u>space-farers</u> of the future will not grow inside a mother's body but will be incubated in a machine.

译文：几百年后，在距离地球数十亿英里处，冷冻的胚胎将会解冻，胎儿的心脏便开始跳动。这些未来的太空旅人，并非在母体内孕育，而是在机器中孵育。

eg. 12   If <u>you</u> know the frequency, <u>you</u> can find the wave length.

译文：如果知道频率，就可求出波长。

这里省略了两个"*you*"，译文简洁明了。

eg. 13   If <u>we</u> should select some sample function $n(t)$, <u>we</u> could not predict the value attained by that same sample function at the time $t+\tau$ with the help of $n(t)$.

译文：即使某样本函数 $n(t)$ 已知，该函数在 $t+\tau$ 时刻的值也不能由 t 时刻的值预测。

这里主从句中都有"we"，在翻译时若将二者都译出，则显重复。

eg. 14 Throughout this text we shall assume that the random processes with which we shall have occasion to deal are ergodic.

译文：在整篇文章中，我们假定要研究的随机过程均为各态历经过程。

本句中介词"with"引导的宾语从句中重复使用了"we"，为了表述逻辑清晰，译文中省略了第二个"we"的翻译。

eg. 15 The jammer covers an operating frequency range from 20~500MHz.

译文：干扰机的工作频段为 20 ~500MHz。

此句省略了"覆盖"一词，但意思一样完整。

eg. 16 Stainless steels possess good hardness and high strength.

译文：不锈钢硬度大、强度高。

"possess"是"占有""拥有"的意思，若将该词直译放在译文中，则表达不符合汉语的习惯，故省略。

eg. 17 The mechanical energy can be changed back into electrical energy by means of a generator or dynamo.

译文：发电机能把机械能转变成电能。

译文省略了"by means of"，原因是"generator or dynamo"就是实现机械能与电能转换的具体工具。如果将"by means of"翻译出来，表达就会有些啰嗦。

eg. 18 Three symbols are used to represent the three types of bus, the symbols for data bus is D. B. , for address bus A. B. , for control bus C. B. .

译文：我们用三种符号来表示三种总线，用符号 D. B. 表示数据总线，用符号 A. B. 表示地址总线，用符号 C. B. 表示控制总线。

这个句子的原文中两处省略了"the symbols"，尽管英语表达含义非常清楚，但是汉语的表达习惯却不做这样的省略，故需要增词。

eg. 19 When being negative, grid repels electrons, and only a fraction of the electrons emitted by the cathode can reach the anode.

译文：当栅极为负时，就会排斥电子，此时只有由阴极发射的小部分电子可以到达阳极。

这个句子省略了一个"grid"，因为当从句的逻辑主语与主句一致时从句的主语可以省去。但在中文翻译时需要将省略的词翻译出来。

eg. 20 The leakage current of a capacitor is an important measure of its quality.

译文：电容器漏电流的大小是衡量电容器质量好坏的重要尺度。

eg. 21 Most DSPs are based on the so-called Harvard architecture, where the data path (including the bus and memory units) is made distinct from the program path, allowing an instruction search to be performed simultaneously with another instruction execution and other tasks.

译文：大部分的 DSP 采用所谓的哈佛体系结构，这种体系结构中数据线（包括总线和存储单元）与程序线相互独立，这样就能在执行某个指令或任务的同时接受其他指令的执行请求。

这里"architecture"的含义应该是"体系结构"，"bus"的含义应该是"总线"，也就是说，在专业英语中一些词汇会有特殊的含义。

eg. 22 Chips require much less space and power and are cheaper to manufacture than an equivalent circuit built by employing individual transistors.

译文：与使用分立的三极管构造的等效电路相比，芯片需要的空间更小，功率更低，更便宜。

"individual"译作"分立"，比译作"独立""各人"更合适。

eg. 23　An electric charge will flow for a short time and accumulate on the plate.

译文：一个电荷在很短的时间内移动并在负极聚集。

"the plate"在该句中应指"负极"，故可以将该词的所指范围确定为"负极"。

eg. 24　When a current passes through the coil, a magnetic field is set up around it.

译文：当电流流过线圈时，就会在线圈周围产生磁场。

由于原文介绍磁场产生的原理，句中的"coil"的含义很明确，指的是"线圈"。

eg. 25　In practice, a relationship is used in which the received power is related to the transmitted power by a factor which depends on the fourth power of the inverse of the distance.

译文：实际上，在接收功率和发送功率之间有一个关系是由距离的倒数的四次幂这个因素决定的。

句中前两个"power"都是功率的含义，第三个"power"是幂、乘方的含义。

eg. 26　Few of these charge carriers combine with the charge (positive in NPN, negative in PNP) in the base.

译文：很少一部分载流子与NPN结基区中的正电荷结合，或与PNP结基区中的负电荷结合。

第一个"charge"指的是"载流子"；第二个"charge"指的是"电荷"。

eg. 27　The motor can feed several machines.

译文：这部电动机可以给几部机器供应动力。

eg. 28　Like charges repel; unlike charges attract.

译文：同性电荷相排斥，异性电荷相吸引。

这句话中"like"是"charges"的定语用作形容词，它与汉语相对应的含义应当是"同性的"，同样"unlike"也是形容词，表示"异性的"。

但在以下各句中"like"又分别属于其他几个不同词类。

eg. 29　Servers are computers exactly like the WS.

译文：服务器是与WS（工作站）非常相似的计算机。

这里的"like"是介词，可译为"相似，像"。

eg. 30　Never do the like again.

译文：不要再做这样的事了。

这句话中的"like"与定冠词"the"组合成名词性词组，相当于汉语中"形似的人或事物"。

eg. 31　Some theorems like regarding noise as Gaussian white noise.

译文：许多理论倾向于将噪声看作高斯白噪声。

这里的"like"用作动词，表示"倾向"。

eg. 32　The sampling theorem shows that all values of a signal can be determined by sampling the signal at a rate equal to at least twice the bandwidth.

译文：采样定理表明信号的抽样频率至少为信号频率的两倍，信号才能全部恢复。

这里"sampling"显然是动词的现在分词，作"theorem"的定语，它与汉语相对应的词义应当是"采样"。

专 业 篇

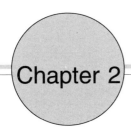

Chapter 2

Circuit System and Design
(电路系统与设计)

2.1 Circuit and System

1. Basic Concepts

Charge and Conductivity

In the Bohr theory of the atom (named after Niels Bohr, 1885—1962), electrons orbit a nucleus containing neutrons and protons. Attraction between the opposite charges of electrons and protons keeps atoms together. Particles with the same charge repel each other.

Electric charge is measured in coulombs (C). An individual electron or proton has much less than one coulomb of charge, -1.6×10^{-19} C on an electron, 1.6×10^{-19} C on a proton. Nature says only that an electron's charge is the opposite of a proton's; there is nothing inherently negative about electrons, they could just as easily be called negative and protons positive.

The electrons of different types of atoms have different degrees of freedom to move around. With some types of materials, such as metals, the outermost electrons in the atoms are so loosely bound that they chaotically move in the space between the atoms of that material by nothing more than the influence of room-temperature heat energy. Because these virtually unbound electrons are free to leave their respective atoms and float around in the space between adjacent atoms, they are often called free electrons.

In other types of materials such as glass, the atoms' electrons have very little freedom to move around. While external forces such as physical rubbing can force some of these electrons to leave their respective atoms and transfer to the atoms of another material, they do not move between atoms within that material very easily.

This relative mobility of electrons within a material is known as electric conductivity. Conductivity is determined by the types of atoms in a material (the number of protons in each atom's nucleus, determining its chemical identity) and how the atoms are linked together with one another. Materials with high electron mobility (many free electrons) are called conductors, while materials with low electron mobility (few or no free electrons) are called insulators.

It should also be understood that some materials experience changes in their electrical properties under different conditions. Glass, for instance, is a very good insulator at room temperature, but becomes a conductor when heated to a very high temperature. Gases such as air, normally insulating materials, also become conductive if heated to very high temperatures. Most metals become poorer conductors when heated, and better conductors when cooled. Many conductive materials become perfectly conductive (this is called superconductivity) at extremely low temperatures.

While the normal motion of "free" electrons in a conductor is random, with no particular direction or speed, electrons can be influenced to move in a coordinated fashion through a conductive material. This uniform motion of electrons is what we call electricity, or electric current. Just like water flowing through the emptiness of a pipe, electrons are able to move within the empty space within and between the atoms of a conductor. The conductor may appear to be solid to our eyes, but any material composed of atoms is mostly empty space! There can be electric current only where there exists a continuous path of conductive material providing a conduit for electrons to travel through. If the path is blocked, the "flow" will not occur.

Electric Circuits, Voltage and Current

An electric circuit is formed when a conductive path is created to allow free electrons to continuously move. This continuous movement of free electrons through the conductors of a circuit is called a current, and it is often referred to in terms of "flow", just like the flow of a liquid through a hollow pipe.

The force motivating electrons to "flow" in a circuit is called voltage, which technically is a measure of potential energy per unit charge of electrons. The most familiar form of potential energy is gravitational potential energy. Because of the gravitational attraction between the earth and the objects on it, lifting objects gives them potential energy. The more mass something has and the higher we lift it, the more potential energy it has. When we speak of a certain amount of voltage being present in a circuit, we are referring to the measurement of how much potential energy exists to move electrons from one particular point in that circuit to another particular point. Without reference to two particular points, the term "voltage" has no meaning.

Voltage is usually indicated by the symbol V, measured in volts (symbol: V), named after Alessandro Volta (1745—1827). One volt is defined as that magnitude of electromotive force required causes a current of one ampere to pass through a conductor having a resistance of one ohm. In digital circuits, we sometimes measure voltage in thousands of a volt, or millivolts (mV). Increasing the voltage of one coulomb of charge by one volt gives it one joule (J) of electrical potential energy, named after James P. Joule (1818—1889). Because electrons have negative charge, we have to take electrons from a higher to a lower voltage to increase their potential energy.

Any source of voltage, including batteries, has two points for electrical contact. We can provide such a path for the battery by connecting a piece of wire from one end of the battery to the other. Forming a circuit with a loop of wire, we will initiate a continuous flow of electrons in a clockwise direction, as shown in Fig. 2-1.

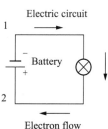

Fig. 2-1　Current in a anti-clockwise direction

So long as the battery continues to produce voltage and the continuity of the electrical path isn't broken, electrons will continue to flow in the circuit. Following the metaphor of water moving through a pipe, this continuous, uniform flow of electrons through the circuit is called a current. So long as the voltage source keeps "pushing" in the same direction, the electron flow will continue to move in the same direction in the circuit. This single-direction flow of electrons is called Direct Current, or DC. When the direction of current switches back and forth, it is called Alternating Current, or AC.

Because electric current is composed of individual electrons flowing in unison through a conductor by moving along and pushing on the electrons ahead, just like marbles through a tube or water through a pipe, the amount of flow throughout a single circuit will be the same at any point. If we were to monitor a cross-section of the wire in a single circuit, counting the electrons flowing by, we would notice the exact same quantity per unit of time as in any other part of the circuit, regardless of conductor length or conductor diameter.

Current flow is represented by the letter symbol I. The basic unit in which current is measured is the ampere (A). One ampere of current is defined as the movement of one coulomb past any point of a conductor during one second of time. The other unit is milliampere (mA) or microampere (μA).

Resistance, Capacitance and Inductance

Free electrons tend to move through conductors with some degree of friction, or opposition to motion. This opposition to motion is more properly called resistance. The amount of current in a circuit depends on the amount of voltage available to motivate the electrons, and also the amount of resistance in the circuit to oppose electron flow. Just like voltage, resistance is a quantity relative between two points. For this reason, the quantities of voltage and resistance are often stated as being "between" or "across" two points in a circuit.

The device to be capable of doing this is called a resistor. The amount of resistance to the flow of current that a resistor causes depends on the material it is made of as well as its size and shape. Some resistors obey Ohm's law, which states that the current density is directly proportional to the electrical field when the temperature is constant.

The resistance of a material that follows Ohm's law is constant, or independent of voltage or current, and the relationship between current and voltage is linear. Modern electronic circuits depend on many devices that deviate from Ohm's law. In devices such as diodes, the current does not increase linearly with voltage and is different for two directions of current. Resistors are often made to have a specific value of resistance so that the characteristics of the circuit can be accurately calculated.

Electrical resistance is represented by the letter symbol R. The unit of resistance is the ohm, a term that is often expressed by using Ω. One ohm is defined as that amount of resistance that will limit the current in a conductor is one ampere when the voltage applied to the conductor is one volt. Larger amounts of resistance are commonly expressed in kiloohm (kΩ) or in megohm (MΩ).

Whenever an electric voltage exists between two separated conductors, an electric field is present within the space between those conductors. Electrical energy can be stored in an electric field. The device to be capable of doing this is called a capacitor or a condenser. Capacitors are components designed by placing two conductive plates (usually metal) in close proximity with each other. A capacitor's ability to store energy as a function of voltage (potential difference between the two leads) results in a tendency to try to maintain voltage at a constant level. In other words, capacitors tend to resist changes in voltage drop. When voltage across a capacitor is increased or decreased, the capacitor "resists" the change by drawing current from or supplying current to the source of the voltage change, in opposition to the change.

If a condenser is connected to a battery, the electrons will flow out of the negative terminal of the battery and accumulate on the condenser plate connected to that side. Thus the condenser is said to be charged. The capacitance is directly proportional to the dielectric constant of the material and to the area of the plates and inversely to the distance of the plates. The larger the plate area, the smaller the space between them, the greater the capacitance.

The measure of a capacitor's ability to store energy for a given amount of voltage drop is called capacitance. Not surprisingly, capacitance is also a measure of the intensity of opposition to changes in voltage (exactly how much current it will produce for a given rate of change in voltage). Capacitance is symbolically denoted with a capital C, and is measured in the unit of the Farad, abbreviated as F. When farad is a too large unit to be used in radio calculation, so microfarad and picofarad are used.

Whenever electrons flow through a conductor, a magnetic field will develop around that conductor. This effect is called electromagnetism. Magnetic energy can be stored in a magnetic field. The device to be capable of doing this is called an inductor. An inductor is simply a coil of wire with or without a magnetic core. Energy storage in an inductor is a function of the amount of current through it. An inductor's ability to store energy as a function of current results in a tendency to try to maintain current at a constant level. In other words, inductors tend to resist changes in current. When current through an inductor is increased or decreased, the inductor "resists" the change by producing a voltage between its leads in opposing polarity to the change.

To store more energy in an inductor, the current through it must be increased. This means that its magnetic field must increase in strength, and that change in field strength produces the corresponding voltage according to the principle of electromagnetic self-induction. When the current through an inductor is increased, it drops a voltage opposing the direction of electron flow, acting as a power load. In this condition the inductor is said to be charging, because there is an increasing amount of energy being stored in its magnetic field. Note the polarity of the voltage with regard to the direction of current.

The measure of an inductor's ability to store energy for a given amount of current flow is called inductance. Not surprisingly, inductance is also a measure of the intensity of opposition to changes in current (exactly how much self-induced voltage will be produced for a given rate of change of current). Inductance is symbolically denoted with a capital L and is measured in the unit of the Henry, abbreviated as H.

2. Circuit and System
Ohm's Law

As stated before, voltage is the measure of potential energy per unit charge available to motivate electrons from one point to another, current is the rate of electric charge motion through a conductor, resistance is the opposition for free electrons to motion through conductors. These units and symbols for electrical quantities will become very important to know as we begin to explore the relationships between them in circuits. The first, and perhaps most important, relationship between current, voltage, and resistance is called Ohm's Law, discovered by Georg Simon Ohm in 1827. Ohm's principal discovery was that the amount of electric current through a metal conductor is directly proportional to the voltage impressed across it, for any given temperature.

Ohm's Law is given by

$$V = IR \qquad (2\text{-}1)$$

where V is the potential difference between two points which include a resistance R, I is the current flowing through the resistance. When the conductance, $g = 1/R$, is used, Ohm's Law in this form is

$$I = gV \qquad (2\text{-}2)$$

If we know the values of any two of the three quantities (voltage, current and resistance) in a circuit, we can use Ohm's Law to determine the third.

Kirchoff's Current Law and Kirchoff's Voltage Law

There are more complicated circuits which cannot be reduced to simply a parallel or series circuit using equivalent resistances. Instead, these need to be solved using two concepts: Kirchhoff's Current Law and Kirchhoff's Voltage Law.

In Fig. 2-2, we see that I_1 is the only current flowing into the node. However, there are three paths for current to leave the node, and these current are represented by I_2, I_3, and I_4.

Once charge has entered into the node, it has no place to go except to leave (this is known as conservation of charge). The total charge flowing into a node must be the same as the total charge flowing out of the node. So,

$$I_2 + I_3 + I_4 = I_1 \qquad (2\text{-}3)$$

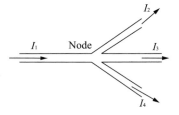

Fig. 2-2 Current flowing into and out of a node

Bringing everything to the left side of the above equation, we get

$$(I_2 + I_3 + I_4) - I_1 = 0 \qquad (2\text{-}4)$$

Then, the sum of all the currents is zero. This can be generalized as

$$\sum I_i = 0 \qquad (2\text{-}5)$$

Note the convention we have chosen here: current flowing into the node is taken to be negative, and currents flowing out of the node are positive.

Kirchhoff's Voltage Law (or Kirchhoff's Loop Rule) is a result of the electrostatic field being conservative. It states that the total voltage around a closed loop must be zero. If this were not the case, then when we travel around a closed loop, the voltages would be indefinite. So,

$$\sum V_i = 0 \qquad (2\text{-}6)$$

Introduction to Network Theorems

In electric network analysis, the fundamental rules are Ohm's Law and Kirchhoff's Laws. While these humble laws may be applied to analyze just about any circuit configuration (even if we have to resort to complex algebra to handle multiple unknowns), there are some "shortcut" methods of analysis to make the math easier.

Superposition Theorem

The strategy used in the Superposition Theorem is to eliminate all but one source of power within a network at a time, using series/parallel analysis to determine voltage drops (and/or currents) within the modified network for each power source separately. Then, once voltage drops and/or currents have been determined for each power source working separately, the values are all "superimposed" on top of each other (added algebraically) to find the actual voltage drops/currents with all sources active.

Thevenin's Theorem

Thevenin's Theorem states that it is possible to simplify any linear circuit, no matter how complex, to an equivalent circuit with just a single voltage source and series resistance connected to a load. The qualification of "linear" is identical to that found in the Superposition Theorem, where all the underlying equations must be linear (no exponents or roots). If we're dealing with passive components (such as resistors, inductors and capacitors), this is true. However, there are some components (especially certain gas-discharge and semiconductor components) which are nonlinear: that is, their opposition to current changes with voltage and/or current. As such, we would call circuits containing these types of components, nonlinear circuits.

Thevenin's Theorem is especially useful in analyzing power systems and other circuits where one particular resistor in the circuit (called the "load" resistor) is subject to change, and re-calculation of the circuit is necessary with each trial value of load resistance, to determine voltage across it and current through it.

Steps to follow for Thevenin's Theorem:

1) Find the Thevenin source voltage by removing the load resistor from the original circuit and calculating voltage across the open connection points where the load resistor used to be.

2) Find the Thevenin resistance by removing all power sources in the original circuit (voltage sources shorted and current sources open) and calculating total resistance between the open connection points.

3) Draw the Thevenin equivalent circuit, with the Thevenin voltage source in series with the Thevenin resistance. The load resistor re-attaches between the two open points of the equivalent circuit.

4) Analyze voltage and current for the load resistor following the rules for series circuits.

Norton's Theorem

Norton's Theorem states that it is possible to simplify any linear circuit, no matter how complex, to an equivalent circuit with just a single current source and parallel resistance connected to a load. Just as with Thevenin's Theorem, the qualification of "linear" is identical to that found in the Superposition Theorem: all underlying equations must be linear (no exponents or roots).

Steps to follow for Norton's Theorem:

1) Find the Norton source current by removing the load resistor from the original circuit and calculating current through a short (wire) jumping across the open connection points where the load resistor used to be.

2) Find the Norton resistance by removing all power sources in the original circuit (voltage

sources shorted and current sources open) and calculating total resistance between the open connection points.

3) Draw the Norton equivalent circuit, with the Norton current source in parallel with the Norton resistance. The load resistor re-attaches between the two open points of the equivalent circuit.

4) Analyze voltage and current for the load resistor following the rules for parallel circuits.

NEW WORDS AND PHRASES

charge　*n.* 负荷，电荷，费用，主管，掌管，充电，充气
conductivity　*n.* 传导性，传导率
insulator　*n.* 绝缘体，绝热器
gravitational　*adj.* 重力的
voltage　*n.* ［电］电压，伏特数
volts　*n.* 直流电压
ampere　*n.* 安培
ohm　*n.* ［物］欧姆
coulomb　*n.* ［电］库仑（电量单位）
diameter　*n.* 直径
inductance　*n.* 感应系数，自感应

condenser　*n.* 冷凝器，电容器
dielectric　*n.* 电介质，绝缘体；*adj.* 非传导性的
farad　*n.* ［电］法拉（电容单位）
picofarad　*n.* ［电］皮（可）法拉，微微法拉，百亿分之一法拉
magnetic core　磁心
polarity　*n.* 极性
potential difference　［电］电位差，电势差
equivalent resistance　等效电阻
Superposition Theorem　叠加定理
Thevenin's Theorem　戴维南定理
Norton's Theorem　诺顿定理

NOTES

1) So long as the battery continues to produce voltage and the continuity of the electrical path isn't broken, electrons will continue to flow in the circuit.

只要电池持续供电，并且导线没有断开，电子将始终在回路中流动。

2) If a condenser is connected to a battery, the electrons will flow out of the negative terminal of the battery and accumulate on the condenser plate connected to that side. Thus the condenser is said to be charged.

当电容与电池相连，电子将从电池的负极流出，并聚集在电容与该端相连的极板上，称电容充电。

3) Whenever electrons flow through a conductor, a magnetic field will develop around that conductor.

只要电子束流过导体，就将在这个导体周围产生磁场。

4) Glass, for instance, is a very good insulator at room temperature, but becomes a conductor when heated to a very high temperature.

例如，玻璃在室温下是一种非常好的绝缘体，但当把它加热到相当高的温度时它就变成一种导体。

5) Whenever an electric voltage exists between two separated conductors, an electric field is present within the space between those conductors.

只要在两个独立的导体间存在电压，它们之间就会产生电场。

6) While the normal motion of "free" electrons in a conductor is random, with no particular direction or speed, electrons can be influenced to move in a coordinated fashion through a conductive material.

通常导体里的自由电子是随机运动的，没有确定的方向或速度，但是电子受力后可沿相同的方向通过导体。

EXERCISES

1. Please translate the following words and phrases into Chinese.
   a) ampere   b) conductivity   c) magnetic core   d) insulator
   e) dielectric   f) Thevenin's Theorem   g) negative terminal   h) charge
   i) inductance   j) polarity

2. Please translate the following words and phrases into English.
   a) 电荷   b) 电感   c) 极性   d) 节点
   e) 电阻器   f) 电容器   g) 绝缘体   h) 等效电阻
   i) 叠加定理   j) 电流

3. Fill in the blanks with the missing word(s).
   a) Electric charge is measured in _____. An individual electron or proton has much less than one coulomb of charge, -1.6×10^{-19} coulomb on an _____, 1.6×10^{-19} on a _____.
   b) Whenever electrons flow through a conductor, a _____ field will develop around that conductor. This effect is called _____.
   c) Magnetic energy can be stored in a magnetic field. The device to be capable of doing this is called an _____.
   d) An inductor is simply a coil of wire with or without a magnetic core. Energy storage in an inductor is a function of the amount of _____ through it.
   e) When current through an inductor is _____ or _____, the inductor "resists" the change by producing a _____ between its leads in opposing _____ to the change.
   f) Once charge has entered into the _____, it has no place to go except to leave.
   g) Kirchhoff's Voltage Law states that the total voltage around a closed loop must be _____.

4. Answer the following questions according to the text.
   a) How the capacitors store energy?
   b) What are the relationship between the voltage and the current?
   c) What is the Ohm's Law?
   d) What are the Kirchhoff's Current Law and Kirchhoff's Voltage Law?
   e) What are the Thevenin's Theorem and Norton's Theorem?

READING

Semiconductor Device

Semiconductors are materials which are neither conductors or insulators, having conductivities intermediate to those of conductors like copper and insulators like wood or plastic. Common semiconductors are Silicon and Germanium. Semiconductor devices such as diodes, transistors and integrated circuits made possible miniaturized electronics, including computers, certain types of medical diagnostic and treatment equipment, and popular telecommunication devices, to name a few applications of this technology. We have come to rely on them and increasingly have come to expect higher performance

半导体器件

半导体是区别于导体和绝缘体的一种材料，其电导率介于铜这样的导体和木头、塑料这样的绝缘体之间。常见的半导体是硅和锗。半导体器件（如二极管、晶体管和集成电路）使得电子设备小型化成为可能，包括计算机、某类医疗诊断和治疗设备、通用的电信设备，这只是这项技术的很少的一些应用。我们越来越依赖这项技术，期望以更低的成本获得更

at lower cost. Behind this revolution in technology stands an even greater revolution in general science: the field of quantum physics. Without this leap in understanding the natural world, the development of semiconductor devices (and more advanced electronic devices still under development) would never have been possible.

1. Diode

Diode, electronic device that allows the passage of current in only one direction, has a low resistance to electric current in one direction and a high resistance to it in the reverse direction. When current flows from the P-type to the N-type material, the positive holes and the negative electrons are forced into close contact at the boundary. At the boundary, the electrons fill the holes across the boundary while the terminals supply new holes and electrons. Thus, in the forward bias case a continual current flows. In the reverse bias case, the charge carriers are pulled apart. There is no longer an easy way for electrons to tunnel through the barrier as there are no longer many empty holes waiting on the opposite side.

The vacuum-tube diodes consist of an evacuated glass or steel envelope containing two electrodes: a cathode and an anode. Because electrons can flow in only one direction, from cathode to anode, the vacuum-tube diode could be used as a rectifier, which can convert Alternating Current (AC) into Direct Current (DC). Fig. 2-3 demonstrates a simple half-wave rectifier.

Since the current only flows one way through the resistor the voltage drop can never be negative. The capacitor serves merely as an extra voltage source to even out the sine wave. Fig. 2-4 demonstrates the resulting voltage V_s.

The term half-wave refers to the fact that in the absence of the capacitor, a voltage exists only during the time when the primary source is positive. One can make a steadier source with a full-wave rectifier as shown in Fig. 2-5.

For the full-wave rectifier the current flows from left to right through the resistor for all parts of the AC cycle. This results in a positive voltage at all time as shown in Fig. 2-6. The addition of capacitors would smooth out the resulting DC current even further.

高的性能。这项技术革命依赖于科学领域的更大的革命:量子物理学领域。没有这种对自然界的理解的飞跃,半导体器件的发展(和仍在开发中的更先进的电子设备)是不可能的。

1. 二极管

二极管是一种只允许单向电流通过的电子设备,对一个方向上的电流电阻低,对相反方向上的电流电阻高。当电流从P型材料到N型材料时,正的空穴和负的电子在边界相遇。在边界上,电子跨越边界填充空穴,产生新的空穴和电子。因此,在正向偏置情况下产生持续电流。在反向偏置情况下,电荷载流子被分开。电子不能穿过屏障,另一侧也不再有空穴。

真空二极管由抽空的玻璃管或金属壳构成,包含两个电极:一个是阴极,一个是阳极。因为电子只能从阴极到阳极单方向流动,所以真空管可用作整流器,将交流电(AC)变成直流电(DC)。图2-3所示为简单的半波整流器。

由于电流流过电阻的电压降不能为负,因此电容器只能作为额外的电压源使正弦波全部为正。图2-4给出了最终产生的电压 V_s 的波形。

半波这个词是指如果没有电容器,只有当电源为正时才有电压存在。图2-5所示为带全波整流器的稳压源。

在整个交流周期,全波整流器的电流从左到右通过电阻。在整个周期内电压均为正,如图2-6所示。加上电容器会使产生的直流电流更平滑。

当加在相反方向上的电压超过一定值时,半导体二极管击穿,在该方向导通且

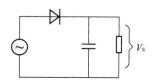

Fig. 2-3 A simple half-wave rectifier

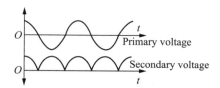

Fig. 2-4 The capacitor serves even out the sine wave

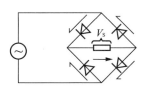

Fig. 2-5　A full-wave rectifier

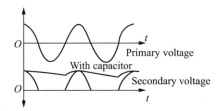

Fig. 2-6　The capacitors smooth out the resulting DC current

When the voltage applied in the reverse direction exceeds a certain value, a semiconductor diode breaks down and conducts heavily in the direction of normally high resistance. When the reverse voltage at which breakdown occurs remains nearly constant for a wide range of currents, the phenomenon is called avalanching. A diode using this property is called a Zener diode. It can be used to regulate the voltage in a circuit.

Semiconductor diodes can be designed to have a variety of characteristics.

One such diode, called a varactor, exhibits a capacitance that is dependent upon the voltage across it.

In another kind, the tunnel diode, the current through the device decreases as the voltage is increased within a certain range; this property, known as negative resistance, makes it useful as an amplifier.

Gunn diodes are negative-resistance diodes that are the basis of some microwave oscillators. Light-sensitive or photosensitive diodes can be used to measure illumination; the voltage drop across them depends on the amount of light that strikes them.

A Light-Emitting Diode (LED) produces light as current passes through it; some LEDs can act as the light source of lasers.

However, some other forms of diode are created by depositing one material onto another, e.g. Schottky diodes are made by placing some metal in contact with a semiconductor. In general, whenever we join two different, very pure, materials we're likely to make some sort of diode.

Diodes are referred to as non-linear circuit elements. Fig. 2-7 shows a schematic symbol for a diode and the current-voltage curve for an ideal diode.

Diode is unidirectional, i.e. current flows in only one direction (anode to cathode internally). When a forward voltage is applied, the diode conducts; and when a reverse voltage is applied, there is no conduction.

Note that the diode conducts a small current in the forward direction up to a threshold voltage, 0.3V for germanium and 0.7V for silicon.

呈现高阻值。当电流在一定范围内变化时，反向击穿电压基本保持不变，这种现象称为雪崩。有这种属性的二极管称为齐纳二极管。它可以用来调节电路中的电压。

半导体二极管具有多种特征。

一种是变容二极管，其电容值依赖于两侧的电压。

另一种是隧道二极管，当电压在一定范围内增加时，流经它的电流减少；这种特点称为负阻，使其可作为放大器。

耿氏二极管是具有负阻效应的二极管，是微波振荡器的基本器件。光电二极管可以用来测量光照；它们的电压降取决于穿过它的光照量。

当电流通过发光二极管（LED）时会发光；一些 LED 可以作为激光光源。

然而，有些二极管通过把一种材料叠加在另一种材料上形成，如肖特基二极管把一些金属叠加在半导体上。通常，当加入两种不同的、纯的材料时，我们就可能会做出某些二极管。

二极管称为非线性电路器件。图 2-7 为理想二极管的原理符号和电流－电压曲线。

二极管是单向的，即电流只能沿一个方向（阳极到阴极的内部）流动。当加正向电压时，二极管导通；当加反向电压时，二极管不导通。

请注意，当电压达到阈值电压时，二极管导通，在正方向产生小电流，锗二极管的阈值电压为 0.3V，硅二极管的阈值电压为 0.7V。

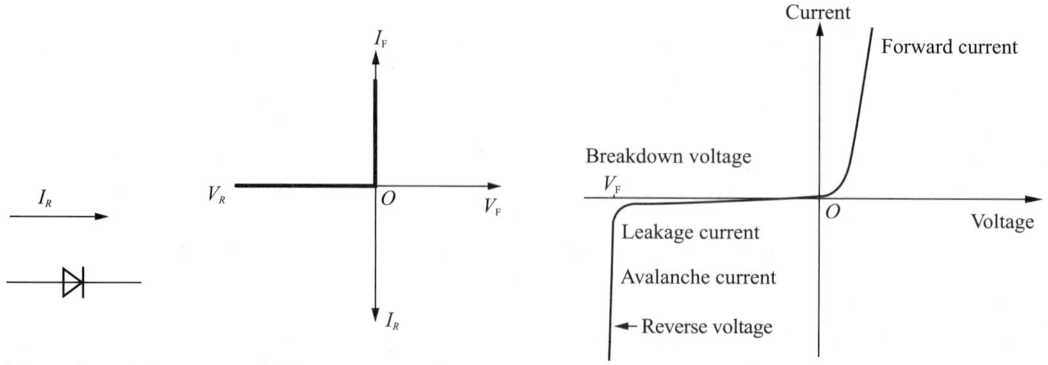

a) Schematic symbol for a diode

b) Current versus voltage for an ideal diode

c) A typical real diode characteristic

Fig. 2-7　Diode

2. Transistors

A transistor (see Fig. 2-8) is the most crucial element in modern electronics. It serves as an amplifier and as a switch. A single transistor will adjust the output according to a small change in the input. Just as light switch can supply many hundreds of watts power by the flick of a finger. Before transistors, amplification and switching were done with vacuum tubes which are enormously bulky and produce a great deal of heat. Since a single microprocessor may hold near 5 million transistors, the advantage to 5 million vacuum tubes is obvious.

A transistor is constructed by sandwiching a layer of N-type semiconductor between two segments of P-type material.

The small battery on the left serves as the switch. Without that portion of the circuit, the large battery can not pump current due to the N-P reverse bias of the right-hand loop. By adding a small voltage V_E, a current flows through the left-hand loop which floods the narrow N-type region with charge which then destroys the ability of the N-P junction to stop the current. Thus a small voltage change in V_E creates a large effect. Thus it can

2. 晶体管

晶体管（见图2-8）是现代电子技术中最重要的器件。它可用作放大器和开关。晶体管将根据输入的微小变化调整输出。就像手指轻轻一按灯的开关就可以提供几百瓦功率。在晶体管出现之前，人们用真空管实现放大和开关，这不仅非常笨重而且会产生大量的热量。因为微处理器可包含近5百万个晶体管，所以其优势是显而易见的。

晶体管在两层P型材料之间夹了一层N型半导体。

左边的小电池作为开关。没有那部分电路，大电池不能产生右侧回路中的穿过N-P反向偏置的电流。加上较低的电压V_E后，左侧回路中产生电流，该电流流过窄的N型区，破坏了N-P结对电流的阻止能力。因此，电压V_E发生小的变化都要产生很大的影响。它可以作为开关或放大器。

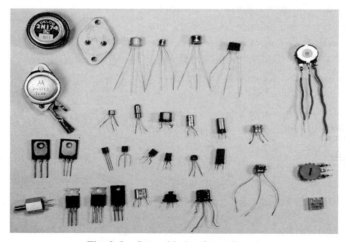

Fig. 2-8　Some kinds of transistors

serve as either a switch or an amplifier. The circuit diagram for the transistor is shown on the left of Fig. 2-9. The upper left lead represents the emitter, the upper right lead represents the collector and the lower lead is the base.

Bipolar Junction Transistors

A bipolar transistor consists of a three-layer "sandwich" of doped (extrinsic) semiconductor materials, either PNP or NPN (see Fig. 2-10). Each layer forming the transistor has a specific name, and each layer is provided with a wire contact for connection to a circuit. Shown here are schematic symbol and characteristic curve of NPN transistor types.

We all know, in theory, the PNP characteristic curves look like the common NPN curves just by rotating the PNP plot by 180°. In swapping N for P so NPN →PNP, we've reversed the direction of current flows (so currents are negative—

晶体管电路图显示在图 2-9 的左边。左上引线表示发射极，右上引线表示集电极，下引线表示基极。

双极结型晶体管

双极结型晶体管是一个由掺杂的半导体材料组成的三层"三明治"（外形），或者 PNP 或者 NPN（见图 2-10）。形成晶体管的每一层都有特定的名称，每一层都设有用于连接到电路的导线。这里给出的是 NPN 型晶体管的原理符号与特性曲线。

我们都知道，在理论上，将 PNP 特性曲线旋转 180°，PNP 的特性曲线与 NPN 的特性曲线看起来一样。交换 N 和 P，NPN 就变成了 PNP，我们把电流流向反向

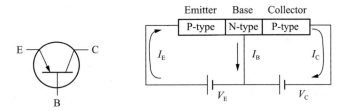

Fig. 2-9 Schematic symbol for a transistor and construct a transistor by sandwiching

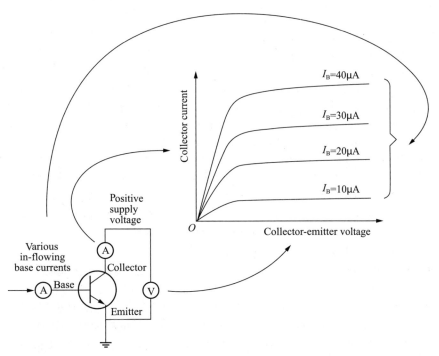

Fig. 2-10 Symbol and characteristic curve of NPN transistor types

flowing out of the collector and base in a PNP) and the required supply voltage becomes negative for a PNP. For any given state of operation, the current directions and voltage polarities for each type of transistor are exactly opposite to each other. Bipolar transistors work as current-controlled current regulators. In other words, they restrict the amount of current that can go through them according to a smaller, controlling current. The main current that is controlled goes from collector to emitter, or from emitter to collector, depending on the type of transistor it is (PNP or NPN, respectively). The small current that controls the main current goes from base to emitter, or from emitter to base, once again depending on the type of transistor it is (PNP or NPN, respectively). According to the confusing standards of semiconductor symbology, the arrow always points against the direction of electron flow, bipolar transistors are called bipolar because the main flow of electrons through them takes place in two types of semiconductor material: P and N, as the main current goes from emitter to collector (or vice versa). In other words, two types of charge carriers (electrons and holes) comprise this main current through the transistor.

As you can see, the controlling current and the controlled current always mesh together through the emitter wire, and their electrons always flow against the direction of the transistor's arrow. This is the first and foremost rule in the use of transistors: all currents must be going in the proper directions for the device to work as a current regulator. The small, controlling current is usually referred to simply as the base current because it is the only current that goes through the base wire of the transistor. Conversely, the large, controlled current is referred to as the collector current because it is the only current that goes through the collector wire. The emitter current is the sum of the base and collector currents, in compliance with Kirchhoff's Current Law. If there is no current through the base of the transistor, it shuts off like an open switch and prevents current through the collector. If there is a base current, then the transistor turns on like a closed switch and allows a proportional amount of current through the collector. Collector current is primarily limited by the base current, regardless of the amount of voltage available to push it.

Junction Field-Effect Transistors

In switching applications, Field Effect Transistors (FET) are preferred because they consume less power. FETs also have a NPN (or PNP) sequence of materials. However, the conductivity is controlled through the so-called gate that is electrically insulated from the device itself. By adjusting the voltage between the gate and the substrate, the width of a

（所以电流是负的——在 PNP 中从集电极和基极流出），并且 PNP 所需的电源电压为负。对于任何给定的工作状态，每种类型的晶体管的电流方向与电压极性完全相反。双极晶体管是电流控制的电流调节器。换句话说，要限制晶体管中电流的大小，使其工作在小的控制电流下。受控的主电流是从集电极到发射极，或者从发射极到集电极，这取决于它的晶体管类型（分别是 PNP 型或 NPN 型）。控制主电流的小电流是从基极到发射极，或者从发射极到基极，同样取决于它的晶体管类型（分别是 PNP 型或 NPN 型）。根据半导体符号学的标准符号，箭头常常指向电子流动的方向，双极晶体管之所以是双极的，是因为流经的主电流主要发生在两种类型的半导体材料中：P 和 N，如从发射极到集电极（反之亦然）。换句话说，两种类型的电荷载流子（电子和空穴）构成主电流通过晶体管。

可以发现，控制的电流和受控的电流总是交织在一起流过发射极的导线，其电子流过的方向总是与晶体管的箭头方向相反。这是使用晶体管的首要规则：所有电流必须要在正确的方向以保证器件用作电流调节器。小的控制电流通常简称为基极电流，因为它是唯一流经晶体管基极导线的电流。相反，大的受控电流称为集电极电流，因为它是唯一流经晶体管集电极导线的电流。发射极电流是基极和集电极电流的总和，遵从基尔霍夫电流定律。如果没有电流流过晶体管的基极，它就像一个打开的开关，防止电流流过集电极。如果有基极电流，晶体管就像一个闭合的开关，允许成正比的电流量流过集电极。集电极电流主要由基极电流控制，忽略加在其上的电压。

结型场效应晶体管

当作为开关使用时，场效应晶体管（FET）因为功耗较小而成为首选。场效应晶体管也有 NPN（或 PNP）材料。然而，其导通性通过所谓的栅极控制，栅极与器件是电绝缘的。通过调整栅极和衬底之间的电压，可以控制源极和漏极之间沟道的

conducting channel between source and drain can be controlled. A FET is a unipolar device, conducting a current using only one kind of charge carrier. If based on an N-type slab of semiconductor, the carriers are electrons. Conversely, a P-type based device uses only holes. Functionally, the following correspondences between BJT and FET exist: base-gate, source-collector, drain-emitter.

At the circuit level, FET operation is simple. A voltage applied to the gate, input element, controls the resistance of the channel, the unipolar region between the gate regions. In an N-channel device, this is a lightly doped N-type slab of silicon with terminals at the ends. The source and drain terminals are analogous to the emitter and collector, respectively, of a BJT. In an N-channel device, a heavy P-type region on both sides of the center of the slab serves as a control electrode, the gate. The gate is analogous to the emitter of a BJT. The unipolar FET is conceptually simple, but difficult to manufacture. Most transistors today are a metal-oxide-semiconductor variety of the FET contained within integrated circuits. However, discrete JFET devices are available.

Metal-Oxide-Semiconductor Field-Effect Transistors (MOSFET)

The most common FET technology is called MOSFET for Metal-Oxide-Semiconductor FET. P-type and N-type MOSFETs are combined to form CMOS (Complementary MOS) logic gates. Today, most transistors are of the MOSFET type as components of digital integrated circuits.

A conceptually similar structure was proposed and patented independently by Lilienfeld and Heil in 1930, but the MOSFET was not successfully demonstrated until 1960. The main technological problem was the control and reduction of the surface states at the oxide-semiconductor interface. A reduction of the surface states enabled the fabrication of devices, which do not have a conducting channel unless a positive voltage is applied. Such devices are referred to as "enhancement-mode" devices. The electrons at the oxide-semiconductor interface are concentrated in a thin (~10nm thick) "inversion" layer. By now, most MOSFETs are "enhancement-mode" devices.

The MOSFET transistor count within an integrated circuit may approach the hundreds of a million. Much larger MOSFETs are capable of switching nearly 100A of current at low voltages; some handle nearly 1000V at lower currents. MOSFETs find much wider application than FETs. However, MOSFET power devices are not as widely used as bipolar junction transistors at this time.

The voltage gain of the MOSFET is caused by the current saturation at higher drain-source voltages, so that a small drain

宽度。场效应晶体管是一种单极型器件，只使用一种电荷载流子。如果场效应晶体管基于 N 型半导体，则载流子是电子。相反，如果场效应晶体管基于 P 型半导体，则载流子是空穴。从功能上讲，BJT 和 FET 之间的对偶关系为：基极对应栅极，源极对应集电极，漏极对应发射极。

就电路性能而言，FET 操作简单。在输入单元栅极加上电压，控制沟道的电阻。N 沟道场效应晶体管是在两极的硅中掺杂少量 N 型杂质。源极和漏极分别类似于 BJT 的发射极与集电极。N 沟道场效应晶体管在中心介质的两侧高参杂 P 型区作为控制电极——栅极。栅极类似于 BJT 的发射极。单极型场效应晶体管的概念很简单，但很难制造。现在集成电路中的晶体管，大多数是金属－氧化物－半导体场效应管。然而，也有分立的 JFET。

金属－氧化物－半导体场效应晶体管 (MOSFET)

最常见的 FET 是金属－氧化物－半导体场效应晶体管（MOSFET）。P 型和 N 型 MOSFET 组合形成 CMOS（互补金属－氧化物－半导体）逻辑门。现在，大多数 MOSFET 型晶体管是数字集成电路中的基本器件。

1930 年 Lilienfeld 和 Heil 分别提出了一个概念相似的结构并申请了专利，但直到 1960 才成功地制成了 MOSFET。主要技术问题是在氧化物－半导体界面控制和减少表面态。表面态的减少，使器件的制造成为可能，当加上正电压时才能形成导电沟道。这种器件称为"增强型"的。在氧化物－半导体界面上的电子集中在一个薄的（约 10nm 厚）"反转"层。现在，大多数的 MOSFET 是"增强型"的。

集成电路中的 MOSFET 晶体管的数目可以多达几百万、几千万。更大的 MOSFET 能够在较低电压达到近 100A 的电流；有一些在较低的电流可得到近 1000V 的电压。MOSFET 的应用比 FET 更广泛。然而，现在 MOSFET 功率器件不如双极结型晶体管应用广泛。

MOSFET 中较高的漏－源电压引起电

current variation can cause a large drain voltage variation.

The behavior of an enhancement N-channel MOSFET (NMOSFET) is largely controlled by the voltage at the gate (usually a positive voltage). For the usual drain-source voltage drops (i.e., the saturation region: positive voltages from a few volts up to some breakdown voltage), the drain current (I_D) is nearly independent of the drain-source voltage (V_{DS}), and instead depends on the gate voltage (V_G). (This is unusual behavior: usually more voltage produces to more current, but here the current only increases slightly with increasing V_{DS}.)

流饱和,从而产生电压增益,因此,小的漏极电流的变化可以引起大的漏极电压的变化。

增强型 N 沟道 MOSFET（NMOSFET）的行为主要由栅极的电压控制（通常是正电压）。对于通常的漏-源电压降（即饱和区：从几伏到击穿电压的正电压），漏极电流（I_D）与漏-源电压（V_{DS}）几乎是无关的,相反却依赖于栅极电压（V_G）。（这是反常的：通常更大的电压产生更大的电流,但这里电流仅随 V_{DS} 的增加而略微增加。）

NEW WORDS AND PHRASES

diode　*n.* 二极管
transistor　*n.* 晶体管
integrated circuit　集成电路
germanium　*n.* ［化］锗
cathode　*n.* ［电］阴极,负极
anode　*n.* ［电］阳极,正极
capacitor　*n.* 电容器
resistor　*n.* 电阻器
Zener　*n.* ［电］齐纳击穿（在半导体中的一种非破坏性击穿）
avalanching　*n.* 磨球崩落
varactor　*n.* ［电］变容二极管,可变电抗器
reverse voltage　反向电压,负极性压
Gunn　*adj.* ［电］耿氏效应的,基于耿氏效应的
oscillator　*n.* 振荡器
Schottky　*n.* 肖特基
bipolar　*adj.* 双极的,有两极的
swapping　*n.* 交换,交换技术
mesh　*n.* 网孔,网眼,圈套,陷阱,［机］啮合;　*vt.* 以网捕捉,啮合,编织;　*vi.* 落网,相啮合
substrate　*n.* 底层,下层,［地］底土层,基础,本源
unipolar　*adj.* ［生］［物］单极的
slab　*n.* 厚平板,厚片,混凝土路面,板层;　*v.* 把……分成厚片,用石板铺
saturation　*n.* 饱和（状态）,浸润,浸透,饱和度
inversion　*n.* 倒置

NOTES

1) They were vacuum-tube diodes, consisting of an evacuated glass or steel envelope containing two electrodes: a cathode and an anode.
   真空二极管由抽空的玻璃管或金属壳构成,包含两个电极：一个是阴极,一个是阳极。

2) A transistor is constructed by sandwiching a layer of N-type semiconductor between two segments of P-type material.
   晶体管在两层 P 型材料之间夹了一层 N 型半导体。

3) By adding a small voltage V_E, a current flows through the left-hand loop which floods the narrow N-type region with charge which then destroys the ability of the N-P junction to stop the current.
   加上较低的电压 V_E 后,左边的回路中产生电流,该电流流过窄的 N 型区,破坏了 N-P 结对电流的阻止能力。

4) In an N-channel device, a heavy P-type region on both sides of the center of the slab serves as a control electrode, the gate.
   N 沟道场效应晶体管在中心介质的两侧高掺杂 P 型区作为控制电极——栅极。

5) A reduction of the surface states enabled the fabrication of devices, which do not have a conducting channel unless a positive voltage is applied.
   表面态的减少,使器件的制造成为可能,当加上正电压时才能形成导电沟道。

2.2 Analog and Digital Circuits Design

Modern circuit design is a "mixed signal" endeavor thanks to the availability of sophisticated process technologies that make available bipolar and CMOS (Complementary Metal-Oxide-Semiconductor), power and signal, passive and active components on the same circuit. It is then up to the circuit designer's creativity and inclination to assemble these components into the analog and/or logic building blocks necessary to develop the intended system on a chip.

1. Analog Circuits

Analog circuits are circuits dealing with signals free to vary from zero to full power supply voltage. This stands in contrast to digital circuits, which almost exclusively employ "all or nothing" signals: voltages restricted to values of zero and full supply voltage, with no valid state in between those extreme limits. Analog circuits are often referred to as linear circuits to emphasize the valid continuity of signal range forbidden in digital circuits, but this label is unfortunately misleading. Just because a voltage or current signal is allowed to vary smoothly between the extremes of zero and full power supply limits does not necessarily mean that all mathematical relationships between these signals are linear in the "straight-line" or "proportional" sense of the word. Many so-called "linear" circuits are quite nonlinear in their behavior, either by necessity of physics or by design.

NPN Transistors

The NPN transistor (see Fig. 2-11) is the king of the traditional bipolar analog integrated circuits world. In fact in the most basic and most cost effective analog IC processes, the chip designer has at its disposal just that: a good NPN transistor. The rest, PNPs, resistors and capacitors are just by-products. For intuitive, back-of-the-envelope type analysis, it is sufficient to model the transistor mostly in DC (Direct Current), keeping in mind that the bandwidth of such an element is finite.

When complexity, like small-signal AC (Alternate Current) behavior, is added to the model, computing simulations should be used since the math quickly becomes hopeless. In Fig. 2-11 the NPN transistor is shown with its symbol (a) and its DC model (b). In this component the current flow enters the collector and base and exits the emitter. Simply stated, the transistor conducts a collector current I_C which is a copy of the base current I_B amplified by a factor of β. It follows that the emitter current I_E is one plus beta times the base current. A typical value for the amplification factor is 100. NPNs have excellent dynamic performance, or bandwidth, measured by their cutoff frequency; easily above 1GHz.

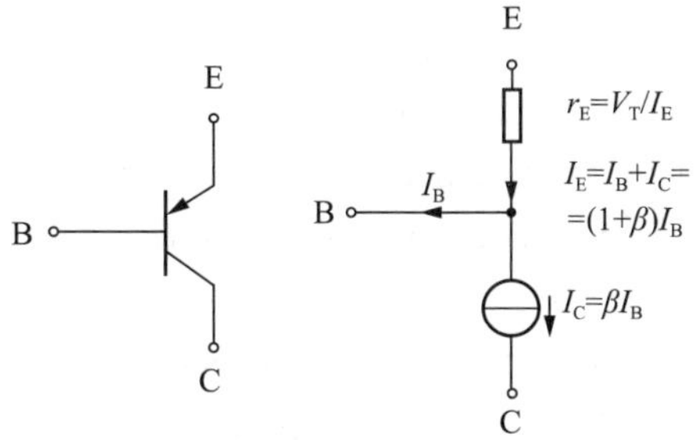

PNP Transistors

The PNP transistor (see Fig. 2-12) is complemen-

a) Symbol   b) Model

Fig. 2-11   NPN transistor

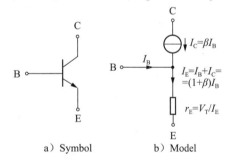

a) Symbol   b) Model

Fig. 2-12   PNP transistor

tary to the NPN, with the current flow entering the emitter and exiting the collector and base, the opposite of what happens in the NPN. Simplicity dictates that PNPs are a by-product of the NPN construction, hence they often have less beta current gain and are slower than NPNs. A typical value for their amplification factor β is 50 and their cutoff frequency (f_T) is generally above 1MHz.

Transistor Equations

The voltage to current relation in a bipolar transistor follows a logarithmic law given by

$$V_{BE} = V_T \ln(I/I_o) \tag{2-7}$$

where V_T is the thermal voltage and I_o is a characteristic current that depends on the specific process. This has some pretty interesting implications; for example, if the transistor from eq. (2-7) carries a current A times higher, we can write

$$V'_{BE} = V_T \ln(AI/I_o) \tag{2-8}$$

The increase in voltage from the factor of A increase in current will be

$$\Delta V_{BE} = V'_{BE} - V_{BE} = V_T \ln(A) = (KT/q)\ln A \tag{2-9}$$

where K is the Boltzman constant, T is the temperature in degrees Kelvin, and q is equal to the electron charge in Coulombs.

Naturally the opposite is true for the current variation as a function of voltage. In fact if we invert the previous equation we have

$$I = I_o \exp(V_{BE}/V_T) \tag{2-10}$$

which shows that the current varies exponentially with the V_{BE}. For a quick estimate of variations in current due to small voltage variations, we can linearize the exponential law and find that the current will vary at roughly 2%/mV. This strong dependence of current on the V_{BE} explains why the transistor is normally driven with current, not voltage.

This also explains how difficult it is to deal with offsets, or small voltage variations between identical transistors. Two identical transistors biased at the same identical voltage will have their current mismatched with a 2% error if their V_{BE} differs by just 1mV.

MOS Transistors

The dual of bipolar NPN and PNP transistors in CMOS technology are the P-channel and N-channel MOS transistors in Fig. 2-13. The general function of the transistors is the same independently as their implementation but there are pros and cons to using both technologies. Generally speaking, the base, the emitter, and the collector of the bipolar transistor are analogous to the gate, source and drain of the MOS transistor, respectively. The bipolar transistors' main problem, which is not present in CMOS, is their need for a base current in order to function. Such current is a net transfer loss from emitter to collector. While the base current is small in small signal operation, in power applications, where the transistor is used as a switch, the base current necessary to keep the transistor on can be very high.

This high base current can lead to implementations with very poor efficiency. With the popularity of portable electronics and the need to extend battery life, it is no wonder that CMOS often tends to have the upper hand

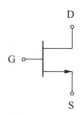

a) N-channel MOS transistor

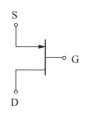

b) P-channel MOS transistor

Fig. 2-13 MOS transistor

over bipolar technologies. The advantage of bipolar over CMOS is that it has better trans-conductance gain and better matching, leading to better differential input gain stages. The best performance processes are mixed-mode BiCMOS (Bipolar and CMOS) or BCD (Bipolar CMOS and DMOS) processes in which the designer can use the best component for the task at hand.

2. Digital Circuits

Boolean Algebra Fundamentals

Unlike other algebras, Boolean algebra allows only two possible values: 0 or 1. The two value representation is often referred to as a bit (binary digit). The bit can represent on or off, true or false, or yes or no. Input variables such as A, B, C are used in logic expressions to represent switches, relay contacts and sensor inputs. The input variables can represent push button switches, limit switches, temperature sensitive switches, pressure switches, level switches, proximity sensors, light sensors, and weight sensors. The results of the logical expression are to perform some action: turn on or off solenoids, relays, motors, lights, buzzers, alarms and other output devices.

The phrase "digital electronics" is used to describe those circuit systems which primarily operate with the use of only two different voltage levels or two other binary states. Analog devices and systems process time-varying signals that can take on any value across a continuous range of voltage, current or other metric. The difference is that we can pretend that they don't.

Boolean algebra has only three basic operations: NOT or Negation, AND (·), and OR (+).

The NOT operation changes the value to the complement of the value. It changes a 1 to a 0, and a 0 to a 1. It can be represented by a bar over the variable. This is also referred to as inversion or negation.

The AND operation is a Boolean multiply and is 1 only when all values are 1. This is represented in Boolean variables as $A \cdot B = Y$ or $AB = Y$. The AND is like the old string of Christmas lights. All the lights have to work to have the stringy light.

The OR operation results in a 1 if any of the values is 1. In Boolean algebra, $1+1=1$ is valid. Logically the statement means if there are one or more true values, the result is true.

As in regular algebra there are mathematical rules that must be followed. There are properties of Boolean operations that are important in working with logic expressions. Using these properties, Shannon showed that logical expression can be expanded and simplified which in turn resulted in simpler logic and reduced the number or relays and switches.

Commutative Law: $A+B=B+A$

Associative Law of Addition: $A+B+C=A+(B+C)$

Associative Law of Multiplication: $A(BC)=(AB)C$

Distributive Law: $A(B+C)=AB+AC$

Identity: $1 \cdot A = A$, $0+A=A$

Complement: $A+\overline{A}=1$, $A \cdot \overline{A}=0$

De Morgan's Theorem: $\overline{A \cdot B} = \overline{A} + \overline{B}$

Logic Gates

The most basic digital devices are called gates. Gates serve as the building blocks to more complex electronic digital logic circuits. They are fundamental to the design of computers. In general, a gate has one or more inputs and produces an output that is a function of the current input value (s). With each logic element there is a "truth table" that explains how the unit works. And there is a symbol to represent every gate.

The three important kinds of gates are:

1) AND gate—produces a 1 output if both of its inputs are 1. The logic expression is $F = A \cdot B$.

2) OR gate—produces a 1 output if one or both of its inputs are 1, produces a 0 output only if both of its inputs are 0. The logic expression is $F = A + B$.

3) NOT gate—more commonly called an inverter, produces an output value that is the opposite of the input value. The logic expression is $F = \overline{A}$.

Three common symbols for every gate are shown in Fig. 2-14 ~ Fig. 2-16 that we can meet in all kinds of references.

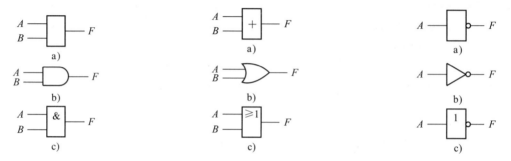

Fig. 2-14　AND gate　　　　Fig. 2-15　OR gate　　　　Fig. 2-16　NOT gate

The basic electronic digital operations are also NOT, AND, OR, but there are combinations of these that are also commonly used: NAND, NOR and EXCLUSIVE NOR (see Fig. 2-17). This is an example of convenient packaging of NAND and AND gates in integrated circuit form.

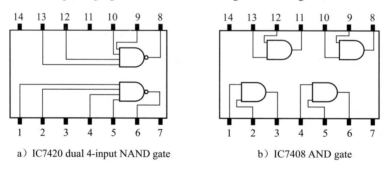

a) IC7420 dual 4-input NAND gate　　　　b) IC7408 AND gate

Fig. 2-17　Integrated circuits of NAND and AND gates

Combinational Logic and Sequential Logic Circuis

Logic circuits are classified into two types: combinational and sequential. A combinational logic is one whose outputs depend only on its current input. A combinational logic circuit may contain an arbitrary number of logic gates and inverters but no feedback loops (a signal path of a circuit that allows the output of a gate to propagate back to the input of that same gate).

When the input is combined with the previous state of the logic circuits, it is referred to as sequential logic. The use of the previous state is called feedback. The outputs of sequential logic circuit depend not only on the current inputs but also on the past sequence of inputs, possibly arbitrarily far back in time. In this sense, a sequential logic circuit can have memory.

In the analysis, use logic diagram and proceed to a formal description of the function performed by that circuit, such as a truth table or a logic expression. In the synthesis, from a formal description and proceeding to a logic diagram. We have learned that there are five possible representations for a combinational logic function:

1) Truth table.
2) An algebraic sum of minterms, the canonical sum.
3) A minterm list using the Σ notation.
4) An algebraic product of maxterms, the canonical product.
5) A maxterm list using the Π notation.

Karnaugh map, like Boolean algebra, is a simplification tool applicable to digital logic. Boolean simplification is actually faster than the Karnaugh map for a task involving two or fewer Boolean variables. It is still quite usable at three variables, but a bit slower. At four input variables, Boolean algebra becomes tedious. Karnaugh maps are both faster and easier. Karnaugh maps work well for up to six input variables, and are usable for up to eight variables. For more than six to eight variables, simplification should be by CAD (Computer Automated Design). It simplifies a logic function by combining pairs of adjacent 1 cells into a Sum-of-Products terms that covers all of the 1 cells. Form groups of 0s to cover all 0s. The Product-of-Sums simplified result is built.

Flip-Flops

"Flip-flop" (see Fig. 2-18) is the common name given to two-state devices which offer basic memory for sequential logic operations. Flip-flops are heavily used for digital data storage and transfer and are commonly used in banks called "registers" for the storage of binary numerical data.

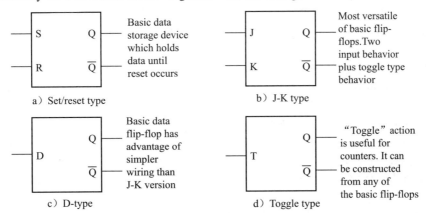

Fig. 2-18 Four types of flip-flop

In an S-R latch, activation of the S input sets the circuit, while activation of the R input resets the circuit. If both S and R inputs are activated simultaneously, the circuit will be in an invalid condition.

The J-K flip-flop is a modified version of an S-R flip-flop with no "invalid" or "illegal" output state. So a J-K flip-flop is nothing more than an S-R flip-flop with an added layer of feedback. This feedback selectively enables one of the two set/reset inputs so that they cannot both carry active signal to the multivibrator circuit, thus eliminating the invalid condition.

The D flip-flop tracks the input, making transitions with match those of the input D. The D stands for "data"; this flip-flop stores the value that is on the data line. It can be thought of as a basic memory cell. A D flip-flop can be made from a S-R flip-flop by tying the set to the reset through an inverter. The result may be clocked.

The T or "toggle" flip-flop changes its output on each clock edge, giving an output which is half the frequency of the signal to the T input. It is useful for constructing binary counters, frequency dividers, and general binary addition devices. It can be made from a J-K flip-flop by tying both of its inputs high.

NEW WORDS AND PHRASES

bipolar *adj.* 双极型的
CMOS *abbr.* Complementary Metal-Oxide-Semiconductor 互补型金属-氧化物-半导体
semiconducting material 半导体材料
integrated circuits 集成电路
transistor *n.* 晶体管
DC *abbr.* Direct Current，直流
AC *abbr.* Alternate Current，交流
digital *adj.* 数字的，计数的
binary *adj.* 具有两个的，二进制的，二变量的
Boolean algebra 布尔代数
positive *adj.* 确实的，积极的，肯定的，现实的，正的，阳性的

negative *adj.* 否定的，否认的，反面的，消极的，反对的，负的，阴极的
hexadecimal *adj.* 十六进制的
number system 计数制
Commutative Law 交换律
Associative Law 结合律
Distributive Law 分配律
inverter *n.* 变换器，倒相器，倒换器，反演器，逆变器，"非"门
truth table 真值表
combinational *adj.* 组合的
sequential *adj.* 时序的
flip-flop *n.* 触发器

NOTES

1) Many so-called "linear" circuits are quite nonlinear in their behavior, either by necessity of physics or by design.
   许多线性电路在工作时呈非线性，或者是由于物理结构造成的，或者是由于电路设计的问题。
2) Simply stated, the transistor conducts a collector current I_C which is a copy of the base current I_B amplified by a factor of β.
   简单地说，晶体管集电极电流 I_C 较基极电流 I_B 放大 β 倍。
3) AND gate——produces a 1 output if both of its inputs are 1.
   与门——输入全1输出1。
4) A combinational logic circuit may contain an arbitrary number of logic gates and inverters but no feedback loops.
   组合逻辑电路可能包括许多逻辑门和反向器，但不包含反馈电路。
5) It simplifies a logic function by combining pairs of adjacent 1 cells into a Sum-Of-Products terms that covers all of the 1 cells.
   卡诺图通过合并相邻项简化逻辑函数，把所有的1项合并成积和式。

EXERCISES

1. Please translate the following words and phrases into Chinese.

a) semiconductor   b) number system   c) IC   d) Commutative Law
e) AC   f) Distributive Law g) binary h) inverter
i) negative   j) sequential

2. Please translate the following words and phrases into English.

a) 双极型的   b) 晶体管   c) N 沟道   d) 线性化

e）布尔代数　　　　　f）真值表　　　　　g）触发器　　　h）组合逻辑电路
i）相邻项　　　　　　j）积和式

3. Fill in the blanks with the missing word(s).

a) _____ circuits are circuits dealing with signals free to vary from zero to full power supply voltage. This stands in contrast to _____, which almost exclusively employ "all or nothing" signals.

b) The PNP transistor is complementary to the NPN, with the current flow _____ the emitter and the collector and base, the opposite of what happens in the NPN.

c) While the base current is small in small signal operation, in power applications, where the transistor is used as a _____, the base current necessary to keep the transistor on can be very high.

d) Logic circuits are classified into two types: combinational and sequential. A _____ is one whose outputs depend only on its current input.

e) A combinational logic circuit may contain an arbitrary number of logic gates and inverters but no _____ (a signal path of a circuit that allows the output of a gate to propagate back to the input of that same gate).

f) When the input is combined with the previous state of the logic circuits, it is referred to as _____. The use of the previous state is called feedback.

g) The outputs of sequential logic circuit depend not only on the current inputs but also on _____, possibly arbitrarily far back in time. A seal-in circuit is an example of a _____.

4. Answer the following questions according to the text.

a) How does a NPN transistor work?

b) What is the advantage of bipolar over CMOS?

c) What are the combinational circuit and the sequential circuit?

d) What is the output/input relationship of NAND gate?

READING

Operational Amplifier

The term operational amplifier or "op-amp" refers to a class of high-gain DC coupled amplifiers with two inputs and a single output. The operational amplifier is arguably the most useful single device in analog electronic circuitry. With only a handful of external components, it can be made to perform a wide variety of analog signal processing tasks. Most existing operational amplifiers are produced on a single semiconductor substrate as an integrated circuit. These integrated circuits are used as building blocks in a wide variety of applications.

1. History

The operational amplifier was originally designed to perform mathematical operations by using voltage as an analogue of another quantity. This is the basis of the analog computer, where op-amps were used to model the basic mathematical operations (addition, subtraction, integration, differentiation, and so on). However, an ideal operational amplifier is an extremely versatile circuit element, with a great many applications beyond mathematical operations. Practical op-amps,

运算放大器

运算放大器或"运放"是指有两个输入端和一个输出端的高增益的直流放大器。实践证明，运算放大器是模拟电子线路中最为有用的器件。只增加一些外部元器件，运算放大器可以完成很多种类的模拟信号处理任务。大多数现存的运算放大器都是集成在单一半导体基底上的集成电路。这些集成电路作为标准模块广泛应用。

1. 发展历史

最初设计运算放大器是为了用电压模拟其他量进行数学运算。这是模拟计算机的基础，计算机采用运放对简单的数学运算（加法、减法、积分、微分等）建模。然而，理想运放是一种用途非常广泛的电路器件，除了数学运算之外，还有非常多的应用。实际的运放具有同理想运放相近的优良性能，它

based on transistors, tubes, or other amplifying components and implemented as discrete or integrated circuits, are good approximations to the ideal.

Op-amps were originally developed in the vacuum tube era, where they were used in analog computers. Op-amps are now normally implemented as integrated circuits (ICs), though versions with discrete components are used when performance beyond that attainable with ICs is required (see Fig. 2-19).

The first integrated op-amp to become widely available, in the late 1960s, was the bipolar Fairchild μA709, created by Bob Widlar in 1965; it was rapidly superseded by the 741, which has better performance and is more stable and easier to use. The μA741 is still in production, and has become ubiquitous in electronics—many manufacturers produce a version of this classic chip, recognizable by part numbers containing "741." Better designs have since been introduced, some based on the FET (late 1970s) and MOSFET (early 1980s). Many of these more modern devices can be substituted into an older 741-based circuit and work with no other changes, to give better performance.

Op-amps usually have parameters within tightly specified limits, with standardized packaging and power supply needs. Op-amps have many uses in electronics. In its ordinary usage, the output of the op-amp is controlled by negative feedback which, because of the amplifier's high gain, almost completely determines the output voltage for any given input. Many standard IC op-amps cost only a few cents in moderate production volume, but integrated or discrete amplifiers with non-standard specifications may cost over $100 in small quantities.

2. Basic Principle of Amplifiers

Electronic amplifiers are often symbolized by a simple triangle shape, where the internal components are not individually represented. As shown in Fig. 2-20, the usual circuit symbol for an op-amp is

V_+: non-inverting input

V_-: inverting input

们常常基于晶体管、电子管或其他放大器件，作为分立或集成电路使用。

运放起源于电子管时代，应用于模拟计算机中。如今，虽然有些分立元件组成的电路在性能上可能会超过集成电路，但运放一般还是以集成电路的形式存在（见图2-19）。

20世纪60年代末期，第一代集成运放双极型Fairchild μA709得到广泛应用，它是Bob Widlar于1965年发明的，但很快被性能更好、更稳定、更简单的μA741所取代。现在μA741仍然在生产，并且在电子产品中无处不在——许多厂家都在生产这个经典芯片的不同版本，并且可以通过部件上标识的"741"来识别。人们已经开发出更好的设计方法，如基于FET（20世纪70年代末）和MOSEFT（20世纪80年代初）的集成运放。许多现代化的元器件可以取代老式的基于电子线路的741型集成运放，它们在使用方面没有任何区别，但能够达到更好的性能。

运放的参数通常具有严格指定的极限值，有标准封装和供电电压。运放广泛用于电子产品中。在正常使用中，运放的输出由负反馈信号控制，因为运放的增益很高，所以无论输入信号如何，负反馈信号都几乎完全决定了输出电压值。由于现代工业批量生产，许多标准化的集成运放都非常便宜，但也有一些集成的或分立的非标准运放会由于产量少，可能花费超过100美元。

2. 运放的基本原理

电子放大器一般都表示成三角形，内部器件并不分别表示出来。如图2-20所示，运放的电路符号一般表示为

V_+: 同相输入端

V_-: 反相输入端

Fig. 2-19　Op-amp ICs in 8-pin Dual In-line Packages (DIPs)

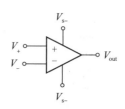

Fig. 2-20　Operational amplifier symbol typically used in circuit diagrams

V_{out}: output

$V_{\text{s+}}$: positive power supply (sometimes also VDD, VCC or VCC+)

$V_{\text{s-}}$: negative power supply (sometimes also VSS, VEE or VCC-)

These amplifier types are called the differential amplifier. Differential amplifiers amplify the voltage difference between two input signals. Voltage output equation is

$$V_{\text{out}} = A[\text{input}(+) - \text{input}(-)] \quad (2\text{-}11)$$

Where A is the open-loop gain of the op-amp. The inputs are assumed to have very high impedance; negligible current will flow into or out of the inputs. Op-amp outputs have very low source impedance. The input (-) is commonly referred to as the inverting input and the (+) as the noninverting input. An increasingly positive voltage on the input (+) tends to drive the output voltage more positive, and an increasingly positive voltage on the input (-) tends to drive the output voltage more negative. When the polarity of the differential voltage matches the markings for inverting and noninverting inputs, the output will be positive. When the polarity of the differential voltage clashes with the input markings, the output will be negative.

If the output is connected to the inverting input, after being scaled by a voltage divider $K = R_1/(R_1 + R_2)$ (see Fig. 2-21), then

$$V_+ = V_{\text{in}}$$

$$V_- = KV_{\text{out}}$$

$$V_{\text{out}} = G(V_{\text{in}} - KV_{\text{out}})$$

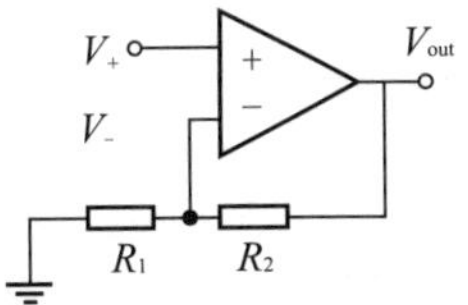

Solving for $V_{\text{out}}/V_{\text{in}}$, we see that the result is a linear amplifier with gain

$$V_{\text{out}}/V_{\text{in}} = G/(1 + GK) \quad (2\text{-}12)$$

If G is very large, $V_{\text{out}}/V_{\text{in}}$ comes close to $1/K$, which equals $1+R_2/R_1$.

This negative feedback connection is the most typical use of an op-amp, but many different configurations are possible, making it one of the most versatile of all electronic building blocks.

When connected in a negative feedback configuration, the op-amp will try to make V_{out} whatever voltage is necessary to make the input voltages equal. These, and the high input impedance, are sometimes called the two "golden rules" of op-amp design (for circuits that use feedback):

1) No current will flow into the inputs.

2) The input voltages will be equal to each other.

The exception is if the voltage required is greater than the op-amp's supply, in which case the output signal stops near

V_{out}：输出端

$V_{\text{s+}}$：正电源端（有时也记作 VDD、VCC 或 VCC+）

$V_{\text{s-}}$：负电源端（有时也记作 VSS、VEE 或 VCC-）

这种放大器称为差分放大器。差分放大器对两个输入端口之间的电压差值进行放大。电压输出为

式中，A 是运放的开环增益。假设运放具有非常高的输入阻抗，那么几乎没有电流由输入端流入或流出运放。运放的输出端具有非常低的电源阻抗。"-"输入称为反相输入端，"+"输入称为同相输入端。增大同相输入端的电压，会使输出电压增大；增大反相输入端的电压，会使输出电压减小。当差分电压的极性与反相输入端和同相输入端的标记一致时，输出端为正；当不一致时，输出端为负。

如果将输出端通过一个分压器 $K=R_1/(R_1+R_2)$ 连接到输入端（见图 2-21），得到

Fig. 2-21 In-phase operation amplifier

通过求解 $V_{\text{out}}/V_{\text{in}}$，可发现结果呈线性放大，其增益为

如果 G 非常大，则 $V_{\text{out}}/V_{\text{in}}$ 将接近 $1/K$，且 $1/K=1+R_2/R_1$。

运放的典型连接采用负反馈形式，但也有许多不同的用法，这就使得运放成为所有电子模块中最为万能的器件之一。

当连接成负反馈形式时，运放将尽量保持 V_{out} 同输入电压之间必要的平衡。这一点连同高输入阻抗，常常被看作运算放大器（采用反馈的）电路设计中的两个"金科玉律"：

1) 输入端无电流流入。

2) 两个输入端的电压相等。

但也有例外，如果所需要的电压大于

the power supply rails, V_{s+} or V_{s-}.

If we connect the output of an op-amp to its inverting input and apply a voltage signal to the noninverting input, we find that the output voltage of the op-amp closely follows that input voltage.

As V_{in} increases, V_{out} will increase in accordance with the differential gain. However, as V_{out} increases, that output voltage is fed back to the inverting input, thereby acting to decrease the voltage differential between inputs, which acts to bring the output down. What will happen for any given voltage input is that the op-amp will output a voltage very nearly equal to V_{in}, but just low enough so that there's enough voltage difference left between V_{in} and the input (-) to be amplified to generate the output voltage.

The circuit will quickly reach a point of stability (known as equilibrium in physics), where the output voltage is just the right amount to maintain the right amount of differential, which in turn produces the right amount of output voltage. Taking the op-amp's output voltage and coupling it to the inverting input is a technique known as negative feedback, and it is the key to having a self-stabilizing system (this is true not only of op-amps, but of any dynamic system in general). This stability gives the op-amp the capacity to work in its linear (active) mode, as opposed to merely being saturated fully "on" or "off" as it was used as a comparator, with no feedback at all.

One great advantage to using an op-amp with negative feedback is that the actual voltage gain of the op-amp doesn't matter, so long as it's very large. If the op-amp's differential gain were 250,000 instead of 200,000, all it would mean is that the output voltage would hold just a little closer to V_{in} (less differential voltage needed between inputs to generate the required output). In the circuit of Fig. 2-22, the output voltage would still be (for all practical purposes) equal to the non-inverting input voltage. Op-amp gains, therefore, do not have to be precisely set by the factory in order for the circuit designer to build an amplifier circuit

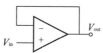

Fig. 2-22　Buffer amplifier

with precise gain. Negative feedback makes the system self-correcting. The circuit as a whole will simply follow the input voltage with a stable gain of 1.

If we add a voltage divider (see Fig. 2-23) to the negative feedback wiring so that only a fraction of the output voltage is fed back to the inverting input instead of the full amount, the output voltage will be a multiple of the input voltage (please bear in mind that the power supply connections to the op-amp have been omitted once again).

运放所能提供的电压，输出信号就会停止变化并接近电源值V_{s+}或V_{s-}。

如果将运算放大器的输出端连接在反相输入端并且给同相输入端加上电压信号，我们就会发现运放的输出电压将跟踪输入电压。

当V_{in}增大时，V_{out}和差分增益一致也增大。而当V_{out}增大时，输出电压将反馈到反相输入端，从而两输入端口之间的差分电压减小，进而使得输出端电压减小。在任何情况下，对于给定的输入电压，运放的输出电压必将近似等于输入电压V_{in}，但其电压差足够小，使得V_{in}和反相输入端之间有足够的电压差，进而对差分电压放大产生输出。

电流将很快达到稳定点（称为物理平衡），这时输出电压达到维持正确差分量的适当值，而这反过来又产生适当的输出电压。我们将运放的输出电压引出并连接在反相输入端的技术称为负反馈，这正是形成自稳定系统的关键所在（不仅在运放电路中，而且在任何常用的动态系统中都是如此）。稳定性使得运放工作在它的线性（有源）模式中，而当运放用于饱和状态下的"开"或"关"时就不同了，如在比较器中，根本不存在反馈。

将负反馈用在运放中的一个非常重要的优点就是不考虑运放实际的放大增益，只要其增益非常大即可。如果运放增益为250 000而不是200 000，也仅仅使得输出电压更接近V_{in}一些（输入端的电压差只需要很小就可以产生所要求的输出）。在图2-22所示的电路中，输出电压将（事实上也是这样）始终等于同相输入端的电压。所以，不必要求生产运放的厂家将运放的增益设定得很精准，不必要求电路设计者设计具有精准增益的放大器电路。负反馈使得系统具有自修正的功能。从整体来看，图2-22中的电路仅仅使输出电压跟随输入电压，它的稳定增益为1。

如果我们在负反馈线上添加分压器（见图2-23），则这样只有输出的一部分而不是全部反馈到反相输入端，输出电压将是输入电压的倍数（为简单起见，此处省略了电源同运放之间的连接）。

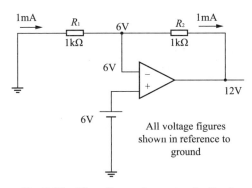

Fig. 2-23 The effects of negative feedback

If R_1 and R_2 are both equal and V_{in} is 6V, the op-amp will output whatever voltage is needed to drop 6V across R_1 (to make the inverting input voltage equal to 6V, as well, keeping the voltage difference between the two inputs equal to zero). With the 2∶1 voltage divider of R_1 and R_2, this will take 12V at the output of the op-amp to accomplish.

Another way of analyzing this circuit is to start by calculating the magnitude and direction of current through R_1, knowing the voltage on either side (and therefore, by subtraction, the voltage across R_1), and R_1's resistance. Since the left-hand side of R_1 is connected to ground (0V) and the right-hand side is at a potential of 6V (due to the negative feedback holding that point equal to V_{in}), we can see that we have 6V across R_1. This gives us 1mA of current through R_1 from left to right. Because we know that both inputs of the op-amp have extremely high impedance, we can safely assume they won't add or subtract any current through the divider. In other words, we can treat R_1 and R_2 as being in series with each other: all of the electrons flowing through R_1 must flow through R_2. Knowing the current through R_2 and the resistance of R_2, we can calculate the voltage across R_2 (6V), and its polarity. Counting up voltages from ground (0V) to the right-hand side of R_2, we arrive at 12V on the output.

3. Integrator and Differentiator

An integrator circuit is shown in Fig. 2-24. Show that the output signal of the amplifier is

$$V_{out} = -\frac{1}{RC}\int V_{in} dt \quad (2-13)$$

Build the circuit with $R = 10\text{k}\Omega$, $C = 0.1\mu\text{F}$ and use square and sinusoidal wave forms to test the predicted behavior. Also place a 100MΩ resistor in parallel with the capacitor. This resistor drains charge to avoid saturation due to very low frequency or DC signals.

A differentiator circuit is shown in Fig. 2-25. Show that the output signal of the amplifier is

如果 R_1 和 R_2 相等，并且 V_{in} 为 6V，无论输出电压是多少，都将使 R_1 两端的压降为 6V（使得反向输入电压等于 6V，同时保持两个输入之间的电压差为 0）。设分压器 R_1/R_2 为 2∶1，运放输出端的电压值为 12V。

还有一种分析这个电路的方法，首先计算通过 R_1 的电流的大小和方向，得出其两端的电压值（用减法计算 R_1 的电压）及 R_1 的电阻值。然后将 R_1 的左侧接地（0V），右侧接到 6V 的电势端（因为反馈使得此处电势等于 V_{in}），我们将看到 R_1 两端的电压差为 6V。我们将得到从左到右流过 R_1 的 1mA 的电流。我们知道运放的两个输入端都有非常高的阻抗，所以可以大胆地假设并没有通过分压器增加或减少电流。换句话说，我们可以认为 R_1 和 R_2 彼此串联，即流过 R_1 的电流一定会流过 R_2。知道了通过 R_2 的电流以及 R_2 的电阻，就可以计算 R_2 两端的电压（6V）及其极性。计算从地（0V）到 R_2 右侧的电压值，可得到输出端电压为 12V。

3. 积分器和微分器

图 2-24 所示为积分器电路。运放输出端信号为

令 $R = 10\text{k}\Omega$，$C = 0.1\mu\text{F}$，用方波和正弦波来测试电路的预测功能。同时把 100MΩ 电阻与电容平行放置。由于频率太低或直流信号，电阻会耗尽电荷以避免饱和。

图 2-25 所示为微分器电路。运放输出端信号为

$$V_{out} = -RC\frac{dV_{in}}{dt}V_{out} = R_f\left(\frac{V_1}{R_1} + \frac{V_2}{R_2} + \cdots + \frac{V_n}{R_n}\right) \quad (2\text{-}14)$$

Build the circuit with $R=10\text{k}\Omega$, $C=0.1\mu\text{F}$ and use triangle and sinusoidal wave forms to test the predicted behavior.

令 $R=10\text{k}\Omega$，$C=0.1\mu\text{F}$，用三角波和正弦波来测试电路的预测功能。

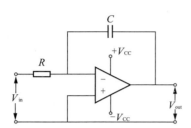

Fig. 2-24　Integrator circuit

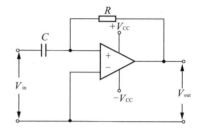

Fig. 2-25　Differentiator circuit

4. Oscillator

An oscillator (see Fig. 2-26) is a device that produces an Alternating Current (AC), or at least pulsing, output voltage. Oscillators are very useful devices, and they are easily made with just an op-amp and a few external components.

When the output is saturated positive, the V_{ref} will be positive, and the capacitor will charge up in a positive direction. When V_{ramp} exceeds V_{ref} by the tiniest margin, the output will saturate negative, and the capacitor will charge in the opposite direction (polarity). Oscillation occurs because the positive feedback is instantaneous and the negative feedback is delayed (by means of a RC time constant). The frequency of this oscillator may be adjusted by varying the size of any component.

5. Low Power Op-Amp-Audio Amp (50 milliwatt)

Fig. 2-27 illustrates using an op-amp as an audio amplifier for a simple intercom. A small 8Ω speaker is used as a microphone which is coupled to the op-amp input through a $0.1\mu\text{F}$ capacitor. The speaker is sensitive to low frequencies and the small value capacitor serves to attenuate the lower tones and produce a better overall response. You can experiment with different value capacitors to improve the response for various speakers. The op-amp voltage gain is determined by the ratio of the feedback resistor to the series input resistor

4. 振荡器

振荡器（见图2-26）用来产生交流（AC）的输出电压，至少是脉冲信号。振荡器应用很广，它可以由运放和少量外围器件简单组成。

当输入是正饱和状态时，V_{ref} 也是正的，并且电容器将正方向充电。当 V_{ramp} 通过不断累积超出 V_{ref} 时，输出就会变为负饱和状态，并且电容器将反向充电。因为正反馈是瞬间发生的且负反馈会发生延迟（以 RC 为时间常数），所以振荡会重复地进行。振荡器的频率可以通过变换元器件的尺寸进行调节。

5. 低功率放大器和音频放大器（50mW）

图2-27所示的是由运放组成的音频放大器，用来做简单的对讲机。一个 8Ω 的扬声器用来做麦克风，通过一个 $0.1\mu\text{F}$ 的电容器连接到运放的输入端。扬声器对低频信号很敏感，小的电容器用来降低低的声调，并且产生更好的综合响应。你可以通过试验使用不同的电容器来改善各种扬声器的响应。运放的增益由反馈电阻和

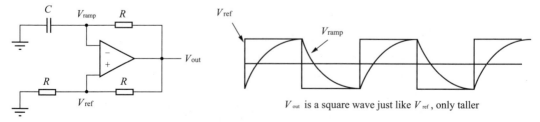

Fig. 2-26　Oscillator circuit with positive feedback

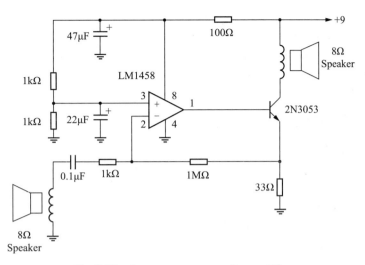

Fig. 2-27 An op-amp as an audio amplifier

which is around one thousand in this case (1MΩ/ 1kΩ). The non-inverting input (pin 3) to the op-amp is biased at 50% of the supply voltage (4.5V) by a couple 1kΩ resistors connected across the supply. Since both inputs will be equal when the op-amp is operating within it's linear range, the voltage at the inverting input (pin 2) and the emitter of the buffer transistor (2N3053) will also be 4.5V. The voltage change at the emitter of the transistor will be around ±2V for a 2mV change at the input (junction of 0.1μF cap and 1kΩ resistor) which produces a current change of about 2/33 = 60mA through the 33Ω emitter resistor and the speaker output. The peak output speaker power is about I^2R or $0.06^2 \times 8 = 28mW$. The 100Ω resistor and 47μF capacitor are used to isolate the op-amp from the power supply and reduce the possibility of oscillation. An additional 22μF cap is used at the non-inverting input to further stabilize operation. These parts may not be needed in such a low power circuit but it's a good idea to decouple the power supply to avoid unwanted feedback. The circuit draws about 1.2W from a 9V source and is not very efficient but fairly simple to put together. The circuit was tested using a couple of 4 inch speakers located a few feet apart (to reduce feedback) and a small pocket transistor radio placed on top of the speaker/microphone as an audio source.

Although an operational amplifier is actually a differential-input voltage amplifier with a very high gain, it is almost never used directly as an open-loop voltage amplifier in linear applications for several reasons. First, the gain variation from one operational amplifier to another is quite high and may vary by ±50% or more from the value specified by the manufacturer. Second, other nonidealities such as the offset voltage

串联输入电阻之比决定，比值为1000 (1MΩ/1kΩ)。由于有两个1kΩ的电阻跨接在电源端，运放的同相输入端（引脚3）有一个50%电源电压（4.5V）的偏置。当运放工作在线性区时，由于两个输入端口的电压相等，因此反向输入端（引脚2）和缓冲晶体管（2N3053）发射器的电压也同样为4.5V。对于输入端（连接0.1μF电容和1kΩ的电阻）发生2mV的电压变化，晶体管发射器的电压变化大约在±2V左右，大约2/33 = 60mA的电流流过33Ω的射极电阻和扬声器，扬声器的峰值输出约为I^2R或者$0.06^2 \times 8 = 28mW$。100Ω的电阻和47μF的电容将运放同电源隔离，并且降低可能产生的振荡。在同相输入端加一个22μF的电容可使其功能更加稳定。这部分在低功率电路中不是必需的，但它是一种解除电源耦合的好方式，以避免不需要的反馈。该电路有一个电压为9V、功率为1.2W的电源，虽然效率不高，但连接很简单。用两个4英寸的扬声器对这个电路进行测试，让几个引脚分开（以减少反馈），将一个小型的晶体管收音机安装在扬声器/传声器的顶部位置作为音频源。

虽然运算放大器实际上是一个高增益的差分输入电压放大器，但由于几种原因，它很少在线性应用中直接用作开环电压放大器。首先，根据制造商的特别说明，运放之间的增益变化非常大，大约±50%，甚至更

make it impractical to stabilize the DC operating point. Finally, performance characteristics such as linearity and bandwidth of the open-loop operational amplifier are poor. In linear applications, the operational amplifier is almost always used in a feedback mode.

大。其次,一些不想要的参数会使其不能稳定地工作在直流平衡点上,如失调电压。最后,运放的一些性能特征参数(如开环运算放大器的线性度和带宽)很差。在线性应用中,运放几乎都采用反馈模式。

NEW WORDS AND PHRASES

operational amplifier   n. 运算放大器
high-gain   n. 高增益
amplifier   n. 扩音器,放大器
integrated circuit   集成电路
versatile   adj. 通用的,万能的,多才多艺的,多面手的
tube   n. 管,管子,<美> 电子管,显像管
discrete   adj. 不连续的,离散的
approximation   n. 接近,走近,[数] 近似值
discrete component   分立元件
bipolar   adj. 有两极的,双极的
be superseded by   被……取代
ubiquitous   adj. 到处存在的,(同时)普遍存在的
negative feedback   负反馈
differential amplifier   差分放大器
configuration   n. 构造,结构,配置,外形
self-stabilizing system   自稳定系统
wiring   n. 配线
input impedance   输入阻抗

fraction   n. 小部分,片断,分数
subtraction   n. 减少
sinusoidal wave   正弦波
square wave   方波
triangle wave   三角波
oscillator   n. 振荡器
pulsing   n. 脉冲调制
exceed   v. 超过
tinily   adv. 极小地,微小地
instantaneous   adj. 瞬间的,即刻的,即时的
milliwatt   n. 毫瓦
intercom   n. 对讲机
emitter   n. 发射极
junction   n. 结,连接点
decouple   v. 分离,减弱
open-loop   n. 开环
manufacturer   n. 制造业者,厂商
offset   vt. 抵消
bandwidth   n. 带宽

NOTES

1) Electronic amplifiers are often symbolized by a simple triangle shape, where the internal components are not individually represented.
电子放大器一般都表示成三角形,内部器件并不分别表示出来。

2) An increasingly positive voltage on the input (+) tends to drive the output voltage more positive, and an increasingly positive voltage on the input (-) tends to drive the output voltage more negative.
增大同相输入端(+)的电压,会使输出电压增大;增大反相输入端(-)的电压,会使输出电压减小。

3) Because we know that both inputs of the op-amp have extremely high impedance, we can safely assume they won't add or subtract any current through the divider.
因为我们知道,运算放大器的两个输入端都有相当高的电阻,所以我们完全可以假设它们没有增加或减少任何电流。

4) In other words, we can treat R_1 and R_2 as being in series with each other: all of the electrons flowing through R_1 must flow through R_2.
换句话说,我们可以认为 R_1 和 R_2 串联,即通过 R_1 的电流一定会通过 R_2。

2.3 Radio Receiver Circuit

RF, the radio frequency portion of the radio spectrum is considered to extend from 3 to 1000MHz (1GHz). At the opposite end of the spectrum, below the High Frequency (HF) band (3~30MHz), the AM radio band extends from 650 to 1650kHz. At these relatively low frequencies the effects of parasitic inductance and capacitance on circuit designs are minimal.

The radio receiver is often a student's first introduction analog electronics. However, today's receivers are amazingly complex structures. The architecture of modern receivers continues to evolve to account not only for improvements in the analog performance of devices but for advance in DSP (Digital Signal Processing) that permit more functions to be programmed in software rather than being hardwired in the circuits themselves.

1. The Superheterodyne Receiver-Analog System

The superheterodyne, or superhet, receiver, is a well-known and almost universal receiver architecture for radio receivers. We will see that such a receiver can provide both good selectivity and sensitivity, because the noise bandwidth can be limited to the channel bandwidth without compromising the receiver's ability to tune across the entire RF band. Its basic components are shown in Fig. 2-28.

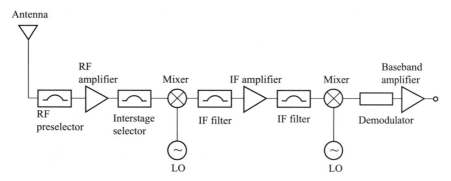

Fig. 2-28 Basic architecture of the analog superheterodyne receiver

RF Preselector

The purpose of this component is to filter out all unwanted signals lying outside the RF band containing the possible channels to be detected. Unwanted signals can include signals fed from the transmitter itself, which might share a common antenna. In this case the preselector is either a diplexer, a filter that allows one frequency band to pass between the antenna and receiver and another (different) band to pass between the transmitter and antenna (as, for example, in CDMA mobile systems), and/or a transmit/receive switch that turns on during the receive phase and off during the transmit phase (as, for example, in GSM systems). Such a circuit thus allows full or half-duplex operation, respectively, and prevents overload of the downstream receiver components from unwanted frequencies. The function of the preselection filter is also to suppress the undesired responses at the output that arise from incoming signals lying at spurious frequencies that the receiver is not tuned to receive (which we will call the tuned frequency f_T). We will see that such spurious frequencies can include the image frequency as well as harmonics of the incoming tuned frequency. Ideally, the preselector will also have a good impedance match in-band to avoid bandpass ripple.

RF Amplifier

The function of the input amplifier is to linearly amplify the input signal and minimize the noise added by the receiver to the signal itself. We will see that such low noise amplification can be achieved by noise matching the input of the amplifier, and is important because it can determine the overall noise matching of the entire receiver. It should have a good input and output match to avoid gain ripple. In addition, the input amplifier must not introduce distortion of the signal, because strong signals may be simultaneously present in adjacent (unwanted) channels, and any nonlinear distortion of the amplifier could swamp a weaker signal in the channel we are trying to detect. To achieve this, it will require a reasonable maximum power-handling capability indicated by its input intercept point. Of course, the RF amplifier can consist of multiple stages in order to provide the necessary gain.

Interstage Selector

The preceding amplifier will provide gain to all the channels within the RF bandwidth, and its gain is likely to roll off slowly beyond it. Furthermore, the amplifier will amplify noise across the entire band, and possibly at the image frequency as well. Therefore, this (optional) component is a filter to suppress any gain of undesired signal responses at spurious frequencies, and in particular at the image frequency. It thus maintains the system noise figure by preventing image noise from entering the mixer. It also helps to minimize LO reradiation from the RF mixer port. This component should have low in-band loss.

Local Oscillator

This is a strong signal that is normally generated by a frequency synthesizer, and is typically tuned across a bandwidth equal to the entire RF bandwidth, but offset from it, to choose any desired channel. Its function is to drive the devices within the mixer into a nonlinear regime for frequency translation (mixing). An important oscillator specification is its phase noise, since any phase fluctuation on the oscillator signal is directly superimposed on the mixer output signal. Its broadband noise should also be low so as not to raise the system noise floor. It will also require a good tuning range or bandwidth, and low spurious and harmonic content.

First Mixer

This component translates all incoming signals in the RF frequency range into signals in some intermediate frequency range, depending on the local oscillator signal frequency. The mixer translates all frequencies linearly, preserving phase information within the new range of frequencies. Within some range of RF signal amplitudes, the amplitude of the output signal is also preserved on the IF. We will also see that the choice of mixer topology (e.g., single balanced, double balanced, and so forth) is important in rejecting unwanted mixer output components. It requires low LO feed through to the RF and IF, and a large spurious-free dynamic range for the incoming RF signal. The selection of the IF frequency is important in ensuring the receiver response to unwanted spurious responses is minimized. A historic rule of thumb for HF/VHF receivers is that signals are upconverted to an IF at twice the highest RF frequency. At microwave frequencies where the tuning range is much less, signals are typically downconverted to a lower frequency. IF frequencies from 45 to 82MHz are common for mobile radio receivers in the 800MHz band, and from 110 to 300MHz for radios in the 1,800MHz band or for both bands.

IF Filter

This component rejects the unwanted signal components generated by the mixer and other components. Its bandwidth must be sufficiently wide to pass the modulation sidebands in the desired channel without distortion. It can be high Q because it is of fixed frequency. The blocking and overload characteristics of the receiver are often determined here in combination with the following.

IF Amplifier

This component should provide adequate gain to the IF signal to drive the following stages. Because it is at a fixed frequency it can provide high gain and be well stabilized.

Second Mixer, Local Oscillator, and Second Filter

Sometimes known as the second IF strip, these components mirror the functions of the first IF strip, but across a different frequency band and with different passband characteristics. The first IF strip is designed to receive the entire RF passband and to reject spurious frequencies and the image frequency in particular, while the function of the second IF strip is to narrow in and select the desired channel from the entire passband, thereby providing additional selectivity to the receiver. For commercial AM radios, 455kHz is a fairly standard second IF frequency, while mobile phone receivers typically use frequencies around 10MHz. In some architecture, the second IF is omitted totally and a single downconversion from RF to a low IF is used instead. In that case, the (first) IF filter also performs channel selection.

Demodulator

This component extracts the modulated signal from the IF signal and converts it to baseband. In the case of an analog system, this information will be either AM or FM; for a digital system, it will typically be symbols having multiamplitude levels that are later decoded. (A symbol is the way a bit or combinations of bits are coded in the waveform.)

Baseband Amplifier

This provides output power to derive drive the relevant output device, which could typically be a speaker, fax output or video screen.

One variation on the standard superheterodyne structure is to fix the (first) LO frequency and downconvert the entire RF band to a wideband IF. This enables a fixed frequency, thus high Q, low-phase noise oscillator to be used for the RF LO, and tuning and channel selection to be performed by varying the IF (second) LO. This can overcome the problem of phase noise introduced by the LO. It can, however, result in do offsets at baseband since the second LO will be at the same frequency as the IF, but this is not a problem unique to this architecture. It does however require a second LO with a broad percentage tuning range, and also exposes the second mixer stage to strong adjacent-channel interferers since now the RF stage has limited ability to select the desired channel.

2. Receiver Characterization

We have already used two terms-receiver sensitivity and receiver selectivity-that turn out to be the two fundamental criteria in evaluating the quality of a receiver. There are other system parameters such as the receiver dynamic range and its maximum input signal, can be determined from the system architecture and a few key parameters of each of the subsystems or components within the architecture. In particular, by configuring the gain, noise figure, power capabilities, and frequency characteristics of each stage, we can derive the overall receiver performance.

Communications Channel

First, however, we will briefly consider the fundamental physical constraints and trade-offs that eventually determine the performance limits of a particular radio system.

Information theory is a complex and well-developed field in its own right. Much emphasis has been given recently to the development of new modulation and coding schemes that conserve bandwidth, power, and minimize the effects of distortion on other systems. This is important because spectrum is a limited, scarce, and consequently expensive resource that needs to be allocated sparingly and used to the benefit of all users.

$$C = B\log_2(1 + \text{SNR}) \tag{2-15}$$

A fundamental result from this theory is Shannon's equation, which predicts the capacity or information throughput of a communications channel. It can be stated in many ways, but for our purposes is a useful form. This states that the channel capacity C (measured as bits per second) is proportional to the channel bandwidth B and to the base-2 log of the Signal-to-Noise Ratio (SNR) at the detector. This equation shows why spectrum is such an expensive resource, because as the signal occupies more bandwidth-assuming signal power and SNR remain the same-more data can be squeezed through it. In practice, modern systems use sophisticated error detection involving the transmission of redundant bits and complex coding schemes in order to approach Shannon's theoretical limit.

A result that can be derived from the above is that for a given channel with some maximum information throughput, the power (or more specifically, the signal-to-noise ratio at the detector) needed to transmit that information through it can be traded off for spectral occupancy or bandwidth B according to

$$\text{SNR}_2 = \text{SNR}_1^{(B_1/B_2)} (\text{SNR} \gg 1) \tag{2-16}$$

Thus if the spectral occupancy B_2 can be increased, the SNR can be lower for the same information transfer rate. A good example of this is to compare the GSM cellular system with CDMA. Both use the same transmission media (free space) and are subject to similar noise sources. Yet the received GSM signal must be several decibels above the noise level to be detectable, whereas the spread CDMA signal can be detected even when buried in the noise. By clever coding that smears the signal across a large bandwidth, the CDMA signal power can be reduced to a level so that the received signal appears like noise to receivers tuned to other channels.

Receiver Noise

We have seen already that noise plays a major role in determining the overall performance of a receiver because, with the signal power, it enters as the SNR into fundamental equations that determine the data rate of the system, and the minimum signal level that can be received.

Noise enters the receiver through a number of sources:
- The channel and into the system through the antenna, where it is usually modeled as additive, white, Gaussian noise and is thermal in nature;
- The RF preselector, which bandlimits the signal but has a finite insertion loss and therefore a thermal noise contribution;
- The active devices, which contribute thermal noise, shot noise, and $1/f$ noise.

These noise components produce a noise floor that sets the minimum signal level that can be detected. The noise is characterized by its power spectral density, and it can be a function of frequency.

Power spectral density is the power contained within a given bandwidth, so has units of watts per hertz. Although we sometimes refer to noise voltage and noise current per hertz, in RF systems we typically measure power into a fixed reference impedance level (usually 50Ω). In this case, the thermal is a function of resistance and a fundamental result of noise power is

$$P_N = KTB \qquad (2\text{-}17)$$

for the total noise power P_N, where K is Boltzmann's constant and T is the temperature in Kelvin. Clearly, the larger the bandwidth, the greater the noise power. It is for this reason that the final IF filter needs to be as narrow as possible, in order to minimize the noise power just prior to demodulation and detection. This final IF filter determines the overall noise bandwidth of the entire receiver since it will be the most narrowband component in the entire chain prior to detection.

In the radio bands below about 30MHz, the external noise is much greater than that calculated, due to both natural and man-made phenomenon. The excess above the thermal floor varies from around 12dB in rural areas at 30MHz to as high as 76dB at a noisy urban site at low megahertz frequencies. This increase in the minimum receiver noise level needs to be considered when determining the weakest signal that can be detected.

Receiver Sensitivity

The noise floor of a receiver, just prior to demodulation and detection of the signal, determines how strong the input signal must be to be correctly interpreted, either as a "1" or a "0" in a digital system, or as a high-quality analog waveform in an analog system. This minimum input signal strength needed to produce a good quality output signal is referred to as the receiver sensitivity. However, just as there are many definitions of what constitutes acceptable quality, there are equally numerous definitions of sensitivity.

The noise floor at the input is accounted not only for thermal noise at the input, but all noise added by the system itself. If we now assume that an input signal must at least equal the noise level in order to be detected, then this input-referred noise floor is sometimes referred to as the Minimum Detectable Signal (MDS). However, most audiophiles believe that a signal-to-noise ratio of at least 10dB is necessary for acceptable sound quality, so that an output signal-to-noise ratio S_o/N_o of 10dB is used to measure the system sensitivity.

System Nonlinearity

The components in any system ultimately reach a point at which they become nonlinear, essentially a component is nonlinear when its output amplitude or phase is no longer linearly proportional to its input amplitude or phase. In most changes active devices, this results predominantly from amplitude-induced in the device transconductance, but the variation of device resistances and capacitances with voltage amplitude also contributes to nonlinear behavior. Gross nonlinearity arises from cutoff and saturation effects that occur as the device exceeds the limits of its normal active momentarily. As a result, we observe effects such as gain distortion and cross modulation such as AM-to-PM conversion.

Receiver Dynamic Range

We have said that at low signal levels the minimum signal that can be detected is limited by the noise floor that results from thermal and other noise sources in passive and active devices. At large signal levels, harmonic and intermodulation distortion components arise, causing compression and interference that ultimately limits the largest signals the receiver can handle. The difference between the minimum detectable signal and the maximum detectable signal is known as the receiver dynamic range. One interpretation of this definition is the difference between the 1dB compressed output power and the output noise floor. But this has limited usefulness because it assumes a single channel system. Instead, the Spurious Free Dynamic Range (SFDR) is a more useful measure. It is defined as the range of input power levels from which the output signal just exceeds the output noise floor, and for which any distortion components remain buried below the noise floor.

In order to increase the useful range of a receiver, the gain of a system can be automatically controlled in order to decrease the gain when strong signals cause overload or distortion. However, the impact of doing this is not always obvious and will require some care in considering the signal-to-noise ratio and making a number of trade-offs. For instance, consider AGC applied to an LNA. Adding attenuation in front of the LNA will hurt noise figure, but it will help reduce the effect of large signals (which may be interferers rather than the desired signal itself). After the LNA an attenuator prevents overload of following stages but reduces the third-order intercept point. Ideally, we would like to reduce the gain, increase power handling capability, and minimally affect the noise figure. Thus, it is necessary to consider both the gain and input intercept point in tandem, since these are the principal trade-offs in setting an AGC level. The effect on system noise figure can then be derived.

AGC is typically applied in an analog receiver as shown in Fig. 2-29. As the desired signal increases in input power, the gain of the system is reduced in order to minimize distortion. The gain of the output stages is ideally reduced first to avoid raising the system noise figure and reducing sensitivity, and as earlier stages begin to distort, AGC is progressively introduced ahead of them. Therefore, the noise floor will eventually rise at the same rate as the input handling capability, since the noise floor is principally set by the loss in the front end.

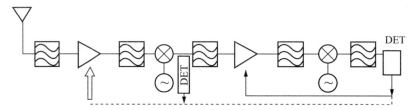

Fig. 2-29 The principle of AGC applied in an analog receiver, showing the points where the signal level is detected and where gain control is applied

The stronger signals may be present as interferers in other channels, and these out-of-band signals must be detected properly by the AGC circuits to sense the distortion and reduce the gain. Because such signals are present in the radio front end and are removed by the selectivity of later stages, it is important that they be detected at the front end, before they are eliminated by filtering downstream. For this reason, dual-stage AGC is sometimes used as shown to ensure proper detection of signal levels not just in the desired channel but also in interfering channels.

For example, consider two strong signals only a few kilohertz away from the desired signal. The receiver's first IF filter may not eliminate these since they are too close to the tuned, or desired signal. As a result they may cause distortion in the RF and IF front end and their third-order intermodulation product will lie on top of the desired signal. However, because adjacent channel signals and their harmonics will be eliminated in the much narrower second or final IF filter, they would not be detected if AGC were controlled only by the power at the output of the receiver. Such interfering signals need to be detected in the first IF stage and reduced prior to any active device in the receiver, possibly by inserting attenuation in the front end. In some older short-wave radios, switches were used to manually insert RF attenuation into the signal flow to reduce strong unwanted signals from saturating the early stages of the radio.

Spurious Responses

Minimizing spurious responses in a receiver is one of the key design criteria behind selecting its frequency architecture. Spurious responses are outputs that arise from unwanted frequency components. In this context, a frequency component that is undesired is one different to that for which the receiver is tuned. For instance, if we desire to demodulate a channel whose carrier is 895MHz, there could be a signal at 890MHz that creates a response in the receiver that interferes with our desired channel at 895MHz. The signal at 890MHz is labeled a spurious frequency if it creates a spurious response. Although modern coding schemes can still detect the desired signal in the presence of interfering signals at the same frequency, spurious responses remain a problem since they reduce the sensitivity to the desired signal.

Spurious responses are caused by distortion products produced in the receiver when the receiver is excited at the spurious frequency. The responses are primarily created by nonlinearities in the mixer and amplifier, although other components such as quartz filters are also nonlinear. The responses can be generated by signals entering, or already within, the receiver. For instance, they can result from leakage paths from the transmuter or from signals in components at the back end of the receiver feeding back to the input. The excitations can occur at the IF itself; its subharmonics, the image frequency, and from higher order mixing products; they all have the property that their spurious responses fall onto the IF frequency. Although we cannot quantitatively predict their amplitude from linear analysis, we can at least predict the spurious frequencies that can cause problems, and take steps where possible to eliminate any voltage or current at these frequencies to avoid them.

NEW WORDS AND PHRASES

parasitic inductance　寄生电感
analog electronics　模拟电子技术
Digital Signal Processing（DSP）　数字信号处理
superheterodyne（superhet）　*n.*［电］超外差式收音机；*adj.* 超外差的
selectivity　*n.* 选择性
sensitivity　*n.* 敏感，灵敏（度），灵敏性
preselector　*n.* 预选器，调谐器
transmitter　*n.* 转送者，传达人发报机，话筒，发射机
the receive phase　接收相位
harmonics　*n.* 谐波
impedance match　阻抗匹配
undesired signal　干扰信号
Local Oscillator（LO）　本机振荡器
Intermediate Frequency（IF）　中频
modulation sideband　调制边带
overload characteristics　过载特性
demodulator　*n.* 解调器
sophisticated error　经验误差
additive, white, Gaussian noise　*n.* 加性高斯白噪声
power spectral density　功率谱密度
megahertz　*n.*［物］兆赫（MHz）
Spurious Free Dynamic Range（SFDR）　无杂散动态范围
AGC　*abbr.* 自动增益控制
spurious responses　（接收机）杂散响应

NOTES

1) We will see that such a receiver can provide both good selectivity and sensitivity, because the noise bandwidth can be limited to the channel bandwidth without compromising the receiver's ability to tune across the entire RF band.

   我们可以看出该接收机具有良好的选择性和敏感性,因为噪声带宽受信道带宽的限制,不影响整个 RF 波段内的接收机的性能。

2) This states that the channel capacity C (measured as bits per second) is proportional to the channel bandwidth B and to the base-2 log of the Signal-to-Noise Ratio (SNR) at the detector.

   这个公式说明信道容量 C (以每秒多少位计量) 与信道带宽 B 和检波处的信噪比的以 2 为底的对数成正比。

3) The channel and into the system through the antenna, where it is usually modeled as additive, white, Gaussian noise and is thermal in nature.

   来源于信道的噪声和经由天线进入系统的噪声,通常以加性高斯白噪声的形式表示,其本质上是一种热量。

4) This component extracts the modulated signal from the IF signal and converts it to baseband.

   本部分的作用是将已调信号从中频信号中分离出来,并将它转换为基带信号。

5) Minimizing spurious responses in a receiver is one of the key design criteria behind selecting its frequency architecture.

   使杂散响应最小化是接收机继选择频率结构之后的一个主要的设计标准。

EXERCISES

1. **Please translate the following words and phrases into Chinese.**

   a) parasitic capacitance   b) channel bandwidth   c) half-duplex
   d) spurious frequency   e) input match   f) tuning range
   g) baseband amplifier   h) noise figure   i) minimum detectable signal
   j) LNA

2. **Please translate the following words and phrases into English.**

   a) 灵敏度   b) 谐波   c) 阻抗匹配
   d) 本机振荡器   e) 过载特性   f) 自动增益控制
   g) 信道   h) 加性高斯白噪声   i) 中频
   j) 基带信号

3. **Fill in the blanks with the missing word (s).**

   a) The function of the input amplifier is to _____ amplify the input signal and _____ the noise added by the receiver to the signal itself.

   b) We will see that such low noise amplification can be achieved by _____ matching the input of the amplifier, and is important because it can determine the overall noise matching of the entire receiver.

   c) It should have a good input and output match to avoid gain _____.

   d) Of course, the RF amplifier can consist of multiple stages in order to _____ the necessary gain.

   e) Clearly, the _____ the bandwidth, the _____ the noise power.

   f) As the desired signal increases in input power, the gain of the system is reduced in order to _____.

   g) Spurious responses are caused by _____ products produced in the receiver when the receiver is excited at the spurious frequency.

4. Answer the following questions according to the text.
a) How many components does the superheterodyne contain?
b) What is the RF amplifier's function?
c) What are the receiver characterization and the system parameters?
d) Please simply describe the theory of AGC.

READING

RF/Microwave Theory
1. Radio-Wave and Microwave Spectrum

The literal meaning of RF is Radio Frequency, but this term is often use in the figurative sense of "anything related to electromagnetic signals". If the Alternating Current (AC) is input to an antenna, an Electromagnetic (EM) field is generated suitable for wireless broadcasting and/or communications. These frequencies cover a significant portion of the electromagnetic radiation spectrum, extending from nine kilohertz (9kHz), the lowest allocated wireless communications frequency (it's within the range of human hearing), to thousands of gigahertz (GHz). Some wireless devices operate at IR or visible-light frequencies, whose electromagnetic wavelengths are shorter than those of RF fields.

When an RF current is supplied to an antenna, it gives rise to an electromagnetic field that propagates through space. This field is sometimes called an RF field; in less technical jargon it is a "radio wave." Any RF field has a wavelength that is inversely proportional to the frequency. In the atmosphere or in outerspace, if f is the frequency in hertz and λ is the wavelength in meters, then

$$\lambda = 3 \times 10^8 / f \tag{2-18}$$

The frequency of an RF signal is inversely proportional to the wavelength of the EM field to which it corresponds. At 9kHz, the free-space wavelength is approximately 33 kilometers (km) or 21 miles (mi). At the highest radio frequencies, the EM wavelengths measure approximately one millimeter (1mm). As the frequency is increased beyond that of the RF spectrum, EM energy takes the form of infrared (IR), visible, ultraviolet (UV), X rays, and gamma rays.

The RF spectrum is divided into several ranges, or bands. With the exception of the lowest-frequency segment, each band represents an increase of frequency corresponding to an order of magnitude (power of 10). Table 2-1 depicts the eight bands in the RF spectrum, showing frequency and bandwidth ranges. The SHF and EHF bands are often referred to as the microwave spectrum.

2. Transmission Line Theory
Many different types of microwave transmission lines have

RF/微波原理
1. 无线电波和微波频谱

RF 是指无线电频率，但是这个词常用来形容"任何与电磁信号有关的"。如果天线馈以交流电，就能够产生电磁（EM）场，可用于无线广播和通信。这些频率覆盖了电磁辐射频谱的重要部分，从最低无线通信频率（人类听觉范围内）9kHz 到几千吉赫兹。一些无线电设备工作在红外线或可见光频率范围内，它们的波长比 RF 波段要短。

当天线中流过 RF 电流时，就会在空间产生能够传播的电磁场。这种场有时称为 RF 场，在某些非专业术语中，也称为"无线电波"。RF 场的波长与传播频率成反比，在大气和外太空中，如果频率的单位是 Hz，波长的单位是 m，那么它们的关系表达式为

RF 信号的频率与对应的 EM 场的波长成反比。当频率为 9kHz 时，自由空间中波长约为 33km 或 21 英里。当以最大的无线电频率传播时，电磁波的波长接近 1mm。在 RF 频谱以外，随着频率的增加，电磁波表现为红外线（IR）、可见光、紫外线（UV）、X 射线和 γ 射线。

射频频谱划分成若干个频率范围或频段。除了最低频率段外，每个频段代表一个数量级所对应的频率范围（10 的次幂）。表 2-1 展示了 RF 频谱中的 8 个频段及其对应的频率和带宽范围。我们常把 SHF（超高频）段和 EHF（极高频）段称为微波频谱。

2. 传输线理论
近年来，我们已经开发了多种不同类

Table 2-1 Frequency and bandwidth ranges in different band of the RF spectrum

Designation	Abbreviation	Frequencies	Free-space wavelengths
Very Low Frequency	VLF	9~30kHz	33~10km
Low Frequency	LF	30~300kHz	10~1km
Medium Frequency	MF	0.3~3MHz	1000~100m
High Frequency	HF	3~30MHz	100~10m
Very High Frequency	VHF	30~300MHz	10~1m
Ultra High Frequency	UHF	0.3~3GHz	1000~100mm
Super High Frequency	SHF	3~30GHz	100~10mm
Extremely High Frequency	EHF	30~300GHz	10~1mm

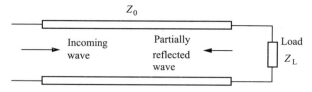

Fig. 2-30 Diagram of lossless transmission line with load showing incident, reflected-transmitted waves

been developed over the years. In an evolutionary sequence from rigid rectangular and circular waveguide, to flexible coaxial cable, to planar stripline, to microstrip line, microwave transmission lines have been reduced in size and complexity. The microstrip transmission line is the technology employed in the current hyperthermia applicator studied.

For fields having a sinusoidal time dependence and steady-state conditions, a field analysis of a terminated lossless transmission line results in the following relations (see Fig. 2-30).

If an incident wave of the form $V_0^+ e^{-j\beta z}$, where β is the phase constant or wave number given by $\beta = \omega\sqrt{\mu\varepsilon}$, is incident from the $-z$ direction then the total voltage on the line can be written as a sum of incident and reflected waves:

$$V(z) = V_0^+ e^{-j\beta z} + V_0^- e^{j\beta z} \quad (2\text{-}19)$$

The total current on the line is

$$I(z) = \frac{V_0^+}{Z_0} e^{-j\beta z} - \frac{V_0^+}{Z_0} e^{j\beta z} \quad (2\text{-}20)$$

where Z_0 is the characteristic impedance of the microstrip line, that is, the impedance the transmission line would have if it were infinitely long or ideally terminated. The incident wave has been written in phasor notation and the common time dependence factor has not been written.

The amplitude of the reflected voltage wave normalized to the amplitude of the incident voltage wave is known as the voltage reflection coefficient, which is

型的微波传输线,从不可弯曲的矩形波导和圆形波导发展到可弯曲的同轴电缆、平面带状线和微带线,微波传输线的尺寸与复杂性已经大大减小。其中,微带线通常采用目前研究的高温蚀刻技术。

对于具有正弦特性和稳态条件的场来说,终端无耗传输线的场分析见图2-30。

设入射波为 $V_0^+ e^{-j\beta z}$,其中 β 为相位常数或波数,$\beta = \omega\sqrt{\mu\varepsilon}$,波从 $-z$ 方向入射,传输线上的总电压可表示为入射波和反射波的叠加:

传输线上的总电流为

式中,Z_0 是微带线的特性阻抗,即传输线无限长或接理想负载时的阻抗。入射波可用矢量表示,通常不写出时间因子。

反射波电压的幅度和入射波电压的幅度的比称为电压反射系数,即

$$\Gamma = \frac{V_0^-}{V_0^+} = \frac{Z_L - Z_0}{Z_L + Z_0} \quad (2\text{-}21)$$

where Z_L is the load impedance.

The total voltage and current waves on the line can then be written in terms of the voltage reflection coefficient as

$$V(z) = V_0^+(e^{-j\beta z} + \Gamma e^{j\beta z}),$$

$$I(z) = \frac{V_0^+}{Z_0}(e^{-j\beta z} - \Gamma e^{j\beta z}) \quad (2\text{-}22)$$

From the previous equations we see that the voltage and current on the line are a superposition of an incident and reflected wave. If the system is static, i.e. if Z_L and Z_0 are not changing in time, the superposition of waves will also be static. This static superposition of waves on the line is called a standing wave.

Because of the complicated shape of this standing wave, the voltage will vary with position along the line, from some minimum value to some maximum value. The ratio of V_{max} to V_{min} is one way to quantify the mismatch of the line. This mismatch is called the Standing Wave Ratio (SWR) or Voltage Standing Wave Ratio (VSWR) and can be expressed as

$$\text{SWR} = \frac{V_{max}}{V_{min}} = \frac{1 + |\Gamma|}{1 - |\Gamma|} \quad (2\text{-}23)$$

The SWR is a real number such as 1 and with a perfect match SWR = 1. By definition, impedance, characteristic or otherwise, is the ratio of the voltage to the current a particular point on the line. The standing waves cause the impedance to fluctuate as a function of distance from the load. The variation in impedance along the transmission line caused by the line/load mismatch can be written as

$$Z_{in} = \frac{V(-l)}{I(-l)} = \frac{V_0^+(e^{j\beta l} + \Gamma e^{-j\beta l})}{V_0^+(e^{j\beta l} - \Gamma e^{-j\beta l})}Z_0 = \frac{1 + \Gamma e^{-2j\beta l}}{1 - \Gamma e^{-2j\beta l}}Z_0 \quad (2\text{-}24)$$

where l is the distance from the load. If we substitute the expression for in terms of the impedances, the generalized input impedance of the load plus transmission line simplifies to

$$Z_{in} = Z_0\frac{Z_L + jZ_0\tan\beta l}{Z_0 + jZ_L\tan\beta l} \quad (2\text{-}25)$$

With this equation the impedance anywhere along the line can be calculated if the load impedance and characteristic impedance are known.

In the most basic sense, then, if the load impedance equals the line impedance, the reflection coefficient is zero and the load is said to be matched to the line. All of the microwave impedance matching techniques can be reduced to this simple idea: minimize the reflection of the incident wave to as nearly zero as possible.

When the load is mismatched to the line and thus there is a reflection of the incident wave at the load, the power delivered to the load is reduced. This loss is called Return Loss (RL) and is equal to

式中，Z_L 为负载阻抗。

传输线上的总电压和总电流可以由电压反射系数表示，即

从上面的等式中，我们可以得出，传输线上的电压和电流都是入射波和反射波的叠加。如果系统是静态的，即 Z_L 和 Z_0 不随时间的变化而变化，那么波的叠加也是静态的。我们把传输线上波的静态叠加称为驻波。

由于驻波波形复杂，传输线上的电压会随着位置的改变而从最小变化到最大。V_{max} 和 V_{min} 的比值可表征传输线的失配程度，这种失配称为驻波比（SWR）或电压驻波比（VSWR），公式为

驻波比是一个实数（如1），当完全匹配时，驻波比为1。根据定义，特性阻抗及其他阻抗参数，都定义为传输线上特定点电压和电流的比值。驻波引起的阻抗是与负载的距离的函数。由此，由于传输线/负载失配引起的传输线上的阻抗变化可写为

式中，l 表示与负载的距离。如果用阻抗替换表达式中的变量，则带负载传输线上输入阻抗可简化为

如果负载阻抗和特性阻抗已知，则可用上式计算传输线上任意一点的输入阻抗。

从最基本的意义上来说，如果负载阻抗等于特性阻抗，则反射系数为0，负载与传输线匹配。所有的微波阻抗匹配技术都基于这个观点：降低入射波的反射系数，使其尽可能接近0。

当负载与传输线不匹配时，负载端将出现入射波的反射，馈给负载的功率降低。这种能量损耗称为回波损耗（RL），公式为

$$RL = -20\log|\Gamma| \quad (\text{dB}) \tag{2-26}$$

3. Microwave Transmission Lines

Three main categories of transmission lines are introduced here: coaxial cables, waveguides and microstrip.

Coax cables have a core wire, surrounded by a non-conductive material (which is called dielectric or insulation), and then surrounded by an encompassing shielding which is often made of braided wires. The dielectric keeps the core and the shielding apart. Finally, the coax is protected by an outer shielding which will generally be a PVC material. The inner conductor carries the RF signal and the outer shield is there to keep the RF signal from radiating to the atmosphere and to stop outside signals from interfering with the signal carried by the core. Another interesting fact is that the electrical signal always travels along the outer layer of the central conductor: the larger the central conductor, the better signal will flow. This is called the skin effect.

A **waveguide** is a conducting tube through which energy is transmitted in the form of electromagnetic waves. The tube acts as a boundary that confines the waves in the enclosed space. The skin effect prevents any electromagnetic effects from being evident outside the guide. The electromagnetic fields are propagated through the waveguide by means of reflections against its inner walls, which are considered perfect conductors. The intensity of the fields is greatest at the center along the X dimension, and must diminish to zero at the end walls because the existence of any field parallel to the walls at the surface would cause an infinite current to flow in a perfect conductor. Waveguides, of course, cannot carry RF in this fashion.

There are an infinite number of ways in which the electric and magnetic fields can arrange themselves in a waveguide for frequencies above the low cutoff frequency. Each of these field configurations is called a mode. The modes may be separated into two general groups. One group, designated TM (Transverse Magnetic), has the magnetic field entirely transverse to the direction of propagation, but has a component of the electric field in the direction of propagation. The other type, designated TE (Transverse Electric) has the electric field entirely transverse, but has a component of magnetic field in the direction of propagation. TM waves are sometimes called E waves, and TE waves are sometimes called H waves, but the TM and TE designations are preferred. The mode of propagation is identified by the group letters followed by two subscript numerals. For example, TE_{10}, TM_{11}, etc. The number of possible modes increases with the frequency for a given size of guide, and there is only one possible mode, called the dominant mode, for the lowest frequency that can be transmitted.

3. 微波传输线

这里介绍三类主要的传输线：同轴电缆、波导和微带线。

同轴电缆的芯线通常由非导电材料（电介质或绝缘材料）包裹，其外层是编织成网状的封闭的屏蔽层。电介质的作用是隔离铜芯和屏蔽层。最终，最外层是由聚氯乙烯（PVC）材料构成的屏蔽外层，其作用是保护同轴电缆。内导体承载射频信号，而外层阻止RF信号辐射到空气中，同时防止外部信号干扰芯线上的载波。有趣的是电信号总是沿着内导体的外表面，内导体越粗，流过的信号就越强。这就是所谓的趋肤效应。

波导是以电磁波形式传送能量的导体管，它将电磁波限制在密封空间内。它的趋肤效应能够有效地阻止电磁感应的泄漏。电磁场通过在波导内壁的反射而传播，将波导称为理想导体。沿X方向中心处的电场强度最大。但是，由于与内壁表面平行的场的存在会导致在理想导体中的电流无限大，因此场强在端壁处减小为0。当然，波导不能用这种方式传播射频信号。

当频率高于截止频率时，波导中的电场和磁场以无限种模式传播。每一种场分布代表一种模式。这些模式分为两大类：一类是指特定的TM波（横磁波），它的磁场与传播方向垂直，在传播方向上有电场分量；另一类是指特定的TE波（横电波），它的电场与传播方向垂直，在传播方向上有磁场分量。TM波有时也称为E波，TE波有时也称为H波，但我们更倾向于TE波和TM波。我们通常用两个下标数字来表示TE波或TM波中的传播模式，如TE_{10}、TM_{11}等。对于给定尺寸的波导，可能传播的模式数会随着频率的增大而增多。以最低频率传输的模式称为主模。

A typical **microstrip line** can be taken as a two-layer PCB, the top layer is chemically etched away to leave copper traces of width W, separated from the ground plane by a dielectric substrate of some thickness d and relative permittivity ε_r.

Because of the anisotropic dielectric geometry, the microstrip line cannot support a true TEM wave for the following reasons: a microstrip line has most of its electric field concentrated in the region between the line and the ground plane; a small fraction propagates in the air above. Because the speed of light c is different in air and dielectric the boundary-value conditions at the air-dielectric interface can not be met with a pure TEM wave and the exact fields constitute a hybrid TM-TE wave. Because the dielectric substrate is electrically very thin ($d \ll \lambda$), for this application, the fields are quasi-TEM. Because the fields are quasi-TEM, good approximations for the phase velocity, propagation constant, and characteristic impedance can be obtained from the static solution.

The phase velocity in microstrip line is given by

典型的**微带线**可以看作双层 PCB，上层经过化学腐蚀形成宽度为 W 的金属贴片，通过厚度为 d、相对介电常数为 ε_r 的介质基片与下层接地板隔离。

由于各向异性电介质的几何构型，这种微带线不能传播 TEM 波，原因如下：这种微带线的绝大多数电场分布在贴片和接地板之间；一小部分电场散射在上层的空气中。因为在空气中和在介质中光的传输速度 c 不同，空气与介质分界面的边界条件与纯 TEM 波不同，其场确切地说是 TM-TE 混合波。因为介质基片非常薄（$d \ll \lambda$），可以近似将其看作准 TEM 波。因为该场是准 TEM 波，所以可以用静态场分析方法近似求解其相速度、传播常数和特性阻抗。

微带线中相速度的表达式为

$$v_p = \frac{c}{\sqrt{\varepsilon_r}} \tag{2-27}$$

and the propagation constant is given by

传播常数的表达式为

$$\beta = k_0 \sqrt{\varepsilon_e} = \omega \sqrt{\mu_0 \varepsilon_0} \sqrt{\varepsilon_e} \tag{2-28}$$

where ε_e is the effective dielectric constant and is given by

式中，ε_e 是有效介电常数，其表达式为

$$\varepsilon_e = \frac{\varepsilon_r + 1}{2} + \frac{\varepsilon_r - 1}{2} \left(\frac{1}{\sqrt{1 + 12d/W}} \right) \tag{2-29}$$

The effective dielectric constant ε_e is the dielectric constant of an equivalent homogenous medium that replaces the air and dielectric layers.

The characteristic impedance of a microstrip line can be calculated, given the width W and substrate thickness d with the result as

有效介电常数 ε_e 是指将空气/介质层等效成均匀介质后的介电常数。

给定贴片宽度 W 和基片厚度 d，可计算微带线的特性阻抗为

$$Z_0 = \begin{cases} \dfrac{60}{\sqrt{\varepsilon_e}} \ln\left(\dfrac{8d}{W} + \dfrac{W}{4d} \right), & \dfrac{W}{d} \leq 1 \\ \dfrac{120\pi}{\sqrt{\varepsilon_e} \left[\dfrac{W}{d} + 1.393 + 0.667 \ln\left(\dfrac{W}{d} + 1.444 \right) \right]}, & \dfrac{W}{d} \geq 1 \end{cases} \tag{2-30}$$

If all microstrip based circuits consisted of a proper width straight feed line terminating in a load, there would not be much need to worry about compensating for discontinuities. Even in this ideal case, the transition from microwave source to microstrip line and from the microstrip to load can be the source of large reflections. Typical microstrip discontinuities are junctions, bends, step changes in width and the coaxial cable to microstrip junction. If these discontinuities are not compensated, they introduce parasitic reactance that can lead

如果基于微带线的电路只包括适当宽度直馈线及终端负载，则不需要考虑其不连续性的补偿问题。即使在理想条件下，波源到微带线和微带线到负载都会造成大的反射。微带线的结点、弯曲、宽度阶跃变化和同轴线与微带线的连接处都会产生不连续性。如果不对这些不连续性进行补偿，将会产生寄生电抗，这些寄生电抗会

to phase and amplitude errors, input and output mismatch, and possibly spurious coupling. The strength of a particular discontinuity is frequency dependent, where the higher the frequency, the larger is the discontinuity.

4. Microwave Networks

A field analysis using Maxwell's equations for many microwave problems would be hopelessly difficult. Circuit and network concepts can be extended to handle many microwave analysis and design problems of practical interest. When we treat various transmission lines and waveguide, we can derive the propagation constant and characteristic impendence. The transition between different transmission lines, or discontinuity on a transmission line, can not be treated as a simple junction between two transmission lines, but is augmented with some type equivalent circuit to account for reactance associated with the transition or discontinuity. This is called Microwave Networks Theory or Equivalent Transmission Line Theory.

For an arbitrary two-conductor TEM transmission line, the voltage and the total current, U and I, can be found as

$$U = \int_{+}^{-} \boldsymbol{E} d\boldsymbol{l}, \quad I = \oint_C \boldsymbol{H} d\boldsymbol{l} \tag{2-31}$$

A characteristic impendence Z_0 can then be defined for traveling wave as

$$Z_0 = \frac{U}{I} \tag{2-32}$$

After having defined and determined the voltage, current, and characteristic impedance, we can proceed to apply the circuit theory for transmission line to characterize this line as a circuit element.

Even though there are many ways to define equivalent voltage, current, and impedance for wave guides, since these quantities are not unique for non-TEM lines, the following considerations usually lead to the useful results:

1) Voltage and current are defined only for a particular waveguide mode, and are defined so that the voltage is proportional to the transverse electric field, and the current is proportional to the transverse magnetic field.

2) In order to be used in a manner similar to voltages and currents of circuit theory, the equivalent voltages and currents should be defined so that their product gives the power flow of the mode.

3) The ratio of the voltage to the current for a single traveling wave should be equal to the characteristic impedance of the line. This impedance may be chosen arbitrarily, but is

导致相位和振幅误差、输入和输出失配以及可能的寄生耦合。一些不连续性的强度与频率有关，频率越高，不连续性越大。

4. 微波网络

利用麦克斯韦方程组的场分析方法求解微波问题非常困难。可以扩展电路和网络的概念来处理微波分析与实际应用中的设计问题。在处理各种传输线和波导时，可以获得传播常数和特性阻抗。不能把不同传输线之间的过渡或传输线上的不连续性，看成是两个传输线的简单连接，而应该当成某种与过渡或不连续性相关的等效电路来处理。这就是所谓的微波网络理论或等效传输线理论。

对于任意双导体 TEM 波传输线，电压和总电流的表达式为

行波中特性阻抗 Z_0 的表达式为

前面定义了电压、电流和特性阻抗，我们进而把电路理论应用到传输线中，以电路元件的形式来表征传输线。

虽然等效电压、电流和波导阻抗的定义有很多种，但是因为在非 TEM 波传输线中这些变量不是唯一的，所以通常做以下约定：

1) 等效电压和电流只针对特定的波导模式，并且电压正比于横向电场，电流正比于横向磁场。

2) 为了能够采用类似电路理论中的电压和电流，定义等效电压和等效电流，从而能够计算出该模式下的功率流。

3) 在行波中，电压/电流比值的大小应该等于传输线上的特性阻抗。这个阻抗值可以任意选择，但在一般情况下，通常

usually selected as equal to the wave impedance of the line, or else normalized to unity.

The most useful networks are impedance and admittance networks, *ABCD* networks, scattering parameters, and so on. For a two-port network, they can be established separately as

选择与传输线阻抗大小相同的阻抗值，或者归一化阻抗值。

几种常用的网络是阻抗矩阵、导纳矩阵、*ABCD* 矩阵网络、散射参数矩阵等。对于两端口网络来说，它们的表达式分别为

$$\begin{bmatrix} U_1 \\ U_2 \end{bmatrix} = \begin{bmatrix} Z_{11} & Z_{12} \\ Z_{21} & Z_{22} \end{bmatrix} \begin{bmatrix} I_1 \\ I_2 \end{bmatrix}, \quad \begin{bmatrix} I_1 \\ I_2 \end{bmatrix} = \begin{bmatrix} Y_{11} & Y_{12} \\ Y_{21} & Y_{22} \end{bmatrix} \begin{bmatrix} U_1 \\ U_2 \end{bmatrix},$$

$$\begin{bmatrix} U_1 \\ I_1 \end{bmatrix} = \begin{bmatrix} A_{11} & A_{12} \\ A_{21} & A_{22} \end{bmatrix} \begin{bmatrix} U_2 \\ -I_2 \end{bmatrix} \quad \begin{bmatrix} \widetilde{U}_{r1} \\ \widetilde{U}_{r2} \end{bmatrix} = \begin{bmatrix} S_{11} & S_{12} \\ S_{21} & S_{22} \end{bmatrix} \begin{bmatrix} \widetilde{U}_{i1} \\ \widetilde{U}_{i2} \end{bmatrix} \quad (2\text{-}33)$$

5. Quarter-Wave Impedance Transformer

A general mismatch in impedance between two points on a transmission line can be compensated with a quarter-wave transformer. The quarter-wave transformer is a very useful matching technique that also illustrates the properties of standing waves on a mismatched line. A quarter-wave transformer in microstrip is shown in Fig. 2-31.

In a quarter-wave transformer, we want to match a load resistance R_L to the characteristic impedance Z_0 through a short length of transmission line of unknown length l and impedance Z_1. The input impedance looking into the matching section of line is given by

5. 四分之一波长阻抗变换器

一般通过四分之一波长变换器来解决传输线上两点之间的阻抗失配。这是一种非常有用的匹配方法，而且也说明了失配传输线的驻波特性。微带线四分之一波长变换器如图 2-31 所示。

在四分之一波长变换器中，我们通过插入一段长度 l 和阻抗 Z_1 都未知的短传输线来实现负载阻抗 R_L 与特性阻抗 Z_0 的匹配。传输线上匹配点的输入阻抗表达式为

$$Z_{in} = Z_1 \frac{R_L + jZ_1 \tan\beta l}{Z_1 + jR_L \tan\beta l} \quad (2\text{-}34)$$

If we choose the length of the line $l = \lambda/4$ then $\beta l = \pi/2$, divide through by $\tan\beta l$ and take the limit as $\beta l = \pi/2$ to achieve

如果我们选择 $l=\lambda/4$，则 $\beta l=\pi/2$，上式中除以 $\tan\beta l$ 且取 $\beta l=\pi/2$ 的极限，可得到

$$Z_{in} = \frac{Z_1^2}{R_L} \quad (2\text{-}35)$$

For a perfect transition with no reflections at the interface between microstrip and load, $\Gamma = 0$, so $Z_{in} = Z_0$ and this gives us a characteristic impedance Z_1 as

对于理想变换器来说，微带线和负载的连接处没有反射，即 $\Gamma=0$，也就是 $Z_{in}=Z_0$。特性阻抗 Z_1 的表达式为

$$Z_1 = \sqrt{Z_0 R_L} \quad (2\text{-}36)$$

which is the geometric mean of the load and source impedances. With this geometry, there will be no standing waves on the feedline although there will be standing waves on the $\lambda/4$ matching section. Why was the value of $l = \lambda/4$ chosen? In fact, any odd multiple $(2n + 1)$ of $l = \lambda/4$ will also work.

When the line length is precisely $\lambda/4$ the reflected wave from the load destructively interferes with the wave reflected

即负载和源阻抗的几何平均值。虽然在 $\lambda/4$ 匹配端存在驻波，但是就馈线而言，不存在驻波。为什么选择 $l=\lambda/4$？事实上，只要长度 l 为 $\lambda/4$ 的 $(2n+1)$ 倍即可。

当插入的传输线长为 $\lambda/4$ 时，来自负载的反射波和 Z_0、Z_1 连接处的反射波产生严重干扰，进而相互抵消。应当注意的是，

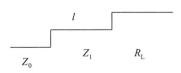

Fig. 2-31 Diagram of quarter-wave impedance transformer

from the Z_0, Z_1 interface and they cancel each other out. It should be noted that this method can only match a real load. If the load has an appreciable imaginary component, it must be matched differently. It can be transformed into a purely real load, at a single frequency, by adding an appropriate length of feed line.

这种方法只能对实负载进行匹配。如果负载有明显的虚部，必须用别的方法进行匹配。在一定频率上，可以适当增加馈线长度进而把带虚部的负载转化为实负载，再进行阻抗匹配。

NEW WORDS AND PHRASES

infrared   *adj.* 红外线的
ultraviolet   *adj.* （光）紫外的
spectrum   *n.* 频谱，范围，系列
microwave   *n.* 微波
inductance   *n.* 感应系数，自感应
shunt   *v.* 分流，并联
coax   *n.* 同轴电缆
waveguide   *n.* 波导
skin effect   趋肤效应
cutoff frequency   截止频率
coefficient   *n.* 协同因素，折算率
wave number   波数
Voltage Standing Wave Ratio   电压驻波比（VSWR）
electromagnetic   *adj.* 电磁的
Return Loss（RL）   回波损耗
transverse   *adj.* 横向的，横断的
dominant mode   主模
relative permittivity   相对介电常数
impendence   *n.* 阻抗
mismatch   *n.* 错配，失谐；*v.* 使搭配不当
microstrip   *n.* 微带线
quasi-TEM   准 TEM 波
sinusoidal   *adj.* 正弦曲线的
phase velocity   相速度
Equivalent Transmission Line Theory   等效传输线理论
scattering parameter   散射参数
feed line   馈线

NOTES

1) Some wireless devices operate at IR or visible-light frequencies, whose electromagnetic wavelengths are shorter than those of RF fields.
   一些无线电设备工作在红外线或可见光频率范围内，它们的波长比射频波段要短。
2) The inner conductor carries the RF signal and the outer shield is there to keep the RF signal from radiating to the atmosphere and to stop outside signals from interfering with the signal carried by the core.
   内导体承载 RF 信号而外部覆盖层阻止 RF 信号发射到大气中以及阻止外部信号干扰芯线上的载波。
3) There are an infinite number of ways in which the electric and magnetic fields can arrange themselves in a waveguide for frequencies above the low cutoff frequency.
   电场和磁场能够以高于截止频率的频率在波导中以无限种模式传播。
4) Voltage and current are defined only for a particular waveguide mode, and are defined so that the voltage is proportional to the transverse electric field, and the current is proportional to the transverse magnetic field.
   等效电压和电流只针对特定的波导模式，并且电压正比于横向电场，电流正比于横向磁场。

课文译文

第 2 章
电路系统与设计

2.1 电路和系统

1. 基本概念

电荷和电导率

根据玻尔的原子理论（以尼尔斯·玻尔命名，1885—1962），电子环绕原子核运转，原子核由质子和中子构成。原子内部带有相反电荷的电子和质子的吸引力使原子聚集在一起。而具有相同电荷的粒子相互排斥。

电荷用库仑（C）进行计量。一个电子或质子所带电荷量远远低于 1C，一个电子带有 -1.6×10^{-19}C 的电荷量，一个质子含有 1.6×10^{-19}C 的电荷量。自然界表明一个电子的电荷量正好与一个质子的电荷量相反；对于电子本身并不存在负电荷量，只是简单地称为电子带负电和质子带正电。

不同类型原子的电子自由移动的程度不同。对于某些类型的材料（如金属），室温时原子外的电子几乎没有束缚，电子在原子间杂乱地运动。因为这些几乎未束缚的电子可以自由地离开各自的原子，在相邻原子间的空间流动，它们通常称为自由电子。

在其他类型的材料（如玻璃）中，原子的电子不能自由移动。虽然外部力量（如物理摩擦）会使这些电子脱离它们相应的原子，转移到另外一种材料的原子上，但是在相同材料的原子间它们不易转移。

电子在材料中相对移动的能力称为电导率。电导率是由材料中的原子类型（每个原子核中质子的数目，决定其化学性质）和原子间的连接决定的。电子迁移率高的材料（自由电子多）称为导体，电子迁移率低的材料（自由电子少或没有）称为绝缘体。

一些材料的电气属性在不同的条件下会发生改变。例如，玻璃在室温下是很好的绝缘体，但当加热到非常高的温度时，它就会成为导体。气体（如空气）通常是绝缘体，如果加热到非常高的温度，它也会成为导体。大多数金属在加热时导电性会变差，而在冷却时导电性较好。多数导电材料在极低的温度下变成完全导电（这称为超导）。

导体中"自由"电子的运动通常是随机的，没有特定的方向或速度，但在受到影响时电子在导电材料中会以一定的方式移动。电子的这种一致运动就是我们所说的电或电流。正如水会在管道的空隙中流动，电子也会在导体的原子内及原子间的空间移动。我们眼前的导体可能是固体，但由原子组成的材料中有很多空间！只有导电材料中存在为电子传输提供通道的连续路径时才会有电流。如果路径被阻断，电流将不会出现。

电路、电压和电流

电路就是自由电子连续移动的导电路径。自由电子通过电路的连续移动就称为电流，而且它通常称为"流"，就像流动的液体通过一条空的管道。

驱动电子在电路中流动的力称为电压，在专业上用每单位电荷的势能来衡量。众所周知，重力势能是最常见的势能。由于地球和地球上物体之间的引力关系，在抬高物体时就会使物体具有势能。物体的重量越大，举得越高，势能就越大。当谈到电路中存在一定量的电压时，我们指的是驱动电子从该电路中一个特定点移动到另一个特定点的势能。如果不指定两个特定点，"电压"这个词就没有任何意义。

电压通常用符号 V 来表示，单位是伏特（符号为 V），以亚历山德罗·伏特（1745—1827）的名字命名。1V 定义为使 1A 的电流通过具有 1Ω 电阻导体所需要的电动势的大小。在数字电路中，我们有时以几千伏或者毫伏（mV）衡量电压。在 1C 的电荷条件下增加 1V 的电压就会增加 1J（焦耳）的电势能，焦耳以 James P. Joule（1818—1889）的名字命名。因为电子带负电荷，所以我们需要把电子从高电压处移到低电压处，以增加其势能。

所有的电压源（包括电池）具有两个电极。所以我们可以用一根导线把电池的一端和另一端连接起来形成回路。用一段导线构成回路，可使电子沿顺时针方向不断地流动起来形成电流，见图 2-1。

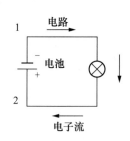

图 2-1 沿逆时针方向的电流

只要电池持续产生电压且电路的连续性不被破坏，电子就将一直在电路中流动。正如通过管道流动的水，电路中电子这种连续的、均匀的流动就称为电流。只要电压源保持相同的"推动"方向，电流就将一直在电路中以相同的方向流动。这种单方向的电流称为直流，或 DC。电流的方向产生交替就称为交流，或 AC。

电子在导体中流动并相互推进形成电流，就像管道中的石子或水的流动一样，所以在电路中任意一点处的电流都相等。如果我们测量一个导线回路的横截面，计算流过的电子，我们会发现单位时间流过回路的电荷量相同，与导体的长度或直径无关。

电流用符号 I 表示，基本单位是安培（A）。1A 电流是指 1s 内通过导线某一点的电荷量为 1C。还有其他的单位，如毫安（mA）和微安（μA）。

电阻、电容和电感

自由电子在导体中移动时往往会遇到一定程度的阻力，这种阻止相对运动的阻力就称为电阻。在电路中电流的大小取决于驱动电子的电压的量和阻止电子流动的电阻的大小。就像电压一样，电阻也是两点之间的相对数量。因此，经常说电路中两点"之间"或"穿过"电路两点间的电压和电阻。

能起到电阻作用的元件叫作电阻器。影响阻值大小的三个因素分别是它的材料、大小和形状。电阻遵循欧姆定律，当温度恒定时，电流密度正比于电场的大小。

由一种材料制成的电阻遵循欧姆定律，是一个常数，或者说和电压和电流无关，电压与电流之间呈线性关系。现代电子电路中的许多元器件是不遵循欧姆定律的。例如二极管，它的电流并不随着电压线性增加而且两个方向的电流也是不同的。电阻器通常有特定的电阻值,从而可以精确地计算电路的特性。

电阻用字母 R 来表示,单位是欧姆,用 Ω 表示。当在导体上加 1V 电压时,产生 1A 的电流,所对应的阻值就是 1Ω。更大的电阻单位是千欧($k\Omega$)或兆欧($M\Omega$)。

当电压加在两个分离的导体之间时,导体之间的空间内就会产生电场。电能就存储在电场中。具备这种能力的元件就称为电容器。把两块导电板(通常是金属)放在相近的位置就形成电容器。电容器存储能量的能力是电压(两个引线之间的电位差)的函数,结果趋向于使电压保持不变。换句话说,电容器阻止产生电压降的变化。当电容器的电压增大或减小时,电容器会通过使电流从电压源流出或流入来阻止这种变化,正好与变化趋势相反。

如果电容器与电池相连接,电子从电池的负极流出,并且积聚在连接到该侧的电容板上,我们称电容器充电。电容值与材料的介电常数和电容板的面积成正比,而与板间距离成反比,即极板面积越大,距离越小,电容越大。

在给定电压降的情况下,电容器存储能量的能力就称为电容。毫无疑问,电容值也是衡量阻止电压变化的强度(准确地说,就是对于给定的电压变化率将产生多大的电流)。电容用大写字母 C 来表示,单位是法拉(F)。在无线电计算中,法拉是一个很大的单位,所以人们也经常使用微法和皮法。

当电流流过导体时,导体周围就会产生磁场。这种效应称为电磁感应。磁场能量存储在磁场中。具备这种能力的元件就称为电感。电感可以简单地由一个有或者没有磁心的线圈构成。电感中存储能量的大小与电流的大小有关且总是试图保持电流为恒定值。换句话说,电感试图阻止电流的变化。当通过电感的电流增大或减小时,电感就会通过产生与引线之间极性相反的电压来"阻止"这种变化。

电感要存储更多的能量,必须加大流经它的电流。这意味着,其周围的磁场也将增大,并根据电磁自感定律,变化的磁场将产生感应电动势。当通过电感的电流增加时,它就会产生相反的电压以阻止电流的变化,此时电感充当电源负载。此时,我们称电感正在充电,此磁场中存储了更多的能量。注意,电压的极性要参考电流的方向。

在给定电流的情况下,电感器储存能量的能力就称为电感。毫无疑问,电感值也是衡量阻止当前电流变化的强度(准确地说,就是对于给定的电流变化率将产生多大的自感电压)。电感用大写字母 L 表示,单位是亨利(H)。

2. 电路与系统

欧姆定律

如前所述,电压是使每单位电荷的电子从一点移到另一点的势能,电流是电荷流经导体的运动速度,电阻阻碍自由电子通过导体。当我们开始探索它们在电路中的关系时,这些电量的单位和符号就很重要。电流、电压和电阻之间的第一个定律是欧姆定律,也是最重要的定律。这个定律由乔治·西蒙·欧姆在 1827 年发现。欧姆最主要的发现就是在给定的温度下,导体中的电流强度与加在它两端的电压成正比。

欧姆定律的计算公式为

$$V = IR \tag{2-1}$$

式中,V 为两点之间的电位差,R 为两点之间的电阻,I 为流过该电阻的电流。当用电导 $g = 1/R$ 来表示欧姆定律时,可以写为

$$I = gV \tag{2-2}$$

如果我们知道电路中三个值(电压、电流和电阻)中的任意两个,就可以使用欧姆定律来计

算第三个值。

基尔霍夫电流定律和基尔霍夫电压定律

许多较复杂的电路不能简化为简单的串联或并联电路。相反，这些电路需要用基尔霍夫电流定律和基尔霍夫电压定律来求解。

在图2-2中，我们可以看到I_1是唯一流进节点的电流。然而，有三条流出节点的电流，这些电流分别是I_2、I_3和I_4。

一旦电荷进入节点，它就只能流出（这就是电荷守恒定律），流进节点的总电流必须等于流出节点的总电流。所以

$$I_2 + I_3 + I_4 = I_1 \tag{2-3}$$

将上式中所有的量都移到式子的左边，可以得到

$$(I_2 + I_3 + I_4) - I_1 = 0 \tag{2-4}$$

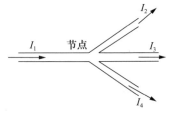

图2-2 流进和流出节点的电流

然后，可以得到总电流是0，这可以用下边的公式来表示：

$$\sum I_i = 0 \tag{2-5}$$

在这里，我们规定流入节点的电流为负值，流出节点的电流为正值。

基尔霍夫电压定律（或基尔霍夫回路准则）体现了静电场是保守场。该定律表明闭合回路的总电压必须为0。若不是这样，当讨论闭合电路时，我们会发现电压是不确定的，所以应该有

$$\sum V_i = 0 \tag{2-6}$$

网络定律

在电路网络分析中，基础定理就是欧姆定律和基尔霍夫定律。然而，这些简单定理可以用于分析任何电路结构（即使我们不得不求助于复杂的代数来处理多个未知数），也有一些捷径可以简化数学问题。

叠加定理

叠加定理所采用的方法是使电路中每次只有一个源，对简化后的电路使用串联/并联的分析方法，确定简化后的网络的电压降（或者电流）。然后，一旦确定了每个源独立工作时的电压降或电流，这些电压降或电流的代数和（算术加）就是所有源一起工作时的实际电压降或电流。

戴维南定理

戴维南定理表明，无论电路有多复杂，都可以将其简化成只有一个电压源和串联到负载的电阻的线性电路。"线性"这一条件同叠加定理中的条件相同：其中所有的基本方程都必须是线性的（没有指数，也没有根号）。如果我们处理的是无源元件（例如，电阻、电感和电容），线性条件一定满足。然而，有些器件（尤其是某些气体放电和半导体器件）是非线性的，也就是说，电流变化与电压不一致，我们把包含这种器件的电路称为非线性电路。

在分析含源的系统和其他电路时，戴维南定理很有用，只需要改变一个特殊阻抗（称为负载电阻），负载电阻的值不同，就要重新计算一次，以确定它两端的电压和流经它的电流。

戴维南定理的步骤如下：

1) 在原始电路中把负载电阻移除，找到戴维南电压源，将曾连接负载电阻的两端开路，计算开路电压。

2) 在原始电路中把所有的电源移除（电压源短路，电流源开路），找出戴维南电阻，计算开路点的总电阻。

3) 通过戴维南电压源与戴维南电阻串联，画出戴维南等效电路。负载电阻重新接在等效

电路的两个开路点。

4）按照串联电路规则分析负载电阻两端的电压和电流。

诺顿定理

诺顿定理表明，无论电路有多复杂，都可以将其简化成只有一个电流源和并联到负载的电阻的线性电路。就像戴维南定理一样，"线性"这一条件也是在叠加定理中表明的：所有的基本方程都必须是线性的（没有指数，也没有根号）。

诺顿定理的步骤如下：

1）在原始电路中把负载电阻移除，找到诺顿电流源，将曾连接负载电阻的两端用短线连接，计算流经该短线的电流。

2）在原始电路中把所有的电源移除（电压源短路，电流源开路），找出诺顿电阻，计算开路点的总电阻。

3）通过诺顿电流源与诺顿电阻并联，画出诺顿等效电路。负载电阻重新接在等效电路的两个开路点。

4）按照并联电路规则分析负载电阻两端的电压和电流。

2.2 模拟与数字电路设计

先进的工艺技术可以将所用到的双极晶体管和 CMOS（即互补金属-氧化物-半导体）、电源和信号、无源和有源器件集成在同一个电路上，正是由于这种复杂工艺技术使得现代电路设计成为一个努力"混合信号"的过程。设计者可以根据自己的思路和喜好，将这些开发集成系统所需的元器件安排在一个模拟或逻辑电路模块上。

1. 模拟电路

模拟电路所处理的信号电压可从零到最大电源电压。这与数字电路不同，数字电路几乎只处理"有或没有"的信号，即电压值仅限于零和最大电源电压两个值，没有定义在这两个极限值中的其他有效值。通常认为模拟电路是线性电路，用来强调在数字电路中被限制的信号范围的有效连续值，这是一种错误的认识。正是因为电压或电流信号可以在极限值零和最大电源电压之间平滑地变动，所以在出现"直线"或"成比例的"之类的情况下并不意味着信号之间的数学关系是线性的。许多线性电路在工作时呈现非线性行为，这要么是由于物理结构造成的，要么是由于设计的问题。

NPN 型晶体管

NPN 型晶体管（见图 2-11）在传统双极型模拟集成电路中占主导地位。事实上，在最基本和最经济

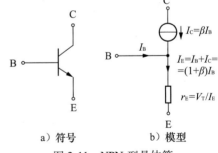

a）符号　　　b）模型

图 2-11　NPN 型晶体管

的模拟 IC 工艺中，电路设计者只需要好的 NPN 型晶体管即可。其余的，如 PNP 型晶体管、电阻器和电容器都只是附属品。直观地说，从底到顶的分析，在直流中对晶体管建模已足够，要知道这些器件的带宽是有限的。

在建模时加上复杂的信号（如小交流信号），由于不能采用快速数学计算，就用到了计算机仿真。如图 2-11 所示，a 为 NPN 型晶体管的符号，b 为直流电模型。在晶体管中，电流流入集电极和基极，然后从发射极流出。简单地说，晶体管集电极电流 I_C 较基极电流 I_B 放大 β 倍。因此，发射极电流 I_E 是基极电流的（$1+\beta$）倍。典型的放大倍数是 100。NPN 型晶体管具有卓

越的动态性能或带宽，它们的截止频率很容易达到 1GHz 以上。

PNP 型晶体管

PNP 型晶体管（如图 2-12 所示）同 NPN 型晶体管是互补的，它的电流由发射极流入，从集电极和基极流出，这与 NPN 型晶体管相反。这决定了它是 NPN 型晶体管的副产品，其电流增益倍数较 NPN 低 β，并且速度比 NPN 慢。PNP 典型的放大倍数为 50，它的截止频率（f_T）一般低于 1MHz。

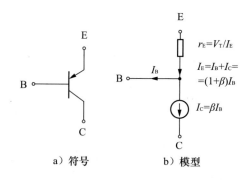

图 2-12 PNP 型晶体管

晶体管方程

双极晶体管的电压和电流之间满足如下对数关系：

$$V_{BE} = V_T \ln(I/I_o) \tag{2-7}$$

式中，V_T 是热电压，I_o 是特征电流，由晶体管的设计工艺决定。这里有一个非常有趣的公式。例如，如果扩大式（2-7）中晶体管电流 A 倍，则有

$$V'_{BE} = V_T \ln(AI/I_o) \tag{2-8}$$

由电流扩大到 A 倍所引起的电压的增加量为

$$\Delta V_{BE} = V'_{BE} - V_{BE} = V_T \ln(A) = (KT/q)\ln A \tag{2-9}$$

式中，K 为玻耳兹曼常数，T 为热力学温度，q 等于电荷量，单位是 C。

当然，反过来将电流的变化作为电压的函数，也是正确的。事实上，如果把上式反过来就得到

$$I = I_o \exp(V_{BE}/V_T) \tag{2-10}$$

上式说明电流随电压 V_{BE} 以指数形式变化。当发生小电压变化时，我们将指数规律线性化以便快速估计电流变化，可发现电流变化大约为 2%/mV。由于电流强烈依赖 V_{BE}，因此晶体管一般作为电流驱动器件，而不是电压驱动器件。

同时，这也说明了处理偏移量或者相同晶体管之间的小电压变化有多么难。两个相同的晶体管具有相同的电压，如果它们的 V_{BE} 相差 1mV，则它们的电流将相差 2%。

MOS 晶体管

在 COMS 技术中双极型 NPN 和 PNP 晶体管对应 P 沟道 MOS 晶体管和 N 沟道 MOS 晶体管，如图 2-13 所示。双极晶体管和 MOS 晶体管在使用时可以独立完成相同的功能，但也各有利弊。一般来说，双极晶体管的基极、发射极、集电极分别相当于 MOS 晶体管的栅极、源极、漏极。双极晶体管最大的问题是其工作时需要基极电流，而 MOS 晶体管则不需要。该电流会造成发射极到集电极的传输损耗。虽然在小信号操作中基极电流很小，但是在电源应用中，双极晶体管用作开关，这时为了确保晶体管导通需要很高的基极电流。

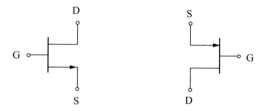

图 2-13 MOS 晶体管

如此高的基极电流会导致双极晶体管的效率非常低。随着便携式电子设备的普及以及电池寿命的延长，毫无疑问 CMOS 技术常常比双极晶体管技术更加有优势。双极晶体管的优点是它具有更好的跨导增益和更好的匹配性能，这使其具有更好的差分输入增益级。性能最好的设

计工艺是混合模式的 BiCMOS（双极型和 CMOS）或 BCD（双极型 CMOS 和 DMOS）工艺，使用这种方法，设计者可以根据手头的任务选择最好的器件。

2. 数字电路

布尔代数基础

与其他代数不同，布尔代数中只允许两个可能的值：0 或 1。这两个值通常称为一位（二进制）。这个位可以表示开或关、真或假、有或无。在逻辑表达式中，输入变量（如 A、B、C）用来表示开关、继电器触点或传感器输入。输入变量可以用来表示按钮开关、限位开关、温度传感器开关、压力开关、液位开关、接近式传感器开关、感光开关和感重开关。逻辑表达式的结果是执行某些操作：打开或关闭电磁铁、继电器、电动机、指示灯、蜂鸣器、报警器和其他输出设备。

"数字电子"用来描述主要处理只有两种不同的电压值或其他二元状态的电路系统。模拟设备和系统用来处理时变信号，可以取电压、电流或其他度量标准量范围内的任何值。区别在于在数字系统中我们可以假设它并不是的那个值。

布尔代数只有三个基本操作：非、与（·）、或（+）。

非运算对所作用的值取补。它将 1 变为 0，将 0 变为 1。它可表示为在变量的上方加横杠，也可以将它看作取反或否。

与运算是一种布尔乘法运算，当且仅当所有量均为 1 时其值为 1。用布尔变量描述就是 $A·B=Y$ 或 $AB=Y$。与运算就像串在一起的老式圣诞节彩灯。所有的灯必须都正常工作才能使这串灯亮起来。

或运算的结果是只要输入值有 1 其值就为 1。在布尔代数中，$1+1=1$。在逻辑上它表示如果有一个或多个真存在，结果就为真。

如同普通代数中有许多必须遵守的数学法则一样，布尔代数中也有许多法则，这些法则在逻辑运算中非常重要。香农证明，使用这些法则可以极大地扩展和简化逻辑描述，从而简化逻辑关系，减少继电器和开关的数量。

交换律：$A+B=B+A$

加法结合律：$A+B+C=A+(B+C)$

乘法结合律：$A(BC)=(AB)C$

分配律：$A(B+C)=AB+AC$

同一性：$1·A=A$，$0+A=A$

互补律：$A+\overline{A}=1$，$A·\overline{A}=0$

摩根定律：$\overline{A·B}=\overline{A}+\overline{B}$

逻辑门

大多数数字器件称作门。门用作构成更复杂的数字逻辑电路的模块。它们是计算机设计的基础。通常一个门电路拥有一个或多个输入，并产生一个输出，这个输出是输入值的函数。每一个逻辑单元都有一个真值表，表明这个单元的工作原理，并且每一个门电路都有对应的符号。

最重要的三种门电路是：

1) 与门——全 1 输出 1。逻辑表达式为 $F=A·B$。

2) 或门——有 1 输出 1，全 0 输出 0。逻辑表达式为 $F=A+B$。

3) 非门——通常称为反转器，输出与输入相反的值。逻辑表达式为 $F=\overline{A}$。

图 2-14~图 2-16 给出了我们可能遇到的三种逻辑门的符号。

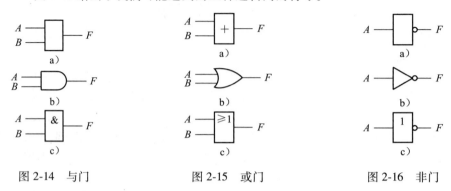

图 2-14 与门　　　　　图 2-15 或门　　　　　图 2-16 非门

基本数字运算包括与、非、或，也包括其他一些常用的组合：与非、或非和异或非。图 2-17 是集成电路形式的与非门和与门的封装示意图。

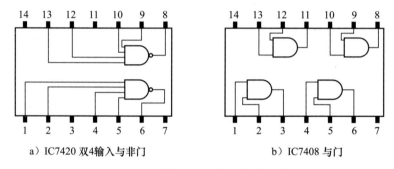

a）IC7420 双4输入与非门　　　　　b）IC7408 与门

图 2-17 与非门和与门的集成电路

组合逻辑电路和时序逻辑电路

逻辑电路分为两类：组合逻辑电路和时序逻辑电路。组合逻辑电路的输出只依赖当前输入。组合逻辑电路可能包括许多逻辑门和反向器，但不包含反馈回路（将门电路的输出信号反向传回该门电路输入端的信号通路）。

时序逻辑电路的输入信号中引入了以前的逻辑状态。以前的逻辑状态称为反馈。时序逻辑电路的输出不仅依赖当前的输入，而且依赖任意过去状态的输入。从这个意义上说，时序逻辑电路具有记忆性。

当电路分析时，可以利用逻辑图或逻辑流程（如真值表或逻辑表达式）来描述这个电路所完成的功能。电路综合就是从形式描述和过程得到逻辑图。我们已经学过 5 种适合描述组合逻辑电路的方法：

1）真值表。
2）最小项之和，标准和。
3）用 Σ 的最小项列表。
4）最大项之积，标准积。
5）用 Π 的最大项列表。

与布尔代数一样，卡诺图也是一种用于数字逻辑的简化工具。在处理涉及两个或更少的布尔变量的情况下，布尔代数确实比卡诺图要快。在处理三个输入变量时，布尔代数仍然可以使用，只是稍慢一点。但是对于 4 个输入变量，布尔代数就变得非常复杂烦琐，而卡诺图既快又容易。当输入变量多于 6~8 个时，就该用 CAD（计算机辅助设计）来简化了。卡诺图通过合并相邻 1

项简化逻辑函数,把所有的 1 项合并成积和式;将所有的 0 项合并,形成和积式。

触发器

"触发器"(见图 2-18)是对时序逻辑运算基本单元的两状态器件的统称。触发器广泛用于数字数据存储和转换中,并且通常用于"寄存器"中,用于存储二进制数字数据。

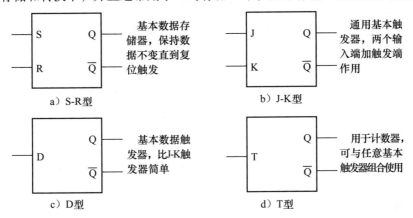

图 2-18 四种类型的触发器

在 S-R 锁存器中,激活 S 输入端实现电路置位,激活 R 输入端实现电路复位。如果 R 和 S 端同时处在高电平状态,电路将处于无效状态。

J-K 触发器是对 S-R 触发器的改进,没有"无效"或"非法"的输出状态。所以 J-K 触发器只是在 S-R 触发器的基础上增加了一个反馈层。这个反馈分别使置位/复位有效,避免两个端口同时置为高电平信号,从而消除了无效状态。

D 触发器的状态紧跟输入端,与输入 D 实现完全匹配。D 端就表示数据,每一个触发器存储数据行中的每一位数据。可以认为 D 触发器是最简单的存储单元。D 触发器可以由 S-R 触发器得到,只要在置位端用反相器将其设置为复位模式即可。结果就可以锁定了。

T 触发器在每一个时钟脉冲边沿到来时改变输出,得到的输出信号的频率是输入端信号频率的一半。T 触发器可以用来构成二进制计数器、分频器以及二进制加法器。将 J-K 触发器的两个输入端都置为高电平,它就变成 T 触发器。

2.3 射频接收机电路

射频是从 3MHz 到 1000MHz(1GHz)的无线电频谱中的一部分。在频谱的末端,即低于 3~30MHz 的高频波段,为 650~1650kHz 的中波波段。由于频率相对低,电路设计中的杂波电感和电容可以忽略不计。

射频接收机通常是学生学习模拟电子技术首先要学习的。然而,现代接收机的体系结构相当复杂。它的体系结构持续演化,不仅涉及模拟电子器件的性能改善,而且包括 DSP(数字信号处理)的性能提升。因此,它不是通过电路的硬件连接,而是通过软件编程来实现更多的功能。

1. 超外差接收机模拟系统

超外差接收机系统简称超外差,是射频接收机中众所周知的常用体系结构。我们可以看出,该接收机具有良好的选择性和敏感性,因为噪声带宽可以限定在信道带宽内,而不影响接收机在整个 RF 波段内的性能。它的基本组成如图 2-28 所示。

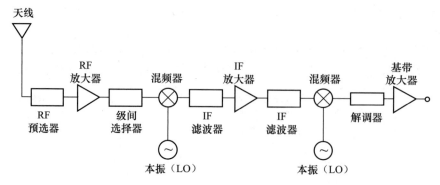

图 2-28　超外差接收机模拟系统的基本组成

RF 预选器

RF 预选器的功能是滤掉包含有用信道的 RF 波段以外的无用信号。无用信号可能是发射机本身通过共用天线产生的。在这种情况下，预选器相当于双工器或滤波器。其功能是，在天线和接收机、天线和发射机之间允许不同的频率波段通过（像 CDMA 移动通信系统一样），或者在接收信号阶段打开发送/接收开关，在发送信号阶段关闭发送/接收开关（像 GSM 系统一样）。因此，这样的电路分别工作在全双工或半双工状态下，并且能够预防后续的接收机组件由于无用频率而造成的过载。预选器也可抑制由于存在杂波频率引入的信号而产生的无用输出端响应（接收机工作频率称为调谐频率 f_T）。我们知道，这样的杂波频率不仅包括镜像频率，还包括入射调谐频率的谐波。在理想情况下，预选器有良好的阻抗匹配，以避免带通波纹。

RF 放大器

RF 放大器的功能是将输入信号线性放大，并将接收机加在自身信号的噪声最小化。由此，我们可以得出，低噪声放大可以实现噪声与放大器输入的良好匹配。低噪声放大很重要，因为它决定整个接收机的整体噪声匹配。因此，RF 放大器有良好的输入和输出匹配，以避免增益波动。此外，RF 放大器不能引起信号失真，因为强信号可能出现在相邻的（不需要的）信道，放大器的任何非线性失真都可能会使我们要检测的弱信号被淹没。为了达到这个目的，RF 放大器应该由多级组成，以提供必要的增益。

级间选择器

前一级放大器提供射频带宽内所有信道的增益，因此在 RF 放大器之外，增益逐渐降低。此外，放大器可能放大了整个频带内的噪声，也可能放大了镜像频率。因此，该级间选择器相当于滤波器，用于抑制杂波频率的无用信号响应的增益，尤其是镜像频率响应。它应该保持系统的噪声系数，防止镜像噪声进入混频器。级间选择器还有助于减少混频器端口的本振再辐射。一般要求它具有较低的带内损耗。

本振

本振频率是由频率合成器产生的强信号，其调谐带宽与整个 RF 带宽一致，但是频率不一样，从而可以选择任意有用的信道。它能使混频器内的元器件进入非线性状态以实现频率转换（混频）。振荡器的一个重要技术参数是它的相位噪声，振荡器信号的任何相位波动都直接叠加在混频器的输出信号上。同时，要求尽可能低的带宽噪声，从而降低系统噪声。在本振中，良好的调谐范围或带宽、低的杂波和谐波分量也是必不可少的。

第一混频器

第一混频器的功能是根据本振信号频率，将 RF 范围内的输入信号转换为中频信号。混频器对频率进行线性转换，在新频率范围内保持其原有的相位信息。在中频输出时一定范围内的 RF 信号振幅得以保留。可以得知，混频器拓扑结构的选择（如单平衡、双平衡等）是非常重要的，它可以滤除无用的混频器输出成分。它要求有较低的 LO 馈给 RF 和 IF，在输入的 RF 信号中一定频率范围内无杂波信号。为了确保接收机对无用信号的响应最小，IF 频率的选择是至关重要的。由 HF/VHF 接收机的历史经验得知，信号上变频为最高 RF 的两倍来转换成中频信号。在微波频率中，由于可调谐范围非常小，信号通常下变频成更低的频率。在 800MHz 波段，45~82MHz 常用于移动无线电接收机的中频，110~300MHz 频率常用于 1800MHz 波段或同时用于这两个频段中。

IF 滤波器

IF 滤波器能够滤掉混频器和其他元器件产生的无用信号。它的带宽很宽，足以使信号在所需信道中无失真地通过调制边带。由于频率保持不变，因此 IF 滤波器有很高的 Q 值。IF 滤波器和下面的器件一起确定了接收机的抑制和过载特性。

IF 放大器

IF 放大器的功能是给中频信号提供足够的增益，以驱动下面的几级。因为频率保持不变，所以它能够提供高增益，具有高稳定性。

第二混频器、本振和第二滤波器

这三个器件有时称为第二 IF 组，虽然和第一 IF 组的功能类似，但是工作在不同的波段，具有不同的通带特性。第一 IF 组覆盖整个射频通带，滤除杂波频率，尤其是镜像频率。而第二 IF 组的功能是从整个通带内缩小范围并选出所需信道，因此，第二 IF 组为接收机提供了额外的选择性。对于商业 AM 广播来说，455kHz 是标准的第二 IF 组频率，而移动通信接收机却通常使用 10MHz 左右的频率。在某些结构中，第二 IF 组被完全忽略了，代之以从射频到低的中频的单个下变频。在这种情况下，（第一）IF 滤波器也具有信道选择的功能。

解调器

解调器的功能是从 IF 信号中提取已调信号，并将其转化为基带信号。在模拟系统中，已调信号要么是 AM 信号要么是 FM 信号。在数字系统中，已调信号通常是能够解码且具有多振幅值的符号（符号是波形编码中一位或几位的组合）。

基带放大器

基带放大器的功能是为相关的输出器件提供输出功率以驱动其工作。这些输出器件通常是扬声器、传真输出或者视频输出。

标准超外差结构的一个变化就是固定了（第一）LO 频率，将整个 RF 波段下变频到 IF 波段。这样就产生了一个固定频率。因此，高 Q 值和低相位噪声的本振用于 RF LO，而且通过改变 IF（或第二）LO，可以实现调谐和信道选择。这可以解决 LO 引入的相位噪声的问题。但是，由于第二 LO 和 IF 有相同的频率，会导致基带偏移，这是这种体系结构特有的。但它确实需要调谐范围宽的第二 LO，而且第二混频器容易受到强相邻信道的严重干扰，这是因为 RF 级在信道选择方面能力有限。

2. 接收机特性

我们将接收机的灵敏度和接收机的选择性作为接收机质量评价的两大基本指标。像接收机的动态范围、最大输入信号等其他系统参数，我们可以通过体系结构或者体系结构中子系统和组件的关键参数获得，尤其是通过设定增益、噪声系数、功率容量以及每一级的频率特性，可以估算出接收机的整体性能。

通信信道

我们首先应该主要考虑信道基本的物理限制和制衡，因为它们最终决定特定无线电系统的性能。

信息论是一门复杂的、快速发展的学科。近年来,我们非常重视新的调制和编码方式的发展,这些措施能够节约带宽、降低功耗,减少其他系统失真所带来的影响。这非常重要。因为频谱资源是非常有限、稀缺的,也就非常昂贵,这就要求我们需要有节制地分配和使用频谱资源。

$$C = B\log_2(1 + SNR) \tag{2-15}$$

信息论的基本公式是香农公式,可通过香农公式预测通信信道的信息传输能力。这个公式也许有很多种形式,但是我们只选取有用的形式。这个公式说明信道容量 C(以每秒多少位衡量)与信道带宽 B 成正比,和检波器的 SNR 的以 2 为底的对数成正比。该公式说明了为什么频谱是一种昂贵的资源,因为如果假设信号的功率和 SNR 仍然相同,随着信号占用更多的带宽,可以放更多的数据。在实践中,现代系统使用发送冗余位和复杂编码方案等检错方法以逼近香农理论的极限。

由上述理论可得,对于一个给定最大信息吞吐量的信道,发送信息的功率(更确切地说是检波器的 SNR)可以由频谱占用率和带宽来得到,即

$$SNR_2 = SNR_1^{(B_1/B_2)} \quad (SNR \gg 1) \tag{2-16}$$

因此,如果频谱占用率 B_2 增加,当信息以相同的比特率传输时,SNR 将会更低。GSM 蜂窝系统与 CDMA 系统的比较便很好地说明了这个问题。两种系统都使用相同的传输介质(自由空间),并且有相似的噪声源。然而,GSM 信号必须比噪声电平高几十分贝才能检测到,而 CDMA 信号即使被淹没在噪声之中,也能检测出来。在大带宽中通过对信号标记进行编码,使得 CDMA 信号功率减少到一定的水平,从而使接收机接收到的信号像调谐在其他信道时所接收到的噪声一样低。

接收机噪声

我们已经看到,噪声在接收机整体性能中起着非常重要的作用。这是因为,与信号功率一起以 SNR 的形式,在香农公式中共同决定着系统的数据传输速率和可接收的最小信号水平。

接收机的噪声来源有很多,如下所示。

- 来源于信道的噪声,经天线进入系统,通常以加性高斯白噪声的形式表示,其本质上是一种热噪声;
- 来源于 RF 预选器,它限制了信号频带,但是叠加了一个有限的插入损耗,因此产生热噪声;
- 来源于有源器件,通常产生热噪声、散粒噪声和 $1/f$ 噪声。

这些噪声分量形成的背景噪声可作为可检测的最小噪声水平。噪声的功率谱密度不同且是频率的函数。功率谱密度表示给定带宽中所包含的功率,单位是 W/Hz。尽管有时我们也指每赫兹的噪声电压和噪声电流,但一般在射频系统中,我们通常以固定的参考阻抗值(通常为 50Ω)来测量功率。在这种情况下,热噪声是电阻的函数,噪声功率表示为

$$P_N = KTB \tag{2-17}$$

式中,P_N 是总的噪声功率,K 为玻耳兹曼常数,T 是热力学温度,单位为 K。显然,宽带越宽,噪声功率越大。因此,最后的 IF 滤波器带宽应尽可能窄,使得在解调和检测信号之前噪声功率最小。因为最后的 IF 滤波器是检测信号之前所有器件中带宽最窄的器件,所以它决定了整个接收机的噪声带宽。

通常在低于 30MHz 的无线电波段中,由于自然现象和人为原因,外部噪声远远大于计算值。在低兆赫兹频率范围内,以 30MHz 的为例,外部噪声与我们测得的噪声相比,在农村地区约高 12dB 左右,在嘈杂的城市中,则高达 76dB 左右。当我们在检测最小信号时,必须考虑提高接收机的最低噪声水平。

接收机灵敏度

由于背景噪声的影响,在解调和检测信号之前,必须保证输入信号的强度以便正确识别。在数字系统中,要保证能区分"1"和"0";在模拟系统中,要保证是高质量的模拟波形。接收机灵敏度指的是系统获得良好的输出信号时所需的最低输入信号强度。然而,由于可接收质量的定义不同,接收机灵敏度的定义也不尽相同。

输入端的背景噪声不仅包括输入端的热噪声,还包括系统本身的所有噪声。如果我们假设输入信号至少和噪声水平相等才能被检测,那么我们可以把输入的噪声参考水平称为最小可辨认信号(MDS)。但是,大多数音响爱好者认为对于能接受的声音质量,其信噪比至少为10dB。因此,我们通常用输出 10dB 的信噪比(S_o/N_o)来检测系统的灵敏度。

系统的非线性特性

对于任何系统的元器件,其性能最终都会到达临界点,从而表现出非线性特性,尤其当输出端的振幅或相位与输入端的振幅或相位不再成正比,它成为非线性元器件。在大多数可变有源器件中,这个结果主要是由于器件互导引起幅度的变化,但是电阻和电容随着电压幅度的变化而变化,也产生非线性特性。当器件超过正常工作极限而进入截止或饱和等状态时,产生的总非线性特性会加剧。结果是,我们会看到诸如增益失真和 AM-PM 转换时的交调等结果。

接收机动态范围

我们已经说过,在小信号情况下,可以检测到的最小信号水平受到背景噪声的限制,背景噪声包括热噪声和其他有源和无源元器件所产生的噪声。对于大信号,由于谐波和交调失真现象的出现,造成了信号的压缩和干扰,最终限制了接收机处理大信号的能力。接收机的动态范围指的是最小可检测信号到最大可检测信号的动态范围。这个定义的一种解释是 1dB 压缩输出功率和输出背景噪声之间的差。因为这个解释假设的是单信道系统,所以它作用有限。相反,无杂散动态范围(SFDR)更有用。我们把它定义成输入功率值的范围。这个范围以输出信号功率刚好超过输出背景噪声功率,任何失真分量都湮没在背景噪声之中为临界点。

为了增加接收机的有用范围,可以使接收机自动调节系统增益,以便减小大信号引发过载或失真时的增益。但是,这样做的影响并不始终明显。我们必须考虑信号的信噪比而且在系统性能方面做一些取舍。例如,在 LNA(低噪声放大器)中应用 AGC(自动增益控制)。在 LNA 之前,增加衰减会降低噪声系数,但是这样会降低大信号(这可能是干扰而不是信号本身)的影响。在 LNA 之后,衰减器能防止后续几级的过载但是同时也会降低三阶截止点。在理想情况下,我们通常希望降低增益,增加功率处理能力同时最小化噪声系数。因此,同时考虑增益和输入互调截点是必要的。这是因为在设置 AGC 水平时,增益和输入截止点是首要因素。对于系统噪声系数的影响可以推导得出。

图 2-29 给出了 AGC 在模拟接收机中的典型应用。随着有用信号输入功率的增加,系统的增益将会降低,以尽量减少失真。在理想情况下,输出级增益的减小首先避免了系统噪声系数的增加和灵敏度的降低。随着前级开始出现失真现象,我们逐步引入 AGC 来消除失真。因此,因为背景噪声主要由系统前端损耗产生,所以背景噪声和输入处理能力具有相同的变化趋势。

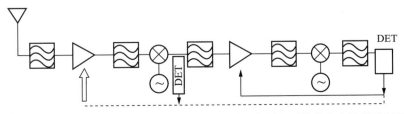

图 2-29 模拟接收机中 AGC 原理的应用,显示了检测信号电平的节点和增益控制的节点

强信号可能以干扰的形式出现在其他信道中，必须通过 AGC 电路来检测这些带外信号，从而发现失真，降低增益。因为这些信号出现在射频前端，由后几级电路的选择性逐渐滤除，所以在后期强信号被滤除之前，必须在前端检测到这些信号。出于这个原因，有时会使用如图 2-29 所示的两级 AGC 电路，以确保不仅在有用信道而且在干扰信道中正确地检测信号水平。

例如，设有两个强信号与有用信号相差仅几千赫兹。因为这些强信号的频率非常接近调谐或者有用信号的频率，所以接收机的第一 IF 滤波器不能滤除这些强信号。结果，这些强信号可能导致在 RF 和 IF 前端产生失真，而且其三阶交调产物将位于有用信号的顶部。但是，在通过更窄的第二或最后的 IF 滤波器后，相邻信道的信号及其谐波将会滤除。如果仅通过接收机输出功率来控制 AGC，将检测不到这些信号。应该在第一 IF 级检测到这些干扰信号，而且通过在前端插入衰减器使得这些信号在进入接收机的有源器件之前被滤除。在一些旧的短波无线电中，通过开关在信号中手动插入 RF 衰减来减少较大的无用信号，而这些无用信号是由接收机前几级的饱和引起的。

杂散响应

最小化杂散响应是接收机继频率选择体系结构之后的主要设计标准。杂散响应是由无用频率分量引起的输出。在这方面，无用频率分量和接收机调谐的频率分量是无关的。例如，如果要对载波为 895MHz 的信道进行解调，则可能有 890MHz 的信号在接收机中产生响应，对载波为 895MHz 的信道产生干扰。如果 890MHz 信号产生了杂散响应，我们就称它为杂散频率。虽然现代编码技术仍然能够在相同频率的干扰信号存在的情况下检测出有用信号，但是由于杂散响应降低了有用信号的灵敏度，因此它们仍旧是我们所面临的难题。

在接收机中，当接收机工作在杂散频率时，失真现象引起杂散响应。虽然诸如石英滤波器等其他器件也是非线性的，但是混频器和滤波器的非线性特性是产生该响应的主要原因。信号输入接收机和进入接收机内部都会产生杂散响应。例如，器件引脚泄漏或者说接收机末端反馈到输入端的信号分量都可能导致杂散响应。IF、次谐波、镜像频率和高阶混频产物都可能激发杂散响应。这些激励源都具有这样的特性：它们的杂散响应都发生在 IF。虽然我们不能从线性分析的角度定量地预测其幅度，但是，至少可以预测产生问题的杂散信号的频率，从而采取相关措施，消除这个频段的电压或电流以免产生杂散信号。

Chapter 3

Signal System and Signal Processing
（信号系统与信号处理）

3.1　Signal and System

The concepts of signals and systems arise in a wide variety of fields, and the ideas and techniques associated with these concepts play an important role in such diverse areas of science and technology as communications, aeronautics and astronautics, circuit design, acoustics, seismology, biomedical engineering, energy generation and distribution systems, chemical process control, and speech processing. In this article, we introduce simply the mathematical representations of continuous-time and discrete-time signals and systems, and the concepts of signal energy and power.

1. Continuous-Time and Discrete-Time Signals

Signals may describe a wide variety of physical phenomena. Although signals can be represented in many ways, in all cases the information in a signal is contained in a pattern of variations of some form. For example, consider the simple circuit in Fig. 3-1. In this case, the patterns of variations over time in the source and capacitor voltages, v_s and v_c, are examples of signals.

Signals are represented mathematically as functions of one or more independent variables. For example, a speech signal can be represented mathematically by acoustic pressure as a function of time, and a picture can be represented by brightness as a function of two spatial variables. For convenience,

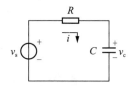

Fig. 3-1　A simple RC circuit with source voltage v_s and capacitor voltage v_c

we will generally refer to the independent variable as time; although it may not in fact represent time in specific applications. For example, in geophysics, signals representing variations with depth of physical quantities such as density, porosity, and electrical resistivity are used to study the structure of the earth. Also, knowledge of the variations of air pressure, temperature, and wind speed with altitude are extremely important in meteorological investigations. Fig. 3-2 depicts a typical example of annual average vertical wind profile as a function of height. The measured variations of wind speed with height are used in examining weather patterns, as well as wind conditions may affect an aircraft during final approach and landing.

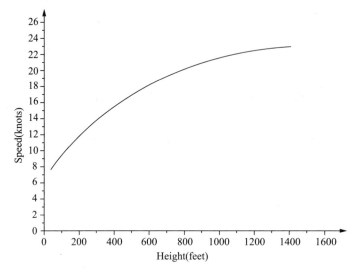

Fig. 3-2　Typical annual vertical wind profile

In this article we will be considering two basic types of signals: continuous-time signals and discrete-time signals. In the case of continuous-time signals the independent variable is continuous, and thus these signals are defined for a continuum of values of the independent variable. On the other hand, discrete-time signals are defined only at discrete time, and consequently, for these signals, the independent variable takes on only a discrete set of values. A speech signal as a function of time and atmospheric pressure as a function of altitude are examples of continuous-time signals. The weekly Dow Jones stock market index, as illustrated in Fig. 3-3, is an example of a discrete-time signal.

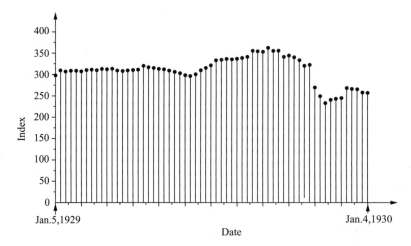

Fig. 3-3　An example of a discrete-time signal

To distinguish between continuous-time and discrete-time signals, we will use the symbol t to denote the continuous-time independent variable and n to denote the discrete-time independent variable. We will also have frequent occasions when it will be useful to represent signals graphically. Illustrations of a continuous-time signal $x(t)$ and a discrete-time signal $x(n)$ are shown in Fig. 3-4. It is important to note that the discrete-time signal $x(n)$ is defined only for integer values of the independent variable.

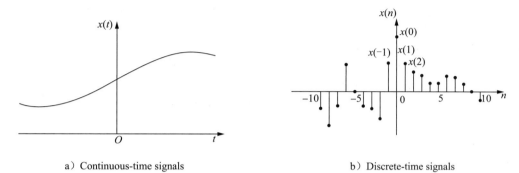

a) Continuous-time signals　　　　　　b) Discrete-time signals

Fig. 3-4　Graphical representations

2. Continuous-Time and Discrete-Time Systems

Physical systems in the broadest sense are an interconnection of components, devices, or subsystems. In context ranging from signal processing and communications to electromechanical motors, automotive vehicles, and chemical-processing plants, a system can be viewed as a process in which input signals are transformed by the system or cause the system to respond in some way, resulting in other signals as outputs. For example, a high-fidelity (hi-fi) system takes a recorded audio signal and generates a reproduction of that signal. If the hi-fi system has tone controls, we can change the tonal quality of the reproduced signal. Similarly, the circuit in Fig. 3-1 can be viewed as a system with input voltage $v_s(t)$ and output voltage $v_c(t)$. An image-enhancement system transforms an input image into an output image that has some desired properties, such as improved contrast.

A continuous-time system is a system in which continuous-time input signals are applied and result in continuous-time output signals. Such a system is represented pictorially as in Fig. 3-5a, where $x(t)$ is the input, $y(t)$ is the output, and $h(t)$ is the system impulse response. Similarly, a discrete-time system-that is, a system that transforms discrete-time inputs into discrete-time outputs-is depicted as in Fig. 3-5b, where $x(n)$ is the input, $y(n)$ is the output, and $h(n)$ is the system unit sample response.

a) Continuous-time system　　　　　　b) Discrete-time system

Fig. 3-5　Time system

We can bring continuous-time and discrete-time systems together through the concept of sampling, and we can develop some insights into the use of discrete-time systems to process continuous-time signals that have been sampled. At present, many digital signal processing methods have been widely used in science and technology fields. So we take digital signal system for example, some system properties are described in next section.

3. Some Properties of Digital Signal System

In general, a system maps an input signal $x(n)$ to an output signal $y(n)$ through a system transformation $T\{\cdot\}$. This definition of a system is very broad. Without some restrictions, when the characterization of a system requires a complete input-output relationship, knowing the output of a system to a certain set of inputs does not allow us to determine the output of the system to other sets of inputs. Two types of restrictions that greatly simplify the characterization and analysis of a system are linearity and time invariance, alternatively referred to as shift invariance. Fortunately, many systems can often be approximated in practice by a linear and time-invariant system.

The linearity of a system is defined through the principle of superposition as

$$T\{ax_1(n)+bx_2(n)\} = ay_1(n)+by_2(n) \tag{3-1}$$

where $T\{x_1(n)\} = y_1(n)$, $T\{x_2(n)\} = y_2(n)$, and a and b are any scalar constants.

Time invariance of a system is defined as

$$T\{x(n-n_0)\} = y(n-n_0) \tag{3-2}$$

where $T\{x(n)\} = y(n)$ and n_0 is any integer.

Linearity and time invariance are independent properties, i.e., a system may have one but not the other property, both or neither.

For a Linear and Time-Invariant (LTI) system, the system output $y(n)$ is given by

$$y(n) = \sum_{k=-\infty}^{+\infty} x(k)h(n-k) = x(n) * h(n) \tag{3-3}$$

The eq. (3-3) is the convolution sum. It meets the addition commutative law, associative law and distributive law:

$$\text{commutative law: } x(n) * y(n) = y(n) * x(n) \tag{3-4}$$

$$\text{associative law: } [x(n) * y(n)] * w(n) = x(n) * [y(n) * w(n)] \tag{3-5}$$

$$\text{distributive law: } x(n) * [y(n) + w(n)] = x(n) * y(n) + x(n) * w(n) \tag{3-6}$$

In continuous-time systems, convolution is primarily an analytical tool. For discrete-time systems, the convolution sum, in addition to being important in the analysis of LTI systems, is important as an explicit mechanism for implementing a specific class of LTI systems.

Two additional system properties that are referred to frequently are the properties of stability and causality. A system is considered stable if and only if a bounded input always leads to a bounded output. A necessary and sufficient condition for a LTI system to be stable is that its unit sample response $h(n)$ be absolutely summable. That is, the eq. (3-7) is met.

$$\sum_{n=-\infty}^{\infty} |h(n)| < \infty \tag{3-7}$$

Thus, an absolutely summable sequence is often referred to as a stable sequence.

A system is referred to as causal if and only if, for each value of n, say n_0, $y(n)$ dose not depend on values of the input for $n > n_0$. A necessary and sufficient condition for an LTI system to be causal is that its unit sample response $h(n)$ be zero for $n < 0$. That is, the eq. (3-8) is met.

$$h(n) = 0 \quad \text{for} \quad n < 0 \tag{3-8}$$

Thus, a sequence that is zero for $n < 0$ is often referred to as a causal sequence.

4. Signal Energy and Power

From the range of examples provided so far, we see that signals may present a broad variety of phenomena. In many, but not all, applications, the signals we consider are directly related to physical quantities capturing power and energy in a physical system. For example, if $v(t)$ and $i(t)$ are, respectively, the voltage and current across a resistor with resistance R, then the instantaneous power is

$$p(t) = v(t)i(t) = \frac{1}{R}v^2(t) \tag{3-9}$$

The total energy expended over the time interval $t_1 \leq t \leq t_2$ is

$$\int_{t_1}^{t_2} p(t)\,dt = \int_{t_1}^{t_2} \frac{1}{R}v^2(t)\,dt \tag{3-10}$$

and the average power over this time interval is

$$\frac{1}{t_2 - t_1}\int_{t_1}^{t_2} p(t)\,dt = \frac{1}{t_2 - t_1}\int_{t_1}^{t_2} \frac{1}{R}v^2(t)\,dt \tag{3-11}$$

It is a common and worthwhile convention to use similar terminology for power and energy for any continuous-time signal $x(t)$ or any discrete-time signal $x(n)$. Moreover, we will frequently find it convenient to consider signals that take on complex values. In this case, the total energy over the time interval $t_1 \leq t \leq t_2$ in a continuous-time signal $x(t)$ is defined as

$$\int_{t_1}^{t_2} |x(t)|^2\,dt \tag{3-12}$$

where $|x(t)|$ denotes the magnitude of the (possibly complex) function $x(t)$. The time-averaged power is obtained by dividing eq. (3-12) by the length t_2-t_1 of the time interval. Similarly, the total energy in a discrete-time signal $x(n)$ over the time interval $n_1 \leq n \leq n_2$ is defined as

$$\sum_{n=n_1}^{n_2} |x(n)|^2 \tag{3-13}$$

And dividing by the number of points in the intervals n_2-n_1+1, yields the average power over the interval. It is important to remember that the terms "power" and "energy" are used here independently of whether the quantities in eqs. (3-12) and (3-13) actually are related to physical energy. Nevertheless, we will find it convenient to use these terms in a general fashion.

Furthermore, in many systems we will be interested in examining power and energy in signals over an infinite time interval, i.e., for $-\infty < t < +\infty$ or for $-\infty < n < +\infty$. In these cases, we define the total energy as limits of eqs. (3-14) and (3-15) as the time interval increases without bound. That is, in continuous-time:

$$E_\infty \stackrel{\Delta}{=} \lim_{T\to\infty} \int_{-T}^{T} |x(t)|^2\,dt = \int_{-\infty}^{+\infty} |x(t)|^2\,dt \tag{3-14}$$

and in discrete-time:

$$E_\infty \stackrel{\Delta}{=} \lim_{N\to\infty} \sum_{n=-N}^{+N} |x(n)|^2 = \sum_{n=-\infty}^{+\infty} |x(n)|^2 \tag{3-15}$$

Note that for some signals the integral in eq. (3-14) or sum in eq. (3-15) might not converge, e.g., if $x(t)$ or $x(n)$ equals a nonzero constant value for all time. Such signals have infinite energy, while signals with $E_\infty < \infty$ have finite energy.

In an analogous fashion, we can define the time-averaged over an infinite interval as

$$P_\infty \stackrel{\Delta}{=} \lim_{T\to\infty} \frac{1}{2T}\int_{-T}^{T} |x(t)|^2\,dt \tag{3-16}$$

and

$$P_\infty \overset{\Delta}{=} \lim_{N\to\infty} \frac{1}{2N+1} \sum_{n=-N}^{+N} |x(n)|^2 \tag{3-17}$$

in continuous-time and discrete-time, respectively. With these definitions, we can identify three important classes of signals.

The first of these is the class of signals with finite total energy, i.e., those signals for which $E_\infty < \infty$. Such a signal must have zero average power, since in the continuous-time case, for example, we see from eq. (3-18) that

$$P_\infty = \lim_{T\to\infty} \frac{E_\infty}{2T} = 0 \tag{3-18}$$

An example of a finite-energy signal is a signal that takes on the value 1 for $0 \leq t \leq 1$ and 0 otherwise. In this case, $E_\infty = 1$ and $P_\infty = 0$.

The second class of signals is those with finite average power P_∞. From what we have just seen, if $P_\infty > 0$, then, of necessity, $E_\infty = \infty$. This, of course, makes sense, since if there is a nonzero average energy per unit time, then integrating or summing this over an infinite time interval yields an infinite amount of energy. For example, the constant signal $x(n) = 4$ has infinite energy, but average power $P_\infty = 16$.

The third class of signals is the signals for which neither P_∞ nor E_∞ are finite. A simple example is the signal $x(t) = t$.

NEW WORDS AND PHRASES

diverse   *adj.* 不同的，变化多的
aeronautics   *n.* 航空学，航空术
astronautics   *n.* 太空航空学
seismology   *n.* 地震学
porosity   *n.* 气隙度
meteorologic   *adj.* 气象的，气象学的
profile   *n.* 剖面，侧面，外形，轮廓
Dow Jones   *n.* 道琼斯
worthwhile   *adj.* 值得做的，值得出力的

convention   *n.* 协定，习俗，惯例
terminology   *n.* 术语学
electromechanical   *adj.* [机] 电动机械的，机电的
automotive   *adj.* 汽车的，自动推进的
vehicle   *n.* 交通工具，车辆
high-fidelity   高保真
tone   *n.* 音调，音质，语调

NOTES

1) The concepts of signals and systems arise in a wide variety of fields, and the ideas and techniques associated with these concepts play an important role in such diverse areas of science and technology as communications, aeronautics and astronautics, circuit design, acoustics, seismology, biomedical engineering, energy generation and distribution systems, chemical process control, and speech processing.
信号与系统的概念出现在多个领域，与之相关的思想和技术在多个科学技术领域发挥着重要的作用，例如，通信、航空航天、电路设计、声学、地震学、生物医学工程、发电与配电系统、化学过程控制和语音处理。

2) Without some restrictions, when the characterization of a system requires a complete input-output relationship, knowing the output of a system to a certain set of inputs does not allow us to determine the output of the system to other sets of inputs.
当系统的特性描述要求完整的输入-输出关系时，如果没有约束条件，即使知道了系统对某些特定输入产生的输出，我们也并不知道系统对其他输入产生的输出。

3) An example of a finite-energy signal is a signal that takes on the value 1 for $0 \leqslant t \leqslant 1$ and 0 otherwise.

举一个有限能量信号的例子：信号在 $0 \leqslant t \leqslant 1$ 内值为1，而在其他时间范围内值为0。

4) This, of course, makes sense, since if there is a nonzero average energy per unit time, then integrating or summing this over an infinite time interval yields an infinite amount of energy.

当然这是有意义的，因为如果单位时间内存在一个非零的平均能量，那么在无限的时间间隔范围内，对其积分或者求和就会产生无限的能量总和。

EXERCISES

1. **Please translate the following words and phrases into Chinese.**
    a) signal and system
    b) aeronautics and astronautics
    c) continuous-time signals
    d) signal energy and power
    e) total energy
    f) complex number
    g) infinite time interval
    h) average power
    i) physical system
    j) automotive vehicle

2. **Please translate the following words and phrases into English.**
    a) 信号处理
    b) 电路设计
    c) 离散时间信号
    d) 非零常数
    e) 独立变量
    f) 瞬时功率
    g) 平均能量
    h) 无限能量
    i) 子系统的相互作用
    j) 图像增强

3. **Fill in the blanks with the missing word(s).**
    a) In this case, the patterns of variations _____ time in the source and capacitor voltages, v_s and v_c, are examples of signals.
    b) For example, a speech signal can be represented mathematically _____ acoustic pressure as a function of time, and a picture can be represented by brightness as a function of two spatial variables.
    c) On the other hand, discrete-time signals are defined only _____ discrete times, and consequently, for these signals, the independent variable takes on only a discrete set of values.
    d) It is important to note that the discrete-time signal $x(n)$ is defined only _____ integer values of the independent variable.
    e) In many, but not all, applications, the signals we consider are directly related _____ physical quantities capturing power and energy in a physical system.
    f) The total energy expended _____ the time interval $t_1 \leqslant t \leqslant t_2$ is $\int_{t_1}^{t_2} p(t) dt = \int_{t_1}^{t_2} \frac{1}{R} v^2(t) dt$.
    g) The time-averaged power is obtained _____ dividing eq. (3-12) by the length $t_2 - t_1$ of the time interval.
    h) In these cases, we define the total energy _____ limits of eqs. (3-14) and (3-15) _____ the time interval increases without bound.
    i) An example of a finite-energy signal is a signal that takes _____ the value 1 for $0 \leqslant t \leqslant 1$ and 0 otherwise.
    j) In context ranging _____ signal processing and communications _____ electromechanical motors, automotive vehicles, and chemical-processing plants, a system can be viewed as a process in which input signals are transformed by the system or cause the system to respond in some way, resulting in other signals as outputs.

4. **Answer the following questions according to the text.**
    a) How many basic types of signals can be divided? Please write out the key features of each type.

b) How to define the total energy over the time interval $t_1 \leqslant t \leqslant t_2$ in a continuous-time system?

c) With the definition of eq. (3-16) and (3-17), how many classes of signal can be identified? Please name each of these.

d) What is a LTI system?

READING

Wavelet Transform

1. Overview

Wavelets are functions that satisfy certain mathematical requirements and are used to represent data or other functions. This idea is not new. Approximation using superposition of functions has existed since the early 1800's, when Joseph Fourier discovered that he could superpose sines and cosines to represent other functions. However, in wavelet analysis, the scale that we use to look at data plays a special role. Wavelet algorithms process data at different scales or resolutions. If we look at a signal with a large "window", we would notice gross features. Similarly, if we look at a signal with a small "window", we would notice small features. The result in wavelet analysis is to see both the forest and the trees.

This makes wavelets interesting and useful. For many decades, scientists have wanted more appropriate functions than the sines and cosines which comprise the bases of Fourier analysis, to approximate choppy signals. By their definition, these functions are non-local (and stretch out to infinity). They therefore do a very poor job in approximating sharp signals. But with wavelet analysis, we can use approximating functions that are contained neatly in finite domains. Wavelets are well-suited for approximating data with sharp discontinuities.

The wavelet analysis procedure is to adopt a wavelet prototype function, called an analyzing wavelet or mother wavelet. Temporal analysis is performed with a contracted, high-frequency version of the prototype wavelet, while frequency analysis is performed with a dilated, low-frequency version of the same wavelet. Because the original signal or function can be represented in terms of a wavelet expansion (using coefficients in a linear combination of the wavelet functions), data operations can be performed using just the corresponding wavelet coefficients. And if you further choose the best wavelets adapted to your data, or truncate the coefficients below a threshold, your data is sparsely represented. This sparse coding makes wavelets an excellent tool in the field of data compression.

小波变换

1. 概述

小波是满足特定数学要求的函数，它用于表示数据或其他函数。这不是新的思想。用叠加函数求近似值早在19世纪早期就出现了，当时，约瑟夫·傅里叶发现他可以将正弦和余弦函数叠加来表示其他函数。然而，在小波分析中，用于观察数据的尺度充当着重要的角色。小波算法用不同的尺度和分辨率处理数据。如果我们通过大窗口来观察信号，则会得到信号的总体特征。同样，如果通过小窗口观察数据，则得到细节特征。从小波分析结果可以看到信号的概况和细节。

这种特性使得小波技术既有意义又实用。几十年来，科学家想要获得比正、余弦函数更适合的函数，用来逼近突变信号，而正、余弦函数是傅里叶分析的基础。根据定义，这些正、余弦函数是非局部的（伸展到无穷大），所以它们在近似尖锐函数时效果很差。但是，当应用小波分析时，我们可以使用近似函数，把它们巧妙地包含在有限区域内。小波非常适合逼近尖锐不连续的数据。

小波分析过程中采用的小波原型函数，称作分析小波或母小波。时域分析是通过紧凑的高频原型小波实现的，频域分析是通过扩展的低频原型小波实现的。因为原始信号或者函数可以通过小波扩展（在小波函数线性组合中使用小波系数）来表示，所以数据操作只需要使用相应的小波系数进行即可。如果选择更适合数据的最优小波，或舍弃低于阈值的系数，那么用稀疏数据就可以代表原数据。这种稀疏编码使得小波在数据压缩领域中成为极佳的工具。

Other applied fields that are making use of wavelets include astronomy, acoustics, nuclear engineering, sub-band coding, signal and image processing, neurophysiology, music, magnetic resonance imaging, speech discrimination, optics, fractals, earthquake-prediction, radar, human vision, and pure mathematics applications such as solving partial differential equations.

2. Wavelet versus Fourier Transforms

Fourier representation of functions as a superposition of sines and cosines has become ubiquitous for both the analytic and numerical solution of differential equations and for the analysis and treatment of communication signals. Fourier and wavelet analysis have some very strong links.

Similarities between Fourier and Wavelet Transforms

The Fast Fourier Transform (FFT) and the Discrete Wavelet Transform (DWT) are both linear operations that generate a data structure that contains $\log_2 n$ segments of various lengths, usually filling and transforming it into a different data vector of length 2^n.

The mathematical properties of the matrices involved in the transforms are similar as well. The inverse transform matrix for both the FFT and the DWT is the transpose of the original. As a result, both transforms can be viewed as a rotation in function space to a different domain. For the FFT, this new domain contains basis functions that are sines and cosines. For the wavelet transform, this new domain contains more complicated basis functions called wavelets, mother wavelets, or analyzing wavelets.

Both transforms have another similarity. The basis functions are localized in frequency, making mathematical tools such as power spectra and scalegrams useful at picking out frequencies and calculating power distributions.

Dissimilarities between Fourier and Wavelet Transforms

The most interesting dissimilarity between these two kinds of transforms is that individual wavelet functions are localized in space. Fourier sine and cosine functions are not. This localization feature, along with wavelets' localization of frequency, makes many functions and operators using wavelets "sparse" when transformed into the wavelet domain. This sparseness, in turn, results in a number of useful applications such as data compression, detecting features in images, and removing noise from time series.

One way to see the time-frequency resolution differences between the Fourier transform and the wavelet transform is to look at the basis function coverage of the time-frequency plane. Fig. 3-6 shows a Windowed Fourier Transform (WFT), where the window is simply a square wave. The

小波在其他领域也得到了应用，包括天文学、声学、核工程、子带编码、信号和图像处理、神经生理学、音乐、磁共振成像、语音识别、光学、分形、地震预报、雷达、人类视觉，以及纯数学的应用，如求解偏微分方程。

2. 小波与傅里叶变换

函数的傅里叶表示是通过正弦和余弦函数叠加而成的，它已经在微分方程的分析和数值解、通信信号的分析与处理中普遍应用。傅里叶和小波分析有着紧密的联系。

傅里叶与小波变换的相同之处

快速傅里叶变换（FFT）和离散小波变换（DWT）都是线性运算，它们产生一个 $\log_2 n$ 级不同长度的数据结构，通常将此数据结构填充和转换为长度为 2^n 的不同数据向量。

变换中包含的矩阵的数学特性也类似。FFT 和 DWT 中的逆变换矩阵是原始矩阵的转置矩阵。这样，两个变换都可以视为从函数空间旋转到不同的域。对于 FFT，这个新域包含的基函数有正弦和余弦函数。对于小波变换，这个新域则包含更多复杂的基函数，叫作小波、母波或者分析小波。

两种变换还有另外的共同之处。它们的基函数都定位于频率，使得功率谱和尺度图等数学工具可以用于提取频率信息和计算功率分布。

傅里叶与小波变换的不同之处

两种变换最显著的不同之处在于，单个小波函数是空间局部化的，而傅里叶的正弦和余弦函数并不是。这种局部化特征伴随着小波频率局部化，使得许多函数和操作在变换到小波域时用到了小波"稀疏"性。这种稀疏性也有很多有用的应用，比如数据压缩、检测图像特征和时间序列去噪。

辨别傅里叶变换和小波变换的时频分辨率不同的一种方法，是看基函数所覆盖的时频面。图 3-6 表示加窗傅里叶变换（Windowed Fourier Transform，WFT），这里的窗为一个简单的方波。方波窗截断正弦

square wave window truncates the sine or cosine function to fit a window of a particular width. Because a single window is used for all frequencies in the WFT, the resolution of the analysis is the same at all locations in the time-frequency plane.

An advantage of wavelet transforms is that the windows vary. In order to isolate signal discontinuities, one would like to have some very short basis functions. At the same time, in order to obtain detailed frequency analysis, one would like to have some very long basis functions. A way to achieve this is to have short high-frequency basis functions and long low-frequency ones. This happy medium is exactly what you get with wavelet transforms. Fig. 3-7 shows the coverage in the time-frequency plane with one wavelet function, the Daubechies wavelet.

One thing to remember is that wavelet transforms do not have a single set of basis functions like the Fourier transform, which utilizes just the sine and cosine functions. Instead, wavelet transforms have an infinite set of possible basis functions. Thus wavelet analysis provides immediate access to information that can be obscured by other time-frequency methods such as Fourier analysis.

3. The Discrete Wavelet Transform

Dilations and translations of the "Mother function", or "analyzing wavelet" $\Phi(x)$ define an orthogonal basis, our wavelet basis:

或余弦函数来适应特定宽度的窗口。因为一个窗用于 WFT 中的所有频率，所以分析的分辨率在时频面中处处相同。

小波变换的优势在于窗可变。为了分离信号的不连续性，希望用一些很短的基函数。同时，为了得到详细的频率分析，希望用某些很长的基函数。达到此目的的方法既需要短的高频基函数又需要长的低频基函数，一个很好的折中正是小波变换。图 3-7 表示了小波函数（Daubechies 小波）在时频面的特性。

记住一点，小波变换不像傅里叶变换那样只有一个基函数集，即正弦和余弦函数，它有无限可能的基函数集。因此，小波分析提供瞬时信息访问，其他的时频分析法方法（如傅里叶分析）是无法做到的。

3. 离散小波变换

"母函数"或者"分析函数" $\Phi(x)$ 的伸缩和平移定义正交基，小波基为

$$\Phi_{(s,\ l)}(x) = 2^{-\frac{s}{2}} \Phi(2^{-s} x - l) \qquad (3\text{-}19)$$

The variables s and l are integers that scale and dilate the mother function $\Phi(x)$ to generate wavelets, such as a Daubechies wavelet family. The scale index s indicates the wavelet's width, and the location index l gives its position. Notice that the mother functions are rescaled, or "dilated" by powers of two, and translated by integers. What makes wavelet bases especially interesting is the self-similarity caused by the

变量 s 和 l 是整数，用来伸缩和平移母函数形成小波，例如 Daubechies 小波族。尺度因子 s 表示小波宽度，平移因子 l 确定小波位置。值得注意的是，母函数重新调整，用 2 次幂扩宽，用整数转换位置。小波基最有意义的性质是它由尺度变换和扩张而引起的自相似性。一旦确定了母函数，

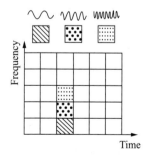

Fig. 3-6 Fourier basis functions, time-frequency tiles, and coverage of the time-frequency plane

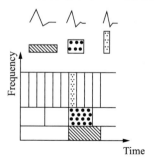

Fig. 3-7 Daubechies wavelet basis functions, time-frequency tiles, and coverage of the time-frequency plane

scales and dilations. Once we know about the mother functions, we know everything about the basis.

To span our data domain at different resolutions, the analyzing wavelet is used in a scaling equation:

$$W(x) = \sum_{k=1}^{N-2} (-1)^k c_{k+1} \Phi(2x+k) \qquad (3\text{-}20)$$

where $W(x)$ is the scaling function for the mother function $\Phi(x)$, and c_k are the wavelet coefficients.

The wavelet coefficients must satisfy linear and quadratic constraints of the form:

$$\sum_{k=0}^{N-1} c_k = 2, \quad \sum_{k=0}^{N-1} c_k c_{k+2l} = 2\delta_{l,0} \qquad (3\text{-}21)$$

where δ is the delta function and l is the location index.

One of the most useful features of wavelets is the ease with which a scientist can choose the defining coefficients for a given wavelet system to be adapted for a given problem.

It is helpful to think of the coefficients $\{c_0, \cdots, c_k\}$ as a filter. The filter or coefficients are placed in a transformation matrix, which is applied to a raw data vector. The coefficients are ordered using two dominant patterns, one that works as a smoothing filter (like a moving average), and one pattern that works to bring out the data's "detail" information. These two orderings of the coefficients are called a quadrate mirror filter pair in signal processing. A more detailed description of the transformation matrix can be found elsewhere.

To complete our discussion of the DWT, let's look at how the wavelet coefficient matrix is applied to the data vector. The matrix is applied in a hierarchical algorithm, sometimes called a pyramidal algorithm. The wavelet coefficients are arranged so that odd rows contain an ordering of wavelet coefficients that act as the smoothing filter, and the even rows contain an ordering of wavelet coefficient with different signs that act to bring out the data's detail. The matrix is first applied to the original, full-length vector. Then the vector is smoothed and decimated by half and the matrix is applied again. Then the smoothed, halved vector is smoothed, and halved again, and the matrix applied once more. This process continues until a trivial number of "smooth-smooth-smooth..." data remain. That is, each matrix application brings out a higher resolution of the data while at the same time smoothing the remaining data. The output of the DWT consists of the remaining "smooth" components, and all of the accumulated "detail" components.

4. Wavelet Applications
Computer and Human Vision

In the early 1980s, David Marr began to work at MIT's

Artificial Intelligence Laboratory on artificial vision for robots. He is an expert on the human visual system and his goal was to learn why the first attempts to construct a robot capable of understanding its surroundings were unsuccessful.

Marr believed that it was important to establish scientific foundations for vision, and that while doing so, one must limit the scope of investigation by excluding everything that depends on training, culture, and so on, and focus on the mechanical or involuntary aspects of vision. This low-level vision is the part that enables us to recreate the three-dimensional organization of the physical world around us from the excitations that stimulate the retina. Marr asked the questions: How is it possible to define the contours of objects from the variations of their light intensity? How is it possible to sense depth? How is movement sensed? He then developed working algorithmic solutions to answer each of these questions.

Marr's theory was that image processing in the human visual system has a complicated hierarchical structure that involves several layers of processing. At each processing level, the retinal system provides a visual representation that scales progressively in a geometrical manner. His arguments hinged on the detection of intensity changes. He theorized that intensity changes occur at different scales in an image, so that their optimal detection requires the use of operators of different sizes. He also theorized that sudden intensity changes produce a peak or trough in the first derivative of the image. These two hypotheses require that a vision filter have two characteristics: it should be a differential operator, and it should be capable of being tuned to act at any desired scale. Marr's operator was a wavelet that today is referred to as a "Marr wavelet".

Denoising Noisy Data

In diverse fields from planetary science to molecular spectroscopy, scientists are faced with the problem of recovering a true signal from incomplete, indirect or noisy data. Can wavelets help solve this problem? The answer is certainly "yes", through a technique called wavelet shrinkage and thresholding methods, which David Donoho has worked on for several years.

The technique works in the following way. When you decompose a data set using wavelets, you use filters that act as averaging filters and others that produce details. Some of the resulting wavelet coefficients correspond to details in the data set. If the details are small, they might be omitted without substantially affecting the main features of the data set. The idea of thresholding, then, is to set to zero all coefficients that are less than a particular threshold. These coefficients are used in an inverse wavelet transformation to reconstruct the data set. The technique is a significant step forward in handling noisy

省理工学院人工智能实验室工作,研究机器人的人工视觉。他是一名人眼视觉系统专家,他研究的目的是弄明白为什么首次制作的机器人对它的环境理解是不成功的。

Marr 认为,建立科学的视觉基础是非常重要的,与此同时,必须通过排除那些与训练、文化等有关的因素来限制研究的范围,重点集中到视觉机理或自然属性方面。视觉的低级研究目标是通过视网膜刺激能够重塑我们周围的三维物理世界。Marr 提出几个问题:能否从物体光强度的改变来确定物体的外部轮廓?如何感知深度?运动是如何感觉到的?之后,他研究开发了相应的算法解决了这些问题。

Marr 的理论认为人眼视觉系统的图像处理过程是一个涉及多层处理的复杂分级结构。在每一个处理层,视网膜系统提供一个以几何方式逐级扩展的视觉表示形式。他的理论取决于检测到的光强度变化。他论证了在图像中强度变化发生在不同尺度下,这样它们的优化检测需要对不同大小的算子进行运算。同时,他也论证了瞬间强度变化在图像的一阶导数上产生峰值或峰谷。这两个假设要求视觉滤波器有两个特征:第一它应该是微分算子,第二它应该可以调整到所需的任意尺度上。Marr 算子是当今大家所指的"Marr 小波"。

数据去噪

从行星科学到分子光谱的不同领域,科学家面临着从不完整、间接、有噪声数据中恢复出真实信号的问题。小波可以帮助我们解决这个问题吗?答案当然是"可以",通过小波收缩和小波阈值方法可以做到,David Donoho 已经在这方面做了几年的研究。

这个技术运算方法如下。当用小波分解数据集时,用滤波器进行平均滤波并产生其他细节量,得到的某些小波系数对应于数据集中的细节量。如果这些细节量取值小,则可以忽略不计,而不会对数据集中的主要特征产生本质影响。之后,阈值的概念就是把所有小于特定阈值的系数设为 0。这些系数在小波逆变换中用于重建数据集。这个技术在处理噪声数据中有着

data because the denoising is carried out without smoothing out the sharp structures. The result is cleaned-up signal that still shows important details.

进步性的重要作用，因为去噪过程并没有平滑掉尖峰结构。这样，得到的干净信号依然可以保留重要的细节信息。

NEW WORDS AND PHRASES

wavelet　　n. 小浪，小波，子波
approximation　　n. 接近，走近，[数] 近似值
superposition　　n. 重叠，重合，叠合
Joseph Fourier　　约瑟夫·傅里叶（男子名）
scale　　n. 刻度，衡量，比例，数值范围，比例尺，天平，等级；vt. 依比例决定，攀登，测量
resolution　　n. 分辨率，解析度
gross　　adj. 总的，毛重的；n. 总额
appropriate　　adj. 适当的
comprise　　v. 包含，由……组成
choppy　　adj. 波浪起伏的
non-local　　非局部的，非本地的
neatly　　adv. 整洁地，优美地，巧妙地
well-suited　　adj. 适当的，便利的
discontinuity　　n. 断绝，不连续，中断
prototype　　n. 原型
analyzing wavele　　分析小波
mother wavelet　　母小波
contracted　　adj. 收缩了的，已定约的，契约的
dilated　　adj. 加宽的，扩大的
adapted　　adj. 适合的
truncate　　v. 截去，修剪，把……截短；adj. 截短的，（羽，叶）平截的，平头的
threshold　　n. 上限，下限，阈值
sparsely　　adv. 稀疏地，稀少地
astronomy　　n. 天文学
sub-band coding　　子带编码
neurophysiology　　n. 神经生理学
magnetic resonance　　磁共振
discrimination　　n. 辨别，区别，识别力，辨别力，歧视
fractal　　n. 不规则碎片形，分形
ubiquitous　　adj. 到处存在的，（同时）普遍存在的
transpose　　vt. 调换，颠倒顺序，移项；vi. 进行变换；n. [数] 转置（矩）阵
rotation　　n. 旋转
power spectra　　能量谱
interval　　n. 间隔，距离，时间间隔
scalegram　　n. 尺度图

dissimilarity　　n. 不同，相异点，相异性
in turn　　反过来
Windowed Fourier Transform（WFT）　　加窗傅里叶变换
tile　　n. 瓦片，瓷砖
coverage　　n. 覆盖
isolate　　vt. 使隔离，使孤立，使绝缘，离析；n. 隔离种群
happy　　adj. 恰当的
medium　　n. 媒体，方法，媒介
immediate　　adj. 直接的，紧接的，紧靠的，立即的
access　　n. 通路，访问，入门；vt. 存取，接近
dilation　　n. 膨胀，扩张，扩大
translation　　n. [数] 平移
orthogonal　　adj. 直角的，直交的
dilate　　vi. 扩大，详述，膨胀；vt. 使扩大，使膨胀
rescale　　v. 重新缩放，重新调节
self-similarity　　自相似性
span　　v. 横越
scaling equation　　尺度方程
quadratic　　adj. 二次的；n. 二次方程式
constraint　　n. 约束，强制，局促
dominant　　adj. 有统治权的，占优势的，支配的
smoothing filter　　平滑滤波器
quadrate mirror filter　　正交镜像滤波器
parlance　　n. 谈话，说法，用法
hierarchical　　adj. 分等级的
pyramidal　　adj. 金字塔形的，锥体的
decimate　　vt. 骤减，在数量上显著减少
trivial　　adj. 琐细的，价值不高的，微不足道的
accumulate　　v. 积聚，堆积
retina　　n. [解] 视网膜
involuntary　　adj. 自然而然的，无意的，不知不觉的，偶然的，不随意的
hierarchical　　adj. 分等级的
progressively　　adv. 日益增多地
spectroscopy　　n. [物] 光谱学，波谱学

NOTES

1) If we look at a signal with a large "window", we would notice gross features. Similarly, if we look at a signal with a small "window", we would notice small features. The result in wavelet analysis is to see both the forest and the trees.

如果我们通过大窗口来观察信号，则会得到信号的总体特征。同样，如果通过小窗口观察数据，则得到细节特征。从小波分析结果可以看到信号的概况和细节。

2) An advantage of wavelet transforms is that the windows vary. In order to isolate signal discontinuities, one would like to have some very short basis functions. At the same time, in order to obtain detailed frequency analysis, one would like to have some very long basis functions. A way to achieve this is to have short high-frequency basis functions and long low-frequency ones. This happy medium is exactly what you get with wavelet transforms.

小波变换的优势在于窗可变。为了分离信号的不连续性，希望用一些很短的基函数。同时，为了得到详细的频率分析，希望用某些很长的基函数。达到此目的的方法既需要短的高频基函数又需要长的低频基函数，一个很好的折中正是小波变换。

3) What makes wavelet bases especially interesting is the self-similarity caused by the scales and dilations. Once we know about the mother functions, we know everything about the basis.

小波基最有意义的性质是小波的自相似性，它是通过母小波的尺度变换和扩张得到的。一旦确定了母函数，我们就知道了这个小波基的所有性质。

4) The coefficients are ordered using two dominant patterns, one that works as a smoothing filter (like a moving average), and one pattern that works to bring out the data's "detail" information. These two orderings of the coefficients are called a quadrate mirror filter pair in signal processing.

我们可以使用两种主要模式对小波系数排序，一种是平滑滤波器的模式（类似于滑动平均），另一种是产生数据细节信息的模式。这两种系数排序模式在信号处理中叫作正交镜像滤波器对。

5) Some of the resulting wavelet coefficients correspond to details in the data set. If the details are small, they might be omitted without substantially affecting the main features of the data set.

得到的某些小波系数对应于数据集中的细节量。如果这些细节量取值小，则可以忽略不计，而不会对数据集中的主要特征产生本质影响。

3.2 Digital Signal Processing

1. Introduction

Digital Signal Processing (DSP) is one of the most powerful technologies used in science and engineering in the twenty-first century. Revolutionary changes have already been made in a broad range of fields: communications, medical imaging, radar & sonar, high fidelity music reproduction, and oil prospecting, to name just a few. Each of these areas has developed a deep DSP technology, with its own algorithms, mathematics, and specialized techniques.

Digital signal processing is distinguished from other areas in computer science by the unique type of data it uses: signals. In this modern world we are surrounded by all kinds of signals in various forms. Some of the signals are natural, but most of the signals are man-made. Some signals are necessary (speech), some are pleasant (music), while many are unwanted or unnecessary in a given situation. In most cases, these signals originate as sensory data from the real world: seismic vibrations, visual images, sound waves, etc. DSP is the mathematics, the algorithms, and the techniques used to manipulate these signals after they have been converted into a digital form. This includes a wide variety of goals, such as enhancement of visual images, recognition and generation of speech, compression of data for storage and transmission, etc.

In engineering context, signals are carriers of information, both useful and unwanted. Therefore extracting or enhancing the useful information from a mix of conflicting information is a simplest form of signal processing. The distinction between useful and unwanted information is often subjective as well as objective. Hence signal processing tends to be application dependent. Fourier analysis and filter design are the methods often used in signal processing. Thus, their principles are described simply as followings.

2. Fourier Analysis

Fourier representation of functions as a superposition of sines and cosines has become ubiquitous for both the analytic and numerical solution of differential equations and for the analysis and treatment of communication signals.

The Fourier transform's utility lies in its ability to analyze a signal in the time domain for its frequency content. The transform works by first translating a function in the time domain into a function in the frequency domain. The signal can then be analyzed for its frequency content because the Fourier coefficients of the transformed function represent the contribution of each sine and cosine function at each frequency. An inverse Fourier transform does just what you'd expect, transform data from the frequency domain into the time domain.

The Discrete Fourier Transform (DFT) estimates the Fourier transform of a function from a finite number of its sampled points. The sampled points are supposed to be typical of what the signal looks like at all other times.

The DFT has symmetry properties almost exactly the same as the continuous Fourier transform. In addition, the formula for the inverse discrete Fourier transform is easily calculated using the one for the discrete Fourier transform because the two formulas are almost identical.

If $f(t)$ is a nonperiodic signal, the summation of the periodic functions (such as sine and cosine) does not accurately represent the signal. You could artificially extend the signal to make it periodic but it would require additional continuity at the endpoints. The Windowed Fourier Transform (WFT) is one solution to the problem of better representing the nonperiodic signal. The WFT can be used to give information about signals simultaneously in the time domain and in the frequency domain.

With the WFT, the input signal $f(t)$ is chopped up into sections, and each section is analyzed for its frequency content separately. If the signal has sharp transitions, it is necessary to window the input data, so that the sections converge to zero at the endpoints. This windowing is accomplished via a weight function that places less emphasis near the interval's endpoints than in the middle. The effect of the window is to localize the signal in time.

To approximate a function by samples, and to approximate the Fourier integral by the discrete Fourier transform, requires applying a matrix whose order is the number sample points n. Since multiplying an $n \times n$ matrix by a vector costs on the order of n^2 arithmetic operations, the problem gets quickly worse as the number of sample points increases. However, if the samples are uniformly spaced, then the Fourier matrix can be factored into a product of just a few sparse matrices, and the resulting factors can be applied to a vector in a total of order $n\log n$ arithmetic operations. This is the so-called Fast Fourier Transform or FFT.

3. FIR Digital Filter Design

A filter is a system that is designed to alter the spectral content of input signals in a specified manner. Common filtering objectives include improving signal quality, extracting information from signals, or separating signal components that have been previously combined. A digital filter is a mathematical algorithm implemented in hardware, firmware, and software that operates on a digital input signal to produce a digital output signal for achieving filtering objectives. A digital filter can be classified as being linear or nonlinear, time invariant or varying. This section is focused on the design of Linear, Time-Invariant (LTI) Finite Impulse Response (FIR) filters.

The process of deriving the digital filter transfer function $H(z)$ that satisfies the given set of specifications is called digital filter design. A variety of techniques have been proposed for the design of FIR filters. There are two direct design methods which are often used. The first method is based on truncating the Fourier series representation of the desired frequency response. The method offers a very simple and flexible way of computing FIR filter coefficients, but it does not allow the designer adequate control over the filter parameters. The second method is based on specifying equally spaced frequency samples of the frequency response of the desired filter. The main attraction of the frequency-sampling method is that it allows recursive realization of FIR filters, which can be computationally efficient. However, it lacks flexibility in specifying or controlling filter parameters. The Fourier series (window) method is discussed as follows.

The basic idea of Fourier series method is to design an FIR filter that approximates the desired frequency response of filter by calculating its impulse response. This method utilizes the fact that the frequency response $H(\omega)$ of a digital filter is a periodic function with period 2π. Thus it can be expanded in a Fourier series as

$$H(\omega) = \sum_{n=-\infty}^{\infty} h(n) e^{-j\omega n} \tag{3-22}$$

where

$$h(n) = \frac{1}{2\pi} \int_{-\pi}^{\pi} H(\omega) e^{j\omega n} d\omega, \quad -\infty \leqslant n \leqslant \infty \tag{3-23}$$

This equation shows that the impulse response $h(n)$ is double-sided and has infinite length. If $H(\omega)$ is an even function in the interval $|\omega| \leqslant \pi$, we can show that

$$h(n) = \frac{1}{\pi} \int_{0}^{\pi} H(\omega) \cos(\omega n) d\omega, \quad n \geqslant 0 \tag{3-24}$$

and the impulse response is symmetric about $n=0$. That is,

$$h(-n) = h(n), \quad n \geqslant 0 \tag{3-25}$$

For a given desired frequency response $H(\omega)$, the corresponding impulse response $h(n)$ can be calculated for a non-recursive filter if the integral (3-23) or (3-24) can be evaluated. However, in practice there are two problems with this simple design technique. First, the impulse response for a filter with any sharpness to its frequency response is infinitely long. Working with an infinite number of coefficients is not practical. Second, with negative values of n, the resulting filter is non-causal, thus is non-realizable for real-time applications.

A finite-duration impulse response $\{h'(n)\}$ of length $L=2M+1$ that is the best approximation (minimum mean-square error) to the ideal infinite-length impulse response can be simply obtained by truncation. That is,

$$h'(n) = \begin{cases} h(n), & -M \leqslant n \leqslant M \\ 0, & \text{otherwise} \end{cases} \quad (3\text{-}26)$$

Note that in this definition, we assume L to be an odd number otherwise M will not be an integer. On the unit circle, we have $z=e^{j\omega}$ and the system transfer function is expressed as

$$H'(z) = \sum_{n=-M}^{M} h'(n) z^{-n} \quad (3\text{-}27)$$

It is clear that this filter is not physically realizable in real time since the filter must produce an output that is advanced in time with respect to the input. A causal FIR filter can be derived by delaying the $h'(n)$ sequence by M samples. That is, by shifting the time origin to the left of the vector and re-indexing the coefficients as

$$b'_l = h'(l - M), \quad l = 0, 1, \cdots, 2M \quad (3\text{-}28)$$

The transfer function of this causal FIR filter is

$$B'(z) = \sum_{l=0}^{L-1} b'_l z^{-l}, \quad l = 0, 1, \cdots, 2M \quad (3\text{-}29)$$

This FIR filter has $L(=2M+1)$ coefficients b'_l, $l=0,1,\cdots,L-1$. The impulse response is symmetric about b'_M due to the fact that $h(-n)=h(n)$ given in eg. (3-25). The duration of the impulse response is $2MT$, where T is the sampling period.

From eq. (3-27) and (3-29), we can show that

$$B'(z) = z^{-M} H'(z) \quad (3\text{-}30)$$

and

$$B'(\omega) = e^{-j\omega M} H'(\omega) \quad (3\text{-}31)$$

Since $|e^{-j\omega M}| = 1$, we have

$$|B'(\omega)| = |H'(\omega)| \quad (3\text{-}32)$$

This causal filter has the same magnitude response as that of the non-causal filter. If $h(n)$ is real, then $H'(\omega)$ is a real function of ω. If $H'(\omega) \geqslant 0$, then the phase of $B'(\omega)$ is equal to $-M\omega$. If $H'(\omega) < 0$, then the phase of $B'(\omega)$ is equal to $\pi - M\omega$. Therefore the phase of $B'(\omega)$ is linear function of ω and thus the transfer function $B'(z)$ has a constant group delay.

As shown in Fig. 3-8, the causal FIR filter obtained by simply truncating the impulse response coefficients of the desired filter exhibits an oscillatory behavior (or ripples) in its magnitude response. As the length of the filter is increased, the number of ripples in both passband and stopband increases, and the width of the ripples decrease. The ripple becomes narrower, but its height remains almost constant. The largest ripple occurs near the transition discontinuity and their amplitude is independent of L. This undesired effect is called the Gibbs phenomenon. This is an unavoidable consequence of truncating impulse response in time domain. The truncation operation described in eq. (3-26) can be considered as multiplication of the infinite-length sequence $\{h(n)\}$ by the rectangular sequence $\{w(n)\}$. That is,

$$h'(n) = h(n) w(n), \quad -\infty \leqslant n \leqslant \infty \quad (3\text{-}33)$$

where the rectangular window $w(n)$ is defined as

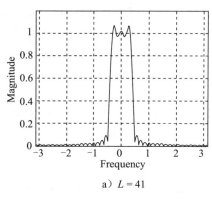
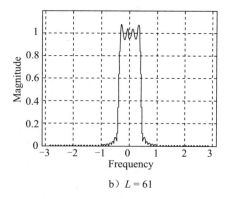

a) $L = 41$ b) $L = 61$

Fig. 3-8 Magnitude responses of lowpass filters designed by Fourier series method

$$w(n) = \begin{cases} 1, & -M \leq n \leq M \\ 0, & \text{otherwise} \end{cases} \tag{3-34}$$

The Discrete-Time Fourier Transform (DTFT) of $h'(n)$ defined in eq. (3-33) can be expressed as

$$H'(\omega) = H(\omega) * W(\omega) = \frac{1}{2\pi} \int_{-\pi}^{\pi} H(\varphi) W(\omega - \varphi) \mathrm{d}\varphi \tag{3-35}$$

where $W(\omega)$ is the DTFT of $w(n)$ defined in eq. (3-34). Thus the designed filter $H'(\omega)$ will be a smeared version of the desired filter $H(\omega)$.

Eq. (3-35) shows that $H'(\omega)$ is obtained by the convolution of the desired frequency response $H(\omega)$ with the rectangular window's frequency response $W(\omega)$. If

$$W(\omega - \varphi) = 2\pi\delta(\omega - \varphi) \tag{3-36}$$

we have the desired result $H'(\omega) = H(\omega)$. Eq. (3-36) implies that if $W(\omega)$ is a very narrow pulse centered at $\omega = 0$ such as a delta function $W(\omega) = 2\pi\delta(\omega)$, then $H'(\omega)$ will approximate $H(\omega)$ very closely. This condition requires the optimum window function as

$$w(n) = 1, \quad |n| < \infty \tag{3-37}$$

4. Window Functions

In practice, the length of the window should be as small as possible in order to reduce the computational complexity of the FIR filter. Therefore we have to use sub-optimum windows that have the following properties:

1) They are even functions about $n = 0$.

2) They are zero in the range $|n| > M$.

3) Their frequency responses $W(\omega)$ have a narrow mainlobe and small sidelobes as suggested by eq. (3-36). A large number of tapered windows have been developed and optimized for different applications. There are four commonly used windows of length $L = 2M+1$. That is, $w(n)$, $n = 0$, $1, \cdots, L-1$ and is symmetric about its middle, $n = M$. In FIR filter design, there are two parameters of the window functions are very important. They are mainlobe width and the relative sidelobe level. To ensure a fast transition from the passband to the stopband, the window should have a small mainlobe width. On the other hand, to reduce the passband and stopband ripples, the area under the sidelobes should be small. Unfortunately, there is a trade-off between these two requirements.

The Hanning window function is one period of the raised cosine function defined as

$$w(n) = 0.5\left[1 - \cos\left(\frac{2\pi n}{L-1}\right)\right], \quad n = 0, 1, \cdots, L-1 \tag{3-38}$$

Note that the Hanning window has an actual length of $L-2$ since the two end values given by eq. (3-38) are zero. For a large L, the peak-to-sidelobe ratio is approximately 31dB, an improvement of 17.5dB over the rectangular window. However, since the width of the transition band corresponds roughly to the mainlobe width, it is more than twice that resulting from the rectangular window.

The Hamming window function is defined as

$$w(n) = 0.54 - 0.46\cos\left(\frac{2\pi n}{L-1}\right), \quad n = 0, 1, \cdots, L-1 \tag{3-39}$$

which also corresponds to a raised cosine, but with different weights for the constant and cosine terms. The Hamming function does not taper the end values to 0, but rather to 0.08. The mainlobe width is about the same as for the Hanning window, but has an additional 10dB of stopband attenuation. In designing a lowpass filter, the Hamming window provides low ripple over the passband and good stopband attenuation. Thus it is usually more appropriate for FIR filter design than the Hanning window.

The Blackman window function is defined as

$$w(n) = 0.42 - 0.5\cos\left(\frac{2\pi n}{L-1}\right) + 0.08\cos\left(\frac{4\pi n}{L-1}\right), \quad n = 0, 1, \cdots, L-1 \tag{3-40}$$

The addition of the second cosine term in eq. (3-40) has the effect of increasing the width of the mainlobe (50%), but at the same time improving the peak-to-sidelobe ratio to about 57dB. The Blackman window provides 74dB of stopband attenuation, but with a transition width six times that of the rectangular window.

The Kaiser window function is defined as

$$w(n) = \frac{I_0\left[\beta\sqrt{1 - \frac{(n-M)^2}{M^2}}\right]}{I_0(\beta)}, \quad n = 0, 1, \cdots, L-1 \tag{3-41a}$$

where β is an adjustable (shape) parameter and

$$I_0(\beta) = \sum_{k=0}^{+\infty}\left[\frac{\left(\frac{\beta}{2}\right)^k}{k!}\right]^2 \tag{3-41b}$$

is the zero-order modified Bessel function. In practice, it is sufficient to keep only the first 25 terms in the summation of eq. (3-41b). Because $I_0(0) = 1$, the Kaiser window has the value $1/I_0(\beta)$ at the end points $n=0$ and $n=L-1$, and is symmetric about its middle $n=M$. This is a useful and very flexible family of window functions. The Kaiser window is nearly optimum in the sense of having the most energy in the mainlobe for a given peak sidelobe level. Providing a large mainlobe width for the given stopband attenuation implies the sharpness transition width. This window can provide different transition widths for the same L by choosing the parameter b to determine the trade-off between the mainlobe width and the peak sidelobe level.

In practice, we can select different window function according to different demands.

The procedures of designing FIR filters using windows are summarized as follows:

1) Determine the window type that will satisfy the stopband attenuation requirements.

2) Determine the window size L based on the given transition width $w(n)$, $n = 0, 1, \cdots, L-1$.

3) Calculate the window coefficients.

4) Generate the ideal impulse response $h(n)$ using eq. (3-24) for the desired filter.

5) Truncate the ideal impulse response of infinite length using eq. (3-26) to obtain $h'(n)$, $-\infty \leqslant n \leqslant \infty$.

6) Make the filter causal by shifting the result M units to the right using eq. (3-28) to obtain b'_l, $l = 0, 1, \cdots, L-1$.

7) Multiply the window coefficients obtained in step 3 and the impulse response coefficients obtained in step 6 sample-by-sample. That is, $b_l = b'_l \cdot w(l)$, $l = 0, 1, \cdots, L-1$.

Applying a window to a FIR filter's impulse response has the effect of smoothing the resulting filter's magnitude response. A symmetric window will preserve a symmetric FIR filter's linear-phase response. The advantage of the Fourier series method with windowing is its simplicity. It does not require sophisticated mathematics and can be carried out in a straightforward manner. However, there is no simple rule for choosing M so that the resulting filter will meet exactly the specified cut-off frequencies. This is due to the lack of an exact relation between M and its effect on leakage.

NEW WORDS AND PHRASES

fidelity　*n.* 保真度，（收音机、录音设备等的）逼真度，保真度，重现精度
sensory　*adj.* 感觉的，感官的
seismic　*adj.* ［地］地震的
vibrations　*n.* 振动，颤动，摇动，摆动
storage　*n.* 储藏（量），储藏库，存储
conflict　*n.* 斗争，冲突；*vi.* 抵触，冲突
superposition　*n.* 重叠，重合，叠合
ubiquitous　*adj.* 到处存在的，（同时）普遍存在的
utility　*n.* 效用，有用
symmetry　*n.* 对称，匀称
chop up　切开，割断（历史），切细
localize　*v.* （使）局部化，（使）地方化，停留在某个地方
weight function　权函数
approximate　*v.* 近似，接近，估计
integral　*n.* ［数］积分，完整，部分
sparse matrice　稀疏矩阵
uniformly　*adv.* 一律地，均一地
invariant　*adj.* 无变化的，不变的
truncate　*v.* 把……截短

Fourier series　傅里叶级数
recursive　*adj.* 回归的，递归的
even function　偶函数
interval　*n.* 间隔
non-recursive　回归的，非递归的
finite-duration　有限长时间
physical　*adj.* 自然的，物理的
delay　*v.* 耽搁，延迟，延期，迟滞
re-indexing　改变符号
oscillatory　*adj.* 摆动的
ripple　*n.* 波纹
transition　*n.* 转变，转换，跃迁，过渡，变调
Gibbs phenomenon　Gibbs 现象
smeared　*adj.* 拖尾的
sub-optimum　*adj.* 未达最佳标准的，次理想的，次适宜的，次满意的
mainlobe　*n.* 主瓣
sidelobe　*n.* 旁瓣
tapered　*adj.* 锥形的，渐缩的
trade-off　*n.* 交换，协定，交易，平衡
taper　*v.* 逐渐变细，逐渐减少
attenuation　*n.* 衰减

NOTES

1) In most cases, these signals originate as sensory data from the real world: seismic vibrations, visual ima-

ges, sound waves, etc. DSP is the mathematics, the algorithms, and the techniques used to manipulate these signals after they have been converted into a digital form.

在多数情况下,这些信号来源于对真实世界的感知数据:地震震动、视觉图像、声波等。DSP 是处理转换为数字形式的信号的一种数学、算法和技术。

2) Fourier representation of functions as a superposition of sines and cosines has become ubiquitous for both the analytic and numerical solution of differential equations and for the analysis and treatment of communication signals.

函数的傅里叶表示,即将函数表示成正弦和余弦信号的叠加,这种方法已经广泛用于微分方程的解析法和数值法求解过程以及通信信号的分析与处理。

3) If $f(t)$ is a nonperiodic signal, the summation of the periodic functions, such as sine and cosine, does not accurately represent the signal. You could artificially extend the signal to make it periodic but it would require additional continuity at the endpoints.

如果 $f(t)$ 是非周期信号,那么用周期函数(例如正弦与余弦)的和,并不能精确地表示该信号。你可以人为地拓展这个信号使其具有周期性,但是这要求在端点处附加连续性。

4) If the signal has sharp transitions, it is necessary to window the input data, so that the sections converge to zero at the endpoints.

如果信号有急剧的过渡,就有必要对输入信号加窗,这样信号在端点处就会收敛于零。

5) A digital filter is a mathematical algorithm implemented in hardware, firmware, and/or software that operates on a digital input signal to produce a digital output signal for achieving filtering objectives.

数字滤波器是一种数学算法,它可以用硬件、固件以及软件来实现。它作用于数字输入信号产生数字输出信号,从而达到滤波目标。

6) The basic idea of Fourier series method is to design an FIR filter that approximates the desired frequency response of filter by calculating its impulse response.

用傅里叶级数设计 FIR 滤波器的基本思想是计算出此滤波器的单位冲激响应来逼近滤波器所期望的频率响应。

7) To ensure a fast transition from the passband to the stopband, the window should have a small mainlobe width. On the other hand, to reduce the passband and stopband ripples, the area under the sidelobes should be small. Unfortunately, there is a trade-off between these two requirements.

为确保从通带到阻带的快速转换,窗需要有小的主瓣宽度。另外,为了降低通带和阻带波纹,旁瓣下的面积就要小一些。遗憾的是,这就需要在这两个要求间找到折中点。

8) Providing a large mainlobe width for the given stopband attenuation implies the sharpness transition width. This window can provide different transition widths for the same L by choosing the parameter b to determine the trade-off between the mainlobe width and the peak sidelobe level.

对于给定的阻带衰减,提供一个较宽的主瓣宽度意味着锐化的过渡带宽。对相同的 L,这个窗口可以通过选择参数 b 来确定主瓣带宽和旁瓣峰值的折中值以提供不同的过渡带宽。

9) However, there is no simple rule for choosing M so that the resulting filter will meet exactly the specified cut-off frequencies. This is due to the lack of an exact relation between M and its effect on leakage.

然而,并没有一个简单的规则来选择 M,以使设计的滤波器能精确满足给定的截止频率。这是由于还缺少 M 值和它的泄漏效应之间的准确关系。

EXERCISES

1. Please translate the following words and phrases into Chinese.

   a) DSP
   b) symmetry properties
   c) time domain
   d) frequency domain
   e) chop up
   f) weight function

g) uniformly spaced   h) sparse matrices   i) fast Fourier transform
j) Fourier series

2. Please translate the following words and phrases into English.
   a) 线性相位
   b) 偶函数
   c) 传递函数
   d) Gibbs 现象
   e) 通带
   f) 阻带
   g) 主瓣
   h) 旁瓣
   i) 线性非时变有限冲激响应滤波器
   j) 非递归的

3. Fill in the blanks with the missing word(s).
   a) Digital signal processing is distinguished _____ other areas in computer science by the unique type of data it uses: signals.
   b) In engineering context, signals are carriers _____ information, both useful and unwanted.
   c) The Fourier transform's utility lies in its ability to analyze a signal in the time domain _____ its frequency content.
   d) With the WFT, the input signal $f(t)$ is chopped up _____ sections, and each section is analyzed _____ its frequency content separately.
   e) Common filtering objectives _____ improving signal quality, extracting information from signals, or separating signal components that have been previously combined.
   f) A finite-duration impulse response $\{h'(n)\}$ _____ length $L = 2M+1$ that is the best approximation (minimum mean-square error) to the ideal infinite-length impulse response can be simply obtained by truncation.
   g) The Hamming window function is defined as $w(n) = 0.54 - 0.46\cos\left(\frac{2\pi n}{L-1}\right)$, $n = 0, 1, \cdots, L-1$ which also corresponds to a raised cosine, but with different weights _____ the constant and cosine terms.
   h) In designing a lowpass filter, the Hamming window provides low ripple _____ the passband and good stopband attenuation. Thus it is usually more appropriate for FIR filter design than the Hanning window.
   i) The addition of the second cosine term in eq. (3-40) has the effect of increasing the width of the mainlobe (50%), but at the same time improving the peak-to-sidelobe ratio _____ about 57dB.
   j) Applying a window _____ a FIR filter's impulse response has the effect of smoothing the resulting filter's magnitude response.

4. Answer the following questions according to the text.
   a) What is the fast Fourier transform?
   b) Which two methods are often used in digital filter designing?
   c) Please tell us what is the Gibbs phenomenon.

READING

Compressive Sensing

1. The Introduction of Compressive Sensing

Compressive Sensing (Compressed Sensing, or Compressed Sampling, CS) is a new direction between mathematics and information science, which is popular in recent years. It brought revolutionary breakthrough for signal acquisition technology. It adopts the non-adaptive linear projection to

压缩感知

1. 压缩感知概述

压缩感知(Compressive Sensing, Compressed Sensing, 或 Compressed Sampling, CS), 是近几年流行起来的介于数学和信息科学之间的新方向。它为信号采集技术带来了革命性的突破。它采用非自适应线性投影

preserve the original structure of the signal, captures signals at a rate significantly below the Nyquist rate, and reconstructs the original signal accurately by using a numerical optimization algorithm.

Literally, the compressive sensing looks like data compression. But actually it is different. Classic data compression technology, whether audio compression (such as MP3), image compression (such as JPEG), video compression (MPEG), or the general coding compression (ZIP), they start from the characteristics of the data itself to find and eliminate redundancy of hidden in the data, so as to achieve the purpose of compression. This compression has two characteristics: first, it occurs after the data has been fully collected; second, it needs a complex algorithm to complete the operation. By contrast, in generally speaking, the calculation of decoding process is simpler, such as audio compression, the calculated amount of compressing a MP3 files is much more than playing (decompression) a MP3 file.

It will be found by a little thought that the asymmetry of compression and decompression is contrary to the people's needs. In most cases, the equipment of data acquisition and processing is often the portable devices that are cheap and power saving, low computing power, such as automatic camera, voice recorder and remote monitor and so on. The process of handling (decompression) information is often conducted on large computer instead, it has higher computing power, is often not portable and save electricity demands. That is to say, people are using cheap energy-saving equipment to handle complex computing tasks, and large efficient equipment to handle relatively simple computing tasks. In some cases, this contradictory may even be more acute. Such as in field operations or military operations, data acquisition equipment is often exposed in the nature environment. It may lose its energy supplies or partial performance at any time. In this case, the traditional data acquisition -compression-transmission-uncompression mode will basically fail.

The concept of compressive sensing is produced to solve the contradiction. Because its redundancy will be compressed after the data acquisition, and the process of compression is relatively difficult, so why don't we just acquisition the compressed data? If so, the acquisition task not only is much lighter, but the trouble of compression also will be left out. This is the so-called compressive sensing, that is, the sensing and compression will be finished in one step.

2. The Core Ideas of Compressive Sensing

The core ideas of compressive sensing mainly include two points.

来保持信号的原始结构，以远低于奈奎斯特频率的采样率对信号进行采样，通过数值最优化算法准确重构出原始信号。

从字面上看起来，压缩感知好像是数据压缩的意思，而实际不然。经典的数据压缩技术，无论是音频压缩（例如 MP3）、图像压缩（例如 JPEG）、视频压缩（MPEG），还是一般的编码压缩（ZIP），都是从数据本身的特性出发，寻找并剔除数据中隐含的冗余度，从而达到压缩的目的。这样的压缩有两个特点：第一，它发生在数据已经被完整采集之后；第二，它本身需要复杂的算法来完成运算。一般来说，解码过程反而在计算上比较简单，以音频压缩为例，压缩一个 MP3 文件的计算量远大于播放（即解压缩）MP3 文件的计算量。

稍加思量就会发现，这种压缩和解压缩的不对称性正好同人们的需求是相反的。在大多数情况下，采集并处理数据的设备往往是廉价、省电、计算能力较低的便携设备，例如自动照相机或者录音笔或者遥控监视器等。而负责处理（即解压缩）信息的过程却反而往往在大型计算机上进行，它有更强的计算能力，也常常没有便携和省电的要求。也就是说，人们在用廉价节能的设备来处理复杂的计算任务，而用大型高效的设备处理相对简单的计算任务。这一矛盾在某些情况下甚至会更为尖锐。例如，在野外作业或者军事作业的场合，采集数据的设备往往暴露在自然环境之中，它随时可能失去能源供给或者丧失部分性能。在这种情况下，传统的数据采集-压缩-传输-解压缩的模式就基本上失效了。

压缩感知的概念就是为了解决这样的矛盾而产生的。既然采集数据之后要压缩掉其中的冗余度，而这个压缩过程又相对比较困难，那么我们为什么不直接"采集"压缩后的数据？这样采集的任务要轻得多，而且还省去了压缩的麻烦。这就是所谓的"压缩感知"，也就是说，感知和压缩在同一个步骤内完成。

2. 压缩感知的核心思想

压缩感知的核心思想主要包括两点。
第一点是信号的稀疏性。传统的香农

The first point is the sparsity of signal. Traditional Shannon signal processing method only uses the most little prior information of sampling signal, which is the bandwidth of signal. However, in real life, many high-profile signals itself has some structure characteristics. Relative to the freedom degree of the bandwidth information, the structure characteristics are determined by a smaller part of the signal freedom degrees. In other words, in case of loss information rarely, the signal can be expressed in a few digital coding. So, in this sense, the signal is a sparse signal (or approximate sparse signal, compressible signal).

The second point is the irrelevant feature of signal. The useful information of sparse signal can be achieved by a nonadaptive sampling method that compresses the signal into a smaller sample data collection. It is proved by theory that sampling method of compressive sensing is only simply method that makes signal operating associated with a group of determined waveforms. These waveforms are required irrelevant to the sparse space which is located by signal. Compressive sensing method abandoned redundant information in the current signal sampling. It can directly get the compressive samples from the transform of continuous time signal. And then, the compressed samples can be handled by using optimization methods in digital signal processing. The optimization algorithms used to reconstruct the signal are often the underdetermined linear inverse problems of a known sparse signal.

3. The Basic Theory of Compressive Sensing
Compressible Signals

Consider a real-valued, finite-length, one-dimensional, discrete-time signal x, which can be viewed as an $N \times 1$ column vector in $\mathbf{R}^N$ with elements $x[n]$, $n = 1, 2, \cdots, N$. (We treat an image or higher-dimensional data by vectorizing it into a long one-dimensional vector.) Any signal in $\mathbf{R}^N$ can be represented in terms of a basis of $N \times 1$ vector $\{\psi_i\}_{i=1}^N$. For simplicity, assume that the basis is orthonormal. Using the $N \times N$ basis matrix $\boldsymbol{\Psi} = [\psi_1 | \psi_2 | \cdots | \psi_N]$ with the vectors $\{\psi_i\}$ as columns, a signal x can be expressed as

$$x = \sum_{i=1}^{N} s_i \psi_i \quad \text{or} \quad x = \boldsymbol{\Psi} s \tag{3-42}$$

where s is the $N \times 1$ column vector of weighting coefficients $s_i = <x, \psi_i> = \psi_i^T x$, and T denotes transposition. Clearly, x and s are equivalent representations of the signal, with x in the time or space domain and s in the $\boldsymbol{\Psi}$ domain.

The signal x is K-sparse if it is a linear combination of only K basis vectors; that is, only K of the s_i coefficients in (3-42) are nonzero and ($N-K$) are zero. The case of interest is when

信号处理方法只利用了被采样信号最少的先验信息,即信号的带宽。但是,现实生活中很多广受关注的信号本身具有一些结构特点。相对于带宽信息的自由度,这些结构特点由信号的少量自由度所决定。换句话说,在很少的信息损失的情况下,这种信号可以用很少的数字编码表示。所以,在这种意义上,这种信号是稀疏信号(或者近似稀疏信号、可压缩信号)。

第二点是信号的不相关性。稀疏信号的有用信息的获取可以通过非自适应的采样方法将信号压缩成较小的样本数据集合来完成。理论证明压缩感知的采样方法只是一个简单地将信号与一组确定的波形进行关联的操作。要求这些波形是与信号所在的稀疏空间不相关的。压缩感知方法抛弃了当前信号采样中的冗余信息。它直接从连续时间信号变换得到压缩样本,然后在数字信号处理中采用优化方法处理压缩样本。这里恢复信号所需的优化算法常常是一个已知稀疏信号的待定线性逆问题。

3. 压缩感知的基本理论
可压缩信号

考虑一个一维有限长的实值离散时间信号 x,能把它看作一个 $N \times 1$ 的列向量,在 $\mathbf{R}^N$ 域用元素 $x[n]$,$n=1,2,\cdots,N$ 表示(我们可以将一幅图像或一个高维数据通过矢量量化变成一个长的一维向量)。在 $\mathbf{R}^N$ 域中的任何信号能通过一个 $N \times 1$ 的向量 $\{\psi_i\}_{i=1}^N$ 的基来表示。为了简化,认为这个基是正交的。使用以向量 $\{\psi_i\}$ 作为列的 $N \times N$ 的基矩阵 $\boldsymbol{\Psi} = [\psi_1 | \psi_2 | \cdots | \psi_N]$,信号 x 能表示为

式中,s 是加权系数 $s_i = <x, \psi_i> = \psi_i^T x$ 形成的 $N \times 1$ 的列向量,T 表示转置。显然,x 和 s 对信号是同等的表示,只是 x 是在时域或空域,s 是在 $\boldsymbol{\Psi}$ 域。

如果 x 是仅有的 K 个基向量的线性组合,那么信号 x 是 K 稀疏的,即在式(3-42)中只有 K 个 s_i 系数是非零的,($N-K$)个是

$K \leq N$. The signal x is compressible if the representation (3-42) has just a few large coefficients and many small coefficients.

Transform Coding and Its Inefficiencies

The fact that compressible signals are well approximated by K-sparse representations forms the foundation of transform coding. In data acquisition systems (for example, digital cameras) transform coding plays a central role: the full N-sample signal x is acquired; the complete set of transform coefficients $\{s_i\}$ is computed via $s = \Psi^T x$; the K largest coefficients are located and the $(N-K)$ smallest coefficients are discarded; and the K values and locations of the largest coefficients are encoded. Unfortunately, this sample-then-compress framework suffers from three inherent inefficiencies. First, the initial number of samples N may be large even if the desired K is small. Second, the set of all N transform coefficients $\{s_i\}$ must be computed even though all but K of them will be discarded. Third, the locations of the large coefficients must be encoded, thus introducing an overhead.

The Compressive Sensing Problem

Compressive sensing addresses these inefficiencies by directly acquiring a compressed signal representation without going through the intermediate stage of acquiring N samples. Consider a general linear measurement process that computes $M<N$ inner products between x and a collection of vectors $\{\varphi_j\}_{j=1}^{M}$ as in $y_i = <x, \varphi_j>$. Arrange the measurements y_i in an $M \times 1$ vector y and the measurement vectors φ_j^T as rows in an $M \times N$ matrix Φ. Then, by substituting Ψ from (3-42), y can be written as

$$y = \Phi x = \Phi \Psi s = \Theta s \quad (3\text{-}43)$$

where $\Theta = \Phi \Psi$ is an $M \times N$ matrix. The measurement process is not adaptive, meaning that Φ is fixed and does not depend on the signal x. The problem consists of designing a) a stable measurement matrix Φ such that the salient information in any K-sparse or compressible signal is not damaged by the dimensionality reduction from $x \in \mathbf{R}^N$ to $y \in \mathbf{R}^M$ and b) a reconstruction algorithm to recover x from only $M \approx K$ measurements y (or about as many measurements as the number of coefficients recorded by a traditional transform coder).

For the two points said as above, firstly, a fixed measurement matrix has to be designed. The measurement matrix must allow the reconstruction of the length-N signal x from $M<N$ measurements (the vector y). Since $M<N$, this problem appears ill-conditioned. If, however, x is K-sparse and the K locations of the nonzero coefficients in s are known, then the problem can be solved provided $M \geq K$. Secondly,

零,对此有意义的情况是$K \leq N$。如果式(3-42)恰好有少数的大系数而有许多小系数,则信号x是可压缩的。

变换编码及其缺陷

可压缩信号能用K稀疏近似表示,这就形成了变换编码的基础。在数据采集系统(例如数码相机)中变换编码扮演了重要的角色:得到信号x的全部的N个采样;通过$s = \Psi^T x$计算变换系数$\{s_i\}$的完备集;定位K个最大的系数,忽略$(N-K)$个最小的系数;对这K个最大系数的值和位置编码。遗憾的是,这种采样-压缩架构存在三个固有的缺陷:第一,即使所期望的K很小,初始的采样数N也可能很大;第二,所有的N个变换系数$\{s_i\}$的集必须要计算,即使除了其中K个值其他的都要丢弃;第三,大系数的位置必须编码,由此带来了开销。

压缩感知问题

压缩感知解决这些缺陷通过直接获得一种压缩信号的表示而不通过得到N个采样值的中间过程。考虑一个一般的线性测量过程,计算$M<N$个x和一个矢量集$\{\varphi_j\}_{j=1}^{M}$的内积,得到$y_i = <x, \varphi_j>$。将测量值y_j写成$M \times 1$的矢量y,测量向量φ_j^T按行排列形成一个$M \times N$的矩阵Φ,那么用Ψ代入式(3-42)中,y能写为

式中,$\Theta = \Phi \Psi$是一个$M \times N$的矩阵。这个测量过程不是自适应的,这意味着Φ是固定的,并不依赖信号x。这个问题包含设计:①一个固定的测量矩阵Φ,在对任意K稀疏或可压缩信号中的主要信息不因维数从$x \in \mathbf{R}^N$到$y \in \mathbf{R}^M$减小而受到破坏;②一种重构算法,从仅有的$M \approx K$个测量值y(或者是大约和由一个传统的变换编码器记录的系数的数量同样多的测量值)中恢复x。

对应以上两点,首先需要设计一个固定的测量矩阵,测量矩阵必须允许长度为N的信号从$M<N$个测量值(矢量y)中重建。由于$M<N$,这个问题是病态的。然

it is necessary to design a reconstruction algorithm. It can reconstruct signal from K-sparse samples. The signal reconstruction algorithm must take the M measurements in the vector $\boldsymbol{y}$, the random measurement matrix (or the random seed that generated it) and the basis $\boldsymbol{\Psi}$, and reconstruct the length-N signal $\boldsymbol{x}$ or, equivalently, its sparse coefficient vector $\boldsymbol{s}$. For K-sparse signals, since $M < N$ in eq. (3-43) there are infinitely many $\boldsymbol{s}'$ that satisfy $\boldsymbol{\Theta s}' = \boldsymbol{y}$. This is because if $\boldsymbol{\Theta s} = \boldsymbol{y}$ then $\boldsymbol{\Theta}(\boldsymbol{s}+\boldsymbol{r}) = \boldsymbol{y}$ for any vector $\boldsymbol{r}$ in the null space $\mathbf{R}(\boldsymbol{\Theta})$ of $\boldsymbol{\Theta}$. Therefore, the signal reconstruction algorithm aims to find the signal's sparse coefficient vector in the $(N-M)$-dimensional translated null space $\boldsymbol{H} = \mathbf{R}(\boldsymbol{\Theta}) + \boldsymbol{s}$. The detail of reconstruction problems are described in other reference literatures, we don't go into here.

4. The Application of Compressive Sensing Technology

The basic idea of compressive sensing is that the much more information can be extracted from the data of less as far as possible. It is an extension of traditional information theory, but also transcends the traditional compression theory. It becomes a new branch and has wide application prospect.

Broadband Spectrum Sensing

Broadband spectrum sensing technology is the emphasis and difficulty in cognitive radio application. It can provide the spectrum access opportunities for users using cognitive radio through a rapid search for wireless spectrum not used in the range of monitoring frequency spectrum. The detection of traditional broadband filter group needs a lot of RF front-end devices, and can't adjust flexibly system parameters. Ordinary broadband receiving circuit requires very high sampling rate. This brings challenge to the A/D converter. In addition, a large amount of data processing work is a heavy burden to the digital signal processor. The problems can be resolved by using the compressive sensing method in the broadband spectrum sensing. A broadband digital circuit is used, and the undersampling random samples can be obtained at relatively low frequency spectrum. And then the broadband spectrum sensing results can be gained with the estimation algorithm of sparse signal in the digital signal processor.

Analog Information Conversion

For the signals with very high bandwidth, such as the RF signal in radar signal processing system, in order to obtain the complete signal information, the A/D converter must have a

而，如果 $\boldsymbol{x}$ 是 K 稀疏的并且在 $\boldsymbol{s}$ 中的 K 个非零系数的位置是已知的，那么当 $M \geqslant K$ 时，这个问题能够解决。其次，需要设计一个信号重构算法，能够从 K 稀疏样本中恢复重建信号。信号重构算法必须采用向量 $\boldsymbol{y}$ 中的 M 个测量值，随机测量矩阵 $\boldsymbol{\Phi}$（或从其中产生的随机种子）和基 $\boldsymbol{\Psi}$，重构长度为 N 的信号 $\boldsymbol{x}$，或等同地，重构它的稀疏系数向量 $\boldsymbol{s}$。对 K 稀疏信号，由于在式（3-43）中 $M<N$，有无穷多的 $\boldsymbol{s}'$ 满足 $\boldsymbol{\Theta s}' = \boldsymbol{y}$。这是因为如果 $\boldsymbol{\Theta s} = \boldsymbol{y}$，那么 $\boldsymbol{\Theta}(\boldsymbol{s}+\boldsymbol{r}) = \boldsymbol{y}$ 对任意向量 $\boldsymbol{r}$ 在 $\boldsymbol{\Theta}$ 的零空间 $\mathbf{R}(\boldsymbol{\Theta})$。因此，信号重构算法的目标是在 $N-M$ 维的转移零空间 $\boldsymbol{H} = \mathbf{R}(\boldsymbol{\Theta}) + \boldsymbol{s}$ 找到信号的稀疏系数向量。重构问题的细节在其他文献里有描述，这里不赘述了。

4. 压缩感知技术的应用

压缩感知的基本思路是从尽量少的数据中提取尽量多的信息。它是传统信息论的延伸，但是又超越了传统的压缩理论，成为一门崭新的分支，具有广泛的应用前景。

宽带谱感知

宽带谱感知技术是认知无线电应用中的难点和重点。它通过快速寻找监测频谱中没有利用的无线频谱，从而为认知无线电用户提供频谱接入机会。传统滤波器组的宽带检测需要大量的射频前端器件，并且不能灵活调整系统参数。普通的宽带接收电路要求很高的采样率，它给 A/D 转换器带来挑战。另外，获得的大量数据处理给数字信号处理器带来负担。针对宽带谱感知的难题，将压缩感知方法应用到宽带谱感知中：采用一个宽带数字电路，以较低的频谱获得欠采样的随机样本，然后在数字信号处理器中采用稀疏信号估计算法得到宽带谱感知结果。

模拟信息转换

对于带宽非常高的信号，例如雷达信号处理系统涉及的射频信号，根据香农采样定理，要获得完整的信号信息，所采用

high sampling frequency based on the Shannon sampling theorem. However, because of the performance limitation of sensor and converter hardware, the signal bandwidth obtained is far below the actual signal bandwidth. This will result in a large amount of information losing. In this regard, researchers design the analog information converter based on compressive sensing theory. The reconstructed complete signal can be obtained from measurement signal according to the principle of compressive sensing theory. First the linear measurements matrix of original signal can be obtained, and then the original signal will be reconstructed by using the back-end DSP or the direct calculation of the original signal statistic and other information.

的 A/D 转换器必须有很高的采样频率。然而，由于传感器及转换器硬件性能的限制，获得的信号带宽远远低于实际信号的带宽，由此引起较大的信息丢失。对此研究人员设计了基于压缩传感理论的模拟信息转换器。根据压缩传感理论中从测量信息可以得到重构完整信号的原理，首先获得原始信号的线性测量矩阵，再利用后端 DSP 重构原始信号或直接计算原始信号的统计数据等信息。

NEW WORDS AND PHRASES

compressive sensing　压缩感知
linear projection　线性投影
redundancy　n. 过多，冗余，多余
asymmetry　n. 不对称，不均匀
portable　adj. 可携带的，可移动的，可搬运的
automatic camera　自动照相机
data acquisition　数据采集
sparsity　n. 稀疏性
freedom degree　自由度
sparse signal　稀疏信号
irrelevant　adj. 不恰当的，不相关的，无关系的

underdetermined　待定的
weighting coefficient　加权系数
column vector　列向量
orthonormal　adj. 正交的
transposition　n. 调换，转置
adaptive　adj. 自适应的
ill-conditioned　adj. 病态的
transcend　v. 超越，胜过，优于
radio　n. 无线电通信，无线电广播设备，无线电接收装置
theorem　n. 定理，法则

NOTES

1) It adopts the non-adaptive linear projection to preserve the original structure of the signal, captures signals at a rate significantly below the Nyquist rate, and reconstructs the original signal accurately by using a numerical optimization algorithm.
它采用非自适应线性投影来保持信号的原始结构，以远低于奈奎斯特频率的采样率对信号进行采样，通过数值最优化算法准确重构出原始信号。

2) In most cases, the equipment of data acquisition and processing is often the portable devices that are cheap and power saving, low computing power, such as automatic camera, voice recorder and remote monitor and so on.
在大多数情况下，采集并处理数据的设备往往是廉价、省电、计算能力较低的便携设备，例如自动照相机、录音笔或者遥控监视器等。

3) However, in real life, many high-profile signals itself has some structure characteristics. Relative to the freedom degree of the bandwidth information, the structure characteristics are determined by a smaller part of the signal freedom degrees.
但是，现实生活中很多广受关注的信号本身具有一些结构特点。相对于带宽信息的自由度，这些结构特点由信号的少量自由度所决定。

4) It is proved by theory that sampling method of compressive sensing is only simply method that makes signal

operating associated with a group of determined waveforms.

理论证明压缩感知的采样方法只是一个简单地将信号与一组确定的波形进行关联的操作。

5) The optimization algorithms used to reconstruct the signal are often the underdetermined linear inverse problems of a known sparse signal.

这里恢复信号所需的优化算法常常是一个已知稀疏信号的待定线性逆问题。

6) The signal x is K-sparse if it is a linear combination of only K basis vectors; that is, only K of the s_i coefficients in (3-42) are nonzero and ($N-K$) are zero.

如果 x 是仅有的 K 个基向量的线性组合,那么信号 x 是 K 稀疏的,即在式(3-42)中只有 K 个 s_i 系数是非零的,($N-K$) 个是零。

7) Compressive sensing addresses these inefficiencies by directly acquiring a compressed signal representation without going through the intermediate stage of acquiring N samples.

压缩感知通过直接获得一种压缩信号的表示而不通过得到 N 个采样值的中间过程来解决这些缺陷。

8) It can provide the spectrum access opportunities for users using cognitive radio through a rapid search for wireless spectrum not used in the range of monitoring frequency spectrum.

它通过快速寻找监测频段中没有利用的无线频谱,从而为认知无线电用户提供频谱接入机会。

3.3 Speech Signal Processing

1. The Speech Signal

The purpose of speech is communication. There are several ways of characterizing the communications potential of speech. One highly quantitative approach is in terms of information theory ideas as introduced by Shannon. According to information theory, speech can be represented in terms of its message content, or information. An alternative way of characterizing speech is in terms of the signal carrying the message information, i.e., the acoustic waveform. Although information theoretic ideas have played a major role in sophisticated communications system, but it is the speech representation based on the waveform, or some parametric model, which has been most useful in practical application.

In considering the process of speech communication, it is helpful to begin by thinking of a message represented in some abstract form in the brain of the speaker. Through the complex process of producing speech, the information in that message is ultimately converted to an acoustic signal. The message information can be thought of as being represented in a number of different ways in the process of speech production. For example, the message information is first converted into a set of neural signals which control the articulatory mechanism (that is, the motions of the tongue, lips, vocal cords, etc.). The articulators move in response to these neural signals to perform a sequence of gestures, the result of which is an acoustic waveform which contains the information in the original message.

The information that is communicated through speech is intrinsically of a discrete nature; i.e., it can be represented by a concatenation of elements from a finite set of symbols. The symbols from which every sound can be classified are called phonemes. Each language has its own distinctive of phonemes, typically numbering between 30 to 50. For example, English can be represented by a set of around 42 phonemes.

A central concern of information theory is the rate at which information is conveyed. For speech a crude estimate of the information rate can be obtained by noting that physical limitations on the rate of motion the articulators require that humans produce speech at an average rate about 10 phonemes per second. If each phoneme is represented by a binary number, then a six-bit numerical code is more than sufficient to represent all of the phonemes of English. Assuming an average rate of 10 phonemes per second and neglecting any correlation between pairs of adjacent phonemes we get an estimate of 60bits/sec for the average information rate of speech. In other words, the written equivalent of speech contains information equivalent to 60bits/sec at normal speaking rates. Of course a lower bound on the "true" information content of speech is considerably higher than this rate. The above estimate does take into account factors such as the identity and emotional state of the speaker, the rate of speaking, the loudness of the speech, etc.

In speech communication systems, the speech signal is transmitted, stored, and processed in many ways. Technical concerns lead to a wide variety of representations of the speech signal. In general, there are two major concerns in any system: one is preservation of the message content in the speech signal. Another is representation of the speech signal in a form that is convenient for transmission or storage, or in a form that is flexible so that modification may be made to the speech signal without seriously degrading the message content.

The representation of the speech signal must be such that the information content can easily be extracted by human listeners, or automatically by machine. Representations of the speech signal (rather than message content) may require from 500 to upwards of 1 million bits per second. In the design and implementation of these representations, the methods of signal processing play a fundamental role.

2. Signal Processing

The general problem of information processing is depicted in Fig. 3-9. In the case of speech signals the human speaker is the information source. The measurement or observation is generally the acoustic waveform.

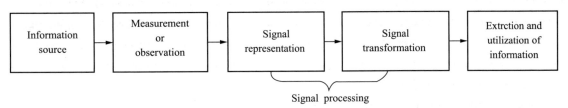

Fig. 3-9　General view of information manipulation and processing

Signal processing involves first obtaining a representation of the signal based on a given model and then the application of some higher level transformation in order to put the signal into a more convenient form. The last step in the process is the extraction and utilization of information. This step may be performed either by human listeners or automatically by machines. By way of example, a system whose function is to automatically identify a speaker from a given set of speakers might use a time-dependent spectral representation of the speech signal. One possible signal transformation would be to average spectra across an entire sentence, compare the average spectrum to a stored averaged spectrum template for each possible speaker, and then based on a spectral similarity measurement choose the identity of speaker. For this example the "information" in the signal is the identity of the speaker.

Thus, processing of speech signals generally involves two tasks. First, it is a vehicle for obtaining a general representation of a speech signal in either waveform or parametric form. Second, signal processing serves the function of aiding in the process of transforming the signal representation into alternate forms which are less general in nature, but more appropriate to specific applications.

3. Digital Signal Processing

We will explore the role of digital techniques in processing speech signals. Digital signal processing is concerned both with obtaining discrete representations of signals, and with the theory, design, and implementation of numerical procedures for processing the discrete representation. The objectives in digital signal processing are identical to those in analog signal processing. Therefore, it is reasonable to ask why digital signal processing techniques should be singled out for special consideration in the context of speech communication. A number of very reasons can be cited. First, and probably the most important, is the fact that extremely sophisticated signals processing function can be implemented using digital techniques. In addition, the algorithms used commonly in speech signal processing are intrinsically discrete-time, signal processing systems. For the most part, it is not appropriate to view these systems as approximations to analog systems, indeed in many cases there is no realizable counterpart available with analog implementation.

Digital signal processing techniques were first applied in speech processing problems, as simulations of complex analog systems. The point of view initially was that analog systems could be simulated on a computer to avoid the necessity of building the system in order to experiment with choices of parameters and other design considerations. When digital simulations of analog systems were first applied, the computations required a great deal of time. For example, as much as an hour might have been required to process only a few seconds of speech. In the mid 1960's a revolution in digital signal processing occurred. The major catalysts were the development of faster computers and rapid advances in the theory of digital signal processing techniques. Thus, it became clear that digital signal processing systems had virtues for beyond their ability to simulate analog systems. Indeed the present attitude toward laboratory computer implementations of speech processing systems is to view them as exact simulations of a digital system that could be implemented either with special purpose digital hardware or with a dedicated computer system.

In addition to theoretical developments, concomitant developments in the area of digital hardware have led to further strengthening of the advantage of digital processing techniques over analog systems. Digital systems are reliable and very compact. Integrated circuit technology has advanced to a state where extremely complex systems can be implemented on a single chip. Logic speeds are fast enough so that the tremendous number of computations required in many signal processing functions can be implemented in real-time at speech sampling rates.

There are many other reasons for using digital techniques in speech communication systems. For example, if suitable coding is used, speech in digital form can be reliably transmitted over very noisy channels. Also, if the speech signal is in digital form it is identical to data of other forms. Thus a communication network can be used to transmit both speech and data with no need to distinguish between them except in the decoding. Also, with regard to transmission of voice signals requiring security, the digital representation has a distinct advantage over analog systems. For secrecy, the information bits can be scrambled in a manner which can ultimately be unscrambled at the receiver. For these and numerous other reasons digital techniques are being increasingly applied in speech communication problems.

4. Digital Speech Processing

In considering the application of digital signal processing techniques to speech communication problems, it is helpful to focus on three main topics: the representation of speech signals in digital form, the implementation of sophisticated processing techniques, and the classes of applications which rely heavily on digital processing.

The representation of speech signals in digital form is, of course, of fundamental concern. In this regard we are guided by the well-known sampling theorem which states that a bandlimited signal can be represented by samples taken periodically in time-provided that the samples are taken at a high enough rate. Thus, the process of sampling underlies all of the theory and application of digital speech processing. There are many possibilities for discrete representations of speech signals. As shown in Fig. 3-10, these representations can be classified into two broad groups, namely waveform representations and parametric representations. Waveform representations, as the name implies, are concerned with simply preserving the "wave shape" of the analog speech signal through a sampling and quantization process. Parametric representations, on the other hand, are concerned with representing the speech signal as the output of a model for speech production. The first step in obtaining a parametric representation is often a digital waveform representation; that is, the speech signal is sampled and quantized and then further processed to obtain the parameters of the model for speech production. The parameters of this model are conveniently classified as either excitation parameters (i.e., related to the source of speech sounds) or vocal tract response parameters (i.e., related to the individual speech sounds).

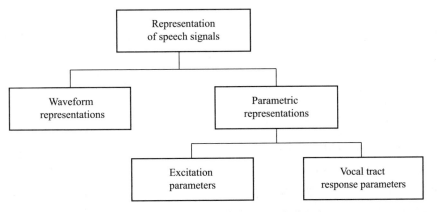

Fig. 3-10 Representations of speech signals

Fig. 3-11 shows a comparison of a number of different representations of speech signals according to the data rate required. The dotted line, at a data rate of about 15,000 bits per second, separates the higher data rate waveform representations at the left from the lower data rate parametric representations at the right. This figure shows variations in data rate from 75 bits per second (approximately the basic message information of the text) to data rates upward of 200,000 bits per second for simple waveform representations. This represents about a 3000 to 1 variation in data rates depending on the signal representation. Of course the data rate is not the only consideration in choosing a speech representation. Other considerations are cost, flexibility of the representation, quality of the speech, etc.

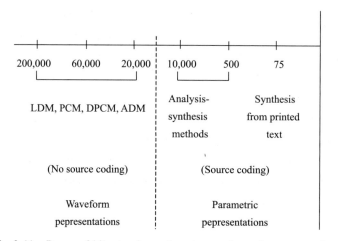

Fig. 3-11 Range of bit rates for various types of speech representations

The ultimate application is perhaps the most important consideration in the choice of a signal representation and the methods of digital signal processing subsequently applied. Fig. 3-12 shows just a few of the many applications areas in speech communications. We have already referred to several of these areas, it is worthwhile giving a brief discussion of each of these areas.

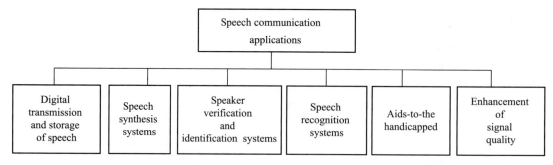

Fig. 3-12 Some typical speech communication applications

Digital Transmission and Storage of Speech

One of the earliest and most important applications of speech processing was the vocoder or voice coder, invented by Homer Dudley in the 1930's. The purpose of the vocoder was to reduce the bandwidth required to transmit the speech signal. The need to conserve bandwidth remains, in many situations, in spite of the increased bandwidth provided by satellite, microwave, and optical communication systems. Furthermore, a need has arisen for systems which digitize speech at as low a bit rate as possible, consistent with low terminal cost for future applications in the all-digital telephone plant. Also, the possibility of extremely sophisticated encryption of the speech signal is sufficient motivation for the use of digital transmission in many applications.

Speech Synthesis Systems

Much of the interest in speech synthesis systems is stimulated by the need for economical digital storage of speech for computer voice response systems. A computer voice response system is basically an all-digital, automatic information service which can be queried by a person form a keyboard or terminal, and which responds with the desired information by voice. Since an ordinary Touch-Tone telephone can be the keyboard for such a system, the capabilities of such automatic information services can be made universally available over the switched telephone facilities without the need for any additional specialized equipment. Speech synthesis systems also play a fundamental role in learning about the process of human speech production.

Speaker Verification and Identification Systems

The techniques of speaker verification and identification involve the authentication or identification of a speaker from a large ensemble of possible speakers. A speaker verification system must decide if a speaker is the person he claims to be. Such a system is potentially applicable to situations requiring control of access to information or restricted areas and to various kinds of automated credit transactions. A speaker identification system must decide which speaker among an ensemble of speakers produced a given speech utterance. Such systems have potential forensic applications.

Speech Recognition Systems

Speech recognition is, in its most general form, a conversion from an acoustic waveform to a written equivalent of the message information. The nature of the speech recognition problem is heavily dependent upon the constraints placed on speaker, speaking situation and message context. The potential applications of speech recognition systems are many and varied; e. g. a voice operated typewriter and voice communication with computers. Also, a speech recognition system combined with a speech synthesis system comprises the ultimate low bit rate communication system.

Aids-to-the-Handicapped

This application concerns processing of a speech signal to make the information available in a form which is better matched to a handicapped person than is normally available. For example variable rate playback of prerecorded tapes provides an opportunity for a blind "reader" to proceed at any desired pace through given speech material. Also a variety of signal processing techniques have been applied to design sensory aids and visual displays of speech information as aids in teaching deaf persons to speak.

Enhancement of Signal Quality

In many situations, speech signals are degraded in ways that limit their effectiveness for communication. In such cases digital signal processing techniques can be applied to improve the speech quality. Examples include such applications as the removal of reverberation (or echos) from speech, or the removal of noise from speech.

NEW WORDS AND PHRASES

characterize　vt. 表现……的特色，刻画……的性格
abstract　adj. 抽象的，深奥的，理论的
ultimately　adv. 最后，终于，根本，基本上
articulatory　adj. 分节的，关节的
articulator　n. 发音之人或物，音节分明之人，发音矫正器，接骨的人
gesture　n. 姿态，手势，表示；v. 做手势，以手势表示
intrinsically　adv. 本质地，固有地
phoneme　n. [语] 音位，音素
concatenation　n. 串联，连接
distinctive　adj. 与众不同的，有特色的
vehicle　n. 媒介物，传达手段
single out　挑选
counterpart　n. 副本，极相似的人或物，配对物
catalyst　n. 催化剂

virtue　n. 德行，美德，优点，功效，效力
dedicated　adj. 专用的，为某一特定用途或功能而设计的
concomitant　adj. 伴随的；n. 伴随物
compact　adj. 紧凑的，紧密的，简洁的
scramble　vt. 搅乱，使混杂
ultimately　adv. 最后，终于，根本，基本上
underlie　vt. 位于……之下，成为……的基础
encryption　n. [计] 加密术，密码术
conserve　vt. 保存，节俭
query　v. 询问，表示怀疑
touch-tone　adj. 按键式的
transaction　n. 办理，交易，事务，处理事务
forensic　adj. 法院的，适于法庭的，公开辩论的
constraint　n. 约束，强制，局促
handicapped　n. 残疾人，身体有缺陷的人；adj. 残疾的

NOTES

1) Assuming an average rate of 10 phonemes per second and neglecting any correlation between pairs of adjacent phonemes we get an estimate of 60bits/sec for the average information rate of speech. In other words, the written equivalent of speech contains information equivalent to 60bits/sec at normal speaking rates.

设平均速率为每秒 10 音素，并且忽略相邻音素对之间的相关性，可以估计出语音的平均信息速率为 60bit/s。换句话说，在正常的讲话速率下，与话音等效的书面文字包含 60bit/s 的信息。

2) Thus, processing of speech signals generally involves two tasks. First, it is a vehicle for obtaining a general representation of a speech signal in either waveform or parametric form. Second, signal processing serves the function of aiding in the process of transforming the signal representation into alternate forms which are less general in nature, but more appropriate to specific applications.

因此，语音信号处理通常涉及两个任务：第一，它是获得语音信号一般表示的一种工具，这种表示既可以用波形的形式，也可以用参数的形式；第二，在把信号从一种表示形式变换到另一种表示形式的过程中信号处理起着辅助作用，变换后的表示形式从本质上讲其普遍性可能较窄，但更适合于特定应用。

3) A number of very reasons can be cited. First, and probably the most important, is the fact that extremely sophisticated signals processing function can be implemented using digital techniques. In addition, the algorithms used commonly in speech signal processing are intrinsically discrete-time, signal processing systems. For the most part, it is not appropriate to view these systems as approximations to analog systems, indeed in many cases there is no realizable counterpart available with analog implementation.

可以列出很多理由。首先，也是最重要的，是利用数字技术可以实现极其复杂的信号处理工作。此外，语音信号处理中常用的算法本质上具有离散时间信号处理系统的性质。从很多方面，不能把这些系统看成是模拟系统的近似。实际上，在许多情况下，无法实现和它们对应的模拟设备。

4) This represents about a 3000 to 1 variation in data rates depending on the signal representation.
这代表了大约3000∶1数据率的变化范围，而数据率依赖于信号的表示形式。
5) The need to conserve bandwidth remains, in many situations, in spite of the increased bandwidth provided by satellite, microwave, and optical communication systems.
在许多情况下，尽管卫星、微波和光纤通信系统能够提供的带宽增大了，但是依然需要节省带宽。

EXERCISES

1. **Please translate the following words and phrases into Chinese.**
   a) quantitative approach
   b) sophisticated communication systems
   c) a number of different ways
   d) take into account
   e) digital techniques
   f) single out
   g) bandlimited signal
   h) parametric representations
   i) vocal tract response parameters
   j) speech synthesis systems

2. **Please translate the following words and phrases into English.**
   a) 信息论
   b) 参数化模型
   c) 发音机制
   d) 信息源
   e) 语音信号处理
   f) 集成电路技术
   g) 波形表式
   h) 激励参数
   i) 说话人确认和辨认
   j) 语音增强

3. **Fill in the blanks with the missing word(s).**
   a) Through the complex process of producing speech, the information in that message is ultimately converted _____ an acoustic signal.
   b) The symbols _____ which every sound can be classified are called phonemes.
   c) _____ general, there are two major concerns in any system.
   d) _____ way of example, a system whose function is to automatically identify a speaker from a given set of speakers might use a time-dependent spectral representation of the speech signal.
   e) Digital signal processing is concerned both _____ obtaining discrete representations of signals, and _____ the theory, design, and implementation of numerical procedures for processing the discrete representation.
   f) In addition to theoretical developments, concomitant developments in the area of digital hardware have led to further strengthening of the advantage of digital processing techniques _____ analog systems.
   g) Also, if the speech signal is in digital form it is identical _____ data of other forms.
   h) Although we have already referred _____ several of these areas, it is worthwhile giving a brief discussion of each of these areas as a means for motivating the techniques to be discussed in subsequent chapters.
   i) Furthermore, a need has arisen for systems which digitize speech at _____ low a bit rate _____ possible, consistent with low terminal cost for future applications in the all-digital telephone plant.
   j) _____ such cases digital signal processing techniques can be applied to improve the speech quality.

4. **Answer the following questions according to the text.**
   a) In general, what are the major concerns in speech communication systems?
   b) Talk about the speech communication applications.
   c) Talk about representations of speech signals.
   d) What is the nature of the speech recognition problem?

READING

Speech Emotion Recognition

1. Introduction

There are many ways of communication but the speech signal is one of the fastest and most natural methods of communications between humans. Therefore the speech can be also the fast and efficient method of interaction between human and machine. Humans have the natural ability to use all their available senses for maximum awareness of the received message. Through all the available senses people actually sense the emotional state of their communication partner. The emotional detection is natural for humans but it is a very difficult task for machine. Therefore the purpose of emotion recognition system is to use emotion related knowledge in such a way that human-machine communication will be improved.

With the development of science and technology, speech emotion recognition is becoming more and more relevant to people's daily life. It has been widely used in various fields such as communication, education, criminal investigation and medical treatment. For example, we can combine speech emotion recognition technology with audio and video communication so that the semantics of speech can match with emotion. It makes people can get a better service experience. In the field of education, speech emotion recognition technology can monitor in real time students' emotional states in class so that the targeted teaching plans can be made to improve students' efficiency in class. In criminal investigation, speech emotion recognition technology is helping to know accurately the suspect's state of mind and emotion. In the medical field, a therapist can use the intelligent diagnostic tool with emotion recognition to treat disease for helping patients to relieve their tension and depression.

2. Speech Emotion Recognition System

A speech emotion recognition system is a pattern recognition system. This shows that the various stages present in a pattern recognition system are also present in a speech emotion recognition system. The speech emotion recognition system contains three main modules: emotion speech database, feature extraction and speech emotion recognition models, as shown in Fig. 3-13. These three modules correspond to the key techniques of speech emotion recognition, and their basics are briefly described below.

语音情感识别

1. 引言

人类之间的交流方式有很多，但语音信号是最快和最自然的交流方式之一。因此，语音也可以成为人机交互的快速、高效的方法。人类有一种天生的能力，能够利用所有可用的感官，最大限度地感知所接收到的信息。通过所有可用的感官，人们能实际感受到他们的交流伙伴的情绪状态。情感检测对人类来说是很自然的，但对机器来说是非常困难的任务。因此，情感识别系统的目的就是利用与情感相关的知识，从而提高人机沟通能力。

随着科学技术的发展，语音情感识别与人们的日常生活越来越密切相关。它已广泛应用于通信、教育、刑侦、医疗等各个领域。例如，在通信领域，我们可以将语音情感识别技术与音/视频通信相结合，使语音语义与情感相匹配，让人们获得更好的服务体验。在教育领域，语音情感识别技术可以实时监控学生在课堂上的情绪状态，制定有针对性的教学计划，提高学生的课堂效率。在刑事侦查领域，语音情感识别技术有助于准确地了解犯罪嫌疑人的心理状态和情感状态。在医疗领域，治疗师可以使用带有情绪识别的智能诊断工具来治疗疾病，帮助患者缓解紧张和压抑的情绪。

2. 语音情感识别系统

语音情感识别系统是一种模式识别系统。这表明在模式识别系统中存在的各个阶段在语音情感识别系统中也存在。语音情感识别系统主要包括情感语音数据库、特征提取和语音情感识别模型三大模块，如图 3-13 所示。这三个模块对应的是语音情感识别的关键技术，下面将简要介绍它们的基础知识。

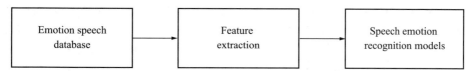

Fig. 3-13 Block diagram of a speech emotion recognition system

Emotion Speech Database

It is a main concern in speech emotion recognition system to find out a set of the significant emotions to be classified by an automatic emotion recognizer. A typical set of emotions contains 300 emotional states. Therefore it is very complex to classify such a great number of emotions. According to palette theory any emotion can be decomposed into primary emotions similar to the way that any color is a combination of some basic colors. Primary emotions are anger, disgust, fear, joy, sadness and surprise.

The evaluation of the speech emotion recognition system is based on the level of naturalness of the database which is used as an input to the speech emotion recognition system. If the inferior database is used as an input to the system then incorrect conclusion may be drawn. The database as an input to the speech emotion recognition system may contain the real world emotions or the acted ones. It is more practical to use database that is collected from the real life situations.

Feature Extraction

Any emotion from the speaker's speech is represented by the large number of parameters which is contained in the speech, and the changes in these parameters will result in corresponding change in emotions. Therefore an extraction of these speech features which represents emotions is an important task in speech emotion recognition system. The speech features can be divide into two main categories that is long term and short term features. The region of analysis of the speech signal used for the feature extraction is an important issue which is to be considering in the feature extraction. The speech signal is divided into small intervals which are referred as a frame.

The prosodic features are known as the primary indicator of the speakers emotional states. Research on emotion of speech indicates that pitch, energy, duration, formant, Mel Frequency Cepstrum Coefficient (MFCC), and Linear Prediction Cepstrum Coefficient (LPCC) are the important features. For the different emotional state, corresponding changes occurs in the speak rate, pitch, energy, and spectrum. Typically anger has higher pitch mean value and variance, and higher energy mean value. In the happy state there is an improvement in pitch mean value, variation range and variance,

情感语音数据库

在语音情感识别系统中,通过自动情感识别器找出一组有意义的情感是主要的关注点。一组典型的情绪包含了300个情感状态。因此,对如此多的情感进行分类是非常复杂的。根据调色板理论,任何情感都可以分解成基本情感,类似于任何颜色都是一些基本颜色的组合。基本情感是愤怒、厌恶、恐惧、快乐、悲伤和惊喜。

语音情感识别系统的评价基于数据库的自然程度,这个数据库就是语音情感识别系统的输入。如果将低级数据库用作系统的输入,那么可能会得出不正确的结论。数据库作为语音情感识别系统的输入,可能包含真实世界的情感或扮演的情感。从现实生活中收集的数据库更真实。

特征提取

说话人语音中的任何一种情感都是通过语音中所包含的大量参数来表示的,这些参数的变化会导致相应的情感变化。因此,提取这些代表情感的语音特征是语音情感识别系统的重要任务。语音特征可以分为两大类,即长时特征和短时特征。语音信号用于特征提取的分析区域是特征提取中需要考虑的重要问题。语音信号被分成若干小间隔,这些小间隔称为帧。

韵律特征被认为是说话人情绪状态的主要指示器。对语音情感的研究表明,基音、能量、持续时间、共振峰、梅尔频率倒谱系数(MFCC)和线性预测倒谱系数(LPCC)是语音情感的重要特征。对于不同的情感状态,语速、基音、能量和频谱都会发生相应的变化。通常,愤怒具有更高的基音平均值和方差,以及更高的能量平均值。在快乐状态下,基音平均值、变化范围和方差以及能量平均值均有改善;而在悲伤状态下,基音平均值、变化范围

and energy mean value. On the other hand the pitch mean value, variation range and variance are decreases in sadness, also the energy is weak, speak rate is slow and decrease in spectrum of high frequency components. The pitch feature of fear has a high mean value and variation range, improvement of spectrum in high frequency components. Therefore statistics of pitch, energy and some spectrum feature can be extracted to recognize emotions from speech.

One of the main speech features which indicate emotion is energy and the study of energy is depends on short term energy and short term average amplitude. As the arousal level of emotions is associated with the short term speech energy therefore it can be used in the field of emotion recognition. The pitch signal which is also referred as the glottal wave form is one more main feature which indicates emotion in speech. The pitch signal depends on the tension of the vocal folds and sub glottal air pressure, and it is produced from the vibration rate of the vocal cord. The pitch signal is characterized by the two features that is pitch frequency, and glottal air velocity at the vocal fold opening time instant. The number of harmonics present in the spectrum is directly get affected by the pitch frequency.

Linear Prediction Cepstrum Coefficient (LPCC) gives the details about the characteristics of particular channel of any individual person, and this channel characteristic will get change in accordance with the different emotions, so by using these features one can extract the emotions in speech. The merits of using the LPCC is that it involves less computation, its algorithm is more efficient and it could describe the vowels in better manner. Mel Frequency Cepstrum Coefficient (MFCC) is extensively used in speech recognition and speech emotion recognition systems, and the recognition rate of MFCC is very good. In the low frequency region better frequency resolution and robustness to noise could be achieved with the help of MFCC rather than that for high frequency region.

In feature extraction all of the basic speech, feature extracted may not be helpful and essential for speech emotion recognition system. If all the extracted features give as an input to the classifier this would not guarantee the best system performance which shows that there is a need to remove some redundancy features from the base features. Therefore there is a need of systematic feature selection to reduce these features. Forward feature selection method could be used to select the best feature subset. In the initial stage forward selection initializes with the single best feature out of the whole feature set. The remaining features are further added which increases the classification accuracy. If the added number of features attained the preset number, the selection process should stop.

和方差降低，能量较弱，说话速度较慢，频谱中高频成分减少。恐惧的基音特征具有较高的平均值和变化范围，改善了高频部分的频谱。因此，我们可以通过提取基音、能量和某些频谱特征的统计值来识别语音中的情感。

表示情感的主要语音特征之一是能量，而对能量的研究依赖于短时能量和短时平均振幅。由于情感的唤醒水平与语音短时能量相关，因此可以将其应用于情感识别领域。基音信号也被称为声门波形，它是另一个反映语音情感的主要特征。基音信号取决于声带的张力和声门下的气压，由声带的振动速率产生。基音信号由两个特征来表征，它们是基音频率和声带开启瞬间的声门气流速度。频谱中存在的谐波数直接受到基音频率的影响。

LPCC给出了任何个体特定信道的特征细节，该信道特征会随着不同的情感而发生变化，因此利用这些特征可以提取语音中的情感。LPCC的优点是计算量少，算法效率高，可以更好地描述元音。MFCC在语音识别和语音情感识别系统中得到了广泛的应用，其识别率非常高。MFCC在低频区域比在高频区域具有更好的频率分辨率和对噪声的鲁棒性。

在对所有基本语音进行特征提取的过程中，提取的特征有可能对语音情感识别系统的作用不是很大。如果所有提取的特征都作为分类器的输入，并不能保证系统性能最好，则表明有必要从基本特征中删除某些冗余特征。因此，我们需要系统化的特征选择来减少这些特征，可以采用前向特征选择方法选择最佳特征子集。在初始阶段，前向选择以整个特征集中的最佳特征初始化，再逐步增加能提高分类精度的其余特征。如果添加的特征数量达到预设数量，则选择过程应该停止。

Speech Emotion Recognition Models

In the speech emotion recognition system after calculation of the features, the best features are provided to the speech emotion recognition models to classify emotions. Thus, the speech emotion recognition models also called classifiers. A speech emotion recognition model recognizes the emotion in the speaker's speech utterance. Various types of recognition models have been proposed for the task of speech emotion recognition. The following statistical models and recognition algorithms are available: Dynamic Time Warping (DTW), Hidden Markov Model (HMM), Gaussian Mixture Model (GMM), Support Vector Machine (SVM) and Artificial Neural Network (ANN). DTW uses template matching for recognition, HMM and GMM use probabilistic statistics for recognition, and ANN and SVM are based on discriminative model approaches. Each recognition model has some advantages and limitations over the others.

DTW is an early model training and pattern matching technique, which takes the whole word as a recognition unit and stores the feature vector sequence templates of all words in the vocabulary in a template library, the feature vector sequences of the speech to be recognized are compared with each template in the language library, and the most similar template is output as the recognition result. The DTW method has successfully solved the problem of unequal duration of signal feature parameter sequences and has good performance in small vocabulary and isolated word speech recognition. However, as it is not suitable for continuous speech and large vocabulary speech recognition systems, it has been gradually replaced by HMM and ANN models.

In speech recognition system like isolated word recognition and speech emotion recognition, HMM is generally used; the main reason is its physical relation with the speech signals production mechanism. In speech emotion recognition system, HMM has achieved great success for modeling temporal information in the speech spectrum. The HMM is doubly stochastic process consist of first order Markov chain whose states are buried from the observer. For speech emotion recognition typically a single HMM is trained for each emotion and an unknown sample is classified according to the model that illustrates the derived feature sequence best. HMM has the important advantage that the temporal dynamics of speech features can be caught, so the recognition framework can be optimized by establishing well procedure. The main problem in building the HMM based recognition model is the features selection process. Because it is not enough that features carry information about the emotional states, but it must fit the

语音情感识别模型

在语音情感识别系统中,通过对特征的计算,为语音情感识别模型提供最佳特征,从而对情感进行分类。因此,语音情感识别模型也称为分类器。语音情感识别模型对说话人话语中的情感进行识别。针对语音情感识别的任务,人们提出了各种类型的识别模型。统计模型和识别算法有:动态时间规整(DTW)、隐马尔可夫模型(HMM)、高斯混合模型(GMM)、支持向量机(SVM)和人工神经网络(ANN)。DTW采用模板匹配进行识别,HMM和GMM采用概率统计进行识别,ANN和SVM采用判别模型方法进行识别。每种识别模型都有各自的优点和局限性。

DTW是一种早期的模型训练和模式匹配技术,它以整个单词为识别单元,将词汇表中所有单词的特征向量序列模板存储在模板库中,将待识别语音的特征向量序列与语言库中的每个模板进行比较,输出最相似的模板作为识别结果。DTW方法成功地解决了信号特征参数序列持续时间不等的问题,在小词汇量和孤立词语音识别中具有良好的性能。但由于它不适用于连续语音和大词汇量语音识别系统,因此逐渐被HMM和ANN模型所取代。

在孤立词识别、语音情感识别等语音识别系统中,HMM被广泛使用,主要原因是其与语音信号产生机理的物理关系。在语音情感识别系统中,HMM在对语音频谱中的时间信息进行建模方面取得了很大的成功。HMM是由一阶马尔可夫链组成的双随机过程,其状态隐藏在观测器中。对于语音情感识别,通常针对每种情感训练单个HMM,并根据最能充分体现所导出特征序列的模型对未知样本进行分类。HMM的一个重要优点是可以捕捉语音特征的时间动态,因此可以通过建立良好的程序来优化识别框架。建立基于HMM的识别模型的主要问题是特征选择过程,因为特征仅携带情感状态信息是不够的,还必须适合HMM结构。与其他分

HMM structure as well. HMM provides better recognition accuracies for speech emotion recognition as compared with the other classifiers. HMM classifiers using prosody and formant features have considerably lower recall rates than that of the classifiers using spectral features. Only when the global features are extracted from the training utterances, Gaussian Mixture Model (GMM) is more suitable for speech emotion recognition. All the training and testing equations are based on the supposition that all vectors are independent therefore GMM cannot form temporal structure of the training data.

Other recognition model that is used for the emotion classification is an ANN, which is used due to its ability to find nonlinear boundaries separating the emotional states. Out of the many types, feedforward neural network is used most frequently in speech emotion recognition. Multilayer perceptron neural networks are relatively common in speech emotion recognition as it is easy for implementation and it has well defined training algorithm.

Transforming the original feature set to a high dimensional feature space by using the kernel function is the main thought behind the SVM recognition model, which leads to get optimum classification in this new feature space. The kernel functions like linear, polynomial, Radial Basis Function (RBF) can be used in SVM model for large extent. In the main applications like pattern recognition and classification problems, SVM classifier are generally used, and because of that it is used in the speech emotion recognition system. SVM has much better classification performance compared to other classifiers. An original SVM classifier was designed only for two class problems, but it can be use for more classes. Because of the structural risk minimization oriented training SVM has high generalization capability.

3. Deep Learning-Based Speech Emotion Recognition

Most of the deep learning algorithms are based on ANN hence they are commonly referred to deep neural networks. The term "deep" comes from the number of hidden layers as it can reach to hundreds of layers, whereas a traditional neural network contains two or three hidden layers. In recent years, performance of the deep learning algorithms surpasses the traditional machine learning algorithms, hence the focus on research changed direction towards them and the current trend in speech emotion recognition research is no different. The advantage of some of these algorithms is that there is no need for feature extraction and feature selection steps. All features are automatically selected with deep learning algorithms. Most

类器相比,HMM 对语音情感识别的准确率更高。使用韵律和共振峰特征的 HMM 分类器比使用谱特征的 HMM 分类器有较低的召回率。只有当能从训练语句中提取全局特征时,GMM 才更适用于语音情感识别。所有的训练和测试方程都建立在假设所有向量都是独立的基础上,因此 GMM 不能形成训练数据的时间结构。

用于情感分类的其他识别模型是 ANN,它的使用是因为它能够找到分离情感状态的非线性边界。在众多的语音情感识别类型中,前馈神经网络应用最为广泛。多层感知器神经网络是语音情感识别中比较常见的一种方法,因为它易于实现,并且具有良好的训练算法。

SVM 识别模型的主要思想是利用核函数将原始特征集转化为高维特征空间,从而在新的特征空间中获得最优分类。在 SVM 模型中,线性、多项式、径向基函数(RBF)等核函数被经常使用。在模式识别和分类等主要应用中,SVM 分类器被广泛使用,因此在语音情感识别系统中也被采用。与其他分类器相比,SVM 具有更好的分类性能。原始的 SVM 分类器只针对两类问题设计,但它可以用于多分类问题。由于面向结构风险最小化的训练,SVM 具有较高的泛化能力。

3. 基于深度学习的语音情感识别

深度学习算法大多基于人工神经网络,因此通常被称为深度神经网络。"深度"一词来源于隐藏层的数量,它可以达到数百层,而传统的神经网络只有 2~3 层隐藏层。近年来,深度学习算法的性能超过了传统的机器学习算法,因此研究的重点转向了深度学习算法,目前语音情感识别的研究趋势也不例外。这些算法的优点是不需要特征提取和特征选择步骤。所有的特征都是通过深度学习算法自动选择的。在语音情感识别领域应用最广泛的深度学习算法是递归神经网络(RNN)和卷

widely used deep learning algorithms in speech emotion recognition domain are Recurrent Neural Networks (RNN) and Convolution Neural Networks (CNN).

RNNs are a family of neural networks which are specialized in processing sequential data. By the usage of internal memory, they can remember the received input data and make a precise prediction about what is coming next. Because of their nature, RNNs are successfully used for sequential data such as time series, speech, text and video. When a unit of RNN produces an output, it forwards data to the next unit and also loops the output back itself. As a result, it has two types of input: present input and input from the recent past. The input from the recent past is important because the sequence of the data contains important information about what is coming next. RNNs have a short time memory. However, by using Long-Short Time Memory (LSTM) architecture, RNN can gain access to long term memory. LSTM-RNNs are a kind of gated RNN which are the most effective models used in practical applications that solves the long term dependency problem of the RNN. LSTM-RNNs have special "LSTM cells" that have internal recurrence besides the outer recurrence of RNN. In addition to standard input and output of the RNN, it has more parameters and gating units with sigmoid nonlinearity that control the flow of information. LSTM has three types of gates: input gate, forget gate and remember gate. By opening and closing these gates, LSTM cell makes decisions about what to store, and when to allow inputs, outputs, and deletions.

CNNs are particular types of neural networks which are designed to process data that has a grid-like topology, such as images. Through applications of several relevant filters, CNN can successfully capture temporal and spatial dependencies from an input source. The inputs are reduced into a form without loss of feature so that computational complexity decreases and the success rate of algorithm is increased. A CNN is composed of several layers: convolution layer, pooling layer, and fully-connected layer. A convolution layer is used to extract high-level features from the input. Mathematically a convolution means combining two functions to obtain a third one. In CNN, the input is taken and, then a kernel is applied to it. The resulting output is a feature map. The pooling layer is used to reduce the size of convoluted features to decrease computational complexity through dimensionality reduction. It is useful for extracting dominant features of the input data. After passing input from several convolution and pooling layers and extracting the high-level features, the resulting features are the 2D data. And then, that are flatted to a column array used as an input to a fully-connected layer. The fully-connected layer is similar to a feedforward network that operates as an ordinary neural network.

积神经网络（CNN）。

RNN 是一类专门处理序列数据的神经网络。通过使用内部存储器，它们可以记住接收到的输入数据，并对接下来的事情做出准确的预测。由于这个性质，RNN 被成功地用于时序数据，如时间序列、语音、文本和视频。当 RNN 的一个单元产生输出时，它将数据转发给下一个单元，并将输出循环回自身。因此，它有两种类型的输入：现在的输入和来自最近过去的输入。来自最近过去的输入很重要，因为数据序列包含了关于接下来会发生什么的重要信息。RNN 有一个短时存储器，但它通过使用长－短时间记忆结构，可以访问长时存储器。LSTM-RNN 是一种门控式 RNN，是解决 RNN 长时依赖问题的最有效的实际应用模型。LSTM-RNN 具有特殊的"LSTM 单元"，除了 RNN 的外部递归外，还存在内部递归。RNN 除了标准的输入和输出外，还具有更多的参数和 sigmoid 非线性控制信息流的门控单元。LSTM 有三种类型的门：输入门、遗忘门和记忆门。通过打开和关闭这些门，LSTM 单元可以决定存储什么，以及何时允许输入、输出和删除。

CNN 是一种特殊类型的神经网络，用于处理具有网格状拓扑结构的数据，如图像。通过应用几个相关的滤波器，CNN 可以成功地从输入源捕获时间和空间相关性。在不丢失特征的情况下，它将输入简化为一种形式，从而降低了计算复杂度，提高了算法的成功率。CNN 由几层组成：卷积层、池化层和全连接层。卷积层用于从输入中提取高级特征。数学上的卷积意味着结合两个函数来得到第三个函数。CNN 对输入施加卷积核，输出结果是一个特征映射。池化层用于减少卷积输出特征的大小，通过降维来降低计算复杂度。这对于提取输入数据的主要特征是很有用的。在输入经过几个卷积层和池化层传递并提取高级特征后，得到的特征是 2D 数据。然后，将 2D 数据按纵向排成列，用作全连接层的输入。全连接层类似于前馈网络，作为普通的神经网络运行。

4. Concluding Remarks

Emotion recognition of speech signals is an important research topic in the field of artificial intelligence. A number of systems have been developed to recognize emotions from speech signals. Three main modules including emotion speech database, feature extraction and speech emotion recognition models have been the focus of much research. This paper briefly introduces the traditional methods for these three components, on the basis of which the currently popular deep learning models LSTM and CNN for speech emotion recognition are briefly introduced, which not only automatically can extract high-level emotion features from speech but also can realize end-to-end speech emotion recognition. Deep learning algorithms play an important role in improving the performance of speech emotion recognition systems.

4. 结论

语音信号的情感识别是人工智能领域的重要研究课题。人们已经开发了许多从语音信号中识别情感的系统。情感语音数据库、特征提取和语音情感识别模型三个主要模块一直是研究的重点。本文简要介绍了这三个部分的传统方法，在此基础上简要介绍了目前流行的语音情感识别深度学习模型 LSTM 和 CNN，它们不仅可以自动提取语音中的高级情感特征，还可以实现对语音情感的端到端识别。深度学习算法在提高语音情感识别系统的性能方面发挥着重要作用。

NEW WORDS AND PHRASES

semantics *n.* 语义，语义学
therapist *n.* 治疗专家
tension *n.* 紧张；*v.* 使……紧张
depression *n.* 抑郁，沮丧
prosodic feature 韵律特征
pitch *n.* 基音，音高
harmonics *n.* 谐波
probabilistic statistics 概率统计
discriminative *adj.* 区别的，有识别力的
isolated word 孤立词
Markov chain 马尔科夫链
prosody *n.* 韵律学，韵律
formant *n.* 共振峰
kernel function 核函数
sequential data 序列数据
grid *n.* 网格
relevant *adj.* 相关的，切题的
temporal *adj.* 时间的

spatial *adj.* 空间的
high-level *adj.* 高级的，高层的
pooling layer 池化层
flattening *v.* （flatten 的 ing 形式）压扁
feedforward *adj.* 前馈的
Mel Frequency Cepstrum Coefficient（MFCC） 梅尔频率倒谱系数
Linear Prediction Cepstrum Coefficient（LPCC） 线性预测倒谱系数
Dynamic Time Warping（DTW） 动态时间规整
Hidden Markov Model（HMM） 隐马尔可夫模型
Gaussian Mixture Model（GMM） 高斯混合模型
Support Vector Machine（SVM） 支持向量机
Artificial Neural Network（ANN） 人工神经网络
Long Short Term Memory（LSTM） 长短时记忆
Convolution Neural Network（CNN） 卷积神经网络
Recurrent Neural Network（RNN） 递归神经网络

NOTES

1) Humans have the natural ability to use all their available senses for maximum awareness of the received message.
人类有一种天生的能力，能够使用所有可用的感官，最大限度地感知所接收到的信息。

2) With the development of science and technology, speech emotion recognition is becoming more and more relevant to people's daily life.
随着科学技术的发展，语音情感识别与人们的日常生活越来越密切相关。

3) Any emotion from the speaker's speech is represented by the large number of parameters which is contained in the speech, and the changes in these parameters will result in corresponding change in emotions.
说话人语音中的任何一种情感都是通过语音中所包含的大量参数来表示的，这些参数的变化会导致

Chapter 3 Signal System and Signal Processing（信号系统与信号处理）

相应的情感变化。

4) Therefore statistics of pitch, energy and some spectrum feature can be extracted to recognize emotions from speech.
因此，我们可以通过提取基音、能量和某些频谱特征的统计值来识别语音中的情感。

5) As the arousal level of emotions is associated with the short term speech energy therefore it can be used in the field of emotion recognition.
由于情感的唤醒水平与语音短时能量相关，因此可以将其应用于情感识别领域。

6) The pitch signal is characterized by the two features that is pitch frequency, and glottal air velocity at the vocal fold opening time instant.
基音信号由两个特征来表征，它们是基音频率和声带开启瞬间的声门气流速度。

7) In the low frequency region better frequency resolution and robustness to noise could be achieved with the help of MFCC rather than that for high frequency region.
MFCC 在低频区域比在高频区域具有更好的频率分辨率和对噪声的鲁棒性。

8) If all the extracted features give as an input to the classifier this would not guarantee the best system performance which shows that there is a need to remove some redundancy features from the base features.
如果所有提取的特征都作为分类器的输入，并不能保证系统性能最好，则表明有必要从基本特征中删除某些冗余特征。

9) DTW uses template matching for recognition, HMM and GMM use probabilistic statistics for recognition, and ANN and SVM are based on discriminative model approaches.
DTW 采用模板匹配进行识别，HMM 和 GMM 采用概率统计进行识别，ANN 和 SVM 采用判别模型方法进行识别。

10) HMM has the important advantage that the temporal dynamics of speech features can be caught, so the recognition framework can be optimized by establishing well procedure.
HMM 的一个重要优点是可以捕捉语音特征的时间动态，因此可以通过建立良好的程序来优化识别框架。

11) Multilayer perceptron neural networks are relatively common in speech emotion recognition as it is easy for implementation and it has well defined training algorithm.
多层感知器神经网络是语音情感识别中比较常见的一种方法，因为它易于实现，并且具有良好的训练算法。

12) Because of the structural risk minimization oriented training SVM has high generalization capability.
由于面向结构风险最小化的训练，SVM 具有较高的泛化能力。

13) The term "deep" comes from the number of hidden layers as it can reach to hundreds of layers, whereas a traditional neural network contains two or three hidden layers.
"深度"一词来源于隐藏层的数量，它可以达到数百层，而传统的神经网络只有 2~3 层隐藏层。

14) LSTM-RNNs are a kind of gated RNN which are the most effective models used in practical applications that solves the long term dependency problem of the RNN. LSTM-RNNs have special "LSTM cells" that have internal recurrence besides the outer recurrence of RNN.
LSTM-RNN 是一种门控式 RNN，是解决 RNN 长时依赖问题的最有效的实际应用模型。LSTM-RNN 具有特殊的"LSTM 单元"，除了 RNN 的外部递归外，还存在内部递归。

15) After passing input from several convolution and pooling layers and extracting the high-level features, the resulting features are the 2D data. And then, that are flatted to a column array used as an input to a fully-connected layer. The fully-connected layer is similar to a feedforward network that operates as an ordinary neural network.
在输入经过几个卷积层和池化层传递并提取高级特征后，得到的特征是 2D 数据。然后，将 2D 数据按纵向排成列，用作全连接层的输入。全连接层类似于前馈网络，作为普通的神经网络运行。

第 3 章
信号系统与信号处理

3.1 信号与系统

信号与系统的概念出现在多个领域，与之相关的思想和技术在多个科学技术领域发挥着重要的作用，例如，通信、航空航天、电路设计、声学、地震学、生物医学工程、发电与配电系统、化学过程控制和语音处理领域。本节简单介绍连续时间和离散时间信号与系统的数学表示，以及信号能量和功率的概念。

1. 连续时间信号和离散时间信号

信号可以描述多种多样的物理现象。虽然信号表示有很多方式，但在所有的情况下，信号中包含的信息总是以某种物理量的变化来表现。例如，图 3-1 中的简单电路，v_s 与 v_c 是电源电压和电容电压信号，是随时间变化的变量。

信号可以用含有一个或者多个自变量的数学函数来表示。例如，语音信号可以用声压来表示，而声压是时间的函数；一幅图像可以用亮度表示，而亮度是两个空间变量的函数。为了方便起见，我们通常用时间作为自变量，尽

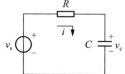

图 3-1　简单的 RC 电路，含电源电压 v_s 和电容电压 v_c

管在某些具体应用中自变量可能并不是时间。比如，在地球物理学研究中，用于研究地球结构的一些物理量（如密度、气隙度和电阻率等）就是随地球深度变化的信号；同样，在气象研究中，空气压力、温度和风速随高度而变化也是很重要的一类信号。图 3-2 描述了典型的年平均风速沿垂直方向随高度变化的分布图，测出的风速随高度的变化用于研究气象图，同时，风力情况可能会影响飞机接近机场和着陆情况。

本节研究两种基本类型的信号：连续时间信号和离散时间信号。对于连续时间信号，自变量是连续的，从而这些信号自变量的值是连续的。相反，离散时间信号只研究离散时间的情况，因此，信号自变量表示离散值的集合。语音信号是时间的函数，大气压力是高度的函数，二者都是连续时间信号的例子；每周的道琼斯（Dow Jones）股市指数是离散时间信号的例子，如图 3-3 所示。

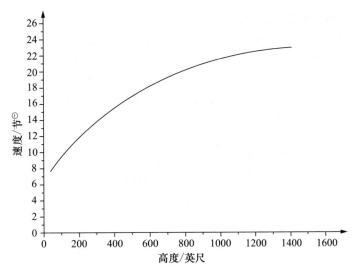

图 3-2 典型的年平均风速沿垂直方向随高度变化的分布图

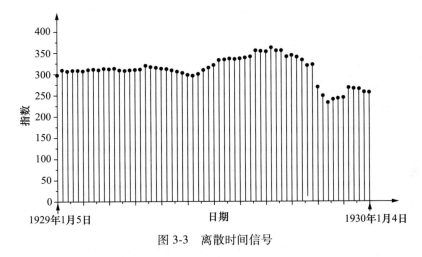

图 3-3 离散时间信号

为了区分连续时间信号和离散时间信号,用符号 t 表示连续时间变量,而用 n 表示离散时间变量。很多情况下,用图形表示信号是很有效的。图 3-4 就给出了连续时间信号 $x(t)$ 和离散时间信号 $x(n)$ 的例子。值得注意的是,离散时间信号 $x(n)$ 自变量只在整数值处有定义。

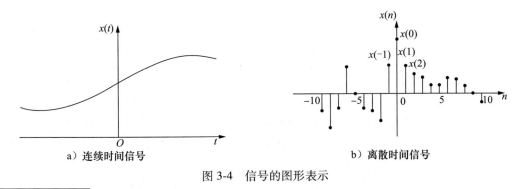

图 3-4 信号的图形表示

⊖ 1 节 = 1 海里/小时,节指地球子午线上纬度 1 分的长度。

2. 连续时间系统和离散时间系统

从广义的角度来看，物理系统都是元件、设备、子系统的互连。从信号处理和通信到电机、各种机动车和化学处理工厂等这些方面来看，系统可看作对输入信号的变换过程或以某种方式使系统产生响应，得到其他的输出信号。例如，一个高保真的系统录制一段音频信号并再现原信号。如果高保真系统的音调可控，我们可以改变录制信号的音调质量。同理，图 3-1 的电路可以看成是输入电压为 $v_s(t)$ 和输出电压为 $v_c(t)$ 的系统。图像增强系统可以将输入图像变换为具有某些所需特性的输出图像，如改善对比度等。

连续时间系统是输入为连续信号，输出同样是连续信号的系统。该系统如图 3-5a 所示，其中 $x(t)$ 是输入，$y(t)$ 是输出，$h(t)$ 是系统冲激响应。同样，离散时间系统将离散时间输入转换为离散时间输出，如图 3-5b 所示，其中 $x(n)$ 是输入，$y(n)$ 是输出，$h(n)$ 是系统单位样值响应。

图 3-5 时间系统

我们利用采样的概念可以将连续时间系统和离散时间系统联系起来，通过深入理解离散时间系统来处理采样后的连续时间信号。如今，许多数字信号处理方法已经广泛应用于科学技术领域，因此，下面我们以数字信号系统为例介绍一些系统的属性。

3. 数字信号系统特性

通常，系统通过变换 $T\{\cdot\}$ 将输入信号 $x(n)$ 映射到输出 $y(n)$，这样的系统定义很广泛。当系统的特性描述要求完整的输入-输出关系时，如果没有约束条件，即使知道了系统对某些特定输入产生的输出，我们也并不知道系统对其他输入产生的输出。两种约束性条件，即线性和时不变性（或者称为平移不变性），极大地简化了系统的特性和分析方法。幸运的是，许多系统在实际中接近线性时不变系统。

线性系统满足叠加原理：

$$T\{ax_1(n) + bx_2(n)\} = ay_1(n) + by_2(n) \tag{3-1}$$

式中，$T\{x_1(n)\} = y_1(n)$，$T\{x_2(n)\} = y_2(n)$，a 和 b 是任意标量常数。

系统时不变性定义为

$$T\{x(n-n_0)\} = y(n-n_0) \tag{3-2}$$

式中，$T\{x(n)\} = y(n)$，n_0 是任意整数。

线性和时不变性是各自独立的性质，即一个系统可能具备其中一种性质、两种都有，或者都不具备。

对于线性时不变（LTI）系统，系统输出 $y(n)$ 为

$$y(n) = \sum_{k=-\infty}^{+\infty} x(k)h(n-k) = x(n) * h(n) \tag{3-3}$$

式 (3-3) 是卷积和，它满足交换律、结合律和分配律：

$$\text{交换律：} \quad x(n) * y(n) = y(n) * x(n) \tag{3-4}$$

$$\text{结合律：} \quad [x(n) * y(n)] * w(n) = x(n) * [y(n) * w(n)] \tag{3-5}$$

$$\text{分配律：} \quad x(n) * [y(n) + w(n)] = x(n) * y(n) + x(n) * w(n) \tag{3-6}$$

在连续时间系统中，卷积是重要的分析工具。在离散时间系统中，除了在分析 LTI 系统中

很重要之外，卷积对于清楚地描述实现特定 LTI 系统的机理也很重要。

系统的另外两个属性——稳定性和因果性也常提到。当且仅当系统的有界输入对应有界输出时，系统才稳定。LTI 系统稳定的充要条件是它的单位样值响应 $h(n)$ 是绝对可和的，满足式（3-7）：

$$\sum_{n=-\infty}^{\infty} |h(n)| < \infty \tag{3-7}$$

因此，一个绝对可和序列通常视为一个稳定序列。

对于每个 n 值，比如 n_0，当且仅当输出 $y(n)$ 的值与 $n>n_0$ 的输入无关时，系统才是因果的。LTI 系统是因果系统的充要条件是它的单位样值响应 $h(n)$ 在 $n<0$ 时为 0，即满足式（3-8）：

$$h(n) = 0, \quad n < 0 \tag{3-8}$$

因此，当 $n<0$ 时为 0 的序列通常视为因果序列。

4. 信号能量与功率

从之前提供的例子看出，信号可以表示多种现象。在很多应用但不是全部应用中，我们考虑的信号直接与物理系统的能量和功率这些物理量相关。例如，如果 $v(t)$ 和 $i(t)$ 分别是电阻 R 的电压与流过的电流，那么此时的瞬时功率为

$$p(t) = v(t)i(t) = \frac{1}{R}v^2(t) \tag{3-9}$$

在 $t_1 \leq t \leq t_2$ 时间内，产生的总能量为

$$\int_{t_1}^{t_2} p(t)\,\mathrm{d}t = \int_{t_1}^{t_2} \frac{1}{R}v^2(t)\,\mathrm{d}t \tag{3-10}$$

且此时间间隔内的平均功率为

$$\frac{1}{t_2-t_1}\int_{t_1}^{t_2} p(t)\,\mathrm{d}t = \frac{1}{t_2-t_1}\int_{t_1}^{t_2} \frac{1}{R}v^2(t)\,\mathrm{d}t \tag{3-11}$$

对任意连续时间信号 $x(t)$ 或离散时间信号 $x(n)$ 应用与功率和能量同样的处理方法是普遍和值得关注的。进一步我们会经常发现对于复信号，这将非常有用。在这种情况下，$t_1 \leq t \leq t_2$ 内连续时间信号 $x(t)$ 的能量总和定义为

$$\int_{t_1}^{t_2} |x(t)|^2 \mathrm{d}t \tag{3-12}$$

式中，$|x(t)|$ 指函数 $x(t)$（可能是复数）的幅度，时间平均功率通过式（3-12）与时间间隔 t_2-t_1 相除得到。同理，离散时间信号 $x(n)$ 在 $n_1 \leq n \leq n_2$ 间隔内的能量总和为

$$\sum_{n=n_1}^{n_2} |x(n)|^2 \tag{3-13}$$

能量和除以间隔数 n_2-n_1+1，得到此间隔内的平均功率。值得注意的是，无论式（3-12）和式（3-13）中的物理量是否与实际能量有关，这里的"能量"和"功率"是独立应用的。我们将发现这两个术语应用方便且广泛。

另外，在许多系统中，我们会检测一段无限时间区间内信号的能量及功率，如 $-\infty < t < +\infty$ 或者 $-\infty < n < +\infty$。在这些情况下，我们定义无限时间内的总能量的极限，如式（3-14）和式（3-15）所示，即在连续时间内：

$$E_\infty \triangleq \lim_{T \to \infty} \int_{-T}^{T} |x(t)|^2 \mathrm{d}t = \int_{-\infty}^{+\infty} |x(t)|^2 \mathrm{d}t \tag{3-14}$$

在离散时间内：

$$E_\infty \stackrel{\Delta}{=} \lim_{N\to\infty} \sum_{n=-N}^{+N} |x(n)|^2 = \sum_{n=-\infty}^{+\infty} |x(n)|^2 \tag{3-15}$$

对于有些信号,式(3-14)中的积分或式(3-15)中的和是不收敛的,例如,若 $x(t)$ 或者 $x(n)$ 对所有时间是非零常数,这样的信号就有无限能量,但对于 $E_\infty < \infty$ 时的信号而言,它是能量有限的。

用类似的方式,我们定义一段无限间隔内连续时间和离散时间的时间平均功率分别为

$$P_\infty \stackrel{\Delta}{=} \lim_{T\to\infty} \frac{1}{2T} \int_{-T}^{T} |x(t)|^2 dt \tag{3-16}$$

和

$$P_\infty \stackrel{\Delta}{=} \lim_{N\to\infty} \frac{1}{2N+1} \sum_{n=-N}^{+N} |x(n)|^2 \tag{3-17}$$

有了这些定义,我们可以把信号分为三大类。

第一类为有限能量信号,即 $E_\infty < \infty$ 的信号。这种信号的平均功率必须为0,在连续时间的情况下为

$$P_\infty = \lim_{T\to\infty} \frac{E_\infty}{2T} = 0 \tag{3-18}$$

举一个有限能量信号的例子:信号在 $0 \leq t \leq 1$ 内其值为1,而在其他时间范围取值为0。这样,$E_\infty = 1$ 且 $P_\infty = 0$。

第二类是具有有限平均功率 P_∞ 的信号。从之前所述可知,如果 $P_\infty > 0$,则必要条件为 $E_\infty = \infty$。当然这是有意义的,因为如果单位时间内存在一个非零的平均能量,那么在无限的时间间隔范围内,对其积分或者求和就会产生无限的能量总和。例如,常数信号 $x(n) = 4$ 就有无限能量,但平均功率为 $P_\infty = 16$。

第三类信号是 P_∞ 和 E_∞ 都无限的信号。一个简单的例子,信号 $x(t) = t$ 就是这样的信号。

3.2 数字信号处理

1. 简介

数字信号处理(DSP)是21世纪在科学与工程领域功能最强大的技术之一。它在广泛的领域中已经引发了革命性的变化,例如,通信、医疗成像、雷达和声呐、高保真音乐再现以及石油勘探。这些应用已经开发了深度DSP技术,拥有它们各自的数学算法和专业技术。

数字信号处理有别于其他计算机科学的标志是其独特的数据类型:信号。在当今世界中,我们被各种不同形式的信号包围着。有些信号是自然的,但大多是人为制造的。一些信号是必需的(语音),一些是令人愉快的(音乐),而很多信号在特定情况下是不希望出现或者没必要出现的。在多数情况下,这些信号来源于对真实世界的感知数据:地震震动、视觉图像、声波等。DSP是处理转换为数字形式信号的一种数学、算法和技术,可以达到很多不同的目的,例如,视觉图像增强、语音识别与生成、用于存储和传输的数据压缩等。

在工程中,信号承载着信息,包括有用信息和无用信息。因此,从混合信息里提取或增强有用信息是信号处理最简单的形式。有用和无用信息的区别往往既主观又客观。因此,信号处理依赖于应用需求。傅里叶分析和滤波器设计是常用的信号处理方法。下面简单介绍它们的原理。

2. 傅里叶分析

函数的傅里叶表示,即将函数表示成正弦和余弦信号的叠加,这种方法已经广泛用于微分

方程的解析法和数值法求解过程以及通信信号的分析与处理。

傅里叶变换的实用性在于它为了获得频率内容能够在时域上分析信号。傅里叶变换首先将时域函数变换为频域函数，之后可以分析信号的频率信息。因为变换函数的傅里叶系数表示在每个频率下每个正弦和余弦函数的贡献。正如你预想的那样，傅里叶逆变换将数据从频域变回到时域。

离散傅里叶变换（DFT）使用有限的采样点估计函数的傅里叶变换。采样点应该是信号在任意其他时刻的典型值。

离散傅里叶变换与连续傅里叶变换一样具有对称特性。此外，通过离散傅里叶变换的公式很容易计算出离散傅里叶逆变换的公式，因为二者几乎是一致的。

如果 $f(t)$ 是非周期信号，那么用周期函数（例如正弦与余弦）的和，并不能精确地表示该信号。你可以人为地拓展这个信号使其具有周期性，但是这要求在端点处附加连续性。加窗傅里叶变换（WFT）可以很好地解决非周期信号的表示问题。加窗傅里叶变换可以同时得到信号的时域信息和频域信息。

在 WFT 中，将输入信号 $f(t)$ 截成段，对每一段信号分别分析它的频率信息。如果信号有急剧的过渡，就有必要对输入信号加窗，这样信号在端点处就会收敛于零。可以通过加权函数来实现加窗处理。相对于某段信号的中间部分，端点处的权重要小。加窗的效果是在时域使信号局部化。

为了用样本来逼近函数，用离散傅里叶变换来逼近傅里叶积分，需要一个以采样点数 n 为维数的矩阵。一个 $n×n$ 维矩阵与一个向量相乘是一个 n^2 级的算术运算。随着采样点数的增加，计算量的问题变得尤为突出。然而，如果均匀划分采样点，则傅里叶矩阵就可以被分解成一些稀疏矩阵的积，并且得到的因子可以应用到向量中，这样总的算术运算量为 $n\log n$ 级，这就是所谓的快速傅里叶变换（FFT）。

3. FIR 数字滤波器设计

滤波器是一个系统，用于以特定方式改变输入信号的频谱内容。普通滤波器的目的包括提升信号质量、提取信号信息或分离先前合成的信号分量。数字滤波器是一种数学算法，它可以用硬件、固件以及软件来实现。它作用于数字输入信号，产生数字输出信号，从而达到滤波的目标。数字滤波器可以分为线性和非线性的，时变和时不变的。这一节内容主要介绍线性时不变（LTI）有限冲激响应（FIR）滤波器的设计。

设计出满足特定技术参数的数字滤波器传递函数 $H(z)$ 的过程叫作数字滤波器设计。人们已经提出许多技术来设计 FIR 滤波器。现有两种常用的直接设计方法。第一种方法基于对期望频率响应的傅里叶级数表示进行截断。这种方法提供了一个非常简单又灵活的方法来计算 FIR 滤波器的系数，但是不允许设计者适当控制滤波器参数。第二种方法基于对期望滤波器的频率响应进行频率样本的等距采样。频率采样方法的主要特点是允许递归实现 FIR 滤波器，这样能提高计算效率。然而，这种方法在确定和控制滤波器参数方面缺乏灵活性。因此，下面介绍傅里叶级数（窗）法。

傅里叶级数法的基本思想是通过计算滤波器的冲激响应，设计出逼近该滤波器期望频率响应的 FIR 滤波器。这种方法利用了这样的事实，数字滤波器的频率响应 $H(\omega)$ 是一个以 2π 为周期的周期函数。这样，用傅里叶级数展开得到

$$H(\omega) = \sum_{n=-\infty}^{\infty} h(n) e^{-j\omega n} \tag{3-22}$$

式中，

$$h(n) = \frac{1}{2\pi} \int_{-\pi}^{\pi} H(\omega) e^{j\omega n} d\omega, \qquad -\infty \leq n \leq \infty \tag{3-23}$$

该式显示，冲激响应 $h(n)$ 是双边且无限长的。如果 $H(\omega)$ 是偶函数，则在区间 $|\omega| \leq \pi$ 内，可以得出

$$h(n) = \frac{1}{\pi} \int_0^\pi H(\omega) \cos(\omega n) d\omega, \quad n \geq 0 \tag{3-24}$$

冲激响应关于 $n=0$ 对称，即

$$h(-n) = h(n), \quad n \geq 0 \tag{3-25}$$

对给定的期望频率响应 $H(\omega)$，如果可以计算出积分式（3-23）或式（3-24），那么对非递归滤波器就可以计算出对应的冲激响应 $h(n)$。但是，实际设计中使用这种简单的设计方法有两个问题。第一，对频率响应具有任意尖锐度的滤波器，其冲激响应的长度是无限的，计算无限个系数是不切实际的。第二，当 n 取负数时，得出的滤波器就是非因果的，这样无法在实时应用中实现。

一个有限长度为 $L=2M+1$ 的冲激响应 $\{h'(n)\}$ 是理想无限长度冲激响应的最佳逼近，可以简单地通过截断来实现，即

$$h'(n) = \begin{cases} h(n), & -M \leq n \leq M \\ 0, & \text{其他} \end{cases} \tag{3-26}$$

注意，在定义中我们设定 L 是奇数，否则 M 为非整数。在单位圆上有 $z = e^{j\omega}$，系统转移函数表达式为

$$H'(z) = \sum_{n=-M}^{M} h'(n) z^{-n} \tag{3-27}$$

显然，此滤波器实际是物理不可实现的，因为要求滤波器必须提前产生与输入对应的输出。一个因果 FIR 滤波器可以通过延迟 $h'(n)$ 序列 M 个采样点得到，即通过向左时移向量重新得到响应系数：

$$b'_l = h'(l - M), \quad l = 0, 1, \cdots, 2M \tag{3-28}$$

则因果 FIR 滤波器的转移函数为

$$B'(z) = \sum_{l=0}^{L-1} b'_l z^{-l}, \quad l = 0, 1, \cdots, 2M \tag{3-29}$$

这个 FIR 滤波器有 $L(=2M+1)$ 个系数 b'_l，$l = 0, 1, \cdots, L-1$。冲激响应关于 b'_M 对称，b'_M 取决于式（3-25）中指定的 $h(-n) = h(n)$。冲激响应持续时间为 $2MT$，其中 T 是采样周期。

从式（3-27）和式（3-29）看出：

$$B'(z) = z^{-M} H'(z) \tag{3-30}$$

$$B'(\omega) = e^{-j\omega M} H'(\omega) \tag{3-31}$$

由于 $|e^{-j\omega M}| = 1$，因此

$$|B'(\omega)| = |H'(\omega)| \tag{3-32}$$

这个因果滤波器与非因果滤波器有同样大小的幅度响应。如果 $h(n)$ 是实数，则 $H'(\omega)$ 为 ω 的实函数。如果 $H'(\omega) \geq 0$，则 $B'(\omega)$ 的相位为 $-M\omega$；如果 $H'(\omega) < 0$，则 $B'(\omega)$ 的相位为 $\pi - M\omega$。因此，$B'(\omega)$ 的相位是关于 ω 的线性函数，从而转移函数 $B'(z)$ 有恒定的群延迟。

如图 3-8 所示，通过简单地截断期望滤波器的冲激响应系数而得到因果 FIR 滤波器，呈现出振荡（或者波纹状）的幅度响应。随着滤波器长度的增加，通带和阻带的谐波数就会增加，而谐波宽度降低。虽然谐波越变越窄，但其高度几乎保持不变。最大波纹出现在不连续过渡段附近且幅度与 L 无关。这种不被期望的效应叫作 Gibbs 现象。这是在时域范围内截断冲激响应方法不可避免的结果。式（3-26）所描述的截断方法可以看成有限长度序列 $\{h(n)\}$ 与矩形序列 $\{w(n)\}$ 相乘：

$$h'(n) = h(n)w(n), \quad -\infty \leqslant n \leqslant \infty \quad (3\text{-}33)$$

式中，矩形窗口 $w(n)$ 定义为

$$w(n) = \begin{cases} 1, & -M \leqslant n \leqslant M \\ 0, & \text{其他} \end{cases} \quad (3\text{-}34)$$

式（3-33）中定义的 $h'(n)$ 的离散时间傅里叶变换（DTFT）可以表示为

$$H'(\omega) = H(\omega) * W(\omega) = \frac{1}{2\pi} \int_{-\pi}^{\pi} H(\varphi) W(\omega - \varphi) d\varphi \quad (3\text{-}35)$$

式中，$W(\omega)$ 是式（3-34）中 $w(n)$ 的 DTFT 表示。这样，所设计的滤波器 $H'(\omega)$ 就是期望的滤波器 $H(\omega)$ 的修改版。

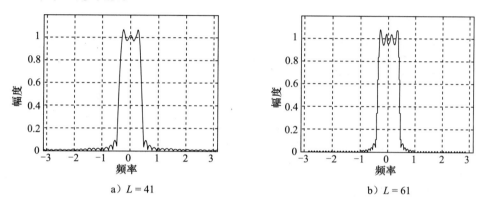

a) $L = 41$ b) $L = 61$

图 3-8 通过傅里叶级数法设计的低通滤波器的幅度响应

式（3-35）所示 $H'(\omega)$ 是通过期望频率响应 $H(\omega)$ 和矩形窗口频率响应 $W(\omega)$ 卷积而成的。如果

$$W(\omega - \varphi) = 2\pi\delta(\omega - \varphi) \quad (3\text{-}36)$$

我们得到预期结果 $H'(\omega) = H(\omega)$。式（3-36）意味着，如果 $W(\omega)$ 是一个中心为 $\omega = 0$ 的窄带脉冲，比如脉冲函数 $W(\omega) = 2\pi\delta(\omega)$，则 $H'(\omega)$ 将会非常接近 $H(\omega)$。这种情况需要优化的窗函数为

$$w(n) = 1, \quad |n| < \infty \quad (3\text{-}37)$$

4. 窗函数

在实际应用中，为了减少 FIR 滤波器的计算复杂度，窗长应越小越好。因此，我们必须用到次优窗函数，它们具有以下性质：

1）关于 $n = 0$ 是偶函数。

2）当 $|n| > M$ 时为 0。

3）由式（3-36）可知频率响应 $W(\omega)$ 具有窄的主瓣和小的旁瓣。已开发和优化大量的锥形窗口用于许多不同的应用中。有 4 种常用的窗，长度为 $L = 2M+1$，窗函数为 $w(n)$，$n = 0$, $1, \cdots, L-1$，关于中心 $n = M$ 是对称的。在 FIR 滤波器设计中，有两个窗函数的参数非常重要，它们是主瓣宽度和旁瓣相对强度。为确保从通带到阻带的快速转换，窗需要有小的主瓣宽度。另外，为了降低通带和阻带波纹，旁瓣下的面积就要小一些。遗憾的是，这就需要在这两个要求间找到折中点。

汉宁窗是一个周期的升余弦函数，定义为

$$w(n) = 0.5 \left[1 - \cos\left(\frac{2\pi n}{L-1}\right) \right], \quad n = 0, 1, \cdots, L-1 \quad (3\text{-}38)$$

注意，汉宁窗实际长度为 $L-2$，因为式（3-38）给出两边末尾值为 0。对于大的 L 值，峰值-旁瓣比大概为 31dB，高于矩形窗的 17.5dB。但它的过渡带宽度大致对应主瓣宽度，是矩形窗的 2 倍。

汉明窗函数定义为

$$w(n) = 0.54 - 0.46\cos\left(\frac{2\pi n}{L-1}\right), \quad n = 0,1,\cdots,L-1 \qquad (3-39)$$

它同样对应升余弦函数，但是常数项和余弦函数项的权值不同。汉明窗函数末尾值不是 0，而是 0.08，主瓣宽度大致与汉宁窗相同，但有另外 10dB 的阻带衰减。在设计低通滤波器时，汉明窗在整个通带有低的波纹和好的阻带衰减。相较汉宁窗，它通常更适合于设计 FIR 滤波器。

布莱克曼窗定义为

$$w(n) = 0.42 - 0.5\cos\left(\frac{2\pi n}{L-1}\right) + 0.08\cos\left(\frac{4\pi n}{L-1}\right), \quad n = 0,1,\cdots,L-1 \qquad (3-40)$$

式（3-40）中第二个余弦项的增加，作用是增加了主瓣宽度（50%），但同时也增加了峰值-旁瓣比大约到 57dB。布莱克曼窗提供 74dB 的阻带衰减，但过渡带宽是矩形窗的 6 倍。

凯撒窗函数定义为

$$w(n) = \frac{I_0\left[\beta\sqrt{1-\frac{(n-M)^2}{M^2}}\right]}{I_0(\beta)}, \quad n = 0,1,\cdots,L-1 \qquad (3-41a)$$

式中，β 是（波形）可调参数，且

$$I_0(\beta) = \sum_{k=0}^{+\infty}\left[\frac{(\beta/2)^k}{k!}\right]^2 \qquad (3-41b)$$

它是零阶修正的贝塞尔函数。在实际中，在对式（3-41b）求和时只保留前 25 项即可。因为 $I_0(0)=1$，凯撒窗在点 $n=0$ 和 $n=L-1$ 时的值为 $1/I_0(\beta)$，是关于 $n=M$ 中心对称的。这是一个既有用又灵活的窗函数族。当给定旁瓣峰值时，凯撒窗在获得主瓣最大能量方面接近最优。对于给定的阻带衰减，提供一个较宽的主瓣宽度意味着锐化的过渡带宽。对相同的 L，这个窗口可以通过选择参数 b 来确定主瓣带宽和旁瓣峰值的折中值以提供不同的过渡带宽。

在实际中，我们可以根据不同的需求选择不同的窗函数。

用窗函数设计 FIR 滤波器的过程总结如下：
1）确定满足阻带衰减要求的窗类型。
2）基于给定过渡带宽 $w(n)$，$n=0,1,\cdots,L-1$，选择窗长 L。
3）计算窗系数。
4）对期望滤波器用式（3-24）生成理想脉冲响应 $h(n)$。
5）用式（3-26）截断有限长度的理想冲激响应，得到 $h'(n)$，$-\infty \leq n \leq \infty$。
6）用式（3-28）将结果向右移动 M 个单位，形成因果滤波器，得到 b'_l，$l=0,1,\cdots,L-1$。
7）将第 3 步得到的窗口系数和第 6 步所得冲激响应系数逐个采样点相乘，即 $b_l = b'_l \cdot w(l)$，$l=0,1,\cdots,L-1$。

将窗应用于 FIR 滤波器的冲激响应有平滑所得滤波器幅度响应的效果。对称窗可以保持对称 FIR 滤波器的线性相位响应。加窗傅里叶级数这种方法的好处在于它的简易性。它不需要复杂的数学计算，可以用直接的方式实现。然而，并没有一个简单的规则来选择 M，以使设计的滤波器能精确满足给定的截止频率。这是由于我们还缺少 M 值和它的泄漏效应之间的准确关系。

3.3 语音信号处理

1. 语音信号

语音的目的就是通信。对语音通信潜在能力的表征方法有好几种。一种高度定量的方法是依据香农提出的信息论的方法。根据信息论，语音可以用它的消息内容或信息来表示。另一种表征语音的方法是利用携带消息信息的信号（即语音波形）来表示。虽然在一些复杂的通信系统中信息论的概念已经起主要作用，但在实际应用中最有用的是基于波形或某些参量模型的语音表示。

在考虑语音通信的过程时，我们对这个过程做如下设想是很有帮助的。首先设想有一条消息以某种抽象的形式表现在说话人的头脑中。在经过复杂的语音产生过程后，这些消息的信息最终转换成声学信号。在这个语音产生的过程中，可以把消息信息想象成使用很多方法表示的。例如，消息信息首先转换成一组神经信号，这些信号控制发音器官（舌、唇、声带等的运动），发音器官按照这些神经信号完成一系列的动作，最后的结果是一个包含原始消息中所有信息的声波。

通过语音进行交流的信息本质上具有离散性质，这就是说，它可以用一连串的单元符号来表示，这些单元符号来源于一个有限的符号集合。根据这些符号可以把所有的音进行分类，这些符号就是所谓的音素。每种语言都有它自己特定的音素集合，其总数一般在30～50之间。例如，英语可以用大约42个音素的集合来表示。

信息论的中心问题是信息传递的速度。对于语音，信息的传输速度可以粗略估计，因为发音器官的运动速度受到物理限制，所以人产生语音的平均速度大约是每秒10个音素。假若每个音素用一个二进制数来表示，那么英语中的全部音素用6位数码就完全足够表示了。假设平均速率是每秒10个音素，并忽略相邻音素对间的相关性，这样就可以估计出语音的平均信息速率为60bit/s。换句话说，在正常的说话速度下，与话音等效的书面文字包含60bit/s的信息。当然，语音的"实际"信息内容的下限远高于这一速度。很多因素在以上的估计中未加考虑，例如，说话人的个性和情绪、说话的速度和语音的强度等。

在语音通信系统中，语音信号以多种方式进行发送、存储和处理。从技术方面考虑语音信号有多种表示方法。一般来说，在任何系统中主要考虑两点：一是要保存语音信号中的消息内容；另一个是语音信号的表示形式应该便于传输和存储，或者十分灵活，以便在不使其消息内容受到严重损失的情况下对它进行各种变换。

语音信号的表示必须使其中的信息内容很容易被听的人提取或自动地被机器提取。语音信号（不是消息内容）的表示可能要求500bit/s～1Mbit/s的传输速率。在设计和实现这些表示方式时，信号处理的方法起着重要的作用。

2. 信号处理

信号处理示意图见图3-9。在语音信号的具体情况下，说话的人是信息源，测量或观察的一般是语音声学波形。

图3-9 信号处理示意图

信号处理包括下面几个内容，首先根据给定的模型得到信号表示，然后再用某种高级的信号变换把信号变成一种更加方便的形式。信号处理的最后一步是消息的提取和使用，这一步可以由听的人来完成，也可以用机器自动完成。例如，有一个系统，其功能是从一组给定的说话人中自动辨认出某个说话人。它所用的语音信号表示可以是时间依赖谱。一种可能的信号变换是计算整个句子的平均谱，把这个平均谱与预先保存的每个可能的说话人的平均谱模板进行比较，最后根据谱的相似度辨认说话人。在这个例子中，信号的"信息"是说话人的个性。

因此，语音信号的处理一般涉及两个任务：第一，它是得到语音信号一般表示的一种工具，这种表示既可以用波形的形式也可以用参数的形式；第二，在把信号从一种表示形式变换到另一种表示形式的过程中信号处理起着辅助的作用，变换后的表示形式虽然从本质上讲其普遍性可能较差，但更适合特定的应用。

3. 数字信号处理

我们将探讨数字技术在语音信号处理中的作用。数字信号处理关心的是如何获得信号的离散表示以及在处理这一离散表示时所用的数值方法的理论、设计和实现。数字信号处理的目的与模拟信号处理是相同的。那么，人们自然会问：在语音通信的书籍中为什么要把数字信号处理技术单独提出来加以考虑呢？对此我们可以列出很多理由。首先并且最重要的一点，是利用数字技术可以实现极其复杂的信号处理工作。此外，通常在语音信号处理中应用的算法本质上具有离散时间信号处理系统的性质。从很多方面，我们都不能把这些系统看成模拟系统的近似。实际上，在很多情况下，根本无法实现和它们相对应的模拟设备。

数字信号处理技术在最初是为仿真复杂的模拟系统而应用到语音处理问题中来的。最初的观点是把模拟系统在计算机上进行仿真，这避免了在进行参数选择或其他设计考虑的试验时需要把系统搭建起来的必要性。当首次使用数字仿真时，模拟系统要求大量的计算时间。例如，只持续几秒的语音需要多于一个小时的处理时间。到 20 世纪 60 年代中期，数字信号处理发生了重大变化。促成这一重大变化的主要因素是快速计算机的发展以及数字信号处理技术在理论上的巨大进展。这时人们开始看到数字信号处理系统所具有的能力远远超过了对模拟系统的仿真。实际上，现代水平的实验室中语音处理系统的计算机实现都被看成某种数字系统的精确仿真，这种数字系统可以由专用数字硬件或专用计算机系统实现。

除了理论上的进展外，数字硬件领域也获得了巨大的进展，这一进展使得数字处理技术与模拟系统相比时的优点更加明显。数字系统可靠且非常紧凑，集成电路工艺的进展已经达到了可以将一个极其复杂的系统在单块芯片上实现的水平。逻辑电路的工作速度也已足够快，所以在语音的采样速率下信号处理工作所要求的大量计算可以实时实现。

在语音通信系统中利用数字技术还有其他一些理由。例如，如果使用适当的编码，数字形式的语音就可以在强干扰的信道中可靠地传输。同时，数字形式的语音与其他形式的数据是相同的。这样，通信网就既可以用来传输语音也可以传输数据，除了译码以外，不需要对它们加以区别。至于要求保密的语音信号的传输，数字的表示方式较模拟系统就有更显著的优势。出于保密的需要，信息码可以用某种方法进行加密，在接收端又可以完全解密。由于这些以及其他各种原因，数字技术在语音通信中将得到日益广泛的应用。

4. 数字语音处理

在考虑数字信号处理技术在语音通信中的应用时，重点集中在三个主题比较好，这三个主题就是：语音信号的数字表示、复杂处理技术的实现以及紧密依赖数字处理的各类应用。

语音信号的数字表示当然是基本的问题。在这个问题上我们以熟知的采样定理作为依据，这个定理告诉我们只要采样的速率足够高，一个限带的信号可以用时域上周期采取的样点来表示。所以,采样过程为数字语音处理的所有理论打下了基础。语音信号的离散表示有很多种可能。如图 3-10 所示,这些表示可以分成两大类,分别称为波形表示和参数表示。顾名思义,波形表示是通过采样和量化的过程仅仅保存模拟语音信号的"波形",而参数表示则是把语音信号表示成某种语音产生的模型的输出。为了得到参数表示,第一步一般是将语音用数字波形表示,也就是对语音信号进行采样和量化,然后再进行进一步的处理以得到语音产生模型的参数。这些参数可以方便地分为两类:一类是激励参数(即有关语声源的),另一类是声道响应参数(即有关单个语声的)。

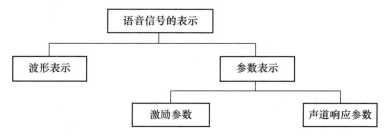

图 3-10 语音信号的表示方法

图 3-11 根据语音信号的不同表示方法对数据率的要求做了比较。在数据率约为 15 000bit/s 处的一条虚线把所有表示方法分成两部分,在其左边的是高数据率的波形表示,在其右边的是低数据率的参数表示。从这张图可以看到数据率的变化范围从 75bit/s(接近书面文字的基本消息的信息)一直到简单波形表示中的 200 000bit/s。这说明随着不同的信号表示方法,数据率的变化可以达到 3000∶1。当然,在选择语音表示方法时,数据率并不是唯一的考虑因素,还有很多其他的考虑因素,比如价格、表示的灵活性、语音的质量等。

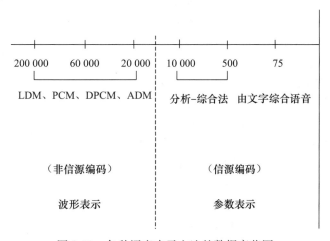

图 3-11 各种语音表示方法的数据率范围

在选择信号表示以及随后所用的数字信号处理方法时,最重要的考虑可能是应用本身。图 3-12 给出了语音通信中的若干典型应用。这里对这些领域逐个加以简要的讨论。

语音的数字传输和存储

语音处理最早和最重要的一种应用是 Homer Dudly 在 20 世纪 30 年代发明的声码器。声码器的目的是减少传输语音信号所需要的带宽。尽管卫星、微波和光通信系统提供了很宽的频带,但在很多情况下仍需要节省带宽。而且,为了适应全数字电话设备中今后要使用的低廉终端,就需要用尽可能低的比特率把语音数字化,对这种系统的需求日益突出。同时,对语音信号进行非常复杂的加密的可能性也极大地推动了数字传输在很多方面的应用。

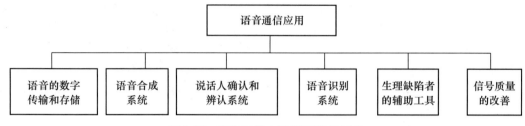

图 3-12　语音通信中的若干典型应用

语音合成系统

人们对语音合成系统的兴趣主要是由在计算机语声应答系统中需要对语音进行经济的数字存储的需求引起的。计算机语声应答系统基本上就是一个全数字的自动信息服务系统，人们可以用键盘或终端对它提出询问，而它则用语音告诉人们所要的信息。因为普通的按键电话就可以作为这样一个系统的键盘，所以这样的自动信息服务系统可以在电话交换设备上普遍使用而不需要增加专门的设备。在研究人类语音产生的过程中语音合成系统也起着重要的作用。

说话人确认和辨认系统

说话人确认和辨认技术涉及从大型的可能的说话人集合中证实或辨别出一个说话人。说话人确认系统必须确定某一说话人是否是它声称的那个，这样的系统可以应用于对信息的访问要求加以控制或限制范围的场合，还可以用于各种自动的信贷交易中。说话人辨认系统必须在说话人的集合中确定某一特定语调的语音是哪一个说话人说的，这种系统可用于法庭审讯。

语音识别系统

语音识别最一般的形式是把语音波形变换成等价的书面消息。语音识别问题的本质在很大程度上依赖于对说话人、说话的情景以及消息内容的限制。语音识别系统可能的应用是多种多样的，例如，语音操作打字机和对计算机的语音通信。此外，语音识别系统与语音合成系统相结合可以构成比特率极低的通信系统。

生理缺陷者的辅助工具

该应用涉及语音信号处理中提供可用信息的一种形式，这种形式相对于一般情况更适用于在生理上有缺陷的人。例如，预录磁带的可变速重放为盲人读者提供了一种机会，使他可以按照任何希望的速度去阅读给定的语音材料。此外，各种各样的信号处理技术也已经用来设计语音信息的知觉辅助器和视觉显示装置，利用这些来教聋哑人讲话。

信号质量的改善

在很多情况下，质量太差的语音信号会影响通信的有效性。在这种情况下我们可以用数字信号处理技术来改善语音的质量。属于这类应用的例子有：语音信号中混响（或回音）的消除或语音信号中噪声的消除。

Chapter 4

Communication Technology

(通信技术)

4.1 Electromagnetic Fields Theory

Franklin, Coulomb, Ampere, Faraday and other scientists have the curiosity of natural phenomena, perseverance to explore and indomitable study, guide them to discover electrical and magnetic phenomena and laws. The spirit of seeking truth and being pragmatic, daring to practice and daring to innovate is worth learning.

In 1864, James Clerk Maxwell presented nine equations summarizing all known laws on electricity and magnetism. This was one of the most successful theories in the history of science. By postulating the need for an additional term to make the set of equations self-consistent, Maxwell was able to put forth what is still considered a complete theory of macroscopic electromagnetism. To form a complete field theory we need a source field, a mediating field, and a set of field differential equations. This allows us to mathematically describe the relationship between effect (the mediating field) and cause (the source field). In a well-posed postulate we must also include a set of constitutive relationships and a specification of some field relationship over a bounding surface and at an initial time. If the electromagnetic field is to have physical meaning, we must link it to some observable quantity such as force. Finally, to allow the solution of problems involving mathematical discontinuities we must specify certain boundary, or "jump" conditions.

In Maxwell's equations, the source field consists of the vector field $\boldsymbol{J}(r,t)$ (the current density) and the scalar field $\rho(r,t)$ (the charge density), the mediating field is the electromagnetic field consisting of the set of four vector fields $\boldsymbol{E}(r,t)$, $\boldsymbol{D}(r,t)$, $\boldsymbol{B}(r,t)$ and $\boldsymbol{H}(r,t)$.

$\boldsymbol{E}$ = electric field intensity (vector), volts/meter (V/m)

$\boldsymbol{H}$ = magnetic field intensity (vector), amperes/meter (A/m)

$\boldsymbol{D}$ = electric flux density (vector), coulombs/meter^2 (C/m^2)

$\boldsymbol{B}$ = magnetic flux density (vector), webers/meter^2 (Wb/m^2)

$\boldsymbol{J}$ = current density (vector), amperes/meter^2 (A/m^2)

ρ = charge density (scalar), coulombs/meter^3 (C/m^3)

All the above quantities, in time-varying fields, are arbitrary real functions of space, i.e. the position vector r(m) and time t(s) while they are just functions of r in the static fields.

Two new concepts should be built: the electric field can be produced by changing magnetic field and the magnetic field produced by changing electric field. So we call it electromagnetic field.

1. Maxwell's Equations

Maxwell's equations are the most important and fundamental equations of electromagnetic theorem. They are described as follows.

$$\oint_C \boldsymbol{H} \cdot d\boldsymbol{l} = \int_S \left(\boldsymbol{J} + \frac{\partial \boldsymbol{D}}{\partial t}\right) \cdot d\boldsymbol{S} \quad \text{(Generalized Ampere's Law or Maxwell's first equation)} \quad (4\text{-}1)$$

Its left side is the closed-loop or line integral (the integral along the closed-path line C) of a magnetic field intensity $\boldsymbol{H}$. Its right side is the surface integral of the total current density, i.e. the sum of the current density $\boldsymbol{J}$ due to the flow of electric charge (commonly, it is just the conduction current) and the displacement current whose density is equal to the time derivative of electric flux density (electric displacement density).

$$\boldsymbol{J}_d = \frac{\partial \boldsymbol{D}}{\partial t} \quad (4\text{-}2)$$

The integral is taken over any surface bounded by contour C.

$$\oint_C \boldsymbol{E} \cdot d\boldsymbol{l} = -\int_S \frac{\partial \boldsymbol{B}}{\partial t} \cdot d\boldsymbol{S} \quad \text{(Faraday's Law or Maxwell's second equation)} \quad (4\text{-}3)$$

This law states that the emf ε induced in the closed-path by a changing magnetic field is equal to the time rate of decrease of the magnetic flux linking the loop.

$$\oint_S \boldsymbol{B} \cdot d\boldsymbol{S} = 0 \quad \text{(Gauss' Law for Magnetic Field or Maxwell's third equation)} \quad (4\text{-}4)$$

The law says that the magnetic flux through any closed surface is equal to zero.

$$\oint_S \boldsymbol{D} \cdot d\boldsymbol{S} = \int_V \rho dV \quad \text{(Gauss' Law for Electric Field or Maxwell's forth equation)} \quad (4\text{-}5)$$

The law tells us that the outward flux of density $\boldsymbol{D}$ through a closed surface is equal to the charge enclosed within the surface.

These equations are in integral forms. Two fundamental theorems are used to rewrite Maxwell's equations into differential forms. Stokes theorem relates the line integral of an arbitrary vector $\boldsymbol{A}$ with the surface integral of the curl of this vector:

$$\oint_C \boldsymbol{A} \cdot d\boldsymbol{l} = \int_S (\nabla \times \boldsymbol{A}) \cdot d\boldsymbol{S} \quad (4\text{-}6)$$

where the direction of the closed line integral C follows the right-hand rule of the normal direction of the surface S. Similarly, by Divergence theorem (or Gauss'Law), the close surface integral of $\boldsymbol{A}$ over a surface S is equal to the volume integral of the divergence of $\boldsymbol{A}$ over the volume V enclosed by S:

$$\oint_S \boldsymbol{A} \cdot d\boldsymbol{S} = \int_V \nabla \cdot \boldsymbol{A} \cdot dV \quad (4\text{-}7)$$

where the normal direction of S is outward.

The differential forms of Maxwell's equations are listed below:

$$\nabla \times \boldsymbol{H} = \boldsymbol{J} + \frac{\partial \boldsymbol{D}}{\partial t}, \quad \nabla \times \boldsymbol{E} = -\frac{\partial \boldsymbol{B}}{\partial t}, \quad \nabla \cdot \boldsymbol{B} = 0, \quad \nabla \cdot \boldsymbol{D} = \rho \qquad (4\text{-}8)$$

These four equations explain the total relationships between electromagnetic sources and the fields:
①The conduction current and the displacement current are the curl sources of the magnetic fields.
②Time varying magnetic field produces an electric field.
③The magnetic fields are solenoidal fields.
④The electric charges are the divergence sources of the electric fields.

These equations describe the motion law of the time-varying electromagnetic field and reveal the philosophical idea of the unity of opposites, that electricity and magnetism excite and restrict each other in nature.

2. Current Continuity Equation

Although it isn't given in Maxwell's equations, we can get it from Maxwell's equations. For example:

$$\nabla \cdot (\nabla \times \boldsymbol{H}) = \nabla \cdot \left(\boldsymbol{J} + \frac{\partial \boldsymbol{D}}{\partial t}\right), \quad \text{div curl } \boldsymbol{H} = 0, \quad \text{div } \boldsymbol{D} = \rho$$

then the equation of continuity can be concluded as

$$\nabla \cdot \boldsymbol{J} = -\frac{\partial \rho}{\partial t} \qquad (4\text{-}9)$$

3. Constitutive Relations

The vector equations and the scalar equations are equivalent to eight scalar equations for twelve scalar unknowns (three component for every field vector $\boldsymbol{E}, \boldsymbol{D}, \boldsymbol{B}, \boldsymbol{H}$), even if we consider the charge density ρ and the current density $\boldsymbol{J}$ as given quantities.

To allow a unique determination of the field vectors, Maxwell's equations must be supplemented by relations describing the behavior of the medium under the influence of the field. These subsidiary relations are called constitutive relations that are established by experimentation or deduced from atomic theory.

If the field vectors are linearly related so that the principle of superposition applies, the medium is said to be linear. A combination of Maxwell's equations and linear constitutive relations forms the basis of linear electrodynamics.

In free space, the constitutive relations take the simplest forms:

$$\boldsymbol{D} = \varepsilon_0 \boldsymbol{E}, \quad \boldsymbol{B} = \mu_0 \boldsymbol{H} \qquad (4\text{-}10)$$

where $\varepsilon_0 = 8.854 \times 10^{-12} \text{F/m} \approx \frac{1}{36\pi} \times 10^{-9} \text{F/m}$, $\mu_0 = 4\pi \times 10^{-7} \text{H/m}$.

A medium is said to be isotropic if the electrical and magnetic properties at a given point are independent of the direction of the field at the point. For example, in simple matter:

$$\boldsymbol{D} = \varepsilon \boldsymbol{E}, \quad \boldsymbol{B} = \mu \boldsymbol{H}, \quad \boldsymbol{J} = \sigma \boldsymbol{E} \qquad (4\text{-}11)$$

where the dielectric constant ε, the relative permeability μ, and the conductivity σ are scalars. If ε, μ and σ have the same values at every point in space, the medium is said to be homogeneous.

On the other hand, if the electrical and magnetic properties of a medium depend upon the directions of field vectors, the medium is called anisotropic. For example:

$$\boldsymbol{D} = \varepsilon_0 \varepsilon_r \boldsymbol{E}, \quad \boldsymbol{B} = \mu_0 \mu_r \boldsymbol{H} \qquad (4\text{-}12)$$

where ε and μ are respectively the dielectric and permeability tensors.

When the constitutive relations are used in the Maxwell's equations, the unknown vectors are just E, H or D, B.

4. Boundary Conditions

The Maxwell's equations are valid in regions where the physical properties of the medium vary continuously. However, across any surface which bounds one medium from another the constitutive parameters such as ε, μ or σ may change abruptly, and we may expect corresponding change in the field vectors. In order to continue the solution of Maxwell's equations from one region to another so that the resulting solution is unique and valid everywhere, we need boundary conditions to impose on the field vectors and the interface. The boundary conditions between these two sets of fields at the interface S can be derived from the integral form of Maxwell's equations. Consider two different media with material properties $(\varepsilon_1, \mu_1, \sigma_1)$ and $(\varepsilon_2, \mu_2, \sigma_2)$ respectively separated by an interface S as shown in Fig. 4-1. Let the electromagnetic fields in these two media be denoted as (E_1, H_1, D_1, B_1) and (E_2, H_2, D_2, B_2).

Denote the unit vector n of S as the normal direction from medium 1 to medium 2 and take the surface integral in Maxwell's equations over the closed surface of a small cylinder. The contribution from the curved surface of the cylinder is directly proportional to Δh, and, for a sufficiently small cross-sectional area ΔS of the cylinder, B may be constant over each end. In the limit as $\Delta h \to 0$, the ends of the cylinder lie just on either side of S and the contribution from the curved surface becomes vanishingly small. Thus we obtain

$$n \cdot (B_1 - B_2) = 0 \tag{4-13}$$

which states that the normal component of B across a boundary surface of two media must be continuous.

Similary, carrying out the integral of D, we obtain

$$n \cdot (D_1 - D_2) = \rho_{sf} \tag{4-14}$$

which states that in the presence of layer of surface charge density ρ_{sf} on S, the normal component of D changes abruptly across the interface, and the amount of discontinuity is equal to the surface charge density. If there is no surface charge ($\rho_{sf} = 0$) on S as in the case of two different dielectrics, the normal component of D must be continuous.

Turning next to the behavior of the tangential components, we replace the cylinder by a small rectangular loop of area ΔA bounded by sides of length Δl, parallel to the interface S, and ends of length Δh, perpendicular to S as shown in Fig. 4-2. When $\Delta h \to 0$, we have

$$n \times (E_1 - E_2) = 0 \tag{4-15}$$

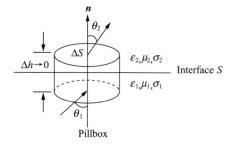

Fig. 4-1 Pillbox used in obtaining boundary conditions for D, B

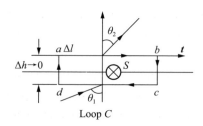

Fig. 4-2 Rectangular loop used in obtaining boundary conditions for E, H

which states that the tangential component of E across a boundary surface of two media must be continuous. It can be expressed in terms of the unit tangent vector t as

$$(E_1 - E_2) \cdot t = 0 \tag{4-16}$$

then we can get

$$n \times (H_1 - H_2) = J_{sf} \tag{4-17}$$

which states that the tangential component of H across any boundary surface of two media is discontinuous, and the amount of discontinuity is equal to the surface current density. If the current density J is finite, as it must be in any medium of finite conductivity, then we have

$$n \times (H_1 - H_2) = 0 \tag{4-18}$$

As a special case, if medium 1 is a perfect electric conductor ($\sigma_1 \to \infty$) and medium 2 is a perfect dielectric ($\sigma_2 \to 0$), surface conduction electric current and charge densities may exist, then all the field vectors in medium 1 vanish identically and the boundary conditions become

$$n \times H_2 = J_{sf}, \quad n \times E_2 = 0, \quad n \cdot B_2 = 0, \quad n \cdot D_2 = \rho_{sf} \tag{4-19}$$

Note that the surface electric charge density and electric current density are also governed by the continuity equation.

5. Power and Energy

From the Maxwell's equations we may formulate the law of conservation of energy for the electromagnetic system. We start from the vector identity

$$\nabla \cdot (E \times H) = H \cdot (\nabla \times E) - E \cdot (\nabla \times H) \tag{4-20}$$

and make use of Maxwell's equations differential form. We obtain the following relation:

$$\nabla \cdot (E \times H) = -H \cdot \frac{\partial B}{\partial t} - E \cdot \frac{\partial D}{\partial t} + E \cdot J \tag{4-21}$$

Then by performing a volume integral over V bounded by the closed surface S and Gauss theorem, we obtain the following relation:

$$-\oint_S (E \times H) \cdot dS = \frac{1}{2} \int_V \left(H \cdot \frac{\partial B}{\partial t} + E \cdot \frac{\partial D}{\partial t} \right) dV - \int_V E \cdot J dV \tag{4-22}$$

Therefore, this equation is nothing but the conservation of energy within a volume V and is known as the integral form of Poynting theorem. It is a power theorem. The time rate of increase of the electromagnetic energy over an arbitrary volume V is equal to the sum of the power crossing the closed surface S and the dissipation of heat inside the volume V. It applies even if the medium is inhomegeneous.

We can define the Poyting vector (power density, measured in W/m^2) as $S = E \times H$ which represents the amount of power crossing a unit area in the direction perpendicular to both E and H, and

$$P = \int_V J \cdot E dV \tag{4-23}$$

is the joule heat which represents the energy dissipated in a medium per unit volume per second.

We may interpret w as the electromagnetic energy density measured in joules per cubic meter (J/m^3). Let us assume that in the remote past, there is no stored energy because the fields are zero. We obtain the total instantaneous energy density as

$$w = w_e + w_m \tag{4-24}$$

where

$$w_e = \int E \cdot \frac{\partial D}{\partial t} dt \tag{4-25}$$

is the instantaneous electric energy density and

$$w_m = \int \boldsymbol{H} \cdot \frac{\partial \boldsymbol{B}}{\partial t} \, dt \tag{4-26}$$

is the instantaneous magnetic energy density.

Let us consider an isotropic, nondispersive, lossless medium, the electric and magnetic energy densities are

$$w_e = \frac{1}{2} \boldsymbol{E} \cdot \boldsymbol{D} = \frac{1}{2} \varepsilon E^2 \tag{4-27}$$

$$w_m = \frac{1}{2} \boldsymbol{H} \cdot \boldsymbol{B} = \frac{1}{2} \mu H^2 \tag{4-28}$$

Note that these quantities are in general functions of both position and time.

NEW WORDS AND PHRASES

vector　n.　[数] 向量，矢量；vt. 无线电导引
scalar　n.　数量，标量；adj. 梯状的，分等级的，数量的，标量的
position vector　位矢，方位向量，位置矢量
flux　n.　[物] 流量，通量，涨潮，变迁；vi. 熔化，流出；vt. 使熔融，用焊剂处理
contour　n.　轮廓，周线，等高线
emf　abbr.　电动势（electromotive force）
Stokes theorem　斯托克斯定理
divergence theorem　散度定理
conduction current　传导电流
displacement current　位移电流
solenoidal field　螺线管磁场，无散场
continuity equation　连续性方程
constitutive relation　本构关系
isotropic　adj.　等方向性的，各向同性的
dielectric constant　介电常数
relative permeability　相对磁导率
conductivity　n.　传导性，传导率
anisotropic　adj.　各向异性的
tensor　n.　张量，张肌

NOTES

1) The conduction current and the displacement current are the curl sources of the magnetic fields.
   传导电流和位移电流之和是磁场的旋度源。
2) A medium is said to be isotropic if the electrical and magnetic properties at a given point are independent of the direction of the field at the point.
   若给定点的电磁特性与场在该点的方向无关，则称媒质为各向同性的。
3) If the electrical and magnetic properties of a medium depend upon the directions of field vectors, the medium is called anisotropic.
   若媒质的电磁场特性与场矢量的方向有关，则该媒质是各向异性的。
4) The boundary conditions between these two sets of fields at the interface S can be derived from the integral form of Maxwell's equations.
   两组场在分界面 S 上的边界条件可通过麦克斯韦方程组的积分形式得到。

EXERCISES

1. Please translate the following words and phrases into Chinese.

   a) time-varying field　　b) displacement current　　c) divergence source
   d) emf　　　　　　　　　e) vector field　　　　　　 f) differential
   g) equation　　　　　　　h) flux　　　　　　　　　　i) boundary condition

j) integral form

2. **Please translate the following words and phrases into English.**

   a) 传导率　　　　　　　b) 介电常数　　　　　　c) 磁场强度
   d) 闭合回路　　　　　　e) 电通量密度　　　　　f) 面积分
   g) 传导电流　　　　　　h) 各向异性的　　　　　i) 相对磁导率
   j) 本构关系

3. **Fill in the blanks with the missing word(s).**

   a) Its right side is the _____ of the total current density, i. e. the sum of the _____ J due to the flow of electric charge (commonly, it is just the _____) and the displacement current whose density is equal to the time derivative of _____ (electric displacement density).

   b) The boundary conditions between these two sets of fields at the interface S can be derived from the _____ form of Maxwell's equations.

   c) Faraday's Law states that the emf ε induced in the closed-path by a changing magnetic field is equal to the time rate of _____ of the magnetic flux linking the loop.

4. **Answer the following questions according to the text.**

   a) What are the basic equations of Maxwell's equations, including the integral and differential forms?
   b) What kind of medium is isotropic and what is anisotropic?
   c) What are the relationships between the sources and the fields?
   d) What are the boundary conditions of Maxwell's equations?
   e) Why do Maxwell's equations must be supplemented? What are the subsidiary relations?

READING

Antennas

An antenna is a device that converts RF power applied to its feed point into electromagnetic radiation and intercepts energy from a passing electromagnetic radiation, which then appears as RF voltage across the antenna's feed point. The official IEEE definition of an antenna as given by Stutzman and Thiele follows the concept: "That part of a transmitting or receiving system that is designed to radiate or receive electromagnetic waves." An antenna acts as a transitional structure between the guiding device (e.g. waveguide, transmission line) and the free space. Antennas can be considered as one of the most important parts of the radio-communication chain.

1. How an Antenna Radiates

In order to know how an antenna radiates, let us first consider how radiation occurs. A conducting wire radiates mainly because of time-varying current or an acceleration (or deceleration) of charge. If there is no motion of charges in a wire, no radiation takes place, since no flow of current occurs. Radiation will not occur even if charges are moving with uniform velocity along a straight wire. However, charges moving with uniform velocity along a curved or bent wire will produce radiation. If the charge is oscillating with time, then

天线

天线是将馈电点的射频能量转换为电磁辐射,将接收到的电磁辐射能量转化为天线的馈电点的 RF 电压设备。Stutzman 和 Thiele 给出了 IEEE 关于天线概念的官方定义:天线是一种发射或接收系统,旨在发射或接收电磁波。天线充当一个在导行设备(如波导、传输线)和自由空间之间的过渡结构。天线可被视为无线通信链最重要的一部分。

1. 天线是如何辐射的

为了了解天线是如何辐射的,首先我们来考虑一下辐射是如何产生的。导线产生辐射主要是因为时变电流或者电荷的加速(或减速)。一根导线如果没有电荷的运动,就不能产生辐射,因为没有电流产生。如果电荷沿直导线匀速直线运动,那么也不会产生辐射。但是,如果电荷沿曲线或折线匀速运动,则会产生辐射。

radiation occurs even along a straight wire.

When a sinusoidal voltage is applied across the transmission line, an electric field is created which is sinusoidal in nature and this result in the creation of electric lines of force which are tangential to the electric field. The magnitude of the electric field is indicated by the bunching of the electric lines of force. The free electrons in the conductors are forcibly displaced by the electric lines of force and the movement of these charges causes the flow of current which in turn leads to the creation of a magnetic field.

Due to the time varying electric and magnetic fields, electromagnetic waves are created and these travel between the conductors. As these waves approach open space, free space waves are formed by connecting the open ends of the electric lines. Since the sinusoidal source continuously creates the electric disturbance, electromagnetic waves are created continuously and these travel through the transmission line, through the antenna and are radiated into the free space. Inside the transmission line and the antenna, the electromagnetic waves are sustained due to the charges, but as soon as they enter the free space, they form closed loops and radiate.

2. Basic Antenna Parameters

An antenna is a device that is made to efficiently radiate and receive radiated electromagnetic waves. There are several important antenna characteristics that should be considered when choosing an antenna for our applications.

Antenna Radiation Patterns

Antenna radiation pattern, shown as Fig. 4-3, is a graphic representation of directional properties of the antenna. Directional properties are usually expressed in the form of the absolute value of the radio of electric intensity of the radiated wave in a given direction and its maximum value (computation is performed for the far field of the antenna). Directivity pattern is usually drawn for a certain plane (e.g., plane perpendicular to the dipole, plane containing the dipole). An antenna radiation pattern can be displayed in two kinds of graphics: those displaying the E-plane (or E-field for electric field) and the H-plane (or H-field for magnetic field).

如果电荷随时间振荡,则沿直线运动也会产生辐射。

当正弦电压加在传输线上时,自然将产生正弦电场,该电场电力线的方向是电场的切线方向。电场的幅度表示电力线的最大值。导体中的自由电荷被迫分离,电荷的移动产生电流,电流产生磁场。

时变电场和时变磁场产生电磁波,且在导体中流动。当电磁波遇到开放的空间时,导线的开放端形成自由空间波。由于正弦波不断地产生电磁干扰,电磁波不断地产生,通过传输线、天线最后辐射到自由空间。在传输线和天线内部,电磁波的持续存在是由于电荷,只要电磁波进入自由空间,就形成封闭的环路并进行辐射。

2. 天线的基本电参数

天线是有效地接收和辐射电磁波的设备。在应用中选择天线时需要考虑几个重要的天线特性参数。

天线的辐射方向图

图 4-3 为天线的辐射方向图,天线的方向图是用图形表示天线方向性的一种方法。方向性通常以给定方向上辐射波电场强度绝对值和它的最大值表示(以天线的远场计算)。方向图通常画在一个特定的平面(如垂直于偶极子的平面和包含偶极子的平面)。有两种天线辐射方向图:E 面(或电场)方向图和 H 面(或磁场)方向图。

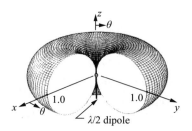

Fig. 4-3 Antenna radiation pattern

From the field pattern, we can get the following parameters of antenna:
- HPBW: the Half Power Beamwidth (HPBW) can be defined as the angle subtended by the half power points of the main lobe.
- Main lobe: this is the radiation lobe containing the direction of maximum radiation.
- Minor lobe: all the lobes other than the main lobe are called the minor lobes. These lobes represent the radiation in undesired directions. The level of minor lobes is usually expressed as a ratio of the power density in the lobe in question to that of the major lobe. This ratio is called as the side lobe level (expressed in decibels).
- Back lobe: this is the minor lobe diametrically opposite to the main lobe.
- Side lobes: these are the minor lobes adjacent to the main lobe and are separated by various nulls. Side lobes are generally the largest among the minor lobes.

In most wireless systems, minor lobes are undesired. Hence a good antenna design should minimize the minor lobes.

Directivity

The directivity of an antenna has been defined as "the ratio of the radiation intensity in a given direction from the antenna to the radiation intensity averaged over all directions". In other words, the directivity of a nonisotropic source is equal to the ratio of its radiation intensity in a given direction, over that of an isotropic source:

$$D = \frac{U}{U_i} = \frac{4\pi U}{P} \quad (4\text{-}29)$$

where D is the directivity of the antenna, U is the radiation intensity of the antenna, U_i is the radiation intensity of an isotropic source, P is the total power radiated.

Sometimes, the direction of the directivity is not specified. In this case, the direction of the maximum radiation intensity is implied and the maximum directivity is given as

$$D_{max} = \frac{U_{max}}{U_i} = \frac{4\pi U_{max}}{P} \quad (4\text{-}30)$$

where D_{max} is the maximum directivity, U_{max} is the maximum radiation intensity.

Directivity is a dimensionless quantity, since it is the ratio of two radiation intensities. Hence, it is generally expressed in dB. The directivity of an antenna can be easily estimated from the radiation pattern of the antenna. An antenna that has a narrow main lobe would have better directivity, then the one which has a broad main lobe, hence it is more directive.

通过场图，我们能得到如下天线参数。
- HPBW：半功率波瓣宽度，定义为主瓣半功率点的夹角。
- 主瓣：包含最大辐射方向的辐射瓣。
- 副瓣：除了主瓣外的所有波瓣都称为副瓣。这些波瓣代表在不需要的方向上的辐射。副瓣电平通常表示为主瓣与副瓣功率密度的比值。这个比值称为旁瓣电平（用dB表示）。
- 后瓣：指与主瓣相对的波瓣。
- 旁瓣：指与主瓣相邻的副瓣，中间有零辐射点分开。旁瓣通常是副瓣中最大的。

在大多数无线系统中，副瓣都是不需要的。因此一个性能良好的天线设计应该将副瓣最小化。

方向性系数

天线的方向性系数定义为给定方向上天线的辐射功率密度与所有方向上的平均辐射功率密度之比。换句话说，非各向同性源的方向性等于在给定方向上其辐射强度与各向同性源辐射强度的比：

式中，D是天线的方向性系数，U是天线的辐射强度，U_i是各向同性源的辐射强度，P是总辐射功率。

有时，没有指定方向性系数的方向。这种情况意味着最大辐射强度方向，最大方向性系数定义为

式中，D_{max}是最大方向性系数，U_{max}是最大辐射强度。

方向性系数是一个无纲量的量，因为它是两个辐射强度的比值。因此，它通常用dB表示。我们能够容易地从辐射方向图中估计出天线的方向性。主瓣窄的天线有较好的方向性，主瓣宽的天线会覆盖较宽的方向。

Input Impedance

The input impedance of an antenna is defined as "the impedance presented by an antenna at its terminals or the ratio of the voltage to the current at the pair of terminals or the ratio of the appropriate components of the electric to magnetic fields at a point." Hence the input impedance of the antenna can be written as

$$Z_{in} = R_{in} + jX_{in} \tag{4-31}$$

where Z_{in} is the antenna impedance at the terminals, R_{in} is the antenna resistance at the terminals, X_{in} is the antenna reactance at the terminals.

Gain

Antenna gain is a parameter which is closely related to the directivity of the antenna. We know that the directivity is how much an antenna concentrates energy in one direction in preference to radiation in other directions. Hence, if the antenna is 100% efficient, then the directivity would be equal to the antenna gain and the antenna would be an isotropic radiator. All antennas will radiate more in some direction than in others. The gain is always related to the main lobe and is specified in the direction of maximum radiation unless indicated. It is given as

$$G(\theta,\varphi) = e_{cd}D(\theta,\varphi) \tag{4-32}$$

where G is expressed in dB (10 times the common logarithm of the power ratio or 20 times the common logarithm of the voltage ratio).

Antenna Polarization

Polarization of a radiated wave is defined as "that property of an electromagnetic wave describing the time varying direction and relative magnitude of the electric field vector." The polarization of an antenna refers to the polarization of the electric field vector of the radiated wave. In other words, the position and direction of the electric field with reference to the earth's surface or ground determines the wave polarization. The most common types of polarization include the linear (horizontal or vertical), circular (Right Hand Circular Polarization (RHCP) or the Left Hand Circular Polarization (LHCP)), Elliptical Right Hand and Elliptical Left Hand. An antenna erected vertically is said to be "vertically polarized" while an antenna erected horizontally is said to be "horizontally polarized." Other specialized antennas exist with "cross polarization", having both vertical and horizontal components and we can have circular polarization.

Polarization is important if you are trying to get the maximum performance from the antennas. For best performance you will need to match up the polarization of the transmitting antenna and the receiving antenna. When a signal is transmitted at one polarization but received at a different polarization there exist a great many decibels of loss.

输入阻抗

天线的输入阻抗定义为天线输入端的阻抗值,或者在天线输入端的输入电压与电流之比,或者某一点上电磁与磁场的比值。因此天线的输入阻抗表达式为

$$Z_{in} = R_{in} + jX_{in} \tag{4-31}$$

式中,Z_{in} 为输入阻抗,R_{in} 为输入电阻,X_{in} 为输入电抗。

增益

天线的增益是与天线的方向性密切相关的参数。我们知道方向性系数是天线集中在一个方向上的能量,此方向的能量大于其他方向的能量。因此,如果天线的效率是100%,那么方向性系数等于天线的增益,天线是一个各向同性辐射器。所有天线在某方向上辐射的能量要比其他方向上多。增益与主瓣有关,通常指最大辐射方向,除非另有说明。增益的表达式为

$$G(\theta,\varphi) = e_{cd}D(\theta,\varphi) \tag{4-32}$$

式中,G 用 dB 表示(功率比常用对数的10倍,电压比常用对数的20倍)。

天线的极化

辐射波的极化定义为"用电场矢量随时间变化的方向和相对幅值所描绘的电磁波的特性"。天线的极化指辐射波的电场矢量的极化。换句话说,与地球表面或地面一致的电场的方向和位置决定了波的极化。常见的极化类型包括线极化(水平或垂直)、圆极化(右旋圆极化或左旋圆极化)、右旋椭圆极化和左旋椭圆极化。垂直架设的天线称为"垂直极化",水平架设的天线称为"水平极化"。一些特殊的天线存在"交叉极化",既有垂直极化分量,也有水平极化分量,我们称其为圆极化。

如果你想让天线达到最佳性能,那么极化是很重要的。发射天线和接收天线的极化匹配才能达到最佳性能。当发射端是一种极化而接收端是不同的极化时,会产生很大的损耗。

Bandwidth

The bandwidth of an antenna is defined as "the range of usable frequencies within which the performance of the antenna, with respect to some characteristic, conforms to a specified standard." The bandwidth can be the range of frequencies on either side of the center frequency where the antenna characteristics like input impedance, radiation pattern, beamwidth, polarization, side lobe level or gain, are close to those values which have been obtained at the center frequency. The bandwidth of a broadband antenna can be defined as the ratio of the upper to lower frequencies of acceptable operation. The bandwidth of a narrowband antenna can be defined as the percentage of the frequency difference over the center frequency. These definitions can be written in terms of equations as follows:

$$BW_{broadband} = \frac{f_H}{f_L} \qquad (4\text{-}33)$$

$$BW_{narrowband}(\%) = \frac{f_H - f_L}{f_0} \qquad (4\text{-}34)$$

where f_H = upper frequency, f_L = lower frequency, f_0 = center frequency.

An antenna is said to be broadband if $\frac{f_H}{f_L} = 2$. One method of judging how efficiently an antenna is operating over the required range of frequencies is by measuring its VSWR. A VSWR ≤ 2 ensures good performance.

The Near and Far Field

The field patterns, associated with an antenna, change with distance and are associated with two types of energy: radiating energy and reactive energy. Hence, the space surrounding an antenna can be divided into two regions.

The Near Field is an electromagnetic field that exists within ~ $\lambda/2$ of the antenna. It temporarily stores power and is related to the imaginary term of the input impedance. The Far Field is an electromagnetic field launched by the antenna that extends throughout all space. This field transports power and is related to the radiation resistance of the antenna.

3. Antennas Types

Antennas come in different shapes and sizes to suit different types of wireless applications. The characteristics of an antenna are very much determined by its shape, size and the type of material that it is made of. Antennas can be divided into two categories: wire antennas and aperture antennas. Some of the commonly used antennas are briefly described below (see Fig. 4-4).

Half Wave Dipole

The length of this antenna $2l$ is equal to half of its wavelength as the name itself suggests. Dipoles can be shorter or

带宽

天线的带宽定义为"天线的某些特性符合具体标准的可用频率范围"。天线的带宽是中心频率两边的频率范围,天线的特性(如输入阻抗值、辐射方向图、波瓣宽度、极化特性、旁瓣电平或增益)接近中心频率处的值。宽带天线的带宽定义为可接受工作范围内的上限频率与下限频率的比值。窄带天线定义为超过中心频率的频率差的比率。这些定义以方程式表示如下:

式中,f_H 为上限频率,f_L 为下限频率,f_0 为中心频率。

当 $\frac{f_H}{f_L} = 2$ 时,称天线是宽带天线。判断天线工作在所需频率范围的有效性方法之一是测量其驻波比。驻波比小于或等于 2 是良好性能的保证。

近场和远场

天线的辐射场随距离变化,并与两种类型的能量有关:辐射能量和感应能量。因此,天线周围的空间分为两个区域。

近场是在天线约 $\lambda/2$ 以内的电磁场。它暂时存储功率,并与输入阻抗的电抗部分有关。远场是通过天线激发并延伸到整个空间的电磁场。该场传输功率,并与天线的辐射电阻有关。

3. 天线类型

针对不同类型的无线应用,天线有不同的形状和尺寸。天线的特性完全由它的形状、尺寸和制作材料决定。天线可分为两类:线天线和口径天线。下面简要介绍一些常用的天线(见图4-4)。

半波偶极子天线

顾名思义,这种天线长 $2l$,等于波长的一半。偶极子天线可以比半个波长短,

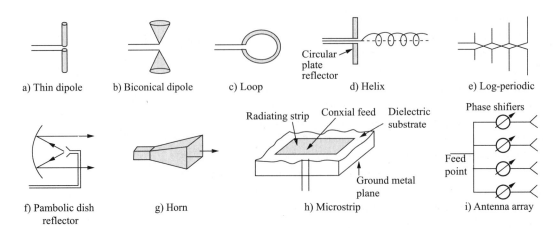

Fig. 4-4　Different kinds of antennas

longer than half the wavelength, but a tradeoff exists in the performance and hence the half wave dipole is widely used.

　　The dipole antenna is fed by a two-wire transmission line, where the two currents in the conductors are of sinusoidal distribution and equal in amplitude, but opposite in direction. Hence, due to canceling effects, no radiation occurs from the transmission line. The currents in the arms of the dipole are in the same direction and they produce radiation in the horizontal direction. Thus, for a vertical orientation, the dipole radiates in the horizontal direction. The typical gain of the dipole is 2dB and it has a bandwidth of about 10%. The half power beamwidth is about 78 degrees in the E plane and its directivity is 1.64 (2.15dB) with a radiation resistance of 73Ω.

Monopole Antenna

　　The monopole antenna results from applying the image theory to the dipole. According to this theory, if a conducting plane is placed below a single element of length $L/2$ carrying a current, then the combination of the element and its image acts identically to a dipole of length L except that the radiation occurs only in the space above the plane.

　　For this type of antenna, the directivity is doubled and the radiation resistance is halved when compared to the dipole. Thus, a half wave dipole can be approximated by a quarter wave monopole ($L/2 = \lambda/4$). The monopole is very useful in mobile antennas where the conducting plane can be the car body or the handset case. The typical gain for the quarter wavelength monopole is 2-6dB and it has a bandwidth of about 10%. Its radiation resistance is 36.5Ω and its directivity is 3.28 (5.16dB).

Loop Antenna

　　The loop antenna is a conductor bent into the shape of a closed curve such as a circle or a square with a gap in the conductor to form the terminals as shown in Fig. 4-4c. There are

也可以比半个波长长，但从性能上来权衡，半波偶极子应用广泛。

　　偶极子通过两条传输线来馈电，导体中的电流呈正弦分布，方向相反。因此，由于相互抵消，传输线没有产生辐射。偶极子两臂的电流方向相同，可产生水平方向的辐射。因此，垂直放置的偶极子天线在水平方向辐射电磁波。偶极子天线典型的增益是 2dB，波瓣宽度为 10%。E 平面半功率波瓣宽度大约为 78°，方向性系数为 1.64(2.15dB)，辐射阻抗为 73Ω。

单极子天线

　　单极子天线来源于偶极子镜像理论。根据这一理论，如果把一个导体平面置于一个载有电流的、长度为 $L/2$ 的单导体下面，则单导体及其镜像组合在一起可当作长度为 L 的偶极子，只是辐射仅产生于导体平面上方的空间。

　　对于这种类型的天线，方向性系数是偶极子的 2 倍，辐射阻抗是偶极子的一半。因此，一个四分之一波长的单极子（$L/2 = \lambda/4$）接近一个半波偶极子。单极子天线在移动天线领域很有用，导体平面可以是车身或手持设备。四分之一波长单极子天线的典型增益为 2~6dB，带宽约 10%，辐射阻抗为 36.5Ω，方向性系数为 3.28(5.16dB)。

环形天线

　　环形天线是弯曲成封闭曲线的导体，如圆形或方形，且在导体中有一个间隙形成终端，如图 4-4c 所示。有两种类型的环

two types of loop antennas-electrically small loop antennas and electrically large loop antennas. If the total loop circumference is very small as compared to the wavelength ($L \ll \lambda$), then the loop antenna is said to be electrically small. An electrically large loop antenna typically has its circumference close to a wavelength. The far-field radiation patterns of the small loop antenna are insensitive to shape.

The performance of the loop antenna can be increased by filling the core with ferrite. This helps in increasing the radiation resistance. When the perimeter or circumference of the loop antenna is close to a wavelength, then the antenna is said to be a large loop antenna.

The radiation pattern of the large loop antenna is different then that of the small loop antenna. For a one wavelength square loop antenna, radiation is maximum normal to the plane of the loop (along the z axis). In the plane of the loop, there is a null in the direction parallel to the side containing the feed (along the x axis), and there is a lobe in a direction perpendicular to the side containing the feed (along the y axis). Loop antennas generally have a gain from -2dB to 3dB and a bandwidth of around 10%. The small loop antenna is very popular as a receiving antenna. Single turn loop antennas are used in pagers and multiturn loop antennas are used in AM broadcast receivers.

Helical Antenna

A helical antenna or helix is one in which a conductor connected to a ground plane, is wound into a helical shape. The antenna can operate in a number of modes, however the two principal modes are the normal mode (broadside radiation) and the axial mode (endfire radiation). When the helix diameter is very small as compared to the wavelength, then the antenna operates in the normal mode. However, when the circumference of the helix is of the order of a wavelength, then the helical antenna is said to be operating in the axial mode.

In the normal mode of operation, the antenna field is maximum in a plane normal to the helix axis and minimum along its axis. This mode provides low bandwidth and is generally used for hand-portable mobile applications.

In the axial mode of operation, the antenna radiates as an endfire radiator with a single beam along the helix axis. This mode provides better gain (up to 15dB) and high bandwidth ratio (1.78 : 1) as compared to the normal mode of operation. For this mode of operation, the beam becomes narrower as the number of turns on the helix is increased. Due to its broadband nature of operation, the antenna in the axial mode is used mainly for satellite communications.

形天线,即电小环形天线和电大环形天线。如果总环路周长远小于波长($L \ll \lambda$),那么环形天线就是电小的。电大环形天线的长度通常接近天线波长。电小环形天线的远场辐射方向图与环的形状有关。

通过填充铁氧体可以提高环形天线的性能。这有助于提高环形天线的辐射阻抗。当外围或环形天线的周长接近波长时,就可以说天线是大环形天线。

电大环形天线与电小环形天线的辐射方向图不同。对于一个波长的方环形天线,通常在环形平面上辐射是最大的(沿z轴)。在环形平面上,在平行于含有馈源一边的方向(沿x轴)上是没有辐射的,在垂直于含有馈源一边的方向(沿y轴)上有一个波瓣。环形天线的增益一般为 -2~3dB,带宽为10%左右。电小环形天线作为接收天线非常有用。单圈环形天线用于传呼机,多圈环形天线用于 AM 广播接收器。

螺旋天线

螺旋天线弯成螺旋形且导体接地。螺旋天线可以工作在很多模式下,但两个主要模式是法向模式(边射)和轴向模式(端射)。当螺旋直径相比波长非常小时,天线工作在法向模式;当螺旋周长接近波长时,天线工作在轴向模式。

在法向模式下,天线辐射场在垂直于螺旋轴的平面上有最大值,在平行于螺旋轴的平面上有最小值。这种模式的带宽较窄,广泛用于手持便携式移动设备。

在轴向模式下,天线是一个端射辐射源,在沿着螺旋轴方向有单波束。相比于法向模式,这种模式提供了更好的增益(高达15dB)和高带宽比(1.78:1)。对于这种工作模式,随着螺旋圈数的增加,波束变窄。由于其宽带特性,轴向模式天线主要用于卫星通信。

Horn Antenna

Horn antennas are used typically in the microwave region (gigahertz range) where waveguides are the standard feed method, since horn antennas essentially consist of a waveguide whose end walls are flared outwards to form a megaphone like structure.

Horns provide high gain, low VSWR, relatively wide bandwidth, low weight, and are easy to construct. The aperture of the horn can be rectangular, circular or elliptical. However, rectangular horns are widely used. These horns are fed by a rectangular waveguide which have a broad horizontal wall. For dominant waveguide mode excitation, the E-plane is vertical and the H-plane horizontal. If the broad wall dimension of the horn is flared with the narrow wall of the waveguide being left as it is, then it is called an H-plane sectoral horn antenna. If the flaring occurs only in the E-plane dimension, it is called an E-plane sectoral horn antenna. A pyramidal horn antenna is obtained when flaring occurs along both the dimensions. The horn basically acts as a transition from the waveguide mode to the free-space mode and this transition reduces the reflected waves and emphasizes the traveling waves which lead to low VSWR and wide bandwidth. The horn is widely used as a feed element for large radio astronomy, satellite tracking, and communication dishes.

喇叭天线

喇叭天线通常用于微波区域（千兆赫兹范围内），在该区域波导是标准的馈电方法。这是由于喇叭天线本质上是由波导终端向外逐渐张开形成喇叭形状而构成的。

喇叭天线增益高，驻波比低，带宽相对较宽，重量轻，结构简单。喇叭天线的口径可以是矩形、圆形或椭圆形。然而，矩形喇叭天线广泛使用。喇叭天线通过一个矩形波导来馈电，矩形波导的横向壁宽。垂直的 E 平面和水平的 H 平面是主要波导模式的激励。如果波导的宽壁扩展而窄壁保持不变，就叫作 H 平面扇形喇叭天线。如果只在 E 平面（窄壁）方向扩展，这就是 E 平面扇形喇叭天线。如果将宽壁和窄壁同时扩展，就可以获得锥形喇叭天线。喇叭天线本质上是从波导模式到自由空间模式的过渡，这一过渡减小了反射波，增强了传输波，从而降低了驻波比并增加了带宽。喇叭天线广泛用作大型无线天文台、卫星跟踪和通信天线的阵元。

NEW WORDS AND PHRASES

antenna *n.* 天线，触角
radiate *vt.* 放射，辐射，传播，广播；*vi.* 发光，辐射，流露；*adj.* 有射线的，辐射状的
electromagnetic *adj.* 电磁的，电磁学的
oscillate *vi.* 振动，振荡，摇摆，发杂音，（银利率等）在中间值上下波动
sinusoidal *adj.* 正弦曲线的
tangential *adj.* ［数］切线的，正切的，略微触及的，附带的
conductor *n.* 指挥家，指导者，售票员，导体，导线
perpendicular *adj.* （常与 to 连用）成直角的，垂直的，陡的（坡）
dipole *n.* 偶极子，对称振子，偶极天线，双合价
beamwidth *n.* 波束宽度
horizontal *adj.* 地平线的，水平的，平放的，横的（与 vertical 相对）
directivity *n.* 定向性，指向性，方向性
terminal *n.* 终端，终点，极限，接头，引线，电极，终端设备，终点站

resistance *n.* 反抗，抵抗，抵抗力，阻力，电阻，阻抗
impedance *n.* 阻抗，电阻抗，交流电阻
reactance *n.* 反应性，反作用力，电抗
component *n.* 元件，分量
gain *n.* 增益
polarization *n.* ［物］偏振（现象），极化（作用），两极化，分化
vector *n.* 矢量，向量
elliptical *adj.* 椭圆的，省略的
frequency *n.* 频率，周率，发生次数
transport *v.* 传送，运输，流放，放逐
transmission *n.* 播送，发射，传动，传送，传输，转播
current *adj.* 当前的，通用的，流通的；*n.* 涌流，趋势，电流，水流，气流
amplitude *n.* 振幅
element *n.* 要素，元素，成分，元件
mobile *adj.* 可移动的，易变的，机动的；*n.* 运动物体

wavelength *n.* 波长
insensitive *adj.* 感觉迟钝的，无感觉的（to），不机敏的，低灵敏度的
null *adj.* 无效力的，无效的，无价值的，等于零的；*n.* 零，空
parallel *adj.* 平行的，类似的，并联的；*n.* 平行线，平行面，相似物；*v.* 相应，平行
helix *n.* 螺旋，螺旋状物
waveguide *n.* 波导
aperture *n.* 孔，穴，缝隙，（照相机、望远镜等的）光圈，孔径
rectangular *adj.* 矩形的，长方形的，直角的
geometry *n.* 几何学
excitation *n.* 刺激，激励，鼓舞，［物］激发，励磁，［植］激感（现象）
dimension *n.* 尺寸，尺度，维（数），度（数），元
IEEE *abbr.* 电气与电子工程师协会

NOTES

1) That part of a transmitting or receiving system that is designed to radiate or receive electromagnetic waves.
（天线是）一种发射或接收系统，旨在发射或接收电磁波。

2) A conducting wire radiates mainly because of time-varying current or an acceleration (or deceleration) of charge.
导线产生辐射主要是因为时变电流或者电荷的加速度（或减速度）。

3) Antenna radiation pattern is a graphic representation of directional properties of the antenna.
天线的方向图是用图形表示天线方向性的一种方法。

4) Antenna gain is a parameter which is closely related to the directivity of the antenna.
天线的增益是与天线的方向性密切相关的参数。

5) Polarization of a radiated wave is defined as "that property of an electromagnetic wave describing the time varying direction and relative magnitude of the electric field vector."
辐射波的极化定义为"用电场矢量随时间变化的方向和相对幅值所描绘的电磁波的特性"。

6) The characteristics of an antenna are very much determined by its shape, size and the type of material that it is made of.
天线的特性完全由它的形状、尺寸和制作材料决定。

4.2 Development of Mobile Communication

Nowadays, cell phones have become an indispensable and important tool in people's life. In addition to regular communication needs, the ever-growing array of apps for chatting on WeChat, mobile payments, watching videos on the way to and from work, playing games and getting the latest news have all been squeezed into a palm-sized screen. It is the mobile Internet that presents the colorful network world in front of us.

1. The Concept of Communication

Communication is the transmission of information from one place to another. It is difficult to trace back to the time when humans first exchanged information, but it is certain that with man came the exchange of information. In ancient times, there were drum transmission, beacon fire smoke, hongyan transmission, courier station and other forms of communication, while in modern times, there were telegraph transmission of written symbols, telephone transmission of sound, facsimile transmission of still images, television transmission of active images plus sound, data communication transmission of information processed by electronic computers.

2. Basic Principles and Characteristics of Communication

Any communication behavior can be regarded as a communication system (see Fig. 4-5), mainly including sender, transmitter, channel, receiver and recipient. The sender (information source) converts the information into electrical signals, and the modulator performs some transformation on the information signal to make it suitable for transmission to the receiving end in the channel, and converts the received signal to the original information through the demodulator, which is sent to the receiver. This is the basic principle of the communication system. No matter the ancient beacon post communication, the modern telegraph and telephone communication, or the modern mobile digital communication, the principle is not different. Ancient post communication through sporadic, scattered post to achieve; modern telephone communications were realized by telephone lines; modern mobile communication is achieved through an invisible network, with each mobile phone merely a node in a vast aerial network. Sustains the ancient communication pivot is a lot of manpower and material resources, the support of modern communication is fast and efficient data transmission between the machine and external network into the internal network, physical network into invisible network, support the communication "relay" gradually reduce, degradation, until you become one with the recipient, as a single point in the communication network.

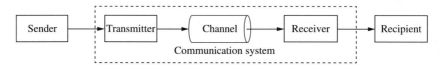

Fig. 4-5 The structure of the communication system

Interestingly, ancient and modern mobile communications share two characteristics in common. One is that they're all wireless. In ancient times, information carriers such as sound, fire and light, such as drumming, beacon, fire and smoke, and flag, etc. were used to realize the long-distance transmission of messages, which was transmitted through relay stations layer by layer and finally reached the receiver. Modern mobile communication is transmitted through electromagnetic wave information carrier in space, instead of passing through current information carrier in metal wire like modern telephone and telegraph. Modern mobile communication tools such as mobile phones enable people to get rid of the limitation of "lines" completely. The second is that they are "real time." The earliest information exchange was face-to-face, the most real-time information exchange. In the same way, the current mobile phone is extremely convenient for real-time communication. With the improvement of CPU speed, switching equipment information conversion speed, source codec speed, channel transmission speed and channel capacity, the "real-time" of communication system has been greatly improved.

3. The Breakthrough in Wireless Communication Theory

The nature and propagation of signal are the foundation of wireless communication. In 1865 James Clerk Maxwell, a British physicist, produced a pair of equations whose solution predicted the existence of electromagnetic waves propagating at the speed of light. In 1888, German physicist Heinrich Rudolf Hertz proved the existence of electromagnetic waves. Maxwell's prediction of electromagnetic wave and the confirmation of Hertz have prepared theoretically and experimentally the communication mode from wired to wireless, and laid the scientific foundation for the generation of communication technology. Maxwell himself did not come up with the word radio, but his theory did suggest that electricity could be transmitted wirelessly. Hertz also did not foresee the possibility of radio communication. In 1889, when a friend of him asked if it was possible to communicate by means of electric waves, he said, "To communicate by means of electromagnetic waves through different wires, you would need a giant mirror with an area about the size of the European continent." But the Hertz experiment greatly inspired scientists around the world and opened the door to radio communication technology. In 1893, Nikola Tesla, a Serbian American scientist, demonstrated the feasibility of radio communication for the first time in public in St. Louis, Missouri. In 1896, an Italian named Guglielmo Marconi made the first successful long-distance radio communication on board the Sao Paulo, a slow sailing ship in the Atlantic Ocean. In 1901, he completed transatlantic radio communications. In 1909, Marconi won the Nobel Prize in physics and was called "the father of radio."

Signal reception is another key link in wireless communication. In 1901, Canadian inventor Reginald Fessenden proposed the idea of heterodyne reception. In 1912, American electrical engineer Armstrong Edwin Howard put forward the "superheterodyne reception principle", that is, the local oscillator frequency is always one Intermediate Frequency (IF) higher than the carrier frequency, which exceeds the audio signal. Later, Armstrong made a major improvement in field reception, inventing the superheterodyne circuit that allowed the receiver to receive any radio wave. The development of communication technology and the breakthrough of radio receiving principle from "heterodyne" to "superheterodyne" created conditions for the rise of TV broadcasting, microwave communication and satellite communication.

4. The History and Present Situation of Mobile Communication

Mobile communication refers to the communication between two or more parties in motion, including land mobile communication, aviation communication, maritime communication and satellite communication.

In 1896, Marconi's successful experiment with long-range radio communications on a drifting Atlantic ship was considered the beginning of "mobile communication." In fact, modern mobile communication began in the 1920s. In 1928, students from Purdue University invented the superheterodyne vehical-mounted radio receiver working in 2MHz, and it was put into use in the Detroit police department soon. It was the first mobile communication system in the world that was used on land and could work effectively.

In the late 1930s, a more efficient mobile communication system, frequency-modulated, was introduced. In 1940s, this kind of FM mobile communication system gradually occupied the mainstream position, and realized the small capacity dedicated mobile communication system, but this was only a work in the experimental sense. During the Second World War, the military needs made mobile communication develop rapidly, and the public mobile communication system came into being. In 1946, St. Louis first developed the manual transfer of small capacity car telephone system. In 1947, Bell Laboratories in the United States proposed the concept of "small cells." In 1950s, America and some European countries have successfully developed the public mobile phone system, which has realized the communication between the mobile phone system and the public telephone network in technology, and has been widely used. In 1960s, mobile communication technology gradually improved. In 1964, the United States developed a new medium-capacity car telephone system that automatically selected the channel of each call. In 1969, the performance of U. S. mobile phone automation was extended to the 450MHz band, and the IMTS became the standard for U. S. mobile phone systems. In the same year, Japan also began to develop the 800MHz honeycomb High Capacity Mobile Telephone System (HCMTS).

In order to make more effective use of the limited spectrum resources, Bell Laboratories proposed the landmark theory of cell system and cellular network, which paved the way for the wide application of mobile communication system in the world. In 1978, Bell Laboratories in the United States developed the Advanced Mobile Phone System (AMPS), which became the first cellular mobile communication system with the capability of anytime and anywhere communication in the real sense, and officially opened the curtain of competition for modern mobile communication. At the end of 1983, AMPS with large capacity was established in Chicago, which brought mobile communication to a new stage of development. Since the mid-1980s, the development of terrestrial cellular mobile communications has reached its peak, and Europe and Japan have also established their own cellular mobile communications. In 1985 there were 553,000 subscribers to cellular mobile phones worldwide. By May 1990, the total number of users had exceeded 8.22 million, of which the United States accounted for 47%. In October 1985, the number of mobile phone users in the United States was 235,000. By May 1990, the number had reached 3.9 million, an increase of 16.6 times, with an average monthly increase of more than 60,000 users. The development of cellular mobile communication in European countries is also rapid, and the number of users accounts for 33.1% of the world total. Japan's cellular system already covers 90% of cities and 70% of major highways, with an average annual growth rate of 150%.

The nearly 100-year development history of modern mobile communication system can be roughly divided into the following four development stages.

The first stage is the early development stage from the 1920s to the 1940s. Itwas characterized by special system development, low working frequency, working mode is simplex or half duplex mode.

The second stage is from the mid-1940s to the early 1960s. This stage was characterized by the transition from the dedicated mobile network to the public mobile network, and the connection mode was manual, the network capacity was small.

The third stage is from the mid-1960s to the mid-1970s. Itwas characterized by adopting large area system, small and medium capacity, using 450MHz frequency band, and realizing automatic frequency selection and automatic connection.

The fourth stage is from the middle and late 1970s till now. Itwas characterized by the rapid increase of communication capacity, the emergence of new services, the continuous improvement of system performance, and the trend of technology development.

At present, mobile communication has been developing rapidly all over the world. The International Telecommunication Union's 2013 annual report shows that there are 6.8 billion mobile phone users out of 7.1 billion people in the world. By the end of 2014, the number of mobile phone users in the world will exceed the world's population, according to a United Nations research agency. At present, 2G, 3G and 4G commercial mobile communication networks are in the coexistence stage and will coexist for a considerable period of time to serve various users and meet different business needs. At the same time, the fifth generation mobile communication system (5G), as a new generation of mobile communication system for the development of mobile communication needs after 2020, the ITU named it as IMT-2020, and its research and development work has been carried out worldwide.

5. The Development of Cellular Mobile Communication Technology

The fourth stage of cellular mobile communication system can be divided into several development stages. If according to the multiple access mode to divide, thenanalog Frequency Division Multiple Access (FDMA) system is the first generation of mobile communication system (1G); digital Time Division Multiple Access (TDMA) or Code Division Multiple Access (CDMA) systems using circuit switching are second generation mobile communication systems (2G); CDMA systems using packet/circuit switching are third generation mobile communication systems (3G); systems using different advanced access technologies and all-IP (Internet Protocol) network are called fourth generation mobile communication systems (4G). According to the typical technology of the system, the simulation system is 1G; digital voice systems are 2G; digital voice/data system is super second generation mobile communication system (B2G); broadband digital system is 3G; the very high data rate system is 4G.

Martin Cooper, an engineer at Motorola during 1970s working on a handheld device capable of two-way communication wirelessly, invented the first generation mobile phone. It was initially developed to use in a car, the first prototype was tested in 1974. This invention is considered as a turning point in wireless communication which led to an evolution of many technologies and standards in future. Since then, mobile phone communication technology has advanced from 1st generation to the 5th generation. It is said that mobile phone communication technology changes from present generation to the next generation every decade.

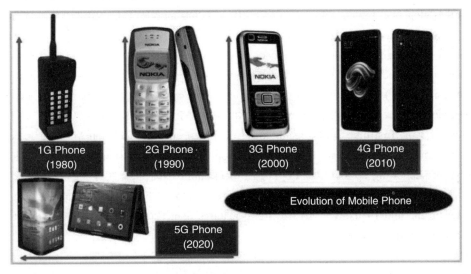

Fig. 4-6 History of mobile phone communication technology

1G: First Generation Mobile Communication System

The emergence of AMPS marked that mobile communication technology had entered the 1G era. The first generation of commercial cellular mobile network was deployed in Japan by Nippon Telegraph and Telephone (NTT) company in Tokyo during 1979. In the beginning of 1980s, it gained popularity in the US, Finland, and UK. During 1980s, the most popular 1G systems included Advanced Mobile Phone System (AMPS), Nordic Mobile Telephone System (NMTS), Total Access Communication System (TACS), and European Total Access Communication System (ETACS).

A cellular network is a network of wireless links. An area on earth is divided into cells. Shape of these cells can be hexagonal, square, rectangular, circular or any other shapes. But hexagonal shape is most preferred to create cells of a cellular network. Each of these cells has their own base transceiver stations. These base stations provide wireless network coverage to the cell. These wireless frequencies can be used for transmission of voice, data, FM radio content etc. Different set of frequencies are used by each cell to avoid conflict with the neighboring cells.

When a number of cells are joined together, they provide wireless radio frequency coverage to a large area. This is how wireless devices or transceivers (transmitter and receiver) like mobile phone, tablets, smart phones, modem etc. work.

In November 1987, Guangzhou opened China's first cellular mobile communication system. Subsequently, Shenzhen, Zhuhai, Shanghai, Beijing, Shenyang, Qinhuangdao and Tianjin also set up cellular mobile communication systems, and the Pearl River Delta region took the lead in networking.

The typical frequency band of the first generation mobile communication system was 800/900MHz and was mainly used for making telephone calls. Therefore, it was essentially a voice transmission technology, and 1G was often referred to as the voice age. 1G was based on analog transmissions and Frequency Division Multiple Access (FDMA) technology. Its disadvantages included low voice quality, unstable signal, insufficient coverage, and large security problems. Even so, subscribers were super excited with the new mobile technology now that they didn't have to rely on stationary telephones or landlines at home or in the office. For the first time, cellular technology had cut the cord from the telephone, giving users the flexibility of being mobile while still staying connected!

2G: Second Generation Mobile Communication System

Second generation of mobile communication system was launched in Finland in 1991. It introduced a new digital technology for wireless transmission also known as Global System for Mobile communication (GSM). In addition to digital voice, data could also be transmitted, such as SMS (Short Message Service), photos or pictures (Multimedia Messaging Service, MMS), and allowed users to roam for the first time. GSM technology was based on Time Division Multiple Access (TDMA) and became the base standard for further development in wireless standards later. This standard was capable of supporting up to 14.4 to 64kbps (maximum) data rate.

Code Division Multiple Access (CDMA) system developed by Qualcomm also introduced and implemented in the mid 1990s. CDMA had more features than GSM in terms of spectral efficiency, number of users, and data rate.

The later versions of this generation, which were called 2.5G using GPRS (General Packet Radio Service) and 2.75G using EDGE (Enhanced Data rates for GSM Evolution) networks. It provided better quality and capacity. Another popular technology CDMA2000 was also introduced to support higher Data rate for CDMA networks. This technology had the ability to provide up to 384kbps (maximum) data rate.

Although 2G had many advantages and had added new functions such as sending and receiving E-mail, and browsing the Internet, it still had disadvantages such as slow transmission speed, nearly exhausted frequency resources, and low voice quality.

3G: Third Generation Mobile Communication System

Third generation mobile communication started with the introduction of UMTS-Universal Mobile Telecommunication System which was introduced in early 2000s. The 3G technology added multimedia facilities to 2G phones by allowing video, audio, and graphics applications to be transmitted over the network. 3G was like the puberty of mobile network standards. On 3G phones, you could stream video or had video telephony. The idea behind 3G was to have a single network standard instead of the different types adopted in the US, Europe, and Asia. A 3G cell-phone system depended on Code Division Multiple Access (CDMA) and spread spectrum radio technology, which allowed many users to share both time and frequencies.

There were three main standards for 3G mobile communication systems: WCDMA, CDMA2000, and TD-SCDMA. TD-SCDMA was developed and submitted by China, but the technology was not mature enough due to its late start. In 2008, the Ministry of Industry and Information Technology issued 3G licenses, with China Mobile holding TD-SCDMA, China Unicom WCDMA, and China Telecom CDMA2000.

The 3G mobile communication system still had many disadvantages, such as system incompatibility, low frequency utilization, and low speed.

After the introduction of 3G mobile communication system, smart phones became popular across the globe. Specific applications were developed for smartphones to handle multimedia chat, E-mail, video calling, games, social media and healthcare. The transmission rate of data was increased up to 2Mbit/s.

4G: Fourth Generation Mobile Communication System

Technical testing of the fourth generation mobile communication system began in 2007. As early as 2010, Germany began to auction 4G licenses in bundles in Europe. Since then, 4G had been put into commercial use in Western Europe, North America, and Japan. Soon, the global mobile communication system entered the era of 4G. The 4G mobile communication technology was a high-speed mobile communication network based on IP protocol, which was a major revolution in the development history of mobile communication technology. It had a larger transmission capacity and a faster rate than 3G. LTE (Long Term Evolution) communication technology was adopted to realize the evolution of wideband wireless system and wireless wideband system. It was capable of providing 100Mbps to 1Gbps speed with high QoS (Quality of Service) and high security.

On December 4, 2013, Ministry of Industry and Information Technology of the People's Republic of China officially issued TD-LTE business license to China Mobile, China Telecom, and China Unicom, marking the beginning of the era of 4G mobile communication in China. 4G communication could realize the original image and video high-definition transmission on the picture and video transmission, and its transmission quality was similar to the computer picture quality. Applications, files, pictures, audio and video downloads could reach speeds of up to tens of megabits per second, which 3G communication technology cannot achieve. In a word, 4G system has higher data transmission rate, security, intelligence, flexibility and service quality.

5G: Fifth Generation Mobile Communication System

In 2017, people began to study the 5G communication technology. The 5G era will officially kick off in 2020. The key technologies for 5G include large-scale antenna arrays, ultra-dense networking, new types of multiple access, full spectrum access, and new network architectures. Compared with the existing 4G system, the performance of 5G system will be improved 1000 times in three aspects: first is the transmission speed will be increased 1000 times, the average transmission rate will reach 100Mbps~1Gbps; next is a 1000-fold increase in total data traffic; and then spectrum efficiency and energy efficiency increased by 1000 times.

The features of 5G are as follows.

1) While promoting technological change, 5G research will pay more attention to user experience. Network average throughput rate, transmission delay and support capacity for emerging mobile services such as virtual reality, 3D experience and interactive games will become key indicators to measure the performance of 5G system.

2) Different from the traditional concept of mobile communication system, 5G system research will not only bring the classic technology as the core goal, for example, physical transmission level of point-to-point, channel encoding and decoding, but improve system performance greatly on architecture from extensive multi-point, more multiple users, multiple antennas, collaborative network as a focal point of breakthrough.

3) The indoor mobile communication service has occupied the dominant position in the application. The indoor wireless coverage performance and business support capability of 5G will be the priority design goal of the system, thus changing the traditional mobile communication system's design concept of "focusing on large-scale coverage and considering indoor".

4) High frequency spectrum resources will be more applied to 5G mobile communication system, but due to the limitations of high frequency radio wave penetration, wireless and wired fusion, optical wireless networking and other technologies will be more widely used.

5) The "soft" configuration of 5G wireless network will become an important research direction in the future. Operators can adjust network resources in real time according to the dynamic changes of business traffic and effectively reduce the cost of network operation and energy consumption.

5G network is no longer just mobile network in the traditional sense, but deeply integrated with the Internet and the Internet of Things, extending the connection between people to the Internet of everything, and providing personalized and intelligent services for users. It is a fusion network in the real sense. Ultra-high speed, ultra-high capacity and ultra-low latency networks will revolutionize people's lives.

Table 4-1 summarizes the comparison results of 1G to 5G mobile communication technology in terms of speed, technology and key features.

Table 4-1　Comparison results of 1G to 5G

Generation	Speed	Technology	Key features
1G (1970s-1980s)	14.4Kbps	AMPS, NMT, TACS	Only voice service
2G (1990-2000)	9.6/14.4Kbps	TDMA, CDMA	Voice and data services
2.5G/2.75G (2001-2004)	171.2Kbps, 20-40Kbps	GPRS	Voice, data, web mobile internet, low speed streaming services and E-mail services

（续）

Generation	Speed	Technology	Key features
3G（2004-2005）	3.1Mbps, 500-700Kbps	CDMA2000（1Xrtt, EVDO), UMTS, EDGE	Voice, data, multimedia, support for smart phone applications, faster web browsing, video calling and TV streaming
3.5G（2006-2010）	14.4Mbps, 1-3Mbps	HSPA	All the services from 3G network with enhanced speed and more mobility
4G（2010-2020）	100-300Mbps, 3-5Mbps, 100Mbps（Wi-Fi）	WiMax, LTE, Wi-Fi	High speed, high quality voice over IP, HD multimedia streaming, 3D gaming, HD video conferencing and worldwide roaming
5G（2020-）	1-10Gbps	LTE-Advanced, OMA, NOMA	Super fast mobile internet, low latency network for mission critical applications, Internet of Things, security and surveillance, HD multimedia streaming, autonomous driving, smart healthcare applications

6. Conclusion

Wireless technology has been continuously evolving to meet increasing demands and higher specification requirements. Since the deployment of first generation mobile networks, telecommunication industry is facing a lot of new challenges in terms of technology, efficient utilization of spectrum and most importantly security to end users. Future wireless technologies will provide ultra fast, feature rich and highly secure mobile networks. The Mobile Internet and the Internet of Things are two major driving forces for the development of the next generation of mobile communication system. The Mobile Internet subverts the traditional mobile communication business model, while the Internet of Things expands the service scope of mobile communication.

NEW WORDS AND PHRASES

heterodyne　*v.* 使（交变无线电信号）混合以产生外差效果；*adj.*（无线电传播中）外差的，外差法的

superheterodyne　*adj.* 超外差的；*n.* 超外差式收音机，超外差式接收机

codec　*n.* 编解码

cellular mobile communication　蜂窝移动通信

hexagonal shape　六角形

Advanced Mobile Phone System（AMPS）　高级移动电话业务

simplex mode　单工模式

half duplex mode　半双工模式

Frequency Division Multiple Access（FDMA）　频分多址

Time Division Multiple Access（TDMA）　时分多址

Code Division Multiple Access（CDMA）　码分多址

Nippon Telegraph and Telephone（NTT）　日本电报电话公司

Short Message Service（SMS）　短消息服务

packet switching　分组交换

circuit switching　电路交换

Long Term Evolution（LTE）　长期演进

spread spectrum radio technology　扩频无线电技术

NOTES

1) Maxwell's prediction of electromagnetic wave and the confirmation of Hertz have prepared theoretically and experimentally the communication mode from wired to wireless, and laid the scientific foundation for the generation of communication technology.
   麦克斯韦关于电磁波的预言和赫兹的证实,为通信方式从有线到无线做了理论上和实验上的准备,奠定了通信技术产生的科学基础。

2) For the first time, cellular technology had cut the cord from the telephone, giving users the flexibility of being mobile while still staying connected!
   蜂窝技术第一次切断了电话的连接,给了用户移动的灵活性,同时还能保持连接!

3) Different from the traditional concept of mobile communication system, 5G system research will not only bring the classic technology as the core goal, for example, physical transmission level of point-to-point, channel encoding and decoding, but improve system performance greatly on architecture from extensive multi-point, more multiple users, multiple antennas, collaborative network as a focal point of breakthrough.
   与传统的移动通信系统理念不同,5G系统研究不仅仅把点到点的物理层传输与信道编译码等经典技术作为核心目标,而是将更为广泛的多点、多用户、多天线、多小区协作组网作为突破重点,力求在体系结构上获得系统性能的大幅度提高。

4) 5G network is no longer just mobile network in the traditional sense, but deeply integrated with the Internet and the Internet of Things, extending the connection between people to the Internet of everything, and providing personalized and intelligent services for users.
   5G网络不再仅仅指传统意义上的移动网络,而是与互联网及物联网深度融合,将人与人之间的连接拓展至万物互联,可以为用户提供个性化和智能化的服务。

EXERCISES

1. Please translate the following words and phrases into Chinese.
   a) superheterodyne
   b) cellular mobile communication
   c) simplex mode
   d) half duplex mode
   e) Frequency Division Multiple Access
   f) Time Division Multiple Access
   g) Code Division Multiple Access
   h) Short Message Service
   i) packet switching
   j) circuit switching
   k) spread spectrum radio technology

2. Please translate the following words and phrases into English.
   a) 编解码
   b) 中频
   c) 载波
   d) 频分多址
   e) 调频
   f) 蜂窝技术
   g) 物理层传输
   h) 信道编译码
   i) 物联网
   j) 智能化服务

3. Fill in the blanks with the missing word(s).
   a) Any communication behavior can be regarded as a communication system, mainly including _____, _____, _____, _____, and _____.
   b) In 1865 _____ produced a pair of equations whose solution predicted the existence of electromagnetic waves propagating at the speed of light. In 1888, _____ proved the existence of electromagnetic waves.
   c) In 1947, Bell Laboratories in the United States proposed the concept of "_____."
   d) If according to the multiple access mode to divide, then analog _____ system is 1G; digital _____

or CDMA systems using _____ are 2G; CDMA systems using _____ are 3G; systems using different advanced access technologies and _____ network are called 4G.

e) _____ shape is most preferred to create cells of a cellular network.

f) The idea behind 3G was to have a _____ network standard instead of the different types adopted in the US, Europe, and Asia.

g) The key technologies for 5G include _____, _____, _____, _____, and _____.

h) Ultra-high speed, _____ and _____ networks will revolutionize people's lives.

4. Answer the following questions according to the text.

a) What is the structure of the communication system?

b) Describe the history of the development of mobile communication briefly.

c) What was considered the beginning of mobile communications?

d) How many stages the fourth stage of cellular mobile communication system can be divided into?

READING

Global Navigation Satellite System

1. Introduction

Since the Internet of Things (IoT) was proposed in 1999, it has formed a complete concept, and its application based on the ground network has gradually developed and matured. However, in some areas, such as the harsh environment across a large area, the Internet of Things is powerless due to the space environment and other restrictions, resulting in a mismatch between service capacity and demand. Mobile cellular networks cannot cover more than 80% of the world's land and 95% of its ocean. Therefore, in some remote mountainous areas and extremely cold areas, it is almost impossible to receive network signals. All of these urge us to construct the integrated environment of heaven and earth, that is, the association of heaven and earth. That is to say, it relies on space-based information network to achieve global coverage through satellites and realize the trans-regional transmission of IoT information (see Fig. 4-7). The most important part of

全球导航卫星系统

1. 引言

物联网（IoT）自1999年提出以来，已经形成了完整的概念，基于地面网络的应用也逐渐发展成熟。但是，在一些领域（比如大范围的恶劣环境），物联网由于空间环境等限制而无能为力，导致服务能力与需求不匹配。移动蜂窝网络无法覆盖全球80%的陆地和95%的海洋。因此，在一些偏远山区和极端寒冷地区，我们几乎不可能收到网络信号。这些都促使我们构建天地的整体环境，即天地的结合。依托天基信息网络，通过卫星实现全球覆盖，实现IoT信息跨区域传输（见图4-7）。天基物联网最重要的组成部分是导航卫星，未

Fig. 4-7 IoT and space-based information network

the space-based Internet of Things is the navigation satellite, which will have a profound impact on the whole industry chain in the next two to three years.

In satellite navigation and positioning technology, the radio signals transmitted by navigation satellites are received by the user terminal. By measuring the time delay of the signal propagated from the navigation satellite to the receiver, navigation, positioning and timing services can be realized. Compared with conventional navigation and positioning techniques, satellite navigation and positioning technology can provide precise three-dimensional positions, velocity and time for users. It is an all-weather, all-time and globally available technology. Great progress has been made in recent decades, and many countries and consortia have established their own global navigation satellite systems. Global satellite navigation and positioning technology has been widely applied in navigation for vehicles, offshore ships, aero crafts and aerospace vehicles and in the fields of geodesy, oil exploration, precision agriculture, precise time transfer, and earth and atmospheric sciences.

2. Composition of GNSS

Global Navigation Satellite Systems (GNSS) is mainly composed of space segment, ground control segment and user segment (see Fig. 4-8).

The space segment of GNSS is made up of working satellites and spare satellites. The satellites are evenly distributed over multiple orbits. The distribution of satellites enables more than four satellites to be observed anywhere in the world at any time, and the navigation information can be stored in the satellites. GNSS satellite due to atmospheric friction and

来两三年将对整个产业链产生深远影响。

在卫星导航定位技术中，导航卫星发射的无线电信号由用户终端接收，通过测量信号从导航卫星传播到接收机的时延，实现导航、定位和授时业务。与传统的导航定位技术相比，卫星导航定位技术可以为用户提供精确的三维位置、速度和时间。它是一种全天候、全天时、全球可用的技术，近几十年来取得了很大进展，许多国家和地区建立了自己的全球导航卫星系统。全球卫星导航定位技术已广泛应用于车辆、船舶、航空飞行器和航天飞行器的导航，以及大地测量、石油勘探、精密农业、精确时变、地球和大气科学等领域。

2. GNSS 的组成

全球导航卫星系统（GNSS）主要由空间段、地面控制段和用户段组成（见图 4-8）。

空间段由工作卫星和备用卫星组成。卫星均匀地分布在多个轨道上。卫星的分布使人们可以在任何时间和世界任何地方观测到 4 颗以上的卫星，而导航信息可以

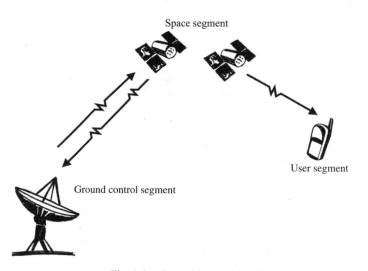

Fig. 4-8　Composition of GNSS

other problems, with the passage of time, the navigation accuracy will decrease gradually.

The ground control segment is composed of a monitor station, a master monitor station and a ground antenna. The ground control station is responsible for collecting information from the satellite and calculating the satellite ephemeris, relative distances, atmospheric correction and other data.

The user segment mainly refers to the terminal facilities of some satellite navigation system users, namely the signal receiver. Its main function is to be able to capture the satellite to be measured according to a certain cut-off angle of the satellite and track the operation of these satellites.

3. Four Major Navigation Satellite Positioning Systems

The satellite navigation system was initially designed for military requirements. With the end of the Cold War, the growing demand for civil and commercial navigation became increasingly strong. Many countries in the world began to develop independent GNSS, including the GPS developed by the US, the Globalnaya Navigatsionnaya Sputnikovaya Sistema (GLONASS) developed by Russia, the Galileo Satellite Navigation System (GSNS) established by the European Union (EU), and the BeiDou navigation satellite System (BDS) developed by China. Each of these GNSS systems employs a constellation of orbiting satellites working in conjunction with a network of ground stations.

GPS

It is a new generation of navigation satellite positioning system based on the Navy Navigation Satellite System (NNSS). In December 1958, the United States Navy developed the NNSS in order to provide global navigation for the Polaris nuclear submarine. NNSS composed of three parts: meridional satellite, ground monitoring system and Doppler receiver. In December 1973, after summarizing the pros and cons of NNSS, a new generation of satellite navigation system, Navigation Satellite Timing and Ranging Global Positioning System, or GPS for short, was approved to be developed by the US Department of Defense.

GPS system consists of three parts: aerial satellites (including 21 GPS working satellites and 3 standby satellites), ground monitoring system (controlling the whole system and time, responsible for orbit monitoring and prediction, and composed of master control station, monitoring station and injection station), and user receivers (mainly various types of receiver).

储存在这些卫星中。由于大气摩擦等问题，随着时间的推移，GNSS 卫星的导航精度会逐渐下降。

地面控制段由监控站、主监控站和地面天线组成。地面控制站负责从卫星收集信息，计算卫星星历、相对距离、大气校正等数据。

用户段主要是指某些卫星导航系统用户的终端设施，即信号接收器。它的主要功能是捕获被测卫星的某一截角，并跟踪这些卫星的运行情况。

3. 四大导航卫星定位系统

卫星导航系统最初用于军事需求。随着冷战的结束，人们对民用和商业航行的需求日益强烈。世界上许多国家和地区开始开发独立的全球导航卫星系统（GNSS），包括美国的全球定位系统（GPS）、俄罗斯的 Globalnaya Navigatsionnaya Sputnikovaya Sistema（GLONASS）、欧盟的伽利略卫星导航系统（GSNS）和中国的北斗卫星导航系统（BDS）。每一个 GNSS 系统都使用了一个与地面站网络协同工作的轨道卫星星座。

GPS

GPS 是在美国海军导航卫星系统（Navy Navigation Satellite System，NNSS）基础上建立起来的新一代导航卫星定位系统。1958 年 12 月，美国海军为了给北极星核潜艇提供全球性导航，研制了 NNSS。NNSS 由三部分组成：子午卫星、地面监控系统以及多普勒接收机。美国国防部在总结了 NNSS 的优劣以后，于 1973 年 12 月批准研制新一代的卫星导航系统——导航卫星定时测距全球定位系统（Navigation Satellite Timing and Ranging Global Positioning System），简称 GPS。

GPS 系统由三大部分组成：空中卫星（包括 21 颗 GPS 工作卫星和 3 颗备用卫星）、地面监控系统（控制整个系统和时间，负责轨道监测和预报，又由主控站、监测站和注入站组成）和用户接收机（主要是各种型号的接收机）。

GLONASS

This system was first developed in the Soviet Union, and the project was continued by Russia. Russia began building its own global navigation satellite system alone in 1993 and began operating in 2007. At that time, Russia was only allowed to provide satellite positioning and navigation services. By 2009, the service scope had expanded to the whole world. The main services of the system included determining the coordinates and moving speed information of land, sea and air targets.

GSNS

This system was developed and established by the European Union, was announced by the European commission in February 1999. The system consists of 30 satellites with an orbital altitude of 236,16km, of which 27 are working stars and 3 are backup stars. The satellite orbits at an altitude of approximately 24,000km and is located in three orbital planes with an inclination of 56 degrees.

BDS

In 2003, China's Beidou 1 was completed and put into operation. Unlike GPS, the BDS command and terminal can communicate in both directions. It consists of 5 satellites in geostationary orbit and 30 satellites in non-geostationary orbit.

With the modernization of GPS and GLONASS, and the deployment of BDS and GSNS, the GNSS constellation has developed from approximately 30 GPS satellites in the early stage to more than 100 GNSS satellites in September 2016, summarized in Table 4-2.

GLONASS

这个系统最初是在苏联发展起来的,这个项目后来由俄罗斯继续进行。俄罗斯从1993年开始建造自己的全球导航卫星系统,并于2007年开始运行。当时,俄罗斯只被允许提供卫星定位和导航服务。到2009年,服务范围已经扩展到全球。该系统的主要功能包括确定陆海空目标的坐标和移动速度等信息。

GSNS

该系统由欧盟开发和建立,并于1999年2月由欧洲委员会宣布。该系统由30颗卫星组成,轨道高度为23 616km,其中27颗为工作卫星,3颗为备用卫星。该卫星在大约24 000km的高度运行,位于三个轨道平面上,倾角为56°。

BDS

2003年,中国的北斗一号完成并投入运行。与GPS不同,BDS命令端和终端可以双向通信。它由5颗静止轨道卫星和30颗非静止轨道卫星组成。

随着GPS和GLONASS的现代化,以及BDS和GSNS的部署,GNSS星座从早期的约30颗GPS卫星发展到2016年9月的100多颗GNSS卫星,总结见表4-2。

Table 4-2 Summary of GPS/ GLONASS/ GSNS / BDS

	GPS	GLONASS	GSNS	BDS
First launch	1978-02-22	1982-10-12	2005-12-28	2017-11-05
Service type	Military/civil	Military/civil	Commercial/open	Military/civil
No. of designed satellites	24	24	30	30
No. of orbital planes	6	3	3	3 (MEO)
Orbital inclination	55°	64.8°	56°	55° (MEO)
Orbital altitude (km)	20,200	19,100	23,222	21,528 (MEO)
Orbital period	11h 58m	11h 15m	14h 04m	12h 53m (MEO)
Coordinate system	WGS84	PZ-90	GTRF	BDCS
Time system	GPST	UTC (SU)	GST	BDT
Modulation mode	CDMA	FDMA	CDMA	CDMA
Frequencies (MHz)	L1: 1575.42 L2: 1227.60 L5: 1176.45	G1: 1602.00 G2: 1246.00 G3: TBD	E1: 1575.42 E5a: 1176.45 E5b: 1207.14 E6: 1278.75	B1: 1575.42 B2: 1176.45 B3: 1268.52

As can be seen from the table, in terms of positioning accuracy, these navigation systems are capable of realizing civil 10m. GPS in the United States and GLONASS in Russia have a wide range of applications and fields. They are also the two positioning systems with the highest commercial penetration rate, which are closely related to their advanced layout, attention and huge investment.

By August 2019, the United States had launched 74 GPS satellites, of which 31 were operational, nine were on standby, two were being tested, 30 had retired and two were missing. The core constellation needs at least 24 operational satellites and 33 for normal global networking.

Since the technical reserve and capital investment required for the GNSS development is rather large, some countries began to develop Regional Navigation Satellite Systems (RNSS) to meet the navigation and positioning demands in their own territory and the surrounding areas, for example, the Quasi-Zenith Satellite System (QZSS) of Japan. QZSS can be used even in the Asia-Oceania regions with longitudes close to Japan, so its usage will be expanded to other countries in these regions as well. Japan plans to increase the number of navigation satellites in QZSS to seven by 2023, when it will no longer rely on the U.S. GPS to provide location information. India is also making steady progress in building its own Navigation with Indian Constellation (NavIC) system.

4. Main Components of Satellite Navigation Messages

GNSS satellite receiver receives modulated wave signal, which includes carrier (L1, L2, etc.), ranging code (C/A code and P code) and data code (also called navigation message). Therefore, after receiving satellite signal by antenna, carrier reconstruction and data decoding are needed to separate navigation message from modulated wave. GNSS satellite navigation message (also called data code or D code) mainly includes satellite ephemeris, clock correction, ionospheric delay correction, working status information and P code captured by C/A code. The satellite ephemeris in GNSS navigation messages are also called broadcast ephemeris, which are obtained and injected into the satellite by the ground control system of the system. It consists of 17 parameters (6 orbital roots, 9 perturbation correction parameters, and 2 time reference parameters).

5. Two Positioning Principles of GNSS

GNSS positioning can be understood as a dynamic aerial rear distance rendezvous. After the known satellite position and the distance between more than four satellites and the receiver is measured at the same time, the positioning distance can be measured.

从表中可以看出，在定位精度方面，这些导航系统能够实现民用10m。美国的GPS和俄罗斯的GLONASS有着广泛的应用领域。它们也是商业渗透率最高的两个定位系统，这与它们先进的布局、关注度和巨大的投入密切相关。

到2019年8月，美国共发射了74颗GPS卫星，其中31颗处于运行状态，9颗处于待命状态，2颗正在测试中，30颗退役，2颗失踪。核心星座至少需要24颗运行卫星，正常的全球网络需要33颗。

由于发展GNSS所需的技术储备和资金投入较大，一些国家开始发展区域导航卫星系统（RNSS），以满足本国及周边地区的导航定位需求，如日本的准天顶卫星系统（QZSS）。QZSS甚至可以在与日本经度相近的亚洲－大洋洲地区使用，因此它的使用也将扩展到这些地区的其他国家。日本计划到2023年将QZSS的导航卫星数量增加到7颗，届时日本将不再依赖美国的GPS提供位置信息。印度也通过印度区域导航卫星系统（NavIC）在建设自己的导航系统方面取得稳步进展。

4. 卫星导航电文的主要组成

GNSS卫星接收机接收到的是调制波信号，它包含了载波（L1、L2等）、测距码（C/A码和P码）和数据码（也叫导航电文）。因此，卫星信号经天线接收后需要进行重建载波和数据解码等工作，将导航电文从调制波中分离出来。GNSS卫星的导航电文（又叫数据码或D码）主要内容包括卫星星历、时钟校正、电离层时延校正、工作状态信息以及由C/A码捕获的P码信息。GNSS导航电文中的卫星星历也称广播星历，它是由系统的地面控制系统求得并注入卫星的。它由17个参数组成（6个轨道根数、9个摄动改正参数和2个时间参考参数）。

5. GNSS的两种定位原理

GNSS定位可理解成动态空中后方距离交会，在已知卫星位置又同时测定到四颗以上卫星至接收机的距离后，即可进行定位距离测量。

GNSS positioning mainly adopts two methods: one is to measure the pseudo distance (non-geometric distance due to the existence of various errors) of ranging code signal to the receiver, that is, pseudo distance measurement; the second is to measure the phase difference between the satellite carrier signal and the reference signal of the receiver, which is carrier phase measurement.

According to different distance measurement principles, GPS positioning methods can be divided into two types: pseudometric positioning method, which realizes 5-10m dynamic real-time single point absolute positioning navigation, and real-time pseudometric differential 1m; carrier phase measurement positioning method, which achieves a few mm± (1-2) ppm static relative positioning.

6. BDS

The BeiDou navigation satellite System (BDS), formerly known as COMPASS, is an independent global navigation satellite system developed and operated by China. As the third mature satellite navigation system after GPS and GLONASS, BDS provides high-quality positioning, velocity measurement, timing and short message services for global users. BDS has evolved from active positioning to passive positioning. A global passive positioning system will be established by 2020.

Compared with the other existing GNSS, the BDS has the following features:

First, implement in stages, from pilot system to regional coverage (Asia-Pacific region) to global coverage gradually;

Second, the whole system of three-frequency civil signal, multi-frequency signal combination to improve the service precision, and the use of passive positioning and navigation system similar to GPS and GSNS (passive positioning, CDMA signal system);

Third, short message communication function, inheriting the short message communication function of Beidou-1 system, with 1200 Chinese characters communication capacity;

Fourth, the high and middle orbits are arranged in layers, which are divided into high orbit synchronous orbit (GEO and IGSO) and middle orbit (MEO);

Fifth, the inter-satellite link system is used for self-correction between satellite orbits.

The service performances of BDS are summarized in Table 4-3.

According to the results of actual measurement, the BDS service capabilities have achieved and are better than above indicators in an all-round way.

GNSS 定位主要采用两种方法：一是测量测距码信号到达接收机的伪距（由于存在各种误差，为非几何距离），即伪距测量；二是测量卫星载波信号与接收机参考信号之间的相位差，即载波相位测量。

根据距离测定原理的不同，GPS 定位方法可分为两种：伪距定位法，实现 5~10m 的动态实时单点绝对定位导航，实时伪距差分 1m；载波相位测量定位法，实现几 mm±（1~2）ppm 的静态相对定位。

6. BDS

北斗卫星导航系统（BDS）的前身是 COMPASS，是中国自主研发运行的全球导航卫星系统。BDS 是继 GPS 和 GLONASS 之后第三个成熟的卫星导航系统，为全球用户提供高质量的定位、测速、授时和短信服务。BDS 已经从主动定位发展到被动定位。全球被动定位系统将于 2020 年建成。

与其他现有的 GNSS 相比，BDS 具有以下特点：

第一，分阶段实施，由试验系统至区域覆盖（亚太地区）逐渐转向全球覆盖；

第二，全系统三频民用信号，多频信号组合提高业务精度，并采用类似于 GPS 和 GSNS 的被动定位导航体制（被动定位，CDMA 信号体制）；

第三，短报文通信功能，继承北斗-1 系统的短报文通信功能，具有 1200 个汉字的通信容量；

第四，高中轨分层布设，分为高轨同步轨道（GEO 和 IGSO）和中轨道（MEO）两层；

第五，星间链路系统，用于卫星轨道之间的自校正。

BDS 的服务性能见表 4-3。

从实际测量结果来看，BDS 的服务能力已经达到并全面优于上述指标。

Table 4-3 Service performances of BDS

	BDS-1	BDS-2 (regional)	BDS-3 (global)
Service coverage	China and neighboring areas	Longitude: 84°–160° Latitude: 55°S–55°N	Global
Positioning accuracy	<20m	Horizontal 25m, elevation 30m	<10m (three-dimensional)
Velocity accuracy	/	0.2m/s	<0.2m/s
Timing accuracy	100ns for one-way, 20ns for two-way	50ns	20ns

The 3rd geosynchronous satellite of the BDS was launched from Xichang Satellite Launch Center on June 23, 2020. It is also the last global networking satellite of the Beidou-3, so far all 30 Beidou-3 satellites have been put in place, and the deployment of the Global Navigation Satellite System constellation has been completed. In the future, BDS will continue to improve service performance, expand service functions, and guarantee continuous and stable operation. Beidou services will be available to all parts of the world.

Since provision of services, BDS has been widely used in transportation, agriculture, forestry, fisheries, hydrological monitoring, meteorological forecasting, communication and other fields, and has been serving national significant infrastructures, thereby resulting in remarkable economic and social benefits. By the end of 2019, 155 framework network benchmark stations and more than 2,200 regional network benchmark stations had been built in China. The BDS navigation products, including chips, modules, high-precision OEM boards and antenna, have been exported to more than 100 countries and regions.

With the arrival of the 5G commercial era, the high bandwidth and low delay of 5G can greatly improve the efficiency of Beidou location navigation service. The Beidou ground-based enhancement system can provide services at the meter level, sub-meter level, and even centimeter level. The combination of Beidou's high precision and 5G speed will greatly improve the quality of people's lives.

7. Conclusion

The construction and application of GNSS have brought a revolutionary change to navigation and positioning technology. With "land, sea, air and sky" all-round real-time navigation, positioning accuracy of 1-10m, satellite navigation industry has become a global high-tech industry, providing information support for intelligent driving, lane navigation, Internet of Things and so on, and will change people's social life. Location is everywhere. Using GPS for high-precision timing and punctuality (observatories, radio data communications, etc.), users can obtain clock corrections of 10ns

2020年6月23日，BDS第三颗同步卫星在西昌卫星发射中心发射升空。这是北斗3号的最后一颗全球联网卫星，目前已全部建成30颗北斗3号卫星，完成了全球导航卫星系统的星座部署。未来，BDS将不断提升服务性能，拓展服务功能，确保持续稳定运行。北斗服务将面向世界各地。

BDS自提供服务以来，广泛应用于交通、农林渔业、水文监测、气象预报、通信等领域，服务国家重要基础设施，产生了显著的经济效益和社会效益。截至2019年底，中国已建成155个框架网基准站和2200多个区域网基准站。BDS导航产品包括芯片、模块、高精度OEM板、天线等，已出口到100多个国家和地区。

随着5G商业时代的到来，5G的高带宽、低延迟可以大大提高北斗定位导航服务的效率。北斗地基增强系统可提供米级、亚米级，甚至厘米级的服务。北斗的高精度和5G速度的结合将大大提高人们的生活质量。

7. 结论

GNSS的建成和应用给导航和定位技术带来了一场革命性的变化。"陆海空天"全方位实时导航，定位精度可达1~10m，卫星导航产业已成为全球性的高技术产业，为智能驾驶、车道导航、物联网等提供信息支持，并将改变人们的社会生活。位置信息无处不在。利用GPS进行高精度的授时和守时（天文台站、无线电数据通信等领域），用户能获得10ns的时钟校正数

(relative to GPS time), up to 0.1 to 1μs ($10^{-7} \sim 10^{-6}$s) relative to UTC. In the field of surveying and mapping it almost replace the conventional geodesy, and is widely used in aerial survey, land survey, demarcation and other fields.

China will further promote the technological integration between BDS and mobile communication, cloud computing, Internet of Things, industry internet, big data and block chain, promote the integration between the satellite navigation industry and high-end manufacturing, software, integrated data and modern service industries, and continue to promote the BDS applications and industrial development, so as to serve the country's modernization construction and daily life of the people, and to make contributions to the global scientific, technological, economic and social development.

With the arrival ofthe 5G era, the Internet of everything becomes possible, and the application of GNSS+5G is limited only by people's imagination!

（相对于 GPS 时间），相对于 UTC 可达 0.1~1μs（$10^{-7} \sim 10^{-6}$s）。在测绘领域几乎取代常规大地测量，在航测、土地调查、勘界等领域应用广泛。

中国将进一步促进 BDS 与移动通信、云计算、物联网、工业互联网、大数据和区块链之间的技术集成，促进卫星导航产业与高端制造业、软件、集成数据和现代服务业之间的集成，并继续推动 BDS 应用和工业的发展，为国家的现代化建设和人民的日常生活，以及全球科技、经济和社会的发展作出贡献。

随着 5G 时代的到来，万物互联将成为可能，GNSS+5G 的应用将超越人们的想象！

NEW WORDS AND PHRASES

Internet of Things（IoT）　物联网　　　　　　　导航卫星系统
space-based Internet of Things　天基物联网　　　pseudo distance measurement　伪距测量
Global Navigation Satellite System（GNSS）　全球　carrier phase measurement　载波相位测量

NOTES

1) The ground control station is responsible for collecting information from the satellite and calculating the satellite ephemeris, relative distances, atmospheric correction and other data.
地面控制站负责从卫星收集信息，计算卫星星历、相对距离、大气校正等数据。

2) GNSS satellite navigation message (also called data code or D code) mainly includes satellite ephemeris, clock correction, ionospheric delay correction, working status information and P code captured by C/A code.
GNSS 卫星的导航电文（又叫数据码或 D 码）主要内容包括卫星星历、时钟校正、电离层时延校正、工作状态信息以及由 C/A 码捕获的 P 码信息。

3) With the arrival of the 5G era, the Internet of everything becomes possible, and the application of GNSS+5G is limited only by people's imagination!
随着 5G 时代的到来，万物互联将成为可能，GNSS+5G 的应用将超越人们的想象！

4.3 Optical Fiber Communication

As shown in Fig. 4-9, optical fiber communication is a method of transmitting information from one place to another by sending pulses of light through an optical fiber. The light forms an electromagnetic carrier wave that is modulated to carry information. First developed in the 1970s, fiber-optic communication systems have revolutionized the telecommunications industry and have played a major role in the advent of the Information Age.

1. Applications

Optical fiber is used by many telecommunications companies to transmit telephone signals, Internet communication, and cable television signals. Due to much lower attenuation and interference, optical fiber has large advantages over existing copper wire in long-distance and high-demand applications. However, infrastructure development within cities was relatively difficult and time-consuming, and fiber-optic systems were complex and expensive to install and operate. Due to these difficulties, fiber-optic communication systems have primarily been installed in long-distance applications, where they can be used to their full transmission capacity, offsetting the increased cost.

Fig. 4-9　Optical fiber

Fiber optics have become the industry standard for the terrestrial transmission of telecommunication information. Fiber optics will continue to be a major player in the delivery of broadband services. Today more than 80 percent of the world's long-distance traffic is carried over optical-fiber cables. Telecommunications applications of fiber-optic cable are widespread, ranging from global networks to desktop computers. These involve the transmission of voice, data, and video over distances of less than a meter to hundreds of kilometers. Carriers use optical fiber to carry analog phone service. Cable television companies also use fiber for delivery of digital video services. Intelligent transportation systems and biomedical systems also use fiber-optic transmission systems. Optical cable is also the industry standard for subterranean and submarine transmission systems.

Since 2000, the prices for fiber-optic communications have dropped considerably. The price for rolling out fiber to the home has currently become more cost-effective than that of rolling out a copper based network.

2. History

In 1880 Alexander Graham Bell and his assistant Charles Sumner Tainter created a very early precursor to fiber-optic communications-the photophone, at Bell's newly established Volta Laboratory in Washington, D. C.. Bell considered it as his most important invention. The device allowed for the transmission of sound on a beam of light.

By 1964, a critical and theoretical specification was identified by Dr. Charles K. Kao for long-range communication devices, the 10 or 20dB of light loss per kilometer standard. In 1966 Charles K. Kao and George Hockham proposed optical fibers at STC Laboratories (STL) at Harlow, England, when they showed that the losses of 1000dB/km in existing glass (compared to 5-10dB/km in coaxial cable) was due to contaminants, which could potentially be removed. Dr. Kao also illustrated the need for a purer form of glass to help reduce light loss.

Optical fiber was successfully developed in 1970 by Corning Glass Works, with attenuation low enough (about 20dB/km) for communication purpose.

The first wide area network fiber optic cable system in the world seems to have been installed in Hastings, East Sussex, UK in 1978. The cables were placed in ducting throughout the town, and had over 1000 subscribers, they were used at that time for the transmission of television channels. The system is still in place, but disused.

The second generation of fiber-optic communication was developed for commercial use in the early 1980s, operated at 1.3μm, and used InGaAsP semiconductor lasers. These early systems were initially limited by multi mode fiber dispersion, and in 1981 the single-mode fiber was revealed to greatly improve system performance, however practical connectors capable of working with single mode fiber proved difficult to develop. By 1987, these systems were operating at bit rates of up to 1.7Gbit/s with repeater spacing up to 50km.

The third generation of fiber-optic systems operated at 1.55μm and had losses of about 0.2dB/km. Engineers overcame earlier difficulties with pulse-spreading at that wavelength using conventional InGaAsP semiconductor lasers. Scientists overcame this difficulty by using dispersion-shifted fibers designed to have minimal dispersion at 1.55μm or by limiting the laser spectrum to a single longitudinal mode. These developments eventually allowed third-generation systems to operate commercially at 2.5Gbit/s with repeater spacing in excess of 100km.

The fourth generation of fiber-optic communication systems used optical amplification to reduce the need for repeaters and Wavelength-Division Multiplexing (WDM) to increase data capacity. These two improvements caused a revolution that resulted in the doubling of system capacity every 6 months starting in 1992 until a bit rate of 10Tbit/s was reached by 2001.

The focus of development for the fifth generation of fiber-optic communications is on extending the wavelength range over which a WDM system can operate. The conventional wavelength window, known as the C band, covers the wavelength range 1.53-1.57μm, and dry fiber has a low-loss window promising an extension of that range to 1.30-1.65μm. Other developments include the concept of "optical solitons", pulses that preserve their shape by counteracting the effects of dispersion with the nonlinear effects of the fiber by using pulses of a specific shape.

3. Optical Fiber

Structure

Typical optical fibers are composed of core, cladding and buffer coating. The core is the inner part of the fiber, which guides light. The cladding surrounds the core completely (see Fig. 4-10).

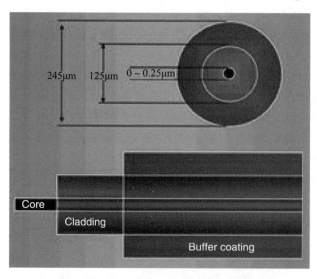

Fig. 4-10 The structure of an optical fiber

For the most common optical fiber types, which includes 1550nm single mode fibers and 850nm or 1300nm multimode fibers, the core diameter ranges from 8μm to 62.5μm. The most common cladding diameter is 125μm. The material of buffer coating usually is soft or hard plastic such as acrylic, nylon and with diameter ranges from 250μm to 900μm. Buffer coating provides mechanical protection and bending flexibility for the fiber.

Operational Principle

Optical fibers are based entirely on the principle of total internal reflection. The refractive index of the core is higher than that of the cladding. So light in the core that strikes the boundary with the cladding at an angle larger than critical angle will be reflected back into the core by total internal reflection. Fig. 4-11 illustrates the operational principle of optical fiber.

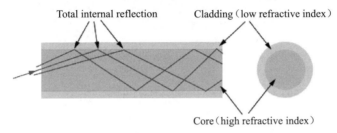

Fig. 4-11   Operational principle of optical fiber

Mode

An optical fiber guides light waves in distinct patterns called modes. Mode describes the distribution of light energy across the fiber. We can take a look at large-core step-index fibers. Light rays enter the fiber at a range of angles, and rays at different angles can all stably travel down the length of the fiber as long as they hit the core-cladding interface at an angle larger than critical angle. These rays are different modes.

Two main types of optical fiber used in optic communications include multi-mode optical fibers and single-mode optical fibers. Fibers that carry more than one mode at a specific light wavelength are called multi-mode fibers. A multi-mode optical fiber has a larger core (≥50μm), allowing less precise, cheaper transmitters and receivers to connect to it as well as cheaper connectors. However, a multi-mode fiber introduces multi-mode distortion, which often limits the bandwidth and length of the link. Furthermore, because of its higher dopant content, multi-mode fibers are usually expensive and exhibit higher attenuation. Some fibers have very small diameter core that they can carry only one mode which travels as a straight line at the center of the core. These fibers are single-mode fibers. The core of a single-mode fiber is smaller (<10μm) and requires more expensive components and interconnection methods, but allows much longer, higher-performance links. This is illustrated in Fig. 4-12.

Index Profile

Index profile is the refractive index distribution across the core and the cladding of a fiber. Some optical fiber has a step-index profile, in which the core has one uniformly distributed index and the cladding has a lower uniformly distributed index. Other optical fiber has a graded-index profile, in which refractive index varies gradually as a function of radial distance from the fiber center. Fig. 4-13 shows some common types of index profiles for single-mode and multi-mode fibers.

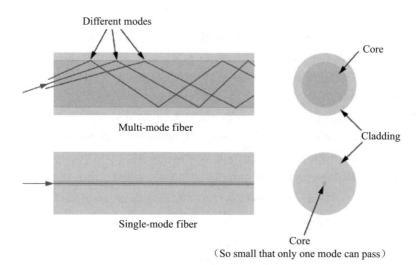

Fig. 4-12 Multi-mode fiber and single-mode fiber

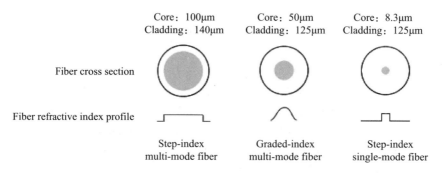

Fig. 4-13 Common types of index profiles

Numerical Aperture

Multi-mode optical fiber will only propagate light that enters the fiber within a certain cone, known as the acceptance cone of the fiber. The half-angle of this cone is called the acceptance angle, θ_{max}, as shown in Fig. 4-14.

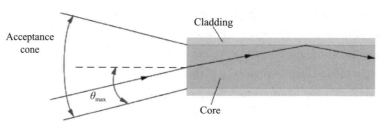

Fig. 4-14 Optical fiber's acceptance angle

For step-index multi-mode fiber, the acceptance angle is determined only by the indices of refraction:

$$\mathrm{NA} = n\sin\theta_{max} = \sqrt{n_f^2 - n_c^2} \tag{4-35}$$

where n_f is the refractive index of the fiber core, n_c is the refractive index of the cladding.

4. Optical Fiber System

The process of communicating using optical fiber system involves the following basic steps: creating the optical signal involving the use of a transmitter, relaying the signal along the fiber, ensuring that the signal does not become too distorted or weak, receiving the optical signal, and converting it into an electrical signal.

Modern fiber-optic communication systems generally include an optical transmitter to convert an electrical signal into an optical signal to send into the optical fiber, a cable containing bundles of multiple optical fibers that is routed through underground conduits and buildings, multiple kinds of amplifiers, and an optical receiver to recover the signal as an electrical signal. A typical optical communication system is shown as Fig. 4-15. The information transmitted is typically digital information generated by computers, telephone systems, and cable television companies.

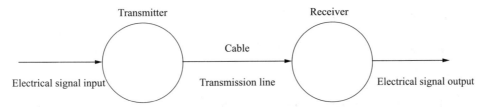

Fig. 4-15 A typical optical communication system

Transmitters

The most commonly used optical transmitters are semiconductor devices such as Light-Emitting Diodes (LED) and laser diodes. The difference between LEDs and laser diodes is that LEDs produce incoherent light, while laser diodes produce coherent light. For use in optical communications, semiconductor optical transmitters must be designed to be compact, efficient, and reliable, while operating in an optimal wavelength range, and directly modulated at high frequencies.

The basic unit of the LED is a forward-biased PN junction, emitting light through spontaneous emission, a phenomenon referred to as electroluminescence. LED light transmission is also inefficient, with only about 1% of input power, or about 100 microwatts, eventually converted into launched power which has been coupled into the optical fiber. However, due to their relatively simple design, LEDs are very useful for low-cost applications.

Commonly used classes of semiconductor laser transmitters used in fiber optics include VCSEL (Vertical Cavity Surface Emitting Laser), Fabry-Pérot (an interferometer invented by Fabry and Pérot) and DFB (Distributed Feed Back).

Laser diodes are often directly modulated, that is the light output is controlled by a current applied directly to the device. For very high data rates or very long distance links, a laser source may be operated continuous wave, and the light modulated by an external device such as an electro-absorption modulator or Mach-Zehnder interferometer.

Receivers

The main component of an optical receiver is a photodetector, which converts light into electricity using the photoelectric effect. The primary photodetectors for telecommunications are made from Indium Gallium Arsenide. The photodetector is typically a semiconductor-based photodiode. Several types of photodiodes include P-N photodiodes, P-I-N photodiodes, and avalanche photodiodes.

Metal-Semiconductor-Metal (MSM) photodetectors are also used due to their suitability for wavelength-division multiplexers and circuit integration in regenerators.

Transmission Windows

Each effect that contributes to attenuation and dispersion depends on the optical wavelength. The wavelength bands (or windows) that exist where these effects are the weakest are the most favorable for transmission. These windows have been standardized, and the currently defined transmission windows of fiber are listed in Table 4-4.

Table 4-4 Transmission windows of fiber

Band	Description	Wavelength range
O band	Original	1260nm to 1360nm
E band	Extended	1360nm to 1460nm
S band	Short wavelength	1460nm to 1530nm
C band	Conventional	1560nm to 1565nm
L band	Long wavelength	1565nm to 1625nm
U band	Ultralong wavelength	1625nm to 1675nm

Historically, there was a window used below the O band, called the first window, at 800-900nm; however, losses are high in this region so this window is used primarily for short-distance communications. The current lower windows (O and E) around 1300nm have much lower losses. This region has zero dispersion. The middle windows (S and C) around 1500nm are the most widely used. This region has the lowest attenuation losses and achieves the longest range. It does have some dispersion, so dispersion compensator devices are used to remove this.

5. Advantages of Optical Fiber

The choice between optical fiber and electrical (or copper) transmission for a particular system is made based on a number of trade-offs. Optical fiber is generally chosen for systems requiring higher bandwidth or spanning longer distances than electrical cabling can accommodate.

The followings are the advantages of optical fiber communication.

1) Wider bandwidth: the information carrying capacity of a transmission system is directly proportional to the carrier frequency of the transmitted signals. Thus the optical fiber yields greater transmission bandwidth than the conventional communication systems and the data rate or number of bits per second is increased to a greater extent in the optical fiber communication system. Further the wavelength division multiplexing operation by the data rate or information carrying capacity of optical fibers is enhanced to many orders of magnitude.

2) Low transmission loss: due to the usage of the ultra-low loss fibers and the erbium doped silica fibers as optical amplifiers, one can achieve almost lossless transmission. In the modern optical fiber telecommunication systems, the fibers having a transmission loss of 0.002dB/km are used. Further the repeater spacing is more than 100km. Since the amplification is done in the optical domain itself, the distortion produced during the strengthening of the signal is almost negligible.

3) Signal security: the transmitted signal through the fibers does not radiate. Further the signal cannot be tapped from a fiber in an easy manner. Therefore optical fiber communication provides a hundred percent signal security.

4) Eliminating spark hazards: in some cases, transmitting signals electrically can be extremely dangerous. Most electric potentials create small sparks. The sparks ordinarily pose no danger, but can be really bad in a chemical plant or oil refinery where the air is contaminated with potentially explosive vapours. One tiny spark can create a big explosion. Potential spark hazards seriously hinder data and communication in such facilities. Optical fibers are made from silica which is an electrical insulator, and fiber optic cables do not produce sparks since they do not carry current.

5) Ease of installation: increasing transmission capacity of wire cables generally makes them thicker and more rigid. Such thick cables can be difficult to install in existing buildings where they must go through walls and cable ducts. Fiber optic cables are developed with small radii, and they are flexible, compact and lightweight. The fiber cables can be bent or twisted without damage.

NEW WORDS AND PHRASES

Information Age 信息时代
attenuation *n.* 衰减
interference *n.* 干扰，干涉
photophone *n.* 光线电话机
pulse-spreading *n.* 脉冲扩展
dispersion-shifted fiber 色散位移光纤
longitudinal mode 纵模
optical amplification 光放大
Wavelength-Division Multiplexing (WDM) 波分复用
data capacity 数据容量
nonlinear effect 非线性效应

total internal reflection 全内反射
refractive index 折射率
index profile 折射率分布
numerical aperture 数值孔径
cable television 有线电视
laser diode 激光二极管
incoherent light 非相干光
coherent light 相干光
electroluminescence *n.* 电致发光
launched power 发射功率
erbium doped silica fiber 掺铒石英光纤

NOTES

1) Due to much lower attenuation and interference, optical fiber has large advantages over existing copper wire in long-distance and high-demand applications.
   由于光纤相比于现有的铜线具有低得多的衰减和干扰，因此在长距离和高需求的应用领域具有很大的优势。

2) Light rays enter the fiber at a range of angles, and rays at different angles can all stably travel down the length of the fiber as long as they hit the core-cladding interface at an angle larger than critical angle.
   光线以一定范围的角度进入光纤内，只要入射到纤芯与包层交界面的角度大于临界角，就能够在光纤中以不同的角度平稳行进。

3) Some optical fiber has a step-index profile, in which the core has one uniformly distributed index and the cladding has a lower uniformly distributed index.
   某些光纤具有阶跃折射率分布，其中纤芯具有均匀分布的折射率，同时包层也具有比纤芯低且均匀分布的折射率。

4) Modern fiber-optic communication systems generally include an optical transmitter to convert an electrical signal into an optical signal to send into the optical fiber, a cable containing bundles of multiple optical fibers that is routed through underground conduits and buildings, multiple kinds of amplifiers, and an optical

receiver to recover the signal as an electrical signal.

现代光纤通信系统一般包括：光发射器——将电信号转换成光信号并将光信号送入光纤，光缆——包含多组沿地下管道和建筑物传输的光纤，多种放大器和光接收器——将光信号恢复为电信号。

5) Due to the usage of the ultra-low loss fibers and the erbium doped silica fibers as optical amplifiers, one can achieve almost lossless transmission.

由于超低损耗光纤和掺铒石英光纤作为光放大器的使用，人们可以实现几乎无损耗的传输。

EXERCISES

1. Please translate the following words and phrases into Chinese.
   a) electromagnetic
   b) internal reflection
   c) mode
   d) transmission window
   e) dopant content
   f) numerical aperture
   g) coherent light
   h) laser diode
   i) optical solitons
   j) acceptance angle

2. Please translate the following words and phrases into English.
   a) 电子通信
   b) 干涉
   c) 临界角
   d) 掺铒石英光纤
   e) 调频
   f) 带宽
   g) 折射率
   h) 衰减
   i) 光放大
   j) 波分复用

3. Fill in the blanks with the missing word(s).
   a) First developed in the 1970s, fiber-optic communication systems have revolutionized the telecommunications industry and have _____ a major role _____ the advent of the Information Age.
   b) Optical fiber is used _____ many telecommunications companies _____ transmit telephone signals, Internet communication, and cable television signals.
   c) Due to these difficulties, fiber-optic communication systems have primarily been installed _____ long-distance applications, where they can be used _____ their full transmission capacity, offsetting the increased cost.
   d) Today more than 80 percent _____ the world's long-distance traffic is carried over optical-fiber cables.
   e) _____ 1964, a critical and theoretical specification was identified _____ Dr. Charles K. Kao for long-range communication devices, the 10 or 20dB of light loss _____ kilometer standard.
   f) The material _____ buffer coating usually is soft or hard plastic such as acrylic, nylon and with diameter ranges _____ 250μm _____ 900μm.
   g) Optical fibers are based entirely _____ the principle of total internal reflection.
   h) Two main types _____ optical fiber used _____ optic communications include multi-mode optical fibers and single-mode optical fibers.
   i) Multi-mode optical fiber will only propagate light that enters the fiber _____ a certain cone, known as the acceptance cone of the fiber.
   j) Each effect that contributes _____ attenuation and dispersion depends _____ the optical wavelength.

4. Answer the following questions according to the text.
   a) What is the structure of the optical fiber?
   b) Describe the history of the development of optical fiber communication briefly.
   c) What does typical optical communication system consist of?
   d) What are the advantages of optical fiber communication?

READING

Ultra-wideband Communication

Ultra-wideband (UWB) radio is a fast emerging technology with uniquely attractive features inviting major advances in wireless communications, networking, radar, imaging, and positioning systems. By its rule-making proposal in 2002, the Federal Communications Commission (FCC) in the United States essentially unleashed huge "new bandwidth" (3.6~10.1GHz) at the noise floor, where UWB radios overlaying coexistent RF systems can operate using low-power ultra-short information bearing pulses. With similar regulatory processes currently under way in many countries worldwide, industry, government agencies, and academic institutions responded to this FCC ruling with rapidly growing research efforts targeting a host of exciting UWB applications: short-range very high-speed broadband access to the Internet, covert communication links, localization at centimeter-level accuracy, high-resolution ground-penetrating radar, through-wall imaging, precision navigation and asset tracking, just to name a few.

1. Introduction

UWB characterizes transmission systems with instantaneous spectral occupancy in excess of 500MHz or a fractional bandwidth of more than 20%. (The fractional bandwidth is defined as B/f_c, where $B = f_H - f_L$ denotes the -10dB bandwidth and center frequency $f_c = (f_H + f_L)/2$ with f_H being the upper frequency of the -10dB emission point, and f_L the lower frequency of the -10dB emission point. UWB systems with $f_c > 2.5$GHz need to have a -10dB bandwidth of at least 500MHz, while UWB systems with $f_c < 2.5$GHz need to have fractional bandwidth at least 0.20.) Such systems rely on ultra-short (nanosecond scale) waveforms that can be free of sine-wave carriers and do not require IF processing because they can operate at baseband. As information-bearing pulses with ultra-short duration have UWB spectral occupancy, UWB radios come with unique advantages that have long been appreciated by the radar and communications communities: i) enhanced capability to penetrate through obstacles; ii) ultra high precision ranging at the centimeter level; iii) potential for very high data rates along with a commensurate increase in user capacity; and iv) potentially small size and processing power. Despite these attractive features, interest in UWB devices prior to 2001 was primarily limited to radar systems, mainly for military applications. With bandwidth resources becoming increasingly scarce, UWB radio was "a

超宽带通信

超宽带（UWB）无线电是一种独具魅力的快速新兴技术，它能推动无线通信、网络、雷达、成像和定位系统等方面的重大进步。美国联邦通信委员会（FCC）在 2002 年制定了规则建议，在噪声层规划了巨大的"新带宽"（3.6~10.1GHz）。在这带宽内，UWB 无线电与射频系统可以在低功率超高频下运作。目前世界上许多国家、行业、政府机构和学术机构采用相似的方式针对 FCC 的规则进行了大量关于 UWB 应用的研究工作：短距离的高速宽带接入互联网、隐蔽通信链路、厘米级精度的定位、高分辨率探地雷达、穿墙成像、精确导航和资产跟踪等。

1. 引言

UWB 的特征是传输系统的瞬时频谱带宽超过 500MHz 或者相对带宽超过 20%（相对带宽定义为 B/f_c，其中 $B = f_H - f_L$ 表示 -10dB 带宽，中心频率 $f_c = (f_H + f_L)/2$，上限频率 f_H 和下限频率 f_L 是 -10dB 的发射点。$f_c > 2.5$GHz 的 UWB 系统需要有至少为 500MHz 的 -10dB 带宽，而 $f_c < 2.5$GHz 的 UWB 系统的相对带宽至少为 0.20）。这些系统依赖于由正弦波发生器发出的超短（纳秒级）波形，并且它们可以在基带操作，所以不需要进行中频处理。由于持续时间极短的信息承载脉冲具有 UWB 频谱，UWB 无线电在雷达和通信方面一直具有独特的优势：①穿透障碍物能力强；②厘米级范围的超高精度；③与随着用户容量增加相称的高数据传输速率；④小尺寸和强大的处理能力。尽管 UWB 设备有这么多吸引人的特点和优势，但是在 2001 年之前主要限于雷达系统，主要用于军事方面。随着带宽资源的日益稀缺，UWB 无线电是"一个仲夏夜的梦"，等待我们去完

midsummer night's dream" waiting to be fulfilled. But things changed drastically in the spring of 2002, when the FCC released a spectral mask allowing (even commercial) operation of UWB radios at the noise floor, but over an enormous bandwidth (up to 7.5GHz).

This huge "new bandwidth" opens the door for an unprecedented number of bandwidth-demanding position-critical low-power applications in wireless communications, networking, radar imaging, and localization systems. It also explains the rapidly increasing efforts undertaken by several research institutions, industry, and government agencies to assess and exploit the potential of UWB radios in various areas. These include short-range high-speed access to the Internet, accurate personnel and asset tracking for increased safety and security, precision navigation, imaging of steel reinforcement bars in concrete or pipes hidden inside walls, surveillance, and medical monitoring of the heart's actual contractions.

For wireless communications in particular, the FCC regulated power levels are very low (below −41.3dBm), which allows UWB technology to overlay already available services such as the Global Positioning System (GPS) and the IEEE 802.11 Wireless Local Area Networks (WLAN) that coexist in the 3.6~10.1GHz band. Although UWB signals can propagate greater distances at higher power levels, current FCC regulations enable high-rate (above 110Mbit/s) data transmissions over a short range (10~15m) at very low power. Major efforts are currently under way by the IEEE 802.15 Working Group for standardizing UWB wireless radios for indoor (home and office) multimedia transmissions. Similar to the frequency reuse principle exploited by wireless cellular architectures, low-power, short-range UWB communications are also potentially capable of providing high spatial capacity, in terms of bits per second per square meter. In addition, UWB connectivity is expected to offer a rich set of software-controllable parameters that can be used to design location-aware communication networks flexible to scale in rates and power requirements.

To fulfill these expectations, however, UWB research and development have to cope with formidable challenges that limit their Bit Error Rate (BER) performance, capacity, throughput, and network flexibility. Those include high sensitivity to synchronizing the reception of ultra-short pulses, optimal exploitation of fading propagation effects with pronounced frequency-selectivity, low-complexity constraints in decoding high-performance multiple access protocols, and strict power limitations imposed by the desire to minimize interference among UWB communicators, and with coexisting legacy systems, particularly GPS, Unmanned Air Vehicles (UAV), aircraft radar, and WLAN. These challenges call for advanced

成。在2002年的春天，事情发生了巨大的变化，FFC宣布在噪声层允许（甚至是商业）使用UWB无线电，覆盖了更大的带宽（达到7.5GHz）。

这个巨大的"新带宽"为带宽要求大、精度要求高、功率要求低的无线通信、网络、雷达成像和定位系统等领域打开了一扇大门。这也解释了多个研究机构、行业和政府为评估与开发UWB无线电在多个领域的潜力方面所做的快速增长的努力的原因，包括短距离高速接入互联网、准确的人员和资产跟踪以增加安全保卫、精确导航、混凝土中的钢筋或墙内管道的成像、监视，以及心脏实时收缩的医疗监控。

尤其是对于无线通信，FCC的稳压电平非常低（低于−41.3dBm），这允许UWB技术可叠加应用于多种服务，如在3.6~10.1GHz频带共存的全球定位系统（GPS）和IEEE 802.11无线局域网络（WLAN）。尽管UWB信号可以以更高的功率传播更远的距离，但目前FCC规定短距离（10~15m）高速率（超过110Mbit/s）数据传输的功耗必须非常低。目前IEEE 802.15工作组的主要工作是规范室内（家庭和办公室）多媒体传输的UWB无线设备。与无线蜂窝体系结构利用的频率复用原则相类似，低功耗、短距离UWB通信也能够提供高空间容量，以bit/(s·m^2)衡量。此外，UWB连接预计将提供一组丰富的软件控制参数，这组参数可以用来设计柔性的位置感知通信网络，以提升速度和功耗要求。

然而，为了满足这些期望，UWB的研究和开发不得不应对严峻的挑战，例如，限制误比特率（BER）、容量、吞吐量和网络灵活性，其中包括超短脉冲同步接收的高灵敏度，有明确频率选择性的衰减传播效应的最优开发，解码高性能多址接入协议的低复杂性约束，降低UWB通信器之间的干扰需求而导致的严格功耗限制，与已有系统的共存，尤其是GPS、无人驾驶飞行器（UAV）、飞机雷达和WLAN。这些

Digital Signal Processing (DSP) expertise to accomplish tasks such as synchronization, channel estimation and equalization, multi-user detection, high-rate high-precision low-power Analog/Digital Conversion (ADC), and suppression of aggregate interference arising from coexisting legacy systems. As DSP theory, algorithms, and hardware advanced narrowband and broadband technology, DSP is expected to play a similar role in pushing the frontiers of emerging UWB applications. To this end, it is important to understand features and challenges that are unique to UWB signaling from a DSP perspective.

2. History and Background

The recent rapid growth in technology and the successful commercial deployment of wireless communications are significantly affecting our daily lives. The transition from analog to digital cellular communications, the rise of the third and fourth generation radio systems, and the replacement of wired connections with Wi-Fi and Bluetooth are enabling consumers to access a wide range of information from anywhere and at any time. As the consumer demand for higher capacity, faster service, and more secure wireless connections increases, new enhanced technologies have to find their place in the overcrowded and scarce Radio Frequency (RF) spectrum. This is because every radio technology allocates a specific part of the spectrum; for example, the signals for TVs, radios, cell phones, and so on are sent on different frequencies to avoid interference to each other. As a result, the constraints on the availability of the RF spectrum become more and more strict with the introduction of new radio services.

Ultra-wideband (UWB) technology offers a promising solution to the RF spectrum drought by allowing new services to coexist with current radio systems with minimal or no interference. This coexistence brings the advantage of avoiding the expensive spectrum licensing fees that providers of all other radio services must pay (the United Kingdom's spectrum auction for next-generation wireless applications generated $35.4 billion in April 2000).

Ultra-wideband communications is fundamentally different from all other communication techniques because it employs extremely narrow RF pulses to communicate between transmitters and receivers. Utilizing short-duration pulses as the building blocks for communications directly generates a very wide bandwidth and offers several advantages, such as large throughput, covertness, robustness to jamming, and coexistence with current radio services.

Ultra-wideband communications is not a new technology; in fact, it was first employed by Guglielmo Marconi in 1901

挑战需要先进的数字信号处理（DSP）专业知识来完成以下工作，如同步、信道估计与均衡、多用户检测、高速率高精度低功耗的模拟/数字转换（ADC），以及由于传统系统共存产生的总干扰抑制。由于DSP理论、算法以及先进的窄带和宽带硬件技术，DSP预计将在推动新兴UWB应用发展方面发挥类似的作用。为此，从DSP的角度来理解UWB信号的特点和挑战是非常重要的。

2. 历史与背景

无线通信技术和成功商业部署的快速发展，大大影响我们的日常生活。从模拟过渡到数字蜂窝通信、第三代和第四代无线系统的崛起，以及从有线连接变为Wi-Fi和蓝牙连接，消费者能够在任意地方和任意时间访问更广泛的信息。随着消费者要求更大的容量、更快的服务、更安全的无线连接，新的先进技术必须在拥挤不堪和稀缺的射频（RF）频谱中找到自己的位置。这是因为每一种无线电技术都需要分配一个特定的频谱，例如电视、收音机、手机等的信号在不同频率上发送，以避免相互干扰。其结果是，随着新的无线服务的引入，RF频谱的使用约束将变得越来越严格。

超宽带（UWB）技术为RF频谱资源的短缺提供了一种可行的解决方案，它通过允许新的服务在很少或没有干扰的情况下与现有无线电系统共存来解决问题。这种共存带来的好处是避免了无线服务供应商所必须支付的昂贵的频谱使用许可费用（2000年4月，英国为下一代无线应用的频谱拍卖达35.4亿美元）。

与其他通信技术根本不同的是，超宽带通信在发射器和接收器之间采用极窄的RF脉冲通信。利用短脉冲作为通信的基础模块将直接产生很宽的带宽，并且有很多优点，如大的吞吐量、隐蔽性、抗干扰性，以及可以与当前的无线服务共存。

超宽带通信并不是新的技术。事实上，它最早可追溯到马可尼（Guglielmo Marconi）

to transmit Morse code sequences across the Atlantic Ocean using spark gap radio transmitters. However, the benefit of a large bandwidth and the capability of implementing multiuser systems provided by electromagnetic pulses were never considered at that time.

Approximately fifty years after Marconi, modern pulse-based transmission gained momentum in military applications in the form of impulse radars. Some of the pioneers of modern UWB communications in the United States from the late 1960s are Henning Harmuth of Catholic University of America and Gerald Ross and K. W. Robins of Sperry Rand Corporation (R. Fontana, "A Brief History of UWB Communications"). From the 1960s to the 1990s, this technology was restricted to military and Department of Defense (DoD) applications under classified programs such as highly secure communications. However, the recent advancement in microprocessing and fast switching in semiconductor technology has made UWB ready for commercial applications. Therefore, it is more appropriate to consider UWB as a new name for a long-existing technology.

As interest in the commercialization of UWB has increased over the past several years, developers of UWB systems began pressuring the FCC to approve UWB for commercial use. In February 2002, the FCC approved the first Report and Order (R&O) for commercial use of UWB technology under strict power emission limits for various devices. Fig. 4-16 summarizes the development timeline of UWB.

在1901年使用火花隙发射器横跨大西洋发送莫尔斯码序列。然而，由电磁脉冲实现的大带宽所带来的益处和多用户系统的能力当时人们并没有考虑过。

马可尼之后的大约五十多年，现代基于脉冲的传输主要以脉冲雷达的形式应用在军事方面。美国天主教大学的亨宁·哈穆特和斯佩里兰德公司（Sperry Rand Corporation）的杰拉尔德·罗斯和K. W. 罗宾斯从20世纪60年代末开始研究UWB（R. Fontana，"A Brief History of UWB Communications"），他们是现代UWB通信的先驱。从20世纪60年代到90年代，该技术仅限于军事和美国国防部（DoD）高度安全的通信中应用。然而，最近微加工上的进步和半导体技术的快速发展使得UWB的商业应用变得成熟了。因此，把UWB看作长期存在技术的新名字比较合适。

在过去几年中，随着人们对UWB商业化兴趣的不断提高，以及UWB系统开发人员不断施加压力，FCC批准了UWB用于商业用途。2002年2月，FCC发布了关于商用UWB技术的报告和规范，对各种设备具有严格的功率限制。图4-16总结了UWB的发展历程。

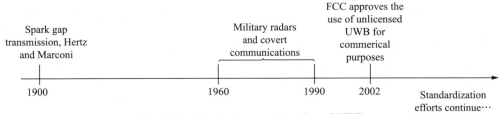

Fig. 4-16　The development timeline of UWB

3. Concepts of UWB

Traditional narrowband communications systems modulate Continuous-Waveform (CW) RF signals with a specific carrier frequency to transmit and receive information. A continuous-waveform has a well-defined signal energy in a narrow frequency band that makes it very vulnerable to detection and interception. Fig. 4-17 represents a narrowband signal in the time and frequency domains.

UWB systems use carrierless, short-duration (picosecond to nanosecond) pulses with a very low duty cycle (less than 0.5 percent) for transmission and reception of the information. A simple definition for duty cycle is the ratio of the time that a pulse is present to the total transmission time. Fig. 4-18

3. UWB 相关概念

传统的窄带通信系统用特定的载波频率来发送和接收信息以调制连续波形（CW）RF信号。连续波形在一个狭窄频段有明确的信号能量，使其很容易被检测和拦截。图4-17表示在时域和频域中的窄带信号。

UWB系统使用持续时间短（皮秒到纳秒）且具有非常低占空比的脉冲（小于0.5%）载波来发送和接收信息。占空比的一个简单定义是脉冲的持续时间占总传输时间的比率。图4-18和式（4-36）表示了

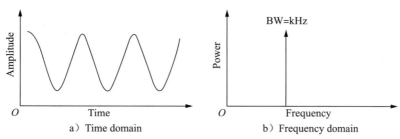

Fig. 4-17　A narrowband signal in the time and frequency domains

Fig. 4-18　A low duty cycle pulse. T_{on} represents the time that the pulse exists and T_{off} represents the time that the pulse is absent

$$\text{Duty cycle} = \frac{T_{on}}{T_{on} + T_{off}} \tag{4-36}$$

and equation (4-36) represent the definition of duty cycle.

Low duty cycle offers a very low average transmission power in UWB communications systems. The average transmission power of a UWB system is on the order of microwatts, which is a thousand times less than the transmission power of a cell phone! However, the peak or instantaneous power of individual UWB pulses can be relatively large (the peak power of UWB pulses in some cases is reported to be about 1W for 1Mbit/s at 1MHz), but because they are transmitted for only a very short time ($T_{on} < 1$ns), the average power becomes considerably lower. Consequently, UWB devices require low transmit power due to this control over the duty cycle, which directly translates to longer battery life for handheld equipment. Since frequency is inversely related to time, the short-duration UWB pulses spread their energy across a wide range of frequencies—from near DC to several gigahertz (GHz)—with very low Power Spectral Density (PSD) (power spectral density is the signals' power in the frequency domain). Fig. 4-19 illustrates a UWB pulse in the time and frequency domains.

The wide instantaneous bandwidth results from the time-scaling property of theoretical Fourier transforms:

占空比的定义。

低占空比为 UWB 通信系统提供了非常低的平均传播功率。UWB 系统的平均传播功率在微瓦级，这低于一部手机传播功率的千分之一！但是，个别 UWB 脉冲的峰值或瞬时功率可以相对较大（在某些情况下，UWB 脉冲的峰值功率在 1MHz 的条件下对于 1Mbit/s 大约是 1W），但是由于发送只需要很短的时间（$T_{on} < 1$ns），平均功率还是相当低的。UWB 设备由于这种可控的占空比，只需要很低的发射功率，从而使手持设备的电池寿命更长。因为频率是相关时间的倒数，所以持续时间较短的 UWB 脉冲可在很宽的频率范围内（从接近 DC 到几 GHz）传播它们的能量，并且具有非常低的功率谱密度（PSD）（功率谱密度是频域中信号的功率）。图 4-19 显示了时域和频域中的 UWB 脉冲。

宽瞬时带宽可从傅里叶变换的时间缩放属性得到：

$$x(at) \leftrightarrow \frac{1}{|a|} X\left(\frac{f}{a}\right) \tag{4-37}$$

The notation on the left side of equation (4-37) shows a signal, $x(t)$, which is scaled in the time domain by a factor a; the right side represents the same signal in the frequency domain, $X(f)$, which is inversely scaled by the same factor a. For example, a pulse with duration T of 500ps can generate a center frequency f_c of 2GHz:

式（4-37）等号的左侧是信号函数 $x(t)$，在时域上有一个缩放因子 a；等号右边表示在频域上的相同信号 $X(f)$，它有相同的反比缩放因子 a。例如，持续时间 T 为 500ps 的脉冲可以生成 2GHz 的中心频率 f_c：

$$f_c = \frac{1}{T} = \frac{1}{500 \times 10^{-12}}\text{Hz} = 2 \times 10^9 \text{Hz} = 2\text{GHz} \tag{4-38}$$

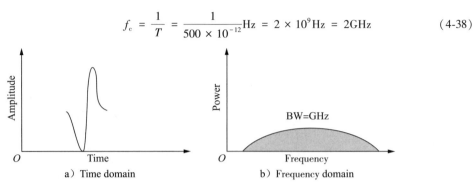

Fig. 4-19　A UWB pulse in the time and frequency domains

4. UWB Signals

As defined by the FCC's first Report and Order, UWB signals must have bandwidths of greater than 500MHz or a fractional bandwidth larger than 20 percent at all times of transmission. Fractional bandwidth is a factor used to classify signals as narrowband, wideband, or ultra-wideband and is defined by the ratio of bandwidth at −10dB points (the −10dB point represents the spectral power of a signal at 10dB lower than its peak power) to center frequency. Equation (4-39) shows this relationship.

4. UWB 信号

根据 FCC 的报告和规范，UWB 信号在任何情况下传输带宽都必须大于 500MHz 或者分数带宽大于 20%。分数带宽是用来把信号归类为窄带信号、宽带信号或超宽带信号的参数，它定义为在 −10dB 点相对于中心频率的带宽比率（−10dB 点表示信号功率谱比它的功率峰值低 10dB）。式（4-39）显示了这种关系。

$$B_f = \frac{BW}{f_c} \times 100\% = \frac{f_H - f_L}{(f_H + f_L)/2} \times 100\% = \frac{2(f_H - f_L)}{f_H + f_L} \times 100\% \tag{4-39}$$

where f_H and f_L are the highest and lowest cutoff frequencies (at the −10dB point) of a UWB pulse spectrum, respectively. A UWB signal can be any one of a variety of wideband signals, such as Gaussian, wavelet, or Hermite-based short-duration pulses. Fig. 4-20 represents a Gaussian monocycle as an example of a UWB pulse in the time and frequency domains. The Gaussian monocycle is the first derivative of a Gaussian pulse and is given by

式中，f_H 和 f_L 分别是 UWB 脉冲频谱的最高和最低截止频率（在 −10dB 点处）。UWB 信号可以是各种宽带信号中的任意一种，例如高斯、小波或者基于厄米的短脉冲。图 4-20 给出了 UWB 脉冲的一种——在时域和频域的高斯单周期信号。高斯单周期是高斯脉冲的一阶导数由下式给出：

$$P(t) = \frac{t}{T} e^{-\left(\frac{t}{T}\right)^2} \tag{4-40}$$

where t represents time and is a time decay constant that determines the temporal width of the pulse.

式中，t 表示时间，是一个时间衰减常数，该时间衰减常数确定脉冲的时间宽度。

As shown in Fig. 4-20, a 500ps pulse generates a large bandwidth in the frequency domain with a center frequency of 2GHz. In Fig. 4-20b, the lowest and highest cutoff frequencies at −10dB are approximately 1.2GHz and 2.8GHz, respectively, which lead to a fractional bandwidth of 80 percent; this is much larger than the minimum B_f required by the FCC:

如图 4-20 所示，一个 500ps 的脉冲将以 2GHz 为中心频率在频域产生一个大的带宽。在图 4-20b 中，−10dB 点的最低和最高截止频率分别是 1.2GHz 与 2.8GHz，这产生了 80% 的分数带宽；这是远远大于 FCC 所要求的最小 B_f：

$$B_f = 2 \times \frac{2.8 - 1.2}{2.8 + 1.2} \times 100\% = 80\%$$

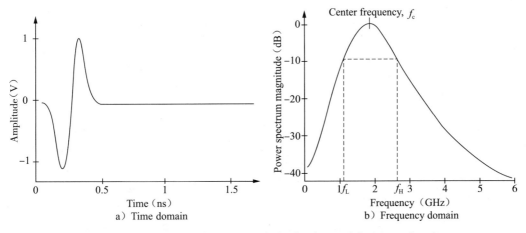

Fig. 4-20 A 500ps Gussian monocycle in the time and frequency domains

Here is the classification of signals based on their fractional bandwidth:

Narrowband $B_f < 1\%$
Wideband $1\% < B_f < 20\%$
Ultra-wideband $B_f > 20\%$

For example, 802.11 and Bluetooth have fractional bandwidths of 0.8 percent and 0.04 percent, respectively.

5. Motivating Applications

Wireless Personal Area Networks（WPANs）

Also known as in-home networks, WPAN address short-range (generally within 10~20m) specific connectivity among portable consumer electronic and communication devices. They are envisioned to provide high-quality real-time video and audio distribution, file exchange among storage systems, and cable replacement for home entertainment systems. UWB technology emerges as a promising physical layer candidate for WPAN, because it offers high-rates over short range, with low cost, high power efficiency, and low duty cycle.

Sensor Networks

Sensor networks consist of a large number of nodes spread across a geographical area. The nodes can be static, if deployed for, e.g., avalanche monitoring and pollution tracking, or mobile, if equipped on soldiers, firemen, or robots in military and emergency response situations. Key requirements for sensor networks operating in challenging environments include low cost, low power, and multifunctionality. High data-rate UWB communication systems are well motivated for gathering and disseminating or exchanging a vast quantity of sensory data in a timely manner. Typically, energy is more limited in sensor networks than in WPAN because of the nature of the sensing devices and the difficulty in recharging their batteries. Studies have shown that current commercial Bluetooth

下面是基于分数带宽的信号分类：

窄带 $B_f < 1\%$
宽带 $1\% < B_f < 20\%$
超宽带 $B_f > 20\%$

例如，802.11和蓝牙的分数带宽分别为0.8%与0.04%。

5. 使用目的

无线个人局域网

无线个人局域网（WPAN）也称为家庭网络，它提供便携式消费电子和通信设备之间的短距离（一般在10~20m之内）特定连接。人们期望它们提供高品质实时的视频和音频、存储系统之间的文件交换以及家庭娱乐系统有线替换。UWB技术的出现为WPAN提供了一种很有前途的连接方法，因为它在短距离范围内具有高速率、低成本、高效率和低占空比的优点。

传感器网络

传感器网络由大量分散在某个地理区域中的节点构成。这些节点可以是静止的，可以用于雪崩监测和污染跟踪或移动，在军事和应急响应的情况下也可以安装到士兵、消防员或机器人上。在挑战性环境下的传感器网络的关键要求包括低成本、低功耗和多功能性。高速率的UWB通信系统可以及时收集和交换大量的传感器数据。通常情况下，传感器网络的功耗要求高于WPAN，这是由传感设备的特性以及更换电池的困难决定的。有研究表明，目前由于能源需求和较高的预期成本，商业化的

devices are less suitable for sensor network applications because of their energy requirements and higher expected cost. In addition, exploiting the precise localization capability of UWB promises wireless sensor networks with improved positioning accuracy. This is especially useful when GPS is not available, e. g., due to obstruction.

Imaging Systems

Different from conventional radar systems where targets are typically considered as point scatterers, UWB radar pulses are shorter than the target dimensions. UWB reflections off the target exhibit not only changes in amplitude and time shift but also changes in the pulse shape. As a result, UWB waveforms exhibit pronounced sensitivity to scattering relative to conventional radar signals. This property has been readily adopted by radar systems and can be extended to additional applications, such as underground, through-wall and ocean imaging, as well as medical diagnostics and border surveillance devices.

Vehicular Radar Systems

UWB-based sensing has the potential to improve the resolution of conventional proximity and motion sensors. Relying on the high ranging accuracy and target differentiation capability enabled by UWB, intelligent collision-avoidance and cruise-control systems can be envisioned. These systems can also improve airbag deployment and adapt suspension/braking systems depending on road conditions. UWB technology can also be integrated into vehicular entertainment and navigation systems by downloading high-rate data from airport of ramp, road-side, or gas station UWB transmitters.

蓝牙设备并不适合传感器网络的应用。此外，UWB 的精确定位功能可以提高无线传感器网络的定位精度。在某些情况下这特别有用，例如由于障碍物使 GPS 装置无法使用时。

成像系统

与传统雷达系统通常把目标看作点散射体不同的是，UWB 雷达脉冲比目标尺寸短。UWB 信号从目标物体反射回来后，不但幅度产生变化、时间产生移位，而且脉冲形状也发生变化。其结果是，与传统雷达信号相比，UWB 信号波形对散射表现出显著的敏感性。该属性已经应用到雷达系统，并可扩展到其他应用，如地下、穿墙和海洋成像，以及医疗诊断和边境监视设备。

车载雷达系统

基于 UWB 的传感具有改善传统接近传感器和运动传感器分辨率的潜力。利用 UWB 的高精度测距和目标分辨能力，我们可以设想智能防撞系统和巡航控制系统。这些系统还可以提高安全气囊的布置并根据路况改进暂停/制动系统。UWB 技术还可以集成到车辆的娱乐和导航系统，使其可以通过机场停机坪、路旁或者加油站的 UWB 发射器下载高速率数据。

NEW WOEDS AND PHRASES

Ultra-wideband（UWB） 超宽带
Federal Communications Commission（FCC） 美国联邦通信委员会
fractional bandwidth 分数带宽
Global Positioning System（GPS） 全球定位系统
Wireless Local Area Network（WLAN） 无线局域网络
indoor multimedia transmission 室内多媒体传输
wireless cellular architecture 无线蜂窝架构
Bit Error Rate（BER） 误比特率
Unmanned Air Vehicle（UAV） 无人驾驶飞行器（无人机）
Digital Signal Processing（DSP） 数字信号处理
synchronization *n*. 校准，同时性，同步
spectrum *n*. 谱，频谱，光谱，射频频谱
Department of Defense（DoD） 美国国防部
Continuous-Waveform（CW） 连续波形
duty cycle 占空比
Fourier transform 傅里叶变换
scatterer *n*. 扩散器（散射体）
border surveillance 边境监视

NOTES

1) As information-bearing pulses with ultra-short duration have UWB spectral occupancy, UWB radios come with unique advantages that have long been appreciated by the radar and communications communities：

i) enhanced capability to penetrate through obstacles; ii) ultra high precision ranging at the centimeter level; iii) potential for very high data rates along with a commensurate increase in user capacity; and iv) potentially small size and processing power.

由于持续时间极短的信息承载脉冲具有 UWB 频谱，UWB 无线电在雷达和通信方面一直具有独特的优势：①穿透障碍物能力强；②厘米级范围的超高精度；③与随着用户容量增加相称的高数据传输速率；④小尺寸和强大的处理能力。

2) The transition from analog to digital cellular communications, the rise of the third and fourth generation radio systems, and the replacement of wired connections with Wi-Fi and Bluetooth are enabling consumers to access a wide range of information from anywhere and at any time.

从模拟过渡到数字蜂窝通信、第三代和第四代无线系统的崛起，以及从有线连接变为 Wi-Fi 和蓝牙连接，消费者能够在任意地方和任意时间访问更广泛的信息。

3) Utilizing short-duration pulses as the building blocks for communications directly generates a very wide bandwidth and offers several advantages, such as large throughput, covertness, robustness to jamming, and coexistence with current radio services.

利用短脉冲作为通信的基础模块将直接产生很宽的带宽，并且有很多优点，如大的吞吐量、隐蔽性、抗干扰性，以及可以与当前的无线服务共存。

4) Since frequency is inversely related to time, the short-duration UWB pulses spread their energy across a wide range of frequencies—from near DC to several gigahertz (GHz)—with very low Power Spectral Density (PSD) (power spectral density is the signals' power in the frequency domain).

因为频率是相关时间的倒数，所以持续时间较短的 UWB 脉冲可在很宽的频率范围内（从接近 DC 到几 GHz）传播它们的能量，并且具有非常低的功率谱密度（PSD）（功率谱密度是频域中信号的功率）。

5) UWB reflections off the target exhibit not only changes in amplitude and time shift but also changes in the pulse shape.

UWB 信号从目标物体反射回来后，不仅幅度产生变化、时间产生移位，而且脉冲形状也发生变化。

第 4 章
通 信 技 术

4.1 电磁场理论

富兰克林、库仑、安培、法拉第等科学家对自然现象的好奇心,以及锲而不舍地探索和不屈不挠地研究,引导他们发现电、磁的现象和规律。求真务实、勇于实践、敢于创新的精神值得我们学习。

1864 年,詹姆斯·克拉克·麦克斯韦提出了九个方程,总结了所有已知的电和磁定律。这是科学史上最成功的理论之一。麦克斯韦通过假定另外一个术语使这组方程式前后一致,提出的理论一直被认为是宏观电磁学的完整理论。我们需要源、媒质和一组微分方程以形成完整的场论,用数学描述作用(媒质中的场)和原因(源场)之间的关系。在特定的假设下,它还应包括完整的本构关系以及在分界面和初始时间上的场量关系。如果电磁场有物理意义,那么还必须将电磁场与其他可观测的量(如力)联系起来。最后为了能够解决涉及数学上不连续性的问题,还必须制定某一边界或"跳跃"条件。

在麦克斯韦方程组中,源场由矢量场 $J(r,t)$ (电流密度) 和标量场 $\rho(r,t)$ (电荷密度) 组成,媒质中的场由电磁场的 4 个矢量组成,即 $E(r,t)$、$D(r,t)$、$B(r,t)$ 和 $H(r,t)$。

E = 电场强度(矢量),伏特/米(V/m)

H = 磁场强度(矢量),安培/米(A/m)

D = 电通量密度(矢量),库仑/米^2(C/m^2)

B = 磁通量密度(矢量),韦伯/米^2(Wb/m^2)

J = 电流密度(矢量),安/米^2(A/m^2)

ρ = 电荷密度(标量),库仑/米^3(C/m^3)

以上所有量均为时变场中任意空间的实函数,即位置矢量 r(m) 和时间 t(s),而在静态场中它们仅仅是 r 的函数。

要建立两个新概念:变化的磁场能产生电场,变化的电场能产生磁场。我们称其为电磁场。

1. 麦克斯韦方程组

麦克斯韦方程组是电磁理论中最重要和最基本的方程组。其描述如下。

$$\oint_C \boldsymbol{H} \cdot \mathrm{d}\boldsymbol{l} = \int_S \left(\boldsymbol{J} + \frac{\partial \boldsymbol{D}}{\partial t} \right) \cdot \mathrm{d}\boldsymbol{S} \quad \text{(扩展的安培环路定律或麦克斯韦第一方程)} \quad (4\text{-}1)$$

等式的左边是磁场强度 $\boldsymbol{H}$ 沿闭合回路或围线的积分（沿着闭合曲线 C 的积分）。等式右边是全电流密度的面积分，即电流密度 $\boldsymbol{J}$ 的总和取决于电荷的流动（通常仅指传导电流）和对电通量密度进行时间求导的位移电流（电位移密度）。

$$\boldsymbol{J}_\mathrm{d} = \frac{\partial \boldsymbol{D}}{\partial t} \quad (4\text{-}2)$$

积分的面以 C 为边界。

$$\oint_C \boldsymbol{E} \cdot \mathrm{d}\boldsymbol{l} = -\int_S \frac{\partial \boldsymbol{B}}{\partial t} \cdot \mathrm{d}\boldsymbol{S} \quad \text{(法拉第电磁感应定律或麦克斯韦第二方程)} \quad (4\text{-}3)$$

该定律表明在闭合曲线上由变化的磁场感应的电动势 ε 等于穿过以该闭合曲线为周界的任意曲面的磁通量变化率的负值。

$$\oint_S \boldsymbol{B} \cdot \mathrm{d}\boldsymbol{S} = 0 \quad \text{(磁场的高斯定律或麦克斯韦第三方程)} \quad (4\text{-}4)$$

该定律表明穿过任意闭合曲面的磁通量为零。

$$\oint_S \boldsymbol{D} \cdot \mathrm{d}\boldsymbol{S} = \int_V \rho \mathrm{d}V \quad \text{(电场的高斯定律或麦克斯韦第四方程)} \quad (4\text{-}5)$$

该定律表明穿过闭合曲面的电通量等于该闭合曲面所包围的电荷。

这些方程组都是积分形式的。用两个基本定理将麦克斯韦方程组转化为微分形式。斯托克斯定理是关于任意矢量 $\boldsymbol{A}$ 的线积分与其旋度的曲面积分的变换定理：

$$\oint_C \boldsymbol{A} \cdot \mathrm{d}\boldsymbol{l} = \int_S (\nabla \times \boldsymbol{A}) \cdot \mathrm{d}\boldsymbol{S} \quad (4\text{-}6)$$

式中，闭合曲线 C 的方向与 S 表面的法向方向满足右手法则。同样，通过散度定理（或高斯定理），矢量 $\boldsymbol{A}$ 在面积 S 上的积分等于矢量 $\boldsymbol{A}$ 的散度在面积 S 所围体积上的体积分：

$$\oint_S \boldsymbol{A} \cdot \mathrm{d}\boldsymbol{S} = \int_V \nabla \cdot \boldsymbol{A} \cdot \mathrm{d}V \quad (4\text{-}7)$$

式中，S 的法向方向向外。

麦克斯韦方程组的微分形式如下：

$$\nabla \times \boldsymbol{H} = \boldsymbol{J} + \frac{\partial \boldsymbol{D}}{\partial t}, \quad \nabla \times \boldsymbol{E} = -\frac{\partial \boldsymbol{B}}{\partial t}, \quad \nabla \cdot \boldsymbol{B} = 0, \quad \nabla \cdot \boldsymbol{D} = \rho \quad (4\text{-}8)$$

这4个方程说明了电磁源和场的全部关系：
①传导电流和位移电流之和是磁场的旋度源。
②时变的磁场产生电场。
③磁场是无散场。
④电荷是电场的散度源。

麦克斯韦方程组描述了时变电磁场的运动规律，揭示了自然界电和磁相互激励、相互制约的对立统一哲学思想。

2. 电流连续性方程

尽管麦克斯韦方程组中没有给出，但是该方程可从麦克斯韦方程组中导出。例如：

$$\nabla \cdot (\nabla \times \boldsymbol{H}) = \nabla \cdot \left(\boldsymbol{J} + \frac{\partial \boldsymbol{D}}{\partial t} \right), \quad \boldsymbol{H} \text{ 的旋度的散度等于零，} \boldsymbol{D} \text{ 的散度等于 } \rho$$

则电流连续性方程为

$$\nabla \cdot \boldsymbol{J} = -\frac{\partial \rho}{\partial t} \tag{4-9}$$

3. 本构关系

即使我们给定了电荷密度 ρ 和电流密度 $\boldsymbol{J}$，在 12 个未知标量方程中，相当于只给了 8 个标量方程（每个场矢量 $\boldsymbol{E}$、$\boldsymbol{D}$、$\boldsymbol{B}$、$\boldsymbol{H}$ 包含三个量）。

为了唯一地确定这些场矢量，麦克斯韦方程组中必须增加描述在场的影响下媒质行为的关系量。这些辅助关系称为本构关系，可以通过试验或原子理论推导建立。

如果场矢量是线性相关的，可应用迭加原理，则媒质称为线性的。麦克斯韦方程组和线性本构关系形成了线性电动力学基础。

在自由空间中，本构关系具有最简单的形式：

$$\boldsymbol{D} = \varepsilon_0 \boldsymbol{E}, \quad \boldsymbol{B} = \mu_0 \boldsymbol{H} \tag{4-10}$$

式中，$\varepsilon_0 = 8.854 \times 10^{-12} \mathrm{F/m} \approx \dfrac{1}{36\pi} \times 10^{-9} \mathrm{F/m}$，$\mu_0 = 4\pi \times 10^{-7} \mathrm{H/m}$。

若给定点的电磁特性与场在该点的方向无关，则称媒质为各向同性的。例如，有简化形式：

$$\boldsymbol{D} = \varepsilon \boldsymbol{E}, \quad \boldsymbol{B} = \mu \boldsymbol{H}, \quad \boldsymbol{J} = \sigma \boldsymbol{E} \tag{4-11}$$

式中，介电常数 ε、相对磁导率 μ 和电导率 σ 均为标量。如果空间的每个点 ε、μ 和 σ 的值都不变，我们称该媒质是均匀的。

另外，若媒质的电磁场特性与场矢量的方向有关，则该媒质是各向异性的。例如：

$$\boldsymbol{D} = \varepsilon_0 \varepsilon_r \boldsymbol{E}, \quad \boldsymbol{B} = \mu_0 \mu_r \boldsymbol{H} \tag{4-12}$$

式中，介电常数 ε 和相对磁导率 μ 为张量。

当将本构关系用于麦克斯韦方程组时，未知向量就只有 $\boldsymbol{E}$ 和 $\boldsymbol{H}$ 或者 $\boldsymbol{D}$ 和 $\boldsymbol{B}$。

4. 边界条件

麦克斯韦方程组适用于介质的物理性质连续变化的区域。然而，当场矢量穿过两种媒质的分界面时，连续的媒质本征参数 ε、μ 或 σ 会发生突变，场矢量产生相应变化。为了继续讨论从一个区域到另一个区域的麦克斯韦方程组的解，在场矢量和分界面上需要增加边界条件，使所得解在任意地方都是唯一且有效的。两组场在分界面 S 上的边界条件可通过麦克斯韦方程组的积分形式得到。设分界面 S 两侧不同的媒质本征参数分别为 $(\varepsilon_1, \mu_1, \sigma_1)$ 和 $(\varepsilon_2, \mu_2, \sigma_2)$，如图 4-1 所示。在这两种媒质中的电磁场定义为 $(\boldsymbol{E}_1, \boldsymbol{H}_1, \boldsymbol{D}_1, \boldsymbol{B}_1)$ 和 $(\boldsymbol{E}_2, \boldsymbol{H}_2, \boldsymbol{D}_2, \boldsymbol{B}_2)$。

定义分界面 S 的法向单位矢量为 $\boldsymbol{n}$，它从媒质 1 指向媒质 2，计算麦克斯韦方程组通过小圆柱体形成的闭合曲面的面积分。圆柱曲面对于积分的贡献直接正比于 Δh，并且当 ΔS 足够小时，每个底面处的 $\boldsymbol{B}$ 是常数。随着 $\Delta h \to 0$，圆柱的底面仅位于分界面 S 的两侧，圆柱曲面对于积分的贡献变得很小，因此得到

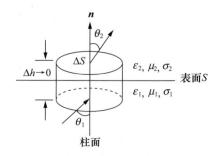

图 4-1 用于得到 $\boldsymbol{D}$、$\boldsymbol{B}$ 边界条件的柱面

$$\boldsymbol{n} \cdot (\boldsymbol{B}_1 - \boldsymbol{B}_2) = 0 \tag{4-13}$$

这表明 $\boldsymbol{B}$ 的法向分量在分界面上是连续的。

同样，通过 $\boldsymbol{D}$ 的积分可得到

$$\boldsymbol{n} \cdot (\boldsymbol{D}_1 - \boldsymbol{D}_2) = \rho_{\mathrm{sf}} \tag{4-14}$$

这表明在分界面 S 上存在面电荷 ρ_{sf}，$\boldsymbol{D}$ 的法向分量通过分界面产生突变且不连续值等于面电荷密度。如果两种不同介质的分界面处没有面电荷（$\rho_{sf}=0$），则 $\boldsymbol{D}$ 的法向分量必然是连续的。

下面讨论切向分量，用以 ΔA 为面积的小的矩形回路来代替圆柱，Δl 平行于分界面 S，Δh 垂直于 S，如图 4-2 所示。当 $\Delta h \to 0$ 时，可得

$$\boldsymbol{n} \times (\boldsymbol{E}_1 - \boldsymbol{E}_2) = 0 \tag{4-15}$$

这表明穿过两种媒质分界面的 $\boldsymbol{E}$ 的切向分量必须是连续的，可用单位正切矢量 $\boldsymbol{t}$ 表示为

$$(\boldsymbol{E}_1 - \boldsymbol{E}_2) \cdot \boldsymbol{t} = 0 \tag{4-16}$$

得到

$$\boldsymbol{n} \times (\boldsymbol{H}_1 - \boldsymbol{H}_2) = \boldsymbol{J}_{sf} \tag{4-17}$$

这表明穿过两种媒质分界面的 $\boldsymbol{H}$ 的切向分量是不连续的，并且不连续值等于面电流密度。如果电流密度 $\boldsymbol{J}$ 是有限值，则在导电性有限的任何媒质中，可得到

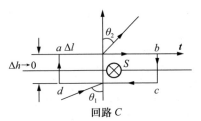

图 4-2　用于得到 $\boldsymbol{E}$、$\boldsymbol{H}$ 边界条件的矩形回路

$$\boldsymbol{n} \times (\boldsymbol{H}_1 - \boldsymbol{H}_2) = 0 \tag{4-18}$$

在特殊情况下，如果媒质 1 是理想导体（$\sigma_1 \to \infty$）且媒质 2 是理想介质（$\sigma_2 \to 0$），存在表面传导电流和面电荷，那么媒质 1 中所有的场矢量恒等于零，边界条件变为

$$\boldsymbol{n} \times \boldsymbol{H}_2 = \boldsymbol{J}_{sf}, \quad \boldsymbol{n} \times \boldsymbol{E}_2 = 0, \quad \boldsymbol{n} \cdot \boldsymbol{B}_2 = 0, \quad \boldsymbol{n} \cdot \boldsymbol{D}_2 = \rho_{sf} \tag{4-19}$$

注意，面电荷密度和面电流密度也遵循连续性方程。

5. 功率和能量

通过麦克斯韦方程组我们能推导出电磁系统的能量守恒定律。我们从矢量恒等式

$$\nabla \cdot (\boldsymbol{E} \times \boldsymbol{H}) = \boldsymbol{H} \cdot (\nabla \times \boldsymbol{E}) - \boldsymbol{E} \cdot (\nabla \times \boldsymbol{H}) \tag{4-20}$$

和麦克斯韦方程组的微分形式开始。我们获得如下关系式：

$$\nabla \cdot (\boldsymbol{E} \times \boldsymbol{H}) = -\boldsymbol{H} \cdot \frac{\partial \boldsymbol{B}}{\partial t} - \boldsymbol{E} \cdot \frac{\partial \boldsymbol{D}}{\partial t} + \boldsymbol{E} \cdot \boldsymbol{J} \tag{4-21}$$

然后，对闭合曲面 S 围成的体积 V 进行体积分，并利用高斯定理，可获得如下关系式：

$$-\oint_S (\boldsymbol{E} \times \boldsymbol{H}) \cdot \mathrm{d}\boldsymbol{S} = \frac{1}{2} \int_V \left(\boldsymbol{H} \cdot \frac{\partial \boldsymbol{B}}{\partial t} + \boldsymbol{E} \cdot \frac{\partial \boldsymbol{D}}{\partial t} \right) \mathrm{d}V - \int_V \boldsymbol{E} \cdot \boldsymbol{J} \mathrm{d}V \tag{4-22}$$

该式为体积 V 中的能量守恒定律，称为坡印廷定理的积分形式。它是功率的定理。任意体积 V 内电磁能量的时间增加量等于进入闭合曲面 S 的能量和体积 V 的热损耗的总和。它在不均匀媒介中也适用。

定义坡印廷矢量（功率密度，单位是 W/m^2）为 $\boldsymbol{S} = \boldsymbol{E} \times \boldsymbol{H}$，代表在垂直于 $\boldsymbol{E}$ 和 $\boldsymbol{H}$ 上穿过单位面积的功率，并且

$$P = \int_V \boldsymbol{J} \cdot \boldsymbol{E} \mathrm{d}V \tag{4-23}$$

为焦耳热，代表单位体积媒质中每秒消耗的能量。

用 w 表示电磁能量密度，单位是 J/m^3。假设在最初，因为场都是零，所以没有能量的存储。总的瞬时能量密度为

$$w = w_e + w_m \tag{4-24}$$

式中，

$$w_e = \int \boldsymbol{E} \cdot \frac{\partial \boldsymbol{D}}{\partial t} dt \tag{4-25}$$

是电场能量密度的瞬时值；

$$w_m = \int \boldsymbol{H} \cdot \frac{\partial \boldsymbol{B}}{\partial t} dt \tag{4-26}$$

是磁场能量密度的瞬时值。

设媒介质是各向同性的、均匀的、无耗的，则电磁能量密度可表示为

$$w_e = \frac{1}{2}\boldsymbol{E} \cdot \boldsymbol{D} = \frac{1}{2}\varepsilon E^2 \tag{4-27}$$

$$w_m = \frac{1}{2}\boldsymbol{H} \cdot \boldsymbol{B} = \frac{1}{2}\mu H^2 \tag{4-28}$$

注意，所有的量都是空间位置和时间的函数。

4.2 移动通信的发展

现今，手机已成为人们生活中不可或缺的重要工具。除了常规的通信需求，聊微信、移动支付、上下班路上刷视频、玩游戏、获取最新新闻等，越来越丰富的应用统统浓缩在尺寸见方的掌上屏幕中。正是移动互联网将异彩纷呈的网络世界呈现在我们面前。

1. 通信的概念

通信就是由一个地方向另一个地方传递信息。人类最早的信息交换的时间很难追述，但有了人类就有了信息交换是可以肯定的。古代就有击鼓传声、烽火狼烟、鸿雁传书、驿站送信等通信形式，近代以来则有电报传递文字符号、电话传递声音、传真传送静止图像、电视传递活动图像加伴音、数据通信传递电子计算机处理的信息等。

2. 通信的基本原理及特征

任何通信行为都可以看成通信系统（见图4-5），主要包括发信者、发送器、信道、接收器、收信者等5个部分。发信者（信源）将信息转换成电信号，调制器对信息信号进行某种变换，使其适合在信道中传输至接收器，并通过解调器将接收到的信号进行与调制器相反的变换，还原为原始的信息，送给收信者即信宿。这就是通信系统的基本原理。无论是古代的烽火驿站通信、近代的电报电话通信，还是现代的移动数字通信，原理并无不同。古代驿站通信通过零星、散落的驿站来实现；近代电话通信通过电话线来实现；现代移动通信则通过无形的网实现，每个手机只不过是庞大空中之网上的一个节点。维系着古代通信支点的是大量的人力、物力，支撑现代通信的是机器间快速高效的数据传输，外在的网变为内在的网，有形的网变为无形的网，支撑通信的"中继站"逐渐减少、退化，直至与收信者成为一体，成为通信网络中的一个点。

图4-5 通信系统组成

有意思的是，古代通信与现代移动通信有两个共同的特点。一是它们都是无线的。古代利用击鼓传声、烽火狼烟、手旗旗语等声音、火、光等信息载体实现消息的远距离传递，通过中

继站层层传递，最终到达接收者。现代的移动通信则通过电磁波信息载体在空间传播，而不是像近代的电话、电报那样通过电流信息载体在金属电线内传递。手机等现代移动通信工具使人们彻底摆脱"线"的限制。二是它们都是"实时"的。最早的信息交换是面对面的交流，是最为实时的信息交换。同样，当前的移动电话则极方便地实现了实时通信。随着 CPU 的运行速度、交换设备的信息转换速度、信源编/解码速度、信道传输速度以及信道容量的提高，通信系统的"实时性"得到了极大提高。

3. 无线通信理论的突破

信号的性质和传播是无线通信的基础。1865 年，英国物理学家麦克斯韦（James Clerk Maxwell）预言了电磁波的存在。1888 年，德国物理学家赫兹（Heinrich Rudolf Hertz）证明了存在以光速传播的电磁波。麦克斯韦关于电磁波的预言和赫兹的证实，为通信方式从有线到无线做了理论上和实验上的准备，奠定了通信技术产生的科学基础。麦克斯韦本人并没有提出无线电这个词，但他的理论确实指出电是可以无线传播的。赫兹也没有预见到无线电通信的可能性。1889 年，他的一个朋友问能否利用电波进行通信时，他说："若要用电磁波进行不同导线的通信，得有一个面积和欧洲大陆面积差不多大的巨型反射镜才行。"但是，赫兹的试验极大地鼓舞了各国的科学家，揭开了无线电通信技术的序幕。1893 年，塞尔维亚裔美籍科学家特斯拉（Nikola Tesla）在美国密苏里州圣路易斯市首次公开展示了无线电通信，证明了无线电通信的可行性。1896 年，意大利人马可尼（Guglielmo Marconi）在一艘缓慢行驶在大西洋上名为"圣保罗"号的邮轮上首次成功实现了远距离无线电通信。1901 年，他完成无线电跨越大西洋的通信。1909 年，马可尼获得了诺贝尔物理学奖，被世人称作"无线电之父"。

信号接收是无线通信的另一个关键环节。1901 年，加拿大发明家费森登（Reginald Fessenden）提出了外差接收法的设想。1912 年，美国电气工程师阿姆斯特朗（Armstrong Edwin Howard）在此基础上提出"超外差接收原理"，即本振频率始终比接收器的接收载波频率信号高出一个中频频率，而这一信号超出音频信号。后来，阿姆斯特朗对外差接收法做了重大改进，发明了超外差电路，使得接收器可以用于接收任何无线电波。通信技术的发展以及无线电接收原理从"外差法"到"超外差法"的突破，为以后的电视广播、微波通信、卫星通信的兴起创造了条件。

4. 移动通信的历史及现状

移动通信是指通信双方有一方、双方或者多方处于运动状态的通信，包括陆地移动通信、航空通信、航海通信和卫星通信等多种形式。

1896 年，意大利人马可尼在大西洋轮船上远距离无线电通信实验的成功，被认为是"移动通信"的开始。事实上，现代意义的移动通信始于 20 世纪 20 年代。1928 年，美国普渡大学学生发明了工作于 2MHz 的超外差式车载无线电接收机，并很快在底特律的警察局投入使用，这是世界上陆地最早使用且可以有效工作的移动通信系统。

20 世纪 30 年代末，比调幅制式更加有效的调频制式移动通信系统诞生。20 世纪 40 年代，这种调频制式移动通信系统逐渐占据主流地位，实现了小容量专用移动通信系统，但这还仅仅是实验意义上的工作。在第二次世界大战期间，军事上的需求使得移动通信得到了快速发展，公众移动通信系统应运而生。1946 年，美国圣路易斯市首先研制出人工转接的小容量汽车电话系统。1947 年，美国贝尔实验室提出"小区"的概念。20 世纪 50 年代，美国和欧洲部分国家相继成功研制了公用移动电话系统，在技术上实现了移动电话系统与公众电话网络的互通，并得到了广泛的使用。20 世纪 60 年代，移动通信技术逐步改进。1964 年，美国研制出新的中容量汽车电话系统，每次呼叫都可以自动选择频道。1969 年，美国移动电话自动化的性能已扩展到 450MHz 频段，改进型移动电话系统（IMTS）成为美国移动电话系统的标准。同年，日本也开始研制 800MHz 蜂窝状大容量移动电话系统（HCMTS）。

为了更加有效地利用有限的频谱资源，美国贝尔实验室提出了具有里程碑意义的小区制和蜂窝组网理论，为移动通信系统在全球的广泛应用开辟了道路。1978 年，美国贝尔实验室开发了高级移动电话业务（Advanced Mobile Phone System，AMPS），成为第一种真正意义上的具有随时随地通信能力的大容量蜂窝移动通信系统，正式拉开了现代移动通信角逐的帷幕。1983 年底，美国在芝加哥建立了大容量的 AMPS，使移动通信进入新的发展阶段。20 世纪 80 年代中期以来，陆地蜂窝移动通信发展进入高峰阶段，欧洲和日本也纷纷建立了自己的蜂窝移动通信。1985 年，全球有 55.3 万移动电话用户。截至 1990 年 5 月，用户总数已超过 822 万，其中美国占 47%。1985 年 10 月，美国的手机用户数量为 23.5 万。到 1990 年 5 月，用户数量达到 390 万，增长了 16.6 倍，平均每月增加 6 万多。欧洲国家的蜂窝移动通信也发展迅速，用户数量占世界总数的 33.1%。日本的蜂窝系统已经覆盖了 90% 的城市和 70% 的主要高速公路，年均增长率为 150%。

现代移动通信系统近百年的发展历史大致可以分为如下 4 个发展阶段。

第一阶段从 20 世纪 20 年代至 40 年代，为早期发展阶段。特点是专用系统开发，工作频率较低，工作方式为单工或半双工方式。

第二阶段从 20 世纪 40 年代中期至 60 年代初期。特点是从专用移动网向公用移动网过渡，接续方式为人工，网络的容量较小。

第三阶段从 20 世纪 60 年代中期至 70 年代中期。特点是采用大区制，中小容量，使用 450MHz 频段，实现了自动选频与自动接续。

第四阶段从 20 世纪 70 年代中后期至今。特点是通信容量迅速增加，新业务不断出现，系统性能不断完善，技术的发展呈加快趋势。

现阶段，移动通信已在全球迅猛发展。国际电信联盟（ITU）2013 年度报告显示世界 71 亿人口中有 68 亿手机用户；据联合国有关调查机构预测，截至 2014 年底，世界上移动通信设备用户总数将超过世界总人口数。目前，2G、3G 和 4G 商用移动通信网络处于共存阶段，并将在相当一段时间内共存下去，为各类用户服务，以满足不同业务需求。与此同时，第五代移动通信系统（5G）作为面向 2020 年以后移动通信需求而发展的新一代移动通信系统（ITU 将其命名为 IMT-2020），其研发工作已在全球范围内展开。

5. 蜂窝移动通信技术的发展

第四阶段的蜂窝移动通信系统又可以划分为几个发展阶段。若按多址方式来分，则模拟频分多址（FDMA）系统是第一代移动通信系统（1G），使用电路交换的数字时分多址（TDMA）或码分多址（CDMA）系统是第二代移动通信系统（2G），使用分组/电路交换的 CDMA 系统是第三代移动通信系统（3G），将使用了不同的高级接入技术并采用全 IP（互联网协议）网络结构的系统称为第四代移动通信系统（4G）。若按系统的典型技术来划分，则模拟系统是 1G，数字话音系统是 2G，数字话音/数据系统是超二代移动通信系统（B2G），宽带数字系统是 3G，极高速数据速率系统是 4G。

20 世纪 70 年代摩托罗拉（Motorola）的工程师马丁·库珀（Martin Cooper）发明了第一代移动电话，他研究的是一种能够无线双向通信的手持设备。它最初用于汽车，第一个原型在 1974 年进行了测试。这项发明被认为是无线通信的转折点，影响了未来许多技术和标准的发展。从此，手机通信技术从第一代一直发展到第五代。据说，移动电话通信技术每十年就会从现在的一代发展到下一代（见图 4-6）。

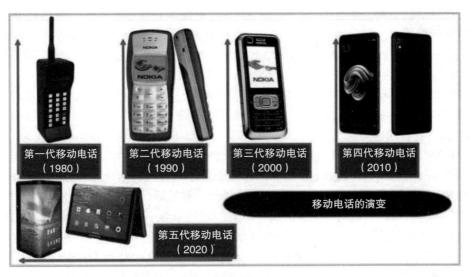

图 4-6　移动电话通信技术的发展历史

1G：第一代移动通信系统

AMPS 的出现标志着移动通信技术进入 1G 时代。1979 年，日本电报电话公司（NTT）在东京部署了第一代商用蜂窝移动网络。20 世纪 80 年代初，它在美国、芬兰、英国等流行开来。20 世纪 80 年代最流行的 1G 系统包括 AMPS、NMTS、TACS 和 ETACS。

蜂窝网络是一种无线连接网络。地球上的区域被分成蜂窝。这些蜂窝的形状可以是六角形、正方形、长方形、圆形或任何其他形状。但是六角形最适合形成蜂窝网络。每个蜂窝都有自己的收发基站。这些基站为小区提供无线网络覆盖。这些无线频率可以用于传输语音、数据、调频广播等内容。每个单元使用不同的频率，以避免与相邻单元冲突。

当许多单元连接在一起时，它们提供大面积的无线射频覆盖。这就是无线设备或收发器（发射器和接收器），如手机、平板电脑、智能手机、调制解调器等的工作原理。

1987 年 11 月，广州开通了我国第一个蜂窝移动通信系统。随后，深圳、珠海、上海、北京、沈阳、秦皇岛和天津等城市也相继建立蜂窝移动通信系统，珠三角地区率先联网运行。

第一代移动通信系统的典型频段为 800/900MHz，主要用途是打电话。因此，其本质上是一种语音传输技术，1G 也常常被称为语音时代。1G 主要采用的是模拟技术和频分多址（FDMA）技术，缺点是语音品质低、信号不稳定、涵盖范围不够全面，安全性也存在较大的问题。尽管如此，用户对这种新的移动技术非常兴奋，因为他们不必在家里或办公室里依赖固定电话或座机。蜂窝技术第一次切断了电话的连接，给了用户移动的灵活性，同时还能保持连接！

2G：第二代移动通信系统

芬兰于 1991 年推出第二代移动通信系统。它引入一种新的数字无线传输技术，也被称为全球移动通信系统（GSM）。除数字语音外，它还可以传输数据，如短消息服务（SMS）、照片或图片（多媒体信息服务，MMS），并首次允许用户漫游。GSM 技术是基于时分多址（TDMA）发展出来的，成为后来进一步发展无线标准的基础标准。该标准可支持 14.4～64kbit/s（最大）的数据速率。

高通公司开发的码分多址（CDMA）系统也是在 20 世纪 90 年代中期引入并实现的。CDMA 在频谱效率、用户数和数据速率方面比 GSM 有更多的特点。

这一代的后期版本，使用 GPRS（通用分组无线电服务）的称为 2.5G，使用 EDGE（GSM 演进的增强数据速率）网络的称为 2.75G。它提供更好的质量和容量。另外还引入了另一种流行技术 CDMA2000，以支持 CDMA 网络的更高数据速率。该技术能够提供高达 384kbit/s（最大）的数据速率。

尽管 2G 有诸多优点，后来又增加了收发电子邮件、浏览互联网等新功能，但是 2G 仍存在传输速度较慢、频率资源已近枯竭、语音质量不高等缺点。

3G：第三代移动通信系统

第三代移动通信开始于 21 世纪初引入的 UMTS——通用移动通信系统。3G 技术为 2G 手机增加了多媒体设施，允许视频、音频和图形应用程序通过网络传输。3G 就像是移动网络标准的发育期。在 3G 手机上，你可以观看视频或进行视频通话。3G 背后的想法是拥有单一的网络标准，而不是在美国、欧洲和亚洲采用不同类型的网络标准。3G 移动电话系统依靠码分多址（CDMA）和扩频无线电技术，允许许多用户共享时间和频率。

第三代移动通信系统的通信标准主要有 WCDMA、CDMA2000 和 TD-SCDMA 三种，其中 TD-SCDMA 是由中国研制提交的，不过由于起步晚，技术不够成熟。2008 年，工信部颁发 3G 牌照，其中中国移动持有 TD-SCDMA，中国联通持有 WCDMA，中国电信则持有 CDMA2000。

第三代移动通信系统还存在系统不兼容、频谱利用率低、速率仍然不高等诸多问题。

随着 3G 移动通信系统的引入，智能手机开始在全球流行起来。专门为智能手机开发的应用程序可以处理多媒体聊天、电子邮件、视频通话、游戏、社交媒体和医疗保健。数据传输速率增加到 2Mbit/s。

4G：第四代移动通信系统

第四代移动通信系统的技术测试始于 2007 年。早在 2010 年，德国就在欧洲开始捆绑式拍卖 4G 牌照，其后 4G 开始在西欧、北美、日本等国家和地区陆续投入商用。很快，全球移动通信系统进入 4G 时代。第四代移动通信技术是基于 IP 的高速移动通信网络，是移动通信技术发展史上的一次重大变革。它比 3G 的传输容量大、速率快，并且具备了 LTE（Long Term Evolution，长期演进）通信技术，实现了系统向宽带无线化和无线宽带化的演进。它能够提供 100Mbit/s～1Gbit/s 的速度，具有高服务质量和高安全性。

2013 年 12 月 4 日，工信部正式向中国移动、中国电信和中国联通发放 TD-LTE 营业执照，标志着中国 4G 移动通信时代的开始。4G 通信可以实现原始图像和视频的高清传输，其传输质量与计算机图像质量相似。应用程序、文件、图片、音频和视频的下载速度可以达到数十 MB/s，这是 3G 通信技术无法实现的。总之，4G 系统具有更高的数据传输速率、安全性、智能化、灵活性和服务质量。

5G：第五代移动通信系统

2017 年起，人们就开始对第五代移动通信技术展开了研究。2020 年，5G 时代正式拉开序幕。5G 的关键技术包括大规模天线阵列、超密集组网、新型多址、全频谱接入和新型网络架构。与现有的 4G 系统相比，5G 系统的性能将在 3 个方面提高 1000 倍：首先是传输速率提高 1000 倍，平均传输速率将达到 100Mbit/s～1Gbit/s；其次是总的数据流量提高 1000 倍；再次就是频谱效率和能耗效率提高 1000 倍。

5G 的特点如下。

1) 5G 研究在推进技术变革的同时将更加注重用户体验，网络平均吞吐速率、传输时延以及对虚拟现实、3D（三维）体验、交互式游戏等新兴移动业务的支撑能力等将成为衡量 5G 系统性能的关键指标。

2）与传统的移动通信系统理念不同，5G 系统研究不仅仅把点到点的物理层传输与信道编译码等经典技术作为核心目标，而是将更为广泛的多点、多用户、多天线、多小区协作组网作为突破重点，力求在体系结构上获得系统性能的大幅度提高。

3）室内移动通信业务已占据应用的主导地位，5G 室内无线覆盖性能及业务支撑能力将作为系统优先的设计目标，从而改变传统移动通信系统"以大范围覆盖为主、兼顾室内"的设计理念。

4）高频段频谱资源将更多地应用于 5G 移动通信系统，但由于受到高频段无线电波穿透能力的限制，无线与有线的融合、光载无线组网等技术将被更为普遍地应用。

5）可"软"配置的 5G 无线网络将成为未来的重要研究方向，运营商可根据业务流量的动态变化实时调整网络资源，有效降低网络运营的成本和能源的消耗。

5G 网络不再仅仅指传统意义上的移动网络，而是与互联网及物联网深度融合，将人与人之间的连接拓展至万物互联，可以为用户提供个性化和智能化的服务，是真正意义上的融合网络。超高速率、超高容量以及超低时延的网络将给人们的生活带来翻天覆地的变化。

表 4-1 归纳了 1G 到 5G 移动通信技术在速率、技术、关键特征方面的对比结果。

表 4-1　1G 到 5G 的对比结果

代际	速率	技术	关键特征
1G（20 世纪 70 年代至 80 年代）	14.4Kbit/s	AMPS、NMT、TACS	只有语音服务
2G（1990 至 2000）	9.6/14.4Kbit/s	TDMA、CDMA	语音及数据服务
2.5G/2.75G（2001 至 2004）	171.2Kbit/s，20~40Kbit/s	GPRS	语音、数据、网络移动互联网、低速流媒体服务和电子邮件服务
3G（2004 至 2005）	3.1Mbit/s，500~700Kbit/s	CDMA2000（1Xrtt、EVDO）、UMTS、EDGE	语音、数据、多媒体，支持智能手机应用程序，更快的网页浏览、视频通话和视频流
3.5G（2006 至 2010）	14.4Mbit/s，1~3Mbit/s	HSPA	所有服务都来自 3G 网络，速度更快，移动性更强
4G（2010 至 2020）	100~300Mbit/s，3~5Mbit/s，100Mbit/s（Wi-Fi）	WiMax、LTE、Wi-Fi	高速高质量的 IP 语音、高清多媒体流媒体、3D 游戏、高清视频会议和全球漫游
5G（2020 至今）	1~10Gbit/s	LTE-Advanced、OMA、NOMA	超高速移动互联网、关键任务应用的低延迟网络、物联网、安全与监控、高清多媒体流媒体、自动驾驶、智能医疗应用

6. 结论

无线技术一直在不断发展，以满足日益增长的需求和更高的规格要求。自第一代移动通信网络部署以来，电信业在技术、频谱的有效利用以及对终端用户的安全等方面都面临着许多新的挑战。未来的无线技术将提供超快、功能丰富和高度安全的移动网络。移动互联网和物联网是下一代移动通信系统发展的两大主要驱动力，其中移动互联网颠覆了传统移动通信的业务模式，而物联网则扩展了移动通信的服务范围。

4.3 光纤通信

光纤通信通过光纤发送光脉冲将信息从一个地方传送到另一个地方，如图4-9所示。光以电磁载波形式通过调制来携带信息。从20世纪70年代开始，光纤通信系统彻底改变了电信业，在信息时代发挥着重要的作用。

1. 应用

许多电信公司使用光纤传输电话信号、网络通信和有线电视信号。由于光纤相比于现有的铜线具有低得多的衰减和干扰，因此在长距离和高需求的应用领域具有很大的优势。然而，城市中基础设施的发展是相当困难和费时的，并且光纤系统的安装和操作也是复杂和昂贵的。因此光纤通信系统主要在长距离应用中使用，这样光纤通信可工作在全容量状态以降低成本。

图4-9　光纤

光纤已成为电信信息地面传输的行业标准。光纤在宽带传输服务中将继续扮演主要角色。如今，世界范围内80%以上的长距离通信通过光缆。光纤通信的应用很广泛，从全球网络到台式计算机。这涉及从距离小于一米到几百公里的语音、数据和视频的传输。运营商采用光纤进行模拟电话服务，有线电视公司也使用光纤进行数字视频服务，智能交通系统和生物医学系统也可以使用光纤传输系统。光缆也是地下和海底传输系统的行业标准。

自2000年以来，光纤通信的价格已经大幅度下降。目前推出的光纤到户的价格已变得比基于铜线的网络更低。

2. 历史

1880年，亚历山大·格雷厄姆·贝尔和他的助手查尔斯·萨姆纳·泰恩特发明了早期的光纤通信设备——光线电话机，地点是在华盛顿贝尔新成立的沃尔特实验室。贝尔认为这是他最重要的发明。该装置可以用于光束通话传输。

1964年，查尔斯·高锟博士定义了关于远距离通信设备的关键理论规范，即10或20dB/km的光损耗的标准。1966年，高锟和乔治·霍克汉姆在英国哈洛的STC实验室提出了光纤。他们发现，现有的玻璃纤维的传输损耗大于1000dB/km（与5~10dB/km的同轴电缆相比）是由于污染物造成的，这是可以消除的。高锟博士还阐述了需要一种更纯净的玻璃，以减少光损耗。

1970年，美国康宁公司成功研制出光纤，其具有足够低的衰减（约20dB/km）以满足通信目的。

世界上第一个广域网光缆系统大概安装于1978年，在英国东苏塞克斯郡的黑斯廷斯。光缆被放置在整个小镇的管道中，并有超过1000个用户，当时它们用来传输电视频道。该系统目前仍然存在，但已废弃。

20世纪80年代初开发的第二代光纤通信用于商业用途，工作波长为1.3μm，使用磷砷化镓铟（InGaAsP）半导体激光器。这些早期系统的建立最初受到多模光纤色散的限制，1981年人们发现单模光纤可以极大提高系统的性能，但是在实际工作中证明单模光纤的连接器难以开发。到1987年，这些系统的中继器间距可达50km，并能以高达1.7Gbit/s的比特率运行。

第三代的光纤系统工作在1.55μm，并且有大约0.2dB/km的损失。科学家克服了使用常规 InGaAsP 半导体激光器在该波长存在脉冲扩展的困难。通过使用在 1.55μm 处具有最小色散或限制激光光谱成为单纵模的色散位移光纤来解决此问题。这些发展最终使得第三代系统的中继器间距超过 100km，比特率为 2.5Gbit/s。

第四代的光纤系统使用光放大器以减少对中继器的需求，并且通过波分复用增加数据容量。这两个方面的改进引起一场革命，使得系统容量每 6 个月增加一倍，从 1992 年开始，直到 2001 年达到 10Tbit/s 的比特率。

第五代光纤通信发展的重点是可以进行扩展的波长范围，其中，WDM（波分复用）系统可以满足该要求。以往的波长范围（称为 C 波段）覆盖的波长范围为 1.53~1.57μm，干纤维具有低损耗的波长范围可以延伸到 1.30~1.65μm。其他发展包括"光孤子"概念，通过使用特定形状的脉冲，利用光纤的非线性效应来抵消色散的影响以保持脉冲形状。

3. 光纤

结构

典型的光纤由纤芯、包层和缓冲涂层组成。纤芯是光纤的内部结构，用于传导光。包层完全包裹着纤芯，如图 4-10 所示。

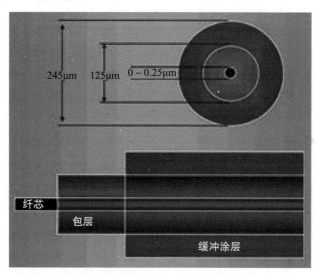

图 4-10　光纤结构

最常见的光纤类型包括 1550nm 的单模光纤和 850nm 或 1300nm 的多模光纤，其纤芯的直径范围为 8~62.5μm。最常见的包层直径为 125μm。缓冲涂层的材料通常是软质或硬质塑料，如直径范围为 250~900μm 的丙烯酸、尼龙。缓冲涂层为光纤提供机械保护和弯曲弹性。

工作原理

光纤完全基于全内反射原理。纤芯的折射率比包层的折射率高，如果光传送到纤芯与包层的临界面的角度比临界角大，那么将通过全内反射把光反射回纤芯。图 4-11 解释了光纤的工作原理。

模式

光纤以不同模式传导光波就叫作模式。模式描述的是光纤中光能量的分布。我们以大纤芯阶跃折射率光纤为例。光线以一定范围的角度进入光纤内，只要入射到纤芯与包层交界面的角度大于临界角，就能够在光纤中以不同的角度平稳行进。这些射线就是不同的模式。

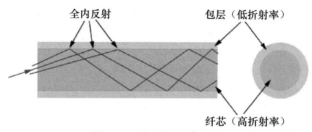

图 4-11 光纤的工作原理

光纤通信中的两种主要类型是多模光纤和单模光纤。如果光纤在特定的光波长下可以传输多种模式，它就称为多模光纤。多模光纤具有较大的纤芯（≥50μm），允许精度较低且较便宜的发射器、接收器以及连接器连接到它。然而，多模光纤会引入多模失真，这往往限制了带宽和链路的长度。此外，由于其较高的掺杂物含量，多模光纤通常是昂贵的，并表现出较高的衰减。某些光纤具有直径非常小的纤芯，它们只有一种传输模式，该模式在纤芯中以一条直线行进。这些光纤称为单模光纤。单模光纤的纤芯较小（<10μm），需要更昂贵的组件和互连方法，但可满足时间更长、性能更高的链接。图 4-12 说明了这一点。

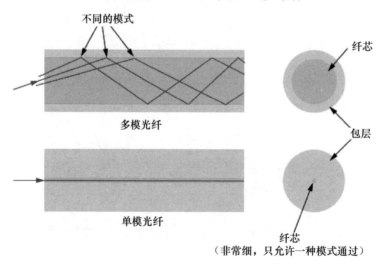

图 4-12 多模光纤和单模光纤

折射率分布

折射率分布是光纤从纤芯到包层的折射率分布。某些光纤具有阶跃折射率分布，其中纤芯具有均匀分布的折射率，同时包层也具有比纤芯低且均匀分布的折射率。其他光纤具有渐变折射率分布，它们的折射率是光纤中心径向距离的渐变函数。图 4-13 展示了单模和多模光纤一些折射率分布的常见类型。

数值孔径

多模光纤只传播以某一特定角度进入光纤的光，这个角度称为光纤的接收光锥区。这个锥半角称为受光角 θ_{max}，如图 4-14 所示。

对于阶跃折射率多模光纤，受光角仅取决于折射率：

$$\text{NA} = n\sin\theta_{max} = \sqrt{n_f^2 - n_c^2} \tag{4-35}$$

式中，n_f 是纤芯的折射率，n_c 是包层的折射率。

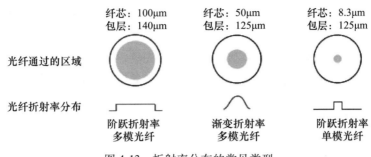

图 4-13 折射率分布的常见类型

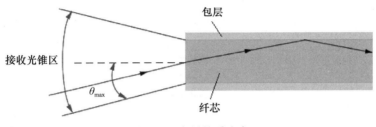

图 4-14 光纤的受光角

4. 光纤系统

光纤系统通信包括以下基本步骤：使用发射器创建光信号源，将信号沿光纤传送，确保信号不会变得太扭曲或太弱，接收光信号，并将其转换成电信号。

现代光纤通信系统一般包括：光发射器——将电信号转换成光信号并将光信号送入光缆，光缆——包含多组沿地下管道和建筑物传输的光纤，多种放大器和光接收器——将光信号恢复为电信号。典型的光纤通信系统如图 4-15 所示。发送的信息通常是由计算机、电话系统和有线电视公司所产生的典型数字信息。

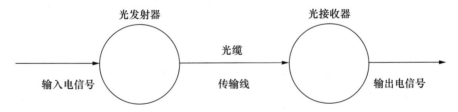

图 4-15 典型的光纤通信系统

光发射器

最常用的光发射器是半导体器件，例如发光二极管（LED）和激光二极管。LED 和激光二极管之间的区别是：LED 产生非相干光，而激光二极管产生相干光。光纤通信半导体光发射器的设计必须紧凑、高效与可靠，可以在最优波长范围内工作，并且在高频率能够被直接调制。

LED 的基本单元是一个正向偏置的 PN 结，通过自发辐射来发光，这种现象称为电致发光。LED 光传输也是低效的，只有约 1% 的输入功率，或约 $100\mu W$，最终转换成已耦合到光纤的发射功率。然而，由于其相对简单的设计，LED 在低成本应用方面是非常有用的。

光纤通信中常用的半导体激光发射器包括：VCSEL（垂直腔表面发射激光器）、法布里-珀罗（法布里和珀罗发明的一种干涉仪）和 DFB（分布式反馈激光器）。

激光二极管往往直接调制，即用加到器件的电流直接对光输出进行控制。对于高数据率或长距离的链接，激光源可以当成连续波，并且用一个外部设备进行光调制，如电吸收调制器或马赫-曾德尔干涉仪。

光接收器

光接收器的主要构成部分是光电探测器,它通过光电效应将光转换成电。用于电信的光电探测器由铟镓砷化物制成。光电探测器是典型的基于半导体的光电二极管。光电二极管包括P-N光电二极管、P-I-N光电二极管以及雪崩光电二极管。也可以使用金属-半导体-金属(MSM)光电探测器,因为它适用于波分复用器以及再生器中的电路集成。

传输窗口

波长决定了衰减和色散的效果。最弱影响波段(或窗口)对于传输是最有利的。这些窗口已经标准化,当前定义的光纤的传输窗口见表4-4。

表4-4 光纤的传输窗口

波段	描述	波长范围/nm
O波段	原始波段	1260~1360
E波段	扩展波段	1360~1460
S波段	短波长波段	1460~1530
C波段	常规波段	1530~1565
L波段	长波长波段	1565~1625
U波段	超长波长波段	1625~1675

历史上,曾使用低于O波段的窗口称为第一窗口,在800~900nm,但是这一范围的损耗很大,因此该窗口主要用于短距离通信。1300nm附近的窗口(O和E)有较低的损耗,该范围具有零色散。1500nm附近的窗口(S和C)是使用最广泛的。该范围有最低的衰减损耗,并且可以达到最长的范围。它有一些色散,因此可使用色散补偿设备去消除。

5. 光纤通信的优点

对于特定的系统,在选择光纤和电气(或铜)传输方面需要做一些权衡。相比于电力电缆,光纤适合在更高的带宽和跨越更长距离的系统中使用。

下面是光纤通信的优点。

1) 更宽的带宽:传输系统的信息承载能力与传输信号的载波频率成正比。因此,光纤比以往的通信系统有更大的传输带宽,光纤通信系统中的数据速率或者每秒的比特数急剧增加。此外,波分复用使得光纤的数据传输速率或者信息承载能力得到了几个数量级的提高。

2) 低传输损耗:由于超低损耗光纤和掺铒石英光纤作为光放大器的使用,人们可以实现几乎无损耗的传输。现代光纤通信系统使用的光纤传输损耗为0.002dB/km。另外,中继器的间距超过了100km。由于光域本身的扩增,在加强信号期间产生的失真几乎可以忽略不计。

3) 信号安全:通过光纤传输的信号不会泄露。此外,信号不能以简单的方式从光纤中被搭线窃听。因此,光纤通信可以提供百分百的信号安全。

4) 消除星火危害:在某些情况下,电传输信号可能是非常危险的。多数电位产生小的火花。火花通常不会造成危险,但在空气可能被爆炸性气体污染的化工厂或炼油厂中火花却是非常糟糕的。一个微小的火花可以产生大爆炸。潜在的火花危险严重危害了此类设施中的数据和通信。光纤由电绝缘体二氧化硅制造,光纤由于不会承载电流,因此不产生火花。

5) 安装方便:传输容量增加通常会使铜线电缆更厚,更坚硬。这种粗电缆在现有建筑物中必须经过墙壁和电缆管道,因此是难以安装的。而光缆不仅半径小,而且灵活、小巧、轻便。光缆弯曲或扭曲之后也不会损坏。

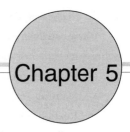

Chapter 5

Artificial Intelligence
（人工智能）

5.1 Pattern Recognition

1. What Are Patterns and Pattern Recognition?

Broadly speaking, a pattern is an observable thing existing in time and space. If we can distinguish whether they are the same or similar, then the information we get from such a thing can be called a pattern. Pattern refers not to the thing itself, but to the information obtained from the thing. Therefore, pattern is often manifested as information with time and space distribution.

In order to grasp objective things, people tend to form categories according to the similarity degree of things. For example, we can easily tell which one is a bicycle, which one is a motorcycle. These seemingly simple processes actually hide a very complex processing mechanism. The basic task of pattern recognition is to understand the mechanism of these mechanisms.

Pattern Recognition (PR) refers to the process of using machine (computer) to imitate human brain to describe, classify, judge and recognize various things in the real world. The goal of PR is to achieve flexible and intelligent computing machines with the ability to perceive, recognize, understand, learn and adapt.

Pattern recognition is related to statistics, psychology, linguistics, computer science, biology, cybernetics and so on. It is intersected with the study of artificial intelligence and image processing. For example, the adaptive or self-organizing pattern recognition system includes the learning mechanism of artificial intelligence. Scenic understanding and natural language understanding in artificial intelligence research also involve pattern recognition. Another example of pattern recognition in the preprocessing and feature extraction link application of image processing technology; pattern recognition is also applied to image analysis in image processing.

With the development of computer technology and artificial intelligence, pattern recognition is widely used in data mining, document classification, financial forecasting, multimedia database organization and retrieval, as well as biometric technology, emotion recognition and other fields.

2. Design of Pattern Recognition System

There are many methods of pattern recognition, mainly used for classification and regression. No matter which one is adopted, pattern recognition generally involves the following two basic processes.

- Learning process (design process): use a certain number of samples (called training set or learning set) to design the classifier;
- Recognition process (realization process): classification decision is made with the classifier designed for the identified samples.

The design of a pattern recognition system essentially involves the following five aspects (see Fig. 5-1): 1) data acquisition; 2) preprocessing; 3) data representation (feature extraction and selection); 4) classification decision; and 5) classifier design. The problem domain dictates the choice of sensor(s), preprocessing technique, representation scheme, decision making model, and the type of classifiers.

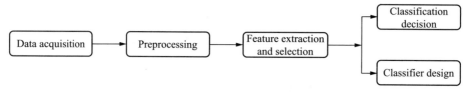

Fig. 5-1 Structure of PR system

The functions of each component of the pattern recognition system are as follows.

1) Data acquisition: capture a considerable amount of biometric data with the help of corresponding sound sensors, image sensors and other hardware devices. The object under study is represented by symbols that can be operated by computer, which corresponds to the transformation from physical space to pattern space. Generally, there are several types of information obtained.

- One-dimensional waveform: electrocardiogram, brain wave, sound wave, vibration waveform, etc;
- 2D images: text, maps, photographs, etc;
- Physical parameters: body temperature, test data, temperature, pressure, current, voltage, etc.

2) Preprocessing: to restore and denoise the information degradation caused by the information acquisition device or other factors and to strengthen the useful information, such as A/D, binarization, and image smoothing, transformation, enhancement, restoration, filtering, etc.

3) Data representation (feature extraction and selection): the raw information obtained from the sensor, its data volume is generally quite large. In order to realize classification and recognition effectively, the preprocessed information should be selected or transformed to obtain the features that can best reflect the essence of classification and constitute the feature vectors. The purpose is to transform the pattern space with higher dimension into the feature space with lower dimension, and select the most helpful feature vectors or the last part of the classification effect for the final classification discrimination of the pattern. Feature selection here is actually an optimization problem.

4) Classification decision: in the feature space, the pattern recognition method (the classification discrimination rules determined by the classifier design) is used to classify the recognition patterns, classify them into a certain category, and output the classification results. This process corre-

sponds to the transformation from feature space to category space.

5) Classifier design: in order to assign the recognized patterns to their respective pattern classes, a set of classification discrimination rules must be designed. The basic approach is to collect a certain number of samples as a training set, on this basis to determine the discriminant function, improve the discriminant function and error test.

3. Measurement of Pattern Similarity

Pattern recognition is an inference process. Since each feature vector represents a pattern, patterns can be classified according to their similarity.

Let $\boldsymbol{X} = [x_1, x_2, \cdots, x_n]^T$ denote a set of n-dimensional eigenvectors of the sample, composed of n eigenvalues. It corresponds to a point in the feature space. The distance function between points in the feature space is used as the measure of pattern similarity, and the "distance" is used as the basis of pattern classification, the smaller the distance, the more "similar" it is.

Hamming Distance

In information coding, the different bits encoded on the corresponding bits of two legal codes are called the code distance, also known as the Hamming distance. Let $\boldsymbol{X}_1$, $\boldsymbol{X}_2$ be n-dimensional binary (1 or -1) mode sample vectors, then the Hamming distance is

$$D_h(\boldsymbol{X}_1, \boldsymbol{X}_2) = \frac{1}{2}\left[n - \sum_{k=1}^{n}(x_{ik} - x_{jk})\right] \quad (5\text{-}1)$$

while $D = n$ indicates the values of each component of the two mode vectors are different, and $D = 0$ indicates they are all the same.

Euclidean Distance

Let $\boldsymbol{X}_1$, $\boldsymbol{X}_2$ be two n-dimensional model samples, and the Euclidean distance between them is

$$D(\boldsymbol{X}_1, \boldsymbol{X}_2) = \|\boldsymbol{X}_1 - \boldsymbol{X}_2\| = [(\boldsymbol{X}_1 - \boldsymbol{X}_2)^T(\boldsymbol{X}_1 - \boldsymbol{X}_2)]^{\frac{1}{2}} \quad (5\text{-}2)$$

The smaller the Euclidean distance, the more similar it is.

Maharanobis Distance

Mahalanobis distance is defined as a square expression:

$$D^2 = (\boldsymbol{X} - \boldsymbol{M})^T \boldsymbol{C}^{-1}(\boldsymbol{X} - \boldsymbol{M}) \quad (5\text{-}3)$$

where $\boldsymbol{X}$ is the mode vector, $\boldsymbol{M}$ is the mean vector, $\boldsymbol{C}$ is the covariance matrix of this model. When $\boldsymbol{C} = \boldsymbol{I}$, the Mahalanobis distance is the Euclidean distance.

Minkowaki Distance

The Minkowaki distance between n-dimensional model sample vectors $\boldsymbol{X}_1$, $\boldsymbol{X}_2$ is expressed as

$$D_m(\boldsymbol{X}_1, \boldsymbol{X}_2) = \left[\sum_{k=1}^{n}|x_{ik} - x_{jk}|^m\right]^{\frac{1}{m}} \quad (5\text{-}4)$$

when $m = 2$, Minkowaki distance is the Euclidean distance; when $m = 1$, it is called the "city block" distance.

Angular Similarity

The angle between two vectors can reflect the difference of two vectors in direction. Define the cosine of the angle between mode vectors $\boldsymbol{X}_1$, $\boldsymbol{X}_2$ as

$$S(\boldsymbol{X}_1, \boldsymbol{X}_2) = \frac{\boldsymbol{X}_1^T \boldsymbol{X}_2}{\|\boldsymbol{X}_1\| \cdot \|\boldsymbol{X}_2\|} \quad (5\text{-}5)$$

when $S=0$, the two vectors are exactly the same.

4. Statistical Pattern Recognition

The known approaches for pattern recognition can be divided in four categories: template matching, statistical, syntactic or structural matching, and neural networks. These models are not necessarily independent and sometimes the same pattern recognition method exists with different interpretations. Attempts have been made to design hybrid systems involving multiple models. A brief description and comparison of these approaches is given below and summarized in Table 5-1.

Table 5-1 Pattern recognition models

Approach	Representation	Recognition function	Typical criterion
Template matching	Samples, pixels, curves	Correlation, distance measure	Classification error
Statistical	Features	Discriminant function	Classification error
Syntactic or structural matching	Primitives	Rules, grammer	Acceptance error
Neural networks	Samples, pixels, features	Network function	Mean square error

Statistical pattern recognition is the most basic pattern recognition method. Statistical pattern recognition relates to the use of statistical techniques for analysing data measurements in order to extract information and make justified decisions. It is a very active area of study and research, which has seen many advances in recent years. Applications such as data mining, web searching, multimedia data retrieval, face recognition, and cursive handwriting recognition, all require robust and efficient pattern recognition techniques. Density estimation (parametric, Bayesian and non-parametric), linear discriminant function analysis, nonlinear discriminant function analysis, decision tree, clustering, support vector machine and so on all belong to statistical pattern recognition.

Linear Discriminant Function

Linear Discriminant Function Analysis (LDFA) was the first multivariate statistical classification method (see Fig. 5-2), invented by R. A. Fisher in 1936. The simplest representation of a linear discriminant function is obtained by taking a linear function of the input vector so that:

$$g(\boldsymbol{x}) = \boldsymbol{w}^T \boldsymbol{x} + w_0 \qquad (5\text{-}6)$$

where $\boldsymbol{x}$ is the D dimensional sample vector, $\boldsymbol{w}$ is called a weight vector, and w_0 is a bias. The negative of the bias is sometimes called a threshold. According to the given training samples of known categories, parameters $\boldsymbol{w}$ and w_0 are determined. An input vector $\boldsymbol{x}$ is assigned to class C_1 if $g(\boldsymbol{x}) > 0$ and to class C_2 otherwise. The corresponding decision boundary is therefore defined by the relation $g(\boldsymbol{x}) = 0$, which corresponds to a $(D-1)$-dimensional hyperplane within the D-dimensional input space.

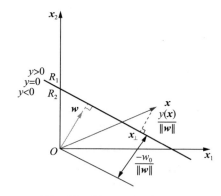

Fig. 5-2 Linear discriminant function analysis

Bayesian Classifier

Accounting for uncertainty is a crucial component in decision making (e.g., classification) because of ambiguity in our measurements. Probability theory is the proper mechanism for accounting for uncertainty. For a random experiment whose result is not certain in advance (e.g., throwing a die), the result is of uncertainty. The set of all possible outcomes (e. g., $\{1,2,3,4,5,6\}$) are the sample space, and a subset of the sample space (e. g., obtain an odd number in the experiment of throwing a die = $\{1,3,5\}$) is an event.

Intuitively, the probability of an event A could be defined as

$$P(A) = \lim_{n \to \infty} \frac{N(A)}{n} \tag{5-7}$$

where $N(A)$ is the number of times that event A happens in n trials. Assumes that all outcomes are equally likely (Laplacian definition). Conditional probabilities are defined as follows:

$$P(A \mid B) = \frac{P(A,B)}{P(B)}, P(B \mid A) = \frac{P(A,B)}{P(A)} \tag{5-8}$$

where $P(A)$ or $P(B)$ is prior probability or marginal probability, $P(A \mid B)$ or $P(B \mid A)$ is posterior probability, and $P(A,B)$ is the joint probability that both A and B occur simultaneously.

The above definitions lead to the chain rule:

$$P(A,B) = P(A \mid B)P(B) = P(B \mid A)P(A) \tag{5-9}$$

Using the definition of conditional probabilities leads to the Bayes' rule:

$$P(A \mid B) = \frac{P(B \mid A)P(A)}{P(B)} \tag{5-10}$$

then allows us to evaluate the uncertainty in A after we have observed B in the form of the posterior probability $P(A \mid B)$.

The quantity $P(B \mid A)$ on the right-hand side of Bayes' theorem is evaluated for the observed data set B and can be viewed as a function of the parameter vector A, in which case it is called the likelihood function. It expresses how probable the observed data set is for different settings of the parameter vector A. We can express the denominator in Bayes' theorem in terms of the prior distribution and the likelihood function:

$$P(B) = \int P(B \mid A)P(A)dA \tag{5-11}$$

Mathematically, Bayes' rule states:

$$\text{posterior probability} = \frac{\text{likelihood function} \times \text{prior probability}}{\text{marginal likelihood}} \tag{5-12}$$

Based on minimum error rate of the Bayes decision rule is: if $P(w_1 \mid x) > P(w_2 \mid x)$, put x classified as w_1; conversely, if $P(w_1 \mid x) < P(w_2 \mid x)$, put x classified as w_2, which can be abbreviated to: if $P(w_i \mid x) = \max P(w_j \mid x)$, $x \in w_i$.

Decision Tree

A decision tree is a graphic flowchart that represents the process of making a decision or a series of decisions (see Fig. 5-3). Leaf nodes represent the class labels or class distribution. Internal node denotes a test on a feature. Branch represents the path of a test outcome. At each node, one attribute is chosen to split the training examples into distinct classes as much as possible. A new case is classified by following a matching path to a leaf node. For a classification problem, it is a top-down, divide-and-conquer process to learn and construct a decision tree from the training samples with known class labels.

Decision tree generation consists of two phases: tree construction and tree pruning. At start, all the training examples are at the root. Then examples are partied recursively based on selected attributes. At last, branches that reflect noise or outliers should be identified and removed.

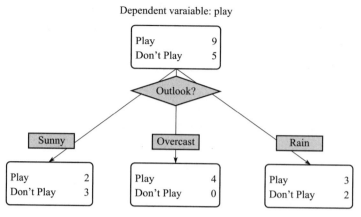

Fig. 5-3 Decision tree

The classification of decision tree is based on information gain. Assume that there are two classes, P and N. Let the set of examples S contain p elements of class P and n elements of class N. The amount of information needed to decide if an arbitrary example in S belongs to P or N is defined as

$$E(S) = -\frac{p}{p+n}\log_2\left(\frac{p}{p+n}\right) - \frac{n}{p+n}\log_2\left(\frac{n}{p+n}\right) \tag{5-13}$$

With an attribute A, data are partitioned into subsets. The information gained by branching on A is as follows:

$$Gain(A) = E(Current\ set) - \sum P(childset)E(childset) \tag{5-14}$$

According to the output result of decision tree, decision tree can be divided into classification tree and regression tree. The output result of classification tree is specific category, while the output result of regression tree is a certain value.

Decision tree construction algorithms mainly include ID3, C4.5 and CART, among which ID3 and C4.5 are classification trees, CART is regression tree, and ID3 is the most basic construction algorithm of decision tree, while C4.5 and CART are optimization algorithms based on ID3.

Support Vector Machine

Support Vector Machine (SVM) was first proposed by Cortes and Vapnik in 1995. It has many unique advantages in solving small sample size, nonlinear and high-dimensional pattern recognition, and can be extended to other machine learning problems such as function fitting.

SVM is based on the VC (Vapnik-Chervonenkis) dimension theory of statistical learning theory and the principle of minimum structural risk. According to the limited sample information, it seeks the best compromise between the complexity of the model (namely, the learning accuracy of specific training samples) and the learning ability (namely, the ability to identify arbitrary samples without error), in order to obtain the best generalization ability.

Typically, a discriminant function $g(x)$ is estimated from a finite set of examples by minimizing an error function, e.g., the MSE. Conventional empirical risk minimization does not imply good generalization performance. To guarantee good generalization performance, the complexity or capacity of the learned functions must be controlled. Functions with high capacity are more complicated (i.e., have many degrees of freedom). In statistical learning, the VC dimension is a popular measure of the capacity of a classifier. The VC dimension can predict a probabilistic upper bound on the generalization error of a classifier. Vapnik has shown that maximizing the margin of separation (i.e., empty space between classes) is equivalent to minimizing the VC dimension. The optimal hyperplane is the one giving the largest margin of separation between the classes (see Fig. 5-4). The margin is defined by the distance of the nearest training samples from the hyperplane. Intuitively speaking, these are the most difficult samples to classify. We refer to these samples as support vectors.

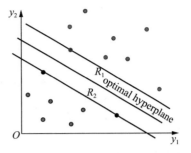

Fig. 5-4　The optimal hyperplane

SVM maps the sample space to a high-dimensional or even infinite-dimensional feature space (Hilbert space) through a nonlinear mapping P, so that the nonlinear separable problem in the original sample space is transformed into a linear separable problem in the feature space. In a nutshell, it's scaling and linearization. Raising dimensions, mapping samples to higher-dimensional spaces, usually adds complexity to calculations and even causes "dimension disaster." However, for classification and regression problems, it is possible to achieve linear partition (or regression) through a linear hyperplane in a high-dimensional feature space for a sample set that cannot be handled linearly in a low-dimensional sample space. General dimension raising will bring complexity to calculation. SVM solves this problem by cleverly applying the expansion theorem of kernel function, so it does not need to know the explicit expression of nonlinear mapping. Since the linear learning machine is built in a high-dimensional feature space, compared with the linear model, it not only hardly increases the complexity of calculation, but also avoids the "dimension disaster" to some extent, thanks to the expansion of kernel function and calculation theory.

Different kernel functions can be selected to generate different SVM. The following four kernel functions are commonly used:

1) Linear kernel function: $K(x,y) = x \cdot y$.
2) Polynomial kernel function: $K(x,y) = [(x \cdot y) + 1]^d$.
3) Radial basis function: $K(x,y) = \exp(-|x-y|^2/d^2)$.
4) Kernel function of bilevel neural network: $K(x,y) = \tanh[a(x \cdot y) + b]$.

SVM is based on exact optimization, not on approximate methods (i.e., global optimization method, no local optima). It appears to avoid overfitting in high dimensional spaces and generalize well using a small training set. Its performance depends on the choice of the kernel and its parameters and its complexity depends on the number of support vectors, not on the dimensionality of the transformed space.

NEW WORDS AND PHRASES

pattern　*n.* 模式，图案，模范，模型，（布或墙纸的）样品；*v.* 用图案装饰，模仿，赋予……以固定（或易辨认）的形式

perceive　*vt.* 认为，理解，察觉，注意到，意识到

feature extraction　特征提取

biometric technology　生物识别技术

emotion recognition　情感识别

classification　*n.* 分类，类别，（动植物等的）分类学，分类系统，编目

regression　*n.* 后退，退化，（疾病或症状的）消

退，(统计) 回归
binarization n. 二值化
image smoothing 图像平滑
enhancement n. 增加，增强，改善
restoration n. 修复，重新实施，返还，(软件程序的) 恢复，还原
eigenvalue n. [数] 特征值，[数] 本征值，固有值
Hamming distance 汉明距离
Euclidean distance 欧氏距离
template matching 模板匹配
statistical classification 统计分类，统计分组
syntactic adj. 句法的，语法的，依据造句法的
neural network 神经网络
discriminant function [数] 判别函数
hyperplane n. [数] 超平面

probability theory [数] 概率论
prior probability [数] 先验概率，事前概率
posterior probability [数] 后验概率，事后概率
joint probability [数] 联合概率
likelihood function [数] 似然函数
decision tree 决策树，决策图表
information gain [计] 信息增益，情报增益
Support Vector Machine (SVM) 支持向量机
structural risk 结构风险
generalization ability 泛化能力
empirical risk 经验风险，试验风险
dimension disaster 维数灾难
kernel function [数] 核函数
polynomial adj. 多项的，多项式的；n. 多项式，表示任何多项式之和

NOTES

1) Let $\boldsymbol{X}=[x_1,x_2,\cdots,x_n]^T$ denote a set of n-dimensional eigenvectors of the sample, composed of n eigenvalues.
   由 n 个特征值组成的 n 维向量 $\boldsymbol{X}=[x_1,x_2,\cdots,x_n]^T$，称为该样本的特征向量。

2) The corresponding decision boundary is therefore defined by the relation $g(\boldsymbol{x})=0$, which corresponds to a $(D-1)$-dimensional hyperplane within the D-dimensional input space.
   相应的决策边界由关系 $g(\boldsymbol{x})=0$ 定义，它对应于 D 维输入空间内的 $(D-1)$ 维超平面。

3) Conventional empirical risk minimization does not imply good generalization performance.
   传统的经验风险最小化并不意味着具有良好的泛化能力。

4) SVM maps the sample space to a high-dimensional or even infinite-dimensional feature space (Hilbert space) through a nonlinear mapping P, so that the nonlinear separable problem in the original sample space is transformed into a linear separable problem in the feature space.
   SVM 通过非线性映射 P 把样本空间映射到高维乃至无穷维的特征空间 (Hilbert 空间)，使得原来样本空间中的非线性可分的问题转化为特征空间中的线性可分的问题。

EXERCISES

1. **Please translate the following words and phrases into Chinese.**

   a) perceive
   b) classification
   c) enhancement
   d) Euclidean distance
   e) hyperplane
   f) prior probability
   g) Support Vector Machine (SVM)
   h) kernel function
   i) discriminant function
   j) eigenvalue

2. **Please translate the following words and phrases into English.**

   a) 特征提取
   b) 统计模式识别
   c) 线性判别函数
   d) 后验概率
   e) 似然函数
   f) 信息增益
   g) 决策树
   h) 经验风险
   i) 泛化能力
   j) 支持向量
   k) 回归
   l) 欧氏距离

3. **Fill in the blanks with the missing word(s).**

   a) Pattern refers not to the thing itself, but to the _____ obtained from the thing.
   b) In order to grasp objective things, people tend to form categories according to the _____ degree of things.

c) The goal of PR is to achieve flexible and intelligent computing machines with the ability to perceive, _____ , understand, _____ and _____ .
d) There are many methods of pattern recognition, mainly used for _____ and _____ .
e) The design of a pattern recognition system essentially involves the following five aspects: 1) _____ , 2) _____ , 3) _____ , 4) _____ , and 5) _____ .
f) Since each _____ represents a pattern, patterns can be classified according to their similarity.
g) The known approaches for pattern recognition can be divided in four categories: _____ , _____ , _____ , and _____ .
h) The mathematic base of Bayesian classifier is _____ .
i) Bayes' rule is _____ .
j) The classification of decision tree is based on _____ .

4. **Answer the following questions according to the text.**
a) What are patterns and pattern recognition?
b) Can the linear discriminant function analysis be used to deal with XOR problem?
c) Please introduce the working process of pattern recognition.
d) How to generate a decision tree? What do the leaf-node, the branch, and the internal node represent?
e) What are the support vectors?

READING

Artificial Neural Network

1. Introduction

An Artificial Neural Network (ANN) is an information processing paradigm that is inspired by the way biological nervous systems, such as the brain, process information. The key element of this paradigm is the novel structure of the information processing system. It is composed of a large number of highly interconnected processing elements (neurones) working in unison to solve specific problems. ANNs, like people, learn by example. An ANN is configured for a specific application, such as pattern recognition or data classification, through a learning process. Learning in biological systems involves adjustments to the synaptic connections that exist between the neurones. This is true of ANNs as well. In more practical terms neural networks are non-linear statistical data modeling tools. They can be used to model complex relationships between inputs and outputs or to find patterns in data. The article will briefly introduce the knowledge about ANN and lay a foundation for further study.

2. The Characteristic of ANN

Neural networks, with their remarkable ability to derive meaning from complicated or imprecise data, can be used to extract patterns and detect trends that are too complex to be

人工神经网络

1. 引言

人工神经网络（ANN）是一种信息处理模式，这种模式受到诸如大脑的生物神经系统处理信息方式的启发。该模式的关键部分是其新颖的信息处理系统结构。这一结构由大量的相互连接的处理单元（神经元）组成，它们共同操作以解决具体问题。ANN 就像人一样，通过实例来学习。一个 ANN 通过对特定的应用进行学习来确定其结构，如模式识别或数据分类。生物系统中的学习包括调整存在于神经元之间的突触的连接，在 ANN 中也是这样，在更多实际情况下，神经网络是非线性的统计数据模型工具。神经网络可以用于模拟复杂的输入与输出间的关系或者在数据中找出模式。下面将简要地介绍 ANN 的知识并为进一步的研究提供基础。

2. ANN 的特征

神经网络具有从复杂或不精确的数据中提取有用信息的显著能力，可以用来建立模型和预测进展趋势，而这些不管是对

noticed by either humans or other computer techniques. A trained neural network can be thought of as an "expert" in the category of information it has been given to analyse. This expert can then be used to provide projections given new situations of interest and answer "what if" questions.

Other advantages of neural networks include.

- Adaptive learning: an ability to learn how to do tasks based on the data given for training or initial experience.
- Self-organization: an ANN can create its own organization or representation of the information it receives during learning time.
- Real time operation: ANN computations may be carried out in parallel, and special hardware devices are being designed and manufactured which take advantage of this capability.
- Fault tolerance via redundant information coding: partial destruction of a network leads to the corresponding degradation of performance. However, some network capabilities may be retained even with major network damage.

3. A Simple Neuron and a Complicated Neuron

A Simple Neuron

An artificial neuron is a device with many inputs and one output, see Fig. 5-5. The neuron has two modes of operation: the training mode and the using mode. In the training mode, the neuron can be trained to fire (or not), for particular input patterns. In the using mode, when a taught input pattern is detected at the input, its associated output becomes the current output. If the input pattern does not belong in the taught list of input patterns, the firing rule is used to determine whether to fire or not.

The firing rule is an important concept in neural networks. A firing rule determines how one calculates whether a neuron should fire for any input pattern. It relates to all the

于人类还是计算机技术来说都过于复杂而无法做到。训练过的神经网络能对要求分析的信息进行分类,可以认为它是信息分类的专家。这样的专家(系统)可以用来对有意义的新的情况提供预测,也可以回答"如果是……怎么样……"的问题。

神经网络的其他优势包括以下几个方面。

- 自适应学习:根据所给定的用于训练的数据或初始经验来学习如何完成任务的能力。
- 自组织:人工神经网络可以创建自身的组织或表示在学习时间内接收的信息。
- 实时操作:人工神经网络可以进行并行计算,并利用该能力设计和制造特定的硬件设备。
- 通过冗余信息编码的容错能力:网络的部分破坏导致相应的性能下降。但是,即使主要网络损害,某些网络能力仍然可以得到保留。

3. 简单神经元与复杂神经元

简单神经元

人工神经元是一个多输入-单输出的系统,如图 5-5 所示。神经元有两种操作模式:训练模式和应用模式。在训练模式中,可以训练神经元是否对特定输入模式触发。在应用模式中,当在输入处检测到已训练的输入模式时,它的相关输出变为当前输出。如果该输入模型不在输入模型的训练列表内,则使用触发规则来确定是否触发。

在神经网络中触发规则是一个重要概念。触发规则决定了对任何输入模式如何计算一个神经元是否应该触发。它与所有

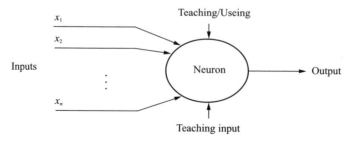

Fig. 5-5　A simple neuron

input patterns, not only the ones on which the node was trained. A simple firing rule can be implemented by using Hamming distance technique. The rule goes as follows.

Take a collection of training patterns for a node, some of which cause it to fire (the 1-taught set) and others which prevent it from doing so (the 0-taught set). Then the patterns not in the collection cause the node to fire, on comparison, they have more input elements in common with the "nearest" pattern in the 1-taught set than with the "nearest" pattern in the 0-taught set. If there is a tie, then the pattern remains in the undefined state.

A Complicated Neuron

The previous neuron doesn't do anything that conventional computers don't do already. A more sophisticated neuron (see) is showed in Fig. 5-6. The difference from the previous model is that the inputs are "weighted", the effect that each input has at decision making is dependent on the weight of the particular input. The weight of an input is a number which when multiplied with the input gives the weighted input. These weighted inputs are then added together and if they exceed a pre-set threshold value, the neuron fires. In any other case the neuron does not fire.

Fig. 5-6 presents a structure of jth neuron. The relationship between output y_j and inputs $X_j = (x_1, x_2, \cdots, x_n)$ is

$$\begin{cases} s_j = \sum_{i=1}^{n} w_{ij} \cdot x_i - \theta_j \\ y_j = f(s_j) \end{cases}$$

输入模式有关,而不仅与训练节点的模式有关。利用汉明距离技术可以实现简单的触发规则,该规则描述如下。

对一个节点取一个训练模式集合作为输入,其中的一些模式会引起触发(记为有导师集1),另外的那些不会引起触发(记为有导师集0)。如果不在这个集合中的模式引起该节点触发,则表明这些模式中与有导师集1最接近的模式数目要多于与有导师集0最接近的模式数目。如果这两种模式数目平衡,则此模式为未定义状态。

复杂神经元

前面讲的神经元不能够完成传统计算机目前不能完成的一些任务。图5-6所示为一个更加复杂的神经元。与之前的模型不同的是神经元的输入是经过加权的,每个输入在决策中的作用取决于特定输入的权重。输入权重是一个数值,它与输入相乘共同作为加权输入。然后,对加权输入求和,如果总和大于设置的阈值,则神经元触发,在其他情况下神经元将不会触发。

图5-6所示为一个j^{th}神经元结构,输出y_j与输入$X_j = (x_1, x_2, \cdots, x_n)$的关系为

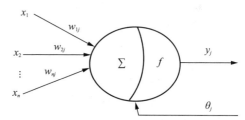

Fig. 5-6 A sophisticated neuron

where θ_j is threshold and $f(\cdot)$ is feature function that has many selectable form.

In mathematical terms, the neuron fires if and only if $xw_{1j} + x_2w_{2j} + \cdots + x_nw_{nj} > \theta_j$. The addition of input weights and the threshold makes this neuron a very flexible and powerful one. The neuron has the ability to adapt to a particular situation by changing its weights and/or threshold. Various algorithms exist that cause the neuron to adapt; the most used ones are the Delta rule and the back error propagation. The former is used in feedforward networks and the latter in feedback networks.

式中,θ_j是阈值,$f(\cdot)$是形式可选择的特征函数。

用数学术语描述,当且仅当$xw_{1j} + x_2w_{2j} + \cdots + x_nw_{nj} > \theta_j$时神经元会触发。输入权重和阈值的加入使得神经元更加灵活和强大。神经元具有通过改变权值或者阈值来适应具体情况的能力。已有大量的算法可以调整神经元使其适应具体情况,其中最常用的是Delta规则和误差反向传播算法。前者用于前馈网络,后者用于反馈网络。

4. Architecture of Neural Networks

Feedforward Networks

Feedforward ANNs allow signals to travel one way only, from input to output. There is no feedback (loops) i. e. the output of any layer does not affect that same layer. Feedforward ANNs tend to be straight forward networks that associate inputs with outputs. They are extensively used in pattern recognition. This type of organization is also referred to as bottom-up or top-down.

Feedback Networks

Feedback networks can have signals traveling in both directions by introducing loops in the network. Feedback networks are very powerful and can get extremely complicated. Feedback networks are dynamic; their state is changing continuously until they reach an equilibrium point. They remain at the equilibrium point until the input changes and a new equilibrium needs to be found. Feedback architectures are also referred to as interactive or recurrent, although the latter term is often used to denote feedback connections in single-layer organizations.

Network Layers

The commonest type of artificial neural network consists of three layers of units: a layer of "input" units is connected to a layer of "hidden" units, which is connected to a layer of "output" units (see Fig. 5-7).

The activity of the input units represents the raw information that is fed into the network.

The activity of each hidden unit is determined by the activities of the input units and the weights on the connections between the input and the hidden units.

The behavior of the output units depends on the activity of the hidden units and the weights between the hidden and output units.

This simple type of network is interesting because the hidden units are free to construct their own representations of the input. The weights between the input and hidden units

4. 神经网络的结构

前馈网络

前馈 ANN 只允许信号单向传输,即由输入到输出。它没有反馈回路,即任意层的输出都不会影响同一层。前馈 ANN 是将输入与输出关联的直接向前网络。它们广泛地应用于模式识别中。这种结构类型也称为自下而上或自上而下。

反馈网络

反馈网络通过在网络中引入环路,信号可以双向传输。反馈网络功能很强大但也很复杂。反馈网络是动态的,其状态也在不停地变换直到达到一个平衡点。它会一直保持在这个平衡点直到输入信号变化,然后需要找到一个新的平衡点。反馈结构也称为交互式的或者递归式的,尽管后者通常用来表示在单层组织中的反馈连接。

网络层

最常见的神经网络结构由三层构成:输入层单元连接着隐层单元,隐层单元又连接着输出层单元(如图 5-7 所示)。

输入层单元的活动表示输入到网络中的原始信息。

每个隐含层单元的活动由输入层单元和连接输入和隐含层单元的权值决定。

输出层单元的活动取决于隐含层单元的活动和隐含层和输出层的权值。

这种简单类型的网络很有意义,因为隐含层单元能够自由地构建输入的表示形式。输入和隐含层单元间的权值决定每个隐含层单元何时激活,继而通过修改这些权重,隐含层单元可以选择它表示什么。

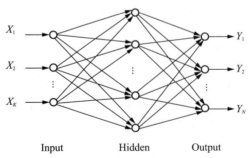

Fig. 5-7 An example of a simple feedforward network

determine when each hidden unit is active, and so by modifying these weights, a hidden unit can choose what it represents.

We also distinguish single-layer and multi-layer architectures. The single-layer organization, in which all units are connected to one another, constitutes the most general case and is of more potential computational power than hierarchically structured multi-layer organizations. In multi-layer networks, units are often numbered by layer, instead of a global numbering.

5. The Learning Process

Information is stored in the weight matrix W of a neural network. Learning is the determination of the weights. According to the way learning is performed, we can distinguish two major categories of neural networks.

- Fixed networks: in which the weights cannot be changed, i.e. $dW/dt = 0$. In such networks, the weights are fixed a priori according to the problem to solve.
- Adaptive networks: which are able to change their weights, i.e. $dW/dt \neq 0$.

All learning methods used for adaptive neural networks can be classified into two major categories.

- Supervised learning: which incorporates an external teacher, so that each output unit is told what its desired response to input signals ought to be. During the learning process global information may be required. Paradigms of supervised learning include error-correction learning, reinforcement learning and stochastic learning. An important issue concerning supervised learning is the problem of error convergence, i.e. the minimization of error between the desired and computed unit values. The aim is to determine a set of weights which minimizes the error. One well-known method, which is common to many learning paradigms is the Least Mean Square (LMS) error convergence.
- Unsupervised learning: uses no external teacher and is based upon only local information. It is also referred to as self-organization, in the sense that it self-organizes data presented to the network and detects their emergent collective properties. Paradigms of unsupervised learning are Hebbian learning and competitive learning.

我们也要区分单层结构和多层结构。单层结构是最一般的情况，其所有的单元是相互连接的，它比多层结构具有更强大的计算潜力。在多层结构中，单元是分层编号的，而不是全局编号。

5. 学习过程

信息储存在神经网络的权值矩阵 W 中。学习的目的是为了决定权值的大小。根据学习方式，可以将神经网络分为两大类。

- 固定网络：在固定网络中，权值的大小固定不变，即 $dW/dt = 0$。在该网络中，根据要解决的问题来固定最优的权值。
- 自适应网络：在该网络中，权值可以改变，即 $dW/dt \neq 0$。

所有自适应神经网络中的学习方法可以分为两大类。

- 有监督学习：该学习方法采用了一个外部老师，以便告知每个输出单元对于输入信号什么是期望的响应。在学习的过程中可能需要全局的信息。有监督学习的范例包括纠错学习、增强学习和随机学习。有监督学习的重要问题是误差收敛问题，即期望值与计算值的最小误差问题。训练的目的是得到一组能使误差最小的权值。最小均方（LMS）误差收敛是最一种众所周知且常用的学习范例。
- 无监督学习：该学习方法不需要外部老师且仅依赖局部信息。这种方法也称作自组织学习方法，从某种意义上说，它自己将数据传输到网络中并检测其出现的集体属性。无监督学习的学习范例有 Hebbian 学习和竞争学习。

We say that a neural network learns off-line if the learning phase and the operation phase are distinct. A neural network learns on-line if it learns and operates at the same time. Usually, supervised learning is performed off-line, whereas unsupervised learning is performed on-line.

Transfer Function

The behavior of an ANN depends on both the weights and the input-output function (transfer function) that is specified for the units. This function typically falls into one of three categories: linear (or ramp), threshold and sigmoid function. For linear units, the output activity is proportional to the total weighted output. For threshold unit, the output is set at one of two levels, depending on whether the total input is greater than or less than some threshold value. For sigmoid units, the output varies continuously but not linearly as the input changes. Sigmoid units bear a greater resemblance to real neurones than linear or threshold units, but all three must be considered rough approximations.

To make a neural network that performs some specific task, we must choose how the units are connected to one another, and we must set the weights on the connections appropriately. The connections determine whether it is possible for one unit to influence another. The weights specify the strength of the influence.

We can teach a three-layer network to perform a particular task by using the following procedure:

1) We present the network with training examples, which consist of a pattern of activities for the input units together with the desired pattern of activities for the output units.

2) We determine how closely the actual output of the network matches the desired output.

3) We change the weight of each connection so that the network produces a better approximation of the desired output.

6. Applications of ANN

Neural networks have broad applicability to real world business problems. In fact, they have already been successfully applied in many industries.

Since neural networks are best at identifying patterns or trends in data, they are well suited for prediction or forecasting needs including:

- sales forecasting
- industrial process control
- customer research

如果神经网络的学习阶段和运行阶段是分开进行的,则我们说这个神经网络是离线学习的。如果神经网络的学习阶段和运行阶段是同时进行的,则我们说这个神经网络是在线学习的。通常情况下,有监督学习是离线学习的,而无监督学习是在线学习的。

传递函数

人工神经网络的特性取决于权值和具体的输入-输出函数(传递函数),这些单元的传递函数是特定的。典型的传递函数包括三类:线性函数、阈值函数和sigmoid函数。对于线性单元,输出的活跃度是与总的加权后的输出成比例的。对于阈值单元,根据总的输入大于或小于某一阈值,输出分为两个级别。对于sigmoid单元,输出根据输入的变化而呈现连续非线性变化。与线性单元和阈值单元相比,sigmoid单元与真实神经元的相似性更大。但是这三类都被认为是粗糙近似。

为了使神经网络完成特定的工作,我们必须选择单元间的连接方式,必须设定合理的连接权重。这种连接决定着一个单元是否可能影响另一个单元,权重确定了影响的强度。

我们可通过以下步骤来训练一个三层神经网络完成指定的任务:

1) 通过训练实例来给出神经网络,该神经网络由输入单元的活动模式和所期望的输出单元的活动模式构成。

2) 决定网络的实际输出与所期望的输出的匹配程度。

3) 改变每个连接的权重,以便网络的输出能更接近期望的输出。

6. 人工神经网络的应用

人工神经网络在解决现实世界中的实际问题方面有着广泛的应用。实际上,它们已经成功地应用到很多行业中。

神经网络在辨识模式和数据趋势方面表现最佳,它们非常适用于需求预测或预报等方向,包括:

- 销售预测
- 工业过程控制
- 客户研究

- data validation
- risk management
- target market

ANN are also used in the following specific paradigms: recognition of speakers in communications, diagnosis of hepatitis, recovery of telecommunications from faulty software, interpretation of multimeaning Chinese words, undersea mine detection, texture analysis, three-dimensional object recognition, hand-written word recognition, and facial recognition.

7. Conclusion

The computing world has a lot to gain from neural networks. Their ability to learn by example makes them very flexible and powerful. Furthermore there is no need to devise an algorithm in order to perform a specific task; i.e. there is no need to understand the internal mechanisms of that task. They are also very well suited for real time systems because of their fast response and computational times which are due to their parallel architecture.

Neural networks also contribute to other areas of research such as neurology and psychology. They are regularly used to model parts of living organisms and to investigate the internal mechanisms of the brain.

Perhaps the most exciting aspect of neural networks is the possibility that some day "conscious" networks might be produced. There are a number of scientists arguing that consciousness is a "mechanical" property and that "conscious" neural networks are a realistic possibility.

ANN 还应用到以下特定的范例中：通信中的说话人识别、肝炎诊断、电信软件故障的修复、汉语多义词的解释、海底矿藏雷探测、文本分析、三维目标识别、手写文本识别、人脸识别等。

7. 结论

计算领域从神经网络中受益颇多，它们从实例中学习的能力使得它们非常灵活和强大。此外，我们没有必要为了实现一个具体的任务而去设计一个算法，即我们没有必要去了解那个任务的内部机制。快速的响应和较短的计算时间使得它们也非常适合实时系统，而这归因于其并行体系结构。

神经网络对其他研究领域也有贡献，比如神经学和心理学。它们常用于模拟生物体的一部分和研究大脑的内部结构。

也许神经网络最令人兴奋的方面是某一天可能会出现"有意识的"网络。有些科学家认为意识是一种"力学"属性，这种"有意识的"神经网络是现实可能的。

NEW WORDS AND PHRASES

ANN 人工神经网络
paradigm n. 范例
inspire vt. 鼓舞，感动，激发，启示，赋予灵感，产生
interconnect vt. 使互相连接
neurone n. [解] 神经细胞，神经元
unison n. 调和，和谐，一致，齐唱，齐奏
configure vi. 配置，设定；vt. 使成形，使具有一定形式
pattern recognition 模式识别
data classification 数据分类
synaptic n. 突触
model n. 模型；v. 模拟
lay a foundation 奠定基础
characteristic adj. 特有的，表示特性的，典型的；n. 特性，特征
remarkable adj. 不平常的，非凡的，值得注意的，显著的
derive vt. 得自；vi. 起源
imprecise adj. 不严密的，不精确的
extract n. 精，汁，榨出物，摘录，选粹；vt. 拔出，榨取，开方，求根，摘录，析取，吸取
category n. 种类，类别
analyse vt. 分析，分解；n. 分析
projection n. 规划，估计，预测
adaptive learning 自适应学习
self-organization n. 自组织
organization n. 组织，机构，团体
real time operation 实时操作
fault tolerance 容错

redundant   *adj.* 多余的
destruction   *n.* 破坏，毁灭
degradation   *n.* 降级，降格，退化
retain   *vt.* 保持，保留
flexibility   *n.* 弹性，适应性，机动性
training mode   训练模式
using mode   应用模式
Hamming distance   汉明距离
tie   *n.* 不分胜负，平局
sophisticated   *adj.* 复杂的
weighted   *adj.* 加权的
threshold   *n.* 极限，阈值
if and only if   当且仅当
back error propagation   反向误差传递
feedforward networks   前馈网络
feedback networks   反馈网络
loop   *n.* 环，回路，回线
equilibrium   *n.* 平衡，平静，均衡，保持平衡的能力，沉着，安静
interactive   *adj.* 交互式的
recurrent   *adj.* 再发生的，周期性发生的，循环的
distinguish   *v.* 区别，辨别

hierarchically   *adv.* 分等级地，分级体系地
fixed networks   固定网络
adaptive networks   自适应网络
prior   *adj.* 优先的，在前的；*n.* 预先
supervised learning   有监督学习
unsupervised learning   无监督学习
error-correction learning   纠错学习
reinforcement learning   增强学习
stochastic learning   随机学习
error convergence   误差收敛
Least Mean Square (LMS) error convergence   最小均方误差收敛
competitive learning   竞争学习
transfer function   传递函数
ramp   *n.* 斜坡，坡道
linear (or ramp), threshold and sigmoid function   线性（或斜坡）函数、阈值函数和 sigmoid 函数
resemblance   *n.* 相似之处
validation   *n.* 确认
hepatitis   *n.* [医] 肝炎
texture   *n.* （织品的）质地，（木材、岩石等的）纹理，（文艺作品的）结构

NOTES

1) Neural networks, with their remarkable ability to derive meaning from complicated or imprecise data, can be used to extract patterns and detect trends that are too complex to be noticed by either humans or other computer techniques.

   神经网络具有从复杂或不精确的数据中提取有用信息的显著能力，可以用来建立模型和预测进展趋势，而这些不管是对于人类还是计算机技术来说都过于复杂而无法做到。

2) A trained neural network can be thought of as an "expert" in the category of information it has been given to analyze. This expert can then be used to provide projections given new situations of interest and answer "what if" questions.

   训练过的神经网络能对要求分析的信息进行分类，被认为是信息分类的专家。该专家（系统）可以用来对有意义的新情况提供预测，也可以回答"如果是……怎么样……"的问题。

3) The firing rule is an important concept in neural networks. A firing rule determines how one calculates whether a neuron should fire for any input pattern. It relates to all the input patterns, not only the ones on which the node was trained.

   触发规则在神经网络中是一个重要的概念。触发规则决定了对任何输入模式如何计算一个神经元是否应该触发。它与所有输入模式有关，而不仅与训练节点的模式有关。

4) Take a collection of training patterns for a node, some of which cause it to fire (the 1-taught set) and others which prevent it from doing so (the 0-taught set). Then the patterns not in the collection cause the node to fire, on comparison, they have more input elements in common with the "nearest" pattern in the 1-taught set than with the "nearest" pattern in the 0-taught set. If there is a tie, then the pattern remains in the undefined state.

对一个节点取一个训练模式集合作为输入,其中的一些模式会引起触发(记为有导师集1),另外的那些不会引起触发(记为有导师集0)。如果不在这个集合中的模式引起该节点触发,则表明这些模式中与有导师集1最近的模式数目要多于与有导师集0最近的模式数目。如果这两种模式数目平衡,则此模式为未定义状态。

5) The addition of input weights and the threshold makes this neuron a very flexible and powerful one. The neuron has the ability to adapt to a particular situation by changing its weights and/or threshold.

输入权重和阈值的加入使得神经元更加灵活与强大。神经元具有通过改变权值或者阈值来适应具体情况的能力。

6) We say that a neural network learns off-line if the learning phase and the operation phase are distinct. A neural network learns on-line if it learns and operates at the same time. Usually, supervised learning is performed off-line, whereas unsupervised learning is performed on-line.

如果神经网络的学习阶段和运行阶段是分开进行的,则我们说这个神经网络是离线学习的。如果神经网络的学习阶段和运行阶段是同时进行的,则我们说这个神经网络是在线学习的。通常,有监督学习是离线学习的,而无监督学习是在线学习的。

5.2 Machine Learning

Artificial Intelligence (AI) is a broad term used to describe systems capable of making certain decisions on their own. Machine Learning (ML), which is the core of artificial intelligence, is to make machines have the same learning ability as human beings. It is specialized in studying how computers simulate or realize human learning behavior to acquire new knowledge or skills and reorganize existing knowledge structure to continuously improve their performance. ML is a multidisciplinary interdisciplinary subject, involving probability theory, statistics, approximation theory, convex analysis, algorithm complexity theory and other disciplines.

1. Definition of Machine Learning

Machine learning is a discipline that specializes in how computers simulate or realize human learning behaviors, so as to acquire new knowledge or skills, and reorganize existing knowledge structures to continuously improve their own performance. Can machines learn as well as humans? In 1959, Samuel designed a chess-playing program that had the ability to learn and improve its skill in constant play. Four years later, the program won out over the designer. Three more years passed, the process defeated an American champion who had been unbeaten for eight years. This program showed the power of machine learning.

But what is learning has long been controversial. Sociologists, logicians and psychologists all have different views. There are some basic common threads, however, and the overarching theme is best summed up by this oft-quoted statement made by Arthur Samuel way back in 1959: "machine learning is the field of study that gives computers the ability to learn without being explicitly programmed."

In 1997, Tom Mitchell, Carnegie Mellon University, gave a "well-posed" definition that has proven more useful to engineering types: "a computer program is said to learn from experience E with respect to some task T and some performance measure P, if its performance on T, as measured by P, improves with experience E." So if you want your program to predict, for example, traffic patterns at a busy intersection (task T), you can run it through a machine learning algorithm with data about past traffic patterns (experience E) and, if it has successfully "learned", it will then do better at predicting future traffic patterns (performance measure P).

In short, machine learning is a computer program that learns from experience and gets better at a specific task.

2. Elements of Machine Learning

There are two aspects of machine learning that are the most important: data and model.

Data

This is the foundation of machine learning, where experience is ultimately translated into data that a computer can understand so that a computer can learn from experience. Data can be collected by sensors such as radar or cameras. It can also be poll data, stock market prices, and so on. Having access to large amounts of high-quality data is the most important capital in machine learning and artificial intelligence.

Model

It provides a mathematical framework for learning. When you have the data, you need to design a model and train the model with the data as input. The trained model eventually becomes the core of machine learning, making the model the decision-making hub. A well-trained model, when a new event is input, responds appropriately and produces a good output.

3. Steps of Machine Learning Application Implementation

The current idea of using machine learning to solve problems is as shown in Fig. 5-8 (take visual perception as an example).

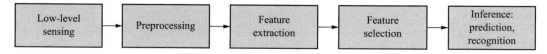

Fig. 5-8 Block diagram of typical machine learning algorithms application implementation

Data is first obtained by sensors (such as CMOS), and then preprocessed, feature extracted, feature selected, and then deduced, predicted, or identified. The last part is the machine learning part.

The core objective of machine learning is learning and inference (see Fig. 5-9). The way the machine learns is similar to the human being. Humans learn from experience. The more we know, the more easily we can predict. Machines are trained the same. Having identified the problem to be solved, to make an accurate prediction, the machine sees an example. The machine learns through the discovery of patterns which is made thanks to the data. One crucial part is to choose carefully which data to provide to the machine. The list of attributes used to solve a problem is called a feature vector. You can think of a feature vector as a subset of data that is used to tackle a problem. Therefore, the learning phase is used to describe the data and summarize it into a model.

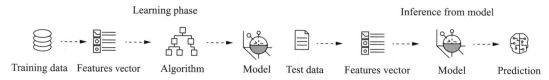

Fig. 5-9 Core steps of machine learning

When the model is built, the never-seen-before data go through the model and give a prediction. There is no need to update the rules or retrain the model. This is all the beautiful part of machine learning.

The life of machine learning programs is straightforward and can be summarized in the following points.

Define a Question

Clarify what problem you want to solve and whether it is appropriate to use machine learning to solve it.

Collect and Label Data

Collect a lot of information about different characteristics, and all the collected data is called training samples, or data sets. In the data acquisition stage, as many features as possible should be collected. The more complete the features and the more data, the more accurate the trained model will be. Data label is necessary for a supervised learning approach. For example, for a spam filtering system, the training sample must contain marked data on whether the message is spam or not.

Clean Data

Check data consistency, and remove duplicate data and noise data. Make the data structured so that it can be easily input to machine learning algorithms.

Select Feature

Analyze the features one by one and finally select the appropriate features as input. The method of feature selection can be either manual selection or automatic selection through the model, such as Principal Component Analysis (PCA) algorithm.

Choose Model

Choose the appropriate model according to various factors such as problem type, data size, training duration and accuracy of the model.

Train and Test the Model

Divide the data set into training data set and test data set, generally according to 8 : 2 or 7 : 3, and then use the training data set to train the model. After the parameters are trained, the test data set is used to test the accuracy of the model. Theoretically, a more reasonable data set partition scheme is divided into three, that is, another cross-validation data set.

Evaluate the Performance and Refine the Algorithm

Evaluate the performance of the model after the model is trained. Performance evaluation generally includes training duration, whether the data set is sufficient, accuracy of the model, etc. If the requirements are not met, the model needs to be refined and then either trained and evaluated, or replaced with another model.

Use the Model to Make a Prediction

Save the parameters of the trained model and load them directly the next time they are used. The result is usually obtained by simply taking the new sample as input and then invoking the model. Once the algorithm gets good at drawing the right conclusions, it applies that knowledge to new sets of data.

4. Classification of Machine Learning

There are many classifications of machine learning, generally based on two points: data types and learning processes. The former is supervised learning, semi-supervised learning and unsupervised learning. The latter includes active learning, reinforcement learning and transduction learning. Most of machine learning (about 70%) is supervised learning and unsupervised learning is about 10% ~ 20%. Sometimes semi-supervised learning and reinforcement learning are also used.

Supervised Learning

Supervised learning algorithm trains machine learning model with instance with classification label, so that the computer can learn rules from it, so as to make reasonable output prediction for a new input. Supervised learning is widely used to predict future events using historical data. There are two categories of supervised learning: regression learning and classification learning.

For instance, we have a lot of price data for houses with different features (size, location, orientation, developer, etc.). The system will be trained from these data to estimate the price of the house with the lowest possible error. When the output is a continuous value, it is regression learning.

Another example, we have a lot of mails, and each mail has been flagged for spam. By studying the marked mail data, a model can be developed to accurately determine whether a new message is spam or not. This is called classification learning, where the output is discrete, such as output 1 to indicate spam or output 0 to indicate non-spam.

Unsupervised Learning

Unsupervised learning analyzes the intrinsic characteristics and structure of data by learning a large amount of unmarked data. The system will not be told the "right answer." The algorithm has to figure out for itself what the data represents. The goal is to explore the data and find some internal structure. Unsupervised learning works well with transactional data. Popular methods include self-organizing mapping, nearest-neighbor mapping, K-means clustering and singular value decomposition. These algorithms are also used to segment text, recommend items and determine outliers for data.

For example, we have a large number of users' shopping history information, and analyze different categories of users from the data. How many categories can we end up with? What are the characteristics of each category? We don't know in advance. So that's clustering.

Special attention should be paid to the difference between categorization in supervised learning: categorization questions are known in advance, and choose one of the known answers. The clustering problem does not know which kinds of categories in advance, so it needs to use the algorithm to dig out the characteristics and structure of the data, and then cluster into several categories.

Semi-supervised Learning

The semi-supervised learning is the same as supervised learning, but usually only a small amount of input data is labeled, and most of it is not (because untagged data is easily available). This type can be learned using methods such as classification, regression, and prediction. Semi-supervised learning can be used when a fully tagged supervised learning process, such as using a webcam to recognize faces, is too expensive due to the associated labels.

Reinforcement Learning

It is often used for robotics, games and navigation. The algorithm maximizes the return through trial and error reinforcement learning. This learning is made up of three main components: agents (learners or decision makers), environments (everything the agents touch) and actions (what agents can do). The goal is to maximize the return on the actions chosen by the agent within a given period of time. With a good strategy, the agent will reach its goals more quickly. Therefore, the goal of reinforcement learning is to get the best strategy.

5. Common Methods of Machine Learning

Fig. 5-10 shows a diagram of common machine learning methods, and Table 5-2 gives a brief description of common machine learning methods.

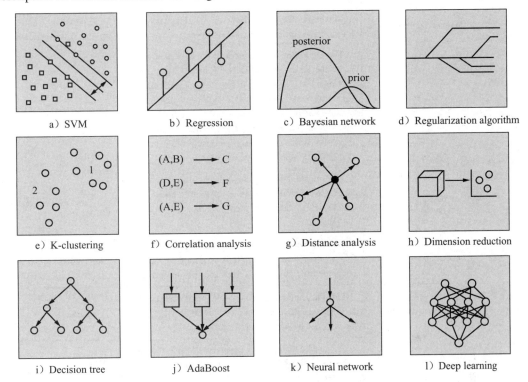

Fig. 5-10   Graphical illustration of common approaches to machine learning

Table 5-2   Commonly used machine learning methods and their description

Category	Algorithm	Description	Type
Supervised learning	Linear regression	Finds a way to correlate each feature to the output to help predict future values	Regression
	Logistic regression	Extension of linear regression that's used for classification tasks. The output variable 3 is binary (e.g., only black or white) rather than continuous (e.g., an infinite list of potential colors)	Classification
	Decision tree	Highly interpretable classification or regression model that splits data-feature values into branches at decision nodes (e.g., if a feature is a color, each possible color becomes a new branch) until a final decision output is made Finds a set of thresholds for a pattern-dependent sequence of features	Regression/Classification
	Naive Bayes	The Bayesian method is a classification method that makes use of the Bayesian theorem. The theorem updates the prior knowledge of an event with the independent probability of each feature that can affect the event	Regression/Classification

（续）

Category	Algorithm	Description	Type
Supervised learning	Radial basis network	Iterative MSE optimization of a feed-forward neural network with at least one layer of neurons using Gaussian-like transfer functions	Regression/Classification
	Support vector machine	Maximizes the margin between the classes by selecting a minimum number of support vectors	Regression (not very common)/Classification
	Random forest	The algorithm is built upon a decision tree to improve the accuracy drastically. Random forest generates many times simple decision trees and uses the "majority vote" method to decide on which label to return. For the classification task, the final prediction will be the one with the most vote; while for the regression task, the average prediction of all the trees is the final prediction	Regression/Classification
	AdaBoost	Classification or regression technique that uses a multitude of models to come up with a decision but weighs them based on their accuracy in predicting the outcome	Regression/Classification
	Gradient-boosting tree	Gradient-boosting tree is a state-of-the-art classification/regression technique. It is focusing on the error committed by the previous trees and tries to correct it	Regression/Classification
Unsupervised learning	K-means clustering	Puts data into some groups (K) that each contains data with similar characteristics (as determined by the model, not by humans in advance)	Clustering
	Gaussian mixture model	A generalization of K-means clustering that provides more flexibility in the size and shape of groups (clusters)	Clustering
	Hierarchical clustering	Splits clusters along a hierarchical tree to form a classification system. Can be used for cluster loyalty-card customer	Clustering
	Recommender system	Help to define the relevant data for making a recommendation	Clustering
	PCA/T-SNE	Mostly used to decrease the dimensionality of the data. The algorithms reduce the number of features to 3 or 4 vectors with the highest variances	Dimension reduction

NEW WORDS AND PHRASES

Machine Learning（ML） 机器学习
Artificial Intelligence（AI） 人工智能
multidisciplinary *adj.*（涉及）多门学科的，有关各种学问的，多专业的
interdisciplinary *adj.* 跨学科的
patterns *n.* 模式（pattern 的复数形式）；*v.* 摹制，用图案装饰，pattern 的第三人称单数形式
feature vector 特征向量
Principal Component Analysis（PCA）［自］［数］
主成分分析
supervised learning 监督学习
semi-supervised learning 半监督学习
unsupervised learning 无监督学习
active learning 主动学习
reinforcement learning 强化学习
transduction learning 转导学习
tag *n.* 标签，称呼，（电子）追踪器，（计算机）标识符；*v.* 给……贴标签，给（计算机程序或

文件）加标记
linear regression　线性回归
logistic regression　逻辑回归
decision tree　决策树
naive Bayes　朴素贝叶斯
radial basis network　径向基网络
Support Vector Machine（SVM）　支持向量机
random forest　随机森林

AdaBoost　集成学习
gradient　*n.* 斜坡，［数］斜率，梯度，梯度率，梯度算子；*adj.* 倾斜的，步行的，能步行的
Gaussian mixture model　高斯混合模型
hierarchical clustering　分层聚类
recommender system　推荐系统
agent　*n.* 代理人，经纪人，间谍，特工，原动力，动因，剂，官员

NOTES

1) ML is a multidisciplinary interdisciplinary subject, involving probability theory, statistics, approximation theory, convex analysis, algorithm complexity theory and other disciplines.
机器学习是一门多领域交叉学科，涉及概率论、统计学、逼近论、凸分析、算法复杂度理论等多门学科。

2) A computer program is said to learn from experience E with respect to some task T and some performance measure P, if its performance on T, as measured by P, improves with experience E.
对于计算机程序来说，给它一个任务 T 和一个性能度量 P，如果在经验 E 的影响下，P 对 T 的测量结果得到了改进，那么就说该程序从 E 中学习。

3) The former is supervised learning, semi-supervised learning and unsupervised learning. The latter includes active learning, reinforcement learning and transduction learning.
前者分为监督学习、半监督学习和无监督学习；后者包括主动学习、强化学习和转导学习。

4) Semi-supervised learning can be used when a fully tagged supervised learning process, such as using a webcam to recognize faces, is too expensive due to the associated labels.
当一个全标记的监督学习过程因其相关标签的成本太高时，我们可以使用半监督学习，例如使用网络摄像头识别人脸。

EXERCISES

1. **Please translate the following words and phrases into Chinese.**
   a) pattern
   b) linear regression
   c) supervised learning
   d) K-means clustering
   e) hierarchical clustering
   f) AdaBoost
   g) PCA
   h) reinforcement learning
   i) agent

2. **Please translate the following words and phrases into English.**
   a) 梯度
   b) 深度学习
   c) 特征向量
   d) 随机森林
   e) 智能体
   f) 径向基网络
   g) 朴素贝叶斯
   h) 主成分分析

3. **Fill in the blanks with the missing word(s).**
   a) _____ is the core of artificial intelligence.
   b) _____ is the foundation of machine learning, _____ provides a mathematical framework for learning.
   c) The more we know, the more easily we can _____.
   d) The machine learns through the discovery of _____ which is made thanks to the data.
   e) After the parameters are trained, the _____ set is used to test the accuracy of the model.
   f) When the output is a continuous value, it is _____.
   g) This is called _____, where the output is discrete, such as output 1 to indicate spam or output 0 to indicate non-spam.

h) The _____ problem does not know which kinds of categories in advance, so it needs to use the algorithm to dig out the characteristics and structure of the data, and then cluster into several categories.

4. Answer the following questions according to the text.
   a) What is machine learning?
   b) What are the main elements of machine learning?
   c) What are the core objective of machine learning?
   d) How to make a machine learning program?
   e) What is supervised learning algorithm?

READING

Deep Learning

1. Introduction

No one knows since when, artificial intelligence has become a hot topic. It is possible that since AlphaGo defeated Ke Jie, or it may be the first robot Sophia with human citizenship, artificial intelligence has been extended unconsciously to healthcare, education, and every aspect of life. The current development of artificial intelligence relies on deep learning, which is a subset of machine learning. The difference is that deep learning algorithms can automatically learn representations from data such as images, videos, or texts, without introducing human domain knowledge. The word "deep" in deep learning refers to a multi-layered algorithm or neural network used to identify patterns in data. Deep learning's highly flexible architecture can learn directly from raw data, similar to how the human brain works, and as more data becomes available, its prediction accuracy improves. AlphaGo used the deep learning algorithm to defeat the human world champion. More importantly, deep learning has promoted the development of other fields of artificial intelligence such as natural language processing and computer vision.

2. Biological Basis of Deep Learning

Deep learning is a machine learning method that relies on artificial neural networks, which allow computer systems to learn from examples. In most cases, deep learning algorithms are based on patterns of information in biological nervous systems. In 1958, David Hubel (an American neurobiologist born in Canada) and Torsten Wiesel studied the correspondence between the pupil area and the neurons in the cerebral cortex. A series of experiments on the back of the cat's skull to measure the activity of neurons have shown that there is a certain correspondence between the different visual neurons

深度学习

1. 引言

不知道从什么时候起,人工智能已经成为一个热门话题,有可能从 AlphaGo 打败柯洁那次起,也有可能是从第一个拥有人类公民身份的机器人 Sophia 起,人工智能已悄然延伸到医疗、教育,以及生活的方方面面。目前的人工智能的发展依赖深度学习,而深度学习是机器学习的一个子集,与众不同之处在于,深度学习算法可以自动从图像、视频或文本等数据中学习表征,无须引入人类领域的知识。深度学习中的"深度"一词表示用于识别数据模式的多层算法或神经网络。深度学习高度灵活的架构可以直接从原始数据中学习,这类似于人脑的运作方式,获得更多数据后,其预测准确度也将随之提升。AlphaGo 正是采用了深度学习算法击败了人类世界冠军,更重要的是,深度学习促进了人工智能其他领域(如自然语言处理和计算机视觉等)的发展。

2. 深度学习的生物学基础

深度学习是一种依靠人工神经网络的机器学习方法,它允许计算机系统通过实例进行学习。在大多数情况下,深度学习算法基于生物神经系统中的信息模式。1958 年,David Hubel(出生于加拿大的美国神经生物学家)和 Torsten Wiesel 通过研究瞳孔区域与大脑皮层神经元的对应关系,通过对猫的后脑头骨的一系列神经元的活跃程度的测量实验证明,位于后脑皮层的不同视觉神经元与瞳孔所受刺激之间

located in the hindbrain cortex and the stimulation of the pupil. When the pupil detects the edge of the object in front of it, and the edge points in a certain direction, a type of neuron cell called a "direction-selective cell" fires.

This finding has stimulated further thinking about the nervous system. The working process of nerve-center-brain may be a process of continuous iteration and continuous abstraction. There are two keywords here, one is abstraction and the other is iteration. From the original signal, do low-level abstraction, and gradually iterate to high-level abstraction. Human logical thinking often uses highly abstract concepts. For example, starting with raw signal ingestion (the pupil ingesting pixels), then doing preliminary processing (cerebral cortex finding edges and directions), and then abstracting (the brain determines that the shape of the object in front of you is circular), then further abstraction (the brain further determines that the object is a balloon).

The information processing of the human visual system is hierarchical (see Fig. 5-11). Extract edge features from the low-level V1 area, to the shape of the V2 area or parts of the target, etc., and then to the higher level, the entire target, the behavior of the target, etc. That is to say, high-level features are a combination of low-level features, and the feature representation from low-level to high-level is more and more abstract, and more and more can express semantics or intentions. The higher the level of abstraction, the less possible guesswork exists, and the better for classification. For

存在某种对应关系。当瞳孔发现眼前的物体的边缘,而且这个边缘指向某个方向时,一种被称为"方向选择性细胞"的神经元细胞就会活跃。

这个发现激发了人们对于神经系统的进一步思考。神经-中枢-大脑的工作过程或许是一个不断迭代、不断抽象的过程。这里的关键词有两个,一个是抽象,另一个是迭代。从原始信号做低级抽象,逐渐向高级抽象迭代。人类的逻辑思维经常使用高度抽象的概念。例如,从原始信号摄入开始(瞳孔摄入像素),接着做初步处理(大脑皮层某些细胞发现边缘和方向),然后抽象(大脑判定眼前的物体的形状是圆形的),然后进一步抽象(大脑进一步判定该物体是只气球)。

人的视觉系统的信息处理是分级的(见图 5-11)。从低级的 V1 区提取边缘特征,再到 V2 区的形状或者目标的部分等,再到更高层(整个目标、目标的行为等)。也就是说,高层特征是低层特征的组合,从低层到高层的特征表示越来越抽象,越来越能表现语义或者意图。抽象层面越高,存在的可能猜测就越少,就越利于分类。例如,单词集合和句子的对应是多对一的,句子和语义的对应也是多对一的,语义和意图的对应还是多对一的,这是个

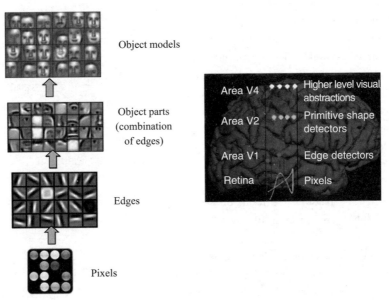

Fig. 5-11 Schematic diagram of hierarchical information processing of the human visual system

example, the correspondence between word sets and sentences is many-to-one, the correspondence between sentences and semantics is many-to-one, and the correspondence between semantics and intent is many-to-one. This is a hierarchical system. That is, the visual cortex is graded, and because of this found that David Hubel and Torsten Wiesel won the 1981 Nobel Prize in Medicine. This physiological discovery led to the breakthrough development of computer artificial intelligence four decades later, and deep learning uses computers to model this process.

3. The Structure of Deep Learning

Deep learning is a type of machine learning based on the structure and function of the human brain. It uses artificial neural networks to perform complex calculations on large amounts of data to interpret data such as images, sounds and text. Deep learning algorithms train machines by learning from examples. Industries such as healthcare, e-commerce, entertainment, and advertising commonly use deep learning.

The essence of deep learning is to learn more useful features by building a machine learning model with many hidden layers and massive training data, thereby ultimately improving the accuracy of classification or prediction. Therefore, "deep models" are the means, and "feature learning" is the end. A multilayer perceptron with multiple hidden layers is a deep learning structure. Deep learning combines low-level features to form more abstract high-level representation attribute categories or features to discover distributed feature representations of data.

There are many similarities and differences between deep learning and traditional neural networks. The similarity between the two is that deep learning adopts a layered structure similar to that of neural networks. The system consists of a multi-layer network including an input layer, a hidden layer (multi-layer), and an output layer. Only the nodes of adjacent layers are connected. Nodes in the same layer and across layers are not connected to each other, and each layer can be regarded as a logistic regression model; this hierarchical structure is closer to the structure of the human brain.

The differences between the two are:

1) Deep learning emphasizes the depth of the model structure, usually with 5, 6, or even 10 layers of hidden layer nodes.

2) Deep learning is a layer-wise training mechanism. If the mechanism of back propagation is used, for a deep network (above 7 layers), the residual propagation to the first layer has become too small, and the so-called gradient diffusion occurs.

层级体系，即可视皮层是分级的。借此发现，David Hubel 和 Torsten Wiesel 获得了 1981 年的诺贝尔医学奖。这个生理学的发现促成了计算机人工智能在四十年后的突破性发展，而深度学习就是利用计算机来对这个过程进行建模的。

3. 深度学习的结构

深度学习是一种基于人脑结构和功能的机器学习。它使用人工神经网络对大量数据执行复杂的计算来解释数据（例如图像、声音和文本）。深度学习算法通过从示例中学习来训练机器。医疗保健、电子商务、娱乐和广告等行业通常使用深度学习。

深度学习的实质是通过构建具有很多隐层的机器学习模型和海量的训练数据来学习更有用的特征，从而提升分类或预测的准确性。因此，"深度模型"是手段，"特征学习"是目的。含有多隐层的多层感知器就是一种深度学习结构。深度学习通过组合低层特征形成更加抽象的高层表示属性类别或特征，以发现数据的分布式特征表示。

深度学习与传统的神经网络之间有相同的地方，也有很多不同的地方。二者的相同点在于深度学习采用了与神经网络相似的分层结构，系统由包括输入层、隐层（多层）、输出层组成的多层网络，只有相邻层的节点之间有连接，同一层以及跨层节点之间相互无连接，每一层可以看作一个逻辑回归模型；这种分层结构比较接近人类大脑的结构。

二者的不同点在于：

1）深度学习强调模型结构的深度，通常有 5 层、6 层，甚至 10 多层的隐层节点。

2）深度学习遵循逐层的训练机制。如果采用反向传播的机制，那么对于深层网络（7 层以上），残差传播到最前面的层已经变得太小，出现所谓的梯度扩散。

3) The importance of feature learning is clearly highlighted, that is, through layer-by-layer feature transformation, the feature representation of the sample in the original space is transformed into a new feature space to obtain features that are more expressive than the input, so that classification can be achieved or easier to predict. Compared with the method of constructing features by artificial rules, using big data to learn features can better describe the rich intrinsic information of the data.

4. Convolutional Neural Networks
The concept of CNN

Convolutional Neural Network (CNN) is a kind of artificial neural network, which has become a research hotspot in the field of speech analysis and image recognition. Its weight sharing network structure makes it more similar to biological neural network, which reduces the complexity of the network model and the number of weights. This advantage is more obvious when the input of the network is a multi-dimensional image, so that the image can be directly used as the input of the network, avoiding the complex feature extraction and data reconstruction process in the traditional recognition algorithm. Convolutional network is a multi-layer perceptron specially designed to recognize two-dimensional shapes. This network structure is highly invariant to translation, scaling, tilting or other forms of deformation.

CNNs are influenced by earlier Time Delay Neural Networks (TDNN). TDNN reduces the learning complexity by sharing weights in the time dimension, and is suitable for processing speech and time series signals. CNNs were the first really successful learning algorithms to train multilayer network structures. It uses the spatial relationship to reduce the number of parameters to be learned to improve the training performance of the general forward BP algorithm. CNNs are proposed as a deep learning architecture to minimize data preprocessing requirements. In CNN, a small part of the image (local receptive area) is used as the input of the lowest layer of the hierarchical structure, and the information is transmitted to different layers in turn, and each layer passes a digital filter to obtain the most salient features of the observation data. This method can capture salient features of observations that are invariant to translation, scaling, and rotation, because the local receptive regions of the image allow neurons or processing units to access the most basic features, such as oriented edges or corners.

The structure of CNN

A CNN is a multi-layer feed-forward neural network, where

3）明确突出特征学习的重要性，也就是说，通过逐层特征变换，将样本在原空间的特征表示变换到一个新特征空间，得到比输入更具有表示能力的特征，从而使分类或预测更加容易。与人工规则构造特征的方法相比，深度学习利用大数据来学习特征，更能够刻画数据丰富的内在信息。

4. 卷积神经网络
卷积神经网络的概念

卷积神经网络（CNN）是人工神经网络的一种，已成为当前语音分析和图像识别领域的研究热点。它的权值共享网络结构使其更类似于生物神经网络，降低了网络模型的复杂度，减少了权值的数量。该优点在网络的输入是多维图像时表现得更为明显，使图像可以直接作为网络的输入，避免了传统识别算法中复杂的特征提取和数据重建过程。卷积网络是为识别二维形状而特殊设计的多层感知器，这种网络结构对平移、比例缩放、倾斜或其他形式的变形具有高度不变性。

CNN 受早期的时延神经网络（TDNN）的影响。TDNN 通过在时间维度上共享权值来降低学习复杂度，适用于语音和时间序列信号的处理。CNN 是第一个真正成功训练多层网络结构的学习算法。它利用空间关系减少需要学习的参数数目以提高一般前向 BP 算法的训练性能。CNN 作为深度学习架构提出是为了最小化数据预处理的要求。在 CNN 中，图像的一小部分（局部感受区域）作为层级结构的最低层的输入，信息依次传输到不同的层，每层通过数字滤波器获得观测数据的最显著特征。这个方法能够获取对平移、比例缩放和旋转不变的观测数据的显著特征，因为图像的局部感受区域允许神经元或者处理单元访问最基础的特征，例如定向边缘或者角点。

卷积神经网络的结构

卷积神经网络是一个多层前馈神经网

each layer consists of multiple two-dimensional planes, and each plane consists of multiple independent neurons (see Fig. 5-12).

CNNs are inspired by biological visual cortical cells, which perform visual cognition through receptive fields. In convolutional neural networks, the function of receptive fields is conceptualized as the convolution kernel realizes the feature extraction of the input information. The composition of CNN generally includes an input layer, a convolution layer, a downsampling layer (pooling layer), a fully connected layer, and an output layer. The convolutional layer and the pooling layer generally appear alternately.

The core idea of convolutional network is to combine three structural ideas: local receptive field, weight sharing (or weight copying), and temporal or spatial subsampling to obtain a certain degree of displacement, scale, and deformation invariance.

In the field of machine learning, ILSVRC (ImageNet Large Scale Visual Recognition Challenge) is one of the most authoritative and popular academic competitions. The project in the competition contains many image-based problems, in which CNN has made synaptic contributions to the problem of image classification, and has achieved remarkable results, proposing a series of typical CNN models. For example, CNN models such as LeNet-5, AlexNet, VGGNet, and GoogleNet.

5. Other Important Deep Learning Models
Long Short-Term Memory Networks

Long Short-Term Memory Networks - often referred to as LSTMs, are a special kind of RNN that are capable of learning long-term dependencies, proposed by Hochreiter and Schmidhuber (1997), and improved and extended by many others in subsequent work. LSTMs have performed extremely well on a wide variety of problems and are now widely used.

LSTMs retain information over time. They are useful in time series forecasting because they remember previous inputs.

络，每层由多个二维平面组成，而每个平面由多个独立神经元组成（见图5-12）。

CNN是受到生物的视觉皮层细胞的启发而来的，生物的视觉皮层细胞是通过感受野来进行视觉认知的，在卷积神经网络中，感受野的功能被概念化为卷积核，实现对输入信息的特征提取。CNN的构成一般都包括输入层、卷积层、下采样层（池化层）、全连接层和输出层。卷积层和池化层一般交替出现。

CNN的核心思想是将局部感受野、权值共享（或者权值复制）以及时间或空间亚采样这三种结构思想结合起来，获得某种程度的平移、比例缩放、旋转不变。

在机器学习领域中，ILSVRC（ImageNet Larege Scale Visual Recognition Challenge）是最权威且最受欢迎的学术竞赛之一。竞赛的项目包含很多图像类的问题，其中CNN在图像分类问题中作出了突出的贡献，并且取得了显著的成果，人们提出了一系列典型的CNN模型，比如LeNet-5、AlexNet、VGGNet和GoogleNet等CNN模型。

5. 其他重要的深度学习模型
长短期记忆网络

长短期记忆（LSTM）网络是一种特殊的RNN，能够学习长期依赖性，由Hochreiter和Schmidhuber于1997年提出，并且在接下来的工作中被许多人改进和推广。LSTM在各种各样的问题上表现非常出色，现在被广泛使用。

LSTM会随时间推移保留信息。它们在时间序列预测中很有用，因为它们会记

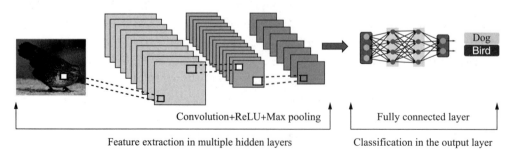

Fig. 5-12 Typical structure of CNN

LSTMs have a chain-like structure where four interacting layers communicate in unique ways. In addition to time series prediction, LSTMs are commonly used in speech recognition, music creation, and drug development.

First, LSTMs forget irrelevant parts of the previous state. Next, they selectively update cell state values. Finally, some parts of the cell state are outputted. Fig. 5-13 is a diagram of how an LSTM works.

Recurrent Neural Networks

The RNN has connections that form a directed loop, allowing the output of the LSTM to be fed as input to the current phase.

RNNs are commonly used for image captioning, time series analysis, natural language processing, handwriting recognition, and machine translation. The expanded RNN is shown in Fig. 5-14. The biggest difference between RNN and traditional neural network is that each time the output of the previous time is brought to the next hidden layer for training together.

Generative Adversarial Networks

GAN (Generative Adversarial Network) is a generative deep learning algorithm used to create new data instances similar to the training data. GAN has two components: a generator (generative model), which captures the distribution of sample data, and generates fake samples to "fool" another discriminator (discriminative model), which is a binary classifier that distinguishes samples from real training. A sample is also a sample generated by a generator.

The principle of GAN is shown in Fig. 5-15.

It works as follows: the discriminator learns to distinguish the generator's fake data from real sample data; during initial training, the generator generates fake data, and the discriminator

住以前的输入。LSTM 具有类似链的结构，其中四个相互作用的层以独特的方式进行通信。除了时间序列预测之外，LSTM 通常用于语音识别、音乐创作和药物开发。

LSTM 首先会忘记前一状态的不相关部分，然后有选择地更新单元格状态值，最后输出单元状态的某些部分。LSTM 的工作原理图如图 5-13 所示。

递归神经网络

RNN 具有形成定向循环的连接，允许 LSTM 的输出作为输入馈送到当前相位。

RNN 通常用于图像字幕、时间序列分析、自然语言处理、手写识别和机器翻译。展开的 RNN 如图 5-14 所示，RNN 与传统神经网络最大的区别在于每次都会将前一次的输出结果带到下一次的隐藏层中一起训练。

生成对抗网络

生成对抗网络（Generative Adversarial Network，GAN）是生成式深度学习算法，用于创建类似于训练数据的新数据实例。GAN 有两个组件：一个是生成器，它捕捉样本数据的分布，生成假样本"骗过"另一个组件——鉴别器，它是一个二分类器，分辨样本是来自真实训练的样本还是生成器生成的样本。

GAN 的运行方式如图 5-15 所示。

其工作原理如下：鉴别器学习区分生成器的假数据和真实的样本数据；在初始训练期间，生成器生成假数据，鉴别器很

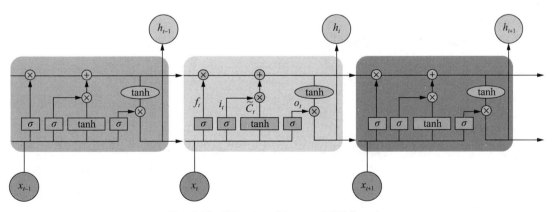

Fig. 5-13 Diagram of how an LSTM works

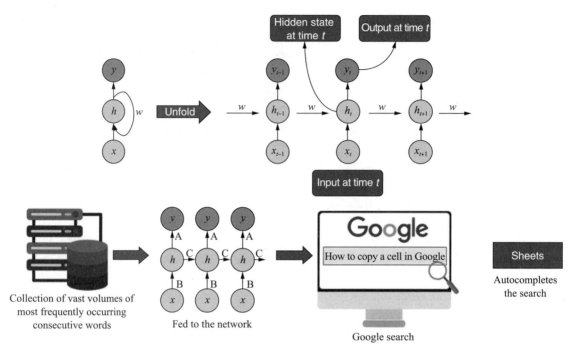

Fig. 5-14 Diagram of the expanded RNN

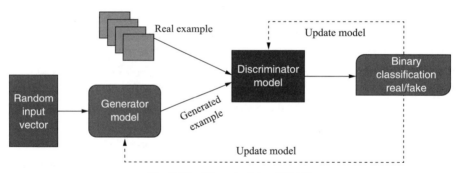

Fig. 5-15 The principle of GAN

quickly learns to judge it to be fake; the GAN sends the results to the generator and discriminator to update the model.

GANs help generate photorealistic images, cartoon characters, photos of faces, render 3D objects, and more.

6. Deep Learning Framework

Business organizations are integrating machine learning and artificial intelligence into their existing systems to derive useful insights and make important decisions. However, this integration requires depth and limits feasibility. With the help of deep learning frameworks, these limitations can be removed.

Deep learning frameworks allow business organizations to integrate machine learning and artificial intelligence with little knowledge about machine learning and deep learning. There

快学会判断它是假的；GAN 将结果发送到生成器和鉴别器以更新模型。

GAN 有助于生成逼真的图像、卡通人物、人脸照片以及渲染 3D 对象等。

6. 深度学习框架

商业组织正在将机器学习和人工智能集成到现有系统中，以得出有用的见解并做出重要决策。但是，这种集成需要深入，并限制了可行性。在深度学习框架的帮助下，它们可以消除这些限制。

深度学习框架允许商业组织在几乎没有关于机器学习和深度学习的知识的情况下集成机器学习和人工智能，以轻松使用多个框架来充分利用深度学习教程。目前

are multiple frameworks that can easily be used to get the most out of deep learning tutorials. At present, the main deep learning frameworks are TensorFlow, Torch, Caffe/Caffe2, Theano, Keras, CNTK, PaddlePaddle (Baidu), etc. These frameworks are widely used in computer vision, speech recognition, natural language processing, medical diagnosis, bioinformatics and other fields. All of these deep learning frameworks have their advantages, advantages, and uses. They also provide the ability to switch back and forth between max.

TensorFlow

TensorFlow is the most commonly used framework in the field of artificial intelligence. It is an open source software for numerical computation using data flow graphs. The framework allows computation on any CPU or GPU, whether it is supported by desktop, server, or mobile devices. The framework uses C++ and Python as programming languages and is easy to learn. TensorFlow makes the implementation of machine learning and deep learning models scalable and easier. TensorFlow is very convenient for creating and experimenting with deep learning architectures, and its schematization also facilitates data integration, e. g. users can input graphs, SQL tables, and images together.

Microsoft's CNTK

CNTK is an open source deep learning toolkit developed by Microsoft Research based on C++. It is a library that improves modularity and maintains separate computing networks, provides learning algorithms and model descriptions, and can utilize multiple servers at the same time, which is faster than TensorFlow. CNTK supports CPU and GPU modes. The CNTK documentation is relatively lacking, and the promotion is not very strong, resulting in fewer users now, but the effect of CNTK in the field of speech recognition is relatively significant.

Theano

Theano is a powerful Python library that uses GPUs to perform data-intensive computations with high operational efficiency and is often used to power large-scale compute-intensive operations. Theano is a grandfather-level existence in the deep learning framework, but it was born in a research institution with a strong academic atmosphere and flawed engineering design. In September 2017, on the occasion of the release of Theano 10.0, Yoshua Bengio, the head of the LISA laboratory and one of the three giants of deep learning,

主要的深度学习框架有 TensorFlow、Torch、Caffe/Caffe2、Theano、Keras、CNTK、PaddlePaddle（百度）等。这些框架广泛地应用于计算机视觉、语音识别、自然语言处理、医疗诊断、生物信息学等领域。所有这些深度学习框架都有其优点、缺点和用途。它们还提供了在最多之间来回切换的功能。

TensorFlow

TensorFlow 是人工智能领域最常用的框架，是使用数据流图进行数值计算的开源软件，该框架允许在任何 CPU 或 GPU 上进行计算，无论是台式机、服务器还是移动设备都支持。该框架使用 C++和 Python 作为编程语言，简单易学。TensorFlow 使机器学习和深度学习模型的实现具有可扩展性且更容易。TensorFlow 对于创建和试验深度学习体系结构非常方便，它的模式化也便于数据集成，例如用户可以将图形、SQL 表和图像一起输入。

CNTK

CNTK 是由微软研究院基于 C++开发的开源深度学习工具包，是一个提高模块化和维护分离计算网络，提供学习算法和模型描述的库，可以同时利用多台服务器，速度比 TensorFlow 快。CNTK 支持 CPU、GPU 模式。CNTK 文档比较缺乏，推广不是很有力，导致现在的使用者较少，但 CNTK 在语音识别领域的效果比较显著。

Theano

Theano 是一个强大的 Python 库，该库使用 GPU 来执行数据密集型计算，操作效率很高，常被用于为大规模的计算密集型操作提供动力。Theano 在深度学习框架中是祖师级的存在，但它诞生于研究机构，学术气息浓厚，工程设计存在缺陷。2017 年 9 月，在 Theano 10.0 发布之际，LISA 实验室负责人、深度学习三巨头之一的 Yoshua Bengio 宣布 Theano 停止开发。尽

announced that the development of Theano was stopped. Although Theano has completed its mission, it has greatly helped the early research of deep learning, and also laid the direction for the later deep learning framework: the core of the framework is the computational graph, and the GPU-accelerated computing is adopted.

Caffe/Caffe2

Caffe is a powerful deep learning framework that mainly uses C++ as the programming language, supports command line, Python and MATLAB interfaces, and can run on both CPU and GPU. Deep learning is very fast, and with Caffe, it is very easy to build convolutional neural networks for image classification. Caffe2 follows a large number of Caffe designs and solves the problems found in Caffe use and deployment. Caffe2 delivers speed and portability, and its Python library and C++ API enable users to prototype, train, and deploy on Linux, Windows, iOS, Android, and even Raspberry and Nvidia Tegra. Because Caffe2 supports all platforms, it is suitable for industrial deployment.

Keras

Keras is an open-source neural network library written in Python. Unlike TensorFlow, CNTK, and Theano, it acts as an interface that provides high-level abstractions to make neural network configuration easy. Keras is a beautifully written API, and the features of the API can completely help users build more novel and complex applications. At the same time, Keras does not block access to the underlying framework. Code written in Keras is more readable and concise. Keras model serialization/deserialization APIs, callbacks, and dataflows using Python generators are very mature.

Torch

Torch is an open source machine learning library for science and numerical value. It mainly uses C language as the programming language. It is a Lua-based library. By providing a large number of algorithms, it is easier for in-depth study and research, and the efficiency and speed are improved. It has a powerful *n*-dimensional array that facilitates operations like slicing and indexing. In addition to this, linear algebra programs and neural network models are provided. PyTorch can be understood as the Python version of Torch.

MXNet

MXNet is the official deep learning platform of Amazon Cloud Computing. MXNet supports languages such as C++,

管 Theano 已经完成了使命，但它为深度学习的早期研究提供了极大帮助，同时也为后来的深度学习框架奠定了方向：以计算图为框架的核心，采用 GPU 加速计算。

Caffe/Caffe2

Caffe 是强大的深度学习框架，主要采用 C++作为编程语言，支持命令行、Python 和 MATLAB 接口，在 CPU 和 GPU 上均可运行。它的深度学习速度非常快，借助 Caffe，我们可以非常轻松地构建用于图像分类的卷积神经网络。Caffe2 沿袭了大量的 Caffe 设计，并解决了 Caffe 在使用和部署上发现的问题。Caffe2 能够提供速度和便携性，其 Python 库和 C++ API 使用户可以在 Linux、Windows、iOS、Android，甚至 Raspberry 和 Nvidia Tegra 上进行原型设计、训练和部署。由于对全平台的支持，Caffe2 适合工业部署。

Keras

Keras 是用 Python 编写的开源的神经网络库，与 TensorFlow、CNTK 和 Theano 不同，它作为接口提供高层次的抽象，让神经网络的配置变得简单。Keras 是一个编写精美的 API，API 的功能特性可以完全帮助用户构建更多新奇复杂的应用。同时，Keras 不会阻止对底层框架的访问。Keras 编写的代码更加可读和简洁。使用 Python 生成器的 Keras 模型序列化/反序列化 API、回调和数据流已经非常成熟。

Torch

Torch 是用于科学和数值的开源机器学习库，主要采用 C 语言作为编程语言，它基于 Lua 的库，通过提供大量的算法，更易于深入学习研究，提高了效率和速度。它有一个强大的 *n* 维数组，有助于切片和索引之类的操作。除此之外，它还提供了线性代数程序和神经网络模型。PyTorch 可以理解为是 Torch 的 Python 版本。

MXNet

MXNet 是亚马逊云计算的官方深度学习平台。MXNet 支持 C++、Python、R、

Python, R, Scala, Julia, MATLAB and JavaScript; supports command line and symbolic programming; can run on CPU, GPU, cluster, server, desktop and mobile devices. MXNet has powerful distributed performance and obvious optimization of video memory and memory. In order to improve the MXNet ecosystem, MXNet launched Gluon designed by PyTorch, and Gluon will also support Microsoft's CNTK in the future. MXNet supports multiple GPUs (optimized computation and fast context switching), with clean and easy-to-maintain code (Python, R, Scala, and other APIs), and the ability to solve problems quickly.

Scala、Julia、MATLAB 以及 JavaScript 等语言；支持命令行和符号编程；可以运行在 CPU、GPU、集群、服务器、台式机和移动设备。MXNet 分布式性能强大，对显存、内存优化明显。为了完善 MXNet 生态圈，MXNet 推出了 PyTorch 设计的 Gluon，未来 Gluon 还将支持微软的 CNTK。MXNet 支持多个 GPU（优化计算和快速上下文切换），具有干净且易于维护的代码（Python、R、Scala 和其他 API），以及快速解决问题的能力。

NEW WORDS AND PHRASES

layer-wise　逐层的
back propagation　反向传播
gradient diffusion　梯度扩散
downsampling　*n.* 下采样
temporal　*adj.* 世俗的，与时间有关的，（语法）表示时态的，暂时的；*n.* 世间万物，暂存的事物，颞部
spatial　*adj.* 空间的，与空间有关的，空间理解能力的
subsampling　*n.* 亚采样
Long Short-Term Memory（LSTM）　长短期记忆

NOTES

1) The higher the level of abstraction, the less possible guesswork exists, and the better for classification.
抽象层面越高，存在的可能猜测就越少，就越利于分类。

2) Deep learning combines low-level features to form more abstract high-level representation attribute categories or features to discover distributed feature representations of data.
深度学习通过组合低层特征形成更加抽象的高层表示属性类别或特征，以发现数据的分布式特征表示。

3) In CNN, a small part of the image (local receptive area) is used as the input of the lowest layer of the hierarchical structure, and the information is transmitted to different layers in turn, and each layer passes a digital filter to obtain the most salient features of the observation data.
在 CNN 中，图像的一小部分（局部感受区域）作为层级结构的最低层的输入，信息依次传输到不同的层，每层通过数字滤波器获得观测数据的最显著特征。

4) The composition of CNN generally includes an input layer, a convolution layer, a downsampling layer (pooling layer), a fully connected layer, and an output layer. The convolutional layer and the pooling layer generally appear alternately.
CNN 的构成一般都包括输入层、卷积层、下采样层（池化层）、全连接层和输出层。卷积层和池化层一般交替出现。

5.3　Computer Vision

1. Definition of Computer Vision

What is Computer Vision, or CV? Here are some different definitions: "the construction of explicit, meaningful descriptions of physical objects from images"; "to make useful decisions about real physical objects and scenes based on sensed images". David Marr said that, the plain man's answer (and Aristotle's too) would be, to know what is where by looking. In other words, vision is the process of discovering from images what is present in the world, and where it is (see Fig. 5-16). He was a British neuroscientist and psychologist, the Marr Prize, one of the most prestigious awards in computer vision, is named in his honor.

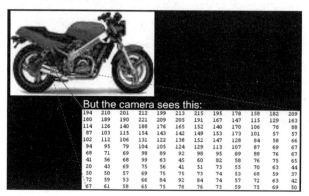

Fig. 5-16 Image and its pixel representation

Computer vision is the science and technology of machine vision, which is concerned with the theory of building artificial systems to obtain information from images. Image data can take many forms, such as video sequences, depth images, views from multiple cameras, or multidimensional data from medical scanners. It is a multidisciplinary study that covers computer science (graphics, algorithms, theoretical research, etc.), mathematics (information retrieval, machine learning), engineering (robotics, NLP, etc.), biology (neuroscience) and psychology (cognitive science).

With these digital images and deep learning models, machines can accurately identify and classify objects, and then react to what they "see." Here are just a handful of them:

1) Face recognition: Snapchat and Facebook use face-detection algorithms to apply filters and recognize you in pictures.

2) Image retrieval: Google Images uses content-based queries to search relevant images. The algorithms analyze the content in the query image and return results based on best-matched content.

3) Gaming and controls: a great commercial product in gaming that uses stereo vision is Microsoft Kinect.

4) Surveillance: surveillance cameras are ubiquitous at public locations and are used to detect suspicious behaviors.

5) Biometrics: fingerprint, iris and face matching remains some common methods in biometric identification.

6) Smart cars: vision remains the main source of information to detect traffic signs and lights and other visual features.

Visual recognition tasks such as image classification, localization, and detection are key components of computer vision. Recent developments in neural networks and deep learning approaches have greatly advanced the performance of these state-of-the-art visual recognition systems.

2. Difference Between Computer Vision and Machine Vision

In fact, they are often confused. The biggest difference between them lies in the technical requirements of the focus, or even very different. Computer Vision (CV) is mainly confrontational analysis, such as classification (this is a cup and that is a dog), or ID identification (face recognition, license plate recognition), or behavioral analysis (intrusions, wandering, leftovers, gathering of people).

Machine Vision (MV) mainly focuses on quantitative analysis, such as measuring the diameter of a part through vision. Generally speaking, it requires high accuracy.

3. Development of Computer Vision

Early experiments in computer vision took place in the 1950s, using some of the first neural networks to detect the edges of an object and to sort simple objects into categories like circles and squares. In the 1970s, the first commercial use of computer vision interpreted typed or handwritten text using optical character recognition. This advancement was used to interpret written text for the blind.

As the internet matured in the 1990s, making large sets of images available online for analysis, facial recognition programs flourished. These growing data sets helped make it possible for machines to identify specific people in photos and videos.

Today, a number of factors have converged to bring about a renaissance in computer vision: mobile technology with built-in cameras has saturated the world with photos and videos; computing power has become more affordable and easily accessible; hardware designed for computer vision and analysis is more widely available; new algorithms like convolutional neural networks can take advantage of the hardware and software capabilities.

The effects of these advances on the computer vision field have been astounding. Accuracy rates for object identification and classification have gone from 50 percent to 99 percent in less than a decade, and today's systems are more accurate than humans at quickly detecting and reacting to visual inputs.

4. Tasks of Computer Vision

Tasks of computer vision can be summed up in one sentence: visual problem solving "what is where?", refers to the use of cameras and computers instead of human eyes to identify, track and measure the target processing, in order to obtain the corresponding scene information (see Fig. 5-17). In the CV field, the main tasks are image classification/localization, target detection, target tracking, image segmentation etc., which are described below.

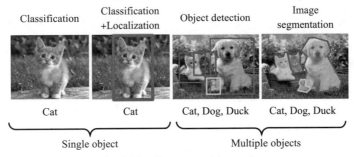

Fig. 5-17　Computer vision tasks

Object Detection

Object detection is the first step of visual perception and an important branch of computer vision. The object of object detection is to mark the position of the object with a box and give the category of the object.

Object detection and image classification is different. Object detection focuses on the search of objects, and the object detection must have a fixed shape and contour. Image classification can be any object, which may be an object, some attributes or scenes.

Object Recognition

The classic problem of computer vision is to determine whether a set of image data contains a particular object, image feature or motion state. This problem can usually be solved automatically by machines, but so far there is no single way to make a wide range of decisions: to identify any object in any environment.

Existing technologies can and only do a good job of identifying specific objects, such as simple geometric shapes, faces, printed or handwritten documents, or vehicles. And these recognition needs to have specific lighting, background and target posture requirements in a specific environment.

Image Classification

The main problem for image classification is "who am I?", such as whether an image contains an object or not, and the characteristic description of the image is the main research content of object classification. In general, object classification algorithms use manual features or feature learning methods to describe the entire image globally, and then use classifiers to determine whether a certain type of object exists.

The image classification problem is the task of assigning labels to input images, which is one of the core problems of CV. Although it is simple, it has a variety of practical applications. Many other seemingly different CV tasks (such as target detection, image segmentation) can be simplified to image classification. This process is often inseparable from machine learning and deep learning.

The most popular method for image classification is Convolutional Neural Network (CNN). The CNN structure is basically composed of a convolutional layer, a pooling layer, and a fully connected layer (see Fig. 5-18). Usually, the input image is fed into a convolutional neural network, feature extraction is performed through the convolutional layer and then the details are filtered by the pooling layer (generally max pooling, average pooling), and finally feature expansion is carried out in the fully connected layer and the corresponding classifier is fed to obtain its classification results.

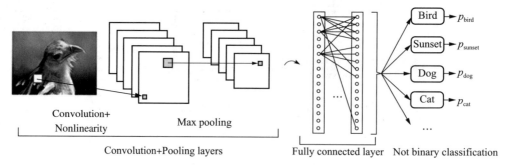

Fig. 5-18　Structure of CNN

Image Localization

If object recognition is to solve "what", then image localization is to solve "where". Computational vision technology is used to find the position of an object in the image, usually in the form of bounding boxes. The localization of object is very important for the application of computer vision in security and automatic driving.

Multi-task learning network has two output branches. A branch is used to do image classification, that is, full connection + softmax to determine the target category, and the difference between pure image classification is that there is an additional "background" class. Another branch is used to determine the target location, that is, the completion regression task outputs four numeric markers to enclose the box position (such as the center point horizontal ordinate coordinate and the enclosing box length and width), and the branch output result is used only if the classification branch is not judged to be "background".

Target Detection

The task of target detection is to find out all the targets of interest in the image and determine their position and size, which is one of the core problems in the field of computer vision (see Fig. 5-19). Target detection has always been the most challenging problem in the field of computer vision because of the different appearance, shape and posture of various targets and the interference of illumination and occlusion during imaging.

The first efficient model was R-CNN (Region-based Convolutional Neural Network), followed by the Fast R-CNN algorithm and the Faster R-CNN algorithm. In recent years, the research trend of target detection has mainly developed into faster and more effective detection systems. There are already a number of other methods available, such as YOLO, SSD, and R-FCN.

Target Tracking

Target tracking refers to the process of tracking specific target or targets of interest in a given scene (see Fig. 5-20). In simple terms, the initial state of the target in the first frame of the tracked video (such as position, size) is given, and the state of the target object in subsequent frames is automatically estimated.

Fig. 5-19 Target detection   Fig. 5-20 Target tracking

The most classic deep network for target tracking using the SAE method is Deep Learning Tracker (DLT), which proposes offline pre-training and online fine-tuning. Typical algorithms for completing target tracking based on CNN are FCNT and MD Net.

Image Segmentation

In the process of image processing, it is sometimes necessary to segment the image to extract valuable parts for subsequent processing, such as screening feature points, or segmentation of one or more images containing specific targets.

Image segmentation refers to the process of subdividing a digital image into multiple image subregions (collections of pixels, also known as superpixels). The purpose of image segmentation is to simplify or change the representation of the image, making the image easier to understand and analyze. To be more precise, image segmentation is a process of labeling each pixel in an image, which makes pixels with the same label have some common visual properties.

Segmentation has two different directions: semantic segmentation andinstance segmentation. The goal of semantic segmentation is to segment the category to which each pixel belongs in the image, regardless of the entity to which it belongs. The instance segmentation is a more refined step by which the pixels belong to different entities.

CNN also demonstrated its excellent performance in this task. The typical approach is FCN. The FCN model inputs an image and obtains a density prediction directly at the output, that is, the category to which each pixel belongs, thus obtaining an end-to-end method to achieve image semantic segmentation.

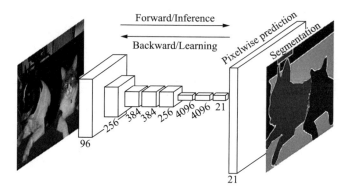

Fig. 5-21 Semantic segmentation

Super-resolution Reconstruction, Style Transfer, and Colorization

Super-resolution reconstruction refers to the process of estimating high-resolution images from low-resolution images and predicting image features at different magnifications, something which the human brain can do almost effortlessly. Originally super-resolution was performed by simple techniques like Bicubic interpolation and nearest neighbor interpolation. In terms of commercial applications, the desire to overcome low-resolution constraints stemming from source quality and realization of "CSI Miami" style image enhancement has driven research in the field.

Style transfer refers to converting the style of image A to image B to get a new B, which contains both the content of image B and the style of image A. Google has also released some interesting work trying to mix styles to produce completely unique image styles.

Colorization is the process of changing monochrome images to new full-color versions. The computer assigns the most likely coloring for images based on its understanding of object location, textures and environment. For example, it learns that skin is pink and the sky is blue. While humans may not accurately represent the true colors of a given scene, their real-world knowledge allows the application of colors in a way which is consistent with the image and another person viewing that image.

5. Conclusion

Computer vision is the creation of artificial models to simulate visual tasks performed by humans.

Its essence is a process of simulating human perception and observation. This process involves not only identification, but a series of processes that can ultimately be understood and implemented in human systems.

NEW WORDS AND PHRASES

Computer Vision（CV） 计算机视觉
surveillance *n.* 监视，监察
fingerprint *n.* 指纹，手印，区别性特征，指纹图谱；*v.* 指纹采样
iris *n.* 虹膜，虹彩光圈，可变光圈，鸢尾，鸢尾属植物；*adj.* 鸢尾属植物的；*v.*（镜头光圈）运用虹彩光圈渐显（或渐隐）
frame *n.* 框架，边框，镜头，画面
semantic segmentation 语义分割
instance segmentation 实例分割
Bicubic interpolation 双三次插值
nearest neighbor interpolation 最近邻插值
super-resolution reconstruction 超分辨率重构
style transfer 风格迁移

NOTES

1) Visual recognition tasks such as image classification, localization, and detection are key components of computer vision.
图像分类、定位和检测等视觉识别任务是计算机视觉的关键组成部分。
2) Machine Vision (MV) mainly focuses on quantitative analysis, such as measuring the diameter of a part through vision.
机器视觉（MV）主要侧重对量的分析，比如通过视觉测量零件的直径。
3) Image segmentation refers to the process of subdividing a digital image into multiple image subregions (collections of pixels, also known as superpixels).
图像分割指的是将数字图像细分为多个图像子区域（像素的集合，也被称作超像素）的过程。
4) Style transfer refers to converting the style of image A to image B to get a new B, which contains both the content of image B and the style of image A.
风格迁移指的是将图像 A 的风格转换到图像 B 中，得到新图像 B，而新图像 B 中既包含图像 B 的内容，也包含图像 A 的风格。

EXERCISES

1. Please translate the following words and phrases into Chinese.

  a) fingerprint   b) semantic segmentation   c) location

  d) style transfer   e) instance segmentation   f) image retrieval

  g) intrusion   h) surveillance

2. Please translate the following words and phrases into English.

  a) 计算机视觉   b) 感知图像   c) 任务

  d) 分割   e) 卷积神经网络   f) 目标检测

  g) 风格迁移   h) 超分辨率

3. Fill in the blanks with the missing word(s).

  a) _____ is the computer vision wants to solve.

  b) _____ is the main problem for image classification.

  c) The most popular method for image classification is _____.

  d) The task of _____ is to find out all the objects of interest in the image and determine their position and size.

e) To be more precise, image segmentation is a process of labeling each _____ in an image, which makes _____ with the same label have some common visual properties.

f) _____ refers to converting the style of image A to image B to get a new B, which contains both the content of image B and the style of image A.

4. Answer the following questions according to the text.
   a) What is computer vision?
   b) What are the tasks of computer vision?
   c) What is the task of object detection?
   d) What is image segmentation?
   e) Which two kinds does image segmentation include?
   f) How to understand the function of convolutional layer, pooling layer, and fully connected layer?

READING

Digital Image Processing

1. Introduction

The 21st century is an era full of information. As the visual basis for human perception of the world, images are an important means for humans to obtain information, express information and transmit information.

Digital image processing is also known as computer image processing. It refers to the method and technology of converting image signals into digital signals and using computers to process them. It is a type of signal dispensation in which input is image, like video frame or photograph and output may be image or characteristics associated with that image. Image processing techniques generally include image compression, noise removal, enhancement, restoration, segmentation, feature extraction, matching, description and recognition. It is one of the rapidly developing technologies, which is applied to agriculture, animal husbandry, forestry, environment, military, industry and medicine. Image processing also forms a core area of study in engineering and computer science disciplines.

Digital image processing technology originated in the 1950s, when electronic computers had developed to a certain level, and people began to use computers to process graphics and image information. Further developed in the 1960s by the Jet Propulsion Laboratory at MIT, Bell Labs at the University of Maryland, and a number of other research institutions for applications in satellite imagery, line photo standard conversion, medical imaging, video telephony, character recognition and photo enhancement. However, due to the backward computing equipment of that era, the cost of processing was

数字图像处理

1. 引言

21世纪是充满信息的时代。图像作为人类感知世界的视觉基础，是人类获取信息、表达信息和传递信息的重要手段。

数字图像处理又称为计算机图像处理，它是指将图像信号转换成数字信号并利用计算机对其进行处理的方法和技术。它是一种信号分配的类型，其中输入是图像（如视频帧或照片），输出可以是图像或与该图像相关的特征。图像处理技术一般包括图像压缩、去除噪声、增强、复原、分割、提取特征、匹配、描述和识别等。它是当今快速发展的技术之一，应用于农牧业、林业、环境、军事、工业和医学等方面。图像处理也成为工程和计算机科学学科的核心研究领域。

数字图像处理技术起源于20世纪50年代，当时的电子计算机已经发展到一定水平，人们开始利用计算机来处理图形和图像信息。20世纪60年代，该技术由麻省理工学院的喷气推进实验室、马里兰大学的贝尔实验室和其他一些研究机构进一步开发，应用于卫星图像、线照片标准转换、医学影像、可视电话、字符识别和照片增强。然而，由于那个时代的计算设备落后，处理的成本相当高。随着图像处理技术的深入发展，从20世纪70年代中期开始，计算机技术、人工智能、思维科学的研究迅速发展，数字图像处理也向更高、

quite high. With the in-depth development of image processing technology, since the mid-1970s, with the rapid development of computer technology, artificial intelligence, and scientific research in thinking, digital image processing has developed to a higher and deeper level. People have begun to study how to use computer systems to interpret images to achieve a similar understanding of the external world to the human visual system, which is called image understanding or computer vision. Digital image processing technology has developed rapidly at home and abroad, and has been widely used, but its discipline construction is still immature, and there is no widely applicable research model and complete quality evaluation system indicators. The applicability of most methods varies with the analysis processing object varies. The research direction of digital image processing is to establish a complete theoretical system.

2. Digital Image Processing Equipment

The equipment needed for digital image processing includes camera, digital image collector (including synchronization controller, analog-to-digital converter and frame memory), image processing computer and image display terminal. The main processing tasks are completed by image processing software. In order to process the image in real time, very high computing speed is needed, which cannot be satisfied by general computers. Special image processing system is needed. This system is composed of many single processors array processor, parallel operation, to improve the realtime processing. With the development of VLSI, high speed chips specially used for various processing algorithms, that is, image processing chips, will form a larger market.

3. Purposes of Digital Image Processing

Generally speaking, the main purpose of image processing (or processing, analysis) has three aspects.

1) Improve the visual quality of the image, such as image brightness, color transformation, enhance and inhibit some components, geometric transformation of the image, etc., to improve the quality of the image.

2) Extract some features or special information contained in the image. These extracted features or information often provide convenience for the computer to analyze the image. The process of extracting features or information is preprocessing of pattern recognition or computer vision. The extracted features can include many aspects, such as frequency domain feature, grayscale or color feature, boundary feature,

更深层次发展。人们已开始研究如何用计算机系统解释图像,以实现与人类视觉系统类似的对外部世界的理解,这被称为图像理解或计算机视觉。数字图像处理技术在国内外发展十分迅速,应用也非常广泛,但是就其学科建设来说,还不成熟,还没有广泛适用的研究模型和齐全的质量评价体系指标,多数方法的适用性都因分析处理对象而异。数字图像处理的研究方向是建立完整的理论体系。

2. 数字图像处理设备

数字图像处理设备包括摄像机、数字图像采集器(包括同步控制器、模-数转换器及帧存储器)、图像处理计算机和图像显示终端。主要的处理任务通过图像处理软件来完成。为了对图像进行实时处理,我们需要非常高的计算速度,通用计算机无法满足,需要专用的图像处理系统。这种系统由许多单处理器组成阵列式处理机,实行并行操作,以提高处理的实时性。随着超大规模集成电路的发展,专门用于处理各种算法的高速芯片(即图像处理专用芯片)将形成较大的市场。

3. 数字图像处理的目的

一般来讲,对图像进行处理(或加工、分析)的主要目的有三个方面。

1) 提高图像的视感质量,如进行图像亮度、彩色的变换,增强、抑制某些成分,对图像进行几何变换等,以改善图像的质量。

2) 提取图像中所包含的某些特征或特殊信息,这些被提取的特征或信息往往为计算机分析图像提供便利。提取特征或信息的过程是模式识别或计算机视觉的预处理。提取的特征可以包括很多方面,如频域特征、灰度或颜色特征、边界特征、区域特征、纹理特征、形状特征、拓扑特

region feature, texture feature, shape feature, topological feature and relational structure, etc.

3) Image data transformation, coding and compression, so as to facilitate image storage and transmission. Regardless of the purpose of image processing, it is necessary to input, process and output image data by the image processing system composed of computer and image special equipment.

4. Types of Digital Images

In computer, images can be divided into binary image, grayscale image, indexed image and true color image according to the number of color and grayscale. Most image processing software supports these four types of images.

Binary Image

A binary image is the simplest digital image, because each pixel is totally black or white, consisting of two values, 0 and 1 respectively, where "0" represents black, and "1" represents white. Since each pixel (each element in the matrix) has only 0 or 1 possible values, the data type of binary image in the computer is usually 1 binary bit. Binary images are usually used for text, line image scanning recognition and mask image storage.

Grayscale Image

Grayscale, also known as brightness, is the variation of light and shade in color. In each pixel, the gray level ranges from of 0-255 (where 0 corresponds to black, and 255 corresponds to white). Therefore, its data type is generally 8-bit unsigned integer (int8), which is often referred to as 256 grayscale images. Grayscale images are frequently used as the input when calculating a gray level histogram or wavelet energy. Binary image can be regarded as a special case of grayscale images.

Indexed Image

The file structure of indexed image is complicated, including a two-dimensional array called color index matrix MAP in addition to the two-dimensional matrix storing the image. When the image is displayed on the screen, the color of each pixel is indexed by the gray value of the pixel stored in the matrix by retrieving the color index matrix MAP. The data type of the index image is generally 8-bit unsigned integer (int8), and the size of the corresponding index matrix MAP is 256×3. Therefore, the indexed image can only display 256 colors at the same time, but the color type can be adjusted by changing the index matrix. Indexed images are generally used to store images with relatively simple color requirements. For

征和关系结构等。

3）图像数据的变换、编码和压缩，以便于图像的存储和传输。无论何种目的的图像处理，都需要由计算机和图像专用设备组成的图像处理系统对图像数据进行输入、加工和输出。

4. 数字图像的类型

在计算机中，按照颜色和灰度的多少可以将图像分为二值图像、灰度图像、索引图像和真彩色图像四种基本类型。大多数图像处理软件都支持这四种类型的图像。

二值图像

二值图像是最简单的数字图像，因为每个像素都是完全黑色或白色的，分别由0和1两个值构成，0代表黑色，1代表白色。由于每个像素（矩阵中每个元素）的取值仅有0和1两种可能，因此计算机中二值图像的数据类型通常为1个二进制位。二值图像通常用于文字、线条图的扫描识别和掩膜图像的存储。

灰度图像

灰度，也称为亮度，它是颜色的明暗变化。在每个像素中，灰度级别范围为0~255（其中0对应黑色，255对应白色），因此其数据类型一般为8位无符号整数（int8），这就是人们经常提到的256灰度图像。灰度图像在计算灰度级直方图或小波能量时经常用作输入。二值图像可以看作灰度图像的特例。

索引图像

索引图像的文件结构比较复杂，除了存放图像的二维矩阵外，还包括一个称为颜色索引矩阵MAP的二维数组。当图像在屏幕上显示时，每个像素的颜色由存放在矩阵中该像素的灰度值作为索引通过检索颜色索引矩阵MAP得到。索引图像的数据类型一般为8位无符号整数（int8），相应的MAP大小为256×3，因此一般索引图像只能同时显示256种颜色，但通过改变MAP，颜色的类型可以调整。索引图像一般用于存放色彩要求比较低的图像，如Windows中色彩构成比较简单的壁纸多采

example, wallpaper with relatively simple color composition in Windows is mostly stored with indexed images. If the color of the image is more complex, true color images should be used.

True Color Image

1) The RGB color model. In a Red, Green, Blue (RGB) color model, each pixel in an image has a color that is represented by the amount of red (R), green (G), and blue (B) primary colors it contains. Each color (R, G, and B) has a range of 0-255. A true color image can be represented by a "stack" of three matrices, with M and N representing the number of rows and columns of the image and three $M \times N$ two-dimensional matrices, representing the R, G and B color components of each pixel.

2) HIS, HSV, and other color models. Hue, saturation and illumination can be used to describe the color space perceived by human eyes. Color vision models that have been developed include HSV (hue, saturation, value), HIS (hue, illumination, saturation), HLS (hue, lightness, saturation), and HVC (hue, value, chroma). Color vision model is a more intuitive method of describing colors, and as the intensity is independent of the color information, this is a very useful model for image processing.

5. Storage of Digital Image Data

Digital image data can be stored in two ways: bitmap and vector.

We usually describe digital images in terms of image resolution (i. e. pixels) and number of colors. For example, a digital image with a resolution of 640×480 and 16-bit color is composed of 307 200 (= 640×480) prime points of 2^{16} = 65 536 colors.

Bitmap method is to convert each pixel of the image into a piece of data. If recorded with 1-bit data, it can only represent 2 colors ($2^1 = 2$); if recorded as 8 bits, 256 colors or hues can be displayed ($2^8 = 256$), so the more bits you use, the more colors you can display. Usually we use 16 colors, 256 colors, enhanced 16 bits, and true color 24 bits. Generally speaking true color refers to the 24-bit (2^{24}) bitmap storage mode and is suitable for complex content of images and real photos. However, as the resolution and the number of colors increase, the image takes up a considerable amount of disk space; in addition, in the process of magnifying the image, the image is bound to become blurred and distorted, and the pixels of the enlarged image actually become pixel "squares". Images taken with digital cameras and scanners

用索引图像存放，如果图像的色彩比较复杂，就要用到真彩色图像。

真彩色图像

1) RGB 颜色模型。在红色、绿色、蓝色（RGB）颜色模型中，图像中的每个像素都有一种颜色，该颜色由它所包含的红（R）、绿（G）、蓝（B）三原色的数量表示。每种颜色（R、G 和 B）的范围为 0~255。真彩色图像可以由三个矩阵组成的"堆栈"表示，M、N 分别表示图像的行列数，三个 $M \times N$ 的二维矩阵分别表示各个像素的 R、G、B 三个颜色分量。

2) HIS、HSV 等颜色模型。色调、饱和度和照度可用于描述人眼感知的色彩空间。已经开发的色觉模型包括 HSV（色调，饱和度，明度）、HIS（色调，照度，饱和度）、HLS（色调，亮度，饱和度）和 HVC（色调，明度，色度）。色觉模型是一种更直观描述颜色的方法，并且由于强度与颜色信息无关，因此对于图像处理非常有用。

5. 数字图像数据的存储

数字图像数据有两种存储方式：位图（bitmap）存储和矢量（vector）存储。

我们平常是以图像分辨率（即像素点）和颜色数来描述数字图像的。例如一张分辨率为 640×480 的 16 位色的数字图像，就由 2^{16} = 65 536 种颜色的 307 200(= 640×480) 个像素点组成。

位图方式就是将图像的每个像素点转换为一个数据。如果用 1 位数据来记录，那么它只能代表 2 种颜色（$2^1 = 2$）；如果以 8 位来记录，便可以表现出 256 种颜色或色调（$2^8 = 256$），因此使用的位元素越多所能表现的色彩就越多。通常我们使用的颜色有 16 色、256 色、增强 16 位和真彩色 24 位。一般所说的真彩色是指 24 位（2^{24}）的位图存储模式，适合内容复杂的图像和真实照片。但随着分辨率以及颜色数的提高，图像所占用的磁盘空间也就相当大；另外由于在放大图像的过程中，其图像势必要变得模糊而失真，放大后的图像像素点实际上变成了像素"方格"。用

are bitmaps.

Bitmap images can produce rich colors and tonal changes of the image, can realistically show the scene of nature, but also can easily exchange files between different software, this is the advantage of bitmap images. The disadvantages are that it can't make true 3D images, and the image can be distorted when zooming and rotating, as well as large files and high demand for memory and hard disk space.

Vector image stores the contour part of the image information rather than every pixel point of the image. For example, a circular pattern simply stores the coordinates of the center and the length of the radius, as well as the edges and interior colors of the circle. The shortcoming of this storage method is that it often takes a lot of time to do some complicated analysis and calculation work, and the image display speed is slow. But image scaling does not distort; images also have much less storage space. Therefore, vector image is more suitable for storing all kinds of charts and projects.

6. Common Methods of Digital Image Processing

Image Transformation

Because the image array is very large, it is directly processed in the spatial domain, which involves a lot of calculation. Therefore, a variety of image transformation methods are often adopted, such as Fourier transform, Walsh transform, discrete cosine transform and other indirect processing technology, to transform the spatial domain processing into transform domain processing, not only reduce the amount of calculation, but also obtain more effective processing (such as Fourier transform can be digital filtering in the frequency domain).

Image Coding Compression

Image coding compression technology can reduce the amount of data (that is, the number of bits) to describe the image, so as to save the image transmission, processing time and reduce the memory capacity occupied. Compression can be achieved without loss of authenticity, or with allowable distortion conditions. Coding is the most important method in compression technology. It is the earliest and mature technology in image processing technology.

There are two kinds of image compression algorithms, namely lossless compression and lossy compression. The most commonly used lossless compression algorithm takes the difference of adjacent pixel values in space or time and encodes them. Run-length codes are examples of such compression codes. Most lossy compression algorithms use image exchange,

数码相机和扫描仪获取的图像都属于位图。

位图图像能够制作出色彩和色调变化丰富的图像，可以逼真地表现自然界的景象，同时也可以很容易地在不同软件之间交换文件，这就是位图图像的优点；而其缺点则是它无法制作真正的3D图像，并且图像缩放和旋转时会产生失真的现象，同时文件较大，对内存和硬盘空间容量的需求也较高。

矢量图像存储的是图像信息的轮廓部分，而不是图像的每一个像素点。例如，一个圆形图案只要存储圆心的坐标位置和半径长度，以及圆的边线和内部的颜色即可。该存储方式的缺点是经常耗费大量的时间做一些复杂的分析演算工作，图像的显示速度较慢；但图像缩放不会失真，图像的存储空间也要小得多。所以，矢量图像比较适合存储各种图表和工程。

6. 数字图像处理的常用方法

图像变换

由于图像阵列很大，直接在空间域中进行处理，涉及的计算量很大，因此往往采用各种图像变换的方法，如傅里叶变换、沃尔什变换、离散余弦变换等间接处理技术，将空间域的处理转换为变换域处理，这不仅可减少计算量，而且可获得更有效的处理（如傅里叶变换可在频域中进行数字滤波处理）。

图像编码压缩

图像编码压缩技术可减少描述图像的数据量（即比特数），以便节省图像传输及处理的时间和所占用的存储器容量。压缩可以在不失真的前提下获得，也可以在允许的失真条件下进行。编码是压缩技术中最重要的方法，它在图像处理技术中是发展最早且比较成熟的技术。

图像压缩有两类压缩算法，即无损压缩算法和有损压缩算法。最常用的无损压缩算法取空间或时间上相邻像素值的差，再进行编码。游程码就是这类压缩码的例子。有损压缩算法大都采用图像交换的途径，例如对图像进行快速傅里叶变换或离散余弦变换。已作为图像压缩国际标准的

such as fast Fourier transform or discrete cosine transform. JPEG and MPEG, which have been regarded as international standards of image compression, belong to lossy compression algorithms. The former is used for static images and the latter for dynamic images.

Image Enhancement and Restoration

The goal of image enhancement is to improve the image quality, such as increasing contrast, removing blur and noise, and correcting geometric distortion. Image restoration is a technique that attempts to estimate the original image on the assumption that a fuzzy or noisy model is known.

According to the methods used, image enhancement can be divided into frequency domain and space domain. The former regards the image as a two-dimensional signal and enhances it based on two-dimensional Fourier transform. Using low-pass filtering (that is, only low frequency signals through), the noise in the figure can be removed. High-pass filtering can enhance high-frequency signals such as edges and make blurred images clear. Representative spatial domain algorithms include local average method and median filtering (taking the median pixel value of local neighborhood), which can be used to remove or attenuate noise.

Image Segmentation

Image segmentation divides the image into some non-overlapping regions, and each region is a continuous set of pixels. The region method, which divides pixels into specific regions, and the boundary method, which seeks the boundaries between regions, are usually used. The region method performs threshold operation according to the contrast between the object to be segmented and the background to separate the object from the background. Sometimes a fixed threshold can not be used to obtain satisfactory segmentation, but the threshold can be adjusted according to the local contrast, which is called adaptive threshold. Boundary method uses a variety of edge detection techniques, that is, according to the image edge has a large gradient value to detect. Both methods can realize image segmentation by taking advantage of the texture characteristics of the image.

Image Description

Image description is the prerequisite of image recognition and understanding. As the simplest binary image, its geometric characteristics can be used to describe the characteristics of the object. The general image description method is two-dimensional shape description, which has two kinds of

JPEG 和 MPEG 均属于有损压缩算法。前者用于静态图像,后者用于动态图像。

图像增强和复原

图像增强的目标是改进图片的质量,例如增加对比度、去掉模糊和噪声、修正几何畸变等;图像复原是在假定已知模糊或噪声的模型时,试图估计原图像的一种技术。

图像增强按所用方法可分成频率域法和空间域法。前者把图像看成一种二维信号,对其进行基于二维傅里叶变换的信号增强。采用低通滤波(即只让低频信号通过)法,可去掉图像中的噪声;采用高通滤波法,则可增强边缘等高频信号,使模糊的图像变得清晰。具有代表性的空间域算法有局部求平均值法和中值滤波(取局部邻域中的中间像素值)法等,它们可用于去除或减弱噪声。

图像分割

图像分割将图像划分为一些互不重叠的区域,每个区域是像素的一个连续集。通常采用把像素分入特定区域的区域法和寻求区域之间边界的境界法。区域法根据被分割对象与背景的对比度进行阈值运算,将对象从背景中分割出来。有时用固定的阈值不能得到满意的分割,可根据局部的对比度调整阈值,这称为自适应阈值。境界法利用各种边缘检测技术,即根据图像边缘处的大梯度值进行检测。这两种方法都可以利用图像的纹理特性实现图像分割。

图像描述

图像描述是图像识别和理解的必要前提。作为最简单的二值图像可采用其几何特性描述物体的特性,一般图像的描述方法采用二维形状描述,它有边界描述和区域描述两类方法。对于特殊的纹理图像可

boundary description and region description methods. The special texture image can be described by two-dimensional texture feature. With the development of image processing, 3D object description has been studied, and volume description, surface description, generalized cylinder description and other methods have been proposed.

Image Classification（Recognition）

Image classification（recognition）belongs to the category of pattern recognition, its main content is the image after some pretreatment（enhancement, restoration, compression）, image segmentation and feature extraction, so as to carry out decision classification. Image classification often adopts classical pattern recognition methods, including statistical pattern classification and syntactic（structural）pattern classification. In recent years, fuzzy pattern recognition and artificial neural network pattern classification have been paid more and more attention in image recognition.

Each content of image processing is related to each other. A practical image processing system often combines several image processing techniques to obtain the desired results. Image digitization is the first step in transforming an image into a form suitable for computer processing. Image coding techniques can be used to transmit and store images. Image enhancement and restoration can be the final goal of image processing or preparation for further processing. The image features obtained by image segmentation can be used as the final result or the basis of the next image analysis.

Image matching, description and recognition compare and register the images, extract the features and mutual relations of the images by classification, get the symbolic description of the image, and then compare it with the model to determine its classification. Image matching attempts to establish geometric correspondence between two images and measure the degree to which they are similar or different. Matching is used for registration between pictures or between pictures and maps, such as detecting the changes of scenery between pictures taken at different times and finding the track of moving objects.

7. Digital Image Processing Application Tools

Digital image processing tools can be divided into three categories.

The first category includes various orthogonal transformation and image filtering methods, whose common ground is to transform the image to other domains（such as frequency

采用二维纹理特征描述。随着图像处理研究的深入发展，人们已经开始进行三维物体描述的研究，提出了体积描述、表面描述、广义圆柱体描述等方法。

图像分类（识别）

图像分类（识别）属于模式识别的范畴，其主要内容是图像经过某些预处理（增强、复原、压缩）后，进行图像分割和特征提取，从而进行判决分类。图像分类常采用经典的模式识别方法，有统计模式分类和句法（结构）模式分类，近年来新发展起来的模糊模式识别和人工神经网络模式分类在图像识别中也越来越受到重视。

图像处理的各个内容是互相联系的。一个实用的图像处理系统往往结合应用几种图像处理技术才能得到所需要的结果。图像数字化是将图像变换为适合计算机处理的形式的第一步。图像编码技术可用以传输和存储图像。图像增强和复原可以是图像处理的最后目的，也可以是为进一步的处理做准备。通过图像分割得出的图像特征可以作为最后结果，也可以作为下一步图像分析的基础。

图像匹配、描述和识别对图像进行比较和配准，通过分制提取图像的特征及相互关系，得到图像的符号化描述，再把它同模型比较，以确定其分类。图像匹配试图建立两张图像之间的几何对应关系，度量其类似或不同的程度。匹配用于图像之间或图像与地图之间的配准，例如检测不同时间所拍图片之间景物的变化，找出运动物体的轨迹。

7. 数字图像处理应用工具

数字图像处理的工具可分为三类。

第一类包括各种正交变换和图像滤波等方法，其共同点是将图像变换到其他域（如频域）中进行处理（如滤波）后，再变换到原来的空间（域）中。

domain) for processing (such as filtering), and then transform to the original space (domain).

The second kind of method is to deal with the image directly in the spatial domain, which includes various statistical methods, differential methods and other mathematical methods.

The third kind is mathematical morphology operation, which is different from the common frequency domain and spatial domain method, and is based on integral geometry and random set theory.

8. Image Processing Database

Image processing is inseparable from massive, rich basic data, including video, static images and other formats. The significance of rich datasets for all facets of machine learning cannot be overstated. To paraphrase Ben Hamner, the CTO and co-founder of Kaggle, "a new dataset can make a thousand papers flourish", that is to say the availability of data can promote new approaches, as well as breath new life into previously ineffectual techniques.

At present, there are many well-known image processing databases, the more famous are as follows.

1) ImageNet is the largest database of image recognition in the world. Used to identify objects from pictures. It currently contains 14,197,122 manually annotated images. These data are freely available to researchers for non-commercial use. This dataset has played an important role in advancing research in computer vision and deep learning. The annual ImageNet competition, the ImageNet Large-Scale Visual Recognition Challenge (ILSVRC), is a dream that draws the hearts of famous schools, large IT companies and network giants at home and abroad, and competes to correctly classify and detect objects and scenes through software programs.

2) Common Objects in COntext (COCO) is a large-scale object detection, segmentation, and captioning dataset. COCO has several features: object segmentation, recognition in context, superpixel stuff segmentation, 330k images (>200k labeled), 1.5 million object instances, 80 object categories, 91 stuff categories, 5 captions per image, 250,000 people with keypoints.

3) CIFAR, which contains 80 million labeled micro-images, is divided into two data subsets, CIFAR-10 and CIFAR-100. The CIFAR-10 dataset consists of 60,000 32×32 color images in 10 classes, with 6,000 images per class. There are 50,000 training images and 10,000 test images.

第二类方法是直接在空间域中处理图像，它包括各种统计方法、微分方法及其他数学方法。

第三类是数学形态学运算，它不同于常用的频域和空间域的方法，是建立在积分几何和随机集合论的基础上的运算。

8. 图像处理数据库

图像处理离不开海量、丰富的基础数据，包括视频、静态图像等多种格式。对于机器学习的所有方面，丰富的数据库的重要性怎么强调也不过分。用 Kaggle 的首席技术官和联合创始人 Ben Hamner 的话来说，"一个新的数据库可以让一千篇论文蓬勃发展"，也就是说，数据的可用性可以促进新的方法，并为以前无效的技术注入新的生命。

目前比较出名的图像处理数据库有很多，比较有名的如下。

1) ImageNet，目前世界上图像识别最大的数据库，用于从图片中识别物体。目前已经包含 14 197 122 张被手动注释过的图像。这些数据可供研究人员免费使用，用于非商业用途。该数据库在推进计算机视觉和深度学习研究方面发挥了重要作用。每年的 ImageNet 大赛即 ImageNet 大规模视觉识别挑战赛（ILSVRC）更是牵动着国内外各个名校和大型 IT 公司以及网络巨头的心，通过软件程序竞相正确分类检测物体和场景。

2) Common Objects in COntext (COCO)，用于图像识别、分割和加字幕标注的数据库。其特点是：目标分割，上下文识别，超像素分割，33 万张图像（>20 万张已标记），150 万个对象实例，80 种对象类别，91 种物品类别，每个图像 5 个字幕，25 万人的关键点。

3) CIFAR，包含被标记的 8000 万张微小图像，分为 CIFAR-10 和 CIFAR-100 两个数据子库。CIFAR-10 由 10 类 60 000 张 32×32 的 RGB 彩色图片构成，训练图像 50 000 张，测试图像 10 000 张（交叉验

The main feature of this dataset is the migration of recognition to universal objects and the application to multiple classifications. The CIFAR-100 dataset is just like the CIFAR-10, except it has 100 classes containing 600 images each. There are 500 training images and 100 testing images per class. The 100 classes in the CIFAR-100 are grouped into 20 superclasses. Each image comes with a "fine" label (the class to which it belongs) and a "coarse" label (the superclass to which it belongs).

4) AFLW is a large-scale face database with multiple poses, multiple perspectives, and each face is labeled with 21 feature points. The database is very informative, including images of various gestures, expressions, lighting, ethnicity and other factors. The AFLW face database contains about 250 million hand-tagged images of faces, 59 percent of which are women and 41 percent of which are men. Most of the images are colored, and only a few are grayscale. This database is very suitable for face recognition, face detection, face alignment and other aspects of the research, has a high research value.

5) KITTI is currently the world's largest computer vision algorithm evaluation data set in autonomous driving scenarios. This dataset is used to evaluate the performance of computer vision techniques such as stereo, optical flow, visual odometry, 3D object detection and 3D tracking in vehicular environment. KITTI consists of 7,481 training images and 7,518 test images collected from urban, rural and highway scenarios. All images are in true color PNG format. With up to 15 cars and 30 pedestrians in each image, and varying degrees of occlusion and truncation, it's definitely a rare dataset for vehicle navigation.

6) The MNIST dataset consists of scans of handwritten. This simple classification problem is one of the simplest and most widely used tests in machine learning research. MNIST has a training set of 60,000 examples, and a test set of 10,000 examples. The digits have been size-normalized and centered in a fixed-size image. The fixed size is 28×28.

7) The MIT StreetScenes is a collection of street images, annotations, location, software and performance measures for object detection. Each image was taken from a DSC-F717 camera at in and around Boston.

证)。这个数据库最大的特点在于将识别迁移到了普适物体,而且应用于多分类。CIFAR-100 数据库与 CIFAR-10 数据库类似,不同之处在于它有 100 个类,每个类包含 600 张图像,其中 500 张用于训练,100 张用于测试。其中这 100 个类别又被分组为 20 个超类。每个图像都带有一个"精细"标签(它所属的类)和一个"粗糙"标签(它所属的超类)。

4) AFLW,一个包括多姿态、多视角的大规模人脸数据库,而且每个人脸都被标注了 21 个特征点。此数据库信息量非常大,包括了各种姿态、表情、光照、种族等因素影响的图片。AFLW 人脸数据库大约包括 2.5 亿张已手工标注的人脸图片,其中 59% 为女性,41% 为男性,大部分的图片都是彩色的,只有少部分是灰度图片。该数据库非常适合用于人脸识别、人脸检测、人脸对齐等方面的研究,具有很高的研究价值。

5) KITTI,目前国际上最大的自动驾驶场景下的计算机视觉算法评测数据库。该数据库用于评测立体图像、光流、视觉测距、3D 物体检测和 3D 跟踪等计算机视觉技术在车载环境下的性能。KITTI 包含市区、乡村和高速公路等场景采集的真实图像数据,共 7481 个训练图像和 7518 个测试图像。所有图像都是真彩色 PNG 格式。每张图像中最多达 15 辆车和 30 个行人,还有各种程度的遮挡与截断,绝对是车载导航不可多得的数据库。

6) MNIST,是一个大型的手写数字数据库,广泛用于机器学习领域的训练和测试。MNIST 包含 60 000 个训练集和 10 000 个测试集,每张图像都进行了尺度归一化和数字居中处理,固定尺寸大小为 28×28。

7) MIT StreetScenes,麻省理工学院街景数据库,该数据库收集用于检测、标注、定位、软件和性能测试的街景图像。所有图像都是使用 DSC-F717 数码相机在波士顿及周边地区拍摄的。

NEW WORDS AND PHRASES

Digital Image Processing（DIP）　［计］数字图像处理

hue　　*n.* 颜色，色调，色度，种类，派别，叫声（hue and cry）

chroma　　*n.*（色彩的）浓度，［光］色度

primary color　　原色

saturation　　*n.* 饱和，饱和状态，（尤指照相的）色饱和度，浸透

illumination　　*n.* 光亮，照明，启迪，阐明，彩灯，灯饰

value　　*n.* 价值，重要性，值，（音乐中的）时值，（色彩）明暗度；*v.* 尊重，重视，给……估价，给……定价

tonal　　*adj.* 色调的，音调的

bitmap　　*n.* ［计］位图，位映像

blur　　*n.* 模糊不清的事物，模糊的记忆，污迹；*v.*（使）看不清楚，记不清，（使）难以区分，玷污

NOTES

1) It is a type of signal dispensation in which input is image, like video frame or photograph and output may be image or characteristics associated with that image.

   它是一种信号分配的类型，其中输入是图像（如视频帧或照片），输出可以是图像或与该图像相关的特征。

2) Bitmap images can produce rich colors and tonal changes of the image, can realistically show the scene of nature, but also can easily exchange files between different software, this is the advantage of bitmap images.

   位图图像能够制作出色彩和色调变化丰富的图像，可以逼真地表现自然界的景象，同时也可以很容易地在不同软件之间交换文件，这就是位图图像的优点。

3) Therefore, a variety of image transformation methods are often adopted, such as Fourier transform, Walsh transform, discrete cosine transform and other indirect processing technology, to transform the spatial domain processing into transform domain processing, not only reduce the amount of calculation, but also obtain more effective processing (such as Fourier transform can be digital filtering in the frequency domain).

   因此，往往采用各种图像变换的方法，如傅里叶变换、沃尔什变换、离散余弦变换等间接处理技术，将空间域的处理转换为变换域处理，这不仅可减少计算量，而且可获得更有效的处理（如傅里叶变换可在频域中进行数字滤波处理）。

4) The goal of image enhancement is to improve the image quality, such as increasing contrast, removing blur and noise, and correcting geometric distortion.

   图像增强的目标是改进图片的质量，例如增加对比度、去掉模糊和噪声、修正几何畸变等。

5) Image matching, description and recognition compare and register the images, extract the features and mutual relations of the images by classification, get the symbolic description of the image, and then compare it with the model to determine its classification.

   图像匹配、描述和识别对图像进行比较和配准，通过分制提取图像的特征及相互关系，得到图像的符号化描述，再把它同模型比较，以确定其分类。

第 5 章
人工智能

5.1 模式识别

1. 什么是模式与模式识别?

广义地说,模式是存在于时间和空间中的可观察的事物,如果我们可以区别它们是否相同或者是否相似,那么我们从这种事物所获取的信息就可以称为模式。模式所指的不是事物本身,而是从事物获得的信息,因此,模式往往表现为具有时间和空间分布的信息。

为了掌握客观的事物,人们往往会按照事物的相似程度组成类别。例如,我们能够轻易地辨别出哪个是自行车,哪个是摩托车。这些看似简单的过程,其背后实际上隐藏着非常复杂的处理机制,而弄清楚这些机制的作用机理正是模式识别的基本任务。

模式识别是指利用机器(计算机)模仿人脑对现实世界各种事物进行描述、分类、判断和识别的过程。其目标是实现具有感知、识别、理解、自学习和自适应能力的灵活和智能的计算机器。

模式识别涉及统计学、心理学、语言学、计算机科学、生物学、控制论等多个领域。它与人工智能、图像处理的研究相交叉。例如,自适应或自组织的模式识别系统包含了人工智能的学习机制。人工智能研究的景物理解、自然语言理解也包含模式识别问题,比如模式识别中的预处理和特征提取需要用到图像处理技术,而图像处理中的图像分析也需要用到模式识别的一些方法。

随着计算机技术和人工智能的发展,模式识别广泛应用于数据挖掘、文档分类、财务预测、多媒体数据库的组织和检索,还有生物识别技术、情感识别等领域。

2. 模式识别系统的设计

模式识别的方法有很多,主要用于分类和回归。无论采用何种方法,模式识别一般都要包括下列两个基本过程。

- 学习过程(设计过程):用一定数量的样本(叫作训练集或学习集)进行分类器设计;
- 识别过程(实现过程):用所设计的分类器对待识别的样本进行分类决策。

模式识别系统的设计主要涉及以下五个方面(见图 5-1):①数据采集;②预处理;③数

据表示（特征提取与选择）；④分类决策；⑤分类器设计。所研究的问题决定了传感器、预处理技术、表示方案、决策模型和分类器的选择等问题。

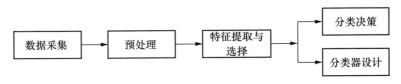

图 5-1 模式识别系统的组成

模式识别系统各组成单元的功能如下。

1) 数据采集：借助相应的声音传感器、图像传感器等硬件设备捕获到相当数量的生物特征数据。利用计算机可以运算的符号来表示所研究的对象，对应于外界物理空间向模式空间转换。通常，获取的信息类型有以下几种。

- 一维波形：心电图、脑电波、声波、振动波形等；
- 二维图像：文字、地图、照片等；
- 物理参数：体温、测试数据、温度、压力、电流、电压等。

2) 预处理：对由于信息获取装置或其他因素所造成的信息退化现象进行复原和去噪，加强有用信息，例如 A/D、二值化，以及图像的平滑、变换、增强、恢复、滤波等。

3) 特征提取与选择：从传感器得到的原始信息，其数据量一般相当大。为了有效地实现分类识别，应对经过预处理的信息进行选择或变换，得到最能反映分类本质的特征，构成特征向量。其目的是将维数较高的模式空间转换为维数较低的特征空间，并从中挑选对模式的最终分类判别最有帮助或者分类效果最好的一部分特征向量。这里的特征选择实际上是一个寻优问题。

4) 分类决策：在特征空间中用模式识别方法（由分类器设计确定的分类判别规则）对待识模式进行分类判别，将其归为某一类别，输出分类结果。这一过程对应于特征空间向类别空间的转换。

5) 分类器设计：为了把待识模式分配到各自的模式类中，必须设计出一套分类判别规则。基本做法是收集一定数量的样本作为训练集，在此基础上确定判别函数，改进判别函数并进行误差检验。

3. 模式相似性的度量

模式识别是一个推理过程。由于每个特征向量代表一个模式，因此可根据模式之间的相似性对模式进行分类。

由 n 个特征值组成的 n 维向量 $\boldsymbol{X}=[x_1,x_2,\cdots,x_n]^T$，称为该样本的特征向量。它对应于特征空间中的一个点，以特征空间中点间的距离函数作为模式相似性的度量，以"距离"作为模式分类的依据，距离越小，越"相似"。

汉明距离

在信息编码中，两个合法代码对应位上编码不同的位数称为码距，又称汉明距离。设 $\boldsymbol{X}_1$，$\boldsymbol{X}_2$ 为 n 维二值（1 或 -1）模式样本向量，则汉明距离为

$$D_h(\boldsymbol{X}_1,\boldsymbol{X}_2)=\frac{1}{2}\left[n-\sum_{k=1}^{n}(x_{ik}-x_{jk})\right] \tag{5-1}$$

$D=n$ 表明两个模式向量的各分量取值均不同，$D=0$ 则表明全相同。

欧氏距离

设 $\boldsymbol{X}_1$，$\boldsymbol{X}_2$ 为两个 n 维模式样本，两者之间的欧式距离为

$$D(\boldsymbol{X}_1,\boldsymbol{X}_2) = \|\boldsymbol{X}_1 - \boldsymbol{X}_2\| = [(\boldsymbol{X}_1 - \boldsymbol{X}_2)^T (\boldsymbol{X}_1 - \boldsymbol{X}_2)]^{\frac{1}{2}} \quad (5\text{-}2)$$

欧氏距离越小,越相似。

马氏距离

马氏距离定义为平方表达式:

$$D^2 = (\boldsymbol{X} - \boldsymbol{M})^T \boldsymbol{C}^{-1} (\boldsymbol{X} - \boldsymbol{M}) \quad (5\text{-}3)$$

式中,$\boldsymbol{X}$ 为模式向量,$\boldsymbol{M}$ 为均值向量,$\boldsymbol{C}$ 为该类模式总体的协方差矩阵。当 $\boldsymbol{C}=\boldsymbol{I}$ 时,马氏距离为欧氏距离。

明氏距离

n 维模式样本向量 $\boldsymbol{X}_1, \boldsymbol{X}_2$ 间的明氏距离表示为

$$D_m(\boldsymbol{X}_1,\boldsymbol{X}_2) = \left[\sum_{k=1}^{n} |x_{ik} - x_{jk}|^m\right]^{\frac{1}{m}} \quad (5\text{-}4)$$

当 $m=2$ 时,明氏距离为欧氏距离;当 $m=1$ 时,称为"街坊"距离。

角度相似性

两个向量的夹角可反映两个向量在方向上的差异性。定义模式向量 $\boldsymbol{X}_1$,$\boldsymbol{X}_2$ 之间夹角的余弦为

$$S(\boldsymbol{X}_1,\boldsymbol{X}_2) = \frac{\boldsymbol{X}_1^T \boldsymbol{X}_2}{\|\boldsymbol{X}_1\| \cdot \|\boldsymbol{X}_2\|} \quad (5\text{-}5)$$

$S=0$ 表明两个向量完全相同。

4. 统计模式识别

已知的模式识别方法可分为四种:模板匹配、统计模式识别、语法及结构匹配和神经网络。这些模型不一定是独立的,有时相同的模式识别方法也存在不同的解释。人们尝试设计涉及多种模型的混合系统。表 5-1 对这些方法进行了简要的描述和比较。

表 5-1 模式识别模型

方法	表征	识别功能	典型准则
模板匹配	样本、像素、曲线	相关,距离测量	分类误差
统计模式识别	特征	判别函数	分类误差
语法及结构匹配	原语	规则,语法	接受误差
神经网络	样本、像素、特征	网络函数	均方误差

统计模式识别是最基本的模式识别方法。统计模式识别涉及使用统计技术分析数据测量,以便提取信息和作出合理的决定。这是一个非常活跃的研究领域,近年来取得了许多进展。数据挖掘、网络搜索、多媒体数据检索、人脸识别和草书笔迹识别等应用都需要健壮、高效的模式识别技术。密度估计(参数、贝叶斯和非参数)、线性判别函数分析、非线性判别函数分析、决策树、聚类、支持向量机等都属于统计模式识别。

线性判别函数

线性判别函数分析(LDFA)是第一个多元统计分类方法(见图 5-2),由 R. A. Fisher 于 1936 年发明。对输入向量取一个线性函数,得到线性判别函数的最简单表示:

$$g(\boldsymbol{x}) = \boldsymbol{w}^T \boldsymbol{x} + w_0 \quad (5\text{-}6)$$

式中,$\boldsymbol{x}$ 为 D 维样本向量,$\boldsymbol{w}$ 为权向量,w_0 为偏差,偏差的负值有时被称为阈值。根据给出的已知类别的训练样本,确定参数 $\boldsymbol{w}$ 和 w_0。如果 $g(\boldsymbol{x}) > 0$,则将输入向量 $\boldsymbol{x}$ 赋给类 C_1,否则

赋给类 C_2。因此，相应的决策边界由关系 $g(\boldsymbol{x})=0$ 定义，它对应于 D 维输入空间内的 $(D-1)$ 维超平面。

贝叶斯分类器

由于我们的测量方法存在随机性，因此作出决策（例如分类）时要考虑不确定性。概率论是解释不确定性的有效机制。对于一个结果事先并不确定的随机实验（如掷骰子），其结果具有不确定性。所有可能结果的集合（例如，{1,2,3,4,5,6}）称为样本空间，样本空间的一个子集（例如在掷骰子={1,3,5} 的实验中得到一个奇数）称为一个事件。

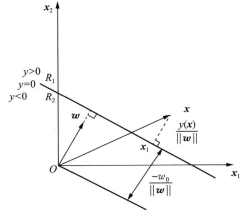

图 5-2　线性判别函数分析

直观上，事件 A 的概率可以定义为

$$P(A) = \lim_{n \to \infty} \frac{N(A)}{n} \tag{5-7}$$

式中，$N(A)$ 是 N 次试验中 A 事件发生的次数。假设所有结果都是等可能的（拉普拉斯定义）。条件概率定义如下：

$$P(A|B) = \frac{P(A,B)}{P(B)}, \quad P(B|A) = \frac{P(A,B)}{P(A)} \tag{5-8}$$

式中，$P(A)$ 或 $P(B)$ 是先验概率或边缘概率，$P(A|B)$ 或 $P(B|A)$ 是后验概率，$P(A,B)$ 是 A 和 B 同时发生的联合概率。

由以上定义得到链式法则：

$$P(A,B) = P(A|B)P(B) = P(B|A)P(A) \tag{5-9}$$

使用条件概率的定义可以得到贝叶斯定理：

$$P(A|B) = \frac{P(B|A)P(A)}{P(B)} \tag{5-10}$$

然后，我们可以在观察到的数据 B 发生概率的基础上，用后验概率 $P(A|B)$ 来评估 A 发生的不确定性。

贝叶斯定理右边的量 $P(B|A)$ 是对观测数据集 B 求值的，可以看作 A 的函数，在这种情况下，它被称为似然函数。它表示观察到的数据集 B 对于 A 的不同设置的可能性有多大。我们可以用先验概率和似然函数来表示贝叶斯定理中的分母：

$$P(B) = \int P(B|A)P(A)dA \tag{5-11}$$

从数学上讲，贝叶斯定理表明：

$$后验概率 = \frac{似然函数 \times 先验概率}{边缘似然} \tag{5-12}$$

基于最小错误率的贝叶斯决策规则为：如果 $P(w_1|x) > P(w_2|x)$，则把 x 归类于 w_1；反之，若 $P(w_1|x) < P(w_2|x)$，则把 x 归类于 w_2。可简写为：如果 $P(w_i|x) = \max P(w_j|x)$，则 $x \in w_i$。

决策树

决策树是表示决策过程或一系列决策的流程图（见图 5-3）。它的每一个叶节点对应着一个分类或类分布，内部节点对应着在某个属性上的划分，分支表示测试结果的路径，根据样本在该属性上的不同取值将其划分成不同的类，新样本通过匹配到叶节点的路径进行分类。对一个分类问题，从已知类标记的训练样本中学习并构造出决策树是一个自上而下、分而治之的过程。

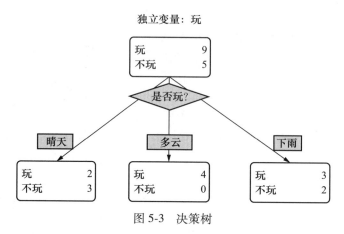

图 5-3　决策树

决策树的生成包括生成树和修剪树两个阶段。开始时，所有的训练样本都在根目录，基于所选属性对样本进行划分，最后识别并删除反映噪声或异常值的分支。

决策树的划分依据信息增益。假设有两个类 P 和 N，设样本集 S 包含 P 类的 p 个元素和 N 类的 n 个元素，定义 S 中任意一个样本属于 P 还是 N，所需信息量为

$$E(S) = -\frac{p}{p+n}\log_2\left(\frac{p}{p+n}\right) - \frac{n}{p+n}\log_2\left(\frac{n}{p+n}\right) \tag{5-13}$$

根据属性 A，数据被划分为不同的子集。在 A 上分支得到的信息如下：

$$增益(A) = E(当前集) - \sum P(子集)E(子集) \tag{5-14}$$

根据决策树的输出结果，决策树可以分为分类树和回归树，分类树输出的结果为具体的类别，而回归树输出的结果为确定的数值。

决策树的构建算法主要有 ID3、C4.5 和 CART 三种，其中 ID3 和 C4.5 是分类树，CART 是回归树，并且 ID3 是决策树最基本的构建算法，而 C4.5 和 CART 是基于 ID3 的优化算法。

支持向量机

支持向量机（Support Vector Machine，SVM）是 Cortes 和 Vapnik 于 1995 年首先提出的，它在解决小样本、非线性及高维模式识别中表现出许多特有的优势，并能够推广应用到函数拟合等其他机器学习问题中。

支持向量机方法建立在统计学习理论的 VC（Vapnik-Chervonenkis）维理论和结构风险最小原理基础上，根据有限的样本信息在模型的复杂度（即对特定训练样本的学习精度）和学习能力（即无错误地识别任意样本的能力）之间寻求最佳折中，以期获得最好的推广能力（或称泛化能力）。

一般来说，判别函数 $g(x)$ 是通过最小化误差函数（例如 MSE），从有限的样本集合中估计出来的。传统的经验风险最小化并不意味着具有良好的泛化能力。为了保证良好的泛化能力，必须控制学习函数的复杂度或容量。具有高容量的函数更复杂（即有许多自由度）。此时的情况便是选择了一个足够复杂的分类函数（它的 VC 维很高），能够精确地记住每一个样本，但对样本之外的数据则一律分类错误。在统计学习中，VC 维是一种常用的衡量分类器能力的方法。VC 维可以预测分类器泛化误差的概率上限，Vapnik 已经证明最大化分离裕度（即类之

间的空隙）等价于最小化 VC 维。最优超平面是一类之间有最大间隔的超平面（见图 5-4），其边缘是由最近的训练样本到超平面的距离定义的。直观地说，这些是最难分类的样本。我们把这些样本称为支持向量。

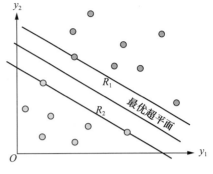

图 5-4　最优超平面

SVM 通过非线性映射 P 把样本空间映射到高维乃至无穷维的特征空间（Hilbert 空间），使得原来样本空间中的非线性可分的问题转化为特征空间中的线性可分的问题。简单地说，就是升维和线性化。升维就是把样本向高维空间做映射，一般情况下这会增加计算的复杂性，甚至会引起"维数灾难"。但是作为分类、回归等问题来说，在低维样本空间无法线性处理的样本集，很可能在高维特征空间中却可以通过线性超平面实现线性划分（或回归）。一般的升维都会带来计算的复杂化，SVM 方法巧妙地应用核函数的展开定理解决了这个难题，就不需要知道非线性映射的显式表达式。由于是在高维特征空间中建立线性学习机，因此与线性模型相比，这不但几乎不增加计算的复杂性，而且在某种程度上避免了"维数灾难"，这一切要归功于核函数的展开定理。

不同的核函数可以生成不同的 SVM，常用的核函数有以下 4 种：
1）线性核函数：$K(x,y) = x \cdot y$。
2）多项式核函数：$K(x,y) = [(x \cdot y) + 1]^d$。
3）径向基函数：$K(x,y) = \exp(-|x-y|^2/d^2)$。
4）二层神经网络核函数：$K(x,y) = \tanh[a(x \cdot y) + b]$。

SVM 基于精确优化，而不是基于近似方法（即全局优化方法，没有局部最优）。该方法避免了高维空间的过拟合现象，并且在较小的训练集下具有较好的推广效果，其性能取决于内核及其参数的选择，它的复杂度取决于支持向量的数量，而不是变换空间的维数。

5.2　机器学习

人工智能（AI）是一个广泛的术语，用来描述能够自己做出某些决定的系统。机器学习就是让机器具备人一样的学习能力，专门研究计算机怎样模拟或实现人类的学习行为，以获取新的知识或技能，重新组织已有的知识结构使其不断改善自身的性能，它是人工智能的核心。机器学习是一门多领域交叉学科，涉及概率论、统计学、逼近论、凸分析、算法复杂度理论等多门学科。

1. 机器学习的定义

机器学习是一门专门研究计算机怎样模拟或实现人类的学习行为，以获取新的知识或技能，重新组织已有的知识结构使其不断改善自身的性能的学科。机器能否像人类一样具有学习能力呢？1959 年美国的 Samuel 设计了一个下棋程序，这个程序具有学习能力，它可以在不断的对弈中改善自己的棋艺。4 年后，这个程序战胜了设计者本人。又过了 3 年，这个程序战胜了美国一个保持 8 年之久的常胜不败的冠军。这个程序向人们展示了机器学习的能力。

但究竟什么是学习，长期以来却众说纷纭。社会学家、逻辑学家和心理学家都各有不同的看法。然而，也有一些基本的共同点，1959 年 Arthur Samuel 将其总结为一句经常被引用的话："机器学习是在不直接针对问题进行编程的情况下，赋予计算机学习能力的研究领域。"

1997 年，卡内基梅隆大学的 Tom Mitchell 给出了经证明更适用于工程类型的"形式化"的定义："对于计算机程序来说，给它一个任务 T 和一个性能度量 P，如果在经验 E 的影响下，P 对 T 的测量结果得到了改进，那么就说该程序从 E 中学习。"如果你想用程序实现预测，如预测一个繁忙十字路口的交通模式（任务 T），你可以用过去的交通模式（经验 E）有关的数据训练机器学习算法，如果它成功地"学习"了，它就会很好地预测未来的交通模式（性能度量 P）。

总之，机器学习是一个计算机程序，针对某个特定任务，从经验中学习，并且越做越好。

2. 机器学习的要素

对机器学习而言，最重要的有两方面内容：数据和模型。

数据

这是机器学习的基础，经验最终要转换为计算机能理解的数据，这样计算机才能从经验中学习。数据可以是传感器（如雷达或照相机）采集的，也可以是民意调查数据、股票市场价格等。掌握高质量的大量的数据是机器学习和人工智能领域最重要的资本。

模型

它为学习提供了数学框架。有了数据之后，你需要设计一个模型，把数据作为输入来训练这个模型。经过训练的模型最终就成了机器学习的核心，使模型成为能产生决策的中枢。当输入新事件时，一个经过良好训练的模型会做出适当的反应，产生优质的输出。

3. 机器学习应用实现的步骤

目前利用机器学习解决问题的思路如图 5-8 所示（以视觉感知为例）。

图 5-8　典型机器学习算法应用实现框图

首先传感器（例如 CMOS）获得数据，然后经过预处理、特征提取、特征选择，再到推理、预测或识别。最后一个部分就是机器学习的部分。

机器学习的核心目标是学习和推理（见图 5-9）。机器学习的方式与人类相似。人类从经验中学习。我们知道得越多，就越容易预测。机器受到的训练也是一样的，确定要解决的问题后，为了做出准确的预测，需要给机器提供一个例子。机器通过数据发现模式来学习。因此，一个关键部分是仔细选择向机器提供哪些数据。用来解决问题的属性列表称为特征向量。我们可以将特征向量视为用于解决问题的数据子集。因此，学习阶段用于描述数据，并将其归纳为模型。

图 5-9　机器学习的核心步骤

当模型建立起来后，新数据输入就可以得出预测，不需要更新规则或再次训练模型。这就是机器学习的美妙之处。

机器学习的流程很简单，可以归纳为以下几点。

定义问题

明确你想要解决的问题是什么,这个问题用机器学习来解决是否合适。

数据采集和标记

采集大量不同特征的信息,所有采集的数据称为训练样本或数据集。数据采集阶段需要收集尽量多的特征。特征越全、数据越多,训练出来的模型才会越准确。数据标记对监督学习方法是必须的。比如,针对垃圾邮件过滤系统,训练样本必须包含该邮件是否为垃圾邮件的标记数据。

数据清洗

检查数据一致性,去掉重复数据及噪声数据,让数据具备结构化特征,以方便作为机器学习算法的输入。

特征选择

逐个分析特征,最终选择合适的特征作为输入。特征选择的方法可以是人工选择,也可以通过模型来自动选择,如主成分分析(PCA)算法。

模型选择

根据问题类型、数据量大小、训练时长、模型准确度等多方面因素选择合适的模型。

模型训练和测试

把数据集分成训练数据集和测试数据集,一般按照 8∶2 或者 7∶3 来划分,然后用训练数据集来训练模型。训练出参数后再使用测试数据集来测试模型的准确度。理论上,更合理的数据集划分方案是分成 3 个,即再分出一个交叉验证数据集。

模型性能评估和优化

模型训练出来后,需要对该模型进行性能评估。性能评估一般包括训练时长、数据集是否足够多、模型准确度等。如果模型不能满足要求,就需要优化,然后继续对模型进行训练和评估,或者更换为其他模型。

使用模型进行预测

训练出来的模型可以把参数保存起来,下次使用时直接加载即可。一般直接把新样本作为输入,然后调用模型即可得出结果。一旦算法能够很好地得出正确的结论,它就会将这些知识应用到新的数据集。

4. 机器学习的分类

机器学习的分类有很多种,一般基于两点:数据类型与学习过程。前者分为监督学习、半监督学习和无监督学习;后者包括主动学习、强化学习和转导学习。大多数(大概 70%)的机器学习是监督学习,无监督学习大概占 10%~20%,有时也会使用半监督学习和强化学习。

监督学习

监督学习算法利用带有分类标签的实例训练机器学习模型,让计算机从中学习出规律,从而能针对新的输入做出合理的输出预测。监督学习方法被普遍应用于使用历史数据预测未来可能发生的事件。监督学习包括回归学习和分类学习。

比如,我们有大量不同特征(面积、地理位置、朝向、开发商等)的房子的价格数据,通过学习这些数据,系统将以最小误差预测一个已知特征的房子的价格。这种输出结果是连续值的学习称为回归学习。

再比如,我们有大量的邮件,每个邮件都已经标记是否为垃圾邮件。通过学习这些已经标记的邮件数据,我们最后得出一个模型,这个模型对新的邮件能准确地判断出该邮件是否为垃圾邮件。这种称为分类学习,即输出结果是离散的,例如要么输出 1 表示是垃圾邮件,要么输出 0 表示不是垃圾邮件。

无监督学习

无监督学习通过学习大量的无标记数据，分析数据本身内在的特点和结构。系统不会被告知"正确答案"。算法必须自己搞明白这些数据呈现了什么，其目标是探索数据并找到一些内部结构。无监督学习对交易（事务性）数据的处理效果很好。流行的方法包括自组织映射、最近邻映射、K-均值聚类和奇异值分解。这些算法也用于对文本进行分段处理、推荐项目和确定数据的异常值。

比如，我们有大量的用户购物的历史记录信息，可以从数据中分析用户的不同类别，最终能划分几个类别？每个类别有哪些特点？这些我们事先是不知道的。这就是聚类。

这里需要特别注意与监督学习中分类的区别：分类问题事先知道有哪几种类别，在已知答案里选一个；聚类问题事先不知道有哪几种类别，需要利用算法挖掘出数据的特点和结构，进而聚成若干个类别。

半监督学习

半监督学习的应用与监督学习相同，但通常只有少量的输入数据被标记，而大多数没有（因为未标记的数据非常容易获得）。这种类型可以使用分类、回归和预测等学习方法。当一个全标记的监督学习过程因其相关标签的成本太高时，我们可以使用半监督学习，例如使用网络摄像头识别人脸。

强化学习

强化学习经常被用于机器人、游戏和导航。算法通过不断地试错进行强化学习，使回报最大化。这种学习分为三个主要组成部分：智能体（学习者或决策者）、环境（智能体所接触到的一切）和行动（智能体可以做的）。其目标是在给定的时间内，使代理选择的行动回报最大化。通过一个好的策略，代理将更快地达到目标。因此，强化学习的目标是得到最好的策略。

5. 机器学习的常用方法

图 5-10 给出了机器学习常用方法的图解，表 5-2 给出了常用的机器学习算法及其描述。

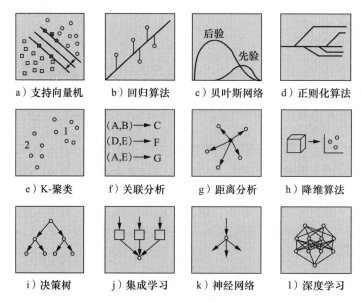

图 5-10　机器学习常用方法的图解

表 5-2 常用的机器学习算法及其描述

类别	算法	描述	类型
监督学习	线性回归	找到一种将每个特征与输出关联起来的方法，以帮助预测未来的值	回归
	逻辑回归	用于分类任务的线性回归的扩展。输出变量 3 是二进制的（例如，只有黑色或白色）而不是连续的（例如，无限可能的颜色列表）	分类
	决策树	高度可解释的分类或回归模型，在决策节点将数据特征值拆分为分支（例如，如果特征是一种颜色，那么每一种可能的颜色都将成为一个新的分支），直到做出最终的决策输出 为模式依赖的特征序列找到一组阈值	回归/分类
	朴素贝叶斯	贝叶斯方法是一种利用贝叶斯定理的分类方法。该定理用每个能影响事件特征的独立概率来更新事件的先验知识	回归/分类
	径向基网络	使用类高斯传递函数的至少有一层神经元的前馈神经网络的迭代均方误差优化	回归/分类
	支持向量机	通过选择最小数量的支持向量来最大化类之间的间隙	回归（不常用）/分类
	随机森林	该算法建立在决策树的基础上，大大提高了算法的精度。随机森林多次生成简单的决策树，并使用"多数投票"的方法来决定返回哪个标签。对于分类任务，最终的预测结果为得票最多的预测结果；而对于回归任务，所有树的平均预测结果就是最终的预测结果	回归/分类
	集成学习	一种分类或回归技术，它使用多种模型来做出决定，但根据预测结果的准确性对它们进行权衡	回归/分类
	梯度提升树	梯度提升树是一种最先进的分类/回归技术。它专注于前面的树所犯的错误，并试图纠正它	回归/分类
无监督学习	K-均值聚类	将数据放入一些组（K），每组包含具有相似特征的数据（由模型确定，而不是由人类预先确定）	聚类
	高斯混合模型	K-均值聚类的一般化，在组（集群）的大小和形状上提供了更大的灵活性	聚类
	分层聚类	沿着层次树分解集群以形成分类系统。可用于集群忠诚卡客户	聚类
	推荐系统	帮助定义相关数据以给出建议	聚类
	PCA/T-SNE	主要用于降低数据的维数。该算法将特征的数量减少到 3 或 4 个具有最大方差的向量	降维

5.3 计算机视觉

1. 计算机视觉的定义

什么是计算机视觉？它有不同的定义，如"从图像中清晰地、有意义地描述物理对象的结构"或者"根据感知的图像做出有关真实物体和场景的有用决策"。大卫·马尔（David Marr）

说，普通人的答案（以及亚里士多德的答案）是通过观察知道哪里是什么。换句话说，视觉是从图像中发现世界上存在的东西以及它在哪里的过程（见图5-16）。他是一名英国神经学家和心理学家，计算机视觉领域最负盛名的奖项之一——马尔奖，就是以他的名字命名的。

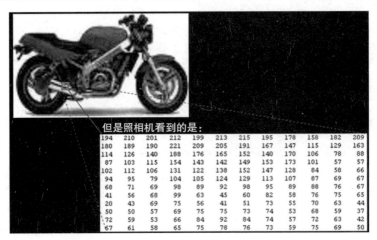

图5-16　图像及其像素表示

计算机视觉是一门研究机器视觉的科学和技术，研究的是建立从图像中获取信息的人工系统的理论。图像数据可以采用多种形式，如视频序列、深度图像、多个摄像机的视图或医疗扫描仪的多维数据。它是一门多学科交叉的研究，涵盖计算机科学（图形学、算法、理论研究等）、数学（信息检索、机器学习等）、工程（机器人、NLP等）、生物学（神经系统科学）和心理学（认知科学）。

通过这些图像数据以及深度学习模型，机器可以准确地识别和分类物体，然后对它们"看到"的东西做出反应。比如：

1）人脸识别：Snapchat和Facebook使用面部检测算法，能够从照片中认出某人的身份。

2）图像检索：谷歌图像使用基于内容的查询来搜索相关图像，算法返回与查询内容最佳匹配的图像。

3）游戏和控制：微软Kinect体感游戏。

4）监控：公共场所随处可见的监控摄像机用来监视可疑行为。

5）生物识别技术：指纹、虹膜和人脸匹配是生物特征识别中常用的方法。

6）智能汽车：视觉仍然是观察交通标志、信号灯及其他视觉特征的主要信息来源。

图像分类、定位和检测等视觉识别任务是计算机视觉的关键组成部分。神经网络和深度学习方法的最新发展极大地提高了这些最先进的视觉识别系统的性能。

2. 计算机视觉与机器视觉的区别

事实上，二者经常被混淆。二者最大的区别在于技术要求的侧重点不一样，甚至差别很大。计算机视觉（CV）主要是对质的分析，比如分类识别（这是一个杯子，那是一条狗）；或者身份确认，比如人脸识别、车牌识别；或者行为分析，比如人员入侵、徘徊、遗留物、聚集等。

机器视觉（MV）主要侧重对量的分析，比如通过视觉测量零件的直径，一般来说，其对准确度的要求很高。

3. 计算机视觉的发展

计算机视觉的早期实验发生在20世纪50年代，使用一些最早的神经网络来检测物体的边缘，并将简单的物体分类为圆形和正方形等类别。在20世纪70年代，计算机视觉的第一次商业用途是使用光学字符识别来解释打字或手写文本。这一进步被用来为盲人解释书面文本。

随着互联网在20世纪90年代的成熟，大量的图像可以在线分析，面部识别程序蓬勃发展。这些不断增长的数据集可帮助计算机识别照片和视频中的特定人物。

今天，许多因素结合在一起带来了计算机视觉的复兴：带有内置摄像头的移动技术已经使世界充满了照片和视频；计算能力变得更加便宜和容易获得；为计算机视觉和分析设计的硬件更广泛地使用；卷积神经网络等新算法可以利用硬件和软件功能。

这些进步对计算机视觉领域的影响是惊人的。在不到十年的时间里，物体识别和分类的准确率从50%上升到99%，今天的系统在快速检测和对视觉输入的反应方面比人类更准确。

4. 计算机视觉的任务

计算机视觉的任务用一句话概括就是：解决视觉问题——"what is where?"，通过摄影机和计算机代替人眼对目标进行识别、跟踪和测量等处理，以获得相应场景的信息（见图5-17）。在计算机视觉领域中，主要任务有图像分类/定位、目标检测、目标跟踪、图像分割等，具体描述如下。

图5-17 计算机视觉的任务

物体检测

物体检测是视觉感知的第一步，也是计算机视觉的重要分支。物体检测的目标就是用框标出物体的位置，并给出物体的类别。

物体检测和图像分类不一样，物体检测侧重于物体的搜索，而且物体检测的目标必须要有固定的形状和轮廓。图像分类可以是任意的目标，这个目标可能是物体，也可能是一些属性或者场景。

物体识别

计算机视觉的经典问题便是判定一组图像数据中是否包含某个特定的物体、图像特征或运动状态。这一问题通常可以通过机器自动解决，但是到目前为止，还没有某个单一的方法能够广泛地对各种情况进行判定：在任意环境中识别任意物体。

现有技术能够也只能够很好地解决特定物体的识别，比如简单几何图形识别、人脸识别、印刷或手写文件识别，或者车辆识别。这些识别需要在特定的环境中，要求指定的光照、背景和姿态。

图像分类

图像分类主要需要解决的问题是"who am I?"，如一张图像中是否包含某种物体，对图像进行特征描述是物体分类的主要研究内容。一般说来，物体分类算法通过手工特征或者特征学习方法对整个图像进行全局描述，然后使用分类器判断是否存在某类物体。

图像分类问题就是给输入图像分配标签的任务，这是 CV 的核心问题之一，尽管它很简单，但具有各种各样的实际应用。许多其他看似不同的 CV 任务（例如目标检测、图像分割）均可以简化为图像分类。这个过程往往与机器学习和深度学习不可分割。

对于图像分类而言，最受欢迎的方法是卷积神经网络（CNN）。CNN 的结构基本由卷积层、池化层以及全连接层组成（见图 5-18）。通常，输入图像送入卷积神经网络中，通过卷积层进行特征提取，之后通过池化层过滤细节（一般采用最大池化、平均池化），最后在全连接层进行特征展开，并送入相应的分类器得到分类结果。

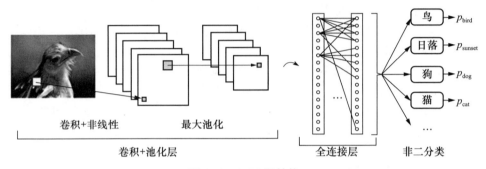

图 5-18　CNN 的结构

图像定位

如果物体识别解决的是 what，那么图像定位解决的则是 where 的问题。图像定位利用计算视觉技术找到图像中某一目标物体在图像中的位置，通常以边界框的形式。目标物体的定位对于计算机视觉在安防、自动驾驶等领域的应用有着至关重要的意义。

多任务学习网络有两个输出分支。一个分支用于图像分类，即全连接+softmax 判断目标类别，与单纯图像分类的区别在于这里还需要另外一个"背景"类。另一个分支用于判断目标位置，即完成回归任务输出四个数字，标记边界框位置（例如中心点横纵坐标和边界框长宽），该分支的输出结果只有在分类分支判断不为"背景"时才使用。

目标检测

目标检测的任务是找出图像中所有感兴趣的目标（物体），确定它们的位置和大小，它是计算机视觉领域的核心问题之一（见图 5-19）。由于各类目标有不同的外观、形状和姿态，加上成像时光照、遮挡等因素的干扰，目标检测一直是计算机视觉领域最具有挑战性的问题。

图 5-19　目标检测

第一个高效模型是 R-CNN（基于区域的卷积神经网络），后来又出现了 Fast R-CNN 算法以及 Faster R-CNN 算法。近年来，目标检测的研究趋势主要向更快、更有效的检测系统发展。目前，已经有一些其他的方法可供使用，比如 YOLO、SSD 以及 R-FCN 等。

目标跟踪

目标跟踪是指在给定场景中跟踪感兴趣的具体对象或多个对象的过程（见图 5-20）。简单来说，给出目标在跟踪视频第一帧中的初始状态（如位置、尺寸），算法自动估计目标物体在后续帧中的状态。

图 5-20 目标跟踪

使用 SAE 方法进行目标跟踪的最经典深层网络是深度学习跟踪器（DLT），它提出了离线预训练和在线微调。基于 CNN 完成目标跟踪的典型算法是 FCNT 和 MD Net。

图像分割

在图像处理过程中，有时我们需要对图像进行分割来提取有价值的用于后续处理的部分（例如筛选特征点），或者分割一幅或多幅图像中含有特定目标的部分等。

图像分割指的是将数字图像细分为多个图像子区域（像素的集合，也被称作超像素）的过程。图像分割的目的是简化或改变图像的表示形式，使图像更容易理解和分析。更精确地说，图像分割是对图像中的每个像素加标签的过程，这一过程使得具有相同标签的像素具有某种共同视觉特性。

分割又有两个不同的方向：语义分割和实例分割。语义分割是像素级的物体识别，即每个像素点都要判断它的类别，但是不关心所属的实体。而实例分割是更精细的步骤，像素属于不同的实体。

CNN 在此项任务中同样展现了优异的性能。典型的方法是 FCN。FCN 模型输入一幅图像后直接在输出端得到密度预测，即每个像素所属的类别，从而得到一个端到端的方法来实现图像的语义分割（见图 5-21）。

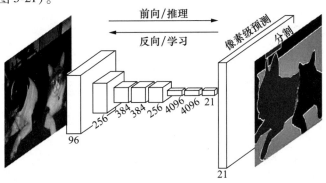

图 5-21 语义分割

超分辨率重构、风格迁移和彩色化

超分辨率重构是指从低分辨率图像中估算出高分辨率图像的过程，也指在不同的放大倍数下预测图像特征的过程，人脑几乎可以毫不费力地做到这一点。最初，超分辨率是通过简单的技术来实现的，比如双三次插值和最近邻插值。在商业应用方面，为了克服来源质量带来低分辨率限制的需求，以及实现"CSI Miami"风格的图像增强，推动了该领域的研究。

风格迁移指的是将图像 A 的风格转换到图像 B 中，得到新图像 B，而新图像 B 中既包含图像 B 的内容，也包含图像 A 的风格。谷歌发布了一些有趣的工作，试图混合多种风格来生成完全独特的图像风格。

彩色化是将单色图像变成新的全彩色版本的过程。计算机根据其对物体位置、纹理和环境的理解，为图像分配最可能的颜色，例如它了解到皮肤是粉红色的，天空是蓝色的。虽然人类可能不能准确地给定场景的真实颜色，但他们拥有的真实世界的知识，使得他们能够以一种与图像和另一个观看图像的人一致的方式来应用颜色。

5. 结论

计算机视觉是通过创建人工模型来模拟本应由人类执行的视觉任务。它的本质是模拟人类的感知与观察的过程。这个过程不止识别，而是包含了一系列的过程，并且最终可以在人工系统中被理解和实现。

应用篇

Chapter 6

Textual Type of Special English
（专业英语文本类型）

6.1 专业原版书文体

外文原版教材的著作者，为了其自己的名誉、学术地位及所在国家的声誉，均会在其出版的著作中客观地反映某一学科领域较新的科研成果。就像产业的优先传递一样，这种知识的优先传递使读者可以站在一个较高的起点上与世界先进水平协调，实现跨越式发展。

2001 年 9 月，在北京的国际图书博览会上，中国图书进出口集团总公司试着设立了一个外国高校原版教材的展区，结果大受欢迎。从中可以看到，随着高等教育事业的发展，对外交流日益频繁，引进国外高质量的原版教材的愿望非常迫切。这也说明传统的全部采用中文版教材、中文讲授的教学方法已无法满足学生的专业培养要求。"双语教学"不仅使学生学到专业知识，而且能大大提高学生的专业英语水平，因此高校图书馆应配合学校的"双语教学"，将英语原版书刊引进"双语教学"的课堂。这不仅能使学生将基础英语知识与专业知识紧密联系在一起，而且能使学生在接受专业知识和提高专业英语水平的同时，直接地了解本专业国际性的科技发展动态及科研成果。英文书刊应用于专业英语教学，从某种程度上说，对教师和学生都能起到积极作用。一方面，老师通过英语书刊的阅读，精选一部分资料作为讲课内容，在提高自身专业素质的同时为自己的科研项目找到了最新的参考资料；另一方面，学生要遵照老师的要求到图书馆阅读本专业的英文资料，使学生从自己的实践中自然提高对英语书刊情报功能的认识，增强情报意识，进而提高专业英语水平。

从目前原版教材引进的形式来看，主要有两种形式：一种是影印版，另一种是翻译版。翻译版图书对翻译人员和编辑都有严格的要求，要求翻译人员既要有专业背景又要有相当的外语水平；对于编辑人员来说，也需要既懂专业，又要具备一定的外语水平。如果出版教材没有专业化的特殊严格要求是很难做好的，这会导致大量的图书质量问题出现。另外，翻译版的出版周期一般比较长，往往译作完成时，原版新版本已问世。由于上述原因，导致有些读者对国内的翻译版不敢问津。影印版的出版周期比较短，因此很多出版社出版的国外教材的原版书都为影印版。

6.2 原版图书结构

英文原版图书一般包括以下部分：封面（cover）、扉页（title page）、版权页（copyright page）、序言（preface）、目录（contents）、正文（text）、附录（appendix）、索引（index）、词汇表（glossary）、参考文献（references）等。

下面以原版教材 *Advanced Digital Signal Processing and Noise Reduction* 为例介绍原版书的结构。

1) 封面：包括书名、版次、作者、编（译）者、出版单位等。
2) 扉页：包括封面的内容，还包括作者简介、出版时间、出版地等。

英文扉页示例

①Advanced
Digital Signal
Processing
and Noise
Reduction
Second Edition
②SAEED V. VASEGHI
Professor of Communications and Signal Processing,
Department of Electronics and Computer Engineering,
Brunet University, UK
③John Wiley & Sons, Ltd
Chichester · New York · Weinheim · Brisbane · Singapore · Toronto

其中，①为书名及版次（现代数字信号处理与降噪，第2版）；

②为著作者及简介（作者——SAEED V. VASEGHI，英国布鲁内尔大学电子与计算机工程系通信与信号处理专业教授）；

③为出版社及出版社在各国的分支机构（出版公司——John Wiley & Sons，各国的分支机构——Chichester · New York · Weinheim · Brisbane · Singapore · Toronto）。

3) 版权页：印有版权所有者及版权声明、版次、印刷者、国际标准图书号、出版公司各分支机构等。

英文版权页示例

First Edition published in 1996 jointly by John Wiley & Sons, Ltd. and B. G. Teubner as Advanced Signal Processing and Digital Noise Reduction.

Copyright ⓒ 2000 by John Wiley & Sons, Ltd
      Baffins Lane, Chichester,
      West Sussex, P019 lUD, England
      National 01243 779777
      International (+44) 1243 779777

E-mail (for orders and customer service enquiries): cs-books@ wiley. co. uk
Visit our Home Page on http://www. wiley. co. uk or http://www. wiley. com

All Rights Reserved. No part of this publication may be reproduced, stored in a retrieval system, or transmitted, in any form or by any means, electronic, mechanical, photocopying, recording, scanning or otherwise, except under the terms of the Copyright Designs and Patents Act 1988 or under the terms of a licence issued by the Copyright Licensing Agency, 90 Tottenham Court Road, London, W1P 9HE, UK, without the permission in writing of the Publisher, with the exception of any material supplied specifically for the purpose of being entered and executed on a computer system, for exclusive use by the purchaser of the publication.

Neither the authors nor John Wiley & Sons Ltd accept any responsibility or liability for loss or damage occasioned to any person or property through using the material, instructions, methods or ideas contained herein, or acting or refraining from acting as a result of such use. The author (s) and Publisher expressly disclaim all implied warranties, including merchantability of fitness for any particular purpose.

Designations used by companies to distinguish their products are often claimed as trademarks. In all instances where John Wiley & Sons is aware of a claim, the product names appear in initial capital or capital letters. Readers, however, should contact the appropriate companies for more complete information regarding trademarks and registration.

Other Wiley Editorial Offices

John Wiley & Sons, Inc., 605 Third Avenue,
New York, NY 10158-0012, USA

Weinheim · Brisbane · Singapore · Toronto

Library of Congress Cataloging-in-Publication Data

Vaseghi, Saeed V.

    Advanced digital signal processing and noise reduction/Saeed V. Vaseghi. —2nd ed.

    p. cm.

    Includes bibliographical references and index.

    ISBN 0-471-62692-9 (alk. paper)

    1. Signal processing. 2. Electronic noise. 3. Digital filters (Mathematics) I. Title.

    TK5102.9.V37 2000

    621.382'2—dc21

    00-032091

本页包含以下一些主要内容：

- 版权：第 1 版为 1996 年 John Wiley & Sons 与 B.G. Teubner 联合公司印刷，2000 年 John Wiley & Sons 有限公司出版。
- 版权声明：版权所有，未经出版者事先书面同意，对本出版物中的任何一部分内容不得以任何形式或方法复制、存储与检索系统或传播，其中包括电子的、机械的、复印、磁带存储等。专用于购书者的计算机配套资料除外。
- 其他说明：作者和 John Wiley & Sons 有限公司对于在使用本书中的程序、方法或导致类似结果时造成的损失或破坏都不承担责任或义务。
- 图书馆出版物数据分类项：主要包括书名、作者名、分类项、国际标准图书号等。

4) 序言：也称前言，每出新版都要重写新的序言。序言概括介绍本书的写作背景、章节内容、适用读者范围、致谢等。

英文序言示例

PREFACE

Signal processing theory plays an increasingly central role in the development of modern telecommunication and information processing systems, and has a wide range of applications in multimedia technology, audio-visual signal processing, cellular mobile communication, adaptive network management, radar systems, pattern analysis, medical signal processing, financial data forecasting, decision making systems, etc. The theory and application of signal processing is concerned with the identification, modelling and utilisation of patterns and structures in a signal process. The observation signals are often distorted, incomplete and noisy. Hence, noise reduction and the removal of channel distortion is an important part of a signal processing system. The aim of this book is to provide a coherent and structured presentation of the theory and applications of statistical signal processing and noise reduction methods.

This book is organised in 15 chapters.

Chapter 1 begins with an introduction to signal processing, and provides a brief review of signal processing methodologies and applications. The basic operations of sampling and quantisation are reviewed in this chapter.

……

Chapter 15 is on blind deconvolution and channel equalisation. This chapter begins with an introduction to channel distortion models and the ideal channel equaliser. Then the Wiener equaliser, blind equalisation using the channel input power spectrum, blind deconvolution based on linear predictive models, Bayesian channel equalisation, and blind equalization for digital communication channels are considered. The chapter concludes with equalisation of maximum phase channels using higher-order statistics.

Saeed Vaseghi
June 2000

参考译文

序　言

信号处理理论逐步成为现代通信和信息处理系统发展的核心技术，并且广泛应用于多媒体技术、音/视频信号处理、蜂窝通信、自适应网络管理、雷达系统、模式分析、医学信号处理、经济数据预测、决策制定系统等方面。信号处理理论及应用与信号处理中的模式和结构的识别、建模、应用紧密相关。而观察到的信号常常是失真的、不完整的和有噪声的。因此，噪声的降低和信道失真的滤除成为信号处理系统的主要部分。本书连贯且结构化地介绍了随机信号处理和噪声降低方法的理论和应用。

本书包括 15 章。

第 1 章以信号处理为始，介绍了信号处理的方法和应用的概况。该章对采样和量化操作进行了概述。

……

第 15 章介绍了盲收敛和信道均衡。该章首先介绍了信道失真的模式和理想信道均衡器；然后讨论了维纳均衡器、采用信道输入功率谱的盲均衡、基于线性预测模式的盲收敛、贝叶斯信道均衡，以及数字通信信道的盲均衡。该章总结了用高阶统计实现的最大相位信道均衡。

Saeed Vaseghi
2000 年 6 月

5）目录：目录即各章节的标题，一般将目录排在序言之后，正文之前。

英文目录示例

CONTENTS

CHAPTER 1	**INTRODUCTION**	1
1.1	Signals and Information	2
1.2	Signal Processing Methods	3
	1.2.1 Non-parametric Signal Processing	3
	1.2.2 Model-Based Signal Processing	4
	1.2.3 Bayesian Statistical Signal Processing	4
	1.2.4 Neural Networks	5
	……	
1.4	Sampling and Analog-to-Digital Conversion	21
	1.4.1 Time-Domain Sampling and Reconstruction of Analog Signals	22
	1.4.2 Quantisation	25
	Bibliography	27
CHAPTER 2	**NOISE AND DISTORTION**	29
2.1	Introduction	30
2.2	White Noise	31
2.3	Coloured Noise	33
	……	
INDEX		**467**

参考译文

目　录

第1章	**概述**	1
1.1	信号与信息	2
1.2	信号处理方法	3
	1.2.1 非参数信号处理	3
	1.2.2 基于模型的信号处理	4
	1.2.3 贝叶斯统计信号处理	4
	1.2.4 神经网络	5
	……	
1.4	采样和模-数转换	21
	1.4.1 时域采样和模拟信号重建	22
	1.4.2 量化	25
	参考文献	27
第2章	**噪声与失真**	29
2.1	引言	30
2.2	白噪声	31
2.3	有色噪声	33
	……	
索引		**467**

6）正文：正文是图书的核心内容，即图书各章节的具体内容。

7）附录、索引、词汇表和参考文献。

英文词汇表示例

FREQUENTLY USED SYMBOLS AND ABBREVIATIONS

AWGN	Additive White Gaussian Noise
ARMA	Auto Regressive Moving Average
AR	Auto Regressive
A	Matrix of predictor coefficients
a_k	Linear predictor coefficients
a	Linear predictor coefficients vector
a_{ij}	Probability of transition from state i to state j in a Markov model
……	

英文索引示例

INDEX

A

Absolute value of error, 374

Acoustic feedbacks, 407

Acoustic noise, 30

Adaptation formula, 212

Adaptation step size, 220, 404

Adaptive filter, 205, 212, 448

Adaptive noise cancellation, 6

Additive white Gaussian noise, 42

Algorithm, 165

Abasing, 23

6.3 专业论文文体

专业论文是一种永久性的科学记录，是科学殿堂的永久建材与库存，具体体现在对国家、对学校、对个人，甚至对世界。它反映科学研究发展的历史，留下研究的痕迹。其作用有：

1）揭示规律，直接为人类带来经济的、文化的或理论的效果。

2）失败的研究可为他人借鉴。

3）科学研究有沉睡再发现的现象，萌芽的理论与观点在初期常不被人重视。

论文写作是全面地、有序地培养锻炼综合思维能力的基本方法，是知识积累升华的主要方法。这是由于论文写作要命题，要翻阅前人研究的观点与结论，要确定研究内容，要选用先进的方法，要做研究设计，要从事研究的实践、得出自己的结论，因此能全面、有序、综合地锻炼思维能力。

在论文写作过程中，为了要论证一个问题和观点，我们就要进行逻辑思维，要有说服力，特别是学术上的争鸣问题，要有理有据，还要客观表达。有的论文要求针锋相对具有战斗性，它强迫你全面、系统、深入地查阅文献进行思维，把头脑中无形无序的思维变为有形有序的文字记录来表达，使那些原本在肯定否定之间的、若明若暗、似是而非、朦朦胧胧的思想明朗化、系统化、成型化、肯定化。因此可以这样说，论文写作（广义）是区别脑力劳动者与体力劳动者的重要标志，甚至是区别科学家与发明家的标志。农民可以选出新品种，工人可以制造出新产品，发明家可能发明出许多实用的东西，但他们往往不是科学家。科学家要对某个研究领域有全面的了解，对某项成果有由理论到实践的系统研究，这些研究都要通过论文反映出来并得到公认。论文写作也是区别大学生与中学生、研究生和本科生学习方法（主动学习与被动学习）与思维成熟度的重要标志。它将集中反映不同学历人员的独立工作与思维能力。

专业论文的类型可包括科技期刊论文、学位论文和会议论文等。虽然这几种专业论文的主要结构类似，但在写作体型与结构等方面各有特点。

1. 科技期刊论文

著名物理、化学家法拉第说过："科学研究有三个阶段，首先是开拓，其次是完成，最后是发表。"很多研究成果都发表在各自的行业期刊上。科技期刊论文既具有一般议论文的特点，由论点、论证、结论构成，又具有与一般议论文不同的特点：科学性和准确性、学术性或理论性、创新性与独创性、规范性与人工语言符号（图表、照片、公式等）的应用。

通常一篇发表在期刊上的科技论文包括以下几项：题目（title）、作者姓名（author name）、作者单位名称地址（author affiliation）、摘要（abstract）、关键词（keywords）、正文（text）、致谢（acknowledgment）、参考文献（references）等。正文包括引言（introduction）、正文论述部分（main part）、结论（conclusion）。

各个部分的写作方法可参考第7章，此处不再做详细的介绍。

2. 学位论文

学位论文（thesis，dissertation）是作者为获得某种学位而撰写的科技论文。thesis通常指硕士毕业论文，而dissertation通常指博士毕业论文，其中博士论文具有较高的参考价值，它内容丰富，一般侧重于理论研究。硕士论文一般侧重于工程应用。

学位论文包括如下几个部分：摘要（abstract）、目录（contents）、前言（preliminary）、正文（text）以及参考文献（references）、致谢（acknowledgment）。有些thesis或dissertation还包括附录（appendix）。下面是一篇论文通常包含的主要部分，以及它们先后出现的顺序。

摘要

摘要在学位论文中很重要，它告诉读者论文讨论的范围以及论文的主题。通常研究者在查找材料时，只读一篇论文的摘要部分，就可以发现该论文是不是与自己的主题相关。因此，摘要必须把重要的发现和方法等叙述清楚。

正文

论文正文的组织和格式应该符合一定的规范。一般来说，正文应该包含：

1）绪论。
2）目前本课题的研究现状与发展。
3）本课题相关的理论研究与发展。
4）对研究中所使用的方法进行描述。
5）记录研究所获得的结果，并讨论所获得的结果对其他研究的意义。
6）研究中所有有意义的发现，并进行总结。
7）对未来研究的建议。

参考文献

参考文献必须包括直接引用的并对论文提供了很多信息的材料，要在正文中引用的位置加上标著序号，并与参考文献一一对应。对论文影响很小的材料不用包括。注意，不要仅仅为了使得这一部分足够长而随意添加原始文献材料。

致谢

致谢是在一篇文章的末尾作者对研究期间曾经给予帮助的人表达谢意。

附录

附录包含一些必需的但不适宜出现在正文中的材料，可以包含以下材料：研究中获得的数据、计算机程序、调查数据、详细的程序流程图，以及一些特别的文献。有可能其他学者希望以此为基础进行更进一步的研究。注意，附录部分必须同正文分开，另起一页。

3. 会议论文

会议论文的要素一般包括标题、作者、单位（或通信地址）、摘要、关键词、正文、注释或参考文献等。这些要素一般是必不可少的，它也是为了规范学术论文，更好地进行交流、统计、索引等。会议论文相对于学位论文内容简练，目的主要是说明自己的观点并进行证实。

下面通过第4届自然计算国际会议（ICNC）和第5届模糊系统与知识发现（FSKD）国际会议的征文通知以及论文格式的要求向读者示明会议论文的投稿过程。

征文通知

从下面给出的征文通知中读者可以得出以下主要内容：

- 会议名称：The 4th International Conference on Natural Computation（ICNC'08）and the 5th International Conference on Fuzzy Systems and Knowledge Discovery（FSKD'08）——第4届自然计算国际会议和第5届模糊系统与知识发现国际会议。
- 会议举办地：中国山东省济南市。
- 会议目标：为智能方法的研究人员提供国际交流，尤其是生物和物理系统方面的智能方法在数据挖掘和控制、设计等各方面的应用。
- 会议发展过程：2005年、2006年和2007年每年有30多个国家的3000多人投稿。
- 会议论文出版及收录情况：所录用的论文由IEEE出版，将被EI和ISTP收录。优秀论文将由 *Soft Computing* 杂志出版，它是SCI收录的国际期刊。
- 会议论文排版要求：全文英文书写，按Latex或MS-Word模板进行排版，转换为PDF格式通过在线投稿系统投稿。
- 会议主办单位：山东大学、IEEE。

The 4th International Conference on Natural Computation
The 5th International Conference on Fuzzy Systems and Knowledge Discovery
25-27 August 2008，Jinan，China
http://www.icnc-fskd2008.sdu.edu.cn

The 4th International Conference on Natural Computation（ICNC'08）and the 5th International Conference on Fuzzy Systems and Knowledge Discovery（FSKD'08）will be jointly held in Jinan, China. Jinan is the capital of Shandong Province, which is known for the home of Confucius, the Taishan Mountain, and the Baotu Spring. ICNC'08-FSKD'08 aims to provide an international forum for scientists and researchers to present the state of the art of intelligent methods inspired from nature, particularly biological and physical systems, with applications to data mining, manufacturing, design, and more. This is an exciting and emerging interdisciplinary area in which a wide range of theory and methodologies are being investigated and developed to tackle complex and challenging problems. Previously, the joint conferences in 2005, 2006 and 2007 each attracted over 3000 submissions from more than 30 countries.

All accepted papers will appear in conference proceedings published by the IEEE and will be indexed by both EI and ISTP. Furthermore, extended versions of selected papers will be published in a special issue of *Soft Computing*: an international journal (SCI indexed).

Submissions of papers describing original work in, but not limited to, the following topics are enthusiastically encouraged.

Prospective authors are invited to submit manuscripts written in English. All submissions will be peer-reviewed by experts in the field based on originality, significance, quality and clarity. Authors should use the Latex style files or MS-Word templates obtained from the conference site to format their papers. Authors should submit PDF files of their manuscripts via the online submission system.

To promote international participation of researchers from outside the country/region where the conference is held (i.e., China), foreign experts are encouraged to propose invited sessions. Each invited session should have at least 4 papers. Invited session organizers will solicit submissions, conduct reviews and recommend accept/reject decisions on the submitted papers. All invited session organizers will be acknowledged in the conference proceedings. Each invited session proposal should include the following information: (1) the name(s) and contact information of invited session organizer(s); (2) the title and a short synopsis of the invited session. Please send your proposal to nc2008@sdu.edu.cn.

征文通知中还应给出会议范围、主要内容以及论文的重要期限，包括论文投稿截止日期、录用通知截止日期和作者注册及终稿截止日期等。其中，这些日期是最重要的，作者要在这些日期前完成相应的工作。

英文征文通知示例

ICNC'08

Neural Computation—Learning algorithms, Neural network architectures, Stability and convergence analysis, Feed forward & recurrent networks, Neurodynamics & spiking neuron systems, Statistical neural network models, Cellular neural networks, Support vector machines, Principal and independent component analysis, Self-organizing maps.

Cognitive Science—Neurobiological systems, Perception, Emotion, Cognition, Selective attention, Vision and auditory models.

Evolutionary Computation—Evolutionary algorithms, Ant colony optimization, Particle swarm optimization, Classifier systems, Multi-objective evolutionary algorithms, Artificial life, Evolutionary intelligent agents, Artificial immune systems, Evolutionary data mining.

Other Types in Natural Computation—Quantum computing, Molecular & DNA computing, Bayesian network, Membrane computing.

FSKD'08

Fuzzy Theory and Foundations—Fuzzy theory and models, Stability of fuzzy systems, Mathematical foundations of fuzzy systems.

Fuzzy Methods and Algorithms—Fuzzy data analysis, Fuzzy image, speech and signal processing, Vision and multimedia, Fuzzy control and robotics, Fuzzy hardware and architectures, Soft computing, Fuzzy systems and the Internet, Fuzzy optimization and modeling, Fuzzy decision and support.

Knowledge Discovery Foundations—Association rules, Classification, Clustering, Privacy preserving data mining, Statistical methods, Parallel/ Distributed data mining, KD process and human interaction, Knowledge management, Knowledge visualization, Reliability and robustness issues.

Knowledge Discovery in Specific Domains—High dimensional data, Temporal data, Biomedical domains, Data streaming, Scientific databases, Semi-structured/unstructured data, Multimedia, Text, Web and the Internet, Graphic model discovery, Software warehouse and software mining.

Applications and Hybrid Systems—Computational intelligence, Bioinformatics, Neuroinformatics, Computer security, Web intelligence, Web-based support systems, Fuzzy neural systems, Evolutionary neural systems, Evolutionary fuzzy systems, Evolutionary neuro-fuzzy systems, Financial engineering.

Deadlines
Paper Submission   25 March 2008
Invited Session Proposal   25 March 2008
Decision Notification   25 April 2008
Author Registration & Final Paper   15 May 2008

参考译文

ICNC'08
神经计算——学习算法，神经网络结构，稳定性与收敛性分析，前馈与递归网络，神经动力学及放电神经元系统，统计神经网络模型，细胞神经网络，支持向量机，主成分和独立成分分析，自组织映射。

认知科学——生物神经系统，感知器，感觉，认知，选择性注意，视觉与听觉模型。

进化计算——进化算法，蚁群优化，粒子群优化，分类器系统，多目标进化算法，人工生命，进化智能体，人工免疫系统，进化数据挖掘。

自然计算的其他类型——量子计算，分子及DNA计算，贝叶斯网络，膜计算。

FSKD'08
模糊理论及基础——模糊理论与模型，模糊系统的稳定性，模糊系统的数学基础。

模糊方法及算法——模糊数据分析，模糊图像、语音及信号处理，视觉与多媒体，模糊控制与机器人，模糊硬件与结构，软计算，模糊系统与互联网，模糊优化与建模，模糊决策与支持。

知识发现基础——关联规则，分类，聚类，隐私保护数据挖掘，统计方法，并行/分布式数据挖掘，知识发现过程与人机交互，知识管理，知识可视化，可靠性与鲁棒性问题。

特殊领域的知识发现——高维数据，时态数据，生物医学领域，数据流，科学数据库，半结构化/非结构化数据，多媒体，文本，Web与互联网，图形模型发现，软件仓库与软件挖掘。

应用与混合系统——计算智能，生物信息学，神经信息学，计算机安全，Web 智能，基于 Web 的支持系统，模糊神经系统，进化神经系统，进化模糊系统，进化模糊-神经系统，金融工程。

截止日期：

论文投稿截止日期	2008 年 3 月 25 日
专题研讨会截止日期	2008 年 3 月 25 日
录用通知截止日期	2008 年 4 月 25 日
作者注册及终稿截止日期	2008 年 5 月 15 日

论文格式

作者在提交论文之前要按照会议通知给出的格式对论文进行排版，通常该格式也就是论文的模板，读者可以通过将论文复制到该模板的方法进行准确的排版，再细读模板了解本会议的具体要求。下面是 ICNC'08 和 FSKD'08 给出的论文格式，本次会议论文格式的要求主要概括如下。

1）摘要为斜体，在论文的左列，作者信息之下。题目标注"Abstract"，12 磅，黑体，居中，首字母大写。摘要内容为 10 磅，单倍行距，不超过 150 字。摘要后空两行，开始正文。关键词为 3 个。

2）原稿为英文，论文页面设置为 A4（18.00cm×22.70cm）。不要超出打印范围。正文为双栏，每栏宽 8.75cm，栏间距为 0.50cm。上 2.5cm，下 4.5cm，左、右各 1.5cm。

3）论文题目居中，16 磅，黑体，名词、代名词、动词、形容词和副词的首字母大写，不要把整个题目大写。题目后空两行 12 磅间隔。

4）作者姓名及联系方式在题目下面，11 磅，非黑体。多个作者时以两列或三列形式给出。可能的话给出 E-mail 地址。作者信息后空两行 12 磅间隔。

5）字体可采用 Times、Times Roman 或 Times New Roman。尽可能不要使用位图。

6）正文为 10 磅，单倍行距，不要采用两倍行距。所有图缩进 1/4 英寸（大约 0.5cm）。调整好左右间距，图之间不要空格。

7）图和表为 10 磅，黑体；编号为 9 磅，非黑体。首字母大写。图标在图的下方，表标在表的上方。

8）一级标题 12 磅，黑体，首字母大写，左对齐，上下各空一行，标题号后采用"."，不能用冒号。二级标题 11 磅，黑体，首字母大写，左对齐，上下各空一行。不赞成出现三级标题，如必须采用三级标题则用 10 磅，黑体，首字母大写，左对齐，上下各空一行。

9）脚注放在页的下方，8 磅，单倍行距。

10）参考文献在论文的最后给出，9 磅，单倍行距，标号采用方括号。

论文终稿

目前，国际会议的终稿一般有三种格式：Word、PDF 和 Latex。对于 Word 格式的文档，可以使用转换工具转换成 PDF 格式。Latex 格式是一种文件编辑语言，类似于 HTML，它的特点是"所见即所得"。在接收到录用通知之后，作者可以根据评阅意见对论文进行修改，并按照会议的要求将相应的论文格式上传至指定网址。一般情况下，上传论文的同时还要进行论文版权的上传。具体事宜根据会议通知逐步进行。

以下是某国际会议的终稿模板。

Author Guidelines for A4 Papers

Author(s) Name(s)
Author Affiliation(s)
E-mail

Abstract

The abstract is to be in fully-justified italicized text, at the top of the left-hand column as it is here, below the author information. Use the word "Abstract" as the title, in 12-point Times, boldface type, centered relative to the column, initially capitalized. The abstract is to be in 10-point, single-spaced type, and up to 150 words in length. Leave two blank lines after the abstract, then begin the main text.

Keywords: word1, word2, word3

1. Introduction

All manuscripts must be in English. These guidelines include complete descriptions of the fonts, spacing, and related information for producing your proceedings manuscripts.

2. Formatting your paper

All printed material, including text, illustrations, and charts, must be kept within a print area of 7 inches (18.00cm) wide by 9 inches (22.70cm) high. Do not write or print anything outside the print area. All text must be in a two-column format. Columns are to be 3-3/8 inches (8.75cm) wide, with a 1/4 inch (0.50cm) space between them. Text must be fully justified.

For A4 papers, that means the margin on the top is 2.5cm, the margin on the bottom is 4.5cm, and the margins on the left and right side are 1.5cm.

3. Main title

The main title (on the first page) should be centered, and in Times 16-point, boldface type. Capitalize the first letter of nouns, pronouns, verbs, adjectives, and adverbs; do not capitalize articles, coordinate conjunctions, or prepositions (unless the title begins with such a word). Leave two 12-point blank lines after the title.

4. Author name(s) and affiliation(s)

Author names and affiliations are to be centered beneath the title and printed in Times 11-point, non-boldface type. Multiple authors may be shown in a two-or three-column format, with their affiliations italicized and centered below their respective names. Include E-mail addresses if possible. Author information should be followed by two 12-point blank lines.

5. Type-style and fonts

Wherever Times is specified, Times Roman or Times New Roman may be used. If neither is available on your word processor, please use the font closest in appearance to Times. Avoid using bit-mapped fonts if possible. True-Type 1 fonts are preferred.

6. Main text

Type your main text in 10-point Times, single-spaced. Do **not** use double-spacing. All paragraphs should be indented 1/4 inch (approximately 0.5cm). Be sure your text is fully justified—that is, flush left and flush right. Please do not place any additional blank lines between paragraphs.

> **Figure and table captions** should be 10-point boldface Helvetica. Callouts should be 9-point non-boldface.
>
> ### 7. First-order headings
>
> For example, "1. Introduction", should be Times 12-point boldface, initially capitalized, flush left, with one blank line before, and one blank line after. Use a period (".") after the heading number, not a colon.
>
> #### 7.1 Second-order headings
>
> As in this heading, they should be Times 11-point boldface, initially capitalized, flush left, with one blank line before, and one after.
>
> ##### 7.1.1 Third-order headings.
> Third-order headings, as in this paragraph, are discouraged. However, if you must use them, use 10-point Times, boldface, initially capitalized, flush left, preceded by one blank line, followed by a period and your text on the same line.
>
> ### 8. Footnotes
>
> Use footnotes sparingly (or not at all) and place them at the bottom of the column on the page on which they are referenced. Use Times 8-point type, single-spaced. To help your readers, avoid using footnotes altogether and include necessary peripheral observations in the text (within parentheses, if you prefer, as in this sentence).
>
> ### 9. References
>
> List and number all bibliographical references in 9-point Times, single-spaced, at the end of your paper. When referenced in the text, enclose the citation number in square brackets, for example [1]. Where appropriate, include the name(s) of editors of referenced books.
>
> Initially capitalize only the first word of each figure caption and table title. Figures and tables must be numbered separately. For example: "Figure 1. Average BER", "Table 1. Input data". Figure captions are to be centered *below* the figures. Table titles are to be centered *above* the tables.
>
> [1] A. B. Smith, C. D. Jones, and E. F. Roberts, "Article Title", *Journal*, Publisher, Location, Date, pp. 1-10.
>
> [2] C. D. Jones, A. B. Smith, and E. F. Roberts, *Book Title*, Publisher, Location, Date.

6.4 产品说明书

随着国际经济的一体化,国际贸易和跨国公司飞速发展。中国加入世界贸易组织以来,国内市场逐步开发,越来越多的产品进入了中国市场,满足了国内消费者多方面的需求。在此过程中,作为产品重要附件之一的说明书引起了人们越来越多的关注。产品说明书(manual、instruction book 或 booklet)主要指随同产品一起附带的说明材料。它主要是对某一产品的所有情况的介绍,诸如其组成材料、性能、存储方式、注意事项、主要用途等。对于电子电气类产品,这类说明书主要包括产品的工作原理、安装、调试、维护、维修等。尽管许多产品已经针对中国市场的需求实现了"汉化",但因为电子电气类相关产业发展迅速,产品更新快,一些新产品仍采用英文说明书,尤其是国外的产品。

英文产品说明书、使用说明书、安装说明书一般采用说明性文字,可根据情况,使用图片、表格等多样的形式,以期达到最好的说明效果。在可能造成产品损坏或危及人身安全的地方,说明书都以醒目的文字或图案提醒用户注意,标注 CAUTION、DANGER、WARNING、IMPORTANT NOTICE 等文字。

下面是 TI 公司的 DSP 芯片数据手册——*TMS320VC5409 Fixed-Point Digital Signal Processor Data Manual*,根据这份材料读者可以总结出英文产品说明书及数据手册的形式、内容和语言特点。

1)封面:包括书名、版次、生产公司等。

英文封面示例

TMS320VC5409 Fixed-Point
Digital Signal Processor
Data Manual

Literature Number:SPRS082E
April 1999-Revised February 2004

PRODUCTION DATA information is current as of publication date. Products conform to specifications per the terms of Texas Instruments standard warranty. Production processing does not necessarily include testing of all parameters.

TEXAS
INSTRUMENTS

---

2)提示页:与版权页类似,说明公司对产品的所有权。

英文提示页示例

IMPORTANT NOTICE

Texas Instruments Incorporated and its subsidiaries (TI) reserve the right to make corrections, modifications, enhancements, improvements, and other changes to its products and services at any time and to discontinue any product or service without notice. Customers should obtain the latest relevant information before placing orders and should verify that such information is current and complete. All products are sold subject to TI's terms and conditions of sale supplied at the time of order acknowledgment.

TI warrants performance of its hardware products to the specifications applicable at the time of sale in accordance with TI's standard warranty. Testing and other quality control techniques are used to the extent TI deems necessary to support this warranty. Except where mandated by government requirements, testing of all parameters of each product is not necessarily performed.

TI assumes no liability for applications assistance or customer product design. Customers are responsible for their products and applications using TI components. To minimize the risks associated with customer products and applications, customers should provide adequate design and operating safeguards. TI does not warrant or represent that any license, either express or implied, is granted under any TI patent right, copyright, mask work right, or other TI intellectual property right relating to any combination, machine, or process in which TI products or services are used. Information published by TI regarding third-party products or services does not constitute a license from TI to use such products or services or a warranty or endorsement thereof.

Use of such information may require a license from a third party under the patents or other intellectual property of the third party, or a license from TI under the patents or other intellectual property of TI. Reproduction of information in TI data books or data sheets is permissible only if reproduction is without alteration and is accompanied by all associated warranties, conditions, limitations, and notices. Reproduction of this information with alteration is an unfair and deceptive business practice. TI is not responsible or liable for such altered documentation.

Resale of TI products or services with statements different from or beyond the parameters stated by TI for that product or service voids all express and any implied warranties for the associated TI product or service and is an unfair and deceptive business practice. TI is not responsible or liable for any such statements.

3）其他产品。

英文其他产品示例

Products		Applications	
Amplifiers	amplifier.ti.com	Audio	www.ti.com/audio
Data Converters	dataconverter.ti.com	Automotive	www.ti.com/automotive
DSP	dsp.ti.com	Broadband	www.ti.com/broadband
Interface	interface.ti.com	Digital Control	www.ti.com/digitalcontrol
Logic	logic.ti.com	Military	www.ti.com/military
Power Mgmt	power.ti.com	Optical Networking	www.ti.com/opticalnetwork
Microcontrollers	microcontroller.ti.com	Security	www.ti.com/security
		Telephony	www.ti.com/telephony
		Video & Imaging	www.ti.com/video
		Wireless	www.ti.com/wireless

4）联系方式。

邮寄地址：Texas Instruments

Post Office Box 655303 Dallas, Texas 75265

5）目录：分列数据手册各部分的主要内容。

英文目录示例

Contents

Section Page

1　**TMS320VC5409 Features**　……………………………………………………………　11
2　**Introduction**　……………………………………………………………………………　12
　2.1　Pin Assignments　……………………………………………………………………　12
　2.2　GGU Package Layout and Pin Assignments　……………………………………　12
　2.3　PGE Package Layout and Pin Assignments　……………………………………　14

3	**Functional Overview**		**15**
	3.1 CPU Core		15
		3.1.1 Software Programmable Wait-State Generator	15
		3.1.2 Programmable Bank-Switching Wait States	17
		3.1.3 CPU Memory-Mapped Registers	19
	3.2 Memory		20
		3.2.1 Memory Map	20
		3.2.2 On-Chip ROM with Bootloader	21
		3.2.3 On-Chip RAM	21
		3.2.4 On-Chip Memory Security	21
		3.2.5 Relocatable Interrupt Vector Table	22
		3.2.6 Extended Program Memory	22
	3.3 On-Chip Peripherals		23
		3.3.1 Parallel I/O Ports	23
		3.3.2 Multichannel Buffered Serial Ports (McBSPs)	26
		3.3.3 Hardware Timer	30
		3.3.4 Clock Generator	30
		3.3.5 DMA Controller	32
		3.3.6 Peripheral Memory-Mapped Registers	39
	3.4 Interrupts		40
	3.5 Terminal Functions		42
4	**Documentation Support**		**48**
	4.1 Device and Development Tool Support Nomenclature		49
5	**Electrical Specifications**		**50**
	5.1 Absolute Maximum Ratings		50
	5.2 Recommended Operating Conditions		50
	5.3 Electrical Characteristics		51
	5.4 Internal Oscillator with External Crystal		52
	5.5 Divide-by-Two/Divide-by-Four Clock Option (PLL Disabled)		53
	5.6 Multiply-by-N Clock Option (PLL Enabled)		54
	5.7 Memory and Parallel I/O Interface Timing		55
		5.7.1 Memory Read	55
		5.7.2 Memory Write	57
		5.7.3 Parallel I/O Port Read	59
		5.7.4 Parallel I/O Port Write	60
	5.8 Ready Timing for Externally Generated Wait States		61
	5.9 HOLD and HOLDA Timings		65
	5.10 Reset, BIO, Interrupt, and MP/MC Timings		66
	5.11 Instruction Acquisition (IAQ) and Interrupt Acknowledge (IACK) Timings		68
	5.12 External Flag (XF) and TOUT Timings		69

5.13　Multichannel Buffered Serial Port（McBSP）Timing ················· 70
　　5.13.1　McBSP Transmit and Receive Timings ····················· 70
　　5.13.2　McBSP General-Purpose I/O Timing ······················ 73
　　5.13.3　McBSP as SPI Master or Slave Timing ···················· 74
5.14　Host-Port Interface Timing ·································· 78
　　5.14.1　HPI8 Mode ······································ 78
　　5.14.2　HPI16 Mode ····································· 82
5.15　GPIO Timing Requirements ·································· 86
6　Mechanical Data ·· 87
　6.1　Ball Grid Array Mechanical Data ····························· 87
　6.2　Low-Profile Quad Flatpack Mechanical Data ····················· 88

6）附录：包括该DSP芯片的封装、内部结构、电气参数、引脚等原理图及数据表格。

英文图列表示例

List of Figures

Figure Page

2-1　GGU Package（Bottom View）······························· 12
2-2　PGE Package（Top View）································· 14
3-1　TMS320VC5409 Functional Block Diagram ······················ 15
3-2　Software Wait-State Register（SWWSR）［Memory-Mapped Register
　　（MMR）Address 0028h］ ·································· 16
3-3　Software Wait-State Configuration Register（SWCR）［MMR Address 002Bh］··· 17
3-4　Bank-Switching Control Register（BSCR）［MMR Address 0029h］ ······· 17
3-5　Memory Map ·· 20
3-6　Extended Program Memory ································· 23
3-7　5409 HPI Memory Map ··································· 24
3-8　Pin Control Register（PCR）································ 26
3-9　Sample Rate Generator Register 2（SRGR2）····················· 29
3-10　TMS320VC5409 DMA Memory Map ··························· 34
3-11　IFR and IMR Registers ··································· 41
······

英文表列表示例

List of Tables

Table Page

2-1　Pin Assignments for the GGU（144-Pin BGA Package）··············· 13
3-1　Software Wait-State Register（SWWSR）Bit Fields ················· 16
3-2　Software Wait-State Configuration Register（SWCR）Bit Fields ········· 17
3-3　Bank-Switching Control Register Fields ························· 18
3-4　CPU Memory-Mapped Registers ······························ 19
3-5　Standard On-Chip ROM Layout ······························ 21

3-6	Bus Holder Control Bits	25
3-7	Pin Control Register（PCR）Bit Field Description	27
3-8	Sample Rate Generator Clock Input Options	29
3-9	Sample Rate Generator Register 2（SRGR2）Bit Field Descriptions	29
……		

通过以上内容的阅读，我们可以总结出电子电气类产品的使用手册（或数据手册）在组成和语言表达等方面的特点：

1）结构与科技图书基本类似，其内容主要包括封面、提示页、目录、各章节内容、索引、封底等。读者可根据需要有选择地阅读。

2）内容以介绍产品的全部信息为主，因此语法上主要采用现在时；大量采用祈使句和被动语句；语言精练、简短、直接。

3）附以大量的图和表，并配以必要的说明文字，用以帮助用户更直观地了解产品的功能、原理、参数设置等信息。

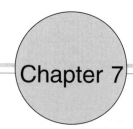

Chapter 7

Writing of English Papers for Science and Technology
（科技英语论文的写作）

科技论文是科技发展及现代化建设的重要科技信息源，是记录人类科技进步的历史性文件。科技论文可从不同的角度，根据不同标准进行分类：按学科性质和功能的不同，可分为基础学科论文、技术学科论文和应用学科论文三大类；按论文内容所属学科、专业的不同，可分为数学论文、物理论文、化学论文、天文学论文、机械工程技术论文、建筑工程技术论文等；按研究和写作方法的不同，可分为理论推导型学术论文、实（试）验研究型学术论文、观测型学术论文、设计计算型学术论文、发现发明型学术论文、争鸣型学术论文、综述型学术论文等；按写作目的和发挥作用的不同，可分成学术性论文、技术性论文和学位论文。科技论文是在科学研究、科学实验的基础上，对自然科学和专业技术领域里的某些现象或问题进行专题研究、分析和阐述，揭示出这些现象和问题的本质及其规律性而撰写的文章。科技论文主要用于科学技术研究及其成果的描述，它是科学技术研究成果的文字体现，是进行成果推广、信息交流、促进科学技术的有力手段。它们的发表标志着研究工作的水平为社会所公认，载入人类知识宝库，成为人们共享的精神财富。科技论文还是考核科技人员业绩的重要标准。

科技论文一般需要附英文摘要。通常是将中文标题、作者、摘要及关键词译为英文，这里的英文摘要泛指以上各项。英文摘要的编写实质上是汉译英的问题，它涉及英文基本功、中文素养以及对论述内容和术语的理解。随着国际交流的日益广泛，国内作者向各种国外期刊和国际会议投稿日益增多，一方面可以推动国际学术交流，促进科学研究工作；另一方面可以加大论文信息传播的力度、速度和广度，吸引读者，拓宽国内外的读者面，提高论文乃至期刊在国内外的被引用频次，还可以提高作者、期刊、工作单位在国内外的学术地位和知名度。若要使论文更高效率地被接受，除了论文的创新性，还需要注意论文的英文写作是否规范。

7.1 标题写作

科技论文的标题是表达论文的特定内容，是反映研究范围和深度的最恰当、最简明的逻辑组合，即应该"以最少数量的单词来充分表述论文的内容"。标题的作用主要有两个方面。

Chapter 7　Writing of English Papers for Science and Technology（科技英语论文的写作）

1）吸引读者。标题相当于论文的"标签"，读者通常根据标题来考虑是否需要阅读摘要或全文，而这个决定往往是在一目十行的过程中做出的。因此，如果标题表达不当，就会失去其应有的作用，使真正需要它的读者错过阅读论文的机会。

2）辅助文献检索。文献检索系统多以标题中的主题词作为线索，因而这些词必须要准确地反映论文的核心内容，否则就有可能产生漏检。此外，图书馆和研究机构大都使用自动检索系统，其中有些是根据标题中的主题词来查找资料的。因此，不恰当的标题很可能会导致论文"丢失"，从而不能被潜在的读者获取。

1. 标题撰写的基本要求

1）准确：标题要准确地反映论文的内容。

作为论文的"标签"，标题既不能过于空泛和一般化，也不宜过于烦琐，使人得不出鲜明的印象。如果标题中无吸引读者的信息，或写得不堪理解，就会失去读者；反之，标题吸引人，读者就可能会进一步阅读摘要或全文，甚至复制并保存。目前，大多数索引和摘要服务系统都已采取"关键词"系统，因此，标题中的术语应是文章中重要内容的"亮点"并且易被理解和检索。

2）简洁：标题的用词应简短、明了，以最少的文字概括尽可能多的内容。

标题最好不超过 10~12 个单词或 100 个英文字符（含空格和标点）；若能用一行文字表达，则尽量不用两行（超过两行可能会削弱读者的印象）。当然，在撰写标题时不能因为追求形式上的简短而忽视对论文内容的反映。标题过于简短，常起不到帮助读者理解论文的作用。例如"Studies on Signal"，读者难以知道论文是关于信号处理的算法、硬件、软件还是仿真的确切信息。若标题偏长，则不利于读者在浏览时迅速了解信息。

3）清楚：标题要清晰地反映文章的具体内容和特色，明确表明研究工作的独到之处，力求简洁有效、重点突出。

模糊不清的标题往往会给读者和索引工作带来麻烦和不便。标题中应慎重使用缩略语，尤其对于有多个解释的缩略语，应严加限制，必要时应在括号中注明全称。对那些全称较长而缩写后已得到科技界公认的，才可使用，并且这种使用还应得到相应期刊读者群的认可。为方便二次检索，标题中应避免使用化学式、上下角标、特殊符号（数字符号、希腊字母等）、公式、不常用的专业术语和非英语词汇（包括拉丁语）等。

2. 标题的句法结构

1）标题的构成：标题通常由名词性短语构成，如果出现动词，多为分词或动名词形式。由于陈述句易使标题具有判断式的语意，同时一般也显得不简洁，因此，大部分编辑和学者都认为标题不应由陈述句构成。有时可以用疑问句作为标题，尤其是在评论性论文的标题中，使用具探讨性的疑问句标题显得比较生动，易引起读者的兴趣。

2）标题的句法规则：由于标题比句子简短，并且不需要主、谓、宾，因此词序也就变得尤为重要。如果词语间的修饰关系使用不当，就会影响读者正确理解标题的真实含义。

科技论文英文标题撰写要准确、简洁、清楚。应特别注意标题中英文句法的正确性，尤其是动词分词和介词的使用。对于标题的长度、眉题、缩写、字母的大小写等应注意参考相关期刊的要求。为突出论文的核心内容，应尽可能地将表达核心内容的最重要的词放在标题的开头，以便引起读者的注意。

3. 英文标题

标题的特点是简短精练，概括性强，一般应控制在 20 个英文单词以内，单词的选择要有助于二次文献编制题录、索引、关键词，为文献检索提供有用信息。英文摘要中的标题不能简单地将中文标题译为英文,要注意英汉表达的差异,要贴切和简练。所谓贴切,不能笼统地理解为英文词语与中文标题词语一一对应或相符,而应使英文本意与中文标题原意相符,做到"信、达、雅"。

1)标题的结构。英文标题以短语为主要形式,尤以名词短语最常见,即标题基本上由 1 个或几个名词加上其前置和(或)后置定语构成。例如,Derivation of Equivalent Capacitance of Active Filter(有源滤波器等效电容的推导),Noise Suppression of Stabilized Switching Supply(开关稳压电源的噪声抑制)。

短语型标题要确定好中心词,再进行前后修饰。各个词的顺序很重要,若词序不当,会导致表达不准确。标题一般不应是陈述句,陈述句容易使标题具有判断式的语义;况且陈述句不够精练和醒目,重点也不易突出。

2)标题的字数。标题不应过长,在能准确反映论文特定内容的前提下,标题词数越少越好。

3)中英文标题的一致性。同一篇论文,其英文标题与中文标题内容上应一致,但不等于说词语要一一对应。在许多情况下,个别非实质性的词可以省略或变动。

4)标题中的冠词。在早年,科技论文标题中的冠词用得较多,近些年有简化的趋势,凡可用可不用的冠词均可不用。

5)标题中的大小写。标题字母的大小写有以下 3 种格式。

a)全部字母大写。例如,A NOVEL TRUE RMS-DC CONVERTER(一种新型真方均根/直流转换器);

b)每个词的首字母大写,但 3 个或 4 个字母以下的冠词、连词、介词全部小写。例如,Research on the Optimal Networking Technology of Anti-Stealth Object in Radar Net(雷达反隐身目标最优组网技术研究);

c)标题第 1 个词的首字母大写,其余字母均小写。例如,Narrowband interference suppression based on Wiener filter(基于维纳滤波器的窄带干扰抑制技术)。

目前第二种格式用得最多,第三种格式的使用有增多的趋势。

6)标题中的缩略词语。已得到整个科技界或本行业科技人员公认的缩略词语,才可用于标题中,否则不要轻易使用。

7.2 摘要写作

1. 摘要的概念和作用

摘要又称概要、内容提要。摘要是以提供文献内容梗概为目的,不加评论和补充解释,简明、确切地记述文献重要内容的短文。国家标准规定:摘要是报告、论文的内容不加注释和评论的简短陈述。摘要的内容包括:研究目的、研究对象、研究方法、研究结果、所得结论、结论的适用范围及意义等 6 项内容。其中,研究对象与结果是每篇摘要必不可少的内容。摘要可按论文的具体内容灵活运用。

摘要应具有独立性和自明性,并且拥有与文献同等量的主要信息,即不阅读全文,就能获得必要的信息。因此摘要是一种可以引用的完整短文。每一篇完整的论文都要写随文摘要,摘要的主要功能有以下两个方面。

1)让读者尽快了解论文的主要内容,以对标题进行进一步的阐述和补充。现代科技文献信息浩如烟海,读者检索到论文标题后是否会阅读全文,主要就是通过阅读摘要来判断的;所以，摘要担负着吸引读者和将文章的主要内容介绍给读者的任务。

2）为科技情报文献检索数据库的建设和维护提供方便。论文发表后，文摘杂志或各种数据库对摘要可以不做修改或稍做修改而直接利用，从而避免他人编写摘要可能产生的误解、欠缺甚至错误。随着电子计算机技术和互联网的迅猛发展，网上查询、检索和下载专业数据已成为当前科技信息情报检索的重要手段，网上各类全文数据库、文摘数据库，越来越显示出现代社会信息交流的水平和发展趋势。同时，论文摘要的索引是读者检索文献的重要工具。所以论文摘要的质量高低，直接影响着论文的被检索率和被引用频次。

2. 摘要的分类

按不同功能来划分，摘要大致有如下3种类型：第一类属于报道性摘要，是指明文献的主题范围及内容梗概的简明摘要，相当于简介，不仅要反映科技论文的主要论据、结论，还要简要介绍主要方法和结果，篇幅以300字左右为宜；第二类是指示性摘要，只简要叙述做的工作和成果，而不涉及具体方法和结果，篇幅以100字左右为宜；第三类是报道-指示性摘要，以报道性摘要的形式表述论文中价值最高的那部分内容，其余部分则以指示性摘要的形式表达，篇幅以100~200字为宜。

一般的科技论文都应尽量写成报道性摘要，用比其他类摘要字数稍多的篇幅，向读者介绍论文的主要内容。而对综述性、资料性或评论性的文章可写成指示性或报道-指示性摘要。论文发表的最终目的是要被人利用。如果摘要写得不好，在当今信息激增的时代论文进入文摘杂志、检索数据库，被人阅读、引用的机会就会少得多，甚至丧失。

3. 摘要写作的注意事项

编写摘要时应注意以下几点。

1）简练准确，以少量字数简练准确地将论文的主要内容概括出来，要求高度浓缩。摘要字数一般不超过正文字数的3%~5%。如一篇5000字的论文，中文摘要以200~300个字为宜，外文摘要不宜超过250个实词。如有特殊需要字数可以略多。学位论文等文献具有某种特殊性，为了评审，可写成变异式的摘要，不受字数的限制。

2）相对完整和独立。读者不需要阅读正文就能揭示论文最本质的要义，使读者判定有无必要去阅读全文。

3）结构严谨，表达简明，语义确切。摘要先写什么，后写什么，要按逻辑顺序来安排。句子之间要上下连贯，互相呼应。摘要慎用长句，句型应力求简单。每句话要表意明白，无空泛、笼统、含混之词，但摘要毕竟是一篇完整的短文，电报式的写法亦不可取。摘要不分段。

4）客观陈述。摘要避免用第一人称主观语气，而应采取第三人称的客观语气阐述，建议采用"对……进行了研究""提出了……算法""进行了……建模"等记述方法标明文献的性质和文献主题，不必使用"本文""作者"等作为主语。不对论文观点进行评价，更不能自封"世界首创""达到了国际最高水平"等，切忌夸张和广告式宣传。

5）要使用规范化的名词术语，不用非公知公用的符号和术语。新术语或尚无合适中文术语的，可用原文或译出后加括号注明原文。

6）除了实在无法变通以外，一般不用数学公式和化学结构式，不出现插图、表格。

7）缩略语、略称、代号，除了相邻专业的读者也能清楚理解的以外，在首次出现时必须加以说明。科技论文写作时应注意的其他事项，如采用法定计量单位、正确使用语言文字和标点符号等，也同样适用于摘要的编写。

4. 英文摘要

英文摘要与中文摘要基本一致，但不一定完全一样，有的刊物还要求前者更详尽些。为使英文摘要更精练地表达出论文的主要内容，在写作时要注意以下几点。

1）应具有相对独立的结构，一般不要引用正文中的图表、公式或参考文献，编写时要注意英文摘要的完整性和独立性。

2）英文摘要的时态。英文摘要时态的运用也以简练为佳，常用一般现在时、一般过去时，少用现在完成时、过去完成时，进行时和其他复合时态基本不用。当说明研究目的、叙述研究内容、描述结果、得出结论、提出建议或讨论等时采用一般现在时；当叙述过去某一时刻（时段）的发现、某一研究过程（实验、观察、调查、医疗等过程）时采用一般过去时；现在完成时把过去发生的或过去已完成的事情与现在联系起来，而过去完成时可用来表示过去某一时间以前已经完成的事情，或在一个过去事情完成之前就已完成的另一过去行为。文摘的时态大都采用一般现在时，个别使用一般过去时，其他时态较少采用。

3）英文摘要的语态。采用何种语态，既要考虑摘要的特点，又要满足表达的需要。一篇摘要很短，尽量不要随便混用，更不要在一个句子里混用。以前强调多用被动语态，理由是科技论文主要说明事实经过，至于那件事是谁做的，无须一一证明。事实上，在指示性摘要中，为强调动作承受者，还是采用被动语态为好。即使在报道性摘要中，有些情况下被动者无关紧要，也必须用强调的事物做主语。现在主张摘要中谓语动词尽量采用主动语态的越来越多，因其有助于文字清晰、简洁及表达有力。

4）避免在摘要中重复标题文字。

5）论文摘要应尽量避免使用人称代词 I、we、you，尽量使用第三人称。

5. 关键词

为了便于读者从浩如烟海的书刊中寻找文献，特别是适应计算机自动检索的需要，国家标准 GB3179/T—92 规定：关键词是为了文献标引工作从报告、论文中选取出来用以表示全文主题内容信息的单词或术语。同时规定：每篇报告、论文选取 3~8 个词作为关键词，以显著的字符另起一行，排在摘要的左下方。如有可能，尽量用《汉语主题词表》等词表提供的规范性词（称叙词或主题词）。对于那些反映新技术、新学科而尚未被主题词表录入的新产生的名词术语，亦可用非规范的自由词标出，以供词表编纂单位在修订词表时参照选用。

关键词是论文信息最高度的概括，是论文主旨的概括体现。因此，选择关键词必须准确恰当，必须真正反映论文的主旨。选择不当就会影响读者对论文的理解，也影响检索效果。选择关键词的方法是：首先，要认真分析论文主旨，选出与主旨一致、能概括主旨、使读者能大致判断论文研究内容的词或词组；其次，选词要精练，同义词、近义词不要并列为关键词；再次，关键词的用语必须统一规范，要准确体现不同学科的名称和术语；最后，关键词的选择大多从标题中产生，但要注意，如果有的标题并没有提供足以反映论文主旨的关键词，则要从摘要或论文中选择。

要强调的一点是：一定不要为了强调反映文献主题的全面性，把关键词写成是一句内容"全面"的短语。

英文关键词一般与中文关键词相对应且应尽量符合《汉语主题词表》或《国防科学技术叙词表》等的规定。如果从词表中可以找到英汉对照的关键词，则把此主题词当作关键词使用；如果没有，则需自译。

6. 实例学习

（1）基于高斯小波滤波器的语音识别特征提取方法

摘要：把小波理论应用于抗噪语音识别特征提取，提出了基于高斯小波滤波器的语音识别特征提取方法，通过对人耳听觉特性的研究，按照人耳临界带宽设计了一组高斯小波带通滤波器。详细讨论了高斯小波滤波器的尺度参数选择方法。使用 RBF 识别网络,仿真实现了使用新特征与原特征的识别结果,证明了新特征具有较高的识别率和优良的抗噪性能。

关键词:特征提取;高斯小波;语音识别

A Feature Extraction Method Based on Gauss Wavelet Filter in Speech Recognition

Abstract:This paper uses wavelet theory in noise robust feature extraction of speech recognition and introduces a feature extraction method based on Gauss wavelet filter. The Gauss wavelet filter with human critical frequency band is obtained by studying human auditory characteristics. This paper also studies the method of scale parameter choosing in designing Gauss wavelet filter. The methods with new and original feature are simulated. The RBF neural net was used in train and recognition course. The results show that new feature has higher recognition rate and better robustness than traditional feature.

Keywords:feature extraction;Gauss wavelet;speech recognition

(2) 基于独立成分分析的单通道语音增强算法

摘要:传统的独立成分分析要求观测信号的个数不能小于源信号的个数,无法直接对单路信号进行独立成分分析。为了能够利用独立成分分析分离加性噪声,须构造一路观测信号。基于语音信号的短时平稳的特性,该文提出一种构造噪声信号的算法,实现了信号与噪声的分离。仿真结果表明,利用该算法可得到很好的消噪结果,提高信号的信噪比。

关键词:独立成分分析;盲源分离;语音增强;单通道

Single Channel Speech Enhancement Algorithm Based on Independent Component Analysis

Abstract:The standard independent component analysis algorithm require that the number of sensors is more than or equal to that of sources, so it is impossible to apply independent component analysis to a single channel signal directly. This paper proposes an algorithm for constructing a noise signal for noise reduction based on ICA, thereby noise and signal can be separated through ICA. Simulation result shows that much better de-noise effect and signal-noise ratio can be obtained by using this algorithm.

Keywords:Independent Component Analysis (ICA);blind sources separation;speech enhancement;single channel

(3) 基于单片机的数字气压表的设计与实现

摘要:为了弥补传统气压表(空盒式、弯管式等)精度低、显示单一的缺点,开发了一种由 Philips 87C552 单片机控制的数字气压表。在开发过程中,利用微控制器强劲的运算能力处理多种数据以实现多个参数的同屏实时显示,采用先进的算法消除硅压力传感器的固有失真以提高测量的精度,采用菜单式人机界面以方便用户操作。该表可以同屏显示被测气体压力、大气压力、真空度、日历,并具有工作参数的调整、报警、密码保护、RS485 网络接口等功能。试用表明,仪表完全克服了传统气压表的缺陷,达到了良好的效果。

关键词:气压表;单片机;真空计

Design and Realization of Digital Barometer based on SCM

Abstract:In order to compensate flaws of traditional barometer (dial barometer, siphon barometer, etc), such as low precision and single display value, a digital barometer controlled by single chip micro-controller of Philips 87C552 is developed. During the development process, multi-data processing is implemented by strong computing power of 87C552 in order to display many parameters on the same LCD screen, advanced algorithm is adopted to compensate silicon pressure transducer's inherent distortion so as to get a high precision, menu man-machine interface is introduced to simplify users' operation. The meter can display the aimed air pressure, atmosphere pressure, vacuum value and calendar accurately at real time. Besides, it has many other functions, such as working parameters' configuration, alarm, password protection, RS485 protocol interface. Probation shows that the meter overcomes traditional barometers' limitations, and worked well.

Keywords：barometer；Single Chip Microprocessor（SCM）；vacuum-meter

7.3 正文写作

科技论文一般包括引言、正文、结果、讨论和致谢五部分。

1. 引言

引言（前言、序言、概述）经常作为论文的开端，主要回答"为什么研究"（why）这个问题。立题的理论或实践依据是什么？拟创新点何在？理论与（或）实践意义是什么？告诉读者你为什么要进行这项研究是引言的主要内容和目的，这其中也包括说明这项研究的理论和（或）实践意义。因此，引言要简明介绍论文的背景、相关领域的前人研究历史与现状（有时亦称这部分为文献综述），以及著者的意图与分析依据，包括论文的追求目标、研究范围和理论、技术方案的选取等。引言应言简意赅，不要等同于摘要，或成为摘要的注释。

大部分情况下，我们所研究的项目是前人开展过的，在引言中对与本文相关的研究进行简要的回顾是十分必要的。研究开始以前就应该对与本研究相关的内容进行系统的回顾，在引言中可以将回顾的结果做简要的概括。

撰写引言时应注意以下几点。

1）引言的内容按国家标准规定，主要是提示内容。所以，引言的写作必须提示写作意图、论题的中心或带有结论性的观点等，以告诉读者这篇论文的写作目的、作者的论题以及基本观点。

2）引言的写作应具有一定的启发性，以开拓读者的思路。

3）内容切忌空泛，篇幅不宜过长。回顾历史择其要点，背景动态只要概括几句即可，引用参考文献不宜过多。根据以往的经验，一篇 3000~5000 字的论文引言字数在 150~250 字较为恰当。

4）引言中不应详述同行熟知的，包括教科书上已有陈述的基本理论、实验方法和基本方程的推导；除非是学位论文，为了反映著者的学业等，允许有较详尽的文献综述段落。如果正文中采用比较专业化的术语或缩写词，最好先在引言中定义说明。

5）引言只起引导作用，可以说明研究的设计，但不要涉及本研究的数据、结果和结论，少与摘要和正文重复。

6）不必强调过去的工作成就。回顾作者以往的工作只是为了交代此次写作的基础和动机，而不是写总结。评价论文的价值要恰如其分，实事求是，慎用"首创""首次发现""达到国际一流水平"等提法。因为首创必须有确切的资料。对此，可以用相对较委婉的说法表达，如"就所查文献，未见报道"等。

2. 正文

正文是科技论文的核心组成部分，主要回答"怎么研究"（how）这个问题。正文应充分阐明论文的观点、原理、方法及具体达到预期目标的整个过程，并且突出"新"字，以反映论文具有的首创性。根据需要，论文可以分层深入，逐层剖析，按层设分层标题。

正文通常占据论文的大部分篇幅。它的具体陈述方式往往因不同学科、不同文章类型而有很大差别，不能牵强地做出统一的规定，一般应包括原理、方法、结果、讨论和结论等几个部分。

试验与观察、数据处理与分析、实验研究结果的得出是正文最重要的成分，应该给予极大的重视。要尊重事实，在资料的取舍上不应该随意掺入主观成分或妄加猜测，不应该忽视偶发性现象和数据。

科技论文不要求华丽的辞藻，但要求思路清晰，合乎逻辑，用语简洁准确、明快流畅；内容务求客观、科学、完备，要尽量让事实和数据说话；凡是用简要的文字能够讲解的内容，应用文字陈述，用文字不容易说明白或说起来比较烦琐的，应由表或图（必要时用彩图）来陈述。表或图要具有自明性，即其本身给出的信息就能够说明欲表达的问题。数据的引用要严谨确切，防止错引或重引，避免用图形和表格重复地反映同一组数据。资料的引用要标明出处。

物理量与单位符号应符合《中华人民共和国法定计量单位》的规定，选用规范的单位和书写符号；不得已选用非规范的单位或符号时应考虑行业的习惯，或使用法定的计量单位和符号加以注解和换算。

教科书式的撰写方法是撰写科技论文的第一大忌。避免重新描述和论证已有的知识，尽量采用标注参考文献的方法；对用到的某些数学辅助手段，应防止过分注意细节的数学推演，需要时可采用附录的形式供读者选阅。

由于具体研究对象的复杂性和差异性，正文写作没有固定的规律可循，但以下几点要引起注意。

1）正文中许多由统计、观察、实验得到的材料可以用图、表来表示，图表要有自明性，即只看图表、图表标题、图例及表注就可明白其所表达的意义。

2）正文中所使用的数学计算公式要居中排列，并尽可能在等号处转行。公式要有编号。

3）正文中若要使用缩略语，则第一次必须要用全称，并注明以下用简称。

4）正文中的数学在以下两种情况下使用汉字：一是数字用作词素，如第一定律、二元方程；二是连用的两数字，如三五天、两三米等。其他用作计量、计数和表示公历年、月、日、年代等时要使用阿拉伯数字。

5）正文的用语要准确、简明和严谨。例如，"基本上""全部""很好"，以及数字前后的"近""多""约""左右"要慎重使用；"大概""可能""众所周知""可想而知"尽量不用；当反映成果水平时，不能言过其实，不能用夸张和奇特的比喻等。

3. 结果

科研的成败与否是根据结果来判断的，结论与推论亦由结果导出。结果部分最能体现论文的学术水平和理论与实用价值。因此，对于这一部分的写作要特别重视。结果部分的写作要做到指标明确可靠，数据准确无误，文字描述言简意赅，图表设计正确合理。

结果的表达通常通过文字、图、表相互结合来完成。下列情况可用文字表达为主或仅用文字表达：①结果中数据较少，能做同类比较的观测项目不多者；②以观察形态特征为主的论文一般不用表格，而以文字描述为主配合形态学图片。能用文字表达的内容不用列表、绘图。已用图表说明的内容，不必再用文字详述，只要强调或概括重点。文字表达主要是陈述本文取得的结果，不必强调过程，也不要重复正文中已交代的资料，更不要将结果提升为理论上的结论，所以一般不引用文献。

表与图设计的基本要求是正确合理，简明清晰。"自明性"是衡量表图的重要标志。所谓"自明性"，是指仅通过表与图就能大体了解研究的内容和结果。

表是简明的、规范化的科学用语。一般主张采用三线表，即表由顶线、标目线和底线这三条横线组成框架，两侧应是开口的。顶线与标目线之间为栏头，标目线与底线之间为表身。栏头左上角不用斜线，但栏头允许再设一条至数条横线。一般表的行头标示组别，栏头标示反应指标。但这种划分并不是固定的，著者可根据情况灵活安排。表的下方还可以加表注。

图是一种形象化的表达方式，它可以直观地表达研究的结果。通常我们用柱图的高度表达非连续性资料的大小，用线图、直方图或散点图表达连续性或计量资料的变化，用点图表示双变量的关系。图的标题应在图的下方，注释可放在柱或线附近。

对于既可用图也可以用表的资料，可根据具体情况选择表达形式。一般来说，要表示变化趋势的资料，尤其是连续的动态资料，宜采用图的形式；要表示确切统计量的资料，宜采用表的形式。

结果的写作一定要采取实事求是的科学态度，遵守全面性和真实性的原则。实验结果无论成功或失败，只要是真实的就是有价值的。切不可为了符合"正常"结果而对实验数据进行任意增删、篡改，这不利于我们全面认识事物和发现新问题。

4. 讨论

讨论是论文的精华部分，是对引言所提出的问题的回答，是将研究结果表象的感性认识升华为本质的理性认识。在讨论中作者通过对研究结果的思考、理论分析和科学推论，阐明事物的内部联系和发展规律，从深度与广度两方面丰富和提高对研究结果的认识。讨论水平的高低取决于作者的理论水平、学术素养以及专业知识的深、广度。讨论的内容大致包括以下几个方面：①概述国内外对本课题的研究近况，以及本研究的结论和结果与国际、国内先进水平相比居于什么地位；②根据研究的目的阐明本研究结果的理论意义和实践意义；③着重说明本文创新点所在，以及本研究结果从哪些方面支持创新点；④对本研究的限度、缺点、疑点等加以分析和解释，说明偶然性和必然性；⑤说明本文未能解决的问题，提出今后研究的方向与问题。并不是每篇论文都必须包括以上内容，应从论文的研究目的出发，突出重点，紧扣论题。

讨论是最能体现论文水平的部分，也是写作难度较高的部分。对于初写者来说，要特别注意以下几点：①讨论是作者阐明自己的学术观点，但并不等于自由论坛，不能泛泛而谈，讨论的内容要从论文的研究结果出发，围绕创新点与结论展开，要做到层次清晰、主次分明，不要在次要问题上浪费笔墨冲淡主题，与文献一致处可一笔带过，重点讨论不一致处，引证必要的文献，切忌进行文献综述；②实事求是、恰如其分地评价，不乱下结论，切忌推理过分外延；③任何研究都有其局限性，如国内的研究结果有待国外验证，体外试验有待体内试验验证，因此讨论要坚持一分为二的观点，对于与他人研究结果不一致处要认真分析原因，要抱有虚心追求真理的态度与其他作者商榷，切勿持"唯我正确"的态度；④并非每篇论文都要有讨论，有的短篇可不写。若结果与讨论关系密切，则可放在一起写，合称结果与分析等。

5. 致谢

科研工作的顺利完成离不开他人的帮助，在正文的最后应向对本研究提供过帮助的人致以谢意。致谢一般单独成段，但它不是论文的必要组成部分。它是对曾经给予论文的选题、构思或撰写以指导或建议，对考察或实验过程中做出某种贡献的人员，或给予过技术、信息、物质或经费帮助的单位、团体或个人致以谢意。一般对例外的劳动可不必专门致谢。

致谢必须实事求是，应防止剽窃掠美之嫌，也勿强加于人，如未经允许写上专家、教授的名字以示审阅来抬高自己。致谢一般要说明被谢者的工作内容，如"技术指导""收集资料""提供资料"等。

7.4 结语和参考文献写作

1. 结语

科技论文的末尾一般要有总结性的文字，称为"结论""结语"或"结束语"。撰写结语的目的：一是便于读者查阅文献时节省时间，当读者看了论文的题目、摘要并读完结语之后，就可以决定是否再阅读全文；二是便于读者做笔记或卡片；三是便于文摘专业工作者撰写摘要。尽管多数科技论文的著者都采用结语的方式作为结束，并通过它传达自己欲向读者表述的主要意向，但它并不是论文的必要组成部分。结语和摘要性质类似，一些内容较简单的论文可以取消这一节，以免与摘要重复。

结语不应是正文中各段小结的简单重复，而应主要回答"研究出什么"（what）。它应该以正文中的试验或考察中得到的现象、数据和阐述分析作为依据，由此完整、准确、简洁地指出：

1）由对研究对象进行考察或实验得到的结果所揭示的原理及其普遍性。
2）研究中有无发现例外或本论文尚难以解释和解决的问题。
3）与先前已经发表过的（包括他人或著者自己）研究工作的异同。
4）本论文在理论上与实用上的意义与价值。
5）对进一步深入研究本课题的建议。

2. 参考文献

科学有继承性。绝大部分研究成果是前人工作的继续，所以学术论文多数引用参考文献。但如果撰写论文时未参考文献也可以不写。在论文的最后列出参考文献，其目的：一是便于查阅原始资料中的有关内容；二是有利于缩短论文的篇幅；三是表明论文有其真实的科学依据；四是尊重他人的劳动成果。列出参考文献的范围应以公开发表过的、作者真正参阅过的、与论文密切相关的或直接引用的为限，未发表过的论文、试验报告、内部资料等不宜列入。

通常，参考文献著录的条目以小于正文的字号编排在文末。当列出参考文献时要按文献在文章中出现的先后，编注数码，依次列出。完整的参考文献写法应列出文献的作者（对于译文注明译者）、名称、出处、页数、出版者、出版时间、版次等。

国内外对文后参考文献的著录方法很多，著录形式也比较复杂，具体执行时请随时查阅国家标准和论文排版规定。

参考文献的类型及其标识

1）根据 GB 7714 规定，以单字母方式标识以下各种参考文献类型。
参考文献类型：普通图书、会议录、报纸、期刊、学位论文、报告、标准、专利。
文献类型标识：［M］、［C］、［N］、［J］、［D］、［R］、［S］、［P］。

2）对于普通图书、会议录中的析出文献，其文献类型标识建议采用单字母"A"；对于其他未说明的文献类型，建议采用单字母"Z"。

3）对于数据库、计算机程序及电子公告等电子文献类型的参考文献，建议以下列双字母作为标识：

电子文献类型标识：DB、CP、EB。
电子资源载体类型及其标识：磁带（magnetic tape）——MT，磁盘（disk）——DK，光盘（CD-ROM）——CD，联机网络（online）——OL。

如：［DB/OL］——联机网络数据库（database online）；
［DB/MT］——磁带数据库（database on magnetic tape）；
［M/CD］——光盘图书（monograph on CD-ROM）；
［CP/DK］——磁盘计算机程序（computer program on disk）；
［J/OL］——联机网络期刊（journal online）；
［EB/OL］——联机网络电子公告（electronic bulletin board online）。

各类参考文献条目的编排格式及示例

1）普通图书、会议录、学位论文、报告。

［序号］主要责任者. 题名：其他题名信息［文献类型标识］. 出版地：出版者，出版年：引文页码.

［1］王小平，曹立明. 遗传算法：理论、应用与软件实现［M］. 西安：西安交通大学出版社，2002：18-21.

［2］XIE G, GAO J L, XIE K M. Fuzzy modeling based on rough sets and mind evolutionary algorithm［C］. In：Proc. of the Sixth International Conference on Electronic Measurement and Instruments，Taiyuan, China, 2003：109-112.

［3］崔艳. 智能模糊 PID 控制系统研究与设计［D］. 太原：太原理工大学，2005.

2）期刊。

［序号］主要责任者. 题名：其他题名信息［J］. 期刊名，年，卷（期）：引文页码.

［4］邱玉霞，谢克明. 一种优化模糊控制规则的新方法［J］. 太原理工大学学报，2004，35（3）：254-256.

［5］杨俊杰，周建中，喻菁，等. 基于混沌搜索的粒子群优化算法［J］. 计算机工程与应用，2005（16）：69-71.

3）国际、国家标准。

［序号］主要责任者. 标准名：标准编号［S］. 出版地：出版者，出版年.

［6］全国电工术语标准化技术委员会. 电工术语 半导体器件和集成电路：GB/T 2900.66—2004［S］. 北京：中国标准出版社，2004.

4）专利。

［序号］专利所有者. 专利题名：专利号［P］. 公告日期或公开日期.

［7］谢克明，阎高伟，谢刚，等. 线性调频雷达物位计非线性进化校正方法：CN1632474［P］. 2005-06-29.

5）电子文献。

［序号］主要责任者. 题名：其他题名信息［电子文献及载体类型标识］.（发表或更新日期）［引用日期］. 获取和访问路径.

［8］刘佳，周广荣，夏志忠. 基于 MSP430F133 和 RFW 模块的短距离无线数据通信［EB/oL］.（2006-08-02）［2008-04-15］. http://www.microcontrol.cn/datasheet/MSP430/MSP430design/基于 F133 和 RFW 模块的短距离无线数据通信.pdf.

6）各种未定义类型的文献。

［序号］主要责任者. 题名：其他题名信息［Z］. 出版地：出版者，出版年.

练习参考答案

2.1 Circuit and System

1. 英译汉

a) 安培

b) 传导率

c) 磁心

d) 绝缘体

e) 电介质

f) 戴维南定理

g) 负极

h) 电荷

i) 感应系数

j) 极性

2. 汉译英

a) charge

b) inductance

c) polarity

d) node

e) resistor

f) capacitor

g) insulator

h) equivalent resistance

i) Superposition Theorem

j) current

3. 填空

a) coulombs, electron, proton

b) magnetic, electromagnetism

c) inductor

d) current

e) increased, decreased, voltage, polarity

f) node

g) zero

4. 根据课文回答问题

a) Whenever an electric voltage exists between two separated conductors, an electric field is present within the space between those conductors. Electrical energy can be stored in an electric field.

b) Ohm's principal discovery was that the amount of electric current through a metal conductor is directly proportional to the voltage impressed across it, for any given temperature.

c) Ohm's Law is given by:

$$V = IR$$

where V is the potential difference between two points which include aresistance R, and I is the current flowing through the resistance.

d) The total charge flowing into a node must be the same as the total charge flowing out of the node. The total voltage around a closed loop must be zero.

e) Thevenin's Theorem states that it is possible to simplify any linear circuit, no matter how complex, to an equivalent circuit with just a single voltage source and series resistance connected to a load. Norton's Theorem states that it is possible to simplify any linear circuit, no matter how complex, to an equivalent circuit with just a single current source and parallel resistance connected to a load.

2.2 Analog and Digital Circuits Design

1. 英译汉

a) 半导体

b) 计数制

c) 集成电路

d) 交换律

e) 交流

f) 分配律

g) 二进制的

h) 倒相器

i) 否定的

j) 时序的

2. 汉译英

a) bipolar

b) transistor

c) N-channel

d) linear

e) Boolean algebra

f) truth table

g) flip-flop

h) combinational logic circuit

i) adjacent cell

j) product-of-sums

3. 填空

a) Analog, circuits

b) entering

c) switch

d) combinational

e) feedback loops

f) sequential logic

g) the past sequence of inputs, sequential logic

4. 根据课文回答问题

a) In this component the current flow enters the collector and base and exits the emitter.

b) The advantage of bipolar over CMOS is that it has better trans-conductance gain and better matching, leading to better differential input gain stages.

c) A combinational logic is one whose outputs depend only on its current input. A combinational logic circuit may contain an arbitrary number of logic gates and inverters but no feedback loops. When the input is combined with the previous state of the logic circuits, it is referred to as sequential logic. The use of the previous state is called feedback. The outputs of sequential logic circuit depend not only on the current inputs but also on the past sequence of inputs, possibly arbitrarily far back in time.

d) NAND gate produces a 0 output if all of its inputs are 1.

2.3 Radio Receiver Circuit

1. 英译汉

a) 寄生电容

b) 信道带宽

c) 半双工

d) 杂散频率

e) 输入匹配

f) 调谐范围

g) 基带放大器

h) 噪声系数

i) 最小可检测信号

j) 低噪声放大器

2. 汉译英

a) sensitivity

b) harmonics

c) impedance match

d) local oscillator

e) overload characteristics

f) AGC

g) channel

h) additive, white, Gaussian noise

i) intermediate frequency

j) baseband signal

3. 填空

a) linearly, minimize

b) noise

c) ripple

d) provide

e) larger, greater

f) minimize

g) distortion

4. 根据课文回答问题

a) 12 components such as RF preselector, RF amplifier, interstage selector, local oscillator, first mixer, IF filter, IF amplifier, second mixer, local oscillator, second filter, demodulator, baseband amplifier and so on.

b) The function of the input amplifier is to linearly amplify the input signal and minimize the noise added by the receiver to the signal itself.

c) We have already used two terms-receiver sensitivity and receiver selectivity-that turn out to be the two fundamental criteria in evaluating the quality of a receiver. There are other system parameters such as the receiver dynamic range and its maximum input signal. In particular, by configuring the gain, noise figure, power capabilities, and frequency characteristics of each stage, we can derive the overall receiver performance.

d) As the desired signal increases in input power, the gain of the system is reduced in order to minimize distortion.

3.1 Signal and System

1. 英译汉

a) 信号与系统

b) 航空航天

c) 连续时间信号

d) 信号能量和功率

e) 总能量

f) 复数

g) 无限时间间隔

h) 平均功率

i) 物理系统

j) 汽车

2. 汉译英

a) signal processing

b) circuit design

c) discrete-time signal

d) nonzero constant

e) independent variable

f）instantaneous power

g）average energy

h）infinite energy

i）interaction between subsystems

j）image enhancement

3. 填空

a）over

b）by

c）at

d）by

e）to

f）over

g）by

h）as

i）on

j）from, to

4. 根据课文回答问题

a）Two basic types of signals: continuous-time signals and discrete-time signals. The key features of each type: at first, the independent variable is different, one is continuous and another is discrete. Then, we use symbol t to denote the continuous-time independent variable and n to denote the discrete-time independent variable.

b）$\int_{t_1}^{t_2} p(t) \, dt = \int_{t_1}^{t_2} \frac{1}{R} v^2(t) \, dt$.

c）Three classes of signals: finite-energy signal, finite average power signal, infinite energy and infinite power signal.

d）A linear and time-invariant system.

3.2　Digital Signal Processing

1. 英译汉

a）数字信号处理

b）对称性

c）时域

d）频域

e）截断

f）权函数

g）均匀划分的

h）稀疏矩阵

i）快速傅里叶变换

j）傅里叶级数

2. 汉译英

a）linear phase

b）even function

c）transfer function

d）Gibbs phenomenon

e）passband

f）stopband

g）mainlobe

h）sidelobe

i）linear time-invariant finite impulse response filter

j）non-recursive

3. 填空

a）from

b）of

c）for

d）into, for

e）include

f）of

g）for

h）over

i）to

j）to

4. 根据课文回答问题

a）If the samples are uniformly spaced, then the Fourier matrix can be factored into a product of just a few sparse matrices, and the resulting factors can be applied to a vector in a total of order $n\log n$ arithmetic operations. This is the so-called fast Fourier transform or FFT.

b）The first method is based on truncating the Fourier series representation of the desired frequency. The second method is based on specifying equally spaced frequency samples of the frequency response of the desired filter.

c）As shown in Fig. 3-8, the causal FIR filter obtained by simply truncating the impulse response coefficients of the desired filter exhibits an oscillatory behavior (or ripples) in its magnitude response. As the length of the filter is increased, the number of ripples in both passband and stopband increases, and the width of the ripples decrease. The ripple becomes narrower, but its height remains almost constant. The largest ripple occurs near the transition discontinuity and their amplitude is independent of L. This undesired effect is called the Gibbs phenomenon.

3.3　Speech Signal Processing

1. 英译汉

a）定量方法

b）复杂的通信系统

c）大量不同的方法

d）考虑

e）数字技术

f）挑选

g）带限信号

h）参数表示

i）声道响应参数

j）语音合成系统

2. 汉译英

a) information theory

b) parametric model

c) articulatory mechanism

d) information source

e) speech signal processing

f) integrated circuit technology

g) waveform representation

h) excitation parameter

i) speaker verification and identification

j) speech enhancement

3. 填空

a) to

b) from

c) In

d) By

e) with, with

f) over

g) to

h) to

i) as, as

j) In

4. 根据课文回答问题

a) In general, there are two major concerns in any system: one is preservation of the message content in the speech signal, another is representation of the speech signal in a form that is convenient for transmission or storage, or in a form that is flexible so that modification may be made to the speech signal without seriously degrading the message content.

b) Digital signal processing and digital simulations of analog systems.

c) The representation of the speech signal must be such that the information content can easily be extracted by human listeners, or automatically by machine. Representations of the speech signal (rather than message content) may require from 500 to upwards of 1 million bits per second. In the design and implementation of these representations, the methods of signal processing play a fundamental role.

d) The nature of the speech recognition problem is heavily dependent upon the constraints placed on speaker, speaking situation and message context.

4.1 Electromagnetic Fields Theory

1. 英译汉

a）时变场

b）位移电流

c）散度源

d）电动势

e）矢量场

f）微分

g）方程

h）通量

i）边界条件

j）积分形式

2. 汉译英

a）conductivity

b）dielectric constant

c）magnetic field intensity

d）closed-loop

e）electric flux density

f）surface integral

g）conduction current

h）anisotropic

i）relative permeability

j）constitutive relation

3. 填空

a）surface integral, current density, conduction current, electric flux density

b）integral

c）decrease

4. 根据课文回答问题

a）The integral forms of Maxwell's equations are listed below:

$$\oint_C \boldsymbol{H} \cdot \mathrm{d}\boldsymbol{l} = \int_S \left(\boldsymbol{J} + \frac{\partial \boldsymbol{D}}{\partial t} \right) \cdot \mathrm{d}\boldsymbol{S} \quad \text{(Generalized Ampere's Law or Maxwell's first equation)}$$

$$\oint_C \boldsymbol{E} \cdot \mathrm{d}\boldsymbol{l} = -\int_S \frac{\partial \boldsymbol{B}}{\partial t} \cdot \mathrm{d}\boldsymbol{S} \quad \text{(Faraday's Law or Maxwell's second equation)}$$

$$\oint_S \boldsymbol{B} \cdot \mathrm{d}\boldsymbol{S} = 0 \quad \text{(Gauss' Law for magnetic field or Maxwell's third equation)}$$

$$\oint_S \boldsymbol{D} \cdot \mathrm{d}\boldsymbol{S} = \int_V \rho \mathrm{d}V \quad \text{(Gauss' Law for electric field or Maxwell's forth equation)}$$

The differential forms of Maxwell's equations are listed below:

$$\nabla \times \boldsymbol{H} = \boldsymbol{J} + \frac{\partial \boldsymbol{D}}{\partial t}, \quad \nabla \times \boldsymbol{E} = -\frac{\partial \boldsymbol{B}}{\partial t}, \quad \nabla \cdot \boldsymbol{B} = 0, \quad \nabla \cdot \boldsymbol{D} = \rho$$

b) A medium is said to be isotropic if the electrical and magnetic properties at a given point are independent of the direction of the field at the point. On the other hand, if the electrical and magnetic properties of a medium depend upon the directions of field vectors, the medium is called anisotropic.

c) Maxwell's equations explain the total relationships between electromagnetic sources and the fields:

①The conduction current and the displacement current are the curl sources of the magnetic fields.

②Time varying magnetic field produces an electric field.

③The magnetic fields are solenoidal fields.

④The electric charges are the divergence sources of the electric fields.

d) $\boldsymbol{n} \cdot (\boldsymbol{B}_1 - \boldsymbol{B}_2) = 0$, $\boldsymbol{n} \cdot (\boldsymbol{D}_1 - \boldsymbol{D}_2) = \rho_{sf}$, $\boldsymbol{n} \times (\boldsymbol{E}_1 - \boldsymbol{E}_2) = 0$, $\boldsymbol{n} \times (\boldsymbol{H}_1 - \boldsymbol{H}_2) = \boldsymbol{J}_{sf}$.

e) To allow a unique determination of the field vectors, Maxwell's equations must be supplemented by relations describing the behavior of the medium under the influence of the field. These subsidiary relations are called constitutive relations that are established by experimentation or deduced from atomic theory.

4.2 Development of Mobile Communication

1. 英译汉

a) 超外差的

b) 蜂窝移动通信

c) 单工模式

d) 半双工模式

e) 频分多址

f) 时分多址

g) 码分多址

h) 短消息服务

i) 分组交换

j) 电路交换

k) 扩频无线电技术

2. 汉译英

a) codec

b) intermediate frequency

c) carrier

d) Frequency Division Multiple Access (FDMA)

e) FM

f) cellular technology

g) physical level transmission

h) channel encoding and decoding

i) Internet of Things

j) intelligent services

3. 填空

a) sender, transmitter, channel, receiver, recipient

b) James Clerk Maxwell, Heinrich Rudolf Hertz

c) small cells

d) FDMA, TDMA, circuit switching, packet/circuit switching, all-IP

e) Hexagonal

f) single

g) large-scale antenna arrays, ultra-dense networking, new types of multiple access, full spectrum access, new network architectures

h) ultra-high capacity, ultra-low latency

4. 根据课文回答问题

a) Any communication system should mainly include sender, transmitter, channel, receiver and recipient.

b) The nearly 100-year development history of modern mobile communication system can be roughly divided into the following four development stages.

The first stage is the early development stage from the 1920s to the 1940s. It was characterized by special system development, low working frequency, working mode is simplex or half duplex mode.

The second period is from the mid-1940s to the early 1960s. This stage was characterized by the transition from the dedicated mobile network to the public mobile network, and the connection mode was manual, the network capacity was small.

The third period is from the mid-1960s to the mid-1970s. It was characterized by adopting large area system, small and medium capacity, using 450MHz frequency band, and realizing automatic frequency selection and automatic connection.

The fourth stage is from the middle and late 1970s till now. It was characterized by the rapid increase of communication capacity, the emergence of new services, the continuous improvement of system performance, and the trend of technology development.

c) In 1896, Marconi's successful experiment with long-range radio communications on a drifting Atlantic ship was considered the beginning of mobile communications.

d) The fourth stage of cellular mobile communication system can be divided into several development stages. If according to the multiple access mode to divide, then analog Frequency Division Multiple Access (FDMA) system is the first generation of mobile communication system (1G); digital Time Division Multiple Access (TDMA) or Code Division Multiple Access (CDMA) systems using circuit switching are second generation mobile communication systems (2G); CDMA systems using packet/circuit switching are third generation mobile communication systems (3G); systems using different advanced access technologies and all-IP (Internet protocol) network structures are called fourth generation mobile communication systems (4G). According to the typical technology of the system, the simulation system is 1G; digital voice systems are 2G; digital voice/data system is super second generation mobile communication system (B2G); broadband digital system is 3G; the very high data rate system is 4G.

4.3 Optical Fiber Communication

1. 英译汉

a）电磁的

b）内反射

c）模式

d）传输窗口

e）掺杂物含量

f）数值孔径

g）相干光

h）激光二极管

i）光孤子

j）受光角

2. 汉译英

a）electronic communications

b）interference

c）critical angle

d）erbium doped silica fiber

e）frequency modulation

f）bandwidth

g）refractive index

h）attenuation

i）optical amplification

j）Wavelength-Division Multiplexing（WDM）

3. 填空

a）played，in

b）by，to

c）in，to

d）of

e）By，by，per

f）of，from，to

g）on

h）of，in

i）within

j）to，on

4. 根据课文回答问题

a）Typical optical fibers are composed of core, cladding and buffer coating. The core is the inner part of the fiber, which guides light. The cladding surrounds the core completely.

b）In 1880 Alexander Graham Bell and his assistant Charles Sumner Tainter created a very early precursor to fiber-optic communications：the photophone.

In 1960s, a critical and theoretical specification was identified by Dr. Charles K. Kao for long-range communication devices. And Charles K. Kao and George Hockham proposed optical fibers at STC Laboratories (STL) at Harlow, England.

In 1970, optical fiber was successfully developed by Corning Glass Works.

The first wide area network fiber optic cable system in the world seems to have been installed in Hastings, East Sussex, UK in 1978.

The second generation of fiber-optic communication was developed for commercial use in the early 1980s. After that, the third, fourth, fifth generation of fiber-optic communication were developed and widely used, the repeater spacing is longer, and the bit rate is higher.

c) A typical optical communication system consists of electrical signal input, transmitter, transmission line, receiver and electrical signal output.

d) Wider bandwidth, low transmission loss, signal security, eliminating spark hazards and ease of installation.

5.1 Pattern Recognition

1. 英译汉

a) 感知

b) 分类

c) 增强

d) 欧氏距离

e) 超平面

f) 先验概率

g) 支持向量机

h) 核函数

i) 判别函数

j) 特征值

2. 汉译英

a) feature extraction

b) statistical pattern recognition

c) linear discriminant function

d) posterior probability

e) likelihood function

f) information gain

g) decision tree

h) empirical risk

i) generalization ability

j) support vector

k) regression

l) Euclidean distance

3. 填空

a) information

b) similarity

c) recognize, learn, adapt

d) classification, regression

e) data acquisition, preprocessing, data representation (feature extraction and selection), classification decision, classifier design

f) feature vector

g) template matching, statistical, syntactic or structural matching, neural networks

h) probability theory

i) $P(A|B) = \dfrac{P(B|A)P(A)}{P(B)}$

j) information gain

4. 根据课文回答问题

a) Broadly speaking, a pattern is an observable thing existing in time and space. Pattern Recognition (PR) refers to the process of using machine (computer) to imitate human brain to describe, classify, judge and recognize various things in the real world.

b) No. XOR isn't a linearly separable problem.

c) The process includes the following five aspects: 1) data acquisition, 2) preprocessing, 3) data representation (feature extraction and selection), 4) classification decision, and 5) classifier design.

d) Decision tree generation consists of two phases: tree construction and tree pruning. At start, all the training examples are at the root. Then examples are partied recursively based on selected attributes. At last, branches that reflect noise or outliers should be identified and removed.

Leaf nodes represent the class labels or class distribution. Internal node denotes a test on a feature. Branch represents the path of a test outcome.

e) The nearest training samples nearest to get the hyperplane are the support vectors.

5.2 Machine Learning

1. 英译汉

a) 模式

b) 线性回归

c) 监督学习

d) K-均值聚类

e) 分层聚类

f) 集成学习

g) 主成分分析

h) 强化学习

i) 智能体

2. 汉译英

a) gradient

b) deep learning

c) feature vector

d) random forest

e) agent

f) radial basis network

g) naive Bayes

h) PCA

3. 填空

a) ML

b) Data, model

c) predict

d) patterns

e) test data

f) regression learning

g) classification learning

h) clustering

4. 根据课文回答问题

a) Machine learning is to make machines have the same learning ability as human beings. It is specialized in studying how computers simulate or realize human learning behavior to acquire new knowledge or skills and reorganize existing knowledge structure to continuously improve their performance.

b) Data and model.

c) The core objective of machine learning is the learning and inference.

d) Define a question; collect and label data; clean data; select feature; choose model; train and test the model; evaluate the performance and refine the algorithm.

e) Supervised learning algorithm trains machine learning model with instance with classification label, so that the computer can learn rules from it, so as to make reasonable output prediction for a new input.

5.3 Computer Vision

1. 英译汉

a) 指纹

b) 语义分割

c) 定位

d) 风格迁移

e) 实例分割

f) 图像检索

g) 入侵

h) 监视

2. 汉译英

a) CV

b) sensed image

c) task

d) segmentation

e) CNN

f) target detection

g) style transfer

h) super-resolution

3. 填空

a) "What is where?"

b) "Who am I?"

c) Convolutional Neural Network (CNN)

d) object detection

e) pixel, pixels

f) Style transfer

4. 根据课文回答问题

a) Computer vision is the science and technology of machine vision, which is concerned with the theory of building artificial systems to obtain information from images.

b) In the CV field, the main tasks are image classification/localization, object detection, object tracking, segmentation etc.

c) The task of object detection is to find out all the objects of interest in the image and determine their position and size.

d) Image segmentation refers to the process of subdividing a digital image into multiple image subregions (collections of pixels, also known as superpixels).

e) Semantic segmentation and instance segmentation.

f) The CNN structure is basically composed of a convolutional layer, a pooling layer, and a fully connected layer. Usually, the input image is fed into a convolutional neural network, feature extraction is performed through the convolutional layer and then the details are filtered by the pooling layer (generally max pooling, average pooling), and finally feature expansion is carried out in the fully connected layer and the corresponding classifier is fed to obtain its classification results.

参 考 文 献

[1] CHANG K. RF and microwave wireless systems [M]. New York: John Wiley & Sons, 2000.
[2] KUPHALDT T R. Lessons in electric circuit: volume Ⅱ (AC) [EB/OL]. (2007-11-06) [2014-03-22]. https://www.ibiblio.org/kuphaldt/electricCircuits/AC/index.html.
[3] POZAR D M. Microwave engineering [M]. 2nd ed. New York: John Wiley & Sons, 1998.
[4] EGAN W F. Practical RF system design [M]. New York: John Wiley & Sons, 2003.
[5] THIDE B. Electromagnetic field theory [M]. New York: Dover Publications, 2011.
[6] LASKAR J, MATINPOUR B, CHARKABORTY S. Modern receiver front-ends systems, circuits, and integration [M]. New York: John Wiley & Sons, 2004.
[7] CARTER B, BROWN T R. Handbook of operational amplifier applications [EB/OL]. (2001-10-01) [2014-03-25]. https://www.ti.com/lit/an/sboa092b/sboa092b.pdf.
[8] WAKERLY J F. Digital design principle & practices [M]. 3rd ed. Upper Saddle River: Prentice Hall, 2005.
[9] 范平志. 专业英语实用教程[M]. 成都: 西南交通大学出版社, 1989.
[10] 方旭明. 新编专业英语[M]. 成都: 西南交通大学出版社, 1997.
[11] 李霞. 电子与通信专业英语[M]. 北京: 电子工业出版社, 2005.
[12] VASEGHI S V. Advanced digital signal processing and noise reduction [M]. New York: John Wiley & Sons, 2000.
[13] Ursinus College. Operational amplifier circuits [EB/OL]. (2000-04-01) [2014-03-27]. http://webpages.ursinus.edu/lriley/ref/circuits/node5.html.
[14] Rice University. Basic electronic [EB/OL]. (1999-09-01) [2014-03-29]. https://www.clear.rice.edu/elec201/Book/basic_elec.html.
[15] Texas Instruments. TMS320VC5409A fixed-point digital signal processor data manual [EB/OL]. (2008-10-01) [2014-04-02]. https://www.ti.com/lit/ds/symlink/tms320vc5409a.pdf.
[16] Wikipedia. Artificial neural network [EB/OL]. (2014-2-25) [2014-04-02]. http://en.wikipedia.org/wiki/Artificial_neural_network.
[17] STERGIOU C, SIGANOS D. Neural networks [EB/OL]. (2011-10-05) [2014-04-02]. https://wiki.eecs.yorku.ca/course_archive/2013-14/F/4403/_media/report.pdf.
[18] 屈乐乐, 方广有, 杨天虹. 压缩感知理论在频率步进探地雷达偏移成像中的应用[J]. 电子与信息学报, 2011, 1(33): 21-26.
[19] BADRAN E F. Optimal channel equalization for filterbank transceivers in presence of white noise [D]. Baton Rouge: Louisiana State University, 2002.
[20] SMITH S W. The scientist and engineer's guide to digital signal processing [M]. 2nd ed. San Diego: California Technical Publishing, 1999.
[21] 张敏瑞, 张红. 通信与电子信息科技英语[M]. 北京: 北京邮电大学出版社, 2003.
[22] 赵淑清. 电子信息与通信专业英语[M]. 哈尔滨: 哈尔滨工业大学出版社, 2002.
[23] KUO S M, LEE B H. Real-time digital signal processing [M]. New York: John Wiley & Sons, 2007.
[24] RABINER L R, SCHAFER R W. Digital processing of speech signals [M]. Upper Saddle River: Prentice Hall, 1978.
[25] Catalyst Development Corporation. Introduction to TCP/IP [EB/OL]. (2002-05-16) [2014-02-15].

https://wenku.baidu.com/view/a538651afc4ffe473368ab5c.html?_wkts_=1720680437090&bdQuery=Introduction+to+TCP%2FIP&needWelcomeRecommand=1.

[26] 倪诗锋, 宋建新. 一种基于压缩感知的视频编解码与传输方案[J]. 信息技术, 2011, 35(1): 39-43.

[27] 单进, 芮贤义. 基于压缩感知的稳健性说话人识别[J]. 电声技术, 2011, 35(2): 61-63.

[28] 中国卫星导航系统管理办公室. 北斗卫星导航系统发展报告[EB/OL]. (2019-12-01)[2023-07-10]. http://www.beidou.gov.cn/xt/gfxz/201912/P020191227337020425733.pdf.

[29] GUO H D, GOODCHILD M F, ANNONI A. Manual of digital earth [M]//SHI C, WEI N. Satellite navigation for digital earth. Berlin: Springer, 2020: 125-160.

[30] 刘健, 曹冲. 全球卫星导航系统发展现状与趋势[J]. 导航定位学报, 2020, 8(1): 1-8.

[31] ZHANG Z T, LI B F, NIE L W, et al. Initial assessment of BeiDou-3 global navigation satellite system: signal quality, RTK and PPP [J]. GPS Solutions, 2019, 23(4): 1-12.

[32] International Civil Aviation Organization. Global Navigation Satellite System (GNSS) manual [EB/OL]. (2012-06-01)[2023-07-12]. https://www.icao.int/Meetings/anconf12/Documents/Doc.%209849.pdf.

[33] YANG Y X, MAO Y, SUN B J. Basic performance and future developments of BeiDou global navigation satellite system [J]. Satellite Navigation, 2020, 1(1): 1-8.

[34] 360百科. 模式识别技术[EB/OL]. (2015-05-12)[2023-07-12]. https://baike.so.com/doc/3581087-3765694.html.

[35] JAIN A K, DUIN R P W, MAO J C. Statistical pattern recognition: a review [J]. IEEE Transactions on Pattern Analysis and Machine Intelligence, 2000, 22(1): 4-37.

[36] OLSSON N A. Lightwave systems with optical amplifiers [J]. Journal of Lightwave Technology, 1989, 7(7): 1071-1082.

[37] PASCHOTTA R. Encyclopedia of laser physics and technology [EB/OL]. (2021-05-01)[2023-07-16]. http://www.rp-photonics.com/peak_power.html.

[38] STEFAN A. Illustrated optical fiber glossary [EB/OL]. (2015-07-15)[2023-07-17]. https://bitesizebio.com/25058/illustrated-optical-fiber-glossary-a-e/.

[39] NTT Group. 14Tbit/s over a single optical fiber: successful demonstration of world's largest capacity [EB/OL]. (2006-09-29)[2014-02-20]. http://www.ntt.co.jp/news/news06e/0609/060929a.html.

[40] Federal Communications Commission. Revision of part 15 of the commission's rules regarding ultra-wideband transmission systems [J]. First Report & Order, 2002, 2: 98-153.

[41] JORDAN M I, MITCHELL T M. Machine learning: trends, perspectives, and prospects [J]. Science, 2015, 349(6245): 255-260.

[42] LE J. The 5 computer vision techniques that will change how you see the world [EB/OL]. (2018-04-22)[2023-07-26]. https://jameskle.com/writes/computer-vision.

[43] DUFFY B F, FLYNN D R. A year in computer vision [EB/OL]. (2018-05-30)[2023-07-29]. https://www.themtank.org/a-year-in-computer-vision.